Ethics and Professional Responsibility for Paralegals

Ethics and Professional Responsibility for Paralegals

Ninth Edition

Therese A. Cannon
Founding President at Minerva University
(retired); Educational Consultant/Attorney

Sybil Taylor Aytch
Adjunct Professor, Phoenix College
Registered Paralegal, Quarles & Brady LLP

Copyright © 2024 Aspen Publishing. All Rights Reserved.

No part of this publication may be reproduced or transmitted in any form or by any means, electronic or mechanical, including photocopy, recording, or utilized by any information storage or retrieval system, without written permission from the publisher. For information about permissions or to request permissions online, visit us at www.AspenPublishing.com.

To contact Customer Service, e-mail customer.service@aspenpublishing.com, call 1-800-950-5259, or mail correspondence to:

> Aspen Publishing
> Attn: Order Department
> 1 Wall Street
> Burlington, MA 01803

Cover image: Sikov/stock.adobe.com

Printed in the United States of America.

1 2 3 4 5 6 7 8 9 0

ISBN 978-1-5438-2054-6

Library of Congress Cataloging-in-Publication Data

Names: Cannon, Therese A, author. | Aytch, Sybil Taylor, author.
Title: Ethics and professional responsibility for paralegals / Therese A Cannon, Sybil Taylor Aytch.
Description: Ninth edition. | Burlington : Aspen Publishing, 2024. | Includes index. | Summary: "College-level textbook on ethics and professional responsibility"-- Provided by publisher.
Identifiers: LCCN 2023058242 | ISBN 9781543820546 (hardcover) | ISBN 9781543820553 (ebook)
Classification: LCC KF320.L4 C37 2024
LC record available at https://lccn.loc.gov/2023058242

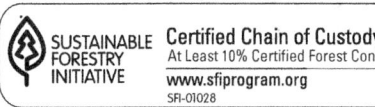

About Aspen Publishing

Aspen Publishing is a leading provider of educational content and digital learning solutions to law schools in the U.S. and around the world. Aspen provides best-in-class solutions for legal education through authoritative textbooks, written by renowned authors, and breakthrough products such as Connected eBooks, Connected Quizzing, and PracticePerfect.

The Aspen Casebook Series (famously known among law faculty and students as the "red and black" casebooks) encompasses hundreds of highly regarded textbooks in more than eighty disciplines, from large enrollment courses, such as Torts and Contracts, to emerging electives, such as Sustainability and the Law of Policing. Study aids such as the *Examples & Explanations* and the *Emanuel Law Outlines* series, both highly popular collections, help law students master complex subject matter.

Major products, programs, and initiatives include:

- **Connected eBooks** are enhanced digital textbooks and study aids that come with a suite of online content and learning tools designed to maximize student success. Designed in collaboration with hundreds of faculty and students, the Connected eBook is a significant leap forward in the legal education learning tools available to students.
- **Connected Quizzing** is an easy-to-use formative assessment tool that tests law students' understanding and provides timely feedback to improve learning outcomes. Delivered through CasebookConnect.com, the learning platform already used by students to access their Aspen casebooks, Connected Quizzing is simple to implement and integrates seamlessly with law school course curricula.
- **PracticePerfect** is a visually engaging, interactive study aid to explain commonly encountered legal doctrines through easy-to-understand animated videos, illustrative examples, and numerous practice questions. Developed by a team of experts, PracticePerfect is the ideal study companion for today's law students.
- The **Aspen Learning Library** enables law schools to provide their students with access to the most popular study aids on the market across all of their courses. Available through an annual subscription, the online library consists of study aids in e-book, audio, and video formats with full text search, note-taking, and highlighting capabilities.
- Aspen's **Digital Bookshelf** is an institutional-level online education bookshelf, consolidating everything students and professors need to ensure success. This program ensures that every student has access to affordable course materials from day one.
- **Leading Edge** is a community centered on thinking differently about legal education and putting those thoughts into actionable strategies. At the core of the program is the Leading Edge Conference, an annual gathering of legal education thought leaders looking to pool ideas and identify promising directions of exploration.

This book is dedicated to the professional paralegals across the country who work diligently every day to deliver quality legal services and uphold the highest standards of professionalism and ethics.

Summary of Contents

Contents	xi
Preface	xxi
1. Regulation of Lawyers	1
2. Regulation of Paralegals and Ethics Guidelines for Paralegals	19
3. Unauthorized Practice of Law	57
4. Confidentiality	127
5. Conflicts of Interest	197
6. Advertising and Solicitation	265
7. Fees and Client Funds	315
8. Competence	387
9. Special Issues in Advocacy	453
10. Professionalism	505
Glossary	527
Table of Cases	533
Index	537

Contents

Preface   xxi

1. Regulation of Lawyers   1

A.	State Courts and Bar Associations	2
B.	American Bar Association	3
C.	Statutes and Other Forms of Regulation	5
D.	Sanctions for Lawyer Misconduct	5
E.	Other Actions for Lawyer Misconduct	6
	Review Questions	7
	Discussion Questions and Hypotheticals	7
	Research Projects and Assignments	8
	Cases for Analysis	8
	Unauthorized Practice of Law Committee v. State Department of Workers' Compensation	8
	Questions about the Case	11
	State Bar of Arizona v. Lang	11
	Questions about the Case	14
	In re: Klitsch, et al.	14
	Questions about the Case	18

2. Regulation of Paralegals and Ethics Guidelines for Paralegals   19

A.	A Brief History of the Paralegal Profession	20
	1. The Beginnings	20
	2. Growth Through the 1970s	20
	3. New Directions in the 1980s and 1990s	21
	4. The Twenty-First Century	21
B.	Regulation of Paralegals: Certification and Licensing	23
	1. Definitions of Terms	23
	2. State Regulation of Lawyer-Supervised Paralegals	24
	3. Voluntary Certification of Paralegals	26
	4. The Arguments about Regulation of Lawyer-Supervised Paralegals	27
	5. Nonlawyer Legal Service Providers	29
	6. Other Legal Professionals	31
	Utah	31
	Arizona	32
	Minnesota	32
	Oregon	33
	Colorado	33
C.	State Guidelines for the Utilization of Paralegal Services	34
D.	Paralegal Association Codes of Ethics and Guidelines	35
E.	Liability of Paralegals as Agents of Lawyers	35
	Review Questions	37
	Discussion Questions and Hypotheticals	38
	Research Projects and Assignments	39
	Cases for Analysis	40
	Musselman v. Willoughby Corp.	41
	Questions about the Case	43
	Supreme Court of Arizona v. Struthers	44
	Questions about the Case	45
	In re Phillips	46
	Questions about the Case	50
	The Florida Bar v. Abrams	50
	Questions about the Case	52
	In re Estate of Divine	52
	Questions about the Case	56

3. Unauthorized Practice of Law 57

A.	A Brief History of Unauthorized Practice of Law	58
	1. The Early Years	58
	2. Recent UPL History: Nonlawyer Legal Service Providers and Access to Legal Services	59
	3. Other Recent UPL Activity	63
B.	Practice of Law Defined	64
C.	The Lawyer's Responsibility to Prevent the Unauthorized Practice of Law	67
D.	What Constitutes the Practice of Law	68
	1. Court Appearances	68
	2. Giving Legal Advice	71
	3. Establishing the Lawyer-Client Relationship and Setting Fees	74
E.	Paralegal Tasks That May Constitute the Unauthorized Practice of Law	75
	1. Common Paralegal Functions	75
	2. Will Executions	75
	3. Real Estate Closings and Related Matters	76
	4. Negotiating Settlements	77
	Review Questions	78
	Discussion Questions and Hypotheticals	79
	Research Projects and Assignments	83
F.	Practice Before Administrative Agencies	86
G.	Disclosure of Paralegal Status and Job Titles	88
H.	Paralegals Working as Independent Contractors	92
	Review Questions	93
	Discussion Questions and Hypotheticals	93
	Research Projects and Assignments	94
	Cases for Analysis	95
	State v. Foster	95
	Questions about the Case	97
	Board of Commissioners of the Utah State Bar v. Petersen	98
	Questions about the Case	100
	In re Finch	100
	Questions about the Case	109
	In re Reynoso	109
	Questions about the Case	111
	People v. Landlords Professional Services	112
	Questions about the Case	115
	Brockey v. Moore	115

	Questions about the Case	117
	In re Morin	118
	Questions about the Case	121
	Cincinnati Bar Ass'n v. Mullaney	121
	Questions about the Case	125

4. Confidentiality 127

A.	The Principle of Confidentiality	128
B.	Attorney-Client Privilege	128
	1. Defined Generally	128
	2. How the Privilege Applies to Paralegals	129
	3. How the Protection of the Privilege Can Be Lost	130
	4. Matters Not Covered by the Privilege	131
	5. Inadvertent Disclosure of Privileged Information	132
	6. Exceptions to the Privilege/Permissive Disclosure	134
	7. The Privilege in the Corporate Setting	135
	8. Asserting the Privilege and Court-Ordered Disclosure	136
C.	Work Product	137
	Review Questions	138
	Discussion Questions and Hypotheticals	139
	Research Projects and Assignments	140
D.	Ethics Rules of Confidentiality	142
E.	Paralegals and the Rules on Confidentiality	143
	1. Application of the Rule to Paralegals	143
	2. Protecting Confidentiality in Daily Practice	144
	3. Special Issues Relating to Technology	147
	4. More on Inadvertent Disclosure	152
	Review Questions	155
	Discussion Questions and Hypotheticals	156
	Research Projects and Assignments	157
	Cases for Analysis	159
	HPD Laboratories, Inc. v. Clorox Co.	159
	Questions about the Case	161
	Genovese v. Provident Life Ins. Co.	162
	Questions about the Case	164
	Victor Stanley, Inc. v. Creative Pipe, Inc.	165
	Questions about the Case	171
	Merits Incentives, LLC v. Eighth Judicial District Court of the State of Nevada	171
	Questions about the Case	174
	Rico v. Mitsubishi Motors Corp.	174

Questions about the Case	180
State v. Lenarz	181
Questions about the Case	185
McDermott Will & Emery LLP v. Superior Court	185
Questions about the Case	191
Guo Wengui v. Clark Hill, PLC	191
Questions about the Case	196

5. Conflicts of Interest 197

A.	Introduction	198
B.	Simultaneous or Concurrent Representation	199
C.	Successive Representation	205
D.	Attorney as Witness	207
	Paralegal as Witness	207
	Review Questions	208
	Discussion Questions and Hypotheticals	209
	Research Projects and Assignments	210
E.	Other Conflicts in Relationships with Clients	211
	1. Business Transactions with Clients	211
	Business Transaction Conflicts Involving Paralegals	212
	2. Publication, Literary, and Media Rights	212
	3. Financial Assistance to Clients	213
	4. Lawyer's Interest in Litigation	213
	5. Gifts from Clients	214
	Gifts from Clients to Paralegals	214
	6. Agreements with Clients Limiting the Attorney's Malpractice Liability	215
	7. Payment of Attorneys' Fees by a Third Party	215
	8. Relatives and Close Friends	216
	Relatives of Paralegals	217
F.	Imputed Disqualification	218
	1. Introduction	218
	2. ABA and State Rules on Imputation of Conflicts and Screening	218
	3. Court Rulings on Imputed Disqualification	219
	4. Use of Screens to Avoid Disqualification	220
	Screening Paralegals and Other Nonlawyer Employees	222
G.	Conflicts Checks	226
	Review Questions	228
	Discussion Questions and Hypotheticals	229
	Research Projects and Assignments	232

Cases for Analysis	233
Phoenix Founders, Inc. v. Marshall	233
Questions about the Case	236
Lamb v. Pralex Corp.	236
Questions about the Case	240
Hayes v. Central States Orthopedic Specialists, Inc.	240
Questions about the Case	242
Leibowitz v. District Court	242
Questions about the Case	247
In re Guaranty Ins. Services, Inc.	247
Questions about the Case	253
Ullman v. Denco, Inc., et al.	253
Questions about the Case	257
Sheppard, Mullin, Richter & Hampton, LLP v. J-M Manufacturing Co.	258
Questions about the Case	263

6. Advertising and Solicitation — 265

A. Advertising	266
1. Background and History	266
2. Case Law on Advertising	268
3. Ethics Rules on Advertising	270
4. Application of the Rules to Electronic Communications	273
B. Solicitation	279
Review Questions	282
Discussion Questions and Hypotheticals	282
Research Projects and Assignments	285
Cases for Analysis	286
Bates v. State Bar of Arizona	286
Questions about the Case	292
Searcy v. The Florida Bar, et. al.	292
Questions about the Case	296
In the Matter of Cartmel	297
Questions about the Case	298
Ohralik v. Ohio State Bar Association	299
Questions about the Case	303
Hunter v. Virginia State Bar	303
Questions about the Case	308
Gibson v. Texas Dept. of Ins. Div. of Workers' Comp.	309
Questions about the Case	313

7. Fees and Client Funds — 315

A.	Fee Arrangements with Clients	316
	1. Fixed Fees	316
	2. Contingency Fees	316
	3. Hourly Fees	318
	4. Alternative Fee Arrangements	318
	5. Billing for Paralegal Time	319
	6. Ethics Rules on Fees	320
B.	Terms and Communication of Fee Arrangements with Clients	324
C.	Court-Awarded Attorneys' Fees	328
	Review Questions	333
	Discussion Questions and Hypotheticals	334
	Research Projects and Assignments	335
D.	Fee Splitting, Referral Fees, and Partnerships Between Nonlawyers and Lawyers	337
E.	Client Funds and Property	341
	Review Questions	345
	Discussion Questions and Hypotheticals	346
	Research Projects and Assignments	347
	Cases for Analysis	348
	Missouri v. Jenkins	348
	Questions about the Case	355
	Richlin Security Service Co. v. Chertoff	355
	Questions about the Case	360
	Taylor v. Chubb	360
	Questions about the Case	363
	Mogck v. UNUM Life Insurance Company of America	363
	Questions about the Case	367
	GreatAmerica Leasing v. Cool Comfort Air Conditioning and Refrigeration, Inc.	367
	Questions about the Case	370
	Perez v. Cate	370
	Questions about the Case	374
	St. Farm Mutual Automobile Ins. Co. v. Edge Family Chiropractic	375
	Questions about the Case	378
	Sanford v. GMRI, Inc.	378
	Questions about the Case	381
	Cincinnati Bar Assn. v. Kathman	381
	Questions about the Case	385

8. Competence — 387

A.	Introduction	388
B.	Legal Education	388
C.	Paralegal Education	389
D.	A Definition of Competency	391
	1. Knowledge	392
	2. Professional Skills	393
	3. Thoroughness and Preparation	393
	4. Diligence and Promptness	393
	5. Communication with Clients	394
E.	Consequences of Failure to Act Competently	394
F.	Current Developments and Issues re: Competence	396
G.	Avoiding Malpractice	399
H.	Factors Affecting Paralegal Competence	401
	Review Questions	404
	Discussion Questions and Hypotheticals	406
	Research Projects and Assignments	407
	Cases for Analysis	409
	In re Gillaspy	409
	Questions about the Case	411
	Mississippi Bar v. Thompson	411
	Questions about the Case	416
	People v. Smith	417
	Questions about the Case	424
	Pincay v. Andrews	424
	Questions about the Case	429
	Tegman v. Accident & Medical Investigations	429
	Questions about the Case	435
	Zamora v. Clayborn Contracting Group, Inc.	435
	Questions about the Case	440
	Official Comm. of Unsecured Creditors of Motors Liquidation Co. v. JPMorgan Chase Bank, N.A. (In re Motors Liquidation Co.)	440
	Questions about the Case	444
	Abbott Laboratories, et al. v. Adelphia Supply USA	445
	Questions about the Case	451

9. Special Issues in Advocacy 453

A.	Introduction	454
B.	Unmeritorious Claims, Delay, and Discovery Abuse	455
C.	Disruption in the Courtroom and Disobeying Court Orders	458
D.	Candor and Honesty	461
	Review Questions	464
	Discussion Questions and Hypotheticals	464
	Research Projects and Assignments	466
E.	Relationships and Communications with Others	467
	1. Judges	467
	2. Jurors	469
	3. Parties and Unrepresented Persons	470
	4. Witnesses	472
F.	Trial Publicity	474
G.	Special Rules for Prosecutors	475
H.	Electronic Resources	476
	Review Questions	479
	Discussion Questions and Hypotheticals	480
	Research Projects and Assignments	481
	Cases for Analysis	483
	Bonda Industrial (HK) Co., Ltd. v. Talbot Group, LLC	483
	Questions about the Case	488
	Massey v. Prince George's County	488
	Questions about the Case	491
	Crane v. State Bar of California	492
	Questions about the Case	494
	Omaha Bank v. Siouxland Cattle Cooperative	494
	Questions about the Case	496
	Eaton v. Fink	497
	Questions about the Case	499
	In re Ositis	499
	Questions about the Case	501
	Sayhers v. Prugh	501
	Questions about the Case	504

10. Professionalism — 505

A.	The State of Professionalism in the Legal Field	506
B.	Professionalism and the Paralegal	512
	1. Commitment to Legal Services	514
	2. Commitment to Education	514
	3. Commitment to the Highest Standards of Ethical Conduct	514
	4. Commitment to Excellence	515
	5. Commitment to the Paralegal Profession	515
	6. Commitment to a Strong Work Ethic	515
	7. Commitment to Acting with Integrity and Honor	515
	8. Commitment to Balance as a Person	515
	9. Commitment to Good Judgment, Common Sense, and Communication	516
C.	Current Issues in Professionalism	516
D.	Pro Bono Work	520
	Review Questions	522
	Discussion Questions and Hypotheticals	523
	Research Projects and Assignments	523

Glossary   527
Table of Cases   533
Index   537

Preface

New to the Ninth Edition

This book was written and first published 30 years ago. This year, the book was primarily authored by Sybil Taylor Aytch with Teri Cannon remaining as a valuable contributor.

Approach

This book is written for paralegal students, working paralegals, and lawyers who use their services. It is intended for use primarily as a text but also as a reference for practicing lawyers and paralegals.

It has been over 50 years since the advent of the paralegal profession. What started as a modest proposal to improve the delivery of legal services has become a reality in the profession. Paralegals are embedded in law practices, serving as integral members of the legal services delivery team. Lawyers in all kinds and sizes of private law firms and those in corporations, government, and the public sector rely heavily on paralegals to accomplish their work. Paralegals are highly educated and competent, engaging in sophisticated work in all areas of law practice.

The paralegal occupation has been one of the fastest growing in the country for over 40 years. It is estimated that there are more than 250,000 paralegals employed across the country. The career is well recognized by the general public, and young people learn of and aspire to it. The roles and functions of paralegals continue to expand into new and exciting areas. The prestige of the occupation has also risen.

We have also witnessed tremendous growth and change in the legal profession generally. The many forces of change include the integration of technology, the use of marketing and advertising, greater competitiveness among firms, increased attorney mobility, the development of mega-firms, the impact of a global economy, more complex laws, legal specialization, and virtual work environments. In the past five years, we have seen a dramatic increase in the number of new lawyers entering the profession and a major re-thinking of law practice, including partnership aspirations and less physical time in the office. These changes have affected legal ethics in ways that probably no one anticipated and have the potential for significant changes in the delivery of legal services and the role of paralegals.

The role of nonlawyers in providing legal services directly to the public continues to be a topic of intense debate as the public and the profession seek ways to increase access to services and control costs. In the past five years, a number of jurisdictions have taken steps to formalize the emerging legal paraprofessional role, which is changing the traditional rules governing the practice of law. New ethics opinions and revisions to rules continue to develop in response to this dynamic environment. Paralegals must have a clear understanding of legal ethics—the concepts and rules that guide them in their work. This grounding is essential for paralegals to function competently and with integrity, to be alert to potential ethical dilemmas in their work, to develop a framework for ethical decision making, and to keep abreast of changes in rules as they develop.

Organization and Coverage of the Ninth Edition

The book is comprehensive and covers all the major areas of legal ethics, placing special emphasis on how the rules affect paralegals. The book begins with a chapter on lawyer regulation because paralegals must understand how the profession is regulated to understand their place in it and the impact of their conduct on the lawyers who employ them. Chapter 2 contains a brief history of the paralegal career, the ways the occupation is regulated, and the growth of voluntary paralegal certification and other moves toward licensing. This chapter examines ethics guidelines for paralegals developed by courts, legislatures, and bar and paralegal associations. Chapter 3 covers the unauthorized practice of law, introducing the history of UPL and definitions of the practice of law, explaining functions that either are prohibited to nonlawyers or are on the borderline. Chapters 2 and 3 both include material on the provision of legal services directly to clients by nonlawyers and updated information on ways to increase access to legal services through other licensed professionals. Chapter 4 covers confidentiality. In discussing the attorney-client privilege, the work product rule, and ethics rules regarding confidentiality, the chapter outlines the duties of paralegals and ways to avoid breaches of confidentiality. Special emphasis is given to inadvertent disclosure and the impact of technology on protected communications.

Chapter 5 covers conflicts of interest, a critical concern given the mobility of lawyers, clients, and paralegals. The chapter includes an in-depth discussion of conflicts rules and how to avoid conflicts, including the use of screens and conflicts checks. Chapter 6 covers rules regarding legal advertising and solicitation, with a discussion of trends in marketing legal services, including the use of social media. Chapter 7 is devoted to financial matters that arise in the representation of clients and between lawyers and paralegals. It discusses billing, fees, statutory fee awards that include compensation for paralegal work, fee splitting, referral fees, partnerships between attorneys and nonlawyers, compensation of paralegals, and handling client funds. Chapter 8 defines the concept of competence specifically in relation to paralegals and includes a discussion of malpractice. Special issues facing litigation paralegals, including communications with clients, courts, parties, and witnesses are covered in Chapter 9. This chapter has been expanded to include technology-related issues, including generative artificial intelligence. Finally, Chapter 10 examines professionalism and issues facing paralegals in today's law firm environment, including titles, overtime, regulation and changing roles, diversity, and *pro bono* work.

Key Features

Each chapter begins with an overview that describes in a few words the main topics of the chapter. The text body of each chapter is divided topically. Key terms are spelled out in italics when first introduced and are highlighted in the margins and included in the glossary. Review questions at the end of each chapter test each student's memory and understanding of the material. Discussion questions and hypotheticals follow the review questions. These may be assigned to students or used for in-class discussion. Research and outside assignments are also included so students apply their knowledge and skills outside of class through legal or factual research or analysis of cases or issues. Cases at the end of the chapters demonstrate how the rules introduced in the chapters are applied specifically to paralegals. Some cases present key principles with which all paralegals should be familiar. Others are landmark cases that involve paralegals. A few new cases in the ninth edition reflect the changes taking place as courts address the application of ethics rules to paralegals.

Recognizing that every paralegal program teaches ethics, but each in its own way, we have chosen a comprehensive approach so that professors may use the entire book in full courses on legal ethics or use only selected parts in programs that teach ethics in several courses or across the curriculum. The accompanying Instructor's Manual provides guidance for instructors who want to incorporate ethics material into their substantive courses.

Acknowledgments

We have many people to thank for their support and assistance with this edition of the book. Recognition must go first to the many entities that are in the forefront of the paralegal profession, including the American Association for Paralegal Education, National Association of Legal Assistants, National Federation of Paralegal Associations, and International Practice Management Association.

Our heartfelt appreciation also goes to the wonderful people at Aspen, especially Denise Clinton, Betsy Kenny, and Sharon Ray. Their patience, warmth, intelligence, and talents made this book possible.

We wish to thank those who have given permission for the use of excerpts from the following:

Ethical Considerations of the American Bar Association, Code of Professional Responsibility and Canons of Judicial Ethics (1970); ABA Informal Opinions (1971; 1976; 1988; 1989); ABA Formal Ethics Opinion 09-455 (2009); ABA Model Rules of Professional Conduct (2022); and material from ABA Standing Committee on Paralegals (2023), copyright © by the American Bar Association. Reprinted with permission. All rights reserved. This information or any portion thereof may not be copied or disseminated in any form or by any means or stored in an electronic database or retrieval system without the express written consent of the American Bar Association.

Ethics and Professional Responsibility for Paralegals

Regulation of Lawyers

This chapter provides basic background on the regulation of lawyers. Paralegals, who work under the supervision of lawyers, need to understand the rules governing lawyer conduct and how those rules affect them. Chapter 1 covers:

- the inherent power of the courts over the practice of law
- the organized bar's participation in lawyer regulation
- the role of the legislature and statutes in governing the conduct of lawyers
- codes of conduct for lawyers
- sanctions for misconduct and other actions against lawyers

A. State Courts and Bar Associations

Like other professions that affect the public interest, the legal profession is subject to regulation by the states. Unlike other regulated professions, however, regulation of the legal profession falls mainly to the judiciary rather than the legislature. Because of the function of lawyers in the court system and the separation of powers, the judiciary has historically asserted inherent authority over lawyers.

The highest court in each state and in the District of Columbia is responsible for making rules related to law practice admission and to lawyers' ethical conduct. The codes of ethical conduct promulgated by the states' highest courts include mechanisms for disciplining lawyers who violate the codes. Most state legislatures have also passed statutes that supplement the ethical rules adopted by the courts. Some states consider legislative authority over the practice of law to be concurrent with judicial authority; others consider legislative action to be only in aid of judicial action. A few state supreme courts have allowed the legislature to assert substantial authority over the practice of law. For example, the New York State Legislature has the power to regulate the legal profession and has vested the power to impose sanctions on lawyers with the intermediate courts (which are called supreme courts in New York, although they are not the highest state courts).

Sometimes the judiciary and the legislature have conflicting ideas about matters affecting the practice of law, and a court will be called on to strike down legislation that attempts to regulate some aspect of the legal profession. Several state supreme courts have held unconstitutional legislation that would have authorized nonlawyers to engage in conduct that the court considered to be the practice of law. (See the *Bennion* and *UPL Committee* cases at the end of this chapter for examples.) Local court rules also govern attorneys' conduct in matters before the courts.

In practice, many state supreme courts rely heavily on state bar associations to carry out their responsibilities for regulating the practice of law. These courts have delegated authority to the bar to alleviate the burden of handling disciplinary cases.

Integrated bar
A bar association in which the mandatory and voluntary aspects of bar activities are combined, and membership is required.

Some state bar associations are ***integrated***, which means that membership is compulsory. In a state with an integrated bar, annual dues to renew the practitioner's law license carry automatic membership in the state bar. Some states have purely voluntary state bar associations; funds to operate the admissions and disciplinary functions in the state are derived from annual licensing or registration fees. Integrated bars generally play a more active role in the admissions and disciplinary functions of the court and in other matters relating to the legal profession. In addition to state bar associations, hundreds of voluntary "specialty" bar associations have been established in the last 15 years as a result of the trend away from lawyers practicing in several areas or "general" law practice to increasingly specialized areas, like probate, real estate, family law, and civil litigation.

Many lawyer disciplinary systems have expanded and reformed in recent years to respond to the growth in complaints about lawyers that has accompanied the growth of the legal profession. Mediation and arbitration are now widely used in disputes between lawyers and clients. Integrated bars and disciplinary authorities also offer or require ethics training for lawyers, conduct random audits of client trust accounts, and some have adopted ethics rules that provide for firm-wide responsibility for ethical breaches. Programs for lawyers with substance abuse and emotional problems have expanded into all jurisdictions. Disciplinary proceedings and records have been made more transparent and open to the public. The courts and the bar understand that to retain control over the legal profession through self-regulation, lawyers must be accountable to the public.

Concerns about the role of lawyers in corporate scandals have resulted in the federal government's adoption of new rules governing the conduct of lawyers advising corporations in matters relating to securities law. The Sarbanes-Oxley Act of 2002 (15 U.S.C. §7201, *et seq*) led to the Securities and Exchange Commission's adoption of rules that require lawyers to report suspected violations of securities laws up the ladder within the corporate governance structure. Not all attempts of the federal government to regulate lawyers have been successful, however.

Some federal cases involve limited application of consumer protection laws to lawyers, in recognition of two important principles: that lawyers are regulated by the states and that lawyers are regulated by the courts. (See *American Bar Ass'n v. F.T.C.*, 430 F.3d 457 (D.C. Cir. 2005).) In another related case, lawyers have successfully asserted that the laws should not apply to them because they are not defined as "financial institutions" or "creditors" under federal laws protecting against identity theft. (See *American Bar Ass'n v. F.T.C.*, 636 F.3d 641 (D.C. Cir. 2011).) However, lawyers may be subject to state and federal laws when they seek to collect debts for clients under state and federal fair debt collection laws. (See, for example, *Heintz v. Johnson*, 514 U.S. 291 (1995).)

B. American Bar Association

All states except one (California) have patterned their ethics rules on the models of the American Bar Association (ABA). The ABA is a national voluntary professional association of lawyers, which currently has about 400,000 members out of almost 1.5 million lawyers in the country. Over 100 years old, the ABA is the chief national professional association for lawyers, asserting a strong voice in matters affecting revision and development of the law, the judiciary, and the administration of justice. Among its many contributions to the profession is the promulgation of model codes of ethics.

The ABA first published the **Canons of Professional Ethics** in 1908. These Canons were patterned after the first code of ethics for lawyers adopted in 1887 by the Alabama State Bar Association. Prior to the adoption of state codes, lawyer conduct was governed largely by common law and some statutes. The 1908 Canons consisted of 32 statements of very general principles about attorney conduct, mainly conduct in the courtroom. Many states adopted these ABA Canons through court rule or statute.

In 1964, the ABA began work on a new set of ethical guidelines at the request of its then-president, Lewis F. Powell, Jr., who later served on the U.S. Supreme Court. This new code, called the **Model Code of Professional Responsibility**, was published in 1969. It was designed as a prototype for states to use in developing their own codes. The Model Code, which was adopted at least in part by every state, contained:

- **Canons**, or statements of general concepts;
- **Disciplinary Rules**, or mandatory rule statements; and
- **Ethical Considerations**, or interpretive comments that are aspirational or advisory.

Although the Model Code was widely adopted, events in the legal field led to a call for a revised code within a very short time. Watergate was one of the most pivotal of these events. The misconduct of lawyers in the Watergate scandal damaged the public image of lawyers. Also during this period, the U.S. Supreme Court decided several cases relating to the legal profession that struck down rules prohibiting lawyer advertising. Further, changes in law practice brought about by economic developments and the proliferation of new laws resulted in more and different kinds of ethical problems that were not addressed effectively in the Model Code.

In 1977, the ABA established a new body to revisit the Model Code. The Commission on the Evaluation of Professional Standards, which came to be known as the Kutak Commission after its chair, developed the Model Rules of Professional Conduct, which were adopted by the ABA in 1983. The Model Rules are formatted differently than the Model Code; the difference between mandatory and aspirational language was eliminated and the rules are written as directives and followed by interpretive comments.

Specific amendments have been made many times to the ABA Model Rules since they were adopted. Recent changes of most interest to paralegals are in the areas of electronic communications and records, confidentiality and conflicts of interest, advertising and solicitation, and nonlawyers outside the law firm. These will be discussed in the relevant chapters of this book. The ABA also publishes several other models, such as the Model Code of Judicial Conduct, Model Rules on Admission by Motion, Temporary Practice by Foreign Lawyers, and Licensing and

C. Statutes and Other Forms of Regulation

Although the state codes of ethics contain most of the rules with which we are concerned in this text, attorney conduct is also governed by **statutes**. For example, some states have statutes that prohibit attorneys from engaging in certain conduct in their professional capacity as lawyers and provide for criminal and civil penalties. As we will see in Chapter 3, several states have laws that make the unauthorized practice of law a crime, usually a misdemeanor. Federal securities law, referred to earlier in Section A, is another example of how legislatures govern the conduct of lawyers.

Usually not binding on attorneys but often consulted when ethical issues arise are ***ethics opinions*** of state and local bar associations and the ABA. Bar associations have ethics committees that consider ethical dilemmas posed to them by attorney-members. The committees write opinions that are published in bar journals and on their websites to give additional guidance to lawyers facing similar dilemmas. Some state and ABA advisory opinions, especially those that involve paralegals, are cited in this text.

Ethics opinions
Written opinions issued by a bar association interpreting relevant ethical precedents and applying them to an ethical dilemma.

D. Sanctions for Lawyer Misconduct

Three main formal sanctions can be imposed on lawyers for ethical misconduct by the state's highest court or other disciplinary body. The most severe sanction is ***disbarment***, in which a lawyer's license to practice law is revoked. Disbarment is only imposed for the most egregious violations or when there is a sustained pattern of serious unethical conduct. Although disbarment is in theory permanent, some admitting authorities allow for re-admission of a disbarred lawyer after some period of time if the lawyer demonstrates complete rehabilitation.

The second most severe sanction is ***suspension***, in which the lawyer is deprived of the right to practice law for a specified period of time. Some disciplinary authorities also exercise the option of imposing ***probation***, under which the disciplined lawyer may continue to practice on the condition that certain requirements are met, such as restitution to injured clients, passing an ethics examination, attending ethics training, or participating in counseling. The suspension is stayed, but the lawyer

Disbarment
Rescinding of a lawyer's license to practice.

Suspension
Lawyer is deprived of the right to practice law for a specified period of time.

Probation
Lawyer can practice, but certain requirements must be met.

remains on probation for some period, during which the disciplinary body may reinstitute the suspension if further ethical violations come to light. Probation may also be imposed following a suspension to allow the disciplinary body ongoing close monitoring of the lawyer.

Reprimand, Reproval, and Admonition
Lawyer is warned that ethical violations have occurred and further violations will warrant a more severe sanction.

The mildest sanction is a ***reprimand***, sometimes called a ***reproval*** or an ***admonition***. This represents a slap on the hand, a warning that the conduct will not be tolerated. Reprimands may be public—placed in the public record—or private—confidentially communicated in writing to the attorney (usually called an admonition). This kind of sanction becomes part of the attorney's record at the court or the state bar. It is considered in determining the appropriate sanction if other violations occur.

In deciding the appropriate sanction, the disciplinary body considers the nature and severity of the offense and whether the attorney has a record of prior misconduct. Other **aggravating and mitigating factors** may be taken into account, such as:

- the extent to which the lawyer cooperated in the investigation and appreciates the seriousness of the matter
- the lawyer's reputation and contributions to the community through public service and professional activities
- the circumstances surrounding the offense and the extent to which these make the lawyer more or less culpable for the conduct
- whether the offense was a one-time incident because of specific circumstances or is likely to be repeated
- the degree to which the lawyer is remorseful and willing to remedy the problems that led to the discipline.

For more information on how sanctions are imposed, see *ABA Standards for Imposing Lawyer Sanctions*, adopted in 1986, revised in 1992, and reaffirmed in 2019.

E. Other Actions for Lawyer Misconduct

Legal malpractice
Improper conduct in the performance of duties by a legal professional, either intentionally or through negligence.

In addition to direct discipline by the court or state bar, a lawyer may be **prosecuted criminally** for violations of statutes governing lawyer conduct or conduct that may relate to a lawyer's practice, such as laws prohibiting solicitation of clients in hospitals and jails and laws limiting the methods that can be used to collect debts. Civil ***legal malpractice*** lawsuits brought by former clients also constitute a major incentive for conforming to ethical requirements and standards of practice. (See Chapter 8 on Competence for more on legal malpractice.) Judges exercise *contempt* **power** to sanction lawyers appearing before them who engage in improper conduct that affects the administration of justice and the smooth functioning of the courts. (See Chapter 9 on Special Issues in Advocacy.) The courts also play a major role in deciding on matters in conflicts of interest because they rule on **motions to** *disqualify* **counsel**, usually brought by the opposing counsel, who claims that a lawyer or law firm has a conflict of interest that jeopardizes client confidentiality. (See Chapter 5 on Conflicts of Interest.)

Contempt
Improper conduct that impairs the administration of the courts or shows disrespect for the dignity or authority of the court.

Disqualification
A court order that a lawyer or law firm may not continue to represent a client in a litigated matter before it.

REVIEW QUESTIONS

1. What branch of government is primarily responsible for regulating attorney conduct? What level of government? State or federal?
2. What role do state bar associations play in governing lawyer conduct?
3. What role do the state and federal legislatures play in governing the conduct of lawyers?
4. What is an integrated bar? How does it differ from a voluntary bar? What is a specialty bar?
5. What is the American Bar Association? What role, if any, does it play in overseeing lawyer conduct? In ethics generally?
6. When did the states first begin to adopt ethics codes?
7. Name and describe the different versions of model ethics rules that have been adopted by the ABA.
8. What are ethics opinions? Who writes them? Are they binding on attorneys?
9. Name and describe the three main direct sanctions for lawyer misconduct that are enforced by the highest state court or state bar.
10. Name some other actions that can be taken to address lawyer misconduct besides those that are imposed by disciplinary authorities.

DISCUSSION QUESTIONS AND HYPOTHETICALS

1. Do you think that lawyers and paralegals should be governed by the states or at the national level? Why? Consider how things have changed since ethics rules were first adopted—in the economy, the practice of law, and the nature of legal work. How does the growing globalization of legal work and law practice affect your thinking?
2. Should there be separate rules that govern lawyers in international practice? How should these interface with state ethics rules and state and federal laws?

RESEARCH PROJECTS AND ASSIGNMENTS

1. Is your state's bar integrated? Does the legislature share in governing lawyers in some way, such as funding for the courts or setting dues for bar membership? Does the judiciary work closely with the bar on matters relating to admission and discipline?
2. What laws in your state govern lawyer conduct? What do these laws say? Where are they found in the state statutes?
3. When were the current rules of ethics in your state adopted? Does your state follow the ABA rules exactly or are some of the provisions different? If some are different, which ones, and why?
4. Does your state or local bar association publish ethics opinions? If so, where do you find them? Are there any ethics opinions relating to paralegals in your state?
5. Has your state's highest court decided any cases in which the authority of the legislature to regulate attorneys was an issue? If so, what did the court decide?
6. Read the SEC rules adopted pursuant to Sarbanes-Oxley that govern the conduct of lawyers (17 C.F.R. Part 205). Do you think that these provisions impinge on the inherent authority of the courts to govern lawyer conduct?
7. Read the two cases brought by the ABA against the FTC, and cited above in this chapter. Do you agree with these decisions? Should lawyers be subject to federal laws such as these? Why? What would have been the impact of the decisions if they had been decided the other way? Be sure to compare and distinguish the two cases.

CASES FOR ANALYSIS

In this case, the state's highest court exercised its exclusive authority over the practice of law to endorse legislation that authorized nonlawyers to assist persons in ways that are typically categorized as the practice of law.

Unauthorized Practice of Law Committee v. State Department of Workers' Compensation
543 A.2d 662 (R.I. 1988)

This case comes before us on appeal by the defendants from a judgment entered in the Superior Court declaring portions of two statutes enacted by the General Assembly (citations omitted) unconstitutional as violative of this court's exclusive power to regulate the practice of law. We reverse. . . .

At its 1985 session the General Assembly enacted a set of comprehensive statutory provisions that created a Department of Workers' Compensation. . . .

The General Assembly, in attempting to implement the scheme of establishing informal hearings within the department as an initial procedure to supplement the formal hearings before the Workers' Compensation Commission, created an office of employee assistants. The function and purpose of these employee assistants are set forth in §42-94-5 as follows:

> The director of the department of workers' compensation shall provide adequate funding for an office of employee assistants and shall, subject to the personnel law, appoint the assistants to the staff of the department. Assistants should, at a minimum, demonstrate a level of expertise roughly equivalent to that of insurance claims analysts or adjusters. The purpose of employee assistants shall be to provide advice and assistance to employees under the workers' compensation act and particularly to assist employees in preparing for and assisting at informal conferences under §28-33-1.1. . . .

In the course of proceedings in the Superior Court, evidence was adduced concerning regulations of the Department of Workers' Compensation and also a position description filed in the department of personnel which defined the duties of employee assistants as follows:

> To provide technical advice and assistance to various parties involving their rights and obligations under the Workers' Compensation Act.
>
> To assist the injured employee in preparation for and at informal Workers' Compensation hearings, and to help in providing the necessary documentation at said hearings.
>
> To provide both routine and technical advice and/or information to the general public regarding rights and responsibilities under the Workers' Compensation Act.
>
> To attempt to settle disputes between injured workers, insurance companies, employers, purveyors of services, and any other interested parties prior to an informal hearing.
>
> To conduct in person interviews; both in office and field.
>
> To gather and prepare information necessary for use at informal hearings.
>
> To do related work as required.

At the conclusion of the presentation of evidence and argument in the Superior Court, the trial justice held that the duties of the employee assistants constituted the practice of law under definitions recognized by this court. . . .

It has long been the law of this state that the definition of the practice of law and the determination concerning who may practice law is exclusively within the province of this court and, further, that the

Legislature may act in aid of this power but may not grant the right to anyone to practice law save in accordance with standards enunciated by this court. (Citations omitted.)

However, it should be noted that since 1935 the General Assembly has without interference by this court permitted a great many services that would have come within the definition of the practice of law to be performed by insurance adjusters, town clerks, bank employees, certified public accountants, interstate commerce practitioners, public accountants (other than certified public accountants), as well as employee assistants. The plain fact of the matter is that each of these exceptions enacted by the Legislature constituted a response to a public need. In each instance the Legislature determined that the persons authorized to carry out the permitted activities were qualified to do so. . . .

We must remember that the practice of law at a given time cannot be easily defined. Nor should it be subject to such rigid and traditional definition as to ignore the public interest. . . .

We are of the opinion that the informal hearings, together with lay representation, may well serve the public interest. We concluded from the evidence introduced that the employee assistants will be adequately trained to carry out the relatively simple and repetitive functions which they will be called upon to perform. We do require, however, that in the event an employee is denied compensation at such a hearing the employee be given an opportunity to consult with an attorney of his choice in order to determine whether he or she will appeal to the Workers' Compensation Commission. This consultation should be paid for at state expense at a reasonable fee to be determined by the director. In the event that an attorney chooses to represent the employee before the commission, such attorney would be paid by the employer if the employee prevails as presently provided by law. See G.L. 1956 (1986 Reenactment) §28-35-32.

In authorizing the employee assistants to carry out the functions authorized by §42-94-5, we are dealing with a question of first impression and are relying to a great extent upon the legislative findings that declare the necessity for an informal prompt hearing in the event of controversy. Therefore, this grant of authorization is made upon a somewhat experimental basis. Consequently we shall leave the matter open for the Unauthorized Practice of Law Committee to come again before the court in the event that the public, and particularly employees, are not adequately protected by the services of the employee assistants. Meanwhile the act may be implemented in the form in which it is presently cast, with the single modification set forth in this opinion.

For the reasons stated, the defendants' appeal is sustained. The judgment of the Superior Court is reversed. The papers in the case may be remanded to the Superior Court with directions to enter judgment for the defendants but without prejudice to the plaintiff to bring a new complaint in the event that the public interest shall so warrant in the future, as indicated heretofore in this opinion.

MURRAY, Justice, dissenting.

I respectfully disagree with the majority. I would affirm the trial justice's decision on the basis that the language in G.L. 1956 (1984 Reenactment) §42-94-5, as amended by P.L. 1986, ch.1, §3, allows a group of nonlicensed employees to perform duties which are equivalent to those reserved for qualified, licensed attorneys. Employee assistants who engage in the unauthorized practice of law serve to the detriment of the public, and this court, by permitting such conduct, compromises established professional standards requisite for the proper administration of justice. . . .

Questions about the Case

1. How did the Rhode Island Supreme Court come to hear this case? What was the lower court's ruling?
2. What system did the Workers' Compensation statute establish that was objectionable to the lower court?
3. Examine the definitions of the practice of law in Chapter 3 and evaluate whether employee assistants functioning under the authority of this statute would be engaging in the "practice of law."
4. What are the reasons that this court decided to endorse the legislation? Are these good reasons? Why was the outcome different from that in *Bennion*, above?
5. What does the court say about other inroads into the practice of law by nonlawyers? Is this important to the court's ruling?
6. Does the court abdicate its exclusive authority over the practice of law?

In the following case, the state's highest court affirmed the ruling of the Superior Court in enjoining a law school graduate who was not admitted to practice law from engaging in the unauthorized practice of law.

State Bar of Arizona v. Lang
No. 1 CA-CV 12-0629 (Ariz. Ct. App. 2014)

Petitioner is a law school graduate and is admitted to practice law in the San Carlos Apache Tribal Court. He has never been admitted to the practice of law by the Arizona Supreme Court and was enjoined from practicing law in Arizona by order of the Maricopa County Superior Court based on evidence that he repeatedly engaged in the unauthorized practice of law. The Arizona Supreme Court affirmed the Superior Court decision, stating that "the injunction is reasonable in its scope."

Pursuant to Ariz. R. Sup. Ct. 32(a), the Bar is tasked with regulating and disciplining persons engaged in the practice of law in Arizona. From 2007 to 2009, the Bar received a series of reports that Lang had engaged in the unauthorized practice of law. After each report was received, Lang was notified by the Bar which demanded that he cease any activity defined under Ariz. R. Sup. Ct. 31 as the practice of law. Lang did not comply with these demands. The Bar commenced an action against him in the Superior Court, alleging five counts of unauthorized practice of law and requested an injunction to prevent Lang from continuing his unlawful conduct. Lang answered and asserted a counterclaim which was later dismissed for lack of prosecution.

In September 2011, the Bar moved for summary judgment on three counts of its complaint and voluntarily withdraw the remaining two counts. Lang objected to the Bar's motion and filed a motion to dismiss Counts 1, 4, and 5 for lack of subject matter jurisdiction.

Count 1—In September 2006, Lang entered an "Attorney-Client Agreement" with T.M., a former professional boxer, "to provide attorney services to Boxer [T.M.] as his personal attorney and counselary on a worldwide basis on all matters concerning Boxer [T.M.]." The agreement was printed on letterhead that showed Lang's name, the name "Integrated Legal Services & Associates," an Arizona address not located on the San Carlos Apache reservation, and Arizona fax and phone numbers, including an "Office" number. Lang signed the contract as "Attorney." Using similar letterhead, Lang again identified himself as T.M.'s "personal attorney" in a letter that he wrote to the Missouri parole board regarding T.M.'s incarcerated brother.

Count 2—In March 2008, Lang met with S.J. in Arizona and agreed to represent S.J., a Washington resident, in a federal employment law matter. In connection with that representation, Lang drafted a notice of appeal in which he identified himself as S.J.'s "Attorney," "Personal Attorney," and "counsel," and indicated that he worked for I.L.S. & Associates in Arizona. I.L.S. & Associates charged S.J. an initial consultation fee and a flat-fee retainer for "Legal Service."

Count 5—In July 2008, Lang entered into an "Attorney-Client Fee Agreement" with J.C., a California resident, by which "DPL, Inc." agreed to provide "legal services." The agreement was prepared by Lang's assistant, who had also helped him to form an Arizona corporation named "Debt Protection, Inc." The agreement was printed on "Debt Protection Legal, Inc." letterhead that showed an Arizona address not on the reservation, toll-free office phone and fax numbers, and an Arizona mobile number for the "Managing Attorney," who was identified in the signature block as Lang.

After oral argument, the Superior Court denied Lang's motion to dismiss and granted summary judgment for the Bar on all three counts. The Court ordered restitution to S.J. and J.C. and entered a permanent injunction restraining Lang from performing acts constituting the practice of law in Arizona. Lang contends that the Superior Court lacked subject matter jurisdiction to consider his conduct, that summary judgment was not warranted based on the undisputed evidence, and that the injunction is overbroad.

Lang entered into a purported "Attorney-Client Agreements" by which he agreed to provide "attorney services" as a "personal attorney" from an office in Arizona located outside the reservation. Lang contends that the agreements were protected commercial speech under the First Amendment. But an attorney's First Amendment interest in commercial speech may yield to the state's interest in regulating the profession, *Gentile v. State Bar of Nev.*, 501 U.S. 1030, 1073 (1991), and "[t]here is 'no constitutional value in false statements of fact.'" *Keeton v. Hustler Magazine, Inc.*, 465 U.S. 770, 776 (1984). Arizona's prohibition against the unauthorized practice of law is not a broad regulation of speech, but a narrowly tailored set of rules aimed at conduct by persons not admitted to the Bar. Lang's speech falls into the zone of speech that the First Amendment allows the state to regulate—his speech was nothing more than an attempt to facilitate unlawful conduct, and he had no First Amendment privilege that could immunize him from the enforcement of the Arizona Supreme Court rules.

The undisputed evidence shows that in his dealings with and for T.M., S.J., and J.C., Lang repeatedly held himself out to be an attorney practicing in an Arizona office. Yet Lang was not admitted to the practice of law by the Arizona Supreme Court. His conduct therefore constituted the unauthorized practice of law under Ariz. R. Sup. Ct. 31(a)(2)(B)(2), 31(b), and 42, E.R. 5.5(b). The Superior Court properly entered summary judgment in the Bar's favor on Counts 1, 4, and 5.

The injunction against Lang is not inconsistent with *Sperry v. Florida*, 373 U.S. 379 (1963). In *Sperry*, the Court held that a practitioner registered to practice before the United States Patent Office, but not licensed to practice law by any state, should not have been enjoined from engaging in his patent practice from Florida. *Id.* at 381, 404. Relying on federal supremacy, *see id.* at 383-85, the Court explained that "the State maintains control over the practice of law within its borders except to the limited extent necessary for the accomplishment of the federal objectives [of the United States Patent Office]" and that "it is entirely reasonable for a practitioner to hold himself out as qualified to perform his specialized work, so long as he does not misrepresent the scope of his license." Id. at 402 & n.47. The San Carlos Apache Tribe is a dependent sovereign nation whose authority to regulate its courts does not enjoy supremacy over the Arizona Supreme Court's authority to regulate the practice of law outside the Tribe's reservation.

Consistent with Ariz. R. Sup. Ct. 31(a)(2)(B)(2), the injunction does not prohibit Lang from referring to his law degree, education, or tribal court admission so long as the reference does not reasonably imply that he is admitted to practice law in Arizona. This limitation is constitutional.

See *Bates v. State Bar of Ariz.*, 433 U.S. 350, 383-84 (1977). Further, the requirement that Lang expressly disclaim admission in Arizona in his letterhead and advertising material is reasonably tailored to prevent client confusion while still recognizing Lang's actual qualifications. We also reject Lang's contention that the injunction should anticipate his future admission to other tribal courts. Should Lang actually become admitted in additional jurisdictions, he may at that time ask the Superior Court to modify the injunction.

Questions about the Case

1. What conduct did Lang engage in that the State Bar alleges constituted the unauthorized practice of law?
2. Is admission to a tribal court analogous to admission to a state supreme court? Why or why not? Identify all necessary steps required by a law school graduate to be admitted to the practice of law by a state supreme court.
3. Did the Superior Court properly grant the State Bar's motion for summary judgment? What was the Court's reasoning for the injunction?
4. What was the basis for Lang's claim that the Superior Court lacked subject matter jurisdiction to consider his conduct?
5. Which rules of the Arizona Supreme Court did the Court primarily rely on in reaching its opinion?
6. Since Lang is enjoined from engaging in the unauthorized practice of law in Arizona, is he precluded from practicing law in another non-tribal jurisdiction in the United States? Is he precluded from practicing law outside of the United States?

In the following case, the court sanctions a lawyer for failure to obtain client signatures prior to filing documents.

In re: Klitsch, et al.
587 B.R. 287 (Bankr. M.D. Pa. 2018)

Law Solutions Chicago LLC, trading as Upright Law LLC ("Upright Law" or "Upright"), is an Illinois-based entity "partnering" with over 400 lawyers nationwide providing consumer bankruptcy services to 6000 plus individuals throughout the country. That entity, and its regional partner, Kevin Tanribilir, (hereinafter "Tanribilir"), are the subject of this sanction motion filed by the bankruptcy Trustee of seven Debtors who have filed in the Middle District of Pennsylvania. The Trustee, William G. Schwab, (hereinafter "Trustee" or "Schwab"), has moved for sanctions against Tanribilir and his so-called partner, Upright, for what the Trustee describes as ethical violations in six cases in which Schwab is Trustee. Schwab seeks a suspension from practice, required attendance at CLE courses, disgorgement of counsel fees, and payment of his own fees in pursuing this sanction motion. More specifically, the Motion predicates relief on 11 U.S.C. § 105 and Local Bankruptcy Rule 2090-2, which reads:

> Rule 2090-2 Attorneys—Discipline and Disbarment.
> (a) Suspension or Disbarment from Practice. This court has the power and authority to govern, control, and discipline the conduct of attorneys appearing before it, including the power to suspend or disbar attorneys from practice before it.
> (b) Failure to Appear. An attorney who fails to appear without just cause on a matter before the court or as counsel for a debtor fails to attend the debtor's § 341(a) meeting, may be subject to discipline by the court.
> (c) Failure to Prepare. An attorney who, without just cause, fails to adequately prepare for any pretrial conference, hearing, or trial may be subject to discipline by the court.

The thrust of Schwab's Motion is that the filings are being made prior to the execution by the clients of the petition and related documents and Tanribilir, individually and as an agent of Upright, is performing subpar work for his clients. Schwab also grouses somewhat about the internet solicitations advanced by Upright, but he makes no direct accusations against the Illinois firm in the Motion except to imply it is allowing unlicensed individuals to provide legal advice.

At hearing, Tanribilir testified and acknowledged that multiple documents were filed without being signed by the Debtors. In fact, Tanribilir admitted in an affidavit . . . that there were no "wet signatures in advance of filing . . . , which I understood to mean that these Debtors simply failed to affix their signatures to these petitions, schedules, and statements in advance of their filings. Tanribilir maintains that the clients authorized him to execute the documents on their behalf. Tanribilir further alleges that advance "wet" signatures were obtained from Shiner, Valukevich, and Ould. Notwithstanding that assertion, Respondents argue that there is no *per se* requirement that a "wet" signature be obtained from a filing debtor. Schwab argues that before a petition, list, schedule, statement, or amendment can be filed with the Court, counsel must obtain a wet-signed (pen to paper) document by the client.

Some districts require that the original signature be "wet ink" signatures. *In re Stomberg*, 487 B.R. 775, 823 (Bankr. S.D. Tex. 2013); *In re Bradley*, 495 B.R. 747, 780 (Bankr. S.D. Tex. 2013); *In re T.H.*, 529 B.R. 112, 124 (Bankr. E.D. Va. 2015), based on a local "CM/ECF Policy Statement"; *Rattan Dev Singh Dhaliwal v. Kavindar Paul Singh (In re Kavindar*

Paul Singh), 2014 WL 842102, at *9 (9th Cir. BAP Mar. 4, 2014); *In re Grimmett*, 2017 WL 2437231, at *11 (Bankr. D.Idaho June 5, 2017); *In re Daw*, 2011 WL 231362, at *3 (Bankr. D.Idaho Jan. 24, 2011). See *In re Nakhuda*, 544 B.R. 886, 904, (9th Cir. BAP 2016), referencing the local rule BLR 5005–2(d) of the Northern District of California.

I believe the effort to convince me that wet signatures are required has been misdirected. The real issue is whether Federal Rules of Bankruptcy Procedure 1008 and 9011 have been complied with. Briefly, those Rules require that every bankruptcy petition be verified or accompanied by an unsworn declaration by the debtor and signed by counsel, if any, prior to filing. Moreover, all lists, schedules, statements, and amendments must be verified or accompanied by an unsworn declaration by the debtor. Traditionally, verifications involve executing a document after first taking an oath before a state or federal official authorized to administer an oath. See, 9 *Collier on Bankruptcy* ¶ 1008.01 (Richard Levin & Henry J. Sommer eds., 16th ed. 2017). The more frequently utilized alternative is signing an unsworn declaration under 28 U.S.C. § 174. If it is not so verified or signed with an unsworn declaration, then clearly the applicable rule has been violated.

Whether that signature must be by "pen to paper" in an era when wet signatures are the exception rather than the rule is problematic. What is critical is that petitions, lists, schedules, statements, and amendments require verifications or unsworn declarations executed by the debtor. Federal Rule of Bankruptcy Procedure 1008. They cannot be filed without that signature. *Ross II. Briggs v. John V. Labarge, Jr. (In re John V. Labarge, Jr.)*, 433 F.3d 1068, 1071 (8th Cir. 2006). Without that simple step, there can be no assurance that the factual allegations contained within those documents are true and correct. A debtor's lawyer cannot endorse those documents for the debtor. *In re Whitehill*, 514 B.R. 687 (Bankr. M.D.Fla. 2014); *In re Stomberg*, 487 B.R. 775, 807 (Bankr. S.D.Tex. 2013), *In re Wenk*, 296 B.R. 719, 727 (Bankr. E.D.Va. 2002).

Tanribilir has acknowledged that the original petition-related documents filed in Klitsch, Lopez, and Mullin were not signed by the clients in advance of their filing. Each one of the petition date filings consists of six separate unsworn declarations, i.e. the Petition, Declaration regarding Schedules, Statement of Financial Affairs, Statement of Intentions, Statement of Monthly Income, and the verification of Creditor Matrix. Each filing bears conformed signatures, that is, the /s/ designation followed by the typed name of the respective Debtor, presumably indicating that Tanribilir had possession of a document signed by the individual Debtors prior to the filing. These conformed signatures were affixed to the documents by Tanribilir or under his instruction. The petition date filings in Klitsch, Lopez, and Mullin were violations of Federal Rule of Bankruptcy Procedure 9011(b)(3) since Tanribilir knew that none of those documents were signed by the Debtors under penalty of perjury or the statutory proscriptions of 18 U.S.C. §§ 152, 1341, 1519 and 3571. . . . Nevertheless, he affixed their conformed signature to those documents. Even Tanribilir's recollection that all his clients authorized the filings in advance was suspect. Tanribilir opted not to bring his files. He offered no explanation why he chose not to bring files for any of the cases in question.

Tanribilir's execution of these filings was tantamount to forgery. Forgery is defined as "[t]he act of fraudulently making a false document or altering a real one to be used as if genuine." FORGERY, Black's Law Dictionary (10th ed. 2014). In each of the cases referenced, the petition has been filed by Tanribilir over the conformed signature of the Debtor as signified by an /s/. The law would thus presume that the respective Debtors had affixed their signatures to the original document verifying that the facts therein were true and correct. . . This Opinion highlights my central concern that Tanribilir falsely certified documents as verified or sworn to by the Debtors when they were not. This is a clear violation of Federal Rule of Bankruptcy Procedure 1008 and the Pennsylvania Rule of Conduct 3.3 . . .

It has been held that, prior to sanctioning an attorney, "particularized notice is required to comport with due process." *Jones v. Pittsburgh Nat. Corp.*, 899 F.2d 1350, 1357 (3d Cir. 1990). While a Rule 9011 violation was not alleged in the sanction Motion, there appears to be a limited exception to the requirement of advance notice of the rule violated. That circumstance is where the respondent has sufficient, advance notice of the conduct alleged to be actionable. *Fellheimer, Eichen & Braverman, P.C. v. Charter Techs., Inc.*, 57 F.3d 1215, 1225 (3d Cir. 1995). I further observe that the exercise of my inherent powers under 11 U.S.C. § 105 require that I make finding of bad faith, while a violation under Rule 9011 merely requires objective unreasonable conduct. . . . Moreover, as indicated earlier, there is no safe harbor provision for the filing of a falsified bankruptcy petition. I am, therefore, willing to utilize the sanctions authorized by Federal Rule of Bankruptcy Procedure 9011(c) against Tanribilir and the Upright firm, who, by agreement, has accepted joint responsibility for all cases filed over their name . . . I find that the violation consisted of filing three falsified bankruptcy petitions.

Moreover, falsely certifying that a Debtor has signed a petition, statement, or schedules and thereafter, at hearing, acknowledging that the Debtors did not so execute those documents, suggests a violation of 18 U.S.C. § 152. The Judicial Code of Conduct, Canon 4.A.(5) requires that I take appropriate action which, in this case, compels a referral to the United States Attorney for the District.

My conclusion is that Tanribilir and Law Solutions Chicago LLC, trading as Upright Law LLC, should be sanctioned for filing three bankruptcy petitions without first securing signatures on those documents from their clients. I find that the minimum sanction needed to deter future violations is the imposition of Movant's attorney's fees against Tanribilir and Upright, jointly and severally. Rule 9011 also authorizes the Court to issue directives of a nonmonetary nature. In order to prevent further occurrences of the shortcomings evidenced by the proceeding before me, I direct Tanribilir and Upright to prepare a 10-page Memorandum of Law on the necessary elements of Federal Rule of Bankruptcy Procedure 1008 and the penalties possible for a violation of that Rule and circulate same to this bankruptcy judge as well as the 400+ "partners" of Upright Law within 30 days of a final Order. Since I award reasonable attorney's fees to the Trustee, whose diligence discovered this shortcoming, I will set a hearing in that regard to determine those fees.

Questions about the Case

1. Which party brought the sanctions motion in this case? What were the party's concerns?
2. Examine the reasons why Tanribilir did not obtain "wet" signatures from his client. Is this in accordance with general legal practice? What constitutes a signature in Bankruptcy Court?
3. What does the Court say about the necessity of "wet" signatures on documents to be filed with the Bankruptcy Court? Do you agree or disagree with the Court's reasoning?
4. How is forgery defined by the Court? What does the court say about the signing of certified documents as verified or sworn to by the Debtors?
5. What was the Court's ruling in this case? Did the Court identify any mitigating factors related to the ruling?
6. What is the Court's intention in mandating a 10-page Memorandum of Law on Federal Rule of Bankruptcy Procedure 1008? Is this an effective sanction to prevent the conduct committed in this case?

Regulation of Paralegals and Ethics Guidelines for Paralegals

This chapter traces the evolution of the paralegal profession, examines initiatives to regulate the profession, and discusses the ways in which paralegals are currently regulated. Chapter 2 covers:

- the development of the paralegal profession since its inception in the late 1960s
- the American Bar Association's involvement in the field
- the role of professional paralegal associations
- past and present efforts to regulate paralegals
- distinctions among kinds of regulation: certification, licensing, and limited licensing
- liability of paralegals as agents of attorneys
- guidelines on the utilization of paralegal services
- ethics codes promulgated by paralegal associations

A. A Brief History of the Paralegal Profession

1. The Beginnings

The use of specifically educated nonlawyers to assist lawyers in the delivery of legal services is a relatively new phenomenon in the history of American law. In the 1960s, the rapidly rising cost of legal services, combined with the lack of access to legal services for low- and middle-income Americans, caused the government, consumer groups, and the organized bar to take a close look at the way legal services were being delivered.

In response to the unmet need for legal services, the federal government established the Legal Services Corporation to provide funding for legal services to the indigent, low-cost legal clinics started to appear, and prepaid legal plans were developed. Practitioners and the organized bar also attempted to develop alternatives to the traditional practice model that would keep costs down without sacrificing quality. The answers they came up with included better management, increased automation, and the use of **legal assistants** or **paralegals**.

In 1967, the American Bar Association (ABA) endorsed the concept of the paralegal and, in 1968, established its first committee on legal assistants, which later was made a standing committee of the ABA under the name Standing Committee on Legal Assistants. Its name was changed to the **Standing Committee on Paralegals** in 2003 in recognition of the growing preference for the title "paralegal." During the late 1960s and early 1970s, the ABA and several state and local bar associations conducted studies on the use of paralegals. Many studies showed initial attorney resistance to paralegals, but actual use was on the rise.

2. Growth Through the 1970s

The first **formal paralegal training** programs were established in the early 1970s. In 1971, there were only 11 programs scattered across the country. In 1974, the ABA adopted guidelines for the paralegal curriculum and, in 1975, began to approve paralegal education programs under those guidelines. There were nine paralegal programs approved that year.

In the mid-1970s, the first professional paralegal associations were formed. Dozens of groups cropped up locally. The **National Federation of Paralegal Associations** (NFPA) and **National Association of Legal Assistants** (NALA) were established. Paralegal educators formed their own organization, the **American Association for Paralegal Education** (AAfPE). In 1976, NALA established its **Certified Legal Assistant** (CLA) program (now called **Certified Paralegal**), a voluntary certification program. It covers general competencies, such as judgment and analytical ability, communications, ethics, legal research, and general substantive law in a range of areas. In 2006, NALA developed the Advanced Certified Paralegal (ACP) credential with exams in specialty areas.

In 1975, the federal government recognized the existence of the paralegal occupation by creating a new job classification. States, counties, and cities soon followed suit. In 1978, the U.S. Bureau of Labor Statistics predicted that the paralegal career would be one of the fastest growing occupations through the year 2000.

3. New Directions in the 1980s and 1990s

Job opportunities expanded and changed dramatically during the late 1970s and into the 1990s. Although the first paralegals were employed primarily in small law firms and legal aid organizations, large private law firms soon became the biggest employers of paralegals. As a result, large firms and corporate law departments developed paralegal manager and supervisor positions so that the large numbers of paralegals they employed could be effectively deployed. In the 1980s, a group of paralegal supervisors and managers started the **Legal Assistant Management Association**, recently known as the **International Paralegal Management Association** and since 2014 as the **International Practice Management Association** (IPMA).

During the 1980s, paralegals began freelancing, handling specialized matters for attorneys on an as-needed, independent-contractor basis. Some worked alone in a specialized area of practice, such as probate, and others worked for full-service paralegal support companies.

Since the 1980s, the United States has experienced tremendous growth of the paralegal profession. Job opportunities have expanded in all sectors of employment. Clients have come to accept paralegals and even to demand that they be included on the legal services delivery team as a way of keeping costs down. Paralegals, like lawyers, have become more specialized, particularly in large law firms, corporate law departments, and government agencies, where most paralegals work in only one area of practice.

Paralegals have been granted recognition by the organized bar and practitioners. Many state bar associations have guidelines for the use of paralegals and along with local bar associations have established paralegal committees or divisions.

4. The Twenty-First Century

Estimates vary on the number of paralegals employed in the United States. Most sources indicate that there are about 300,000. About a thousand paralegal educational programs are operating, nearly 300 of which are approved by the ABA. About 300 are members of the American Association for Paralegal Education. Most surveys show that well over half of paralegals hold a baccalaureate degree and even more have some formal paralegal education.

Voluntary certification by one of the paralegal associations has gradually become more common. In addition to NALA's program mentioned above, the National Federation of Paralegal Associations (NFPA) has offered the **Paralegal Advanced Competency Examination** (PACE) for experienced paralegals since 1996, and added the Paralegal CORE Competency Exam for entry-level paralegals in 2011. The NFPA is an umbrella organization of state and local paralegal associations with more than 30 - member local associations, representing about 8,000 paralegals. At the time of this writing, more than 600 paralegals have earned the Registered Paralegal designation that is granted to those who pass the PACE and over 500 paralegals have earned the CORE Registered Paralegal (CRP) designation.

NALA represents more than 18,000 paralegals, including more than 7,500 individual members and about 90 state and local affiliated associations. Over 19,000 paralegals have been certified by NALA and over 8,000 can use the Certified Paralegal (CP) designation, which has been accredited by the National Commission for Certifying Agencies. In addition, more than 3,500 CPs have obtained advanced certification through a curriculum-based model. NALA offers advanced certification in at least a dozen areas of practice.

IPMA, representing managers and supervisors of paralegals and other practice support managers in law firms, has about 400 members, local chapters in several major cities across the country, and members in other parts of the world. IPMA leads the way in promoting the expanded and effective utilization of paralegal services and other practice support professionals.

Another group that includes paralegals is **NALS**, the Association for Legal Professionals. This group was established many years ago as a group for legal secretaries, but in the 1990s changed its name to reflect its changing mission of representing the interests of all legal support professionals. NALS has about 6,000 members but does not track how many of its members are paralegals. It has long offered a certification program for legal secretaries and also administers a paralegal certification examination called the Accredited Legal Professional (ALP) (formerly known as the PP, or Professional Paralegal examination). More than 600 paralegals have passed this examination.

The job market for paralegals vacillates with the ebb and flow of the economy, but overall has continued to grow. The legal profession is undergoing deep and extensive change in the twenty-first century, especially because of the ever-expanding use of technology, which is eliminating some functions and some jobs. Paralegal employment opportunities are steady and salaries have increased beyond levels of inflation. As has always been the case, small law firms still do not employ paralegals to the same degree as large ones, and the ratio of lawyers to paralegals in most firms has slightly increased to about four or five to one.

Several important trends characterize the paralegal profession at this point in its history. Levels of education for paralegals are increasing every year. Firms often expect a baccalaureate degree and paralegal education. Certification and licensing and the role of nonlawyer legal service providers continue to dominate the discussion of paralegal professional organizations. Opportunities for growth have been developed in new areas of employment and law practice, and exciting alternative and niche paralegal careers are flourishing. All of these trends point to the maturation and evolution of the paralegal profession. As is discussed in more detail below, some experts are predicting a major paradigm shift in the legal services industry, which would have an impact on the role of paralegals. These changes have led to declines in law school enrollments in recent years because of concerns that the need for new lawyers will not return to previous levels. However, law school enrollment once again increased and spiked in 2021.

B. Regulation of Paralegals: Certification and Licensing

1. Definitions of Terms

Certification of an occupation, as used in the context of paralegal regulation, is a form of recognition of an individual who has met specifications of the granting agency or organization. It is usually voluntary, although some proposals for certification of paralegals by courts have been framed as mandatory. NALA's CP/ACP program, NFPA's PACE/PCCE, and NALS's ALP are forms of certification, as are some state bar-sponsored programs, described later in this section.

Licensing is a mandatory form of regulation in which a government agency grants permission to an individual to engage in an occupation, to use a particular title, or both. Only a person who is so licensed may engage in this occupation. There is no licensing of paralegals at the present time in the United States. Lawyers are "licensed" by the state or states in which they practice.

Typically, both licensing and certification require applicants to meet specified requirements regarding education and moral character and to pass an examination. Additional requirements usually include adoption of an ethics code, a mechanism for disciplining licensed persons who violate ethics rules, and requirements for continuing education.

Certification
A form of recognition of an occupation based on a person's having met specific qualifications, usually undertaken voluntarily.

Licensing
Mandatory form of regulation in which a government agency grants permission to engage in an occupation and use a title.

2. State Regulation of Lawyer-Supervised Paralegals

Since the beginning of the paralegal profession, the need for and value of regulating paralegals has been a topic of discussion and debate. The paralegal profession is split, without a clear consensus about regulation. However, the push for regulation has become stronger as paralegals have sought to professionalize the occupation and to distinguish themselves from persons who provide legal services directly to the public.

South Dakota's Supreme Court took a step toward regulation in 1992 when it adopted rules that define legal assistants/paralegals and set qualifications for persons seeking to use that title (South Dakota Supreme Court Rule 92-5, Codified Laws, §16-18-34). Later, Maine became the first state in the country to legislate the use of the titles paralegal and legal assistant. In 1999, **Maine** adopted a state law that defines paralegal or legal assistant as:

> a person qualified by education, training or work experience, who is employed or retained by an attorney, law office, corporation, governmental agency or other entity and who performs specifically delegated substantive legal work for which an attorney is responsible.

M.R.S.A. §921.

The Maine law establishes fines for persons using the title legal assistant or paralegal without meeting the terms of the definition. The intention of this law is to deter nonlawyer practitioners from using these titles.

The efforts of California paralegals to get similar protection for the paralegal occupation led to adoption of the **first regulatory scheme for paralegals** in the country. The **California statutes** create a form of regulation that is neither certification nor licensing. Effective in 2001, California's law requires persons who fit the statutory definition of a paralegal to meet certain education requirements and to engage in specified continuing education. Only persons working under the supervision of a lawyer can use the titles paralegal, legal assistant, and other comparable titles. The statute also makes it unlawful for those not meeting the statutory definition and requirements to hold themselves out as paralegals. Compliance with this law is not monitored by the state in any formal way, as it would be in a full-blown licensing program, but law firms and paralegals in the state generally do comply.

Under the California law, a paralegal, or any other person using one of several similar titles, is defined as:

> A person who holds himself or herself out to be a paralegal, who is qualified by education, training or work experience, who either contracts with or is employed by an attorney, law firm, corporation, governmental agency, or

other entity, and who performs substantive legal work under the direction and supervision of an active member of the State Bar of California . . . that has been specifically delegated by the attorney to him or her.

California Business and Professions Code §6450(a).

It should be noted that one federal court in California has acknowledged this statute is setting the qualifications for paralegal time to be compensated in a fee petition. See *Sanford v. GMRI, Inc.* (CIV-S-04-1535 DFL CMK (E.D. Cal. 2005)), which is excerpted in Chapter 7.

The **Florida Supreme Court** has also limited the use of the titles paralegal, legal assistant, and other similar terms to those persons who work under the direct supervision of a lawyer. It first defined the terms paralegal and legal assistant when it amended its Rules of Professional Conduct in 2000 by adding the definition of paralegal to the general rule on supervision of nonlawyers, which is based on ABA Model Rule 5.3, discussed later (Florida Rule 4-5.3). Later, the definition of paralegal/legal assistant was added to the Rules Governing the Investigation and Prosecution of the Unlicensed Practice of Law, which indicate that it constitutes unauthorized practice for someone who does not meet the definition of a paralegal or legal assistant to use that term in providing legal services. Florida has also adopted a registration program for paralegals; see the discussion below.

The **Arizona Supreme Court** adopted a definition of paralegal/legal assistant as part of its 2003 rules on the unauthorized practice of law, as follows:

> a person qualified by education and training who performs substantive legal work requiring a sufficient knowledge of and expertise in legal concepts and procedures, who is supervised by an active member of the State Bar of Arizona, and for whom an active member of the state bar is responsible, unless otherwise authorized by supreme court rule.

Rules of the Supreme Court of Arizona, Rule V.A.

The **New Mexico** court rules define paralegals and set minimum qualifications, and recommend that lawyers not use the designation of paralegal for persons who do not meet these requirements, falling short of prohibiting the use of the title. This may be seen as an interim step toward the kind of "soft" regulation that has been adopted in states like California.

All these initiatives show some acceptance of the idea that paralegals should be regulated, but efforts to regulate paralegals in a more comprehensive way have been met with substantial resistance by the organized bar, which generally holds to the view that paralegal regulation is unnecessary. Lawyers sometimes also express concerns that regulated paralegals would compete for work with lawyers, especially lawyers who are in solo and small practices and serve individuals in areas such as divorce, bankruptcy, and landlord-tenant matters.

Several jurisdictions have seen unsuccessful initiatives to regulate paralegals. Most recently, in 2011 and 2012, bills were introduced in Florida and New York, but failed to move forward. Earlier, a plan in Hawaii to establish mandatory certification of paralegals by the state supreme court was rejected, even with strong support among influential leaders on the bench. A Wisconsin plan for mandatory licensing of paralegals was finally rejected by the state supreme court in 2008 after having been stalled since 2000. In the 1980s and 1990s, licensing proposals in Minnesota, Montana, Nevada, New Jersey, Oregon, South Carolina, and Utah were shelved.

In Ontario, Canada, under the auspices of the Law Society of Upper Canada, paralegals can perform some functions that would be considered the practice of law in the United States. Ontario started licensing paralegals in 2008 and has about 7,500 paralegal licensees. Requirements include formal education at an accredited program and passing an examination. Paralegals are subject to an ethics code and discipline just as lawyers are.

NFPA continues to promote mandatory regulation, publishing a model act for the licensure of paralegals. While some paralegals across the country continue to promote regulation, several associations have changed strategy and are working to establish state-sponsored programs of voluntary certification.

3. Voluntary Certification of Paralegals

Early in the profession's evolution, **Oregon** adopted a **voluntary certification program** for legal assistants. It was abolished after a few years because of low participation. The second state to venture into certification, Texas, has been more successful. Texas adopted a voluntary certification program for paralegals in 1994. The program is administered through its Board of Legal Specialization. Certification examinations are given in seven practice areas. Certification, valid for five years, is renewable on demonstrated participation in continuing education, employment by a Texas attorney, and substantial involvement in the specialty area. The states of North Carolina, Florida, and Ohio have also adopted voluntary certification or registration programs in the last 10 or 12 years. The North Carolina and Ohio programs were established by the state bar association and both require applicants to meet entrance standards and pass an examination. Florida's was adopted by the state supreme court. North Carolina's certification is designed for paralegals who have met educational requirements or have a specified level of experience, whereas the Ohio plan requires applicants to have designated levels of legal experience in addition to meeting educational criteria. Florida's registration program has two tiers, with paralegals meeting the higher-level requirements eligible to call themselves Florida Registered Paralegals. Over 10,000 paralegals are certified by these states.

As noted above, the national paralegal associations continue to promote voluntary certification and have increased the numbers of paralegals with these credentials substantially in the last decade. On a national level, these organizations want to be poised for regulation when it comes by having proven examinations in place that can be adopted by states.

At the state level, a growing number of statewide paralegal organizations have developed state-specific certification examinations, usually in connection with NALA and designed for CPs. California, Florida, Louisiana, Delaware, Pennsylvania, Kentucky, and New Jersey have such programs.

The ABA Standing Committee on Paralegals continues to hold fast in opposing regulation and maintains a more neutral stance toward voluntary certification, adhering to policy statements on certification and licensing issued in 1975 and 1986. In both instances, the Standing Committee rejected the notion that paralegals need to be licensed, contending that the public is protected by the extensive ethical and disciplinary requirements to which lawyers are subject as the appropriate means to protect consumers. IPMA also opposes licensing of paralegals, asserting that licensing of paralegals who work under lawyer supervision is unnecessary for the protection of the public and would unduly interfere with lawyers' prerogative to hire the best-qualified persons for the job they need done.

The ABA Standing Committee on Paralegals has long had a **definition of paralegal**, which was adopted by the House of Delegates. As revised in 2020, it reads as follows:

> A paralegal is a person, qualified by education, training or work experience, who is employed or retained by a lawyer, law office, corporation, governmental agency or other entity and who performs specifically delegated substantive legal work for which a lawyer is responsible.

4. The Arguments About Regulation of Lawyer-Supervised Paralegals

The issues relating to regulation of paralegals who work under the supervision of attorneys are significantly different from those who sometimes call themselves "independent paralegals" and who seek to provide legal services directly to the public.

The primary arguments **against licensing** of lawyer-supervised paralegals are that it:

- is unnecessary because attorney-employers are already fully accountable to clients;

- would increase the cost of legal services as the costs of employing paralegals would rise;
- would stifle the development of the profession by limiting the functions that paralegals can perform;
- would inappropriately limit entry into the profession;
- would unnecessarily standardize paralegal education; and
- would limit paralegals from moving into new areas of practice or duties.

In addition, opponents cite the practical difficulty of determining exactly what legal tasks and functions could be assigned exclusively to paralegals through a regulatory process. In other words, what could paralegals be authorized to do that other workers in the legal environment could not do? What would prevent lawyers from having other nonlawyers perform those tasks under different job titles?

Arguments **favoring the licensing** of traditional paralegals center mainly on the benefits to the profession, in terms of establishing it as a separate and autonomous allied legal career, one with its own identity and a concomitant increase in societal status and rewards.

Proponents believe regulation would:

- provide appropriate public recognition for paralegals as important members of the legal services delivery team;
- ensure high standards and quality of work by paralegals;
- expand the use of paralegals, thereby expanding access to legal services and lowering costs;
- provide guidance to clients and to lawyers regarding the paralegal role and qualifications; and
- encourage needed standardization in paralegal education.

The most progressive regulatory models would expand the scope of paralegal work into areas where it might not currently be permitted because of unauthorized-practice-of-law rules and statutes, reinforcing the notion that lawyers could provide general oversight and supervision. This model is based on the idea that paralegals can be used to increase access to legal services through lawyers and nonlawyers working hand in hand, as opposed to playing separate but similar roles in the delivery of legal services.

Even among supporters of regulation, there are wide differences about the details of a good regulatory plan. Contentious issues relate to what level and kind of formal education should be required; whether experienced paralegals without formal education should be licensed; the necessity for a competency-based examination, a moral character check, continuing education, and a separate ethics code; whether the legislature or court is the most appropriate entity to regulate; how discipline should be handled; and how the entire process should be funded.

A related and much-debated concern is whether disbarred or suspended lawyers should be able to work as paralegals. Even without regulation, this is a contentious subject. California Rules of Professional Conduct permit disbarred lawyers to work in paralegal-type roles (e.g., legal research, drafting documents) with some specified protections for clients (Rule 1-311). The California courts have made it clear that they will not condone a disbarred lawyer engaging in work that falls within the definition of the practice of law, including representing clients in administrative hearings. See *Benninghoff v. Superior Court*, 38 Cal. Rptr. 3d 759 (2006). Colorado adopted a rule similar to California's, but many other states, such as Illinois, Indiana, and Massachusetts, do not allow disbarred lawyers to work in law firms. See, for example, *In the Matter of Scott*, 739 N.E.2d 658 (S. Ct. Ind. 2000). In 2014, NFPA issued a position statement advocating against the employment of disbarred or suspended lawyers in any capacity related to the practice of law.

5. Nonlawyer Legal Service Providers

In the last 35 years, reforming the legal services delivery system to improve **access to legal services** has been a persistent theme. Study after study has demonstrated that the vast majority of Americans do not have access to legal services, cannot afford a lawyer when they need one, and do not know how to go about finding an attorney. Persons of modest means need access to the legal system and are more frequently than ever representing themselves with or without the assistance of self-help resources and nonlawyers. Barriers to access include not only inadequate financial resources, but language and physical access. As a result of this diverse array of access barriers, nonlawyer practice has developed in virtually every jurisdiction. More than half the states have considered proposals to regulate nonlawyers who provide legal services directly to the public.

Consumer groups and nonlawyer practitioners advocate for legislation or court rules that would authorize nonlawyers to engage in tasks that are otherwise considered the practice of law and therefore are within the exclusive domain of licensed attorneys. Although there is substantial resistance to this concept from many practicing attorneys, there has also been support for it going back to the 1970s, when the paralegal profession was born. Some commentators favor the idea of ***nonlawyer legal service providers*** to perform such tasks as handling simple real estate closings and drafting simple wills. However, opposition is strong from those who believe that the system of limited licensure would establish a second tier of legal services that are not as good as those services that lawyers would provide.

Nonlawyer legal service providers Persons not licensed to practice law who provide legal services directly to the public.

The concept of independent nonlawyer practice has been re-energized in California, Utah, and some other states. The state of Washington has adopted rules described below, and is closest to bringing this idea to life in the United States. This renewed interest is spurred in part by a growing recognition that law practice is changing in ways that require rethinking legal education, entry into the profession, and practice models. This cluster of concerns, together with the continuing challenge of providing access to legal services for low- and middle-income Americans, has commanded the attention of legal commentators and the organized bar. The use of nonlawyers as court facilitators and navigators, bankruptcy preparers, and the like is slowly eroding resistance to the idea of direct nonlawyer practice.

Several important books have been written on the need to reform legal education and to restructure law practice. Richard Susskind's *The End of Lawyers: Rethinking the Nature of Legal Services* explains that technology and the commoditization of legal services demand a new way to practice law, one which calls for streamlined law firms and new roles for both lawyers and nonlawyers (Oxford University Press, 2008). *Failing Law Schools*, by law professor Brian Tamanaha, has brought a clear voice and strong evidence for the idea that the American legal education model needs radical reform (University of Chicago Press, 2012).

In 2012, the ABA Task Force on the Future of Legal Education was charged to study the "key challenges facing the delivery of legal services and the provision of legal education," including the rising cost of legal education, declining employment prospects, practical skills training, and the changing nature of legal work. One of its subcommittees has issued a preliminary call for states to create a common framework for licensing nonlawyers to provide a limited range of legal services and for law schools to provide the requisite educational programs, which the ABA would then accredit. This work has been stalled since 2014. The most recent ABA report, "A Report on the Future of Legal Services in the United States," issued in December 2016, explains the desperate need for greater access to legal services and cites expanded use of nonlawyer personnel working independently or under minimal supervision. In California, the State Bar Board has adopted the resolution of its Limited Licensing Working Group to "study and develop a proposed limited license to practice law. . . ." Other states considering limited licensing are Colorado, Connecticut, Florida, Michigan, New Mexico, Oregon, and Utah. In 2015 the Utah Supreme Court endorsed the recommendations of a task force to adopt an LLLT rule similar to Washington's. The court established a steering committee to work on an implementation plan for Licensed Paralegal Practitioners (LPPs) to offer discrete legal services in three practice areas: (1) temporary separation, divorce, paternity, cohabitant abuse and civil stalking, custody and support, and name change; (2) residential eviction; and (3) debt collection.

Proponents of limited licensure disagree on the appropriate level of regulation. Some favor a simple registration procedure under which practitioners register their names and addresses with an agency or the applicable court. Others want to create higher standards that would protect consumers, favoring educational requirements, a licensing examination, bonding or insurance, and continuing education.

Some states have taken steps to protect consumers from incompetent or unscrupulous providers. In California, **legal document assistants** have been required since 2000 to register with the county or counties in which they work. The California law defines and circumscribes their work, specifying that they may not provide legal advice, and sets up minimum education and experience requirements (California Business and Professions Code §§6400, et seq). Nevada adopted a similar registration and practice statute for documentation preparation services in 2014 (Nevada Revised Statutes 240.A).

In 2003, Arizona's Supreme Court adopted rules governing the activities of **legal document preparers**, defined as nonlawyers who prepare or provide legal documents without lawyer supervision for persons who are representing themselves. Arizona's program sets standards for certification by the court based on education or experience; defines the role of certified LDPs, limiting it to providing and preparing forms, providing information (but not legal advice), filing and arranging for service; and mandates continuing education (Arizona Code of Judicial Administration §7-208).

Legal document assistants/preparers Nonlawyer legal service providers who assist persons in preparing legal documents without giving legal advice; called LDAs under California statutes, these persons are called Legal Document Preparers under Arizona court rules.

6. Other Legal Professionals

After 10 years of advocacy, the state of Washington, through the Washington Supreme Court, adopted the Limited Practice Rule for Limited License Legal Technicians (LLLT) in 2012. The rule established certification requirements, defined the types of activities that a legal technician could engage in, and contained detailed prohibitions and recertification and financial responsibility requirements. In an interesting post-script, in 2015 the Supreme Court of Washington also approved revisions to the Rules of Professional Conduct to allow LLLTs to form partnerships with lawyers and to share fees. As of this writing, the LLLT program has been sunsetted by the Washington Supreme Court. However, Utah, Arizona, Minnesota, Oregon, and Colorado have moved forward in expanding the role of **limited practice legal professionals**.

Limited practice legal professionals Licensed professionals who are not lawyers but are authorized by state statutes and court rules to practice law and represent clients on a limited basis.

Utah

In August 2020, the Utah Supreme Court approved nonlawyer ownership or investment in law firms and permitted legal services providers to try new ways of serving clients during a two-year pilot period. This launched the Office of Legal Services Innovation (the "Innovation Office") and the legal sandbox. Nontraditional legal services entities must seek approval to operate in a regulatory sandbox established by the court. At the conclusion of the two-year pilot period, the court will evaluate whether the core reforms it has approved should continue "based on a review of data collected from those entities and individuals participating in the program." The court also amended Utah's Rules of Professional Conduct to permit attorney fee sharing with nonlawyers as long as there is written notice to the client. (See UT RPC 5.4A.)

In 2023, the Innovation Office moved to the Utah State Bar and the court formed an advisory Legal Services Innovation Committee to direct the Innovation Office's regulatory activities.

Arizona

Effective January 1, 2021, the Arizona Supreme Court eliminated its ethics rule barring nonlawyers from having an economic interest in a law firm or participating in fee sharing. The court also approved a new category of nonlawyer licensee called "Legal Paraprofessionals" who are able to represent clients in court. Both regulatory reforms were recommended by Arizona's Task Force on the Delivery of Legal Services and approved by the Arizona Supreme Court.

Arizona requires proposed alternative business structures to go through a rigorous application process. Nontraditional legal businesses also must comply with a code of conduct that mandates that they have an internal compliance attorney. (See AZ ACJA7-209.) Look for more discussion of this in Chapter 7.

Arizona Legal Paraprofessionals (LPs) practice as affiliate members of the state bar who are subject to the same ethical rules and discipline process as lawyers. Those interested in becoming LPs are required to meet education and experience requirements, pass a professional abilities examination, and pass the character and fitness process. LPs are able to practice in administrative law, family law, debt collection, and landlord-tenant disputes, with limited jurisdiction in civil and criminal matters. (See AZ ACJA 7-210.)

Minnesota

The Minnesota Supreme Court adopted Court Rule amendments authorizing Minnesota's Legal Paraprofessional Pilot Project effective March 1, 2021, through March 31, 2024. The Pilot Project is intended to increase access to civil legal representation in case types where one or both parties typically appear without legal representation. It permits legal paraprofessionals (LPs), under the supervision of a Minnesota attorney, to provide legal advice and, in some cases, represent a client in court in two legal areas: landlord-tenant disputes and family law disputes.

The Legal Paraprofessional Pilot Project Standing Committee, established in November 2020, oversees the Pilot Project and evaluates its success in meeting the goal of improving access to legal services. An interim report issued by the Committee on March 1, 2023, stated that the Pilot Project "continues to have a positive impact overall and demonstrates that legal paraprofessionals can successfully provide quality services to parties." (See MN ADM19-8002.)

Oregon

On July 19, 2022, the Oregon Supreme Court approved a licensed paralegal program that permits paralegals to provide limited legal services to clients. The program went into effect in July 2023. The licensed paralegal program allows licensed paralegals (LPs) to provide limited legal services in family law, including divorce and custody matters, and in landlord and tenant cases. LPs are able to assist clients in drafting and filing forms, observe depositions, represent clients in settlement discussions and mediation, and prepare clients for court appearances. LPs cannot argue on behalf of clients in court.

LPs have specific requirements for education and experience, and are subject to many of the same rules and regulatory requirements that currently apply to lawyers. The LP program is administered by the Oregon State Bar's Paraprofessional Licensing Implementation Committee (PLIC). (See SCO No. 22-033.)

Colorado

In March 2023, the Colorado Supreme Court approved a new paraprofessional program that will allow some non-attorneys to practice limited family law. The Court agreed to create a Licensed Legal Paraprofessional (LLP) program that will allow licensed non-attorneys to represent clients in some divorce and child custody cases. Under the plan, candidates will be required to pass a written exam and meet certain educational requirements in order to become LLPs. Candidates must have completed at least 1,500 hours of "substantive law-related practical experience," including 500 hours focused on family law, during the three years prior to sitting for the exam.

Licensing is projected to begin in Colorado in 2024. LLPs will be allowed to file some pleadings and represent their clients in mediation. The licensed legal paraprofessionals can accompany their clients to court but cannot present argument or examine witnesses. LLPs will be required to complete annual ongoing education and will be disciplined and grieved like attorneys; they will also be subject to professional ethical rules. (See CRCP 207.1.)

C. State Guidelines for the Utilization of Paralegal Services

In an effort to promote the effective and ethical use of paralegals, more than half of the states have adopted **guidelines** to assist attorneys in working with paralegals. At the time of this writing, the following states have guidelines of some kind: Colorado, Connecticut, Georgia, Idaho, Illinois, Indiana, Iowa, Kansas, Kentucky, Michigan, Missouri, Nebraska, New Hampshire, New Mexico, New York, North Carolina, North Dakota, Pennsylvania, Rhode Island, South Carolina, South Dakota, Texas, Utah, Virginia, Washington, and West Virginia.

In Indiana, Kentucky, New Mexico, North Dakota, Rhode Island, and South Dakota, the guidelines have been adopted by the highest court of the state. In other states, the guidelines have been approved by the state bar association, a state bar committee on paralegals, or both.

Some of the states that have adopted guidelines have also prepared accompanying **statements on the effective use of paralegals**. Detailed listings of paralegal job functions accompany the Colorado, Georgia, and New York guidelines.

Nearly all the state guidelines cover several critical areas of ethics that come into play when nonlawyers, not subject to discipline in the way that lawyers are, perform professional-level work and are interacting with clients and the public. These key areas, covered in later chapters of this text, are:

- unauthorized practice of law,
- disclosure of status as a paralegal,
- confidentiality,
- conflicts of interest,
- supervision and delegation,
- financial arrangements between lawyers and paralegals.

The **ABA Model Guidelines for the Utilization of Paralegal Services**, originally adopted in 1991, serve as a model for states and as a guide to help lawyers use paralegal services effectively and appropriately. Many of the jurisdictions with guidelines have adopted all or part of the ABA guidelines.

D. Paralegal Association Codes of Ethics and Guidelines

The two major national paralegal professional associations both have codes of ethics to guide the conduct of their members. NALA first adopted its **Code of Ethics and Professional Responsibility** in 1975. NFPA adopted its first Affirmation of Responsibility in 1977, which is now called the **Code of Ethics and Professional Responsibility**. The current codes of the two organizations are included in Appendix A and Appendix B, respectively.

NALA also publishes **Model Standards and Guidelines for the Utilization of Paralegals**. The dual purposes of these guidelines are to serve as an educational and informational tool for individual attorneys and state bars and to provide a model for states seeking to develop their own guidelines.

NFPA issues ethics opinions on current concerns of interest to practicing paralegals. These opinions have addressed such matters as communications over the Internet, the role of paralegals who work in the corporate setting, outsourcing of legal work, and disbarred lawyers working as paralegals.

Both organizations provide information on ethics on their websites as follows:

The National Association of Legal Assistants—*www.nala.org*
The National Federation of Paralegal Associations—*www.paralegals.org*

In addition to these two national organizations, some local and regional associations have created and adopted their own ethics rules, borrowing from NALA, NFPA, and the ABA.

E. Liability of Paralegals as Agents of Lawyers

Because paralegals are not lawyers who are licensed by the state, they are neither bound directly by state legal ethics codes nor subject to sanctions for breaches of those codes. Without certification, licensing, or some other form of direct regulation of the paralegal occupation, a paralegal is bound to comply with high standards of professional behavior primarily because the attorney for whom the paralegal works is responsible for any lapses in the paralegal's behavior. Lawyers therefore have a strong incentive to ensure that the paralegals they retain and employ are familiar with the state's ethics code and comply with it. Some states specifically require that attorneys take affirmative steps to educate paralegals about ethics and to ensure their compliance.

The ABA Model Rules of Professional Conduct contain an important section on supervision. Rule 5.3 provides as follows:

> With respect to a nonlawyer employed or retained by or associated with a lawyer:
>
> (a) a partner, and a lawyer who individually or together with other lawyers possesses comparable managerial authority in a law firm shall make reasonable efforts to ensure that the firm has in effect measures giving reasonable assurance that the person's conduct is compatible with the professional obligations of the lawyer;
>
> (b) a lawyer having direct supervisory authority over the nonlawyer shall make reasonable efforts to ensure that the person's conduct is compatible with the professional obligations of the lawyer; and
>
> (c) a lawyer shall be responsible for conduct of such a person that would be a violation of the Rules of Professional Conduct if engaged in by a lawyer if:
>
> (1) the lawyer orders or, with the knowledge of the specific conduct, ratifies the conduct involved; or
>
> (2) the lawyer is a partner or has comparable managerial authority in the law firm in which the person is employed, or has direct supervisory authority over the person, and knows of the conduct at a time when its consequences can be avoided or mitigated but fails to take reasonable remedial action.

Although this rule applies to all nonlawyers in the lawyer's office and to outside vendors and independent contractors, it has special application for paralegals, who often work closely with clients and work continuously with sensitive and confidential information. The official **Comments** to this **Model Rule** mandate that lawyers provide appropriate instruction and supervision concerning ethical obligations, highlighting the duty of confidentiality. The Comments also advise managing lawyers to have internal procedures and policies that provide reasonable assurance that nonlawyers will act ethically.

Paralegals have one other very meaningful incentive for complying with high standards of conduct—they are **potential defendants** in civil malpractice suits, which can be brought by clients who believe their attorneys have acted negligently. Paralegals are subject to the same general tort principles that apply to lawyers and other professionals. They are liable for negligent or intentional misconduct that injures a client.

The lawyers for whom they work are also liable under the doctrine of ***respondeat superior*** or **vicarious liability**. Under this principle of agency law, employers are responsible for the acts of their employees carried out in the course and scope of their employment. This responsibility extends to vendors and others to whom lawyers may outsource work, a practice that is the subject of considerable discussion in the last decade as lawyers have outsourced more and more work and retained vendors at locations outside the country.

Because clients always name their attorneys and rarely name paralegals as defendants in malpractice cases, there is little case law available defining the standards of conduct to which paralegals are held. As a general principle, paralegals are held to the same standard of care, skill, and knowledge common to other paralegals so long as they do not hold themselves out as attorneys and they perform typical paralegal tasks.

Three cases provide examples of attorneys being held responsible for the actions of their nonlawyer staff. The *Musselman* case (at the end of this chapter) involves a malpractice action in which a paralegal played a part. In *The Florida Bar v. Lawless*, 640 So. 2d 1098 (Fla. 1994), a lawyer is disciplined as a result of the actions of a paralegal (see this case at the companion website that accompanies this text). *Struthers* (also at the end of this chapter) involves the discipline of a lawyer who abdicated his responsibility to nonlawyers who were really running his "practice."

Across the country, a number of lawyers are disciplined every year for over-delegating and failing to supervise paralegals. The gravity of the paralegals' breaches of ethics in these cases ranges from embezzling client funds, to misinforming a client that he did not need to show up for a hearing in a criminal case, to improperly executing documents, to over-billing. In one recent case, a lawyer hired two paralegals in a row, both of whom embezzled money from his client trust accounts.

REVIEW QUESTIONS

1. When did the paralegal profession begin and what was the impetus for its development?
2. What are the two main professional associations for paralegals?
3. What is certification? What is licensing?
4. What states have some form of direct regulation of paralegals? What entity (court or legislature) adopted the regulation in each case?
5. What states have some form of voluntary certification of paralegals? What entity is responsible for these programs in these states?
6. What are the national associations' programs for paralegal certification called? How do they differ?
7. What is limited licensure? How do nonlawyer legal service providers differ from traditional paralegals who work under lawyer supervision? How do they differ from freelance or independent contractor paralegals? Which states have such a program?

8. What is the status of discussions and initiatives about limited licensing, both nationally and in individual states? What are the reasons for the renewed interest in limited licensing?
9. What are the arguments in favor of the licensing of traditional paralegals? The arguments against?
10. What is the ABA's position on paralegal certification and licensing?
11. How many states have guidelines for the utilization of paralegals? What is their purpose?
12. What are the ABA Model Guidelines for the Utilization of Paralegal Services and what kinds of conduct do they cover?
13. Do NALA and NFPA have rules on the ethical conduct of paralegals? How are these rules enforced?
14. Can a paralegal who is negligent while working on a client's case be sued by the client for malpractice? Can this paralegal's attorney-employer be sued? If so, on what legal basis?
15. Can a lawyer be disciplined for the unethical conduct of a paralegal whom he or she supervises? Can the paralegal be disciplined?
16. What does ABA Model Rule 5.3 say about lawyer responsibility for paralegals?

DISCUSSION QUESTIONS AND HYPOTHETICALS

1. Do you think that paralegals working under the supervision of attorneys should be licensed? Why or why not?
2. Do you think that nonlawyer legal service providers should be licensed? Should they be permitted to give legal advice as they help "customers" who are representing themselves?
3. If you were creating a licensing scheme for nonlawyer legal service providers, what would it include?
4. If nonlawyer legal service providers were licensed in your state, would you be interested in becoming licensed? Why or why not?
5. What methods can you suggest to improve access to legal services for low- and middle-income persons?
6. Do lawyers have an ethical obligation to delegate work to an employee who has the qualifications to do the work and/or to the person who is the most cost-effective to the client?
7. Many law firms outsource work to vendors, sometimes even offshore vendors. What is the ethical duty to supervise in that situation? Is it possible to supervise effectively at this distance? How?
8. What would you do if the lawyer you worked for had a heavy caseload and delegated everything but court appearances to you, including getting clients to sign retainer agreements, conducting intake interviews, and preparing pleadings? Would it make a difference if the lawyer reviewed everything you did late at night?

9. You are offered a job at VCollect, which is a collection agency. VCollect has a relationship with a lawyer, Larry H., who shares office space and also has offices in two other locations. Under the agreement between VCollect and Larry, the VCollect employees, including the paralegals, are paid by VCollect but are "supervised" by the lawyer. New employees undergo training provided by nonlawyer supervisors and approved by Larry. VCollect pays Larry a monthly fee of $5,000. Larry has approved standard form collection letters that are generated by a computer. He does not see or sign them. Is Larry providing adequate supervision of the nonlawyers? Why or why not? Is the arrangement acceptable under MR 5.3? Why or why not? How might the arrangement be revised to be acceptable? Would you accept this position? (See *In the Matter of Hecker*, Docket No. DRB 09-372, decided August 9, 2010 by the Supreme Court of New Jersey Disciplinary Review Board, and affirmed 205 N.J. 263, 15 A.3d 16 (2011).)
10. How might ABA Model Rule 5.3 apply to prosecutors? Who in the office would be considered managerial? What nonlawyers might be subject to lawyer supervision in this setting? What kinds of ethical errors might these nonlawyers make that would be covered by Rule 5.3? What might the consequences be? (See ABA Formal Opinion 467 (2014) for an analysis and some guidelines for preventing ethical lapses in this environment.)
11. How might the new rules in Utah and Arizona related to lawyers being authorized to share fees with paralegals impact legal practice in these states? (See ABA Formal Opinion 484, with an examination of lawyers referring clients to fee financing companies or brokers in which the lawyers have no ownership or other financial interests.)

RESEARCH PROJECTS AND ASSIGNMENTS

1. Is there a local paralegal association in your area? Is it affiliated with NALA or NFPA, or is it independent? What kinds of activities does it have? What are the benefits of membership? How many members does it have? How many are certified by NALA, NFPA, or another entity? Does it have its own ethics code?
2. Does your state or local bar have a committee that addresses paralegal issues? Can paralegals join it? What does it do? Has your state considered licensing of traditional paralegals or independent paralegals who provide services directly to the public?
3. A number of states identified in this chapter have adopted guidelines to assist attorneys in working with paralegals. Research each of these states and locate the related guidelines. Compare these guidelines to the ABA Model Guidelines for the Utilization of Paralegal Services.

Are the state guidelines analogous to the ABA guidelines? How do they differ?
4. Research the status of the work of two jurisdictions that are considering the limited licensing of nonlawyers and report on their activities, hearings, and actions. Compare these efforts with the LP program in Arizona.
5. Has your state bar or court system conducted any studies on access to legal services or access to justice? If so, read the studies and report on the findings about barriers to access and solutions, proposed or implemented. Does the report discuss how paralegals can contribute to solving the access problem?
6. Read and analyze the 2016 ABA *Report on the Future of Legal Services in the United States*. Select two or three paralegal-related ideas from this report and present to the class with updates on any progress in these areas, either within the ABA or in particular states.
7. Search for any legal malpractice cases in your state in which a paralegal was implicated and report to the class.
8. Is voluntary certification through the state bar, statewide paralegal association, NALA, NFPA, or NALS popular in your state or local area? How many paralegals in your state are certified?
9. Has your jurisdiction adopted Model Rule 5.3 or some version of it? Are there any disciplinary cases or ethics opinions interpreting this rule? Are paralegal-related issues addressed?
10. What are your state's rules about disbarred lawyers working as paralegals? Do you think that disbarred lawyers should be able to work as paralegals? What are the risks to the client? Does this affect the paralegal profession or the image of paralegals?
11. As mentioned in this chapter, some law firms outsource work, such as legal research and document management, to vendors outside the country. Is it possible to exercise appropriate supervision under these circumstances? Read ABA Ethics Opinion 08-451 to identify the full array of ethical issues that arise in these circumstances.
12. The legal profession and some other regulated professions were taken by surprise in 2015 by a U.S. Supreme Court decision that struck down actions of the North Carolina Dental Practice Board that purported to prohibit non-dentists from whitening teeth. Read this case and check for any other cases that have followed it. Analyze how its thinking might be applied to the legal profession. North Carolina St. Brd. of Dental Examiners v. FTC, 135 S.Ct. 1101 (2015).

CASES FOR ANALYSIS

The *Musselman* case demonstrates how a paralegal might become involved in a transaction that results in harm to a client, thus becoming the subject of a malpractice suit.

Musselman v. Willoughby Corp.
230 Va. 337, 337 S.E.2d 724 (1985)

This is an attorney malpractice case arising from a real estate transaction. The lawyer represented a corporate client and employed an untrained paralegal who played a significant role in the closing of the transaction.

The relevant facts mainly are undisputed. Appellee Willoughby Corporation, the plaintiff below, was formed in September 1974. . . .

Appellant Robert M. Musselman, a defendant below, represented the bondholders in formation of the Corporation. He became attorney for the Corporation and also served as its Secretary. He was not a member of the Board of Directors. The daily operations of the Corporation were handled from defendant's law office by defendant's employees. . . .

In 1976, aware that the Board of Directors wished to sell a portion of the Willoughby Tract, defendant contracted Thomas J. Chandler, Jr., a local real estate broker, who obtained an offer to purchase Parcel 9. The offer was made by Charles W. Hurt, a medical doctor who had been a real estate developer in the Charlottesville and Albemarle County area for a number of years. . . .

Subsequently, another standard form purchase contract for $215,000 was completed dated May 6, 1976. The purchaser was shown to be "Charles Wm. Hurt or Assigns." . . . The contract was executed by Hurt, by Musselman on behalf of the Corporation as corporate Secretary, and by the realtor. . . .

[Stanley K. Joynes, III,] had been employed by Musselman in June 1977. Joynes had just graduated from college but had no formal training either as a lawyer or a paralegal. His main responsibility, under Musselman's direction, was to "shepherd the Willoughby Project along." Joynes attended his first Board meeting in July 1977 and was chosen Assistant Secretary of the Corporation.

In the course of the September 1977 Board meeting, defendant was directed to close the Hurt transaction "as soon as possible." Three weeks later, Stuart F. Carwile, Hurt's attorney, notified Musselman by letter dated September 22, 1977 that his client desired to take title to Parcel 9 as follows:

> Stuart F. Carwile and David W. Kudravetz, as trustees for the Fifth Street Land Trust, pursuant to the terms of a certain land trust agreement dated 22 September 1977.

Carwile advised that after Musselman submitted a draft of the deed, Carwile would forward the proposed deed of trust and note for defendant's approval.

The paralegal then prepared the deed, with "some assistance" from other employees of defendant, in accordance with Carwile's request showing the Land Trust as grantee. Joynes arranged for Frankel to execute the deed, dated October 5, 1977, and on that day participated with Carwile in the closing of the transaction. Musselman was out of town on business on both October 4th and 5th. In the course of the closing on October 5th, the paralegal accepted the deed of trust, and other closing documents prepared by Carwile, which specifically exculpated Hurt from personal liability in the transaction as beneficiary under the land trust.

At this point, we note several important undisputed facts. First, the Board of Directors, upon being advised that Hurt, a man of substantial wealth, was to be the purchaser of Parcel 9, intended to rely on Hurt's potential personal liability as a part of the security for payment of the deferred purchase price. Second, Musselman maintained in his trial testimony that he was authorized by the Board to execute the contract of the sale on behalf of the Corporation, and this was not contradicted by any witnesses. In addition, Musselman testified that Joynes, the paralegal, represented the Corporation at the closing, acting within his authority as an employee of defendant. Also, none of the Board members, prior to closing, ever examined either the proposed contract of March 26 or the final contract dated May 6. Moreover, no member of the Board knew before closing that the contract showed the purchaser to be "Hurt or Assigns." In addition, Musselman always was of the opinion that the foregoing language in the contract authorized Hurt to escape personal liability under the contract by assigning his rights in the contract to whomever he chose. Also, Musselman never called the language to the Board's attention or explained its meaning to the Board. Finally, the fact that the closing documents exculpated Hurt from personal liability as beneficiary under the land trust was never revealed or explained to the Board of Directors prior to closing. . . .

The Land Trust defaulted under the terms of the $170,000 note in respect to an interest payment due on April 1, 1978. Subsequently, this action to recover the principal sum plus interest, due under the real estate transaction was filed in September 1978 in numerous counts against Hurt and Musselman. The proceeding against Hurt was severed and he was eventually dismissed by the trial court as a party defendant.

The Corporation's action against Musselman was based on alternative theories. The plaintiff charged that defendant breached certain fiduciary duties in his capacity as an officer of the Corporation. In addition, the Corporation alleged that Musselman, in his capacity as attorney for the Corporation, was negligent and breached his fiduciary duty as counsel to the Corporation.

At the March 1982 trial, the jury was permitted, under the instructions, to find against defendant in his capacity either as attorney, or as an officer of the Corporation, or as both attorney and officer. The jury found against defendant in his capacity as attorney only and fixed the damages, which were not in dispute, at $243,722.99. This sum represented the principal amount due on the obligation, plus interest through the last day of trial. The trial court entered judgment on the verdict in June 1982, and we awarded defendant this appeal in July 1983. . . .

Inexplicably, defendant's main contentions on appeal are based on the faulty premise that he lacked corporate authority to act in executing the contract containing the "or Assigns" language and in completing the conveyance to a land trust, while, in the process, exculpating Hurt from personal liability. This argument is totally inconsistent with defendant's trial testimony that he did, in fact, have authority to execute the contract. It is also at odds with the uncontroverted evidence about defendant's "dominant role" in acting for the Corporation. . . .

There is no merit to this argument. Musselman, being authorized to execute the contract and to close the transaction, had the responsibility as counsel to advise his client, immediately upon discovery of the "problem," that it should attempt to rescind the transaction, if we assume an attempt at rescission would have been successful. Instead, defendant at no time advised the Board of Directors that it should pursue rescission. . . .

For these reasons, the judgment of the trial court will be affirmed.

Questions about the Case

1. What functions did the paralegal Joynes perform in this transaction? Do you think any of these duties were inappropriate functions for a paralegal to perform? Were they carried out competently?
2. What were the mistakes made by the attorney Musselman in this case? What should he have done to fulfill his duty to the client without being negligent?
3. Do you think that Musselman adequately supervised Joynes? Why or why not?
4. Why was Joynes not named as a defendant in this action? Did Joynes act negligently? Did the court hold Musselman liable for Joynes's mistakes?
5. How did the fact that Joynes was "untrained" affect the court's thinking? Does a lawyer have a duty to hire a qualified person? A duty to match the person's skills and knowledge to the work that is delegated?

In the following case, a lawyer is disciplined for failure to supervise his "legal assistants," who, like the paralegal in the *Musselman* case, did not have formal paralegal training and education and breached several aspects of the ethics rules.

Supreme Court of Arizona v. Struthers
179 Ariz. 216, 877 P.2d 789 (1994)

Child Support Collections ("CSC"), a debt collection agency, retained Struthers in December 1989 to work with another lawyer who had been handling CSC's cases. The following day, the first lawyer resigned. . . .

When Struthers started with CSC, the agency was owned by Robert Hydrick and run in large measure by John Star, neither of whom was an attorney. . . .

In 1990, at Struthers' suggestion, Hydrick dissolved CSC. This occurred during an investigation by the State Banking Department into allegations of irregularities in CSC's handling of client funds and that Star was holding himself out as an attorney. Struthers knew about and even represented Star and Hydrick in these matters.

When Hydrick dissolved CSC, Struthers superficially converted its operations into a law practice. In reality, however, CSC simply continued to operate. Star and Hydrick formed a new entity called MIROVI Inc., which was supposed to act as a managing company, providing support personnel and services for Struthers' practice. Star and Hydrick became Struthers' "legal assistants."

From the beginning of Struthers' association with CSC, he had a very large case load. At first he took over from his predecessor about 250 cases, but this number later rose to nearly 750. Although Struthers nominally maintained his status as an independent attorney, CSC (now MIROVI) staff ran his office, his accounting system and performed other tasks, such as conducting client interviews. . . . Under these circumstances, many of the formalities of a law firm were abandoned, giving rise to a number of the violations discussed below. [The violations related to client trust accounts, scope of representation, diligence, communication, fees, safekeeping client property, terminating representation, and professional independence.]

We examine in detail some of the more egregious violations . . . in four categories . . . [including supervision of] nonlawyer assistants. . . .

It is important to note that lawyers are often responsible for the actions of their nonlawyer assistants. Ethical Rule 5.3(a) provides that a lawyer in Struthers' position shall "make reasonable efforts to ensure that the firm has in effect measures giving reasonable assurance" that nonlawyer assistants conduct themselves according to the rules for lawyers. . . .

In the present case, however, Struthers virtually abandoned responsibility for running his office to Star and Hydrick. Although Struthers knew that the Banking Department has charged Star and Hydrick with serious improprieties, he gave them total control of his office and unfettered access to his trust fund. . . .

[H]e knew about Star's dishonesty early in their relationship. Struthers admitted to the Committee that although Star told him he was an attorney licensed in other states, Struthers knew from that start this was not true.... Although there may often be some question of what is a reasonable effort to ensure proper conduct by nonlawyer employees, at a minimum the lawyer must screen, instruct, and supervise. [Citation omitted.] Struthers did little but close his eyes.

Moreover, even if Struthers had been unaware that he placed untrustworthy persons in charge of his affairs, he still violated ER 5.3(c) by knowingly ratifying many of their ethical lapses and by failing to mitigate their consequences. For example, although he knew Hydrick had commingled his own funds with those in Struthers' trust account, Struthers did nothing to stop this....

Struthers violated [Rule 43, State Bar Trust Account Guidelines] when he allowed incompetent and untrustworthy employees to manage his trust account, and then failed to properly supervise them to ensure they were complying with the Trust Account Guidelines.... For example, Struthers routinely signed pages of blank checks for his employees to complete in his absence. As a result, Star and Hydrick were free to decide whether and how much to pay clients, and often based their decisions on which clients they favored....

Ethical Rule 5.4(a) provides that a "lawyer ... shall not share legal fees with a nonlawyer...." Struthers' agreement with MIROVI, however, required him to turn over all fees that he received to MIROVI, with any profit left after paying expenses to be "distributed by the agreement of the parties."...

We deal here with a lawyer who, by premeditated scheme, has demonstrated that his practice is not designed to serve the public but, rather, to prey on those most in need of his help. He has demonstrated that he is indeed a danger to the public. To allow him to resume an active practice would be to ignore our obligation to that public....

Accordingly Andrew Leeroy Struthers is disbarred....

Questions about the Case

1. What functions did the nonlawyers perform in the lawyer's office? Can each of these duties be properly delegated to a nonlawyer and supervised?
2. Did these "legal assistants" meet any of the definitions of paralegal or legal assistant in this chapter? If not, what is lacking in their background?
3. Could the lawyer have set up a collections practice with a large caseload and run it in a manner that would comport with ethics rules? Describe how. Note that the court refers to recruiting, delegating, and

supervising paralegals. Define each one of these aspects of a lawyer's responsibility for paralegals.
4. Do you think that the lawyer should have been disbarred? What do you think should have happened to Hydrick and Star? Can you use this case to argue for regulation of paralegals?

In the following case, a supervising lawyer in a high-volume practice is sanctioned for failure to supervise and other ethical breaches.

In re Phillips
26 Ariz. 112, 244 P.3d 549 (2010)

Phillips is the founder and managing attorney of Phillips & Associates ("P & A"), a large law firm based in Phoenix. A self-styled "consumer law firm," P & A handles a high volume of cases, having represented approximately 33,000 clients between 2004 and 2006. At the time of the disciplinary proceedings, P & A employed 250 people, including [38] lawyers. The firm's practice was limited to criminal defense, bankruptcy, and personal injury.

Phillips no longer represents clients, but instead supervises and manages the firm. His duties include setting firm policy on billing, accounting, and intake procedures. Although Phillips has general control over the firm, during the relevant period he had delegated primary responsibility for the criminal division to Robert Arentz, and for the bankruptcy division to Robert Teague.

In 2002, Phillips was the subject of disciplinary proceedings resulting in his conditionally admitting to violations of ERs 5.1, 5.3, and 7.1, and agreeing to a censure and two years' probation. The judgment and order entered in 2002 included detailed probationary terms relating to the management of P & A. . . .

> Bonuses paid to intake personnel cannot be based exclusively on either the number of clients who retain the firm or on the amount of fees received from those clients. The criteria for determining bonuses must be provided to the intake personnel in writing. . . .
>
> All attorneys and other billable staff members who work on criminal cases shall keep contemporaneous time records to enable the firm to conduct a "backward glance" at the conclusion of a case in order to determine whether a refund is due. . . .

Phillips successfully completed his probation in 2004.

Between August 2006 and May 2008, the Bar issued a series of probable cause orders against Phillips and Arentz. The Bar filed a formal complaint against them in October 2007 and, after several amendments, ultimately charged [22] counts, alleging violations of ERs 1.1, 1.2, 1.3, 1.4, 5.1, 5.3, 7.1, and 8.4. . . .

Prospective clients who visit the firm's offices do not immediately meet with an attorney. Instead, they are provided a blank fee agreement and a general questionnaire. After completing the questionnaire, the prospective client meets with a P & A legal administrator, a nonlawyer tasked with retaining clients. Legal administrators are paid a base salary and monthly bonuses, based in part on the number of cases that the legal administrator retains. After obtaining general information from the client, the legal administrator meets with a lawyer who sets the fee. After the fee agreement is prepared, the client speaks with a lawyer to make sure the client understands the fee agreement, who the lawyer will be, and the scope of P & A's representation.

The Hearing Officer found that this process, known as "closing," was often not completed by an attorney knowledgeable in the relevant practice area. . . .

[T]he Hearing Officer found P & A's retention policies, as implemented, impeded potential clients from obtaining the information needed to make informed decisions about retention. With respect to Counts 9 and 12, the Hearing Officer found that a P & A legal administrator gave a client's family member unreasonable expectations about the representation, suggesting that the firm would be able to reduce the client's sentence in criminal proceedings.

In Count 9, the client's father was told that the firm should be able to reduce his son's sentence. An attorney signed a fee agreement describing the scope of the services as "mitigation of sentencing." The client, however, had already entered into a plea agreement with a stipulated sentence, and no one at P & A advised the client or his father of the unlikelihood of mitigating the sentence. Despite the client's expectations, the client's sentence was not reduced.

In Count 12, a client's mother signed a fee agreement after being told by a legal representative that the firm should be able to help reduce her son's sentence. As the firm was aware, however, the client had already stipulated to a particular sentence. The client's mother met with a bankruptcy attorney, who did not know what a stipulated plea agreement was. A criminal attorney did not meet with her until the day of sentencing, when she was informed that her son would receive the sentence stipulated in the plea agreement. . . .

The Hearing Officer found that Phillips and Arentz violated ERs 5.1(a) and 5.3(a) in both counts because the firm's retention practices did not require a knowledgeable attorney to speak with the potential client before entering into a fee agreement, and the firm used nonlawyers in its retention process. Similarly, in Count 17, a client with a suspended driver's license met only with a bankruptcy attorney and a legal administrator before hiring P & A to represent him. The client wanted to have his license reinstated but also had an unadjudicated DUI charge. The scope of services set forth in the fee agreement did not match the client's expectations. The firm did not follow the client's decisions regarding the scope of the representation, and the firm waited weeks before telling the client his driver's license could not be reinstated until the DUI charge was resolved. The firm also failed to inform the client prior to retention that the firm could not accomplish his goals. . . .

The Hearing Officer also found violations of ER 5.3 arising from P & A's providing legal administrators with bonuses based, in part, on the number of clients retained. Count 8 involved a legal administrator who used "high pressure tactics" to attempt to dissuade a client from terminating P & A's representation. Count 19 involved a client who retained the firm for defense of a DUI charge and, as the firm was aware, was also in the process of becoming a United States citizen. When the client asked to terminate P & A's representation after meeting with a legal administrator and a bankruptcy attorney, the client was subjected to intimidation and false statements from a P & A employee. At one point, the employee warned the client that he was "looking to lose his citizenship," and the employee insinuated that if the client stopped payment on the retainer check, the firm could have the police investigate his immigration status. After making several unsuccessful attempts to obtain documents he had furnished to P & A, the client was only able to recover the papers after hiring new counsel. . . .

Although the P & A employees' tactics violated P & A's policies, the Hearing Officer concluded that Phillips and Arentz violated ER 5.3(a) in both counts because legal administrators' bonuses were tied, in part, to client retention. These incentives provided "the motive for the misconduct." The words in the firm's policy manual prohibiting such conduct were insufficient to insulate managers and supervisors from ethical responsibility when the actual ongoing practices were to the contrary. . . .

In Count 11, the Hearing Officer found that P & A employees failed to act promptly on a client's termination request. The firm took more than five months to refund money to the client despite repeated requests for a refund. The Hearing Officer found that both Arentz and Phillips violated ERs 5.1(a) and 5.3(a) for failing to have practices in place to prevent difficulty in obtaining a refund. . . .

Ethical Rule 5.1(a) provides that a partner or an attorney with comparable managerial authority "shall make reasonable efforts to ensure that the firm has in effect measures giving reasonable assurance that all lawyers in the firm conform to the Rules of Professional Conduct." Similarly, ER 5.3(a) provides that a partner or a lawyer with comparable managerial authority must make "reasonable efforts to ensure that the firm has in effect measures giving reasonable assurances that" nonlawyers employed by the firm or associated with the lawyer comply with the professional obligations of the lawyer.

These duties require not only supervision, but also that the supervising attorney establish "internal policies and procedures" providing reasonable assurances that lawyers and nonlawyers in the firm conform to the Rules of Professional Conduct. ERs 5.1 cmt. 2; 5.3 cmt. 2. The size of the firm is relevant in determining what is "reasonable," and in a large firm such as P & A, "more elaborate measures may be necessary." ER 5.1 cmt. 3.

The rules imposing managerial and supervisory obligations, however, do not provide for vicarious liability for a subordinate's acts; rather, they "mandate an independent duty of supervision." *In re Galbasini*, 163 Ariz. 120, 124, 786 P.2d 971, 975 (1990). Nor is a supervising attorney of a nonlawyer assistant "required to guarantee that that assistant will never engage in conduct that is not compatible with the professional obligations of the lawyer." *In re Miller*, 178 Ariz. 257, 259, 872 P.2d 661, 663 (1994).

In contesting the findings that he violated ERs 5.1(a) and 5.3(a), Phillips refers to the "mountain of undisputed evidence" adduced at the hearing of P & A's supervisory efforts and the "relatively rare" occurrence of ethical breaches by other P & A employees. But the prior modification of firm policies, made pursuant to the 2002 judgment and order, did not alleviate Phillips's ongoing duty to ensure that his subordinates complied with the revised policies and ethical rules.

The Hearing Officer found actual injury in each of the client-related counts. P & A clients were misled and improperly advised by unqualified lawyers, had difficulty obtaining refunds, and were misinformed about the reasonable objectives of the representation. Clients were also financially harmed, having paid unreasonable fees or retainers without a full understanding of the likely results of the representation. The record supports these findings. . . .

We also recognize that Phillips, as managing partner of a law firm representing more than 10,000 clients per year, was in a position of greater supervisory authority than Arentz. Phillips, not Arentz, had full power and control over P & A's policies and practices. As such, he was better able to effect positive change and insist on full compliance with ethics standards. Conversely, Phillips's lapses in these areas might potentially cause greater harm. Phillips's apparent delegation of responsibility and hands-off approach does not make his policies any less of a danger. Indeed, the decisions he makes directly affect the public, the profession, and the integrity of the legal system.

Although attorney partners and supervisors are not guarantors of their employees' conduct, they must take reasonable steps to ensure that firm practices, not merely policies, actually comply with ethical rules binding all lawyers practicing law in this state. Phillips's failure to do so, particularly in view of his disciplinary history, warrants a significant period of suspension followed by a lengthy probation term with strict conditions.

A longer suspension for Phillips is therefore justified. . . .

The Hearing Officer and the Commission recommended that Phillips's two-year probation term and conditions of probation begin and take effect after Phillips's suspension is fully served. We accept that recommendation. . . .

Questions about the Case

1. What kind of firm was this? Who were the clients? How many clients were served by this firm? What were the lawyers' roles and the nonlawyers' roles?
2. What was ethically objectionable about what the nonlawyers were doing?
3. Did the firm have the necessary policies and procedures to ensure that matters were handled properly? How could this firm have been run in a manner that comports with the ethics rules?
4. What factors did the court consider in deciding the sanction? Why were these important?

In the following case, a lawyer faces disciplinary charges for the conduct of a paralegal who runs a business providing services in the immigration area.

The Florida Bar v. Abrams
919 So.2d 425 (Fla. 2006)

Suzanne Akbas, a paralegal, formed a corporate entity titled U.S. Entry, Inc. to provide legal services to persons with immigration issues who were seeking to gain entry and establish lawful status in the United States. Attorney Daniel Everett Abrams was employed by U.S. Entry as "Managing Attorney" and was paid for "piecemeal legal work," generally at a rate of one hundred dollars per unit of work. Olga Ulershperger and Abdullah Ziya, who were husband and wife, both entered the United States in November 1999 on tourist visas and then in the spring of 2000 sought assistance from U.S. Entry in obtaining further lawful status. Ulershperger was an accomplished gymnast; Ziya was a Turkish Kurd who had suffered persecution, including torture, in his native land.

Akbas told the couple that instead of seeking political asylum based on Ziya's history of persecution, they should apply for employment visas based on Ulershperger's skills as a gymnast. The couple's applications ultimately were denied and their existing visas expired in May 2001. They did not learn of their unlawful status until March or April of 2002, after consulting with an immigration lawyer in California. That lawyer told the couple that they should not have been counseled to seek employment visas but rather should have been counseled to seek political asylum based on Ziya's persecution and torture, but that the one-year time limit for seeking asylum had expired in November 2000. The couple ultimately sought and were granted asylum under an ineffective representation exception to the one-year time limit, which prompted the present proceeding.

Based on the above matters, The Florida Bar filed a two-count complaint against Abrams, and the referee made the following findings of fact:

> . . . [Ulershperger and Ziya] were not notified of the status of their claim or of the lapse of their lawful status. . . . There was no follow-through by the Respondent — not telephone calls, no letters to the INS. . . .
>
> Respondent violated a number of disciplinary rules. . . . Instead of Akbas being employed by and under the Respondent's supervision, it was the other way around. Akbas was the employer and she used Respondent's license to practice law. . . .
>
> The referee recommended that Abrams be found guilty of violating [several sections of] the Rules Regulating the Florida Bar . . . and that the following disciplinary measures be imposed on Abrams: a one-year suspension; restitution in the amount of $2,400; and payment of the bar's costs. . . .
>
> The present record shows that Abrams was listed as the attorney of record on a status extension application submitted by Ziya and was listed as the "Managing Attorney" on the letterhead of a missive used by U.S. Entry in requesting alien labor certification for Ulershperger. The letter was signed, "Suzanne J. Akbas For Daniel E. Abrams, Esq." At the hearing below, [an] immigration lawyer . . . testified . . . that the proper handling of asylum claims requires substantial intake by a lawyer, not a paralegal. . . . Abrams had no contact whatsoever with Ulershperger and Ziya. . . . We approve the referee's recommendation that Abrams be found guilty of violating of rule 4-1.1 [re competent representation]. . . .
>
> [T]he record shows that even though Akbas worked as a paralegal at U.S. Entry, she actually was the person in control of the corporation's day-to-day operations. She met with clients, conducted client interviews, and made the decisions as to the appropriate course of action for clients. Abrams himself visited the U.S. Entry office only several times a month. Akbas testified that she unsuccessfully tried to get Abrams more involved in the company's operations. We conclude that Abrams's role and course of conduct at U.S. Entry were inconsistent with the title "Managing Attorney," and the title constituted a clear misrepresentation of his status. We approve the referee's recommendation that Abrams be found guilty of violating rule 4-8.4(c) [on dishonesty, fraud, deceit or misrepresentation]. . . .

Based on the foregoing, we approve the referee's findings of fact, recommendations as to guilt, and recommended discipline. . . .

Questions about the Case

1. How would you characterize the relationship of Abrams and Akbas? Who was the employer? Can an employee "supervise" his or her boss?
2. What functions did Akbas perform that might be considered practicing law? Consult Chapter 3 for definitions.
3. Do you think that Abrams should have been held responsible for Akbas's mistakes? Why or why not?
4. Should Akbas have been held responsible for her mistakes? How would this come about?
5. Is there a way for a nonlawyer-run immigration service like U.S. Entry to operate legally and ethically?

In this interesting case, a paralegal who is the recipient of a gift from an elderly client is held not to be a fiduciary to the client by virtue of her status as a paralegal. This case demonstrates the lack of clear and consistent case law about the liability of legal assistants in their professional capacity.

In re Estate of Divine
263 Ill. App. 3d 799, 635 N.E. 2d 581 (1994)

Beginning in approximately 1979, Giancola was employed in Chicago by attorney Samuel Poznanovich as a part-time secretary in his law office. Eventually, she became his full-time secretary. Giancola received a paralegal certificate from Roosevelt University in 1980, and took an H & R Block tax course in 1970. Poznanovich employed one other secretary in addition to Giancola.

In 1981, Richard and his wife, Lila, came to Poznanovich's office for income tax services. The Divines did not have any children and both were retired. Giancola estimated that they were in their "early seventies" in 1981. Giancola interviewed the Divines, took tax information from them such as W-2 forms and copies of their previous tax returns, and introduced them to Poznanovich. After this initial meeting, Poznanovich prepared the Divines' tax returns every year until 1986. Each year, Giancola would interview the Divines and gather their tax information. She never prepared their taxes, but simply gathered information for Poznanovich's use. In 1985, Poznanovich also represented Richard in a personal injury case. Giancola was not involved in that case. Additionally, Richard called Poznanovich occasionally for legal advice on other matters. Before 1986, Giancola and Poznanovich saw the Divines only at the law office, although, according to Poznanovich, the relationship became "more and more friendly" each year.

In December 1986, Lila died. Richard called Giancola at the office to tell her about Lila's death. Giancola stated that Richard had "depended on Lila for just about everything" and was very lonely without Lila. Also, he was "unable to do for himself." Giancola went to visit Richard in his apartment on Coles Avenue "within a day or two" of Lila's death. Richard was afraid to leave the apartment alone and could not walk long distances because "his legs were bad." Richard's relatives and Poznanovich also testified that Richard had physical problems with his legs. Giancola stated that for "the most part," Richard was confined to his apartment. After Giancola's first visit, Richard frequently called her, and she visited his apartment once or twice a week. Richard asked her to assist him in getting his groceries and other necessities. Richard gave Giancola money for the groceries and supplies. She testified that he did not give her a "fee" for her services, but admitted that sometimes he gave her "something for [her]self." He did his own cooking while living in the Coles Avenue apartment.

Giancola believed that the neighborhood around Coles Avenue was too dangerous for Richard, and she did not like going there to visit him. She suggested that he move to a safer area; she also mentioned to Poznanovich that Richard's neighborhood was unsafe. Poznanovich's office is located in a building he and his sister own. There are four residential apartments in that building which are rented by Poznanovich and his sister. Giancola occasionally takes the rent checks from tenants for Poznanovich. When an apartment became vacant in Poznanovich's building, Giancola told Richard it "would be easier" if he moved into that apartment. She did not know that Richard's relatives wanted him to move to Michigan City, Indiana. . . .

In addition to getting his supplies and cooking his meals, Giancola cashed checks for Richard and made bank deposits for him. She wrote out the checks for all his bills. She explained that she would write the checks, he would sign them, and she would mail them. All these transactions involved only Richard's personal checking account. Richard would discuss "personal problems" with Giancola, but did not talk to her about legal matters. . . .

In November 1987, Richard called Poznanovich and asked him to come to his apartment. In the apartment, Richard told Poznanovich that he wanted to "put his affairs in order." First, he handed two bank account passbooks to Poznanovich and said "I want this for my sweetheart." Richard told Poznanovich that his "sweetheart" was Giancola, and that he wanted her to have the two accounts. These two accounts were separate from Richard's personal checking account which Giancola used for his finances. Richard told Poznanovich he did not want to leave the accounts to Giancola in his will because he wanted her "to have them now." Richard explained: "As far as I'm concerned, if it were not for her, I would be dead now." Poznanovich suggested that the accounts be made joint accounts, like the accounts Richard had shared with Lila. When

Poznanovich assured Richard that a joint tenancy would allow Giancola to have the money immediately, Richard told Poznanovich to change the two accounts to joint accounts. Giancola was not present during this discussion. Poznanovich testified that he did not receive any direct or indirect financial benefit from this transaction.

Next, Richard asked Poznanovich to draft a will for him. The will made Poznanovich executor of the estate and gave $3,000 each to Giancola and Poznanovich. Poznanovich testified: "I had a problem with [Richard] inserting me as a beneficiary under the will . . . [and] we agreed that if I were to remain in the will as a beneficiary, I would waive my executor's fee, which I did." The will made one other specific bequest of $2,000, then left one half of the residuary estate to the petitioners and one half to four other family members. After his death, the value of Richard's estate, in addition to the joint accounts, was approximately $150,000.

Poznanovich obtained two signature cards from the bank and had the accounts changed to joint accounts. On November 14, 1987, he asked Giancola to sign these signature cards. Neither Richard nor Poznanovich ever discussed the accounts with Giancola before presenting her with the cards. They also did not discuss the transactions with any members of Richard's family. . . .

At the hearing in the trial court and in this court the petitioners argued that the actions of Poznanovich and Giancola are inextricably intertwined and that because Giancola was a paralegal and an employee of the lawyer, Poznanovich, who was a fiduciary as a matter of law, so also is Giancola a fiduciary as a matter of law. They also repeatedly assert that Poznanovich gained financially from the transactions which benefitted Giancola. Nonetheless, they never requested that Poznanovich or Giancola return the $3,000 bequests and they do not challenge the validity of the will. Additionally, they have never made Poznanovich a party to these proceedings. Essentially, the petitioners argue that Poznanovich's questionable action of drafting a will which gave him a gift and his status as an attorney should be imputed to Giancola and that she should be liable because of his actions.

Under certain circumstances, one person will be charged with liability for the actions of or knowledge given to another person. For example, actions by one partner will be imputed to another partner. [Citation omitted.] Also, an employer will be held liable for certain actions of his employee. [Citation omitted.] There is no case law holding an employee liable for the acts of his employer, however, and the petitioners cite no law to support their position that Giancola should be accountable for Poznanovich's actions. Unfortunately, there also is no case law in Illinois involving the narrower question of a paralegal's fiduciary duty to his employer's client, making this a case of first impression. In fact, we have found no reported case in the United States involving a paralegal's fiduciary responsibility, as a paralegal, to his attorney's client.

Moreover, there is very little case law from Illinois or any jurisdiction generally discussing paralegals. Two cases address the somewhat analogous issue of a paralegal's possible liability for legal malpractice. A divided Nevada Supreme Court, in *Busch v. Flangas* (1992), 108 Nev. 821, 837 P.2d 438, held that an attorney's law clerk or paralegal who attempts to provide legal services can be liable for malpractice to the client. On the other hand, the *Busch* dissent argued that a law clerk or paralegal, as an employee of an attorney, owes no duty to the attorney's client, but is liable only to the attorney. (*Busch*, 837 P.2d at 441 (Springer, J., dissenting).) The Court of Appeals of Ohio, without extensive discussion, determined that a paralegal could not be sued for legal malpractice because she was not an attorney. *Palmer v. Westmeyer* (1988), 48 Ohio App. 3d 296, 549 N.E.2d 1202, 1209.

On the other hand, the idea that an attorney is liable, in malpractice or as an ethical violation, for his paralegal's acts is well-supported in Illinois. . . .

Several Illinois cases support the idea that paralegals are an extension of their employing attorney. For example, the presence of an attorney's employee, such as a secretary or law clerk, does not destroy the attorney-client privilege for material disclosed to the attorney in the employee's presence. [Citations omitted.] Also, in the majority of Illinois cases discussing paralegals, which involve disputed attorney fee petitions, the courts have held that an attorney may recover reasonable fees for time properly spent by his paralegal. . . .

Based on these cases, we refuse to treat Poznanovich and Giancola as a unit for purposes of Giancola's liability. It is clear that Poznanovich, as a licensed attorney and as an employer, could be held liable for Giancola's actions. Nonetheless, holding Giancola liable as if she were an attorney is not consistent with general *respondeat superior* law or with the decisions discussed above treating paralegals as subordinate employees of attorneys. The theme running through all these cases is that paralegals do not independently practice law, but simply serve as assistants to lawyers. They are not equal or autonomous partners. Thus, while supervisors properly are held liable for paralegals' actions, the subordinate paralegals should not be liable for the actions of these supervisors. Therefore, we refuse to find that Giancola owed Richard a fiduciary duty simply because she worked for Richard's attorney, and we refuse to hold that paralegals are fiduciaries to their employers' clients as a matter of law. . . .

We also wish to make it clear that we are not saying that the evidence shows that Poznanovich did anything improper. We have discussed his "actions" only in the general sense to illustrate that, while he was a fiduciary to Richard as a matter of law and if he had been the recipient of the joint account funds, the burden of proof would have been on him to show that the transaction was proper, his fiduciary obligations may not be imposed upon Giancola. Nor are we saying that an improper transfer may never be shown under circumstances like those present in this case. If the petitioners had offered evidence from which it could be inferred that collusion existed between Poznanovich and Giancola or that Poznanovich gained financially in any way from the transfer, our holding would be different. But neither the trial judge nor this court may decide a case on speculation, guess, conjecture, or suspicion.

For these reasons, the judgment of the circuit court is affirmed.

Questions about the Case

1. What was the paralegal's relationship with the client, and how did it evolve over time? Was it professional or personal?
2. What evidence might show that the paralegal took advantage of the client? Discuss the adequacy of this evidence.
3. Did the petitioners sue the lawyer? Why or why not? On what grounds did they sue the paralegal?
4. Under this case, can a paralegal be held liable for the actions of his or her employing lawyer? Could the lawyer be held liable for the actions of the paralegal?
5. Does a paralegal have a fiduciary duty directly to a client in Illinois? How would you state this principle?
6. Review the rules in Chapter 5 about accepting gifts from clients and determine if either the lawyer or the paralegal in this case violated those rules. What should they have done to protect against a lawsuit like this one?

3

Unauthorized Practice of Law

This chapter covers the limitations on the practice of law, including what acts constitute the practice of law and how these restrictions affect and guide paralegal conduct. Chapter 3 covers:

- the history of the unauthorized practice of law
- definitions of the practice of law
- the effect of restrictions on the practice of law on access to legal services
- the lawyer's ethical responsibility to prevent the unauthorized practice of law and to supervise paralegals
- key functions that may constitute the unauthorized practice of law, including:
  - making court appearances and taking depositions
  - preparation and signing of documents and pleadings
  - giving legal advice
  - accepting cases and setting fees
- analysis of functions that may or may not constitute the practice of law
- nonlawyer practice before administrative agencies
- disclosure of the paralegal's nonlawyer status
- paralegals working as independent contractors

A. A Brief History of Unauthorized Practice of Law

1. The Early Years

Limitations on who can practice law in the United States can be traced back to the colonial era. At that time, a proliferation of untrained practitioners caused local courts to adopt rules requiring lawyers who appeared before them to have a license granted by the court. Additional rules adopted during this period limited the amount of fees that could be charged by lawyers and mandated that lawyers could not refuse to take a case. The stated purposes of these rules were to prevent stirring up of litigation by unscrupulous "pettifoggers" and "mercenary" lawyers, to stop incompetence that harmed clients and impaired the administration of justice and dignity of the courts, and to prevent exploitive, excessive fees.

These early limitations on the practice of law evolved to their present state incrementally and not always in a smooth and linear way. Many of these rules, along with later rules that governed the training of lawyers and their admission to the bar, were eliminated during an era of deprofessionalization in the early nineteenth century, only to reemerge in the late nineteenth century. State and local bar associations began to gain strength during this period, in part because of concern over the large numbers of lawyers competing with one another for legal work and with newly developing businesses, such as collection agencies, banks and trust companies, and accounting firms, and the establishment of administrative agencies that permitted nonlawyer appearances. The first unauthorized practice statutes were passed in several states during the 1850s, prohibiting court appearances by anyone not licensed as an attorney and prohibiting the practice of law by court personnel such as bailiffs. The first unauthorized practice prosecutions were also brought during this period. These cases held it improper for an unlicensed person to portray themselves as an attorney and for a nonlawyer to form a partnership with a lawyer.

The definition of the practice of law that was formulated in early cases gradually broadened to cover activities beyond court appearances. Early cases held that the practice of law also includes the preparation of documents by which legal rights are secured. Gradually, new justifications for restricting the right to practice law to licensed lawyers were developed, including the lawyer's professional independence, proven moral character, and special training. Advocates for tight controls over the practice of law also used public protection arguments by pointing out that lawyers are subject to sanctions for breaches of ethics or competence, unlike unlicensed practitioners.

Legal historians believe that the height of unauthorized practice restrictions came during the Depression when lawyers needed most to protect their economic interests from competition. Bar associations became especially powerful trade organizations during this era. Unauthorized practice statutes were passed in virtually all states, making it a crime to practice law without a license. The definition of the practice of law was further expanded to include "all services customarily rendered by lawyers."

In 1930, the American Bar Association created its powerful Special Committee on the Unauthorized Practice of Law, which by the late 1950s had agreements called Statements of Principles with accountants, collection agencies, insurance adjusters, life insurance underwriters, publishers, and realtors, to name a few. These agreements, later rescinded when it became apparent that they would be found illegal under the Sherman Antitrust Act, delineated the legal activities that these other nonlawyer professionals could engage in without stepping into the protected realm of the practice of law. Most state and local bar associations had committees that monitored the activities of competitor organizations, and many also entered into Statements of Principle with nonlawyer legal service providers. The California State Bar, for example, had 20 such agreements, which were rescinded in 1979.

Criminal prosecutions and civil suits to restrain unauthorized practice slowed during the 1960s and 1970s. During this period, the sale of legal self-help kits and books began, and soon most courts determined this activity not to constitute the unauthorized practice of law (UPL). These decisions signaled the beginning of a new movement to expand access to legal services by alternative means.

2. Recent UPL History: Nonlawyer Legal Service Providers and Access to Legal Services

The 1980s saw a **resurgence of unauthorized practice prosecutions** because of the increased number of nonlawyer legal service providers providing low-cost legal services directly to the public. Many factors converged to create the great need for alternative legal service providers: the decrease in federal funding for the Legal Services Corporation, which had supplied legal services to low-income persons; the increase in the need for legal services by every socio-economic group because of the proliferation and complexity of laws; and the rising cost of legal services provided by lawyers, which made it difficult or impossible for most Americans to employ a lawyer when they need one.

Most nonlawyer legal service providers work in areas of law in which low- and moderate-income people need assistance, such as landlord–tenant matters; family law matters, including **divorce**, paternity, domestic violence, and child support; consumer matters, including **bankruptcy**; and **immigration**. Some run "typing services" that assist persons only by typing documents, usually to be filed with the court, after the "customer" fills in the blanks on forms. Others provide more complete information and assistance, helping the customer decide what forms to use, what information to include on the forms, where to file them, and advising the customer on procedural matters and court appearances. Increasingly, these providers use electronic programs to complete standard court forms. Nonlawyer legal service providers call themselves by a variety of titles, including independent paralegals, legal technicians, and document preparers. (Remember from Chapter 2 that in several states, the use of the terms *paralegal* is prohibited to nonlawyers who are not supervised by lawyers.) Some providers are offering their services through We the People (WTP), a national organization that provides help to self-represented persons through offices owned and operated locally. See *In re Finch* at the end of this chapter for a WTP office that crossed the line into UPL.

The unmet need for legal services is well documented, but lawyers are largely opposed to giving up any of their traditional functions to nonlawyers. Clearly, lawyers have both monopolistic, economic reasons for this stance and legitimate professional and societal concerns about the quality of legal services that someone not trained as a lawyer can provide. The debate takes on national proportions as courts throughout the country attempt to address the needs of *pro se* litigants who have no choice but to represent themselves.

Prosecutions of nonlawyer legal service providers have been rising. No formal studies document the exact increase in prosecutions; however, starting in the early 1990s, most states reported criminal prosecutions for UPL and for injunctive relief against nonlawyer legal service providers after decades of virtually no such cases. Most cases are brought against bankruptcy, landlord-tenant, immigration, and family law practitioners where there has been egregious or incompetent conduct that harmed consumers. But some prosecutions have been based on lawyer complaints, rather than from complaints from disgruntled consumers.

Defendants in UPL cases sometimes argue, although unsuccessfully, that they are not giving legal advice but are simply assisting lay persons in the preparation of legal documents; that is, giving legal information. Some defendants in unauthorized practice prosecutions have argued unsuccessfully that a statutory power of attorney from a client gives a nonlawyer the authority to represent the client in litigation. (See, for example, *Whitehead v. Town House Equities, Ltd.*, 8 A.D.3d 369, 777 N.Y.S.2d 917 (2004); and *Drake v. Superior Court of San Diego County*, 21 Cal. App. 4th 1826, 26 Cal. Rptr. 2d 829 (1994).) Similarly, it has been consistently held that nonlawyers who are serving as conservators, executors, and other representatives of estates cannot make appearances in court on behalf of these estates. (See, for example, *Hansen v. Hansen*, 114 Cal. App. 4th 618 (2003).)

Some defendants have claimed, to no avail, a public necessity defense based on the lack of availability of legal services for their clients. For additional justifications on constitutional grounds, see *Board of Commissioners of the Utah State Bar v. Petersen* at the end of this chapter. As we moved into the twenty-first century, several states increased penalties for unauthorized practice of law. Even Arizona, which for many years was the only state without a UPL statute or rule, has adopted a court rule asserting the state supreme court's authority over anyone who practices law, whether authorized or not. In 2000, the American Bar Association's House of Delegates adopted a resolution calling on the states to vigorously investigate, report, and eliminate incidents of UPL.

The tremendous increase in **foreclosures** during the economic recession that began in 2008 gave rise to a new form of unauthorized practice, one that has sometimes drawn in lawyers. Foreclosure consultants and loan modification agencies, which seek to negotiate more affordable loans for homeowners with lenders, have been found by courts to be engaged in the unauthorized practice of law. Some of these firms also hire lawyers or use them as outside counsel, which has resulted in disciplinary action against lawyers for a variety of ethics violations, including aiding in the unauthorized practice of law, unethical solicitation of clients (see Chapter 6), and fee splitting (see Chapter 7). See *The Cincinnati Bar Ass'n v. Mullaney* at the end of the chapter for a disciplinary case on lawyers working with a loan modification company.

Another development of note has been the proliferation of **electronic resources** for persons seeking to represent themselves in various kinds of legal matters. Although one might expect that electronic resources would fall into the protected category of self-help books and materials, some bar associations and courts have challenged this interpretation. For example, in 1997, the Unauthorized Practice of Law Committee of the Supreme Court of Texas investigated the publication of electronic self-help resources, contending that the publication of these resources was tantamount to giving legal advice. These increasingly popular programs guide users to specific options and forms and help them to complete forms by asking them a series of questions that trigger selection and completion of forms. One of the Committee's contentions was that this process constituted legal advice that could only be given in Texas by a lawyer licensed in the state of Texas. The final result of this dispute, after several hearings and much publicity, was that the Texas legislature passed a law allowing self-help companies to publish this material without threat of a UPL prosecution. The use of technology to increase access to legal services through programs like these has grown dramatically despite ongoing controversy over whether it violates UPL rules. See *In* *re Reynoso*, 477 F.3d 117 (9th Cir. 2007), at the end of this chapter for an interesting case in this ongoing debate. (Also see North Carolina House Bill 439, approved in 2016, which resolved a longstanding dispute with LegalZoom and determined that interactive software that generates legal documents based on consumers' responses does not constitute UPL.)

Some states have taken action to regulate nonlawyers who assist persons with **immigration** matters, including Arizona, Illinois, and Oregon. Although federal statutes establish nationwide standards for accredited visa consultants, some immigration "consultants" do not fall within the reach of these federal laws, and widespread abuses of clients have been documented in the immigrant community. In 2011, the U.S. Justice and Homeland Security departments and the Federal Trade Commission initiated a nationwide campaign to target unauthorized immigration practitioners who prey upon immigrant communities. In 2012, the State Bar of Arizona and the U.S. Citizenship and Immigration Services, along with other federal and local agencies, launched an initiative to prohibit the unauthorized practice of law by **notarios**, who often act as legal advisors to Latino immigrants. In most of Latin America, notarios are lawyers, but in the United States, their function is limited to that of a **notary**, whose purpose is to witness and authenticate the execution of documents. A notary cannot represent clients or provide legal advice. Several states have determined that the preparation of **living trust documents** constitutes the practice of law and have prosecuted nonlawyers running companies that market and prepare living trust plans. These decisions hold that the client's decision about having a living trust, the attendant preparation and execution of documents, and the funding of the trust are functions that require a lawyer's judgment and involvement. (See ethics opinions about this topic, for example, Florida Bar re: Advisory Opinion on Nonlawyer Preparation of Living Trusts, 613 So. 2d 426 (Fla. 1992); California State Bar Ethics Opinion 97-148; South Dakota Bar Ethics Opinion 91-14; Colorado 90-87; Pennsylvania 90-65; Kansas Advisory Opinion 96-08; and Texas Prof. Eth. Comm. Opinion 95-498.)

Lawyers in several jurisdictions have been disciplined for aiding the unauthorized practice of law by participating in businesses that promoted and sold **living trusts**. In most of these cases, nonlawyer living trust marketers had all the client contact, and the lawyer did not counsel the clients about the decision to create a living trust or the provisions and funding of the trust. Courts have found that these lawyers have abdicated their responsibility to advise clients and to exercise independent professional judgment. Many lawyers in these cases failed to supervise the work of their employees in counseling clients or preparing the documents for them. The consequences have been disastrous for many elderly people who thought they were protecting their estates from probate, but were setting up these trusts unnecessarily and paying exorbitant commissions to fund the trusts. One such case is *In re Morin*, found at the end of this chapter. A few others of note are *In re Phillips*, 338 Or. 125, 107 P.3d 615

(2005); *In the Matter of Flack*, 272 Kan. 465, 33 P.3d 1281 (2001); and *Doe v. Condon*, 341 S.C. 22, 532 S.E.2d 879 (2000). (See also Texas Ethics Opinion 95-498 and Arizona Ethics Opinion 98-08.)

3. Other Recent UPL Activity

Another category of UPL cases are those in which lawyers have been disciplined for running **large-volume practices** without adequately supervising their paralegals and other employees. In most of these cases, the firms were set up so that paralegals were accepting cases, having clients sign retainer agreements, preparing legal documents for them, and counseling them about their legal rights with little or no lawyer involvement and no direct relationship between the lawyer and the client. In some cases, these violations were coupled with unlawful solicitation of clients by the nonlawyers and compensation arrangements that violate rules against fee splitting and lawyers and nonlawyers entering into a partnership for the practice of law (covered in Chapters 6 and 7, respectively). Finally, in a few cases, lawyers have been hired by nonlawyer legal service provider companies in an attempt to legitimize their work, an arrangement that has repeatedly been found unacceptable by the courts and in advisory opinions. (See, for example, Iowa Ethics Advisory Opinion 96-19 regarding a divorce business, *In re Phillips* in Chapter 2, and *The Cincinnati Bar Ass'n v. Mullaney* regarding a foreclosure consulting business at the end of the chapter.)

The unauthorized practice of law by lawyers who are licensed in one state but practicing in another has been a subject of much discussion within the organized bar in the past two decades. Because of the nature of the economy, which does not recognize neatly drawn **jurisdictional lines**, lawyers often engage in legal work in states other than the one(s) in which they are licensed. Sometimes this work takes place in a bordering state and sometimes across the country. States have become more protective of their authority over the practice of law and have been making it more difficult for lawyers to engage in this kind of work. The California Supreme Court in *Birbower, Montalbano, Condon & Frank, P.C. v. Superior Court*, 17 Cal. 4th 119, 949 P.2d 1, 70 Cal. Rptr. 2d 304 (1998), determined that a New York law firm doing some work in California could not collect its fees because the lawyers were not licensed to practice in California and had therefore engaged in the unauthorized practice of law, a crime that voided the contract with the clients. Similar cases followed in other jurisdictions. To provide exceptions and clear guidance, the ABA adopted Model Rule 5.5, setting up carefully drawn exceptions for limited out-of-state practice.

Another interesting UPL question is whether a corporate officer who is not a lawyer can represent the corporation in legal matters. Few cases have addressed this issue but most allow this practice only in actions in small claims court or in administrative hearings. (See, for example, *Dayton Supply v. Montgomery Bd. of Rev.*, 111 Ohio St. 3d 367 (2006), in which the court allowed a corporate office to appear for the company in a matter concerning the valuation of property.)

Finally, questions have been raised about the **rights of nonlawyers and parents to represent their children** under the federal Individuals with Disabilities Education Act (IDEA). At least two states have found that nonlawyers cannot represent parents or children in administrative hearings (see *In re Arons*, 756 A.2d 867 (Del. 2000) *cert. denied*, 532 U.S. 1065 (2001), and Oklahoma Attorney General Opinion 06-27). The law gives parents the right to advocate for their children in administrative hearings, but the courts are split on whether parents can represent their children in federal court judicial reviews of these administrative decisions. Most federal circuits have found that parents cannot represent their children in IDEA actions in federal court, as this would constitute the unauthorized practice of law. They may, however, represent their own interests in such actions. See *Winkelman v. Parma City School Dist.*, 550 U.S. 516, 127 S. Ct. 1994 (2007), *Cavanaugh v. Cardinal Local School Dist.*, 409 F.3d 753 (6th Cir. 2005), and *Fry v. Napoleon Comm. Sch.*, 580 U.S. 154 (2017).

B. Practice of Law Defined

No one definitive list of activities captures the meaning of the practice of law. As you can see from the foregoing history, the concept is flexible; it changes over time with the push and pull of economics, political and professional activity, public pressure and consumerism, and the complexity of laws. The oft-quoted ABA Model Code of Professional Responsibility (ABA Model Code) EC 3-5 states: "It is neither necessary nor desirable to attempt the formulation of a single, specific definition of what constitutes the practice of law." Efforts to build a national consensus for a definition of the practice of law have been unsuccessful. For example, in 2003, an ABA Task Force on the Model Definition of the Practice of Law had to withdraw its proposed definition when it was met with harsh criticism from the Department of Justice, the Federal Trade Commission, and other organizations that believed that it was overly broad and illegally noncompetitive. States continue to establish their own definitions in statutes and court rules and rely on court decisions that provide tests for determining what defines the practice of law. The traditional tests for determining if an act constitutes the practice of law are found in Charles W. Wolfram's treatise *Modern Legal Ethics* (1986):

1. *The professional judgment test:* whether the activity at issue is one that requires the lawyer's special training and skills. Wolfram suggests that a better version of this test would be "whether the matter handled was

of such complexity that only a person trained as a lawyer should be permitted to deal with it." Id. at 836.
2. *The traditional areas of practice test:* whether the function in question is one that would traditionally be performed by an attorney or is commonly understood to be the practice of law. Id.
3. *The incidental legal services test:* whether the activity is essentially legal in nature or is a law-related adjunct to some business routine or transaction, that is, completing a simple legal document incidental to a banking or real estate transaction, for which no separate fee is charged, would not constitute the practice of law under this definition. Id.

Some scholars add other tests, such as whether the activity in question is characterized by a personal relationship between lawyer and client or whether the activity is one for which the public interest would best be served by limiting it to licensed attorneys.

Examples of definitions of the practice of law in a few major UPL cases may be instructive.

> [I]t embraces the preparation of pleadings and other papers incident to actions of special proceedings, and the management of such actions and proceedings on behalf of clients before judges in courts. However, the practice of law is not confined to cases conducted in court. In fact, the major portion of the practice of any capable lawyer consists of work done outside of the courts. The practice of law involves not only appearance in court in connection with litigation, but also services rendered out of court, and includes the giving of advice or the rendering of any service requiring the use of legal skill or knowledge, such as preparing a will, contract, or other instrument, the legal effect of which under the facts and conclusions involved must be carefully determined.

Davies v. Unauthorized Practice Committee of State Bar of Texas, 431 S.W.2d 590, at 593 (Tex. Civ. App. 1968).

> [O]ne is deemed to be practicing law whenever he furnishes to another advice or service under circumstances which imply the possession and use of legal knowledge and skill. . . . Practice of law includes the giving of legal advice and counsel, and the preparation of legal instruments and contracts of which legal rights are secured. . . . Where the rendering of services for another involves the use of legal knowledge or skill on his behalf — where legal advice is required and is availed of or rendered in connection with such services — these services necessarily constitute or include the practice of law.

In re Welch, 185 A.2d 458, 459 (Vt. 1962).

> [The] definition of law practice has two aspects: exercise of professional judgment and application of legal principles to individual cases. An exercise of professional judgment occurs any time there is "informed or trained

discretion exercise in the selection or drafting of a document to meet the [legal] needs of persons being served"; "an intelligent choice between alternative methods of drafting a legal document"; or advice given that "involves the application of legal principles." [Citations omitted.]

Oregon State Bar v. Taub, 190 Or. App. 280, 78 P.3d 114 (2003). Also see the definitions offered by other courts in each of the cases at the end of this chapter.

States have adopted some definitions that are more specific than those commonly adopted in the past. For example, the Arizona Supreme Court defines the practice of law as follows:

"Practice of law" means providing legal advice or services to or for another by:
 (1) preparing or expressing legal opinions to or for another person or entity;
 (2) representing a person or entity in a judicial, quasi-judicial, or administrative proceeding, or other formal dispute resolution process such as arbitration or mediation;
 (3) preparing a document, in any medium, on behalf of a specific person or entity, for filing in any court, administrative agency, or tribunal;
 (4) negotiating legal rights or responsibilities on behalf of a specific person or entity; or
 (5) preparing a document, in any medium, intended to affect or secure a specific person's or entity's legal rights.

Arizona Supreme Court Rule 31(b).

Hundreds of published opinions on UPL help to define the practice of law. UPL cases come to the courts by a variety of paths:

- criminal prosecutions of a nonlawyer or out-of-state lawyer (UPL is a misdemeanor in more than 30 states and a felony in a few),
- civil contempt proceedings brought when a nonlawyer appears in court on behalf of a client (a remedy in more than 25 states),
- actions for injunctive relief, usually brought by bar associations or courts (a remedy in at least 40 jurisdictions),
- contempt proceedings brought against nonlawyers appearing before a court (a proper remedy in every jurisdiction).

See Rhode, D. L. and Ricca, L. B, "Protecting the Profession or the Public? Rethinking Unauthorized-Practice Enforcement," 82 Fordham L. Rev. 2587 (2014) for an analysis of more than a hundred UPL cases.

Additional deterrents to unauthorized practice include liability for negligent performance, unenforceability of the contract for legal services, court dismissal of an action brought by a nonlawyer for a client, and a court's voiding of a judgment in which a nonlawyer represented the prevailing party.

C. The Lawyer's Responsibility to Prevent the Unauthorized Practice of Law

Rules that prohibit the unauthorized practice of law affect lawyers and nonlawyers alike. Lawyers engage in UPL if they practice in a state in which they are not licensed or practice while they are suspended or after they have been disbarred. Nonlawyers engage in UPL when they perform services for the public that fall under the state's definition of the practice of law, unless specifically authorized by state statutes and court rules to do so. See Chapter 2. As you will see in the next sections, some of the prohibited activities are absolutely prohibited to paralegals, whereas others may be done by a nonlawyer under **lawyer supervision**. In a traditional legal setting where paralegals are supervised by lawyers, paralegals may engage in UPL by overstepping the accepted boundaries.

Lawyers are obligated by various rules not to aid the unauthorized practice of law. In many states, a statute prohibits a lawyer from aiding unauthorized practice. In others, the ethical codes contain such a restriction. See ABA Model Code DR 3-101(A) and ABA Model Rule 5.3(b), also discussed in Chapter 2.

Under ethics rules, lawyers are responsible for the training and supervision of paralegals and for the proper delegation of work to paralegals. The obligation of adequate supervision runs to all areas of ethics — such as confidentiality, conflicts, and competence — but carries special force in the area of unauthorized practice. Cases interpreting ethics rules make clear that lawyers are responsible for the actions of their paralegals and other nonlawyer assistants, including actions that constitute UPL. Further, in nearly all states, lawyers must maintain professional independence and may not form a partnership with a nonlawyer or divide legal fees with a nonlawyer. (See ABA Model Rule 5.4 and exceptions to this rule in the District of Columbia, and the states of Arizona, Utah, and Washington, discussed in more detail in Chapter 7.)

As discussed in Chapter 2, Rule 5.3(b) of the ABA Model Rules requires lawyers to make "reasonable efforts to ensure that the [nonlawyer's] conduct is compatible with the professional obligations of the lawyer" and makes lawyers accountable for the conduct of their paralegals. Guideline 1 of the ABA Model Guidelines for the Utilization of Paralegal Services (ABA Model Guidelines) and all state guidelines on paralegal utilization state that lawyers are responsible for all the professional actions that their paralegals perform at the lawyer's direction. Guidelines typically note the attorney's duty to employ and delegate work to paralegals who are competent for the tasks assigned.

Guideline 2 of the Model Guidelines provides an expansive definition of permissible paralegal functions and notes that lawyers are prohibited from delegating to paralegals those tasks proscribed to one not licensed as a lawyer by statute, administrative rule or regulation, or controlling authority.

See also Guideline V.1-5 of the NALA Model Standards and Guidelines for the Utilization of Paralegals, Canons 1 through 5 of the NALA Code of Ethics and Professional Responsibility, and Section 1.8 of the NFPA Code of Ethics and Professional Responsibility. NALA and NFPA codes are found in this book's Appendices.

D. What Constitutes the Practice of Law

1. Court Appearances

The one function that is universally considered to be the exclusive province of licensed attorneys is the representation of a client in court proceedings. Recall from the brief history of unauthorized practice at the beginning of this chapter that this was the first kind of restriction placed on nonlawyer practitioners in the early days of the United States.

The rationale for this rule is strongly supported by the avowed purposes of unauthorized practice rules generally. Presumably, a court appearance, especially an adversarial one such as a pretrial motion or a trial, requires knowledge and skills that only a lawyer possesses by virtue of specialized education, training, and experience. Many would say that appearing in court on behalf of a client represents one of the highest uses of a lawyer's professional judgment and skills. In addition to benefiting from a lawyer's special competence, the client is protected by ethics and related rules that apply to lawyers only, like the attorney-client privilege, conflicts of interest, and confidentiality. A court appearance is an event that decides a client's rights and responsibilities. The client should have the best representation possible at this critical moment. Further, incompetent representation in a hearing or trial may not only damage the client, but may also impair the administration of justice.

Despite the clear rules and strong rationale for these prohibitions on the nonlawyer's role in court-related matters, a few notable exceptions do exist. Perhaps most important is the general principle of self-representation. The **right of self-representation** in federal courts is guaranteed by statute (28 U.S.C. §1654 (1948)) and was found to be a constitutional right in the landmark case of *Faretta v. California*, 422 U.S. 806 (1975). However, cases in federal and several state courts have determined that the right to self-representation does not encompass a right to be represented by a nonlawyer.

Some states have carved out narrow exceptions for the **marital relationship**. A California statute, for instance, permits one nonlawyer spouse to represent the other if he or she does not wish to represent his or her own interests. (Cal. Code of Civ. Proc. §371). However, parents cannot generally represent their children in actions before the courts (e.g., cases brought under the federal IDEA, discussed above). And nonlawyer plaintiffs cannot represent other nonlawyer co-plaintiffs in the same matter.

All jurisdictions have rules permitting **law students** to engage in limited practice under lawyer supervision, and nearly all allow law students to represent clients in court. This exception has been created for the dual purposes of providing practical training for law students and increasing the availability of legal services. Rules governing law student practice vary from jurisdiction to jurisdiction. Most states' rules identify specific qualifications that the law student must meet (including having taken specific courses like Evidence), require certification of the student by the law school dean and attorney-sponsor, and impose strict limitations on the kind of court appearances that the law student may make without being accompanied by the supervising attorney.

In some local jurisdictions, **paralegals are allowed to make appearances** for their attorney-employers in uncontested matters. Some enlightened courts permit such appearances under local court rules, including courts in the states of Indiana and Washington. For example, Seattle-King County, Washington, has a court rule that permits paralegals who are registered with the local bar association to present stipulated, *ex parte*, and uncontested orders in court when such orders are based solely on the documents in the record. Paralegals must have six months of work experience with an attorney, must devote at least half their work time to paralegal tasks, and must have a certificate from an ABA-approved program or the equivalent.

In Arizona, **legal paraprofessionals**, as authorized by the Arizona Supreme Court, are allowed to appear in courts and tribunals in a limited representation capacity, including mediation, arbitration, and settlement conferences where not prohibited by the rules and procedures of the forum. See Arizona Code of Judicial Administration (ACJA) § 7-210(F).

The rationale for prohibiting nonlawyer representation in court appearances extends to another aspect of the litigation process: the **taking of depositions**. In a ***deposition***, one of the key discovery tools, the lawyer asks questions in person of an opposing or a third party. The responses are given orally under oath and are recorded by a court reporter, who then produces a transcript of the questions and answers. A deposition may be introduced in court. It carries the same weight as testimony given under oath in court. This testimony may be used at trial to impeach the credibility of the deponent or in lieu of direct testimony if the deponent is no longer available.

Deposition
Method of discovery in which a witness or party makes statements under oath, in question-and-answer form.

The lawyer's role in representing a client being deposed includes making objections to questions on evidentiary grounds and preserving these objections for the record. Typically, objections are based on relevancy or privilege. The lawyer who is deposing a party or witness is performing a task similar to that of direct examination in a trial and, therefore, must be familiar with the complex rules of evidence.

During a deposition, the lawyer wants to learn about the facts of the case and to assess the credibility of the deponent as a potential witness. This work requires not only a full understanding of the factual and legal issues but highly developed skills in phrasing questions that will elicit candid and thorough responses, perhaps beyond those the party intends to reveal.

For the foregoing reasons, paralegals may not conduct a deposition. Although this is rarely challenged, two states have issued an ethics opinion on the question. In Opinion 87-127 (1987), the Pennsylvania state bar ethics committee said that a lawyer may not allow a paralegal to conduct a deposition even when she or he has a series of attorney-approved questions. The basis for this opinion was that the paralegal would not be qualified to answer any questions that might arise and to make objections, and may be called on to give legal advice. In 1996, the Iowa Bar issued a similar opinion indicating that paralegals may not ask questions at a deposition even when supervised by an attorney. (Iowa Bar Ethics Opinion 96-3.) See *State v. Foster*, 674 So. 2d 747 (1996) at the end of this chapter for a case involving nonlawyers who were prosecuted for taking depositions.

Almost three-quarters of the paralegals in the country work in **litigation**. Paralegals are involved in all phases of the litigation process, from legal research and drafting of pleadings and motions through the discovery process (including preparing and answering interrogatories, and handling subpoenas *duces tecum* and document productions) and trial preparation to settlement, trial, and post-judgment matters. Paralegals play an active role in the discovery and trial phases of the litigation process. They are often the factual experts in cases and, as such, work with lawyers in preparing for depositions by assisting in identifying areas of questioning. Many also help to prepare clients for the experience of being deposed or testifying at trial. Some accompany clients to independent medical examinations. It is common for paralegals to attend depositions and trials, taking notes, assisting with the introduction of evidence, and otherwise handling a variety of details, functions that generally have been supported by the courts and the organized bar.

Related is the prohibition on paralegals signing a pleading or other document filed with the court on behalf of the client. A ***pleading*** constitutes a written "appearance" in court that only a licensed attorney can make. This includes electronic signatures. The lawyer's failure to sign a pleading may also imply that the lawyer has not properly reviewed the document before it was filed. A few ethics opinions address this matter.

Pleading
A written document filed with a court that sets forth the facts of a party's case or the defendant's grounds for defense.

See, for example, Florida State Bar Ethics Opinion 87-11, warning against allowing a nonlawyer to sign pleadings and notices with the nonlawyer's initials. One state allows a narrow exception: the North Carolina State Bar Ethics Council issued an ethics opinion that allows a lawyer to delegate the signing of a pleading in "exigent circumstances" for the protection of the client (N.C. Formal Ethics Opinion 2006-13). In an unpublished California case, a lawyer was disciplined for misleading the court by authorizing his assistant to simulate his signature on pleadings. (*In re Dowd*, State Bar Court of California Review Department, Case No. 07-O-11955, filed in May 2011.)

2. Giving Legal Advice

The largest and most complex category of conduct that constitutes the practice of law is giving legal advice. (See ABA Model Guideline 3(c).) Similar to representing a client in court, formulating a substantive legal opinion to guide a client's conduct is a core lawyer function that cannot be delegated. A lawyer's legal advice lies at the heart of their value because it requires the application of the lawyer's knowledge of law; judgmental and analytical abilities; and understanding of the client's situation, context, and goals.

Case law and advisory opinions generally indicate that the following actions constitute "giving legal advice":

- recommending a course of conduct or a particular action to a client
- evaluating the probable outcome of litigation, negotiations, or other proposed action for or with a client
- outlining legal rights or responsibilities to a client
- interpreting and applying statutes, decisions, or legal documents to a client.

In practice, many paralegals have frequent **communications with clients**, which creates the potential for the paralegal to give legal advice. Paralegals generally get considerable satisfaction from working with clients and have an important role as a liaison between the lawyer and clients. The benefits to the firm and the client are countless. Paralegals are often easier to reach than lawyers, who are often in court or meetings. Paralegals are sometimes more patient with clients and may use less legal jargon. It is also more cost-efficient for the client and the lawyer to have the client speak with a paralegal.

Clients frequently develop good rapport with paralegals and eventually may ask a paralegal a question that requires a response that would amount to giving legal advice. That the paralegal knows the answer to the question further exacerbates this dilemma. To avoid giving legal advice, the paralegal must first consult with the lawyer before relaying the lawyer's advice to the client. The paralegal may then communicate the lawyer's legal advice, so long as it is the exact legal opinion of the attorney, delivered without expansion or interpretation, and it is clear that the legal advice is coming from the attorney, not the paralegal. In other words, lawyers can delegate to a paralegal the function of communicating legal advice so long as the paralegal is not formulating and giving advice without lawyer approval and the lawyer still maintains a direct relationship with the client, exercising independent professional judgment.

One exception to the prohibition against nonlawyers giving legal advice has been created for so-called *jailhouse lawyers*. In *Johnson v. Avery*, 393 U.S. 484 (1969), the Supreme Court held that a state may not bar inmates from helping one another to prepare post-conviction writs unless the state provides a reasonable alternative. This opinion was upheld and expanded in *Wolff v. McDonnell*, 418 U.S. 539, 94 S. Ct. 2963 (1974), in which the court specifically held that prisons could not prohibit inmates from giving or receiving legal assistance to other inmates without providing a reasonable alternative. The Board of Corrections of the State of Arizona decided to hire paralegals to help inmates with their appeals and writs after a similar opinion in *Lewis v. Casey*, 518 U.S. 343, 116 S. Ct. 2174 (1996). However, there has been a trend toward restricting the exercise of these rights. See *Shaw v. Murphy*, 532 U.S. 223, 121 S. Ct. 1475 (2001).

Jailhouse lawyers
Inmates who help other inmates to prepare post-conviction writs.

The prohibition against nonlawyers giving legal advice has been challenged by persons seeking to aid those representing themselves. As noted above, *self-representation* aids such as do-it-yourself legal kits, books, and most electronic resources do *not* constitute the unauthorized practice of law as long as they are not sold in conjunction with direct personalized assistance in completing the forms or procedures. Whether or not electronic programs that *pro se* litigants use to fill out legal forms is categorized as UPL is something of an open question. (See, for example, *In re Reynoso*, at the end of this chapter.)

Self-representation
The act of representing oneself in legal proceedings before a tribunal.

A related concern is the advent of court-sponsored resources to help *pro se* litigants without the use of an intermediary or adviser. User-friendly **computer programs** have been set up in courthouses in several states, including Arizona, California, Colorado, and Florida, enabling users to prepare court-approved forms in domestic relations, small claims, and landlord-tenant matters. Users answer a series of questions, and forms and instructions are filled in automatically and printed out for filing.

There is a nationwide trend toward expanding the role of nonlawyers in providing legal assistance to *pro se* litigants despite the unauthorized practice prohibitions. Most of the progress in this area has come about as the result of legislation that narrowly circumscribes the role of the nonlawyer within a particular area of practice where there is a great need for access to the civil legal system by persons who cannot afford lawyers and seek to represent themselves. In California, government-employed small claims advisers are authorized by statute to assist litigants in filling out and filing forms and preparing for trial. Legislation in California, Maryland, and a few other states permits private nonlawyer practitioners to assist litigants in unlawful detainer and summary ejection proceedings. In Washington and other jurisdictions, court facilitators assist *pro se* litigants in child support and family law proceedings.

As noted in Chapter 2, two states, California and Arizona, have officially recognized the role of nonlawyer legal service providers in assisting consumers to prepare and file documents. Under California statutes, **legal document assistants** (LDA) are required to meet certain educational or experiential requirements and to register with the county in which they do business. Similarly, but in a more comprehensive system, an Arizona Supreme Court Rule created the category of **legal document preparers** (LDP), who are certified by the court upon completion of a comprehensive exam, payment of minimal fees, and proof of meeting educational or experiential requirements. LDAs and LDPs are required to comply with legal and ethical restrictions. In both states, provisions prohibit them from giving legal advice. In California the related statute on unlawful detainer assistants (UDAs) has been used to prosecute UDAs who failed to register, did not meet the requirements of the law concerning written contracts with clients, and committed UPL. (See *Brockey v. Moore* at the end of this chapter.)

As described in Chapter 2, several states have adopted court rules that created a role for specialized nonlawyer legal practitioners, who are licensed and authorized to provide legal services in designated areas of law.

Another area of interest concerns the dispensing of **legal advice on the Internet**. Whether on a legal website, blog, in a chat room, or on social media sites, nonlawyers are prohibited from giving legal advice on the Internet. Lawyers must take care as well when operating in this medium not to inadvertently establish an attorney-client relationship and not to give legal advice unless a lawyer-client relationship is intended. It is important in this context to keep in mind the distinction between legal information and legal advice. Providing general legal information, such as that given in a self-help resources or in an online column about the law, is encouraged. However, legal advice that is specific to a person's legal matter cannot be given by a person who is not licensed to practice law, including a lawyer who is licensed in one state but gives legal advice to someone about a legal matter in another state.

One final word of warning about nonlawyers who assist persons with their legal matters directly, whether as a legal document preparer or as a jailhouse lawyer: Communications between a person and their nonlawyer adviser are not protected by the ***attorney-client privilege***. This rule applies to all kinds of nonlawyer representatives. Courts have consistently

Attorney-client privilege
Rule of evidence that protects confidential communications between lawyer and client during their professional relationship.

refused to extend the privilege to communications between nonlawyer practitioners and their "clients" or "customers." As you will learn in Chapter 4, if a communication is not protected by the privilege, a court can require the person involved to testify about the contents of the conversation, even if the "customer" or client believed that the communication was privileged.

3. Establishing the Lawyer-Client Relationship and Setting Fees

The last main category of conduct that is reserved exclusively for lawyers is establishing the lawyer-client relationship and setting the fees to be charged for the legal services. As stated in ABA Model Guideline 3, a lawyer may not delegate responsibility for establishing an lawyer-client relationship or the amount of a fee to be charged for the legal service.

The lawyer-client relationship and fee arrangements between lawyer and client are considered sacrosanct. A lawyer should establish a **direct relationship** with a client and not allow a paralegal to make the decision independently about whether or not to undertake the representation. The related matter of what fee to charge for the service should be determined by the lawyer.

This prohibition does not prevent a paralegal from communicating standard or specific fee information to a client at the lawyer's instruction, drafting retainer agreements or engagement letters, or presenting lawyer-approved documents for the client's signature. It should be noted that there are cases and ethics opinions that dictate against a paralegal signing such a document on behalf of the lawyer. (See, for example, *Attorney Grievance Commission of Maryland v. Hallmon*, 343 Md. 390, 681 A.2d 510 (1996), and Pennsylvania Bar Association Formal Opinion 98-75.)

In addressing the question of establishing the lawyer-client relationship and the fee agreement, courts look at the facts of the case to see if the lawyer has a direct relationship with the client, has met with the client, has properly reviewed documents, and has exercised **independent professional judgment** on behalf of the client. If the lawyer has abdicated the exercise of judgment to the nonlawyer employee, the lawyer may be found in breach of ethical obligations and the paralegal may be seen as engaging in the unauthorized practice of law.

The ABA Model Rules and the predecessor Model Code both emphasize the importance of establishing the lawyer-client relationship early on. (See ABA Model Rule 5.4.) NALA Model Standards and Guidelines, and most state guidelines on working with paralegals, also make reference to these matters. (See NALA Guideline V.2; NALA Code of Ethics Canon 3.)

E. Paralegal Tasks That May Constitute the Unauthorized Practice of Law

Throughout this chapter, a number of legal tasks have been discussed as falling within or outside the boundaries of the practice of law. Because the concept of unauthorized practice is vague and changes with time and place, creating a definitive list of functions that fall on either side of the boundary is not really possible. Such a list is likely to be quickly outdated or to be inaccurate for one jurisdiction or another.

1. Common Paralegal Functions

The following is a short list of generic paralegal functions, not specific to any particular area of practice, that are commonly performed by paralegals under the supervision of a lawyer and are not UPL in this context:

- conducting legal and factual research and investigation
- drafting memoranda, pleadings, and other legal documents
- preparing standard form documents
- preparing correspondence for attorney and paralegal signature
- interviewing clients and witnesses
- acting as liaison with clients and others outside the firm
- organizing, analyzing, and summarizing legal documents
- managing electronic document databases
- interviewing and coordinating with legal technology vendors
- filing documents with courts and government agencies
- handling procedural, administrative, and scheduling matters

There is little dispute over the propriety of paralegals performing the above functions under attorney supervision; however, other very specialized tasks present special ethical challenges for paralegals and the lawyers who utilize their services, as the rest of this section describes.

2. Will Executions

A *will execution* is a relatively simple but critical step in the process of estate planning. Whether by case law or statute, very specific rules exist in every state about the signing and witnessing of wills, including the number of witnesses, their relationship to the person making the will, and their presence during the signing. Few states have addressed this issue. In an early ethics opinion, the New York State Bar Association recommended against paralegals handling these proceedings on their own.

Will execution
The formal process of signing and witnessing a will.

NYSBA Ethics Opinion 74-343 concluded that the delegation of the task of supervising a will execution is "tantamount" to "counseling a client" and constitutes the practice of law. Iowa guidelines, adopted in 1988, indicate that "generally, a lawyer should be present for the execution of legal documents." However, newer guidelines, such as those in Connecticut, specifically allow paralegals to attend and supervise will executions so long as the paralegal does not give any legal advice.

Rhode Island and Colorado list witnessing the execution of documents or wills as permissible functions for paralegals. See *In re Morin* at the end of this chapter for an example of the problems that arise when wills are not properly executed.

3. Real Estate Closings and Related Matters

Real estate closing
The consummation of the sale of real estate by payment of the purchase price, delivery of the deed, and finalizing collateral matters.

The role of paralegals and other nonlawyers in the real estate industry in handling ***real estate closings*** has been the subject of ongoing controversy. The jurisdictions that have issued opinions are split. For example, the Illinois State Bar Association reaffirmed its opinion on the subject in a position paper with the following language:

> Attorney assistants may attend real estate closings of all types, but only in the company of the employing attorney and at such closings prepare computations, revisions of agreements and perform similar tasks, but only at the direction of, and under the supervision of, the employing attorney.

Position Paper of the Illinois State Bar Association Real Estate Section Council and Unauthorized Practice of Law Committee Re: Use of Attorney Assistants in Real Estate Transactions, Approved by the State Bar Board of Governors, May 16, 1984.

Georgia, Pennsylvania, and some of the bar associations in New York have issued comparable advisory opinions. (See, for example, Georgia's Formal Advisory Opinions 86-5 and 00-3.) North Carolina Advisory Opinion 00-13 (July 12, 2000) recommends that although a nonlawyer can oversee the execution of documents, a lawyer should be available to confer with clients. Pennsylvania's guidelines, found in Formal Opinion 98-75, state that the closing may involve the "legal interpretation of documents . . . and advice to the clients as to the course of action to be taken. . . ." Other entities, like the Federal Trade Commission and the U.S. Department of Justice, have advocated allowing nonlawyers a greater role in real estate closings to increase competition and lower the cost of services.

As noted in the Pennsylvania opinion, the rationale for this prohibition is that the client might need or want legal advice, particularly an explanation of the meaning and legal consequences of the various legal documents that must be signed. In addition, there is always the potential for a last-minute dispute that may require the services of a lawyer. A paralegal who explains the legal consequences of documents or attempts to resolve a dispute over terms would likely be giving the kind of legal advice that constitutes the unauthorized practice of law.

These concerns are addressed by bar association opinions that endorse the use of paralegals to attend real estate closings unaccompanied by a lawyer. For example, a Florida Bar advisory opinion states that "[a] law firm may permit a paralegal or other trained employee to handle a real estate closing at which no lawyer in the firm is present if certain conditions are met." The conditions listed in the opinion include lawyer supervision and review up to the time of the closing; lawyer availability to give advice during the closing if needed; client consent; a determination that the closing will be purely ministerial and that the client understands the documents in advance; and a prohibition against the paralegal giving legal advice or making legal decisions during the closing. Imposing these limitations on the paralegal role adequately protects the client's interests and prevents the unauthorized practice of law (Florida Professional Ethics Committee Advisory Opinion 89-5 (1989)).

Several states and bar associations have followed this reasoning and adopted similar opinions. See, for example, Virginia State Bar Unauthorized Practice of Law Committee Opinion No. 91-47, New York State Bar Association Ethics Opinion 95-677, Wisconsin Ethics Opinion 95-3, Connecticut Bar Association Ethics Opinion 96-14, Vermont Bar Association Formal Opinion 99-3, Nassau County Bar Association Committee on Professional Ethics, Opinion 02-3, and New York State Bar Association Ethics Opinion 20-1208.

4. Negotiating Settlements

Special mention also needs to be made about one paralegal function that is fairly common in personal injury practices—negotiating settlements. Paralegals in many personal injury firms handle client contact and documentation of cases. "Working up" the case typically involves collecting medical bills, assisting the client with medical insurance claims, and discussing the case with insurance claims adjusters. Paralegals handling these matters often have ongoing communications with adjusters, providing information about the nature and extent of the client's injuries, treatment, and property damage. Adjusters may make offers to settle to the paralegal, who must convey the offer to the lawyer, who in turn is ethically obligated to discuss the offer to settle with the client.

Few jurisdictions have addressed the matter of paralegals negotiating settlements. South Carolina Ethics Advisory Opinion 89-24 indicates that permitting a nonlawyer to do the "actual negotiation, even without authority to settle the case, may be an inappropriate delegation of responsibility by the attorney." The Georgia Bar Guidelines for Attorneys Utilizing Paralegals, found in the State Bar of Georgia Advisory Opinion 77-21, indicate that "[n]egotiation with opposing parties or their counsel on substantive issues in expected or pending litigation" and "[c]ontacting an opposing party or his counsel in a situation in which legal rights of the firm's client will be asserted or negotiated" are both tasks that should not be delegated to paralegals. An early Florida ethics opinion also endorses this view, indicating that lawyers may not delegate to nonlawyers the handling of negotiations with insurance company adjusters (Op. 74-35).

These opinions are very limiting and in practice are not followed in many firms. As long as the paralegal does not commit the client to a particular settlement without client and lawyer approval or argue the legal merits of a case with opposing counsel, the rationale for prohibiting this task is weak. Paralegals who work in this area, however, must take special care to act as the conduit for information in the negotiations, and not to interpret the law or value of a case in a way that would affect the client's position. (See *The Florida Bar v. Neiman*, 816 So. 2d 587 (2002), for a case where a paralegal's involvement in settlement negotiations crossed the line into the practice of law.) Finally, the cases about nonlawyer loan modification services hold that some aspects of negotiating a loan modification do constitute the practice of law. (See *Cincinnati Bar Ass'n v. Mullaney* at the end of this chapter.)

REVIEW QUESTIONS

1. When were the first rules limiting the practice of law passed in the United States? What did the rules limit? What were the purposes of these rules?
2. What is the role of bar associations in limiting the practice of law to licensed attorneys?
3. What kinds of legal functions do most nonlawyer legal service providers perform? Whom do they serve? What areas of law do they work in? How do UPL rules circumscribe their work? What titles do nonlawyer legal service providers use?
4. Give the most complete and accurate definition of the practice of law that you can.
5. What are the potential consequences of engaging in the unauthorized practice of law? Are prosecutions for unauthorized practice of law increasing or decreasing? Why?
6. What are a lawyer's responsibilities to prevent the unauthorized practice of law? What might happen to a lawyer whose paralegal engages in the practice of law?
7. How might a licensed lawyer engage in the unauthorized practice of law? What do ABA rules say about this?

8. Make a list of the specific functions that constitute the practice of law and may not be performed by paralegals. What rationale lies behind each prohibition?
9. What are the exceptions to the general rule against a nonlawyer appearing in court on behalf of a client? Describe each exception and the rationale.
10. Give your best definition of what constitutes giving legal advice. Why are nonlawyers prohibited from giving legal advice? What is the difference between giving legal advice and giving legal information?
11. What are the exceptions to the general prohibition against giving legal advice?
12. Does operating a self-help divorce website constitute giving legal advice? What about developing and selling electronic programs that help someone to prepare a will or complete the forms required to file for divorce?
13. Does answering someone's questions about legal matters constitute giving legal advice? Why or why not? If a lawyer does this, is an attorney-client relationship formed?
14. What kinds of work can nonlawyer legal service providers perform without engaging in the unauthorized practice of law?
15. Why are paralegals prohibited from setting legal fees? From accepting a case? Can a paralegal quote a fee to a prospective client over the phone? Sign a retainer agreement with a client?
16. Should a paralegal supervise a will execution without an attorney present? Why or why not?
17. Should a paralegal supervise a real estate closing without the supervising attorney present? Why or why not?
18. Should a paralegal negotiate a settlement in a case? What steps should the paralegal take to be sure that he or she does not practice law unethically when negotiating?
19. Can parents represent their children in court cases? Are there any statutes that allow parents to represent their children in administrative agencies?
20. Can a nonlawyer set up a service to help people to renegotiate their bank loans and avoid foreclosure? Can a lawyer work for such a company?

DISCUSSION QUESTIONS AND HYPOTHETICALS

1. Do you agree that only licensed lawyers should be able to give legal advice and represent clients in court? Why or why not? What are the consequences of limiting these functions to lawyers only?
2. Do you think that a sole practitioner lawyer who has ten paralegals working in their office can supervise that many paralegals adequately?

Is the answer the same for every area of law practice? What office procedures and policies might ensure adequate supervision under these conditions? What if the lawyer is in court every day and only spends a few hours a week in the office?
3. Do you think that a lawyer who hires a paralegal without any formal paralegal training is violating the duty to supervise and to guard against UPL? Why or why not? How might this depend on the circumstances? What factors would you consider in deciding? Glance back at the *Musselman* and *Phillips* cases in Chapter 2 for some insight.
4. How can a lawyer engage in the unauthorized practice of law? What is multijurisdictional practice? Does state jurisdiction over law practice make sense in today's economy?
5. Why should law students, and not paralegals, be permitted to represent clients in court?
6. Based on *Faretta v. California*, do you think a constitutional argument could be made that citizens should be able to choose their representative in court, even if that person is a nonlawyer? Try to formulate that proposition and then develop the arguments against it.
7. Because it is essential for lawyers to have a direct relationship with their clients and paralegals are prohibited from giving legal advice, why are paralegals allowed to have any client contact at all?
8. Which of the following acts by a paralegal would be permissible and which prohibited under the definitions of legal advice given in this chapter?

   a. interviewing a client to obtain the facts relating to an automobile accident
   b. telling the client that the firm probably would be able to get a $10,000 recovery
   c. explaining to the client what happens at a deposition
   d. discussing the questions that the opposing counsel might ask at the deposition
   e. attending a deposition without the lawyer present
   f. explaining to the client the meaning of an affidavit given to the client for signature
   g. telling a client that their case is likely to settle
   h. telling a client that the best course of action would be to file a small claims action
   i. answering a client's questions about the meaning of terms in a contract
   j. giving a client the legal opinion that the paralegal knows the lawyer would give
   k. relaying a message from the lawyer to the client, which tells the client that it is okay to sign a contract

l. talking with opposing counsel about the legal grounds for the client's case
m. attending a real estate closing without the lawyer present and explaining the purpose of each document to be signed

9. Could you use *Johnson v. Avery* to make an argument that poor people who do not have access to legal services have a right to legal advice from whomever they choose unless the state provides an alternative? Is this argument convincing? Why or why not?
10. The cases that hold self-help resources are not prohibited by unauthorized practice of law statutes also hold that helping customers to use those resources violates unauthorized practice of law statutes. Do you think this an appropriate place to draw this line? Do any of the cases in this chapter help you to decide where to draw the line?
11. Many courts and access-to-justice advocates have promoted the use of technology to increase access to legal services. In what ways might this be a viable solution? What might the barriers to this means of increasing access be? (See Magnuson, E. J. and Frank, N. S., "The High Cost of Efficiency: Courthouse Tech and Access to Justice," 22 The Prof. Lawyer 4 (2014).)
12. What are the policy reasons for permitting nonlawyers to give legal advice in small claims or unlawful detainer cases, or to serve as family court facilitators for *pro per* litigants? Why do these reasons not apply to other kinds of legal matters? How do you reconcile this exception with the policy reasons for prohibiting nonlawyers from giving legal advice?
13. In a personal injury law firm that takes every case that comes to it and that charges the same contingency fee, why should it be necessary for the lawyer to set the fee and establish the relationship with the client? Should this be an ethics rule, or is it really a matter of good practice? Suppose the initial contact between the lawyer and client is a five-minute meeting to formalize the relationship and the client never speaks to the lawyer again because the paralegal "works up" the case, negotiates the settlement, and has all the client contact. Is the lawyer maintaining a direct relationship with the client? Does the *Lawless* case in Chapter 2 help you to decide?
14. What kinds of prohibited tasks might be made permissible for paralegals in the future?
15. Can a paralegal take a statement from a witness, or is this akin to taking a deposition? Compare the two functions and then see *Jackson v. United Artists Theatre Circuit, Inc.*, 278 F.R.D. 586 (D. Nev. 12-5-2011).
16. Nelson contacted Long's office seeking legal representation for a friend, Merritt, who was incarcerated for allegedly violating a protective order. Nelson met with paralegal Scheeler, paid a retainer fee, and signed a flat fee agreement for Long to represent Merritt. Long did not appear at the

initial or the second hearing in Merritt's case. Scheeler told Nelson that he would handle the matter himself "as a mediator." Two days later, Nelson paid an additional sum to resolve Merritt's criminal case. Long received a letter from a lawyer who had been hired by Smith, the individual who filed the protective order in Merritt's criminal case. The letter stated that Smith and Merritt needed to resolve an issue concerning property division but could not contact one another in light of the protective order. Merritt signed a flat fee agreement in which Long agreed to represent him. Scheeler then conducted a mediation between Merritt and Smith and drafted a settlement agreement. Although Long was shown as Merritt's attorney, he did not participate in the mediation or the drafting of the settlement agreement. Nelson submitted a complaint to the bar in which he stated that he thought Scheeler was a lawyer. Long's website listed him as a "legal mediator." Has Scheeler committed UPL? Has Long aided in UPL? Why or why not? See *Long v. Ethics and Discipline Committee*, 2011 UT 32, 256 P.3d 206 (2011).

17. Legal Documentation Company, also known as Divorce Documentation Service, prepares documents for persons representing themselves in all kinds of legal transactions. The company's owner interviews a person who wants to file for divorce, asks this customer questions about the length of the marriage, children, property, and whether or not the customer wants support, and then fills in the blanks on the forms and provides sample testimony for uncontested divorces. Is this UPL? What facts do you need to make this analysis? See *Statewide Grievance Committee v. Zadora*, 772 A.2d 681 (Conn. 2001).

18. An insurance company distributes to claimants a flyer entitled "Do I Need an Attorney?" that apparently attempts to advise claimants about the efficacy and costs of hiring a lawyer. Is this UPL? Is this speech that should be protected under the First Amendment? For an interesting analysis, see *Allstate Ins. Co. v. W. Virginia State Bar*, 233 F.3d 813 (U.S.C.A. 4th Cir. 2000).

19. Hanna is a family law paralegal with ten years of experience. She works very independently and really knows the family law process well. Her friend, Isabel, wants to file for divorce. Isabel and her husband, Jim, did not have any children; both work and have good benefits and own a couple of pieces of property. Isabel asks Hanna to help her do the divorce papers because Isabel and Jim don't want to pay a lawyer to do it. It seems that the situation is not contentious and that the couple will be able to end the relationship without a fight. What should Hanna do? Can she help them fill out the paperwork? Can she fill it out for them? Can she draft a settlement agreement for them? If she helps them and the court finds an error in her work, what are the consequences? If she helps them and the situation becomes contentious between them, what happens? Assume Hanna brings an action for divorce and Jim contests the proposed settlement. Can Hanna be called to testify about what she knows?

20. Paralegal Joan works for the corporate department of a large law firm. The partner in charge, Susan, always introduces Joan to clients and encourages them to call her directly for updates and information. Joan values this client contact and the trust that Susan has placed in her. Joan has developed a good relationship with a client, Ken, who owns several small companies. Ken calls Joan frequently to check on the status of matters that the firm is handling for him. One day, Ken calls asking Joan about a new corporate entity that he wants formed. He is trying to decide in what jurisdiction the corporation should be formed. Joan knows that it would be most favorable to form the corporation in Delaware. Can Joan answer? What might be the consequences of her actions? How should she handle this situation?
21. Lon is a business litigation paralegal for a firm that handles construction litigation. A prospective client, Cathy, who is also a friend of Lon's, comes in to see the lawyer, Mat, who is unexpectedly called away. Mat asks Lon to interview Cathy. Cathy tells a detailed story about the faulty construction on her major house-remodeling job. Cathy asks Lon, "Do I have a good case? Can you represent me? How much do you think I will get?" Lon is 100 percent certain that Mat will want to take the case and that Cathy will get some compensation for damages. How should Lon answer each of the three questions? Can Lon get Cathy to sign an agreement for Mat to represent her? Can Lon tell Cathy what kind of fee agreement Mat would normally make with a client in a case like this? Does it make any difference that Cathy and Lon are friends?
22. Fran has just gone to work for Georgia, a genius litigator and fiery advocate who is notoriously disorganized and hard to get along with. Fran is the third in a series of paralegals who have worked for Georgia in a year. Georgia is away on vacation for two weeks, giving Fran time to get organized and situated. Among other tasks, Fran has taken it upon herself to straighten Georgia's office. While Fran is going through Georgia's desk, she finds a file in the back of the bottom drawer. It appears to relate to a case on which the statute of limitations will run out the next day, and it looks like nothing has been filed. On top of her worries about the case, Georgia did not give permission to Fran to go through her desk. Fran knows how to prepare the complaint and file it and also realizes that it could be amended later. What should Fran do? Can she prepare the complaint? Sign it? File it?

RESEARCH PROJECTS AND ASSIGNMENTS

1. Interview five litigation paralegals in your area and ask them what kinds of tasks they perform. Find out if they attend trials and depositions with the lawyers for whom they work. Ask them if they have client contact and if they are ever asked questions by clients or friends that would require them to give "legal advice."

2. Contact the local legal aid organization in your area and find out how many paralegals and other nonlawyers they employ and use as volunteers, and what these persons do. Do any of the functions they perform cross the line into unauthorized practice under the definition used in this book? If so, why do you think that this situation is permitted?
3. Read the regulations for family law LPs in Arizona and consider the list of duties and prohibited acts. How do these functions compare to the categorization of functions as UPL given in this chapter? In what ways are LPs authorized to do more (or less) than they would be as LDPs under other state rules? (See AJCA §§ 7-208 and 7-210. See also Thomas, S., "Rethinking Unauthorized Practice of Law in Light of the Access to Justice Crisis," 23 The Prof. Lawyer 3 (2016) and "The Overreach on Limits on 'Legal Advice'," 131 Yale L.J. Forum 637 (2022).)
4. What are the rules governing will executions in your state? Does the state or local bar association have an advisory opinion about paralegals supervising will executions without the presence of an attorney? Interview three probate/estate-planning paralegals and find out what the practice is in their firms.
5. Do parties to residential real estate transactions in your state usually utilize the services of lawyers? If not, who represents the parties? If so, are paralegals who work for real estate lawyers permitted to handle closings without an attorney present? Is it common practice? Does the state or local bar have an opinion about it? Do you find the Illinois or the Florida rules most appropriate? Why?
6. Has your state bar or supreme court studied the problem of increasing access to legal services? What are the nature and extent of the problem in your state? What are some of the solutions that have been proposed in your state? See American Bar Association Commission on the Future of Legal Services, *Report on the Future of Legal Services in the United States*, published by the ABA in 2016. What solutions does this report offer? How many of them relate to paralegals? See the resources cited for other good publications on nonlawyer delivery as a means to increase access.
7. Research cases and disciplinary actions in your jurisdiction concerning loan modification services and foreclosure consultants. Have any nonlawyers been prosecuted for UPL in doing this work? Have any lawyers been disciplined? Has an ethics opinion been issued? Given the legitimate need of many homeowners for help in dealing with these issues, what kinds of services should be available and what should be the role of the legal community in providing them? (See *The Cincinnati Bar Ass'n v. Mullaney* at the end of this chapter for an example.)

8. Research the ABA and your state bar's website for information on "unbundling of legal services." What is this concept and how does it work? Do you see a role for paralegals in unbundling? Look at the website of Avvo, which was formerly a legal directory and in 2016 started to offer "limited scope legal services." In what ways does this model hold promise to increase access and lower cost? How might paralegals get involved in a model like this?
9. What do you think of disbarred lawyers working as paralegals? Is this practice permitted in your state? Is it more likely that a disbarred lawyer would engage in the unauthorized practice of law than a paralegal? What do you think about this? Research cases in your state. For a start, see *In re Scott*, 739 N.E.2d 658 (Ind. 2000), where a lawyer is disciplined for hiring a disbarred lawyer and allowing him to serve as the main contact with clients and to prepare and file various legal documents without adequate supervision. Also, see some state ethics rules on disbarred lawyers (California Rules of Professional Conduct 1-311, Georgia Rule 5.3(d), and Louisiana Rule 5.5(e)(1)). Additionally, see NFPA Position Statement on Disbarred Attorneys Working as Paralegals (2014).
10. Read *Ohio State Bar Ass'n v. Burdzinski, Brinkman, Czarzasty & Lanwehr, Inc.*, 112 Ohio St. 3d 107, 858 N.E.2d 372 (2006), which addresses the question of nonlawyer consultants providing advice and counsel in labor election campaigns. What did the court decide? How does this fit with the definitions of UPL in this chapter? Compare this with *In re the Town of Little Compton*, 37 A.3d 85 (R.I. 2012), in which the court is called upon to decide if nonlawyer union representatives can represent union members in labor arbitration hearings.
11. If you are interested in the use of paralegals in criminal cases, read and brief *Mississippi Bar v. Thompson*, 5 So. 3d 330 (Miss. 2008), a disciplinary case about a lawyer who hired a former inmate who then engaged in UPL.
12. To see how a court handles a lawyer who enabled a law school graduate who had not been admitted to the bar to engage in UPL, see *In re Hrones*, 457 Mass. 844 (2010).
13. Go to the website of LegalZoom and research its activities online. Write a report, telling the class about what it does and evaluating what you learn about the LegalZoom model in light of what you have learned about UPL. In what ways are the ethics rules implicated by this delivery model? Are the advertising claims appropriate? See if you can find out the status of lawsuits or other legal actions against the company. Class actions and suits brought by state attorneys general and state bars have sought to enjoin the company from various activities, but it has largely prevailed. In what ways might the LegalZoom model work? How might paralegals be part of this delivery model?

F. Practice Before Administrative Agencies

Administrative agency
A government body responsible for the control and supervision of a particular activity or area of public interest.

Administrative agencies are created by state and federal legislatures to provide for the regulation of certain highly **specialized** fields. A few examples of administrative agencies are the Environmental Protection Agency, the National Labor Relations Board, and the Patent Office at the federal level, and workers' compensation, unemployment insurance, public utility, and disability boards at the state level. Although some agencies oversee very complex areas of law (e.g., patents), many administrative agencies handle an extremely large volume of cases that do not require much more than a mechanical application of rules. The volume of cases and the specialized non-legal subject matter make it impractical and inefficient to adjudicate disputes in these fields through regular court procedures.

Administrative agencies are **quasi-judicial** in nature, meaning that disputes before these agencies are resolved through a hearing, similar to although less formal than a trial, before an administrative law judge or hearing officer or examiner, with advocates representing the parties. Procedures typically include the issuance of subpoenas, testimony under oath, admission of evidence, and oral and written arguments.

Someone representing a client before an administrative agency requires legal skills that are comparable to those needed by a lawyer representing a client in a trial. The advocate must have knowledge of the specialized area of law and of the procedures used by the agency; be able to apply this knowledge to the specific facts and context of the case, using the proper analytical and judgmental abilities in doing so; and be able to advocate the client's case competently in an adversarial setting. Although the area of law might be narrower and the rules of evidence and procedure more informal than in a court, the functions of the advocate and the skills necessary for success in this setting are similar to a trial lawyer's.

Despite the similarities just described, many administrative agencies do not require advocates to be lawyers. The federal government has long permitted nonlawyer practice before many of its administrative agencies. The purpose of doing so is twofold: to allow easy **access** to these agencies and to make the process as informal, efficient, and inexpensive as possible. The Administrative Procedure Act, 5 U.S.C. §555(b) (1994), specifically authorizes individual federal administrative agencies to permit nonlawyer practice. It states that persons appearing before an agency may be "accompanied, represented, and advised by counsel or, if permitted by the agency, by other qualified representative."

This provision leaves the decision about nonlawyer practice to the agency itself. Some agencies require a J.D. degree or a license as a lawyer or certification as a public accountant, or recommendations of others admitted to practice, or passing an exam. A few such federal agencies are the U.S. Patent Office, Internal Revenue Service, and Interstate Commerce Commission. Other agencies allow all nonlawyer representatives without requiring them to meet any specific standards. Examples of these agencies include the Small Business Administration, Social Security Administration, and Bureau of Indian Affairs.

While recognizing the benefits of nonlawyer practice to both consumers and the administrative legal system, some have advocated for competence and ethics requirements for those who practice before federal and state administrative agencies without law degrees. See, for example, "Nonlawyer Practice Before Federal Administrative Agencies Should Be Encouraged," 37 Administrative L. Rev. 363 (1985) and "Are We Our Brother's Keepers? A Discussion of Nonlawyer Representation Before Texas Administrative Agencies and Recommendations for the Future," 8 Texas Tech Administrative L.J. 115 (2007). In addition, see State of Washington Advisory Opinion No. 5 (2014).

Rules about nonlawyer practice before state administrative agencies are inconsistent across the country. Some state statutes authorize representation by nonlawyers before many or all state administrative agencies, and some do not. In states that have a strong judicial history supporting the inherent power of the court to oversee the practice of law, legislation authorizing nonlawyer practice before state administrative agencies has been struck down. (See, for example, *Denver Bar Association v. P.U.C.*, 154 Colo. 273, 391 P.2d 467 (1964), and an opinion of the Illinois State Bar Association, which holds that employers cannot utilize nonlawyer representatives in termination hearings held before the Illinois Department of Employment Security.) Another way of limiting nonlawyer representation without actually banning it is by prohibiting nonlawyers from collecting fees. (See, for example, California Labor Code §§4903 and 5710.) Also recall the case in Chapter 1, *UPL Committee v. State Department of Workers' Compensation*, in which the court upheld legislation that created a job classification for nonlawyer advisers to assist persons filing claims.

There is also some debate about whether paralegals employed by lawyers may represent clients before state administrative agencies that otherwise allow nonlawyer representation. Most states allow it. For example, the State Bar of California opines that "a law firm may delegate authority to a paralegal employee, provided that the employee is adequately supervised, to make appearances at Workers' Compensation Appeals Board hearings." Advisory Opinion 88-103 (1988). For another example, see Michigan Ethics Opinion RI-125 (1992).

There is also periodic conflict between the states' authority to regulate the practice of law and the federal government's authority over its administrative agencies. The key case of *Sperry v. Florida*, 373 U.S. 379 (1963), would seem to have resolved this conflict when it held that the U.S. Patent Office regulations authorizing nonlawyer practice supersede state law by virtue of the U.S. Constitution's Supremacy Clause. However, unauthorized practice charges are still brought occasionally against nonlawyer practitioners who appear before federal agencies. (See, for example, *Unauthorized Practice Committee, State Bar of Texas v. Cortez*, 692 S.W.2d 47 (Tex. 1985).)

G. Disclosure of Paralegal Status and Job Titles

Many paralegals act as the liaison to persons outside the law firm — clients, witnesses, co-counsel, opposing law firms, courts, and so forth. This contact may take the form of telephone conversations, e-mail communications, correspondence, and meetings in person. A key ethical aspect of the liaison role is ensuring that the person with whom the paralegal is dealing is fully aware that the paralegal is not a lawyer.

Disclosure of status fits in this chapter on unauthorized practice of law for two reasons. First, a paralegal **may appear to be engaging in unauthorized practice** if they seem to others to be a lawyer. Not clearly identifying one's status may mislead the other person into believing that the paralegal is a lawyer. It is not difficult to see how someone, especially a lay person such as a client or witness, might misconstrue the paralegal's status because they "sound" like a lawyer. To the other person, a paralegal's inadvertent lack of disclosure may appear to be intentional. A severe consequence is that the paralegal could be charged with holding themself out as a lawyer, which in many states is considered the unauthorized practice of law and is a misdemeanor. Disciplinary action against the supervising lawyer may also result, under the ethics rules prohibiting a lawyer from aiding in the unauthorized practice of law.

The second reason that disclosure fits into the context of the unauthorized practice of law is that a paralegal who is mistaken for a lawyer may be called upon **to give legal advice**. If a client mistakenly believes that a paralegal is a lawyer, the client may ask questions that require the paralegal to respond with legal advice. This situation places paralegals in the uncomfortable position of having to explain why they cannot respond.

ABA Model Guideline 4 and similar state guidelines hold lawyers responsible for **informing clients** and others that the paralegal is not licensed to practice law. Some state guidelines on paralegal utilization advise "routine, early disclosure" or disclosure at the "outset" of the communication with the third party. Using a proper **title** for a paralegal is an important aspect of disclosure. The title must reflect that the person is not a lawyer, and should also accurately designate the role that the person has on the legal services delivery team. The title "associate," for example, is not appropriate for paralegals, as it is commonly used for lawyers who are working for a firm but have not attained partnership status.

The preferred and proper titles for paralegals have changed over time and been debated extensively. In the last 20 years, many firms have adopted the practice of calling legal secretaries legal assistants. This usage accelerated the trend toward use of the title paralegal and away from the title legal assistant. It is noteworthy that this title cannot be used for legal secretaries in California and other states where that title is only for someone who meets specified requirements. It should be noted that the titles **legal assistant** and **paralegal** were historically used interchangeably, and may carry different connotations in different regions of the country. However, paralegal is overwhelmingly the preferred title, as exemplified by the ABA, which in 2020 removed the title legal assistant from its definition of paralegal.

Frequently, a legal specialty is attached to a title to indicate the area of practice in which the paralegal works, for instance, probate or litigation paralegal. As more firms have developed career paths for paralegals, new titles have been created, such as senior paralegal and litigation support specialist. As a general rule, any title that does not potentially mislead a third party into believing that the paralegal is a lawyer is permissible.

Paralegals are permitted to use their **certification designations** with their titles, *e.g.*, Certified Paralegal or Registered Paralegal. Iowa, Mississippi, and New York have opinions that support this practice. (See, for example, Mississippi Ethics Opinion 95-223 and New York State Bar Association Ethics Opinion 97-695.) In another twist on titles, New York issued an opinion endorsing the terms *paralegal* and *senior paralegal*, but finding unacceptable and ambiguous the terms *paralegal coordinator, legal associate, public benefits advocate, family law advocate, housing law advocate, disability benefits advocate*, and *public benefit specialist*. New York State Bar Ethics Opinion 640 (54-92) (1992).

Paralegals are also permitted to **sign correspondence** with their job titles. Many states have ethics opinions or guidelines that endorse the signing of correspondence by paralegals so long as the paralegals use an accurate job title that is not misleading. Early in the development of the paralegal occupation, the ABA issued an informal ethics opinion that supported this practice:

> The lawyers' use of assistants to perform specialized tasks . . . is becoming increasingly common, and, indeed essential to the efficient practice of law. The Committee is of the opinion that it is appropriate for Legal Assistants to sign correspondence which is incidental to the proper conduct of his or her responsibilities but care should be taken to identify accurately the capacity of the person who signs the letter so that the receiver is not misled.

ABA Commission on Ethics and Professional Responsibility, Informal Op. 1367 (1976).

A more problematic practice is communicating legal advice in correspondence signed by the paralegal. In theory, this practice is not different from a paralegal relaying legal advice orally from the lawyer to the client, with the added benefit of the advice being spelled out in writing. The e-mail or letter documents the advice being issued by the lawyer through the paralegal. However, some states have opinions that indicate that allowing a paralegal to sign a letter containing legal advice or threatening legal action constitutes the unauthorized practice of law. (See, for example, Georgia Formal Advisory Opinion 00-2 and the Utah State Bar Legal Assistant Guidelines, which state that paralegals may "[a]uthor and sign letters provided the legal assistant's status is clearly indicated and the correspondence does not contain independent legal opinions or legal advice." Guideline D.8.) Care should be taken in wording letters and e-mails that might contain legal advice to ensure that the client understands that the advice was formulated by the lawyer and is only being communicated by the paralegal. In addition, all e-mail communications should contain an e-mail signature block that clearly indicates the paralegal's nonlawyer status.

State rules on the use of business cards by paralegals and listing of paralegals on law firm letterhead have not been uniform across the country. Some bar associations were initially concerned that **business cards** might be misused to solicit clients (discussed in Chapter 6). Most states have balanced the benefits of disclosure about a paralegal's status in favor of having business cards. The ABA has long supported the use of business cards by paralegals, as indicated in a 1971 opinion:

> The term "legal assistant" appears to be coming into general use as connoting a lay assistant to a lawyer, as evidenced by its use in the title of the American Bar Association's Special Committee on Legal Assistants. . . . Informal Opinion 909 permits the designation on a business card of an employee of a law firm who does investigation work for the firm as an "Investigator." By the same reasoning, it would appear to be proper to designate a legal assistant as such on a business card, provided that the designation is accurate, and the duties involved are properly performed under the direction of the lawyer. . . .

ABA Comm. on Ethics and Professional Responsibility, Informal Op. 1185 (1971).

Related is the question of listing paralegals' **names and titles on law firm letterhead**. The ABA Model Code (in effect from 1969 to 1980), which had been adopted in whole or in part by nearly all jurisdictions, originally prohibited the listing on a lawyer's letterhead of virtually anything other than lawyers' names and the firm's address and phone numbers. ABA Model Code DR 1-102(A)(4) (1969, amended 1980).

G. Disclosure of Paralegal Status and Job Titles

The decision of *Bates v. State Bar of Arizona*, 430 U.S. 350 (1977), raised questions about the constitutionality of these restrictions. This case, which appears in Chapter 6, held that the state could not impose blanket restrictions on lawyer advertising. In its opinion, the Supreme Court emphasized that consumers need information about legal services to make those services more accessible and to help consumers to select a lawyer.

Because of this case and several that followed it, all states and the ABA revised the ethics rules that limited the kind of information that may appear on lawyers' **letterhead**, in announcements, and the like. Several states that prohibited the listing of paralegals on letterhead adopted new rules permitting this practice. All but a few states that have opinions on the subject permit the listing of paralegals on letterhead. For example, Ohio's opinion indicates that it is acceptable for law firms to list the names of nonlawyer employees on letterhead and websites, as long as their status is clear. (Ohio Ethics Opinion 2012-2).

The ABA ethics opinion, adopted after *Bates*, reads in part:

> The listing of nonlawyer support personnel on lawyers' letterheads is not prohibited by these [Model Rules 7.1 and 7.5] or any other Rules so long as the listing is not false or misleading. In order to avoid being misleading, the listing must make it clear that the support personnel who are listed are not lawyers. The listing of support personnel, such as the law firm administrator or office manager, administrative assistants, paralegals or others, appropriately designated may furnish useful information to the public in determining whether to engage the firm and in learning the status of members of the support staff with whom they have contact.
>
> A law firm also may list nonlawyer personnel on business cards, written advertisements and the like, provided the designation is not likely to mislead those who see it into thinking that the nonlawyers who are listed are lawyers or exercise control over lawyers in the firm.

ABA Comm. on Ethics and Professional Responsibility, Informal Opinion 1527 (1989).

The ABA Model Guidelines also conform to this policy. Guideline 5 states that a lawyer "may identify paralegals by name and title on the lawyer's letterhead and on business cards identifying the lawyer's firm."

Hence the general practice permits paralegals to be listed with appropriate job titles on business cards and letterhead, in firm announcements, in firm newsletters, in directory listings, in print advertisements, on firm websites, and so forth. In practice, most law firms provide paralegals with business cards but do *not* list them on the firm letterhead or on the door. Many list them on their websites.

The NFPA Model Code addresses the issue of disclosure in Section 1.7, which requires that titles be fully disclosed. Canon 5 of the NALA Code also requires disclosure "at the outset of any professional relationship. . . ."

H. Paralegals Working as Independent Contractors

Freelance paralegals
Paralegals who work as independent contractors providing services to lawyers on an as-needed basis.

Many paralegals offer their services as **independent contractors**, handling projects for lawyers on an as-needed basis. In the 1970s, the first *freelance paralegals* worked in the probate area, which lends itself well to effective paralegal use because the probate process is highly structured and procedural. In addition, many firms handle only a small amount of probate work, not enough to warrant having a full-time paralegal on staff. Gradually, freelance paralegals came to offer their services in other areas of practice, especially litigation. Many work as litigation support specialists, focusing on discovery management, trial preparation, usually in large civil lawsuits. They aid law firms in organizing and managing the sometimes massive numbers of documents in large cases and assisting in discovery.

The use of independent contractors in the legal field is not limited to paralegals. Contract attorneys and a wide array of support services are now provided to firms in this fashion. Outsourcing to vendors and the use of part-time and freelance workers constitute accepted methods of doing business in today's economy. These practices give businesses more flexibility in meeting their needs and potentially save clients money. Many paralegals find that working as an independent contractor is an attractive career path. Many freelance paralegals work for themselves, running their own businesses. Paralegals with an entrepreneurial spirit often find this kind of work more rewarding than working 9 to 5 (or longer) for a paycheck. They enjoy the added responsibility of working for themselves, the freedom and flexibility of choosing their own hours, the power to decline an assignment if they choose, and the earning potential.

Working as a freelance paralegal presents special ethical concerns in many areas—such as confidentiality and conflicts of interest—and issues are also present in the area of unauthorized practice of law. One concern is to distinguish the independent paralegal who is supervised by a lawyer from a nonlawyer legal service provider who works directly with the public and sometimes uses the title of independent paralegal. The confusion between these two categories of nonlawyers has resulted in legislation and court rules in some states that prohibit nonlawyer legal service providers from calling themselves paralegals. (See more on this earlier and in Chapter 2.)

The ABA Model Rules of Professional Conduct allow lawyers to use the services of all kinds of independent contractors, including paralegals. Rule 5.3, which outlines attorneys' ethical responsibilities regarding nonlawyer assistants, specifically includes nonlawyers "retained by" a lawyer or employed by a lawyer, and the accompanying comment to Rule 5.3 emphasizes that assistants may be "independent contractors."

The 50-year history of the paralegal profession is characterized by a tremendous expansion in the nature and extent of legal tasks that paralegals perform. The trend is toward continued growth into new areas and functions that neither lawyers nor paralegals might have expected when the profession was just beginning. The pressures to expand the functions performed by supervised paralegals and to allow some legal services to be delivered directly to the public by nonlawyers will undoubtedly continue. As we have seen, social and economic forces have changed the way we view the practice of law and will redefine the rules prohibiting the practice of law by nonlawyers.

REVIEW QUESTIONS

1. Why are nonlawyers allowed to practice before some administrative agencies?
2. Name five federal agencies that permit nonlawyer practice.
3. Do states allow nonlawyers to represent clients before their administrative agencies? Discuss.
4. Can paralegals who work under the supervision of a lawyer represent clients before administrative agencies for their lawyer-employers? Discuss.
5. Can a state court prohibit a nonlawyer from practicing before a federal administrative agency within the state on grounds that such representation constitutes the unauthorized practice of law? Why or why not?
6. Why must paralegals be careful to disclose their status as a paralegal?
7. Name three job titles that are appropriate for paralegals to use in identifying their status. Name some titles that are not acceptable.
8. May paralegals sign correspondence on firm letterhead? Why or why not? What limitations might be placed on the form and content of correspondence between paralegals and clients?
9. May paralegals have business cards? How should a card read? How might it be misused?
10. May paralegals' names be listed on law firm letterhead? On websites? Why or why not? Why have policies about this changed? Is this practice common?
11. Are freelance paralegals who work for lawyers engaging in the unauthorized practice of law? How might they be more susceptible to allegations that they have engaged in UPL?

DISCUSSION QUESTIONS AND HYPOTHETICALS

1. How can the prohibition against nonlawyers representing clients in court be reconciled with nonlawyer representation of clients before administrative agencies? Do you think that the differences in these two settings are substantial enough to warrant the differences in policy?

2. How can independent paralegals who work under the supervision of lawyers distinguish themselves from those who serve the public directly? Do different job titles make a difference? For example, nonlawyer direct service providers are called legal document assistants in California and legal document preparers in Arizona. Will this solve the problem in those states?
3. Do you think freelance paralegals who provide services to attorneys are engaged in the practice of law? Might lawyers who use the services of independent contractors be more likely to fail in their responsibility to select, train, supervise, and review the work of these paralegals than those who are employed full-time by a firm? What about other independent contractors who serve lawyers—for example, process servers, investigators, accountants, and experts?
4. A lawyer hires an independent paralegal who will (1) conduct initial interviews of clients that have requested estate planning services, and (2) supervise execution of estate planning portfolios prepared by the lawyer. Is this UPL? What do you need to know to decide? See State Bar of Arizona Ethics Opinion 98-08 (1998) for one state's analysis.

RESEARCH PROJECTS AND ASSIGNMENTS

1. Are there any state administrative agencies in your jurisdiction that permit nonlawyer practice? Do nonlawyers appear before these agencies frequently or infrequently? What about paralegals working under the supervision of lawyers? Are there any state or local bar ethics opinions on this matter?
2. Do any statutes in your state disallow fees for nonlawyer representatives in administrative agencies? Which ones? Do lawyers represent clients in these agencies or do most people represent themselves?
3. Contact ten local law firms, five large and five small, and find out what job titles their paralegals use and if their paralegals:
   a. have business cards
   b. are listed on the law firm letterhead
   c. have individualized letterhead
   d. are listed in advertisements, firm brochures, or newsletters
   e. are listed on the door to the firm
   f. are listed in the directory to the firm in the lobby of the building
   g. are listed on the law firm website
   h. prepare and sign correspondence to clients under their own names and titles
4. Contact your local paralegal association and find out if independent contractors or freelance paralegals are widely used in your area. Interview five freelance paralegals and the lawyers who utilize their services. Ask them what special ethical problems they face. Does the

freelance paralegal work in the lawyer's office or elsewhere? How does a lawyer select an independent contractor? How does the lawyer supervise and review the work of the independent contractor?
5. Contact the paralegal managers of five large law firms in your area and ask if they outsource any paralegal work. If they do, find out if the work is done locally or overseas, and what measures are in place to guard against ethical violations. Are there any state or local ethics rules about outsourcing in your jurisdiction?
6. Is it UPL for a company to represent a debtor in negotiations with a creditor's lawyer? See the Supreme Court of Georgia In re UPL Advisory Opinion 2003-1 (2005) or *Cincinnati Bar Ass'n v. Telford*, 85 Ohio St.3d 111, 707 N.E.2d 462 (1999).
7. Is it UPL for a financial service company to prepare loan documents and charge a fee for their preparation in connection with a mortgage transaction? See *King v. First Capital Financial Services Corp.*, 828 N.E.2d 1155 (Ill. 2005).
8. Read and brief *The Florida Bar v. Neiman*, 816 So. 2d 587 (Florida 2002), for a compelling example of a paralegal engaged in the unauthorized practice of law while employed by lawyers.

CASES FOR ANALYSIS

In this Florida case, the court is faced once again with constitutional arguments about the UPL statute, this time in a prosecution involving two paralegals who took depositions.

State v. Foster
674 So.2d 747 (Fla. 1996)

The State of Florida appeals from orders issued in separate cases (1) dismissing charges against Scott E. Foster, Jr., and his wife, Martha J. Foster, purportedly arising from the unauthorized practice of law and (2) finding [the Florida UPL statute] vague and violative of federal constitutional protections or unconstitutional in its application to the appellees. . . .

Mr. Foster was charged with four counts of unauthorized practice of law for his participation in four depositions by questioning four witnesses in two different cases. . . . [T]he state likewise charged Mrs. Foster for her participation in one deposition by questioning a witness.

The applicable statute provides:

Any person not licensed or otherwise authorized by the Supreme Court of Florida who shall practice law or assume or hold himself out to the public as qualified to practice law in this state, or who willfully pretends to be, or willfully takes or uses any name, title, addition, or description implying that he is qualified, or recognized as qualified, to act as a lawyer in this state, and any person entitled to practice who shall violate any provisions of this chapter shall be guilty of a misdemeanor of the first degree. . . .

Neither of the appellees disputes the fact that each participated in the respective depositions by questioning one or more witnesses. The Fosters are paralegals who own a business that performs paralegal functions. Neither one is a licensed attorney. . . .

The first issue to be resolved is whether taking a deposition constitutes the practice of law. . . . The Supreme Court of Florida considered an analogous question in *Florida Bar v. Riccardi*, 304 So. 2d 444 (Fla. 1974). . . . The court held that Mr. Riccardi's conduct constituted the unauthorized practice of law. . . . [W]e agree that appellee's questioning of witnesses in depositions likewise constituted the unauthorized practice of law in violation of [the Florida statute].

The second issue is whether the lower courts correctly found the statute to be unconstitutionally vague. . . . The Supreme Court of Arizona has described the practice of law as follows: "We believe it sufficient to state that those acts, whether performed in court or in the law office, which lawyers customarily have carried on from day to day through the centuries must constitute 'the practice of law.'" [Citation omitted.]

. . . [T]he definition of the practice of law in Florida is not confined to the language of [the statute], but rather is shaped by decisional law and court rules as well as common understanding and practices. . . . The Supreme Court of Florida has defined various acts as constituting the practice of law, including "appearing in Court or in proceedings which are part of the judicial process,"[citation omitted] and, specifically, active participation in depositions, the conduct for which appellees were charged. *Riccardi*, 304 So. 2d at 445. . . . The appellees have not pointed out, nor have we found, any instance where [the statute] has been found unconstitutional on any of the grounds argued at trial or set forth on appeal. We note that foreign courts that have reviewed comparable "unlicensed practice of law" provisions consistently have found no unconstitutional vagueness. [Citations omitted.] . . .

In supporting its ruling . . . , the trial court noted the Supreme Court of Florida's statement in the *Florida Bar v. Brumbaugh*, 355 So. 2d 1186 (Fla. 1978) that "it is somewhat difficult to define exactly what constitutes the practice of law in all instances." In its very thorough opinion, the trial court reasoned that, if Florida's highest court cannot "define exactly" the practice of law, then the statute addressing the unauthorized practice of law must necessarily be unconstitutionally vague. We respectfully disagree, finding that the quoted language in *Brumbaugh* must be considered within the factual context of that case. . . . We agree that "any attempt to formulate a lasting, all encompassing definition of 'practice of law' is doomed to failure 'for the reasons that under our system of jurisprudence such practice must necessarily change with the ever changing business and social order.'" *Id.* at 1191-92. . . .

The quoted comment was not intended, and should not be construed, to suggest that the practice of law cannot be defined or that an attempt to interpret [the Florida statute] must involve guesswork and chance. Were we to adopt the appellees' suggestion that . . . renders a statute void for vagueness, the State would be effectively precluded from establishing minimum qualifications for practice in the regulated and licensed professions and occupations. . . .

We think that in determining whether the giving of advice and counsel and the performance of services in legal matters for compensation constitute the practice of law it is safe to follow the rule that if the giving of such advice and performance of such services affect[s] important rights of a person under the law and if the reasonable protection of the rights and property of those advised and served requires that the persons giving such advice possess legal skill and a knowledge of the law greater than that possessed by the average citizen, the giving of such advice and the performance of such services by one for another as a course of conduct constitute the practice of law. *State ex rel. The Florida Bar v. Sperry*, 140 So. 2d 587 (Fla. 1962). . . .

A deposition is an important, formal, recorded proceeding in which lawyers must observe the Florida rules of court and must rely on their training and skills to question witnesses effectively. The activities and services involved . . . often implicate ethical questions and strategic considerations of utmost importance. The effectiveness of a person deposing a witness can have a significant impact on whether objectionable information is identified and addressed or waived, whether a case is made, and how the evidence therefore is used in any subsequent proceeding. Depositions are transcribed by a court reporter for possible use later in court. . . .

We conclude that, lacking adequate legal training, a nonattorney participating in the examination of a witness poses . . . dangers of "incompetent, unethical, or irresponsible representation." [Citations omitted.]

The third question is whether [the Florida statute], although facially constitutional, is unconstitutional in its application to the appellees' particular conduct. . . . [W]e decline to apply the overbreadth doctrine to the instant case, where the appellees' active participation in depositions does not lie at the fringe of conduct constituting the practice of law. . . . Reversed. . . .

Questions about the Case

1. What do you think of the language in the Arizona case cited in this case? Does it give notice to the public about what functions fall under the Florida statute?

2. How persuasive is the appellees' argument that if the court cannot define the practice of law, it is necessarily vague?
3. Is a definition in a court opinion sufficient to give notice to nonlawyers who are involved in providing legal services? How might such persons find out about the rule?
4. Did you find the *Sperry* case formulation of the practice of law useful? How might you break down the long sentence cited here into more useful components?

In the following case, a "paralegal" who is prosecuted for the unauthorized practice of law raises multiple defenses.

Board of Commissioners of the Utah State Bar v. Petersen
937 P.2d 1263 (Utah 1997)

Petersen, a nonattorney, has worked in Manti, Utah, since 1991. During that time, he has prepared wills, divorce papers, and pleadings and conducted legal research on behalf of clients for a fee. Petersen also advertised his services in local publications. Just prior to moving to Manti, Petersen had completed a nine-month correspondence course through the N.R.I. Paralegal School. Petersen subsequently registered as a paralegal through the National Paralegal Association, the Pennsylvania organization which offered the correspondence course. However, Petersen was never employed by an attorney, and none of his law-related work was supervised by an attorney. Petersen's activities were brought to the attention of the Board of Bar Commissioners of the Utah State Bar, and the Bar filed a formal complaint in 1993. The Bar claimed that Petersen had engaged in the unauthorized practice of law in violation of section 78-51-25 of the Utah Code and sought a permanent injunction against him. Section 78-51-25 of the Utah Code states in relevant part as follows:

> No person who is not duly admitted and licensed to practice law within this state . . . shall practice or assume to hold himself out to the public as a person qualified to practice or carry on the calling of a lawyer within the state.

Petersen filed two pretrial motions to have section 78-51-25 declared unconstitutional. . . . The trial court denied both motions.

The case was tried to a jury. . . . The jury returned a verdict in favor of the Bar and against Petersen, and the court ordered Petersen to stop the unauthorized practice of law. . . .

On appeal, Petersen argues that section 78-51-25 is constitutionally vague, . . . overbroad, . . . [and that it] violates the separation of powers doctrine . . . by purporting to authorize the legislature to pass a law that regulates the unauthorized practice of law. . . .

Petersen claims that an ordinary reader would not understand . . . section 78-51-25 to prohibit the kinds of activities in which he was engaged. He asserts that the obvious reading of the statute is that a nonlawyer is prohibited from either claiming to be or working as a lawyer, neither of which Petersen did. . . . We disagree. . . . The obvious reading of the statute is that unless a person is licensed to practice law within the state, he cannot practice as a lawyer, act as a lawyer, or even *present himself to the public as a person qualified* to act as a lawyer. . . .

Although "the practice of law" has not been exactly defined, an "ordinary reader" would understand that certain services, when performed on someone else's behalf, are part of such practice. Such services would include not only appearing in court, but also drafting complaints, drafting or negotiating contracts, drafting wills, counseling or giving legal advice on matters, and many other things. . . .

Further, when such services are performed for a fee, it is even more likely that they constitute the practice of law. . . .

Petersen's conduct falls within the clear sanction of section 78-51-25. Although not licensed to practice law, he met with and counseled clients on how best to proceed in their particular cases; with the aid of forms he selected, he drafted such things as complaints, summonses, motions, orders, and findings of fact and conclusions of law for pro se clients; he drafted wills; and he advertised his services in local publications. Thus Petersen held himself out to the public as a person qualified to provide, for a fee, services constituting the practice of law.

Petersen claims that section 78-51-25 is unconstitutionally overbroad . . . because it would make it "illegal for anyone to aid in the legal process" and thus would deprive many individuals, including Petersen, of their right to employment . . . [including] police officers who inform individuals in custody of their *Miranda* rights, nonattorney justice court judges when rendering a judgment, and court clerks who assist in the filing of court documents. . . . Petersen's arguments are without merit. . . . He may work under the supervision of an attorney. In addition, it is absurd to argue that the statute prohibits the activities of policemen, justice court judges, and clerks of court. None of these individuals offer legal advice, draft legal documents, or in any way represent clients for a fee. . . .

Petersen also claims that it is a violation of the . . . Utah Constitution to treat him any differently . . . than a paralegal working under the supervision of an attorney. . . . The legislative objective of section 78-51-25 was to protect the public. . . . As Petersen himself concedes, it is certainly a legitimate objective to want to protect the public from people claiming to be qualified to practice law even though they are not so qualified. . . . [I]t is reasonable to classify individuals based on a license to practice law. There are many safeguards built into the licensing process that offer protection to the public . . . including those laws which hold attorneys responsible for the actions of their paralegals. . . .

Petersen next claims that section 78-51-25 . . . violates the separation of powers doctrine. . . . This court's power over the regulation of the practice of law is a power over "members of the legal profession as officers of the Court." [Citation omitted.] The scope of article VIII, Section 4, does not extend to the unauthorized practice of law. Therefore, section 78-51-25 does not encroach on any exclusive jurisdiction of the Utah Supreme Court and does not violate the separation of powers doctrine. . . .

Therefore, we affirm the trial court's judgment and injunction. . . .

Questions about the Case

1. What were the paralegal's educational credentials? Was Mr. Petersen a paralegal, as that term is commonly understood in your state? Did he work under lawyer supervision?
2. What was Mr. Petersen charged with, and what sanction was imposed by the trial court?
3. What were the three arguments with which he defended himself against the UPL charge? Set forth each argument and the response of the court to each argument. Do you agree with the court's analysis or Mr. Petersen's?
4. Think back to the separation of powers discussion in Chapter 1. Does it make sense to you that the court has authority over the practice of law and the legislature over the "unauthorized" practice of law? Note the court rules about unauthorized practice that are referenced in this chapter. Do most states embrace this distinction?

In this case, a bankruptcy court considers the conduct of the owner-operators of an office of We the People, a company that provides services to people who are representing themselves in court, usually in bankruptcy and family law matters. The case addressed statutory violations as well as negligence, contract, and UPL issues.

In re Finch
Case No. 303-12945 (Bankr. M.D. Tenn. 2004)

All of the debtors involved in these matters consulted We the People [WTP] to prepare bankruptcy petitions. In each case, Chapter 7 petitions were filed, and Vincent Gould was listed as the petition preparer. . . . The trustee found inaccuracies and omissions in the Statements and Schedules of the debtors in *Finch, Toalson,* and *Smith.* Accordingly, the trustee filed dischargeability actions pursuant to 11 U.S.C. §727 seeking to deny the debtors' discharges for omitting or providing inaccurate information on their petitions, Statements, and Schedules.

Each of these debtors filed their petitions *pro se*, but following the dischargeability complaints filed by the Chapter 7 trustee, each debtor retained counsel to defend the adversary proceedings. In all three cases, the debtors filed third-party actions against Vincent and Shannon Gould and WTP alleging that the negligence, breach of contract, and/or violations of 11 U.S.C. §110 led to the omissions and inaccuracies in their bankruptcy filings. Accordingly, in the *Finch, Toalson,* and *Smith* cases, the debtors seek a judgment over Vincent and Shannon Gould and WTP. . . .

Harry David Finch is a former contractor who is in the process of obtaining disability. His wife died in 2001, and he has had no steady income since that time. He has a 10th grade education and difficulty reading. The debtor had been on medication for his multiple medical problems for more than two years prior to filing bankruptcy. He contacted WTP after his friend, Felicia Stevens, saw their advertisement on a bus stop. Stevens testified that she told Finch that WTP advertised bankruptcy filings for $199. Finch remembered WTP's phone number as having "LEGAL" in the number and contacted them. At his WTP meeting, he signed a "Contract for Services" provided by WTP, received information about bankruptcy, and received a "workbook" to fill out and return to WTP.

Finch testified that a WTP employee named Sandy or Cindy told him that they would file everything, and that he thought WTP was representing him. When Finch got to a question asking about real property, he explained to Sandy/Cindy that he had owned some real property, but had sold it and gotten some money for it. The debtor testified that Cindy/Sandy told him that he did not have to list the property. . . .

The debtor paid WTP $199 for their services, and another $199 for the filing fee.

WTP filed the debtor's voluntary petition under Chapter 7 of the Bankruptcy Code on October 9, 2003. The debtor signed his petition, Statements and Schedules indicating that the information contained therein was correct. However, at the 11 U.S.C. §341 Meeting of Creditors, when asked by the trustee, the debtor indicated that he had owned and sold property located at 1066 Chestnut Road, Ashland City prior to filing. Finch indicated he received $15,000.00 from the sale. Upon request of the trustee, the debtor provided bank records showing that the debtor used the money to pay bills from January 2003 until July 2003. The property had not been disclosed in the debtor's Statements and Schedules because Finch had relied on WTP's advice to leave the question blank. . . .

[Finch] hired an attorney after the trustee filed a §727 action against him seeking to deny his discharge. The debtor's attorney then helped him amend his Statements and Schedules to include the property transfer and a pending consumer protection lawsuit that the debtor had brought against Nissan. The debtor testified that he would have told the trustee about the lawsuit if he had been asked about it at the Meeting of

Creditors, and he did not know he should have listed it until consulting his attorney.

The trustee's dischargeability action seeks to deny the debtor's discharge based on the omission of the property transfer and the omission of the lawsuit. The debtor counters that the property transfer was not listed based on advice given by WTP, and that he did not know to list the pending lawsuit until meeting with an attorney. No money is or was remaining from the sale of the property as of the filing of bankruptcy or the Meeting of Creditors.

Michael Scott Toalson has not worked for several years except for a few months in the summer of 2003. He testified that he is disabled due to health issues including cardiovascular problems, back troubles, and foot problems. In 1999, he lived in Fulton, Kentucky on his late parents' property he owned jointly with his brother and sister. He and his brother took out a loan to buy out his sister's 1/3 interest, and Toalson lived in the Fulton, Kentucky home until it was sold in November of 2002 for $45,000. He and his brother divided the sale proceeds evenly after repaying the loan.

Toalson used the sale proceeds to pay living expenses. Although the debtor had receipts documenting some of the expenses paid, he could not account for every dollar received from the sale proceeds. Toalson's testimony was credible, however, that all of the proceeds had been expended on reasonable living expenses. When he was down to his final $200, he decided to file bankruptcy.

Toalson explained that he saw WTP's advertisement in a "Sensible Shopper" flyer stating that if he called "44-LEGAL," he could file bankruptcy for $200. He called WTP and spoke to Cindy and made an appointment. At the first meeting, he met with Cindy for about 10-15 minutes. She gave him a packet of information containing informational brochures about bankruptcy, a WTP Contract for Services, and a bankruptcy "workbook." Toalson testified that Cindy went through some of the workbook highlights, but that Shannon Gould took over when he needed help with Question 10 asking about real property. Toalson explained that Shannon Gould marked through questions that did not pertain to him. . . . Toalson stated that Mrs. Gould told him that because he did not transfer the Fulton, Kentucky property to a creditor or family member, he did not have to list the transfer. This advice was given after Mrs. Gould consulted with Mr. Vincent Gould, who in turn referenced a book source and confirmed the omission. . . .

The debtor returned to WTP to sign his petition, Statements, and Schedules and on October 7, 2003 paid an additional $215 to Mr. Gould to cover the filing fee and copy fee. He was told where to sign, and was not offered an opportunity to compare his workbook with his finalized papers. In fact, under questioning by the UST, the debtor identified several instances where WTP had made changes, such as: (1) WTP marked out questions; (2) WTP inserted corrections without the debtor's permissions; (3) WTP added information without asking the debtor; (4) WTP suggested to Toalson to include such things as exemption statutes; (5) WTP recommended assigning a "yard sale" value for personal property and exemptions; and (6) WTP "helped" with whether a claim was priority, secured, or unsecured. WTP filed the debtor's voluntary petition under Chapter 7. . . . The debtor signed his petition, Statements, and Schedules indicating that the information contained therein was correct. However, the debtor disclosed at his Meeting of Creditors, when asked by the trustee, that he had sold his parents' house seven months prior to filing. The property had not been disclosed in the debtor's Statements and Schedules because Toalson had relied on WTP's advice to leave the question blank.

The trustee told the debtor after his Meeting of Creditors that he might need to consult an attorney because of the omissions in the Statements and Schedules. The debtor returned to WTP with his brother. Toalson testified that Mr. Gould told him that he could do an amendment for $30, and when Toalson stated he had no money, Mr. Gould said he would take care of it, but Toalson never heard from WTP again. . . .

The trustee's dischargeability action seeks to deny the debtor's discharge based on the omission of the property transfer. The debtor counters that the property transfer was not listed based on advice given by WTP. No money is or was remaining from the sale of the property as of the filing of bankruptcy or as of the Meeting of Creditors. . . .

In 2003, Linda Smith and her husband decided to divorce. In the divorce negotiations, Smith quitclaimed her interest in the marital residence in exchange for expediting the divorce. Smith testified that there was no equity in the house, and she received nothing in return for giving up her interest. She got her divorce in June 2003, but continued to suffer from financial problems.

In July of 2003, Smith lost her job at Shoney's Restaurant and testified that five minutes after leaving the restaurant, she called WTP at "44-LEGAL" and talked to a man about how to file bankruptcy. At WTP, she paid the $199 fee, and was given a workbook by Shannon Gould. Smith testified that she had difficulties with the workbook and took it back twice to ask questions. Specifically, she asked about Question 10 regarding transfer of property. According to Smith, Vincent Gould told her that the property transfer "wouldn't matter" and therefore, she left Question 10 blank. Smith testified that she told WTP about her divorce, and that she had left Question 4a, asking for suits or administrative proceeding to which she had been a party within one year, blank as well.

Smith explained that Shannon Gould later called her to discuss the exemptions and the valuation of her car. Mrs. Gould told her Tennessee had a "wildcard exemption." Smith asked her what value to place on the car, and was told by Mrs. Gould that she could not advise her on that issue. When Smith then asked if $3,000 would work because she did not understand what Gould was talking about, she was told by Gould that it would.

When Mrs. Smith went back to sign her bankruptcy petition, she told WTP that she had obtained a job making about $1,400 per month. She thought this information was in the petition, Statements, and Schedules that she signed. Smith paid Mr. Gould $200 for the filing fee and asked WTP to file her petition.

WTP filed the debtor's voluntary petition under Chapter 7. . . . The debtor signed her petition, Statements, and Schedules indicating that the information contained therein was correct. However, at the 11 U.S.C. §341 Meeting of Creditors, upon questioning by the trustee, the debtor indicated that: (1) she had recently divorced; (2) that she had owned and quitclaimed her interest in real property to facilitate her divorce; (3) that she was employed at the time of filing her petition; and (4) that she did own an engagement ring (later valued at $1,000) that was not listed in the petition. Smith thought that she had properly filled out her petition, and she testified that she was completely cooperative with the trustee once she realized the errors and omissions contained in her original petition. . . .

The debtor hired an attorney after the trustee filed a §727 action against her seeking to deny her discharge. The debtor's attorney then refiled her entire petition to accurately reflect the property transfer, her divorce, her employment, and her engagement ring. The debtor provided all information requested of her to both the UST and the chapter 7 trustee. . . .

The trustee contends that these debtors' discharges should be denied pursuant to 11 U.S.C. §§727(a)(2), (a)(3), (a)(4), and/or (a)(5). [These provisions relate to providing false information in the documents filed with the court.] . . . The Section 727 provisions are to be construed liberally in favor of debtor and strictly against the movant. [Citation omitted.] In these cases, the court finds that the trustee is unable to show by a preponderance of the evidence that their discharges should be denied based upon any of the §727 provisions relied upon. Accordingly, the court dismisses all of the trustee's §727 complaints against all three debtors in the *Finch, Toalson*, and *Smith* cases. . . .

Section 110 provides for monetary sanctions and injunctive relief against bankruptcy petition preparers who violate the specific provisions of the statute. For most of these requirements, the statute allows the court to impose a $500 fine for each violation. 11 U.S.C. §§110(b)(2), (c)(3), (d)(2), (e)(2), (f)(2), and (g)(2). The court may also disallow and order the turnover of any petition preparer fee found to be excessive. 11 U.S.C. §110(h)(2). In addition, the Bankruptcy Court shall certify all violations of this section to the District Court, and a debtor, trustee, or creditor may then move that court for actual damages, a penalty of $2,000 or twice the fees paid to the petition preparer, whichever is greater, and attorneys' fees and costs. 11 U.S.C. §110(i)(1). The Bankruptcy Court may enjoin the petition preparer from engaging in further violations of the statute, or may permanently enjoin a petition preparer from preparing any petitions in the future. 11 U.S.C. §110(j)(1). . . .

A bankruptcy petition preparer is defined in section 110(a)(1) to be a "person, other than an attorney, who prepares for compensation a document for filing." In this case, Mr. Vincent Gould testified that he and his wife were co-owners of the franchise "We the People" in Nashville, Tennessee. . . . They owned and operated WTP Nashville for approximately 11 months from April 2003 until March 2004. Both Mr. and Mrs. Gould testified that they accepted compensation for their role as "glorified secretaries" for preparing bankruptcy petitions. Although Mrs. Gould testified that only her husband had actually signed the petitions, the proof was uncontradicted and even acknowledged by the Goulds, that both Mr. and Mrs. Gould prepared documents for filing with the anticipation of compensation.

The court finds that Vincent Gould, Shannon Gould, and We the People Nashville are all bankruptcy petition preparers within the meaning of section 110(a)(1). All of the debtors independently testified that the phone number for WTP was "44-LEGAL." Section 110(f) prohibits a bankruptcy petition preparer from using the word "legal" or "any similar term" in an advertisement. Each violation subjects WTP to a fine of not more than $500 for each violation. This is a strict liability provision. [Citation omitted.] In other words, there is no "reasonable cause" exception, and proof of each violation results in a fine of not more than $500 per violation. . . . Accordingly the court finds that the third-party defendants should be fined $500 for each violation of section 110(f) in each of the three bankruptcy cases. The court finds a total fine of $1,500 shall be assessed jointly and severally among Vincent Gould, Shannon Gould, and WTP Nashville.

Section 110(g) prohibits WTP from collecting or receiving any payment from the debtor for the court fees in connection with filing a petition. Although there is minor disagreement about the scope of this provision, it is clear that a petition preparer accepting money, that is later used to pay court filing fees, is a violation. . . . In all three cases, however, these debtors testified that they paid WTP either in cash or money order made payable to Vincent Gould. . . .

[T]he court finds that Vincent Gould and WTP violated section 110(g). There was absolutely no attempt to comply with the statutory requirements of section 110(g), and therefore, the court finds that a $500 fine for each of the three violations should be imposed. A total fine of $1,500 shall be assessed jointly and severally among Vincent Gould, Shannon Gould, and WTP Nashville.

Section 110(h)(2) prohibits a preparer from charging an excessive fee. This section allows the court to disallow and order the immediate turnover of any fee received within 12 months immediately prior to the filing of the case that is found to be excessive.... In deciding whether fees are excessive, the Court must determine the reasonable value of the services rendered. Courts have found bankruptcy petition preparers' services to be of no value or negative value where those services accomplished little benefit and, in some instances, harmed the debtor or put his or her bankruptcy discharge at risk. [Citations omitted.] . . .

The fee charged by WTP in all three cases was at least $199, exclusive of the filing fee. Because WTP cannot engage in the unauthorized practice of law, the type of services for which WTP is eligible for compensation under state law is limited to its "typing service." . . . Based on the proof in this case, the value of services provided to these debtors is unquestionably negative. WTP's involvement with the debtors has created incredible problems in these debtors' cases. All debtors had dischargeability actions brought against them by the chapter 7 trustee caused by inconsistencies and omissions in the petitions, and all of the debtors were forced to hire bankruptcy counsel to defend the dischargeability actions and to prosecute the third-party actions. Accordingly, the Court finds that the services rendered to these debtors by the Goulds and WTP had no value to the debtors. Pursuant to 11 U.S.C. §110(h)(2), the Court will disallow and order the immediate turnover by Vincent Gould and WTP to the trustee of all fees paid by the debtors. . . .

Section 110(i) provides that if a bankruptcy petition preparer violates this section or commits any fraudulent, unfair, or deceptive act, then this court shall certify the findings of such to the district court. Fraudulent, unfair, or deceptive acts cover a broad spectrum of conduct. . . . [U]nfair acts and deceptive practices include such conduct or omissions that are likely to mislead a reasonable consumer. . . . The proof in all three cases before the court is replete with evidence demonstrating unfair and deceptive practices by the third-party defendants.

All three debtors allege that the third-party defendants' "advice" caused the section 727 actions to be brought by the trustee, and made it necessary to hire counsel to defend those actions and prosecute WTP. The court finds that WTP's "assistance" to these debtors constituted unfair acts and deceptive practices, negligence, and a breach of their contract to provide "typing services." Mr. and Mrs. Gould's testimony was unhelpful in their defense of the section 110(i) allegations. Mrs. Gould had no recollection of dealings with any of the debtors. Mr. Gould remembered only his dealings with Mr. Finch and his testimony was inconsistent with Mr. Finch's version of events. Mr. Gould testified that he would never provide legal advice to the debtors. He explained that based on his WTP cultural training, that he and his wife were provided "scripts" of what to say to the debtors, and that it was office policy not to provide legal advice. Mr. Gould testified that if a debtor had a question, he simply re-read the question to them, and then if a debtor still did not understand, it was office policy to refer the clients to the "supervising attorney." Mr. Gould testified that he does not think he has ever deviated from that office policy.

Mrs. Gould also testified that everything that was said to the debtors was "scripted." She also followed office policy of referring clients to the supervising attorney if they had a question. Although she did not remember any of the debtors specifically, Mrs. Gould testified that she had never provided valuation information. She explained that she and her husband bought the business to help people and making a judgment call might hurt someone; so, she did not do it. . . .

In Tennessee, a claim of common law negligence requires proof of the following elements: a duty of care owed by the defendant to the plaintiff; conduct falling below the applicable standard of care that amounts to a breach of that duty; an injury or loss; cause in fact; and proximate or legal cause. [Citation omitted.] Non-attorneys who attempt to practice law will be held to the same standards of competence demanded of attorneys and will be liable for negligence if these standards are not met. See *Tegman v. Accident & Medical Investigations, Inc.*, 30 P.3d 8, 13 (Wash. Ct. App. 2001), *rev. granted in part*, 43 P.3d 21 (Wash. 2002), *and remanded*, 75 P.3d 497 (Wash. 2003). In all three of these cases, all of the negligence elements are plainly met. If WTP is required to meet the same standard of competence demanded by attorneys, the conduct of the Goulds and WTP fell substantially below that bar.

Examples of the negligence by the third-party defendants are numerous, including instructing Mr. Finch to omit a recent property transfer. Likewise, Mr. Toalson was told by WTP to omit the sale of the Kentucky real property. WTP also marked out questions, suggested property valuations, added exemption statutes, and suggested how to classify claims for Mr. Toalson. In Mrs. Smith's case, WTP instructed her to leave out the recent quitclaim of her marital residence to her soon-to-be ex-husband, excluded her new employment from the petition after being informed of such by Smith, and "helped" the debtor with the valuation of her vehicle for exemption purposes. This course of conduct is actionable as negligence, breach of contract, the unauthorized practice of law, and/or violations of 11 U.S.C. §110(i) as unfair and deceptive.

When the third-party plaintiffs "helped" these debtors by filling in unsolicited answers, supplying relevant code sections, suggesting valuations, determining what court the petitions should be filed in, providing advice on how to answer certain questions, and crossing out questions that should have been answered, they did so negligently. As a direct result of that negligence, all of these debtors had their discharges challenged by the chapter 7 trustee, and were forced to hire counsel to defend themselves and prosecute the third-party defendants. The court finds the third-party defendants were negligent in their conduct as it relates to these debtors, and that negligence was the proximate cause of these debtors' losses. . . .

Several courts have found that the unauthorized practice of law constitutes a fraudulent, unfair, or deceptive act under section 110(i). [Citations omitted.] The Tennessee Attorney General has spoken on the unauthorized practice of law by document preparation services in Tenn. Op. Atty. Gen. No. 94-101, 1994 WL 509446 (Tenn. A.G. 1994). The Opinion provides in relevant part: . . . (a) The "practice of law" is defined to be and is the appearance as an advocate in a representative capacity or the drawing of papers, pleadings, or documents or the performance of any act in such capacity in connection with proceedings pending or prospective before any court, commissioner, referee or any body, board, committee, or commission constituted by law or having authority to settle controversies. (b) The "law business" is defined to be and is the advising or counseling for a valuable consideration of any person, firm, association, or corporation, as to any secular law, or the drawing or the procuring of or assisting in the drawing for a valuable consideration of any paper, document, or instrument affecting or relating to secular rights, or the doing of any act for a valuable consideration in a representative capacity, obtaining or tending to secure for any person, firm, association, or corporation any property or property rights whatsoever.

The provisions of T.C.A. §23-3-101 are mirrored in rules regulating the practice of law adopted by the Tennessee Supreme Court. . . . The purpose of the aforementioned provisions regulating the practice of law is "to prevent the public's being preyed upon by those who, for valuable consideration, seek to perform services which require skill, training and character, without adequate qualifications." [Citations omitted.] . . .

In these cases, WTP stepped over the line. Mr. and Mrs. Gould's general denials that they followed office policy of referring all questions to the supervising attorney are not only self-serving, but pale under the weight of the specific and credible testimony of all three debtors. . . . The court finds that under even the most generous definition of "unauthorized practice of law," WTP has engaged in the practice of law without a license. Whether the court characterizes their conduct as negligent, unauthorized practice of law, or otherwise, the result is the same—"unfair and deceptive" within the meaning of section 110(i). The credible testimony of the debtors amply supports a finding that the third-party defendants have committed unfair and deceptive acts.

The debtors also assert that the third-party defendants breached their services contract by providing legal advice. WTP's obligation to the debtors, as outlined in the Contract for Services, was to "complete a BANKRUPTCY form with information supplied by [the debtor] for the purpose of filing Pro Se (For Self) in the appropriate court." The contract further states that WTP are not attorneys and "will not provide legal advice in any form whatsoever." Clearly this contract was breached by the outpouring of "assistance" given by the Goulds and WTP in all three cases. For all of the same reasons that the third-party defendants were negligent, they also breached their contract. . . .

This matter is CERTIFIED to the United States District Court for the Middle District of Tennessee. Under section 110, upon motion of the debtor, trustee, or a creditor, the district court shall order the payment of damages following a hearing. . . .

Questions about the Case

1. What kinds of activities are bankruptcy preparers allowed to perform and what kinds are they prohibited from performing under the statute? What specific provisions were violated by these preparers? What were the remedies or sanctions?
2. What did the court find about the petitioners' claims of fraud? Breach of contract? Negligence?
3. What definition of the practice of law was used? Which aspects of this definition applied to the facts here?
4. What did WTP say in its defense? Did this defense comport with the claims of Finch and others? How did the court handle this matter?

In this case of first impression, an online program designed for consumers to use in preparing forms to file for bankruptcy was found by a court to be the practice of law.

In re Reynoso
477 F.3d 1117 (9th Cir. 2007)

This appeal arises from an adversary proceeding initiated by the United States Trustee ("Trustee"), during the bankruptcy proceeding of Debtor Jayson Reynoso, against Henry Ihejirika, d/b/a Frankfort Digital Services, Ltd. and Ziinet.com (collectively "Frankfort"). . . .

The United States Bankruptcy Court for the Northern District found that Frankfort . . . acted as a "bankruptcy petition preparer" within the meaning of 11 U.S.C. 110 . . . [and concluded that] Frankfort had committed fraudulent, unfair or deceptive conduct, and had engaged in the unauthorized practice of law. . . . [The decision was affirmed by the Bankruptcy Appellate Panel.]

Frankfort sold access to websites where customers could access browser-based software for preparing bankruptcy petitions and schedules, as well as informational guides promising advice on various aspects of relevant bankruptcy law.

... Reynoso accessed one of Frankfort's websites . . . , [which] represented to potential customers, like Reynoso, that its software system offered expertise in bankruptcy law:

> Ziinet is an expert system and knows the law. Unlike most bankruptcy programs that are little more than customized word processors the Ziinet engine is an *expert system*. It knows bankruptcy law right down to the state in which you live. . . .

It explained that its program would select bankruptcy exemptions for the debtor and would eliminate the debtor's "need to choose which schedule to use for each piece of information."

The site also offered customers access to the "Bankruptcy Vault"—a repository of information regarding "loopholes" and "stealth techniques." For example, according to the site, the Vault would explain how to hide a bankruptcy from credit bureaus and how to retain various types of property.

Reynoso paid $219 for a license to access the Ziinet Engine, including the Vault. . . . The online software prompted Reynoso to enter his personal information, debts, income, assets, and other data into dialog boxes. The program then used the data to generate a complete set of bankruptcy forms. . . .

Reynoso printed the forms and filed his chapter 7 bankruptcy petition. . . . During the first meeting with creditors, the chapter 7 trustee noticed errors in the petition and, upon questioning Reynoso, learned that he had paid for the assistance of an "online bankruptcy engine." . . .

Frankfort argues that the creation and ownership of a software program used by a licensee to prepare his or her bankruptcy forms is not preparation of a document for filing under the statute. Whether a software provider may qualify as a bankruptcy preparer under 11 U.S.C. 110(a)(1) is a question of first impression in the Ninth Circuit. We hold that the software at issue in this case qualifies as such.

Frankfort charged fees to permit customers to access web-based software. Frankfort's software solicited information from the customers. Critically, it then translated that information into responses to questions on the bankruptcy forms, and prepared the bankruptcy forms for filing using those responses. . . .

In sum, for a fee, Frankfort provided customers with complete bankruptcy petitions. . . . This is materially indistinguishable from other cases in which individuals or corporations have been deemed bankruptcy preparers. . . .

Since "bankruptcy petition preparers" are—by definition—not attorneys, they are prohibited from practicing law. [Citations omitted.] . . .

Several features of Frankfort's business, taken together, lead us to conclude that it engaged in the unauthorized practice of law. To begin, Frankfort held itself out as offering legal expertise. Its websites offered customers extensive advice on how to take advantage of so-called loopholes in the bankruptcy code, promised services comparable to those of a "top-notch bankruptcy lawyer," and described its software as an "expert system." . . .

The software did, indeed, go far beyond providing clerical services. It determined where (particularly, in which schedule) to place information provided by the debtor, selected exemptions for the debtor and supplied relevant legal citations. Providing such personalized guidance has been held to constitute the practice of law. [Citations omitted.] . . .

The judgment of the Bankruptcy Appellate Panel of the Ninth Circuit is affirmed.

Questions about the Case

1. Did the court say that a software program can engage in the practice of law? What do you think of this idea?
2. Do you think that the outcome would have been different if the advertising for the software had not made claims about its expertise? Was this an important factor?
3. Under the bankruptcy statutes, petition preparers are required to include their names on petitions. Why do you think that this provision was included in the bankruptcy law?
4. What would a court decide if a bankruptcy petition preparer used another company's software to help petitioners fill in forms? For one court's view of this unsettled area, see *In re Gross*, Bankr. E.D. Va. 8-27-2009, where the court said, "Even though [the preparer] may have relied on a computer program rather than her own knowledge or analysis, she, rather than the debtor, effectively chooses which exemptions [to claim]. The act of selecting exemptions requires 'the exercise of legal judgment.' . . ."
5. What are the ramifications of this decision for other legal software providers? How is this different from software to prepare a will or a divorce? What might companies that provide this software do to protect against UPL claims?

Landlord-tenant law is another area in which nonlawyer legal service providers commonly work. In the following case, an eviction service is prosecuted under the state unauthorized practice and consumer protection statutes.

People v. Landlords Professional Services
215 Cal.App.3d 1599, 264 Cal.Rptr. 548 (1989)

In 1982, the Orange County Apartment News carried an advertisement for the eviction services provided by LPS. The ad stated "Evictions as low as $65" and showed the picture of a purposeful and authoritative looking man, arms folded across his chest, stating: "One low price $65 plus costs uncontested or contested in pro per. Attorney for trial extra if needed." Below the picture were the words "Time to Act!" and "Call & talk to us." The advertisement ended with an address and telephone number.

In 1982, Roberta Spiegel decided to evict the tenants of an apartment she owned. A friend recommended LPS. Roberta spoke to Bill Watts, an employee of LPS, who told her to come to the LPS office and bring all documentation related to the rental. On arrival Roberta was given a booklet with Mr. Watts's business card attached. The card was imprinted with the words "Landlord's Professional Services" and the name Bill Watts. Beneath Mr. Watts's name was the word "Counselor."

The booklet begins with a chronology of an unlawful detainer action as carried out by the eviction service. The chronology was generally factual. However, at the end of the chronology, this bit of advice is imparted concerning what to do after the tenants have been evicted: "*You must change the locks at that time.* If you do not change the locks you may have a problem. The defendant may re-enter and take possession, and the ball game starts from the beginning."

The following pages of the booklet contain examples of the types of forms used in an unlawful detainer action and provide a guide for how those forms should be completed. Often the guidance is purely factual, i.e., where a form requires the name of the city in which the subject property is located the guide states "enter city." The advice given, however, can be more useful. In discussing the "Notice to Pay Rent or Quit," for example, the guide states: "Acceptance of any money after service may void notice. You don't have to accept money after notice expires."

Bill Watts reviewed the normal routine in an unlawful detainer action with Roberta, who was unfamiliar with eviction procedures. Roberta asked questions about the procedure and Bill answered them. Roberta told Bill she had already mailed the tenants a three-day notice. Bill told her this was insufficient and she would have to take another notice to the apartment. Bill asked Roberta questions and completed the documents and forms necessary for the unlawful detainer action and eventually filed them.

On December 7, 1982, Ralph Lopes, an investigator with the Orange County District Attorney's Office, called LPS and stated he was a property owner who was interested in eviction services. . . . The procedure for commencing and carrying through an unlawful detainer action was explained by Jacqueline Sutake, an LPS employee. . . . Lopes asked what it meant in the LPS ad when it stated "pro per." Sutake explained LPS was not an attorney and Lopes would be representing himself. Sutake stated LPS could not represent him in court. If an answer was filed by the tenant, LPS would type up Lopes's testimony and he could read it in court. Lopes asked if he would need an attorney. Sutake stated if an answer is filed by an attorney, LPS recommends its client obtain one as well but that it is possible to prevail without the assistance of counsel.

Lopes asked if he could turn off the utilities at the rental property. Sutake stated he could not. Lopes asked what would occur if he needed an attorney during the process. Sutake stated he could use his own attorney or "we have attorneys here."

Ms. Sutake testified she did not advise her clients on questions of law. She did, however, explain the unlawful detainer procedure and would share with clients her personal experiences as a landlord. If the case presented was more complex than the routine uncontested unlawful detainer action, she would suggest the client contact an attorney Ms. Sutake explained her activities were always supervised by an attorney. When an unfamiliar situation arose she would ask an attorney for help and the attorney would determine if the complexity of the case required the services of a lawyer. In most cases her work was reviewed by an attorney before being filed.

In February 1983, the Orange County District Attorney filed a civil complaint against LPS and five other eviction services, alleging the unauthorized practice of law. (Bus. & Prof. Code. §§6125, 6126.) The complaint sought monetary penalties . . . and injunctive relief. At the conclusion of the hearing below the trial court ordered LPS to pay $8,000 in civil penalties for eight violations of Business and Professions Code section 17200 and $9,000 for nine violations of Business and Professions Code section 17500. . . .

The trial court also granted the following permanent injunction: "Defendants, their agents, officers, employees and representatives are enjoined from engaging in or performing directly or indirectly any and all of the following acts: '1. the preparation, other than at the specific and detailed direction of a person in propria persona or under the direct supervision of an attorney, of written instruments relating to evictions such as: three day notices, summons and complaints, at issue memoranda, judgments, writs of execution or other legal documents relating to evictions.

'2. Explaining orally or in writing, except under the direct supervision of an attorney, to individual clients: (A) the effect of any rule of law or court; (B) advising such persons as to the requirements for commencing or maintaining a proceeding in the Courts of this state; or

(C) advising or explaining to such clients the forms which are legally required or how to complete such forms.

'3. Holding themselves out or allowing themselves to be held out to newspapers, magazines, or other advertising, or representing themselves as being able to provide, except through an attorney, any of the following: legal advice, the preparation of legal documents (other than as a secretarial service), or any explanation of any rules of law or court in relation to evictions or as being qualified to do any of the above activities.

'4. Any employee, agent, officer, or representative of L.P.S., not a licensed member of the California Bar, is prohibited from practicing law in any form or holding themselves out as having the right to practice law in any form.'" . . .

Business and Professions Code section 6125 states: "No person shall practice law in this State unless he is an active member of the State Bar." Business and Professions Code section 6126, subdivision (a), provides: "Any person advertising or holding himself or herself out as practicing or entitled to practice law or otherwise practicing law who is not an active member of the State Bar, is guilty of a misdemeanor."

The code provides no definition for the term "practicing law." In *Baron v. City of Los Angeles* (1970) 2 Cal. 3d 535, 542 [86 Cal. Rptr. 673, 469 P.2d 353, 42 A.L.R.3d 1036], our Supreme Court noted that as early as 1922, before the passage of the State Bar Act, it had adopted a definition of "practice of law" used in an Indiana case: "[A]s the term is generally understood, the practice of law is the doing and performing services in a court of justice in any manner depending therein throughout its various stages and in conformity with the adopted rules of procedure. But in a larger sense it includes legal advice and counsel and the preparation of legal instruments and contracts by which legal rights are secured although such matter may or may not be depending in court." [Citations omitted.] . . .

The eviction service offered by LPS was designed to assist clients in the preparation, filing and resolution of unlawful detainer actions. LPS, therefore, offered to assist clients in advancing their legal rights in a court of law. We believe general California law and the approach taken by other states with respect to divorce services teach that such services do not amount to the practice of law as long as the service offered by LPS was merely clerical, i.e., the service did not engage in the practice of law if it made forms available for the client's use, filled the forms in at the specific direction of the client and filed and served those forms as directed by the client. Likewise, merely giving a client a manual, even a detailed one containing specific advice, for the preparation of an unlawful detainer action and the legal incidents of an eviction would not be the practice of law if the service did not personally advise the client with regard to his specific case.

With these principles in mind, we conclude LPS was engaged in the unauthorized practice of law. The advertisement used by LPS implies its eviction services were not limited to clerical functions. The tenor of the advertisement was that the service accomplished evictions. The advertisement's statement "Call & talk to us" was a general invitation for clients to discuss the matter of eviction with LPS. Bill Watts's LPS business card listed his title as "Counselor." In short, LPS cast about itself an aura of expertise concerning evictions.

While an eviction may not be the most difficult of procedures, it is, nonetheless, a legal procedure carried out before a court with specific legal requirements for its accomplishment. As we have seen, some courts have held that providing advice as to which forms to use, which blanks to fill in with what information or in which courts an action must be filed is itself the practice of law. Here, of course, LPS's eviction advice went further. It provided specific information to its clients concerning eviction procedure. This it did in the context of personal interviews where it was able to provide additional information and advice addressed to the specific problems and concerns of its clients.... Given the aura of expertise created by the business practices of LPS such advice would undoubtedly be relied upon by its clients, perhaps to their serious detriment....

The judgment is affirmed.

Questions about the Case

1. What specific conduct by LPS constituted the unauthorized practice of law? What conduct constituted false or misleading advertising?
2. What definition of the practice of law does this court use? How does it compare to other definitions cited in this chapter?
3. How did the prosecutor's office investigate LPS?
4. Does it make any difference that an eviction is simple and many nonlawyers could file the appropriate papers without any help?
5. Did the court cite any instances where LPS customers were given bad advice or were harmed?

In this California landlord–tenant matter, plaintiffs seek damages and an injunction against a nonlawyer legal service provider who should have been registered under state law as an Unlawful Detainer Assistant. Related UPL and false advertising claims are also covered in the case.

Brockey v. Moore
107 Cal.App.4th 86, 131 Cal.Rptr.2d 746 (2003)

In adopting the Unlawful Detainer Assistants Act (Bus. & Prof. Code 6400 et seq.) the Legislature found in part that "there currently exist numerous unscrupulous individuals . . . who purport to offer protection to tenants from eviction. They represent themselves as legitimate tenants' rights associations, legal consultants, professional legal assistants, paralegals, attorneys or typing services. . . . The acts of these unscrupulous individuals . . . are particularly despicable in that they target low-income and non-English-speaking Californians as victims for their fraudulent practices." [Citation omitted.]

Under names such as "Legal Aid" and "Legal Aid Services" defendant Walter Moore operates a business which purports to offer typing services, particularly in eviction cases. Victims of Moore's deception Brockey [and others] were eventually directed to Legal Services of Northern California's Redding office and obtained representation in the underlying cases and in this action seeking monetary and injunctive relief.

A jury found [that] Moore practiced law in violation of the State Bar Act (Bus. & Prof. Code 6125), violated the Consumer Remedies Act (Civ. Code 1750, et seq.) and awarded damages of $150 to each of the plaintiffs. . . .

Plaintiffs lived in a mobile home park . . . [T]hey received unlawful detainer summonses they wanted to fight. None had the means to hire a lawyer and they tried to obtain free legal help.

The Judicial Council summons form for unlawful detainer actions states . . . "if you do not know an attorney, you may call an attorney referral services or a legal aid office. . . ." The Judicial Council information sheet on waiver of costs states "If you have any questions and cannot afford an attorney, you may wish to consult the legal aid office, legal services office, or lawyer referral services in your county. . . ."

Brockey (who lived with Gayler) looked in his local telephone directory under "Legal Aid" . . . and found a local number which he called. That number was forwarded to Moore's Modesto business. . . . [Moore using the name Jay] told Brockey that he had to wire money. . . . Brockey did not tell [Moore] which boxes to check, that he wanted each party to bear its own fees, or that he wanted to raise an affirmative defense by talking to the judge at the time of trial. Gayler thought that they had contacted a law office "that offered services to low income people, [maybe on] a sliding scale of some sort." . . .

Plaintiff Pavloff called "411" information to get the number for free "Legal Aid Services," which he had used before, and was given Moore's number by the operator. He was told to wire $85, which he did. He did not tell [Moore] how to fill out the forms. . . .

The plaintiffs had to sign an "agreement & disclosure" form for the "Legal Aid Services Processing Center" in Modesto after paying money but before receiving their answers. The form states that "[t]his office is a professional document preparation and typing service only," that it is not a law office and "will not provide any legal advice." It suggests clients contact an attorney. . . .

[Six other persons not participating as plaintiffs had similar experiences in seeking free or low-cost legal services.]

Moore's former employee . . . testified he was told not to tell callers where the company was, to use aliases, and not to refer callers to the "real" legal aid. . . . When [he] worked there . . . , the company received from 60 to 200 calls a day. . . . [Testimony from various nonprofit groups and Legal Aid confirmed Moore's practices. An instruction was given to the jury indicating that the reference to Legal Aid on the Judicial Council forms and instructions refers to a "publicly funded nonprofit law corporation, which provides free legal services to low-income eligible clients."]

Moore was the owner and manager of "Legal Aid" and "Legal Aid Services" and "Premiere Marketing." He was not a lawyer or paralegal, but claimed to have an attorney "on staff," though he did not [at the time that he performed services for the plaintiffs]. [He claimed that he had a business license as Legal Aid and that he only typed what people told him to. Various discrepancies in his testimony came to light, including false statements about his website and the availability of a 900 number. Moore had been sanctioned by the local Bankruptcy Court for using the word "legal" in his advertisements and ordered to disgorge fees.] Moore . . . admitted that he was not registered under the UDAA and had not posted the required bond. . . .

The judgment recites that the jury found Moore practiced law without a license, violated the UDAA and acted with fraud, oppression, or malice. The annexed injunction prohibits Moore in part from using names "Legal Aid Services" or "Legal Aid" or "Legal Services" because these three names signify a non-profit law office providing free legal services to low-income persons and families; using the term "legal" except as a paralegal; and using "local" telephone numbers which forward to his Modesto business. The injunction requires Moore to change his website, tell his customers he is not an attorney, place newspaper advertisements regarding the lawsuit and so forth.

In our view, the way Moore words his telephone book listings is calculated to mislead and is likely to mislead consumers. . . . [The court dismissed various grounds for appeal and affirmed.]

Questions about the Case

1. If Moore had been registered as an Unlawful Detainer Assistant, would the outcome have been different?
2. Which of Moore's acts appear to constitute UPL?
3. Why were the courts at trial and on appeal concerned about the use of the word "legal" in the name of Moore's business?
4. Describe the background of the people that were Moore's "clients." Did this make a difference in the court's analysis?
5. Do you find it troubling that the court does not prohibit Moore from calling himself a "paralegal"? Remember that other California

legislation prohibits the use of the term "paralegal" by anyone who is not working for a lawyer and does not meet the qualifications set forth in the statute.

In recent years, preparing living trusts for consumers has become a popular business for lawyers and nonlawyer practitioners alike. In this case, an attorney working with paralegals was found to have violated several ethics rules in the conduct of his living trust practice.

In re Morin
319 Or. 547, 878 P.2d 393 (1994)

The facts relating to this case are undisputed. The accused was licensed to practice law in California in 1974 and was admitted to practice law in Oregon in 1984. During the spring of 1988, the accused began conducting "living trust" seminars and selling "living trust packages," which included pour-over wills and directives to physicians.

The accused and two of his employees, who were paralegals, travelled throughout Oregon and northern California, conducting seminars and preparing the living trust packages. If a person at a seminar indicated that he or she was interested in discussing a living trust package, the accused or one of the paralegals would make an appointment and return to meet with the client. The accused or the paralegal would gather information from the client and then prepare the documents for the living trust package in the accused's Medford office.

At trial, Monnett, a paralegal employed by the accused, testified that he usually travelled alone, conducted seminars before groups, collected information from prospective clients, and assisted clients in executing the documents contained in the trust packages. He testified that the questions that he answered at the seminars were general and did not apply to individual clients' problems.

Monnett also testified that, during meetings with individual clients, he read their wills and explained to them the operative parts of the will. He also testified that he inquired into the clients' assets and advised them whether or not they needed a trust. He reviewed the trusts and other legal documents with the clients. Some of the clients never met the accused and dealt only with Monnett throughout the process. Both Monnett and the other paralegal employed by the accused, Pesterfield, testified that the accused instructed them to call him if they had legal questions. Both also testified that they believed that the accused reviewed all the documents that were prepared because he signed all of them and because occasionally he discussed the contents of the documents with Monnett.

Ordinarily, after the documents were prepared, the accused or one of the paralegals scheduled an additional appointment with the client to execute the documents. . . .

The accused testified that clients in the Medford and Ashland area ordinarily executed the documents in the living trust packages in the accused's office, where the accused's office staff members served as witnesses. When the accused or the paralegals executed documents at seminar sites, however, it was difficult for them to have the wills and directives to physicians witnessed.

The accused and the paralegals began a practice of taking the wills and directives to physicians back to the accused's office in Medford after they were signed by the clients at the seminar sites and directing the office staff to sign the documents as witnesses. The signatures of the "witnesses" on the wills were notarized either by the accused or by one of his employees. The signatures on the directives to physicians were not notarized. The accused then mailed the signature pages back to the clients. . . .

[T]he accused admitted that he had caused the wills and directives to physicians of approximately 300 clients to be executed outside the presence of the witnesses, who later signed the wills and directives to physicians.

The accused stated before the trial panel that he knew that a will is invalid unless it is either executed or affirmed by the testator in the presence of two witnesses. He also testified that part of the fee he charged his clients was for a valid will and that he understood that his clients believed that they were receiving valid wills as part of the living trust packages. . . . Here, the accused charged his clients a fee for the performance of certain services, including the preparation and execution of a *valid* will and a valid directive to physicians. The accused intentionally failed to provide his clients with the valid documents for which they had paid. The accused intentionally charged clients for services that he knew he would not provide. Accordingly, the fee was excessive and the accused violated DR 2-106(A). . . .

There is insufficient evidence for us to conclude that the paralegals engaged in the unlawful practice of law by giving the seminars on living trusts and by answering general questions about the living trust packages. Disseminating information that is "directed to the general public and not to a specific individual" is not the practice of law. *Oregon State Bar v. Gilchrist*, 272 Or. 552, 558, 538 P.2d 913 (1975). Apparently, the seminars and questions answered by the paralegals in the seminars went to general information about the advantages of living trusts and about the contents of the packages. The dissemination of that information did not involve the practice of law.

It appears, however, that at least Monnett went beyond the mere dissemination of general information to the public. The Bar alleges that it was Monnett's interactions with individuals that constituted the practice of law. In *Gilchrist*, this court held that advertising and selling do-it-yourself divorce kits did not constitute the practice of law. 272 Or. at 557-60, 538 P.2d 913. This court also held, however:

[A]ll personal contact between defendants and their customers in the nature of consultation, explanation, recommendation or advice or other assistance in selecting particular forms, in filling out any part of the forms, or suggesting or advising how the forms should be used in solving the particular customer's marital problems does constitute the practice of law....

Id. at 563-64, 538 P.2d 913....

This court set forth the test for ascertaining what conduct constitutes the practice of law in *State Bar v. Security Escrows, Inc.*, 233 Or. 80, 89, 377 P.2d 334 (1962): "[T]he practice of law includes the drafting or selection of documents and the giving of advice in regard thereto any time an informed or trained discretion must be exercised in the selection or drafting of a document to meet the needs of the persons being served."

In *State Bar v. Miller & Co.*, 235 Or. 341, 347, 385 P.2d 181 (1963), this court held that an insurance salesperson that assisted people in preparing estate plans could:

explain to his prospective customer alternative methods of disposing of assets ... which are available to taxpayers *generally*.... He cannot properly advise a prospective purchaser with respect to his *specific* need for life insurance as against some other form of disposition of his estate, unless the advice can be given without drawing upon the law to explain the basis for making the choice of alternatives. [Emphasis in original.]

In this case, Monnett examined wills and interpreted them for clients of the accused. Moreover, Monnett discussed clients' individual assets with them to determine whether a living trust would be an appropriate device for the particular client to use. Monnett also told the accused's clients his opinion of the usefulness of another trust format, telling them that it "didn't do much." In short, Monnett advised clients and potential clients of the accused on legal decisions specific to them, and he used discretion in selecting between using a trust and a will and among trust forms. Accordingly, Monnett, a nonlawyer, practiced law.

The accused argues that, even if Monnett practiced law, he did not assist Monnett. He argues that he "took pains to tell these paralegals not to practice law at the seminars." He also told them to call him at the office or at home "[i]f any legal questions arose." Furthermore, the accused argues that he did not know of Monnett's conduct nor did he aid in that conduct: therefore, he did not violate the rule.

This court's decision in *In re Jones*, 308 Or. 306, 779 P.2d 1016 (1989), is instructive. In that case, the accused allowed a nonlawyer to use pleading paper and a letterhead stamp with the lawyer's name on it in the nonlawyer's dissolution-processing business.... The accused knew that the nonlawyer had been warned by the Bar not to practice law.... The accused instructed her to bring any legal questions that she had to him.... This court held that the accused aided a nonlawyer in the practice of law because he "took no steps to enforce his instruction or to test her ability to determine when legal help was needed." ...This court also found it to be important that the clients were never required to speak with the accused....

Here, as in *Jones*, although the accused told his paralegals not to practice law, he did not tell them the precise contours of what constituted the practice of law. Moreover, the accused created the situation in which at least one of his paralegals had the opportunity to practice law. The accused sent the paralegals to meet with clients alone, and he failed to supervise them properly. Thus, even if the accused did not intend for the paralegals to practice law, he assisted in that unlawful practice by allowing them too much freedom in dealing with clients, thereby allowing at least Monnett to provide legal advice to those clients. Accordingly, we conclude that the accused assisted in the unlawful practice of law....

Accordingly, considering the ABA Standards and the prior decisions of this court, we conclude that the trial panel's decision of disbarment is correct.

Questions about the Case

1. What exactly did the paralegals do in this case that constitutes the unauthorized practice of law?
2. Could the attorney have run his practice in a way that avoided the ethical violations cited? How?
3. What was wrong with the way the wills were executed? What was the result for the client? Is this legal malpractice? (See Chapter 8.)
4. What did the court say about the attorney charging fees for the invalid wills?
5. Did the court condemn the activities of the paralegals as the unauthorized practice of law?
6. What definition of the practice of law did this court use?

The following case illustrates what can happen when lawyers affiliate with an organization of nonlawyers. This specific scenario involves a foreclosure consulting company and a law firm. Similar cases could be found throughout the country during the economic recession that started in late 2007.

Cincinnati Bar Ass'n v. Mullaney
119 Ohio St.3d 412 (2008)

Respondents Brooking and Moeves are principals in Brooking, Moeves & Halloran, P.L.L.C. ("the Brooking firm"), a law firm established in September 2004....Respondent Mullaney was employed as an associate of the Brooking firm and its predecessors . . . from May 2004 until May 2006. Foreclosure Solutions, L.L.C., is a company located in Ohio that purports to serve homeowners threatened with foreclosure by helping them set up a savings plan, so that after the homeowners follow the plan, Foreclosure Solutions can use the money saved to negotiate with the lenders to reinstate the loan and avoid foreclosure.

In 2003, Moeves . . . worked out a deal with Timothy Buckley, president of Foreclosure Solutions, agreeing to represent Foreclosure Solutions' customers in Kentucky courts. Pursuant to their agreement, Moeves began accepting clients from Foreclosure Solutions, who routinely obtained a limited power of attorney to hire an attorney for its customers, and Moeves collected a flat fee from Foreclosure Solutions of $125 for each client. With the formation of the Brooking firm in the fall of 2004, Moeves and Buckley extended their agreement to include representation of Foreclosure Solutions' customers in Ohio courts. . . .

Foreclosure Solutions' customers paid between $700 and $1,100 for the company's services, the goal of which was to stall pending foreclosure proceedings while trying to negotiate a settlement with the lender. The company is not a licensed or accredited consumer-credit-counseling agency. Nor is Buckley or any of his employees, to the respondents' knowledge, licensed to practice law in any jurisdiction.

Foreclosure Solutions advertised to attract customers and often sent advertisements to defendants listed on court foreclosure dockets. Agents of the company told prospective customers that an attorney and legal services would be furnished to them as part of their fee. The company then hired a lawyer for the customer-client to respond in court to the recently filed foreclosure action. The client had no choice in the lawyer's selection, and after the lawyer was hired, Foreclosure Solutions' agents continued to negotiate directly with the foreclosing creditors.

Foreclosure Solutions' agents met with customers to collect the company's fee and had the customer sign a standardized contract, the "Work Agreement," containing the basic terms and conditions of the engagement. The agent also had the customer sign a standardized limited power of attorney appointing Foreclosure Solutions as the customer's attorney-in-fact, which, in addition to authorizing the hiring of an attorney, allowed company agents to negotiate on the customer's behalf with creditors. Neither the Work Agreement nor the limited power of attorney identified any particular lawyer, established when a lawyer was to be hired, or informed the client of the amount of the lawyer's fee.

As the solution to a customer's foreclosure troubles, the Work Agreement provided for the customer to set up a savings account and deposit a certain amount of money into it on a regular basis; Foreclosure Solutions would then use that money as a bargaining chip in negotiations with the creditor. Foreclosure Solutions determined the amount the client was to periodically deposit in the savings account. The Work Agreement specified that bankruptcy was considered a last resort.

Once the Foreclosure Solutions customer had signed the Work Agreement and limited power of attorney, the agent completed a financial worksheet and determined the savings recommendation. The agent then collected Foreclosure Solutions' fee, none of which was designated as attorney fees. From this $700 to $1,100 fee, Foreclosure Solutions paid the lawyers their flat fee. . . .

Under the arrangement with Foreclosure Solutions, the Brooking firm represented approximately 2,000 clients in Ohio foreclosure proceedings during 2005 and 2006, at first accepting $125 and later $150 for each case. . . . Brooking represented Foreclosure Solutions' customers during the spring and summer of 2006. . . . Respondents did not oversee solicitations or have any other involvement with Foreclosure Solutions' customers before the company sent its customers' files to the Brooking firm. When received by the firm, the files typically contained the Work Agreement, the limited power of attorney, an intake sheet that had been completed by a Foreclosure Solutions' agent, and a copy of the complaint in foreclosure. The intake sheet, another standardized form, contained the client's financial information. The Brooking firm often received several client files at a time, together with one check for all the fees.

When it accepted a new case, the Brooking firm routinely sent the client an informational brochure entitled "The Nuts and Bolts of an Ohio Foreclosure" that Moeves and Mullaney had prepared. As the foreclosure actions went forward, Mullaney, Brooking, or Moeves responded in court with standardized pleadings and other filings, sending copies to the clients. Cases rarely if ever went to trial, and if the parties could not negotiate a resolution, trial courts granted judgment to the lenders and ordered the sale of the property. At that time, Mullaney, Brooking, or Moeves notified the client of the sale date and sent a standardized letter recommending that the client contact a bankruptcy lawyer. . . .

In following its typical procedure, the Brooking firm lawyers did not as a rule meet with the Foreclosure Solutions clients to determine their particular objectives or complete financial situation or to discover facts that could be defenses to foreclosure. The lawyers generally communicated with the clients through boilerplate correspondence, which the lawyers had no indication that the clients understood. As an example, one standard Brooking firm letter asked whether the client knew of any defenses to the foreclosure, relying on the client to guess what factors might be useful in his or her case.

In this way, Mullaney, Brooking, and Moeves failed to determine what action, including filing bankruptcy immediately, was in any one particular client's best interest. Respondents instead simply followed the Foreclosure Solutions "savings plan" strategy and allowed the foreclosure action to proceed until either a settlement could be negotiated with the lender or the court granted judgment in favor of the lender and ordered the property to be sold, with the lawyers filing routine pleadings and motions at critical stages to delay the process. Only when a sale was imminent did Mullaney, Brooking, and Moeves advise the clients to consider another remedy by contacting a bankruptcy attorney. . . .

In restricting a lawyer's use of referral services to those that serve the public interest and otherwise comply with the rule, DR 2-103(C) prohibits lawyers from using "a person or organization to recommend or promote the use of the lawyer's services or those of the lawyer's partner or associate, or any other lawyer affiliated with the lawyer or the lawyer's firm, as a private practitioner." Foreclosure Solutions is not a referral service as described by the rule, yet Mullaney, Brooking, and Moeves accepted clients from that company. We therefore find that respondents violated DR 2-103(C).

DR 3-101(A) prohibits lawyers from aiding nonlawyers in the unauthorized practice of law. We have held that by advising debtors of their legal rights and the terms and conditions of settlement in negotiations to avoid pending foreclosure proceedings, laypersons engage in the unauthorized practice of law. *Cincinnati Bar Assn. v. Telford* (1999), 85 Ohio St. 3d 111, 707 N.E.2d 462. Here, Mullaney, Brooking, and Moeves facilitated nonlawyers' negotiations with the creditors of debtors facing foreclosure by doing business with Foreclosure Solutions. We therefore find that respondents violated DR 3-101(A).

Except in circumstances not relevant here, DR 3-102(A) prohibits lawyers from sharing legal fees with nonlawyers. By accepting a portion of the compensation that the customers paid Foreclosure Solutions for legal services, Mullaney, Brooking, and Moeves shared legal fees with nonlawyers. We therefore find that respondents violated DR 3-102(A).

DR 3-103(A) prohibits a lawyer from forming a partnership with a nonlawyer if any activities of the partnership consist of the practice of law. Brooking and Moeves, principals in the Brooking firm, partnered with Foreclosure Solutions in representing debtors facing foreclosure. We therefore find that these two respondents violated DR 3-103(A).

DR 6-101(A)(2) prohibits a lawyer from handling a legal matter without preparation adequate under the circumstances. DR 7-101(A)(1) prohibits a lawyer from intentionally failing to seek a client's lawful objectives. These rules prohibited Mullaney, Brooking, and Moeves from surrendering their professional judgment to Foreclosure Solutions.

Counseling debtors in financial crisis as to their best course of legal action requires the attention of a qualified attorney. *Columbus Bar Assn. v. Flanagan* (1997), 77 Ohio St. 3d 381, 383, 674 N.E.2d 681. Expert testimony in this case discredited respondents' approach to their foreclosure clients' cases. John Rose, an experienced bankruptcy attorney, explained a few of the adverse consequences that the tactics used by Foreclosure Solutions and respondents could have.

Rose first pointed out that stall tactics usually result in mounting arrearages for the debtor and increased legal fees for the creditor, lessening the debtor's chances of getting ahead financially and of reaching an agreement with the creditor. Moreover, delay in seeking bankruptcy relief may result in lost opportunities to obtain maximum relief. . . . [I]n keeping with Brooking-firm practice, Mullaney did not explore . . . any other legal remedy for the clients referred by Foreclosure Solutions. . . .

Mullaney, Brooking, and Moeves failed to evaluate their clients' situations and develop a strategy to meet their individualized needs, and instead stuck to Foreclosure Solutions' single strategy to obtain relief. By not investigating and evaluating each client's debts and assets and other potential resources in order to assess the opportunities presented by existing law, respondents were inadequately prepared to represent their clients and failed to seek the clients' lawful objectives. We therefore find that respondents violated DR 6-101(A)(2) and 7-101(A)(1). . . .

When imposing sanctions for attorney misconduct, we consider relevant factors, including the duties violated and sanctions imposed in similar cases. . . . Regarding similar cases, we find respondents' misconduct most analogous to that of attorneys sanctioned for providing legal services in affiliation with nonlawyers marketing living trusts and related products to consumers. . . .

As a new attorney, Mullaney devoted many hours trying to assist the clients assigned to him; however, practices in place at the Brooking firm necessarily constrained his efforts. For his part in representing Foreclosure Solutions customers, a public reprimand is appropriate. Brooking, on the other hand, is a seasoned practitioner. . . . [A] one-year suspension of Brooking's license to practice, all stayed on the condition that he commit no further misconduct, is appropriate. Moeves is also a seasoned practitioner but is not admitted to the Ohio bar. Moeves entered into the agreement with Foreclosure Solutions and then put into place the practices that led to all the charges against him and the other respondents. For his integral role in this ill-advised undertaking, an injunction prohibiting his pro hac vice practice in this state for two years is appropriate. . . .

Questions about the Case

1. What were the individual ethics violations, and what facts support the court's findings for each violation?
2. What specific conduct by Foreclosure Solutions constituted the practice of law?
3. What kinds of services could this company have provided to help people in danger of losing their homes without violating the UPL rules?
4. Could this law firm have worked out an arrangement with a foreclosure consulting firm that would be acceptable under the ethics rules? What might this arrangement look like?
5. Also see *Cincinnati Bar Ass'n v. Foreclosure Solutions*, 123 Ohio St. 3d 107 (2009), in which the company and the individuals who established it were found to have violated unauthorized-practice-of-law rules, were enjoined from engaging in further unethical conduct, and were fined $50,000.

4
Confidentiality

This chapter covers confidentiality and the attorney-client privilege, which comprise one of the most fundamental elements of legal ethics. The principles of confidentiality and the privilege are covered with examples of how they are applied, and effective practices to protect confidentiality are discussed. Chapter 4 covers:

- the foundations and basic principles of confidentiality
- the attorney-client privilege and the difference between the evidentiary privilege and the ethics rules on confidentiality
- information that is privileged or protected by the rule of confidentiality
- conditions under which the privilege and the duty of confidentiality may be broken or waived
- the work product rule
- applications of the principles and rules of confidentiality for paralegals
- methods to protect confidentiality of information and records
- special problems in maintaining confidentiality with technology

A. The Principle of Confidentiality

Confidentiality is one of the oldest and most honored precepts of legal ethics, one that is unquestioned in its importance. Issues relating to confidentiality and situations that jeopardize confidentiality face paralegals daily. Ethical dilemmas concerning confidentiality arise in all kinds of law practices from the smallest to the largest law firm, in corporate law settings, and in government.

The principle of confidentiality is based on the notion that a lawyer must know all the facts about a matter to best serve the client and that a client is not likely to provide full disclosure without assurance that incriminating and embarrassing information will not be revealed. The principle of confidentiality is also based on agency law. A lawyer has a fiduciary relationship with the client that requires the lawyer's highest trust, which includes confidence, loyalty, and good faith.

The principle of confidentiality encompasses both ethics rules and evidentiary rules relating to *attorney-client privilege* and **work product**. The attorney-client privilege is a rule of evidence that protects confidential information from being divulged in litigation by way of discovery or testimony. The ethics rules on confidentiality are much broader than the attorney-client privilege, and require a lawyer not to divulge virtually any information about a client in any context.

> **Attorney-client privilege**
> The rule of evidence that protects confidential communications between a lawyer and client made in the course of the professional relationship.

B. Attorney-Client Privilege

1. Defined Generally

All jurisdictions make provisions for the attorney-client privilege by statute, court rule, or common law. The general rule is that a client who seeks a lawyer's advice or assistance may invoke an unqualified privilege not to testify and to prevent the lawyer from testifying as to communications made by the client in confidence to the lawyer. The client is the holder of the privilege; only the client may waive it, by consenting to the disclosure of confidential communications. And although the client is the holder of the privilege, the attorney must advise the client of the existence and protection of the privilege.

Case law and statutes have clarified the meaning of the attorney-client privilege: The privilege covers confidential communications between lawyer and client—whether oral or written—so long as the advice sought by the client is **legal**; other kinds of advice—personal or business, for instance—are not covered. **Initial consultations** are protected by the privilege even if the lawyer does not undertake representation, as are matters in which the lawyer does not charge a fee. The privilege does not cover material or information that is not classified as a communication, such as physical evidence. The privilege lasts indefinitely. It continues after the representation of the client ends. In most states, the privilege is considered to exist even after the death of the client; however, some states, like California, extinguish the privilege upon the final resolution of the client's estate and some allow disclosure if it would be in the best interests of the client. (See *HLC Properties, Ltd. v. Superior Court*, 35 Cal. 4th 54 (2005).) There are very limited reasons for which the privilege will be waived, as noted later.

2. How the Privilege Applies to Paralegals

One of the key aspects of the privilege for paralegals is that it covers communications made directly to or in the presence of the lawyer or the lawyer's agents, a category that includes colleagues and employees in the law firm who are working or may be working on the client matter. The privilege extends to experts, investigators, vendors, and outside agencies working with counsel on a case. For example, the privilege covers contracted companies that provide services to lawyers, such as data processing or management firms that store confidential information.

Some state statutes on the privilege specifically extend its scope to employees of attorneys. Even without such statutory language, the privilege would be defeated were it not extended to persons who work with lawyers on clients' matters as members of the legal services delivery team. In an important case, the Arizona Court of Appeals confirmed this principle in unequivocal language:

> We hold that a lawyer does not forfeit the attorney-client privilege by receiving otherwise privileged client communications through the conduit of a properly supervised paralegal employee.

Samaritan Foundation v. Superior Court, 844 P.2d 593 (Ariz. App. Div. 1 1992) at 599.

After this decision was handed down in 1992, the Arizona attorney-client privilege statute was amended to include paralegals along with other named law office personnel, such as secretaries and clerks. The publicity surrounding the case caused a heightened awareness about paralegals being covered by the privilege. All state and federal courts that have addressed the issue since that time have held that the privilege extends to paralegals and other nonlawyer employees. For an example of an ethics opinion on the subject, see Michigan Opinion Number RI-123, which held that information collected by a paralegal in an interview with a prospective client is protected.

A patent case, *HPD Laboratories, Inc. v. Clorox Co.*, 202 F.R.D. 410 (2001), found at the end of this chapter, raises concerns about the application of the privilege to paralegals working in corporations. In that case, the internal memoranda prepared by an experienced paralegal who worked very autonomously were found not to be protected by the privilege. Paralegals must be cognizant that the privilege derives from the attorney-client relationship and does not exist independently from it. (It should be noted that the reasoning in this case has not been followed in other later cases.)

Paralegals working with lawyers must be distinguished from nonlawyer legal service providers. Because the privilege applies only to the attorney-client relationship, it does not cover nonlawyer legal service providers who do not work under the auspices of a lawyer, even those authorized by states to work as legal document assistants or preparers, or to "jailhouse lawyers" who advise fellow inmates.

3. How the Protection of the Privilege Can Be Lost

Disclosure of confidential information to another person who is not essential to the representation may result in a court's finding that the information has lost the privilege. The client can waive the privilege by implication by repeating the communication to non-confidential third parties or otherwise by intentionally making the confidential information public. For example, if a client tells friends about otherwise protected communications, the privilege covering the information that is revealed may be lost. Likewise, if a lawyer or paralegal does not treat information as privileged, a court may find that it is not privileged. Rules on whether disclosure to third persons results in the loss of the privilege vary from jurisdiction to jurisdiction and depend to a large extent on the status of the person to whom the information was revealed and the purpose of the disclosure. Generally, if the disclosure is made for the purpose of furthering the representation, it will be protected.

Communications must be made in a **confidential setting** to merit the protection of the privilege. This means that the setting must be private—that is, one in which others cannot overhear—and there should not be any other persons present who would not otherwise be covered by the privilege. The presence of a colleague, family member, or friend of the client, for example, can negate the privilege. Under contemporary rules, an eavesdropper who listens in on a confidential communication will not destroy the privilege unless of course the setting was such that the lawyer and client could expect the conversation to be overheard.

New issues have arisen because of the extensive use of e-mail and other forms of electronic communication. Courts have found that the privilege is waived when an otherwise privileged communication with an employee's lawyer is made over the employer's e-mail system when the employer had a policy against using company e-mail for private purposes and made clear that employees' e-mail messages were not private. See *Holmes v. Petrovich Development Co., LLC*, at the end of this chapter. In general, unencrypted e-mail with clients is protected. (See more on this later in the chapter.)

Data breaches at law firms have become more prevalent as the volume of data usage and the sophistication of hacking increase. Network security personnel must determine the cause of the breach and generate a plan for enhanced security to reduce the likelihood of reoccurrences while maintaining the confidentiality of all data. A breach may lead to litigation relating to the requested production of data breach reports. For an example of a discovery dispute concerning the waiver of the privilege and work product protections, see *Guo Wengui v. Clark Hill, PLC*, 338 F.R.D. 7 (D.D.C. 2021), found at the end of this chapter.

Some disclosures are specially protected and do not result in a waiver of the privilege. For example, information disclosed during plea bargaining or settlement negotiations cannot later be admitted at trial to prove guilt or liability.

4. Matters Not Covered by the Privilege

The privilege usually does not extend to the **identity of a client** or to **a client's whereabouts**. In one well-known case, *Baird v. Koerner*, 279 F.2d 623 (9th Cir. 1960), the court held the identity of a client to be privileged when the attorney sent a payment to the Internal Revenue Service anonymously on the client's behalf for underpayment of federal taxes. Because revealing the identity of the client could have led to conviction of a federal crime, the client's identity was protected. A few other cases have followed this reasoning, generally only when revealing the client's identity would lead to a criminal prosecution. Protection of confidential communications about a client's whereabouts is almost never extended. Usually in such cases, the client is a fugitive, so that the attorney's nondisclosure of the client's location would amount to assisting the client in committing a future crime.

The **fee arrangement** between a lawyer and client has historically not been privileged. Exceptions to this rule are triggered when details of the fee arrangement would reveal privileged information, such as the identity of a client when the identity itself is privileged. Government prosecutors, grand juries, and the Internal Revenue Service have subpoenaed information about fee agreements to identify and seize legal fees paid to attorneys with money or assets obtained through illegal activity, such as the drug trade and money laundering. Criminal defense lawyers often challenge the government on the basis of the privilege. They contend that fee arrangements and records as well as client names should be privileged and that the government's actions interfere with the right to counsel.

A client cannot bring a **preexisting document** within the protection of the privilege simply by giving it to his or her lawyer. For example, internal e-mails that are copied to a lawyer have been found not to be privileged and were ordered to be produced. If a preexisting document is covered by another privilege, such as the spousal privilege, it will continue to be privileged while in the lawyer's possession.

Physical evidence of a client's crime is not protected by the privilege, and a lawyer who comes into possession of such evidence is probably required under law to turn it over to the prosecutor. The lawyer may or may not be compelled to testify about the source of the evidence, depending on the attorney's role in obtaining the evidence—if the lawyer obtained the evidence illegally, the court would be more inclined to force such testimony.

5. Inadvertent Disclosure of Privileged Information

In addition to actual client consent to waiver of the privilege and consent implied from the actions of the client, inadvertent disclosure might destroy the privilege. For example, if a protected document is accidentally given to opposing counsel in a document production, a dispute may arise over whether the privilege is lost. The cases across the country are not uniform; a few states consistently hold that such conduct constitutes a waiver of the privilege, but most states hold that inadvertent disclosure does not automatically constitute a waiver. Most cases hold that the disclosure is not tantamount to waiver so long as reasonable, good-faith measures to prevent disclosure were made. Some courts also look at the extent of the disclosure, the timeliness of attempts to rectify it, and the issue of fairness. Courts acknowledge that inadvertent disclosure by the attorney should not result in waiver of the privilege because the client is the holder of the privilege and would not actually or impliedly consent to damaging protected information being revealed. Often counsel enter into agreements, called non-waiver or claw-back agreements, concerning the inadvertent disclosure of privileged information, whereby they agree in advance that they will not review and will return any obviously privileged documents that are disclosed by mistake during discovery.

The Federal Rules of Evidence protect against the loss of the privilege when documents are inadvertently produced during discovery. This section states in part:

(b) Inadvertent Disclosure. When made in a federal proceeding or to a federal office or agency, the disclosure does not operate as a waiver in a federal or state proceeding if:
    (1) the disclosure is inadvertent;
    (2) the holder of the privilege or protection took reasonable steps to prevent disclosure; and
    (3) the holder promptly took reasonable steps to rectify the error, including (if applicable) following Federal Rule of Civil Procedure 26(b)(5)(B).

Federal Rule of Evidence Section 502.

Fed. R. Civ. P. 26(b)(5)(B) provides:

> If information produced in discovery is subject to a claim of privilege or of protection as trial-preparation material, the party making the claim may notify any party that received the information of the claim and the basis for it. After being notified, a party must promptly return, sequester, or destroy the specified information and any copies it has; must not use or disclose the information until the claim is resolved; must take reasonable steps to retrieve the information if the party disclosed it before being notified; and may promptly present the information to the court under seal for a determination of the claim. The producing party must preserve the information until the claim is resolved.

A rare exception to the protection of waiver of privilege because of inadvertent disclosure occurred in a patent infringement case, *VLT, Inc. v. Lucent Technologies, Inc.*, 2003 U.S. Dist. LEXIS 723 (D. Mass. 2003). In this case, a paralegal mistakenly produced privileged documents during a document production. The Court found that the circumstances under which the unintentional production of the privileged documents occurred resulted in a ***subject matter waiver*** under Federal Rule of Evidence 502(a), which in effect vacated the non-waiver provision in the protective order (claw-back agreement) entered into by the parties. Consequently, the receiving party was not required to return the documents. See, for example, *Federal Election Comm'n v. Christian Coalition*, 178 F.R.D. 61, 74 (E.D. Va. 1998) ("Additionally, the Fourth Circuit recognizes the concept of subject matter waiver. That is, when a party waives the attorney-client privilege as to one document or communication, it may waive the attorney-client privilege as to all documents that bear on the same subject matter." (citing *In re Martin Marietta Corp.*, 856 F.2d 619, 623 (4th Cir. 1988)); recognizing the distinction between this concept and the principle of unlimited waiver of the attorney-client privilege), *aff'd in part, modified in part*, 178 F.R.D. 456 (E.D. Va. 1998).

Subject matter waiver
Limits a party from revealing helpful privileged information while withholding less than helpful privileged information, thus requiring the party that produced some privileged information to produce all the remaining privileged information on the same subject matter.

See also *Victor Stanley, Inc. v. Creative Pipe, Inc.* at the end of this chapter for a court's analysis of whether the privilege was waived when otherwise protected documents were disclosed in a document production.

Receiving inadvertently disclosed privileged material creates ethical duties for the recipient. For more on this issue, see Section E.4.

6. Exceptions to the Privilege/Permissive Disclosure

Privileged information may be disclosed by a lawyer when the client calls into question the attorney's **professional competence** through criminal charges, a malpractice suit, disciplinary action, or a claim of ineffective assistance of counsel on appeal from a criminal conviction. See *Mack v. Baker, et al.*, 3:12-cv-00104-RCJ-VPC (D. Nev. 2014), where a convicted criminal used an ineffective assistance of counsel claim against his former lawyers as grounds to seek a new trial.

When a lawyer represents **two clients** who later become adversaries, otherwise privileged communications relating to the joint matter are not protected. Pooled information shared by counsel who represent different clients with common interests generally is protected, although it may be used by the parties in later litigation in which the interests of the parties are adverse.

Also, confidential communications about a **future crime or fraud** that a client is planning are not protected. The basis for this exception is that a lawyer's services should not be used to assist a client in committing a crime. (Note in the discussion of the ethical rules in Section D that the ethics rules provide more protection for this kind of information than does the privilege.) Under the important crime-fraud exception, privileged communications can be disclosed if they were made in furtherance of a crime or fraud. What communications fall into this exception varies from jurisdiction to jurisdiction, but the trend seems to be toward more court-ordered disclosure for plaintiffs in civil lawsuits and prosecutors in criminal cases. For example, in the major tobacco litigation of the 1990s, the crime-fraud exception was used successfully in several cases to gain access to incriminating documents sent between the companies and their lawyers. See, for example, *Haines v. Liggett Group Inc.*, 975 F.2d 81 (3d Cir. 1992), and *American Tobacco Co. v. State of Florida*, 697 So. 2d 1249 (4th Fla. Dist. Ct. App. 1997). Similarly, during the financial crisis of the 2000s, the crime-fraud exception was again used successfully to compel the production of documents related to alleged financial malfeasance. See *In re Grand Jury Proceedings, G.S., F.S.*, 609 F.3d 909 (8th Cir. 2010), and *SEC v. Bernard L. Madoff Investment Securities LLC*, 319 F.R.D. 100 (S.D.N.Y. 2017).

7. The Privilege in the Corporate Setting

Special issues in applying the attorney-client privilege arise in the representation of corporations. Who is the client? What communications are protected? Different jurisdictions use different tests to determine the application of the privilege. On one end of the spectrum is the ***control group test***, which limits the privilege to confidential communications between the lawyer and the management personnel responsible for acting on behalf of the corporate entity in the legal matter at issue. The broader ***subject matter test***, now followed in most jurisdictions, was formulated in *Upjohn Co. v. United States*, 449 U.S. 383 (1981). The Supreme Court in that case extended the privilege to all corporate employees who communicate in confidence with the corporation's lawyer for the purpose of enabling the lawyer to render legal services to the corporation.

Another issue that arises in corporate representation relates to the **holder of the privilege**. The corporation, not the employee, is the client and thus the holder of the privilege; only the corporation may waive it. The employee who communicates the information may object to the corporation's waiver of the privilege because the information implicates or embarrasses the employee, but the corporation is the client and the holder of the privilege and therefore, makes the decision to protect or waive the privilege. See, for example, *U.S. v. Martin*, 278 F.3d 988 (9th Cir. 2002), for a case where a lawyer who represented a corporation revealed information about the criminal activities of a corporate officer to a government agency. See *U.S. v. Nicholas*, 606 F. Supp. 2d 1109 (C.D. Cal. 2009), at the end of Chapter 5, for a case in point.

Paralegals must take great care in discussing legal matters with employees of a corporate client. Employees often believe that the corporation's lawyers and paralegals represent their individual interests. The lawyer represents the interests of the corporation, which may or may not be aligned with those of the employee in any given case. This scenario is further complicated when the employee is no longer employed by the corporation. Most jurisdictions hold that this communication is not privileged. (See, for example, *Newman v. Highland Sch. Dist. No. 203*, 381 P.3d 1188 (2016).)

Another issue that arises in the corporate setting is whether an **internal audit or investigation** conducted by a corporation's lawyers is protected under the attorney-client privilege. Whether a court will extend the protection of the privilege to such audits varies from state to state and depends to a large extent on how carefully the lawyers and their client construct the audit to preserve the privilege.

Finally, a provision of the **Sarbanes-Oxley Act** (15 U.S.C. §7245) mandated the adoption of Securities and Exchange

Control group test
Limits the attorney-client privilege to confidential communications between the lawyer and top management personnel.

Subject matter test
Applies the attorney-client privilege to all corporate employees who communicate in confidence with the lawyer for the purpose of enabling the lawyer to render legal services.

Commission regulations concerning lawyers who practice securities law. The key provisions require lawyers to report evidence of a material violation or breach of fiduciary duty "up the ladder" to the chief legal counsel or chief executive officer; require reporting to the board audit committee if no action is taken; and allow lawyers to reveal confidential information to prevent the corporation from committing a material violation that is likely to cause financial injury, to rectify such an action, or to prevent an illegal action (17 Code of Federal Regulations 205).

8. Asserting the Privilege and Court-Ordered Disclosure

When opposing counsel, in discovery or trial, seeks to discover or introduce privileged information, the lawyer must assert the client's privilege. Disputes often arise about what is privileged. For example, in cases with massive numbers of documents, a lawyer might assert a **blanket privilege** for large categories of documents. Most judges will not allow this; a document-by-document basis for the privilege must be shown. When a paralegal prepares a **log** of documents that are claimed as privileged, the privilege log should state the grounds for the privilege, for example, "Letter seeking advice re: merger discussions," not simply "Letter re: merger." Also, a privilege log should indicate all the senders and recipients. If a document was sent to a number of persons who do not fall within the privilege, the court may find that it is not privileged.

If the court orders the lawyer to testify or to produce documents, the lawyer may do so or may refuse and appeal the ruling. Often, a court will order an *in camera* examination to determine whether to order disclosure in open court.

In camera
Proceedings held in the judge's chambers without the jury or public present.

If a lawyer breaks the privilege without client consent or court order, the client may seek to enjoin or suppress the lawyer's testimony or seek dismissal of the case. And, of course, the client may sue the lawyer for malpractice and file a complaint with the appropriate disciplinary authorities.

Finally, some states have statutes or cases that allow limited disclosure of confidential information for specific purposes, such as a challenge to the validity of a will. In such a case, the lawyer's notes of conversations with a deceased may be sought to prove or disprove the testator's capacity. See, for example, *Eizenga v. Unity Christian School*, 2016 IL App. (3d) 150519.

C. Work Product

Federal and state rules of evidence and discovery provide for the protection of materials prepared by lawyers in anticipation of litigation. This **work product doctrine** was set forth in *Hickman v. Taylor*, 329 U.S. 495 (1947), in which the Court created a qualified immunity from discovery for a lawyer's trial preparation so as to allow each side to prepare fully and in private. Under this case and subsequent cases and statutes, the work product rule encompasses two kinds of trial preparation material: informational material and mental impressions. **Mental impressions**, which are covered by an unqualified privilege, are the lawyer's ideas on how to conduct the case—that is, strategies and theories, including research. **Informational material**, which is protected by a qualified privilege, covers factual research such as witness statements.

> **Work product doctrine**
> Protects the work done by a lawyer and his or her employees and agents in the process of representing a client in litigation.

When the opposition finds informational material critical to its case and does not have an effective substitute, it may ask the court to break the privilege and force the opposing counsel to disclose the material. The work product doctrine as enunciated in *Hickman* is codified in the Federal Rules of Civil Procedure and provides the model for most state rules as well. (See FRCP 26.)

Because only material prepared in **anticipation of litigation** is protected under the work product doctrine, some material, such as investigators' reports, prepared before there was a clear indication that a lawsuit would be filed, may be discoverable. This aspect of the rule creates special problems in litigation with insurance companies. Cases in this area vary widely, some lending protection whenever an insurance investigation is made, some only after an attorney becomes involved and orders the investigation or reports.

The life of the work product protection varies across jurisdictions. Some states hold that the protection terminates with the litigation; others continue it indefinitely; still others terminate it with the end of the litigation except as to future related litigation.

The work product doctrine has special application in **electronic discovery**. Discovery of the opposition's electronic databases under the information prong of the rule is generally permitted if documents are input verbatim. However, paraphrased or summarized documents, selectively input or coded documents, and documents sorted topically by means of an index of issues prepared by an attorney and staff generally are protected because such information relates to case preparation, usually representing both strategic and legal theories the lawyer is developing. (See, e.g., *Bloss v. Ford Motor Co.*, 126 A.D.2d 804, 510 N.Y.S.2d 304 (1987) for an example of a dispute over an index.)

As with the attorney-client privilege, work product protection can be waived by actual or implied consent of the client.

REVIEW QUESTIONS

1. What is the basis for the principle of confidentiality?
2. Define the attorney-client privilege. How does it differ from the ethics duty of confidentiality?
3. A client seeks advice from a lawyer. Give three examples of advice that would be covered by the attorney-client privilege. Give three examples of advice that would not. What is the difference?
4. Are initial consultations covered by the privilege if the lawyer does not undertake the representation?
5. Are conversations that take place between nonlawyer employees and clients covered by the privilege? Under what circumstances?
6. Do privileged communications that are relayed to outside vendors hired by a lawyer retain the protection?
7. Does the privilege cover communications in cases in which the lawyer does not charge a fee, such as *pro bono* matters?
8. Are conversations protected by the privilege if they take place in reception areas? Lobby? Elevator? A restaurant? A cocktail party?
9. Is a nonlawyer who helps a friend prepare divorce papers covered by the privilege? What about an inmate helping another inmate? A legal document preparer/assistant, such as those in California and Arizona?
10. Name three ways in which the privilege may be destroyed.
11. Does the privilege cover information about a client's identity? A client's whereabouts? The fee arrangement made with the attorney?
12. When are a client's written documents protected by the privilege? When are they not?
13. What does a lawyer do when a court requests disclosure of information that the lawyer believes to be privileged?
14. What happens when privileged information is inadvertently disclosed to opposing counsel?
15. What is a claw-back agreement?
16. Name three circumstances under which a lawyer may disclose privileged information.
17. How does the privilege apply when the client is a corporation?
18. Does the privilege apply to a paralegal who works in a corporate setting? In what ways might the privilege be jeopardized in this setting?
19. Who is the holder of the privilege in a corporate setting? Who can waive the privilege?
20. Define the work product doctrine. What is the reasoning behind this rule? What are the two kinds of information covered by the rule, and what kind of privilege attaches to each one?
21. Is an electronic database prepared in litigation protected as work product? Explain why or why not.
22. What is a privilege log?

23. In a federal court case in which privileged material is inadvertently disclosed in discovery, is the privilege waived? What factors might a court consider in deciding?
24. What do regulations adopted under Sarbanes-Oxley require of lawyers who work in securities law?

DISCUSSION QUESTIONS AND HYPOTHETICALS

1. Do you think that the government should be able to access information about clients' identities and their fee arrangements with lawyers? If not, what principles and arguments support your opinion? If so, what is the basis and rationale for your opinion?
2. You discover that opposing counsel has included clearly privileged documents in a document production. What would you do? What rule does your state follow in deciding whether inadvertent disclosure results in a waiver of the privilege?
3. A distressed client comes running into your reception area and demands to see her lawyer. The lawyer is unavailable and you are the assigned paralegal. You greet the client and she begins to tell her story in a loud voice in front of other people waiting in the reception area. What should you do? What might happen if you allow the client to continue?
4. Why is the privilege not extended to nonlawyer legal service providers who may be assisting clients with legal matters? Is this a good policy?
5. A subpoena comes in seeking the following documents. Which are protected by the privilege? Is the privilege absolute or qualified?

    a. Notes of your meeting with a client.
    b. The database of documents that you have compiled in a case.
    c. The database of case law that you have compiled in a case.
    d. Notes of your meeting with a witness.
    e. Notes of your meeting with a witness who is no longer available.

6. What would you suggest if your supervising lawyer instructed you to have all the information on a litigated matter input verbatim in full text into a database to be used in preparation for trial?
7. Juan is a litigation paralegal in a large full-service law firm. Many of the clients are wealthy individuals and corporations. One morning a client named Adam, who is a famous actor, comes into the office unannounced. His lawyer, John, is not in, but the receptionist asks Juan to talk to Adam in the reception area. When Juan sees Adam, he knows something is wrong: he is disheveled and wild-eyed. He immediately erupts in a loud voice about someone dying the night before. He is incoherent, but Juan hears the words "argument" and "gun." What should Juan do? What if Juan cannot get Adam to

stop, and he tells the whole story in the reception area? Is this information privileged? Why or why not? What if one of the paparazzi following Adam overhears the conversation with his ear to the door?
8. Paralegal Anna retires from her 20-year career in several prominent law firms in Los Angeles where she worked with famous clients from the entertainment industry. She decides to take up writing and produces a tell-all book full of interesting stories about the legal escapades of these clients. She self-publishes it and sells it on Amazon. Has she violated the privilege or breached the duty of confidentiality? Why or why not? What might be the consequences of her conduct? What if she were a lawyer? (See if you can find out what happened to Indiana lawyer Joseph Stork Smith who published *Rove-ing Her Way to the White House: Machiavelli's Sexy Twin Sister.*)
9. Are communications between lawyers and their in-house counsel concerning potential malpractice suits by an existing client protected by the privilege? Or can the client gain access to those communications? (Two cases may provide guidance. See *St. Simons Waterfront LLC v. Hunter, Maclean, Exley & Dunn*, 323 Ga. App. 757, 748 S.E.2d 131 (2013) and *RFF Family Partnership LP v. Burns & Levinson*, 465 Mass. 702 (2013)).
10. Lawyer Thea is representing a client in criminal court on a drug charge. The night before she is scheduled to appear, she gets a call from the client's mother who tells her not to expect the client in court because he just left the house "as high as a kite." In court the next day, the judge asks Thea where the client is. What can Thea say? Must she tell the judge what she knows? What ethical duties are in balance here, and which one prevails?

RESEARCH PROJECTS AND ASSIGNMENTS

1. Find the source of the attorney-client privilege in your state. Is it in the statutes? A case or series of cases? A court rule? How does it compare with the general definition of the privilege given in this chapter?
2. Are there any cases in your state relating to paralegals and the privilege? What do they say?
3. Find the rule for the work product doctrine in your state. How does it compare with the provision in the Federal Rules of Civil Procedure?
4. Courts have historically allowed the privilege to stand in situations in which a confidential communication is relayed to a lawyer by a nonlawyer such as an accountant (*United States v. Kovel*, 296 F.2d 918 (2d Cir. 1961)) or a lawyer's public relations firm (*In re Grand Jury Subpoenas*, 265 F. Supp. 2d 321 (S.D.N.Y. 2003)). However, in another case, communications between the client's lawyer and an investment

adviser about a client's prospective transaction were held not to be privileged (*United States v. Ackert*, 169 F.3d 136 (2d Cir. 1999)). Read and compare these cases. What conclusions can you draw?

5. There are many cases in which the government has tried to find the identity of a client, sometimes one who is seeking tax advice. Read some of these cases, starting with *United States v. BDO Seidman*, 225 F. Supp. 2d 918 (2002). Check for other cases on this issue and formulate a rule that reflects these holdings.

6. Read these cases about the protection of fee agreements between lawyers and clients and write a report that summarizes and compares the various rulings: *In re Grand Jury Subpoena for Attorney Representing Reyes-Requena*, 926 F.2d 1423 (5th Cir. 1991); *In re Grand Jury Matter*, 969 F.2d 995 (11th Cir. 1992); *U.S. v. Ellis*, 90 F.3d 447 (11th Cir. 1996); *U.S. v. Ritchie*, 15 F.3d 592 (6th Cir. 1994); *Whitehouse v. U.S. Dist. Ct.*, 53 F.3d 1349 (1st Cir. 1995); *United States v. Goldberger & Dubin*, 935 F.2d 501 (2d Cir. 1991).

7. Read *In re Grand Jury Subpoena Duces Tecum*, 112 F.3d 910 (8th Cir.), *cert. denied*, 521 U.S. 1005 (1997), in which the court held that the presence of White House lawyers during conversations between Hillary Clinton and her lawyers destroyed the privilege. Debate the merits of this decision.

8. Read *Swidler & Berlin v. United States*, 524 U.S. 399, 118 S. Ct. 2081 (1998), in which the Supreme Court held that the privilege survives the death of the client. In this case, Independent Counsel Kenneth Starr sought the notes of the lawyer for Vincent Foster, who committed suicide during the investigation into Whitewater and other matters relating to President Bill Clinton. On what grounds does the Court base its decision? Do you agree with the decision?

9. Does your state provide for permissive disclosure of privileged information in the case of a will contest? Under what other circumstances is disclosure permitted under your state law?

10. Read *Lenz v. Universal Music Corp.*, 2010 WL4789099 (N.D. CA. 2010), where the plaintiff in a copyright infringement case sent e-mails, posted a blog, and engaged in Gmail chat sessions regarding litigation strategy prior to and during the litigation. Defense counsel moved to compel discovery related to these communications, alleging that the plaintiff had waived the attorney-client privilege for the information disclosed. What duty does a lawyer have to inform clients about the potential waiver of the privilege via their use of e-mail, blogs, chats, and social media?

11. A lawyer is seeking to substitute himself for a party that got a default judgment against the lawyer's former client. Should this be allowed? How is the rule of confidentiality implicated? See *Styles v. Mumbert*, 164 Cal. App. 4th 1163, 79 Cal. Rptr.3d 880 (2008).

12. Should e-mails among several lawyers in a law firm concerning the threat of a malpractice action by a client be protected by privilege

if the client later does sue for malpractice? See *Koen Book Distributors v. Powell, Trachtman, et al.*, 212 F.R.D. 283 (E.D. Penn. 2002).
13. An interesting issue concerning whether a waiver has taken place arises in the context of federal investigations and related civil lawsuits. During the 1990s, the Department of Justice adopted a policy that it would consider the cooperation of a corporation in deciding whether or not to indict it on criminal charges, and in making this determination, it considered whether the corporation had waived its privilege during the investigation and produced documents that would otherwise be privileged. The plaintiffs, in a related action, moved to compel production of the documents involved, but the court found that the privilege had not been waived because the disclosure had been coerced. See *Regents of the Univ. of California v. Superior Court*, 165 Cal. App. 4th 672, 81 Cal. Rptr. 3d 186 (2008). After this decision, the Department of Justice revised its policy, which now prohibits forced disclosures. Research the current Department of Justice rules to see what they now say about forcing disclosures.
14. What happens when the attorney-client privilege clashes with another public policy enshrined in statute and favoring transparency? In a recent California case, the privilege conflicted with the California Public Records Act in a dispute over access to billing invoices from a lawyer to a client. Read this case and explain which policy prevailed and why: *Los Angeles County Bd. of Supervisors v. Superior Court*, 212 Cal. Rptr. 3d 107, 2 Cal. 5th 282, 386 P.3d 773 (2016).

D. Ethics Rules of Confidentiality

Broad protection for client confidentiality was included in the earliest codes governing lawyer conduct and is included in the ethics rules in every state. In addition to requiring lawyers to protect client confidences, these rules also provide the most important components of the foundation for conflict of interest rules, discussed in Chapter 5.

Rule 1.6 of the ABA Model Rules of Professional Conduct contains a broad statement obligating the lawyer not to reveal "information relating to the representation of a client unless the client gives informed consent, the disclosure is impliedly authorized . . . or permitted by paragraph (b)." This language means that virtually all information is covered, regardless of when and how it was learned by the attorney. No private setting is required; the information need not have been communicated directly by the client; information learned before or after the representation is covered. Further, the client need not request confidentiality for the attorney to protect against disclosure.

There are exceptions allowing permissive disclosure under 1.6(b). Note that permissive disclosure means that the lawyer is permitted under the Rules to disclose the information but is not required to. The exceptions are: (1) to prevent reasonably certain death or substantial bodily harm; (2) to prevent the client from committing a crime or fraud that is reasonably certain to result in substantial injury to the financial or property interests of another; (3) to prevent, mitigate, or rectify such injury; (4) to secure legal advice about the lawyer's compliance with ethics rules; (5) to establish a lawyer's claim or defense in a dispute between the lawyer and client or a civil or criminal case against the lawyer; (6) to comply with a court order or law; and (7) to detect and resolve a conflict of interest so long as revealing the information does not compromise the client or privilege.

Section (c) importantly calls on lawyers to "make reasonable efforts to prevent inadvertent or unauthorized disclosures of or unauthorized access to" protected information. Comments [18] and [19] to this rule describe the factors that lawyers should consider in deciding the level of measures to protect confidentiality: the sensitivity of the information, the likelihood that it might be disclosed without special safeguards, the costs and difficulty of deploying special safeguards, and the extent to which the safeguards may impair the ability to represent the client. The comment also notes that the client may require additional security measures or agree to less rigorous ones than are advisable. Finally, comment [18] also reiterates the principles of Rule 5.3 indicating that lawyers must act competently to safeguard confidential information against inadvertent or unauthorized disclosure by persons subject to the lawyer's supervision, which, of course, includes paralegals.

Not all states have adopted the rule or its recent addition verbatim, and jurisdictions vary significantly in the way that they approach permissive disclosure related to crime, fraud, and other actions that may harm persons. More than half the states allow disclosure of confidential information to prevent any crime; a few mandate disclosure and a few prohibit disclosure. Some states allow disclosure only if the crime would likely result in death or substantial bodily harm. Some states permit disclosure to prevent a fraud that would result in substantial loss to a person.

E. Paralegals and the Rules on Confidentiality

1. Application of the Rule to Paralegals

Virtually every state that has guidelines on paralegal utilization requires lawyers to ensure that paralegals preserve client confidences. The ABA Model Guidelines for the Utilization of Paralegal Services (ABA Model Guidelines) cover confidentiality in Guideline 6. Most state guidelines speak in terms of the lawyer "instructing" the paralegal to preserve client confidences or to "exercise care" to ensure that paralegals preserve client confidences. One state, Illinois, is more detailed in its statement, calling on the lawyer to ensure that the paralegal's work product "does not benefit the client's adversaries." Illinois State Bar Association Recommendations to Attorneys for the Use of Legal Assistants, Recommendation (A)(3) (1988). The Iowa guidelines remind lawyers that the confidentiality duty covers "casual disclosure (for example, by common gossip) as well as intentional misuse (for example, by such things as insider trading)." Ethical Guidelines for Legal Assistants in Iowa, V.A. (1988).

Finally, at least one state has issued an opinion endorsing the use of freelance paralegals' services so long as the supervising attorney exercises care to prevent disclosure or use of client confidences. Maryland Ethics Opinion 86-83 (1986). The ABA reached a similar conclusion about attorney supervision of freelance lawyers in its Formal Ethics Opinion 88-356 (1988).

NALA Model Guideline V.1 requires paralegals to preserve confidences and secrets, using the terminology of the ABA Model Code. Canon 7 of the NALA Code calls on paralegals to protect client confidentiality and to uphold the laws on the attorney-client privilege. NFPA Model Code Section 1.5 requires paralegals to "preserve all confidential information" and in several subsections details rules prohibiting paralegals from using confidential information to the client's disadvantage or advantage of the paralegal or a third party.

More than other nonlawyer employees in the law firm, paralegals have access to confidential information about clients. They are frequently included in client conferences in which privileged information is revealed, are privy to confidential written communications from and to clients, and work on highly sensitive and private matters for clients.

2. Protecting Confidentiality in Daily Practice

Law firms need to have and follow well-established policies and procedures to prevent inadvertent disclosure of confidential information. Some firms include these in their manuals, orientation programs, or training materials.

ABA Formal Opinion 477 Secured Communication of Protected Client Information (2017) enhances the change to ABA Model Rule 1.1, which states that lawyers should be aware of the benefits and risks associated with relevant technology. The Opinion addresses how lawyers should understand the nature of cyber intrusions, the handling, storage and protection of client confidential information, the reasonable use of electronic security measures, the training of lawyers and paralegals in technology and information security, and the conducting of due diligence on vendors providing communication technology.

Policies should deny unauthorized personnel **access to electronic and hard copy files** and places where files are stored or used. **Code numbers** can be used on client files instead of names. Access to extremely sensitive confidential information should be limited to as few employees and vendors as possible.

Old files and papers (even scratch paper) concerning clients should be disposed of properly, preferably by shredding. Stories of carelessness in disposing of papers abound. One firm was horrified to learn that its confidential drafts of documents had been turned into scratch paper. In one case, the files of a lawyer with financial problems were about to be auctioned off with his other personal assets when another lawyer came to the rescue.

Lawyers are responsible for the proper disposal of client files, including the digital "shredding" of electronic files. See Pennsylvania Bar Association Formal Opinion 2007-10: "A lawyer's retention policy should establish a procedure for file destruction that protects client confidentiality while ensuring complete destruction (e.g., burning, shredding, electronic shredding, etc.)." Electronic files include administrative documents, case and trial documents, voicemails, videos, emails, and time, billing, and accounting records. For destruction of electronic files, lawyers should either (1) use a data destruction program that meets government or military standards and which deletes the content by overwriting it a number of times, or (2) physically destroy the drive. Destruction of any files must be handled in a manner that preserves client confidentiality.

Computer screens should not be visible to those walking through the office. Conversations over the **intercom and speakerphones** should be held behind closed doors or limited to non-confidential matters to prevent unauthorized personnel, clients, or others visiting the office from overhearing. **Remote or virtual** online communications and meetings require safeguards to be enacted to prevent unauthorized access.

Privileged documents should be **labeled** as such when they are created to reduce the risk that they will not be handled carefully. Privileged documents should also be segregated from non-confidential documents in **separate files and databases** whenever possible. Procedures should limit who has access to any privileged documents.

The most common kind of disclosure of confidential information takes place in casual **conversation** about work outside the office. Like everyone else, lawyers and paralegals talk with friends and family about their work. Casual conversations concerning clients that are held with coworkers and people outside the firm are potentially serious breaches of ethics. Participants in these conversations may repeat what they learn to others and conversations may be overheard. Improper disclosures like this are not uncommon and rarely result in sanctions; however, the consequences—losing a client, having a court deny protection to the information, having opposing counsel learn confidential information through the grapevine, or having a client bring a malpractice suit or initiate a disciplinary complaint—are quite serious and should provide a major incentive to exercise great discretion when discussing client matters. In another example of the consequences of sharing confidential information, the husband of a lawyer paid a fine for insider trading after purchasing stock because of confidential information he learned from his wife, who learned it from the general counsel of the company.

There are many commonsense practices that paralegals should live by to prevent disclosure. One set of practices centers on the importance of keeping communications between the client and the lawyer and staff sufficiently private to withstand a challenge under the attorney-client privilege by demonstrating that the communication was intended to be confidential. Lawyers and paralegals must not carry on a conversation in the **presence of persons** who are not necessary to the representation. Conversations with clients should take place in the privacy of a **closed office, conference room**, or virtual private meeting, not the reception or secretarial area, lunchroom, hallway, elevator, or restaurant. Cell phones present special risks, as many people talk in public places on cell phones even though their side of the conversation can be overheard. As noted later in the technology section below, e-mail recipients should be carefully limited to those within the scope of the privilege, and statements asserting the privilege of the communication should be included on all e-mails that pertain to protected information.

The presence of others during confidential discussions should also be limited to those lawyers and nonlawyer employees who are working on the client's case. This automatically excludes such law firm employees as receptionists, file clerks, and mailroom personnel. Although these people are covered by the privilege, it is wise to limit the staff members who have confidential information to as few people as possible. Paralegals should not take calls from a client while meeting with another client because the client present might learn confidential information by hearing part of the conversation. Likewise, when seeing a client or anyone else from outside the firm, paralegals should not have any other client documents in view or an active computer screen visible to the visitor.

The work product rule is the primary means of protecting information in databases, especially those used for litigation support. To ensure that a **database** is protected, lawyers must be involved in the design and planning of the database. Headnotes should include their legal theories, opinions, conclusions, and strategies. Clients, witnesses, and others should not have access to the database. Full-text databases are most likely to be found discoverable. To prevent this, only selected material should be included, and lawyers and paralegals should develop headings or annotations to assist with searches cooperatively.

Confidentiality agreements are another means to guard against disclosure of protected information. A confidentiality agreement between a law firm and a vendor or employee should require the signer not to disclose and to prevent any disclosure of confidential information. It should require the signer to return all documents acquired or developed during the course of work and admonish the signer not to remove any documents from the workplace. Such agreements should be signed by all employees, independent contractors, vendors, and outside agencies with access to privileged information.

> **Confidentiality agreement**
> An agreement entered into between a law firm and an employee or other agent in which the employee or agent agrees to keep client information confidential.

Finally, steps should be taken to prevent anyone in the law firm from using confidential information **for their own gain**. For example, if a paralegal learns that a real estate development being handled by a firm will result in dramatic increases in property values in the surrounding area, she or he may not misuse this information to buy property. Similarly, using confidential information to benefit on the stock market is forbidden by insider trading rules. In addition to the individual's liability under securities law, the firm is also liable. Fines may be levied against a law firm whose employee uses confidential or inside information to engage in unlawful securities transactions if the firm did not exercise appropriate supervision to prevent the unlawful trading.

In one case, a paralegal at a prominent New York law firm turned in a lawyer from another firm who tried to bribe her to obtain inside information on mergers and acquisitions that the firm was working on. In another, a stock trader who learned about a big merger from a friend who was a second-year associate at a San Francisco law firm reaped more than $40,000 in profits before he pleaded guilty to felony charges. In another case, a summer intern and paralegal at a large New York plaintiff's firm was arrested when he stole the firm's 400-page trial plan in a large asbestos case and tried to sell the plan to the defendants' lawyers for $2 million.

3. Special Issues Relating to Technology

The use of technology creates challenges for the protection of confidential client information, challenges that continue to evolve rapidly as technology advances. Electronic records are more portable and accessible than paper; are easier to retrieve, copy, and transmit; are easier to alter and intercept; and are more difficult to delete. Technology-mediated communications necessitate that firms take special security measures to preserve confidentiality and to protect against potential claims that the privilege has been waived because communications were not treated as private and confidential.

Most firms no longer use freestanding **fax** machines because the fax function is built into an integrated technology system. If a firm still uses faxes, care should be taken to avoid breaches of confidentiality.

When faxing confidential material, one must ensure that the client is on the receiving end so that third parties who are not covered by the privilege do not have access to the communication, which could give rise to a claim that the communication was not treated as privileged. An appropriate notice of the privileged or confidential nature of the material should accompany the transmission and the word *confidential* or *privileged* should appear on every page.

Calls made on some **cellular and cordless telephones** can be intercepted by special scanners, making them less secure for sensitive conversations than ordinary land-based telephone lines. Under the Federal Electronic Communications Privacy Act and state statutes, an interception of any kind of communication made through these media does not destroy the privilege if the communication is otherwise protected by the attorney-client privilege. Despite these statutes, caution must be exercised when using cordless and some cellular telephones for privileged communications.

Some state and local bar associations have issued opinions recommending that lawyers not use such telephones for confidential communications because of the risk of interception and the lowered expectation of privacy. Many of these opinions were rendered before the current technology developed. The risk of interception on most cell phones is slim; however, it is still good practice to be especially careful about sensitive conversations and messages on cell phones, especially because of advances in technology, such as devices that can surreptitiously access other people's text messages. It is wise for lawyers to inform clients of the risks of using cell phones and to obtain their consent to use this means of communication to discuss confidential matters. The safest practice is to communicate about especially sensitive privileged matters only on a secure land-based phone.

Special protections must be in place to ensure that privileged material stored electronically is not vulnerable. Physical security of computers and network servers is essential. Servers should be in a secure, locked room and should be secured to the furniture or floor. New concerns about security relate to the increased use of **cloud computing**, where data are stored by vendors at remote locations, resulting in multiple copies of the data, sometimes in multiple locations. Storing confidential information in the cloud is considered acceptable as long as there are adequate safeguards to protect confidentiality and the lawyer knows how to verify that the information is protected. Firms should be sure that vendors have strong security systems and will provide notification of any breaches. (See the ABA website for a compilation of more than 25 ethics opinions on cloud computing.) Firms also need good security to screen email for malware, and employees should not click on any suspicious messages. In a 2016 cautionary tale, an employee in a Pennsylvania prosecuting attorney's office clicked on a link in an email and the associated malware ring got access to all the firm's files, which it held for ransom.

Likewise, using **unsecured wireless networks** (Wi-Fi) can expose confidential communications and information. For example, if a paralegal accesses law firm files remotely through an unprotected wireless router, confidential information will be exposed. Devices are now available that mimic a Wi-Fi connection and can access any computer within range that is seeking a Wi-Fi connection. Avoiding public Wi-Fi hotspots is best practice.

Several bar associations have issued ethics opinions about the lawyer's duty to protect confidentiality when using technology. ABA Formal Opinion 11-459 states that the lawyer must warn the client about the risk where there is a significant risk that a third party will gain access. The opinion gives the example of an employee-client using the employer's e-mail system or computer to communicate with the employee's lawyer.

The State Bar of California Standing Committee on Professional Responsibility and Conduct provides useful guidelines on the duty to protect confidentiality using technology. Responding to a question about working in cafes and at home, the opinion provides that the duties depend on the technology being used and the circumstances and indicate that a lawyer must take steps to evaluate:

1. The level of security attendant to the use of that technology, including whether reasonable precautions may . . . increase the level of security;
2. The legal ramifications to a third party who intercepts, accesses or exceeds authorized use of the electronic information;
3. The degree of sensitivity of the information;
4. The possible impact on the client . . . ;
5. The urgency of the situation; and
6. The client's instructions and circumstances, such as access by others to the client's devices and communications.

Formal Opinion 2010-179.

Passwords should be carefully chosen so that they are not obvious (i.e., do not use initials, birthdates, and the like) and should be regularly changed. They should not be written down and left in an accessible place and employees should be admonished not to reveal their passwords to anyone except their supervisor. Obvious passwords, like spouse's, children's, and pet's names or birthdates should not be used, and the same passwords should not be used for all electronic accounts. Users should log out when they will be away from their computers for any period of time. Two-step authentication processes for accessing emails and shared drives should be used. Some firms use **electronic identification cards** ("smart cards") in conjunction with passwords. Most firms restrict what passwords can log on at remote locations.

Security systems, **antivirus software**, and regular **backups** should be in place. Special software must be used to **delete material**;

otherwise, it may be subject to retrieval. Software to ensure complete redaction of material in documents is available and can prevent serious breaches of confidential information. The number of persons serving as network administrators should be small, and these persons should be especially screened and trained; policies that prohibit their access to materials except to service the network should be adopted. **Laptop** computers and smart phones should require passwords, two-step authentication, and protective software so that if they are stolen, confidential information and the firm network cannot be accessed. Purging data before replacing computers and other devices is advisable and is critical for leased equipment.

Electronic mail communications are protected by federal and state statutes, in the same way that telephone conversations are. In other words, if a communication is privileged, it does not lose the privilege simply by being made through e-mail. In the early days of e-mail, some state bars issued advisory opinions warning lawyers not to communicate by e-mail with clients. Many people did not trust the technology and believed that e-mail was not secure and did not meet their duty to protect confidentiality. However, in 1999, the ABA issued an advisory opinion that endorsed the use of unencrypted e-mail "because the mode of transmission affords a reasonable expectation of privacy from a technological and legal standpoint." This opinion recommends that lawyers consult with clients about transmitting highly sensitive information by e-mail and warns lawyers to follow their clients' instructions about the appropriate method of transmission (ABA Formal Opinion 99-413). This opinion effectively put an end to the debate about the ethics of e-mailing with clients.

To guard against inadvertent disclosure of confidential information and to meet the duty of confidentiality, firms must take steps to ensure security of e-mail communications. Many firms have **firewalls** and **closed networks** with key clients, which make messages less vulnerable to interception. Some use **encryption** software that encodes messages at the sending end so that they can be opened at the receiving end only with a matched decoding program. Some companies offer **digital courier** service that provides secure document delivery services.

Firms should take special steps when sending documents electronically to opposing counsel. Embedded **metadata** can be tracked so that earlier drafts of documents can be accessed, including the names and dates of revisions and comments that may have been included on earlier drafts. An ABA opinion (Ethics Opinion 06-442) recommends that electronic documents be scrubbed or sent by a method that ensures that metadata cannot be revealed, such as scanning the document to create a PDF. Importantly, this opinion indicates that metadata can be used by the recipient. (See more on metadata later under the discussion of inadvertent disclosure.)

Finally, programs are available to **track e-mail** that is forwarded to others. For example, opposing counsel using such programs can see what happens to an e-mail that he or she sent after it is received. The tracker will show if it was forwarded to the client or someone else, including the cover e-mail that accompanies it. The Alaska and New York State Bar Associations have issued ethics opinions finding that "web bug" tracking is unethical. (See also Alaska Bar Association Ethics Opinion No. 2016-1.)

Firms need good procedures and practices to protect the confidentiality and privileged status of e-mail communications. Paralegals should follow these practices:

- Do not use e-mail for highly sensitive communications with clients.
- Inform clients about the risks involved in electronic communications and obtain their written consent to use electronic mail.
- Label all confidential communications as privileged and include a statement telling the reader what to do if the communication is inadvertently sent to the wrong person (i.e., not to read it and to contact the sender).
- Limit the recipients of a privileged e-mail to those who are absolutely essential to the privileged communication and warn recipients not to send such communications on to other persons, e.g., by including DO NOT FORWARD in the subject line.
- Do not send e-mail to a client e-mail inbox that can be accessed by persons not covered by the privilege.
- Do not send documents that have been drafted electronically to opposing counsel without "scrubbing" them of metadata through software and the creation of a clean PDF.
- Do not forward e-mails directly if they are received from opposing counsel or others outside the group of individuals covered by the privilege.
- Be especially careful about "replying to all" when responding to e-mail; check to be sure that all of the recipients are covered by the privilege before you click Send.
- Beware of misdirecting an e-mail when you use the "auto-fill" function, which automatically fills in the e-mail address once you type in the first few letters.

In addition, firms should have internal policies of which employees are informed and to which they agree to in writing. Policies should:

- prohibit employees from misusing e-mail to send personal, sexually explicit, or harassing material
- prohibit accessing another person's e-mail
- stress the importance of sending confidential material only to those who need to have it
- remind employees not to leave their e-mail access open and unattended or to share their passwords

- establish procedures for sending and storing privileged material
- establish the rights of the employer and employee regarding e-mail, including when the employer has the right to review an employee's e-mail messages.

Finally, the use of social media has created new risks to client confidentiality. The widespread use of LinkedIn, Facebook, Instagram, Snapchat, TikTok, and blogs poses serious threats to the privilege and has implications in other areas of ethics as well. A few examples illustrate some of the potential problems. An experienced public defender in Illinois was terminated and disciplined by the bar when she was found to have described clients in her blog in a way that allowed their identification, through her use of first names or derivatives of first names or jail identification numbers. She revealed, among other things, that clients had lied to the court. Another lawyer was sanctioned by a court after posts on Facebook showed him partying when he was supposed to be at a family funeral. Lawsuits have been brought against lawyers and others who are alleged to have defamed lawyers or criticized judges in their blogs or on their social networks. Other risks relate to client conduct, such as clients claiming to have injuries who post photos or videos of themselves engaging in activities that would not be possible if their claims were true. Finally, the police and prosecutors routinely search YouTube and other sites for evidence of crimes (e.g., videos of illegal auto racing). Sound firm-wide policies regarding social networking and blogs are a must.

4. More on Inadvertent Disclosure

Lawyers and paralegals have a duty to guard against inadvertent disclosure of confidential information to unintended recipients. As noted above, ABA Model Rule 1.6 and the comments to it indicate that lawyers do not need to take special security precautions if the method of transmission affords a **reasonable expectation of privacy**, but warns lawyers to consider several factors, including the sensitivity of the information and the extent to which its privileged status might be protected by the law or an agreement.

Unfortunately, incidents of inadvertent disclosure are not uncommon. Large-scale discovery, the discovery of electronically stored information, the extensive use of e-mail, and the widespread utilization of e-discovery all contribute to the ease with which information can be disclosed by mistake.

Examples of inadvertent disclosure are everywhere in the legal media and cases. For example, a lawyer in a large law firm accidentally released sealed documents to a magazine; another firm inadvertently placed sealed records in an appellate file to find them later published in a magazine; a staff member for a defense firm accidentally sent a long, detailed memorandum outlining legal strategy to the plaintiff's lawyer; and a lawyer accidentally handed over to opposing counsel a memorandum from a paralegal to witnesses in a case when the memo was stuck to another document with a paper clip. A trial judge in a Baltimore case dismissed a panel of prospective jurors in a major asbestos case when a staffer working for a defense firm inadvertently faxed a privileged document on jury selection strategy to the plaintiff's firm. A lawyer in a prominent firm accidentally released a confidential internal memo about opposing counsel to more than a dozen reporters. Another common error is sending confidential information by mistake to a listserv. In more than a few cases, a lawyer has hit the wrong e-mail address in his or her mailbox and sent a confidential client communication to hundreds of people.

Paralegals often have extensive responsibility for discovery, including responding to subpoenas duces tecum and handling **document productions**. When thousands of pages of documents are requested by opposing counsel, the paralegal is usually the one to review, organize, and examine these documents, to prepare privilege logs, and to see that the documents are purged of privileged material before they are provided to the opposing counsel. In addition to needing guidance from the supervising attorney as to what documents to look for, the paralegal needs a clear understanding of the privilege so that he or she can flag documents that may be protected and bring them to the lawyer's attention. Increasingly important are the methods by which electronically stored documents are screened for removal before a document production. See *Victor Stanley, Inc. v. Creative Pipe, Inc.* at the end of this chapter for a case in which the lawyers' actions resulted in waiver of the privilege because of their failure to conduct an adequate review of electronically stored information.

In addition to the ethical breach involved in inadvertently disclosing documents, paralegals need to know how to meet ethical obligations when they come into possession of privileged documents through the error of the opposition. ABA Model Rule 4.4(b) states that:

> a lawyer who receives a document or electronically stored information relating to the representation of the lawyer's client and knows or reasonably should know that the document or electronically stored information was inadvertently sent shall promptly notify the sender.

Comment [2] to this rule says that further actions to remedy the breach are outside of the "scope of the rule" and are subject to the relevant state law or legal opinions. Comment [3] indicates that lawyers may determine whether to return or delete the material in question as a matter of professional judgment. This provision applies to all electronically stored information (commonly referred to as ESI), including metadata.

This rule stops far short of two ABA ethics opinions that were issued in the 1990s but withdrawn in 2006. ABA Formal Ethics Opinions 92-368 and 94-382, superseded by Ethics Opinion 06-440, stated that the lawyer who receives privileged material should:

1. upon recognizing the privileged or confidential nature of the materials,
    a. either refrain from reviewing such materials or
    b. review them only to the extent required to determine how appropriately to proceed . . .
2. notify her adversary's lawyer that she has such materials and . . .
3. either
    a. follow instructions of the adversary's lawyer with respect to the disposition of the materials, or
    b. refrain from using the materials until a definitive resolution of the proper disposition of the materials is obtained from a court.

Although these opinions have been withdrawn, several cases still enforce them and several states have adopted similar opinions that have not been withdrawn. Courts have held that lawyers are obligated not to examine such materials and either to return them to the lawyer who disclosed them or to seek a court resolution. See, for example, *Rico v. Mitsubishi Motors Corp.* at the end of this chapter. This opinion endorses the earlier appellate court case of *State Compensation Insurance Fund v. Telanoff*, 70 Cal. App. 4th 644, 82 Cal.Rptr.2d 799 (1999), which follows the reasoning of the earlier ABA Formal Opinions. Similarly, some ethics opinions warn against exploiting unsolicited breaches of confidentiality. See New York State Bar Association Commission on Professional Ethics, Opinion 98-700. Finally, as noted above, state and federal rules on discovery may protect against waiver of the privilege and allow a claim of privilege to be made after inadvertent production of a privileged document in discovery (see Federal Rule of Evidence 502(b) and Federal Rule of Civil Procedure 26(b)(5)).

Finally, the ABA has issued another ethics opinion that seeks to address this question in a narrowly drawn factual scenario. ABA Formal Opinion 11-460 indicates that when a lawyer receives copies of an employee's private e-mail communications, found in the employer's e-mail files or on the employee's work computer, the lawyer is not required by Rule 4.4(b) to notify opposing counsel. The opinion goes on to state that if no applicable law requires notification, the lawyer should explain the alternatives to the employer-client and allow the client to make an informed decision.

The disclosure of privileged information by sharing documents with embedded **metadata** is still somewhat unsettled. As noted above,

ABA Formal Ethics Opinion 06-442 indicates that the sending lawyer has a duty to prevent such disclosure, but it does not provide definitive guidance on whether the receiving lawyer is required to give notice to opposing counsel, as would be required in other kinds of inadvertent disclosures under Model Rule 4.4(b). The opinion does indicate that the recipient is not prohibited from examining and using the embedded information. At the time of this writing, 18 bar associations have issued ethics opinions concerning metadata. Although all impose a duty of reasonable care on the sender to prevent disclosure and all but a few require the recipient to inform the sender, there is a split on the question of whether the recipient can use the metadata, with a slight majority in favor of allowing such use. (See, for example, Alabama Bar Association Ethics Opinion 07-02, which prohibits use of the metadata; Florida Bar Ethics Opinion 06-02; Arizona Bar Ethics Opinion 07-03, which prohibits examination of the metadata and advises the recipient to notify the sender; and several others, including District of Columbia Ethics Opinion 2007-341; Maine Ethics Opinion 08-196; Maryland Ethics Opinion 07-09, that align with the ABA opinion allowing examination and use of the metadata. Some opinions like New Hampshire Bar Ethics Opinion 08-09/4 advise lawyers not to search for metadata, and New York City Bar Ass'n Ethics Opinion 08-738 and New York Ethics Opinion 01-749 advise against mining for metadata. Pennsylvania Bar Ethics Opinion 07-500 and Vermont Bar Ethics Opinion 2009-01 indicate that searching for metadata is acceptable but notification upon finding it is required.) See also *Lake v. City of Phoenix*, 218 P.3d 1004 (2009), for an example of how metadata is handled in electronic versions of public records. Paralegals are often the first ones to discover that a document has been inadvertently disclosed. The safest approach for the paralegal is to refrain from examining the documents and to communicate the situation to the supervising attorney to handle.

REVIEW QUESTIONS

1. Under what circumstances may an attorney reveal protected information pursuant to the ethics rules?
2. What are a lawyer's responsibilities in preventing the disclosure of confidential information by their employees?
3. What do the state guidelines on paralegal utilization say about the paralegal's role in client confidentiality? What do the ABA Guidelines for the Utilization of Paralegal Services say? What about paralegal associations' rules? Are these sources in accord?
4. Name ten procedures or policies that would help a firm prevent disclosure of confidential information.

5. How can inadvertent disclosure of confidential information be avoided? What should you do if you receive privileged information in error?
6. What procedures and practices should be in place to guard against disclosures of confidential information via faxes, cellular phones, and computer databases? What about when using the cloud to store and access ESI?
7. What are the risks of disclosure through e-mail communications? How should these communications be protected?
8. What are confidentiality agreements? Who should use them? What provisions should they contain?
9. What is metadata? How might it reveal privileged client information? What are a lawyer's or paralegal's duties concerning metadata? What are the duties if one receives a document with metadata in it? Can the paralegal look for metadata? Use it? Does the lawyer have to notify the sender?
10. What is "misuse" of confidential information? Give examples of how confidential information can be misused. What might be the ramifications of such misuse?
11. What conduct should lawyers and paralegals be wary of when blogging or posting to social network sites?

DISCUSSION QUESTIONS AND HYPOTHETICALS

1. What would you do if a lawyer at your firm introduced you during a social event to a client, who then proceeded to tell you the whole sordid story that led to his being represented by the firm?
2. What would you do if while attending a local paralegal association meeting you overheard a group of paralegals talking about a case on which you worked for opposing counsel? Would your answer be any different if you weren't working on the opposite side of the case?
3. What would you do if you overheard a paralegal in your firm discussing confidential information about a client with a person in another firm? Would your answer be different if a lawyer were doing the talking?
4. What would you do if you caught a client going through other clients' files on your desk while you were momentarily out of the room?
5. What should you do with handwritten notes of a confidential conversation once they have been typed up and put into a client's file?
6. What would you do first if you were assigned to respond to a document production but knew nothing about the case?

7. Lawyers from opposing firms were on a conference call. Lawyers from the ABC firm hung up and lawyers from the XYZ firm remained on the line talking. The call was recorded through an automatic conference call system and the ABC lawyers got a recording of the conversation. Can they listen to it? What should they do about it? What if the conversation reveals that the ABC lawyers were planning something fraudulent with their client? For one court's opinion, see *Jasmine Networks, Inc. v. Marvell Semiconductors, Inc.*, 117 Cal. App. 4th 794, 12 Cal. Rptr.3d 13 (2004).
8. A law firm finds a document produced by opposing counsel that is marked privileged but is not privileged. Should the privilege attach to the document? What should the recipient do about this? See *Asousa Partnership v. Smithfield Foods, et al.*, Adversary No. 04-1012 [Dkt. 35] (Bankr. E.D. Pa. Nov. 17, 2005) for one court's opinion.
9. A disgruntled client posts negative information about a lawyer's services on Yelp. Can the lawyer respond? What might happen if the lawyer responds and includes information that might be considered confidential? If the client decides to sue the lawyer for malpractice based on dissatisfaction with the services, can the lawyer reveal confidential information to defend the case?

RESEARCH PROJECTS AND ASSIGNMENTS

1. Find the ethics rule of confidentiality in your state. Does it vary from the ABA model? How? Which do you think is the best formulation of the rule?
2. Does your state mention confidentiality in its guidelines for paralegals? In any ethics opinions concerning paralegals and confidentiality?
3. Research your state bar's ethics opinions related to protecting the confidentiality of information, including confidentiality agreements and protections for e-mail, metadata, and cloud computing.
4. Research the kinds of electronic software available to protect the confidentiality and security of documents and e-mail, including software used for encryption, redaction, deletion, couriers, scrubbing of documents, and prevention of e-mail tracking. Evaluate the value of these in protecting client confidentiality.
5. Have any cases on inadvertent disclosure been decided in your jurisdiction? What about ethics opinions issued by the state bar? What are the rules in your jurisdiction about waiver and about receipt of inadvertently disclosed information?
6. Does your jurisdiction have an opinion about metadata? What do you think the rules on metadata should be? Should recipients be permitted to mine these data? Use this information in discovery? Should the recipient be required to notify the sender upon receiving metadata?

7. Using the ABA website, which shows all the state and local ethics opinions about metadata, conduct an analysis of the ethical actions that should be taken when receiving metadata. Is there a predominant point of view? If so, what is it? How do the nuances differ among the states? Do you see a trend more in favor of protecting the confidential information or being able to use it?
8. Research model policies concerning social networking sites and blogs available through state or local bar associations or included in legal ethics publications. Draft a model policy.
9. In Chapter 3 you read about lawyers entering into relationships with nonlawyer service companies that prepared living trusts and sold insurance policies to "clients" to fund the trusts. Read the case of *In re Phillips*, 338 Or. 125, 107 P.3d 615 (2005), to see how this scenario results in a breach of client confidentiality.
10. Can a lawyer or paralegal use privileged information that has been obtained illegally and then passed on by someone else? To start your research, see Florida Bar Ethics Opinion 07-01 and District of Columbia Bar Ethics Opinion 02-318.
11. If a paralegal sues her employer, can she take any or all of the e-mails and other documents that relate to her employment? See *Bedwell v. Fish & Richardson P.C.*, Case No. 07-CV-0065-WQH (S.D. Cal. 12-3-2007).
12. Assuming that the attorney-client privilege and work product rule apply to paralegals, under what circumstances might a court allow a paralegal to be deposed? See *Wal-Mart Stores, Inc. v. Dickinson*, 29 S.W.3d 796 (Ky. 2000).
13. For an example of how the California courts apply the work product rule to witness statements, see *Coito v. Superior Court*, 182 Cal. App. 4th 758, 106 Cal. Rptr. 3d 342 (2010). In this wrongful death action, the plaintiff sought statements of four juveniles who were interviewed by state investigators after the drowning that led to the action.
14. For a high-profile case on waiver of the privilege, see *U.S. v. Stewart*, 03 Cr. 717 (MGC) (S.D.N.Y. 2003). This decision involves the prosecution of Martha Stewart for securities law violations. Ms. Stewart had forwarded to her daughter an otherwise privileged e-mail that she had sent to her lawyer. The court had to decide if the e-mail was privileged.
15. For a case in which the court allowed access to e-mails of an employee-client who was suing the employer, see *Holmes v. Petrovich Development Co., LLC*, 191 Cal. Rptr. 878 (2011). Read this case and see if there are others like it in other jurisdictions. Compare it to the ABA Ethics Opinion on the subject.
16. Research court decisions about whether metadata must be included in documents that are produced in discovery. See, for example, *Williams v. Sprint/United Management Co.*, 230 F.R.D. 640 (D. Kan. 2005).

17. What duty does a lawyer have to protect confidentiality when withdrawing from the representation? See ABA Formal Ethics Opinion 16-476 for guidance.

CASES FOR ANALYSIS

This case involves the application of the attorney-client privilege to a paralegal who works in the legal department of a corporation. As an experienced and highly specialized paralegal, she functions very autonomously. The court must decide if the nature of her work takes her communications with other employees out of the attorney-client privilege.

HPD Laboratories, Inc. v. Clorox Co.
202 F.R.D. 410 (2001)

This discovery dispute presents an interesting question about the scope of the attorney-client privilege. Plaintiff, HPD Laboratories, Inc. ("HPD"), seeks to compel defendant, The Clorox Company ("Clorox") to turn over documents that contain statements to and from Karen Peeff ("Ms. Peeff"), a longtime paralegal in Clorox's in-house legal department. Clorox objects and contends that the documents are covered by the attorney-client privilege, as defined by California law. HPD disagrees and reasons that, under federal law, the attorney-client privilege does not encompass Ms. Peeff's communications because she acted independently rather than in conjunction with or at the discretion of an attorney. . . .

To facilitate its operations, Clorox maintains an in-house legal team. Karen Peeff has been a part of the team since 1985. She currently serves as a "legal specialist" for advertising and regulatory matters. Her duties include (1) reviewing prospective product labels, packages, and advertisements; (2) assessing whether those items comply with apposite state and federal statutes and regulations; and (3) advising Clorox's marketing department on compliance issues. Ms. Peeff's immediate supervisor is Patrick Meehan, an attorney. Notably, Ms. Peeff admits that she does not regularly consult with her supervisor, or other in-house counsel, prior to dispensing advice. . . .

HPD filed this suit. . . . It accused Clorox of . . . infringing the 330 Patent by selling Bleach & Blue . . . ; falsely advertising Rain Clean . . . ; committing unfair competition . . . and tortious interference with business relations. . . . Discovery ensued. . . .

Ms. Peeff is an important source of information at Clorox, no doubt due to her longevity and experience. Employees routinely confer with her on marketing and other issues. Notably, Ms. Peeff took part in many discussions concerning Rain Clean. She raised several questions for consideration and provided advice in her capacity as a Legal Specialist on advertising and regulatory matters. Her statements are embodied in several documents. . . .

Strictly speaking, none of the documents in controversy reflect communications between attorney and client. That fact is not determinative however, as statements to and from non-attorneys may warrant protection on occasion. The question is, thus, whether Ms. Peeff's statements deserve attorney-client protection even though she is not an attorney. . . .

To varying degrees, each of the subject documents contains statements from Clorox employees to Ms. Peeff. Those employees clearly sought legal advice on a variety of issues associated with labeling and marketing Rain Clean. . . .

These communications are not protected merely because they solicited legal advice or because they were directed to a paralegal. To invoke the attorney-client privilege, a client's statement must at minimum "be made in confidence for the purpose of obtaining legal advice *from the lawyer.*" [Citation omitted.] Clorox proffers no evidence that its employees approached Ms. Peeff to obtain advice from in-house or outside counsel. In fact, the opposite is true. The disputed documents convey statements and questions to Ms. Peeff herself. They do not, on their face, seek anything from Clorox's team of lawyers. This is not an oversight. In her more than fifteen years at Clorox, Ms. Peeff developed significant familiarity with marketing and regulatory matters. Recognizing her expertise, Clorox employees often sought out her opinions. Indeed, one of Clorox's project leaders averred that he routinely reviews all of his legal and substantiation issues with Ms. Peeff even though he knows that she is not a lawyer.

While there is nothing wrong with Clorox employees using Ms. Peeff as a legal resource, there is also nothing privileged about their communications to her in this instance. . . . Moreover, although not dispositive, Clorox has provided no evidence that its employees thought that their statements were privileged and that they would not have spoken to Ms. Peeff otherwise. . . .

The record also lacks evidence that Ms. Peeff relayed these statements to her supervisors in order to obtain legal advice for interested employees. In fact, Ms. Peeff actually admits that she did not discuss or pass on the disputed documents — or the concerns raised in them to in-house counsel. This admission confirms that she did not function as a conduit of information for Clorox's lawyers. . . .

Ms. Peeff's statements are not privileged simply because she expressed legal advice or works in Clorox's legal department. Federal courts expand attorney-client privilege to third-party communications for one reason: to facilitate the attorney's provision of legal advice to the client. . . . Moreover, federal law does not recognize a freestanding "paralegal privilege." . . .

A paralegal's statements may assist an attorney because they pass on that attorney's advice to the client. In this instance, however, Ms. Peeff did not function as a go-between. . . .

A paralegal's statements may also be privileged because they convey advice formulated "under the supervision and at the direction of an attorney." [Citation omitted.] Courts do not, however, safeguard advice that paralegals develop and disseminate on their own. . . . Ms. Peeff admits that she did not consult with the lawyers before answering questions about Rain Clean. This admission, standing alone, constitutes a sufficient basis for concluding that her statements are not privileged because it shows that she acted independently. . . .

Clorox has not presented any evidence . . . that would even suggest that Ms. Peeff acted either at the direction or under the actual supervision of a lawyer. Given the absence of such evidence, the Court finds that Ms. Peeff conveyed her own advice. That advice, while legal in nature, is not privileged. . . .

Clorox attempts to avoid this conclusion by pointing out that Ms. Peeff works within its legal department under attorney supervision. It further highlights that, over time, she received training from lawyers to deal with diverse legal and regulatory issues and used the basic knowledge she acquired to provide the specific advice in question. Finally, Clorox notes that Ms. Peeff meets with attorneys when "unusual or novel" compliance issues arise. . . .

Clorox's position is flawed for several reasons. First, although Ms. Peeff may function under theoretical direction of an attorney, she did not receive any discernible supervision or guidance. . . . Second, Ms. Peeff's statements are not inherently privileged merely because she is a legal employee. . . . Her activities, not her job title, determine whether protection is warranted. . . . Third, the documents at issue are not protected simply because Ms. Peeff received generalized legal training, which she subsequently used to advise Clorox's employees. A non-lawyer's statements do not automatically become privileged simply because, at some point, that person interacted with or learned from an attorney. . . .

ORDERED that HPD's discovery application to compel Clorox to produce statements to and from Ms. Peeff is GRANTED. . . .

Questions about the Case

1. What was the title used by the paralegal in this case? Did this make a difference?
2. What kind of supervision and direction did the lawyers in the Clorox legal department give to the paralegal Peeff? How did this factor into the court's reasoning?

3. What should a paralegal in this employment situation do to ensure that communications she has with employees are protected by the attorney-client privilege?
4. Do you agree with the court's decision? What does it mean for the concept of lawyers having "general" instead of "direct" supervision over paralegals? What impact would this decision have on paralegal utilization in the corporate sector if it were widely known?
5. Did the paralegal engage in the unauthorized practice of law in carrying out her duties at Clorox? Did the lawyers to whom she reported assist in UPL?

The following case demonstrates the differences between the attorney-client privilege and the work product rule.

Genovese v. Provident Life Ins. Co.
74 So.3d 1064 (Fla. 2011)

Peter Genovese brought a statutory first-party bad faith action against Provident Life and Accident Insurance Company ("Provident") after Provident terminated the monthly payments under Genovese's disability income policy. Following commencement of the bad faith suit, Genovese requested production of Provident's entire litigation file including all correspondence and communications made between the attorneys representing Provident and Provident's agents regarding Genovese's claims for benefits. The trial court issued an order compelling production of the documents. Subsequently, Provident filed a petition for writ of certiorari, asking the Fourth District to quash the trial court's order. Provident argued in part that this Court's decision in *Ruiz* did not allow for the discovery of documents protected by the attorney-client privilege.

The certified question asks whether our holding in *Allstate Indemnity Co. v. Ruiz*, 899 So.2d 1121 (Fla. 2005), permitting the discovery of work product in first-party bad faith actions brought pursuant to section 624.155, Florida Statutes (2010), also applies to attorney-client privileged communications in the first-party bad faith context.

Section 624.155, Florida Statutes, enacted in 1982, created a statutory bad faith cause of action for first-party insureds. The enactment of section 624.155 "essentially extended the duty of an insurer to act in good faith and deal fairly in those instances where an uninsured seeks first-party coverage or benefits under a policy of insurance." [Citations omitted.] Thus, an insured may bring a civil action against an insurer who does not attempt "in good faith to settle claims when, under all the circumstances, it could and should have done so, had it acted fairly and honestly toward its insured and with due regard for her or his interests."§624.155(1)(b)(1), Fla. Stat. (2010).

In *Ruiz*, we held that in first-party bad faith actions brought pursuant to section 624.155, work product materials were discoverable. At the outset, the first sentence of our opinion in *Ruiz* makes it clear that the only issue involved in that case was the work product doctrine. . . . In concluding that work product materials were discoverable in first-party bad faith actions, we then defined such work product as materials "contained in the underlying claim and related litigation file material that was created up to and including the date of resolution of the underlying disputed matter and pertain in any way to coverage, benefits, liability, or damages." Id. at 1129-30. . . . Thus, based on a reading of our language in *Ruiz*, it is clear that the only issue being decided in *Ruiz* was the discovery of work product pertaining to the underlying claim in first-party bad faith actions. However, Genovese suggests that . . . we held broadly that both attorney-client communications and work product should be discoverable in first-party bad faith claims against insurers. . . .

The attorney-client privilege and work product doctrine are two distinct concepts. The attorney-client privilege is provided for in section 90.502, Florida Statutes (2010), which states that "[a] client has a privilege to refuse to disclose, and to prevent any other person from disclosing, the contents of confidential communications when such other person learned of the communications because they were made in the rendition of legal services to the client."§90.502(2), Fla. Stat. (2010). "The purpose of the [attorney-client] privilege is to encourage clients to make full disclosure to their attorneys."[Citations omitted.] However, the privilege "protects only those disclosures necessary to obtain informed legal advice." Id. "[I]f a communication with a lawyer is not made with him in his professional capacity as a lawyer, no privilege attaches." [Citation omitted.]

On the other hand, the work product doctrine is outlined in Florida Rule of Civil Procedure 1.280(b)(3), which states that a party may obtain discovery of documents and tangible things otherwise discoverable under subdivision (b)(1) of this rule and prepared in anticipation of litigation or for trial by or for another party or by or for that party's representative, including that party's attorney, consultant, surety, indemnitor, insurer, or agent, only upon a showing that the party seeking discovery has need of the materials in the preparation of the case and is unable without undue hardship to obtain the substantial equivalent of the materials by other means. . . .

Issues regarding the discovery of work product and attorney-client privileged materials in the context of bad faith claims have arisen because of the requirements a party must satisfy to pursue a bad faith action against an insurance company. In order for a party to bring a bad faith claim against an insurer, there must be an "underlying claim for coverage or benefits or an action for damages which the insured alleges was handled in bad faith by the insurer." *Ruiz*, 899 So.2d at 1124. Consequently, the underlying claim materials are the evidence needed to determine whether an insurer acted in bad faith, which raises the issue of what materials are discoverable in bad faith actions. Because the underlying claim materials are "necessary to advance [a first-party bad faith] action . . . [and] evaluate the allegations of bad faith," see *Ruiz*, 899 So.2d at 1128-29, the materials fall within the confines of the exception to the work-product doctrine, and thus are discoverable.

On the other hand, the attorney-client privilege, unlike the work-product doctrine, is not concerned with the litigation needs of the opposing party. . . . Instead, the purpose of the privilege is to "encourage full and frank communication" between the attorney and the client. [Citations omitted.] This significant goal of the privilege would be severely hampered if an insurer were aware that its communications with its attorney, which were not intended to be disclosed, could be revealed upon request by the insured. Moreover, we note that there is no exception provided under section 90.502 that allows the discovery of attorney-client privileged communications where the requesting party has demonstrated need and undue hardship.

Therefore, although we held in *Ruiz* that attorney work product in first-party bad faith actions was discoverable, this holding does not extend to attorney-client privileged communications. Consequently, when an insured party brings a bad faith claim against its insurer, the insured may not discover those privileged communications that occurred between the insurer and its counsel during the underlying action.

Although we conclude that the attorney-client privilege applies, we recognize that cases may arise where an insurer has hired an attorney to both investigate the underlying claim and render legal advice. Thus, the materials requested by the opposing party may implicate both the work product doctrine and the attorney-client privilege. Where a claim of privilege is asserted, the trial court should conduct an in-camera inspection to determine whether the sought-after materials are truly protected by the attorney-client privilege. If the trial court determines that the investigation performed by the attorney resulted in the preparation of materials that are required to be disclosed pursuant to *Ruiz* and did not involve the rendering of legal advice, then that material is discoverable. . . .

For the reasons explained above, we answer the certified question in the negative and hold that the attorney-client privilege is applicable in the first-party bad faith context. . . .

Questions about the Case

1. What kind of lawsuit was this? Why is this relevant to the case?
2. What is the difference between the attorney-client privilege and the work product rule? What is the underlying purpose of each, and why does that matter in this case?

3. What other instances might give rise to the discovery of work product?

In the following case, the court has to decide whether the disclosure of electronically stored information in a document production resulted in a waiver of the privilege. The opinion sets forth the three tests that have been used by the courts and applies the intermediate test to the facts. The opinion provides guidance for lawyers and paralegals seeking to guard against disclosure of protected electronically stored information.

Victor Stanley, Inc. v. Creative Pipe, Inc.
250 F.R.D. 251 (D. Md. 2008)

The plaintiff, Victor Stanley, Inc. ("VSI" or "Plaintiff"), filed a motion seeking a ruling that five categories of electronically stored documents produced by defendants Creative Pipe, Inc. ("CPI") and Mark and Stephanie Pappas ("M. Pappas," "S. Pappas" or "The Pappasses") (collectively, "Defendants") in October, 2007, are not exempt from discovery because they are within the protection of the attorney-client privilege and work-product doctrine, as claimed by the Defendants. VSI argues that the electronic records at issue, which total 165 documents, are not privileged because their production by Defendants occurred under circumstances that waived any privilege or protected status. . . . Defendants acknowledge that they produced all 165 electronic documents at issue to VSI during Rule 34 discovery, but argue that the production was inadvertent, and therefore that privilege/protection has not been waived. . . .

The following facts are not subject to dispute. The Defendants' first Rule 34 response was a "paper production," not ESI [electronically stored information], made in May 2007. Plaintiff objected to its sufficiency, and following a hearing, the court ordered the parties' computer forensic experts to meet and confer in an effort to identify a joint protocol to search and retrieve relevant ESI responsive to Plaintiff's Rule 34 requests. This was done and the joint protocol prepared. The protocol contained detailed search and information retrieval instructions including nearly five pages of keyword/phrase search terms. It is noteworthy that these search terms were aimed at locating responsive ESI, rather than identifying privileged or work-product protected documents within the population of responsive ESI. After the protocol was used to retrieve responsive ESI, Defendants reviewed it to locate documents that were beyond the scope of discovery because of privilege or work-product protection. Counsel for Defendants had previously notified the court on March 29, 2007, that individualized privilege review of the responsive documents "would delay production unnecessarily and cause undue expense." To address this concern, Defendants gave their computer forensics expert a list of keywords to be used to search and retrieve privileged and protected documents from the population of documents that were to be produced to Plaintiff. However, Defendants' counsel also acknowledged the possibility of inadvertent disclosure of privileged/protected documents, given the volume of documents that were to be produced, and requested that the court approve a "clawback agreement" fashioned to address the concerns. . . . However, on April 27, 2007, Defendants' counsel notified the court that because Judge Garbis recently had extended the discovery deadline by four months, Defendants would be able to conduct a document-by-document privilege review, thereby making a clawback agreement unnecessary. Accordingly, Defendants abandoned their efforts to obtain a clawback agreement and committed to undertaking an individualized document review. Following their privilege review, Defendants made their ESI production to Plaintiff in September 2007. . . . [B]y the time of this production, Defendants had discharged their local attorneys . . . and brought in new counsel. . . . Plaintiff's counsel began their review of the materials. They soon discovered documents that potentially were privileged or work-product protected and immediately segregated this information and notified counsel for Defendants of its production, following this same procedure each time they identified potentially privileged/protected information. Defendants' Counsel, Mr. Schmid, responded by asserting that the production of any privileged or protected information had been inadvertent. Defendants also belatedly provided Plaintiff with a series of privilege logs, purportedly identifying the documents that had been withheld from production pursuant to Fed. R. Civ. P. 26(b)(5).

The parties disagree substantially in their characterization of how Defendants conducted their review for privileged and protected documents before the ESI productions were made to Plaintiff. Defendants contend that after the joint ESI search protocol was implemented and the responsive ESI identified, their computer forensics expert, Ms. Genevive Turner, "conducted a privilege search using approximately seventy different keyword search terms . . . [that] had been decided upon previously by Mr. Pappas, his former attorney, Christopher Mohr, and another attorney, F. Stephen Schmid. . . . All documents which were returned during the keyword search were segregated and provided to one of Mr. Pappas' attorneys, John G. Monkman, Jr. for the first phase of the pre-production privilege review." This characterization, however, is somewhat misleading. In actuality, after the joint retrieval protocol had been executed, Ms. Turner determined that there were some ESI files (4.9 gigabytes) that were in text-searchable format and others (33.7 gigabytes) that were not. Turner conducted a search for privileged material on the text-searchable files using the seventy keywords developed by

M. Pappas, Mohr, and Schmid. As to the non-text-searchable files, she produced them to Monkman for manual privilege review. Monkman reviewed each of the files identified as privileged/protected by Turner based on her keyword searches. Additionally, Monkman and M. Pappas teamed up to begin doing a "page-by-page" manual privilege review of the non-text-searchable ESI files. "[D]ue to the compressed schedule and time constraints in reviewing these tens of thousands of documents within the time permitted, this review was undertaken by reviewing the page titles of the documents. Documents whose page titles indicated that the privilege might be applicable were reviewed in their entirety by Mr. Pappas or me. This was the only way for us to complete the unwieldy review of these documents within the time permitted." . . .

The implied conclusion that the court is invited to draw, from the limited information provided by the Defendants, is that the 165 documents that are the subject of the present motion were contained within the population of non-text-searchable ESI files that were produced by the Defendants to the Plaintiff, making their production inadvertent. However, this inference is not so easily drawn.

First, the Defendants are regrettably vague in their description of the seventy keywords used for the text-searchable ESI privilege review, how they were developed, how the search was conducted, and what quality controls were employed to assess their reliability and accuracy. . . . [N]othing is known from the affidavits provided to the court regarding their qualifications for designing a search and information retrieval strategy that could be expected to produce an effective and reliable privilege review. As will be discussed, while it is universally acknowledged that keyword searches are useful tools for search and retrieval of ESI, all keyword searches are not created equal; and there is a growing body of literature that highlights the risks associated with conducting an unreliable or inadequate keyword search or relying exclusively on such searches for privilege review. Additionally, the Defendants do not assert that any sampling was done of the text-searchable ESI files that were determined not to contain privileged information on the basis of the keyword search to see if the search results were reliable. Common sense suggests that even a properly designed and executed keyword search may prove to be over-inclusive or under-inclusive, resulting in the identification of documents as privileged which are not, and non-privileged which, in fact, are. The only prudent way to test the reliability of the keyword search is to perform some appropriate sampling of the documents determined to be privileged and those determined not to be in order to arrive at a comfort level that the categories are neither over-inclusive nor under-inclusive. There is no evidence on the record that the Defendants did so in this case. Rather, it appears from the information that they provided to the court that they simply turned over to the Plaintiff all the text-searchable ESI files that were identified by the keyword search Turner performed as non-privileged, as well as the non-text-searchable files that Monkman and M. Pappas' limited title page search determined not to be privileged. . . .

VSI vigorously disputes Defendants' assertion that the text-searchable ESI received by Defendants' computer forensic expert, Turner, following the execution of the joint search and retrieval protocol was in a format that was difficult to search for privileged or protected materials. Plaintiff contends that it was able to do a keyword search of the text-searchable ESI produced by Defendants in about one hour using a "readily-available desktop search tool." VSI further contends that the non-text-searchable files that Monkman and M. Pappas reviewed by looking at the title pages consisted primarily of image files, such as photographs, catalogs, and drawings, which are not likely to contain privileged or protected information. Most importantly, however, the Plaintiff argues that the Defendants' complaint—that they could not effectively conduct a privilege review of the non-text-searchable files because there were so many of them—is a red herring because "the privileged materials [that are the subject of this motion] were all in text and thus were all searchable using standard text search tools. Contrary to Mr. Pappas' assertion, a majority of the .PDF files in the ESI were searchable using readily available search tools . . . within Adobe Acrobat."

Thus, according to the Plaintiff, the Defendants have waived any claim to attorney-client privilege or work-product protection for the 165 documents at issue because they failed to take reasonable precautions by performing a faulty privilege review of the text-searchable files and by failing to detect the presence of the 165 documents, which were then given to the Plaintiff as part of Defendants' ESI production. . . .

As this court discussed in some detail in *Hopson*, 232 F.R.D. at 235-38, courts have taken three different approaches when deciding whether the inadvertent production to an adversary of attorney-client privileged or work-product protected materials constitutes a waiver. Under the most lenient approach there is no waiver because there has not been a knowing and intentional relinquishment of the privilege/protection; under the most strict approach, there is a waiver because once disclosed, there can no longer be any expectation of confidentiality; and under the intermediate one, the court balances a number of factors to determine whether the producing party exercised reasonable care under the circumstances to prevent against disclosure of privileged and protected information, and if so, there is no waiver. . . .

The intermediate test requires the court to balance the following factors to determine whether inadvertent production of attorney-client privileged materials waives the privilege: (1) the reasonableness of the precautions taken to prevent inadvertent disclosure; (2) the number of inadvertent disclosures; (3) the extent of the disclosures; (4) any delay in measures taken to rectify the disclosure; and (5) overriding interests in justice. [Citations omitted.] The first of these factors militates most strongly in favor of a finding that Defendants waived the privilege in this case. . . .

Defendants, who bear the burden of proving that their conduct was reasonable for purposes of assessing whether they waived attorney-client privilege by producing the 165 documents to the Plaintiff, have failed to provide the court with information regarding: the keywords used; the rationale for their selection; the qualifications of M. Pappas and his attorneys to design an effective and reliable search and information retrieval method; whether the search was a simple keyword search, or a more sophisticated one, such as one employing Boolean proximity operators; or whether they analyzed the results of the search to assess its reliability, appropriateness for the task, and the quality of its implementation. While keyword searches have long been recognized as appropriate and helpful for ESI search and retrieval, there are well-known limitations and risks associated with them, and proper selection and implementation obviously involves technical, if not scientific knowledge. [Citations omitted.] . . .

Use of search and information retrieval methodology, for the purpose of identifying and withholding privileged or work-product protected information from production, requires the utmost care in selecting methodology that is appropriate for the task because the consequence of failing to do so, as in this case, may be the disclosure of privileged/protected information to an adverse party, resulting in a determination by the court that the privilege/protection has been waived. Selection of the appropriate search and information retrieval technique requires careful advance planning by persons qualified to design effective search methodology. The implementation of the methodology selected should be tested for quality assurance; and the party selecting the methodology must be prepared to explain the rationale for the method chosen to the court, demonstrate that it is appropriate for the task, and show that it was properly implemented. . . .

Further, the Defendants' attempt to justify what was done, by complaining that the volume of ESI needing review and time constraints presented them with no other choice is simply unpersuasive. Defendants were aware of the danger of inadvertent production of privileged/protected information and initially sought the protections of a non-waiver agreement. . . . Had they not voluntarily abandoned their request for a court-approved non-waiver agreement, they would have been protected from waiver. . . . According to Defendants' version of the facts, when they undertook an individualized review of the non-text-searchable ESI and determined that they could only review the title pages, they neither sought an extension of time from the court to complete an individualized review nor reinstated their request for a court-approved non-waiver agreement. . . . In these circumstances, Defendants' protests that they did their best and that their conduct was reasonable rings particularly hollow.

The remaining factors to be assessed under the intermediate test may be quickly disposed of. The Defendants produced 165 asserted privileged/protected documents to the Plaintiff, so this case does not present an instance of a single document slipping through the cracks. Further, the court's *in camera* review of the documents reflects that many of them are e-mail and other communications between the Defendants and their various attorneys, as well as draft discovery responses, documents relating to settlements in unrelated litigation, comments from M. Pappas to counsel regarding discovery responses, and e-mail correspondence between M. Pappas and Ms. Turner, the ESI forensic expert retained by the Defendants. Thus, the disclosures were substantive—including numerous communications between defendants and their counsel. . . . [A]ny order issued now by the court to attempt to redress these disclosures would be the equivalent of closing the barn door after the animals have already run away. [Citations omitted.] And, while the precise dates of the disclosures of the documents at issue are not clear . . . it is noteworthy that the Defendants did not discover the disclosure, but rather the Plaintiff made the discovery and notified the Defendants that potentially privileged/protected ESI had been produced. Therefore, this is not an instance in which a party inadvertently produced privileged information to an adversary, discovered the disclosure promptly, and then took immediate steps to inform the adversary that they had received the information inadvertently, thus demanding that it be returned.

While Defendants' counsel did assert privilege and inadvertent production promptly after being notified by the Plaintiff of the production of possible privileged/protected information, the more important period of delay in this case is the one-week period between production by the Defendants and the time of the discovery by the Plaintiff of the disclosures—a period during which the Defendants failed to discover the disclosure. Finally, the Defendants have pointed to no overriding interests in justice that would excuse them from the consequences of producing privileged/protected materials. The Plaintiff is blameless, but the Defendants are not, having failed to take reasonable precautions to prevent the disclosure of privileged information, including the voluntary abandonment of the non-waiver agreement that the Plaintiff was willing to sign. Every waiver of the attorney-client privilege produces unfortunate consequences for the party that disclosed the information. If that alone were sufficient to constitute an injustice, there would never be a waiver. The only "injustice" in this matter is that done by Defendants to themselves. [Citations omitted.] . . .

For the reasons stated, the court finds that the Defendants waived any privilege or work-product protection for the 165 documents at issue by disclosing them to the Plaintiff. Accordingly, the Plaintiff may use these documents as evidence in this case, provided they are otherwise admissible. . . .

Questions about the Case

1. What kind of information was contained in the documents that were inadvertently produced by the defendants' counsel? Would this information have ordinarily been protected by the attorney-client privilege?
2. What kind of review did the defendants' lawyers perform to guard against privileged documents being produced to opposing counsel? What did the court say about the adequacy of this review?
3. What is a "clawback" agreement? Why did the parties not have one? Would the outcome have been different if there had been one?
4. What are the three kinds of tests that courts can use when deciding whether the privilege has been waived when there has been an inadvertent disclosure? Which test did this court use? What are the factors that will be considered under this test?
5. Federal Rule of Evidence 502 provides that a disclosure "does not operate as a waiver . . . if (1) the disclosure is inadvertent; (2) the holder of the privilege or protection took reasonable steps to prevent disclosure; and (3) the holder promptly took reasonable steps to rectify the error, including (if applicable) following Federal Rule of Civil Procedure 26(b)(5)(B)." Would the outcome have been different if this rule had been in effect at the time of the disclosure? See *Amobi v. Dist. of Columbia Dep't of Corrections*, 262 F.R.D. 45 (D.C. 2009), where the court found waiver for inadequacy of precautions after the adoption of Fed. R. Evid. 502.

The following case involves a lawyer who received and used confidential/privileged information from an anonymous source in litigation.

Merits Incentives, LLC v. Eighth Judicial District Court of the State of Nevada

262 P.3d 720, 127 Nev. Adv. Op. 63 (2011)

Petitioners Merits Incentives, LLC, Ramon DeSage, and Cadeau Express, Inc. (collectively, "petitioners"), contracted with Bumble & Bumble, LLC (Bumble) to distribute Bumble's products to the Wynn Hotel in Las Vegas, Nevada. After entering into the contract with petitioners, Bumble discovered that some of its products were being sold at unauthorized retailers such as CVS, Rite Aid, and Walgreens. Bumble sued petitioners for breach of contract, fraud, and injunctive relief because of the alleged distribution of Bumble products by petitioners to entities other than those authorized by the parties' contract.

After filing suit, one of Bumble's lawyers, John H. Mowbray, received an anonymous package from Lebanon containing a disk with confidential/privileged information regarding the distributor. The disk was from an anonymous source who subsequently was discovered to be a fired former logistics engineer for distributor Cadeau Express. Bumble's lawyer notified petitioners that he had received the information and petitioners did not immediately object. Later, petitioners filed a motion to disqualify Mowbray based on his use of the information.

The anonymous package was received by Mowbray on September 24, 2009. On October 15, 2009, less than one month later, Mowbray served on petitioners a supplemental NRCP 16.1 mandatory pretrial discovery disclosure (16.1 disclosure). The third of three disclosures identified a "[d]isk received by Bumble and Bumble on September 24, 2009, from an unidentified source." The Rule 16.1 disclosure also included a copy of the disk and a copy of the envelope it arrived in, which bore Lebanese stamps and the phrase "[h]ighly [c]onfidential." On October 19, 2009, Bumble served an amended supplemental Rule 16.1 disclosure on petitioners and provided another identical copy of the disk. At the time, petitioners did not inform Bumble that they objected to Bumble having the disk, and they did not file any motions with the court to preclude Bumble's use of the disk or its contents. Most documents on the disk were not privileged. Mowbray did not review the one privileged document (a draft affidavit).

The Eighth Judicial District Court, Clark County, Nevada opined that the "opposing party did not show any prejudice resulting from affidavit's disclosure, and client would suffer prejudice if it had to retain new counsel due to complexity of litigation."

The court "concluded that petitioners failed to show that any of the documents, except a draft affidavit, contained on the disk were privileged. The court excluded the use of the draft affidavit, but otherwise allowed the use of the documents contained on the disk. Despite the one privileged document on the disk, the court concluded that Mowbray 'acted reasonably and in accordance with the Nevada Rules of Professional Conduct with respect to the documents and the Disk.' . . ." Petitioners then sought a writ of mandamus to compel the judge to disqualify Mowbray but did not seek dismissal of the underlying case.

The Nevada Supreme Court denied the writ and clarified the proper analysis for disqualification. The Court held that: "1. attorney did not violate any ethical duties; 2. as a matter of first impression, an attorney who receives documents regarding a case from an anonymous source must promptly notify opposing counsel or risk being in violation of ethical duties and of being disqualified as counsel; 3. attorney was not subject to disqualification; and 4. as a matter of first impression, in determining whether to disqualify an attorney who through no wrongdoing of his or her own received an opponent's privileged materials, court considers the nonexhaustive list of factors listed in *In re Meador*, 968 S.W.2d 346 (Tex.1998)."

The opinion first noted that Mowbray did not violate any ethical rules and that Nevada Bar Rule 4.4(b), which governs inadvertent disclosures in Nevada (and is similar to Florida Bar Rule 4-4.4(b)), did not apply because the disclosure was from an anonymous third party, not the opposing party/counsel, and was intentional rather than inadvertent. Nevada Bar Rule 4.4(a) (prohibiting methods of obtaining evidence that violate the rights of a third person), and Nevada Bar Rule 8.4(d) (prohibiting conduct prejudicial to the administration of justice), also did not apply because those rules require some affirmative action by the lawyer but Mowbray had passively received the information.

Absent any controlling authority, the opinion analogized to Nevada Bar Rule 4.4(b) and imposed a requirement that lawyers who receive anonymous information regarding a case must promptly notify opposing counsel. Failure to do so could result in an ethical violation and/or disqualification of the lawyer. The opinion also found that the trial court did not abuse its discretion by refusing to disqualify Mowbray because he had promptly notified opposing counsel of the anonymous disclosure and had declined to review the privileged document.

The opinion adopted the *Meador* multifactor analysis used by the Texas Supreme Court for the trial court's determination of the disqualification question. The list of factors includes but is not limited to: 1. whether the lawyer knew or should have known that the material was privileged; 2. the promptness with which the lawyer notified the opposing side of the receipt of the privileged information; 3. the extent to which the lawyer reviewed and digested the privileged information; 4. the significance of the privileged information; *i.e.*, the extent to which the disclosure may prejudice the moving party's claim or defense, and the extent to which the return of the documents will mitigate any prejudice; 5. the extent to which the moving party may be at fault for the unauthorized disclosure; and 6. if and to what extent the non-moving party will suffer prejudice from the disqualification.

The court concluded that although there is no Nevada Rule of Professional Conduct that specifically governs an attorney's actions under these facts, the attorney in this case fulfilled any ethical duties by giving prompt notification to opposing counsel, soon after his receipt of the disk from an unidentified source, through an NRCP 16.1 disclosure.

Questions about the Case

1. How did the Nevada Supreme Court come to hear this case? What was the lower court's ruling?
2. What was the basis for the petitioners' writ of mandamus? Why did the petitioners seek to disqualify the lawyer?
3. Should a lawyer or paralegal review information or documents received from an anonymous source during the course of litigation?
4. Did the lower court abuse its discretion by refusing to disqualify the lawyer?
5. What factor analysis did the Nevada Supreme Court consider in its decision? Examine how each of these factors relates to the court's decision.
6. What does the court say about the proper grounds for disqualification? Which rules are applicable to the court's ruling?
7. What requirements does the court impose on lawyers who receive anonymous information?

In the following case, a lawyer tried to use a copy of the inadvertently disclosed notes of opposing counsel to impeach experts at a deposition. The notes were prepared in part by a paralegal.

Rico v. Mitsubishi Motors Corp.
42 Cal. 4th 807, 171 P.3d 1092, 68 Cal. Rptr. 3d 758 (2007)

Here we consider what action is required of an attorney who receives privileged documents through inadvertence and whether the remedy of disqualification is appropriate.

Two Mitsubishi corporations (collectively Mitsubishi or defendants), and the California Department of Transportation (Caltrans), were sued by various plaintiffs after a Mitsubishi Montero rolled over while being driven on a freeway. Subsequently, Mitsubishi representatives met with their lawyers, James Yukevich and Alexander Calfo, and two designated defense experts to discuss their litigation strategy and vulnerabilities. Mitsubishi's case manager, Jerome Rowley, also attended the meeting. Rowley and Yukevich had worked together over a few years. Yukevich asked Rowley to take notes at the meeting and indicated specific areas to be summarized. The trial court later found that Rowley, who had typed the notes on Yukevich's computer, had acted as Yukevich's paralegal. At the end of the six-hour session, Rowley returned the computer and never saw a printed version of the notes. Yukevich printed only one copy of the notes, which he later edited and annotated. Yukevich never intentionally showed the notes to anyone, and the court determined that the sole purpose of the document was to help Yukevich defend the case.

The notes are written in a dialogue style and summarize conversations among Yukevich, Calfo, and the experts. They are dated, but not labeled as "confidential" or "work product." The printed copy of these compiled and annotated notes is the document at issue here.

Less than two weeks after the strategy session, Yukevich deposed plaintiffs' expert witness, Anthony Sances, at the offices of plaintiffs' counsel, Raymond Johnson. Yukevich, court reporter Karen Kay, and Caltrans counsel Darin Flagg were told that Johnson and Sances would be late for the deposition. After waiting in the conference room for some time, Yukevich went to the restroom, leaving his briefcase, computer, and case file in the room. The printed document from the strategy session was in the case file. While Yukevich was away, Johnson and Sances arrived. Johnson asked Kay and Flagg to leave the conference room. Kay and Flagg's departure left only the plaintiffs' representatives and counsel in the conference room. Yukevich returned to find Kay and Flagg standing outside. Yukevich waited approximately 5 minutes, then knocked and asked to retrieve his briefcase, computer, and file. After a brief delay, he was allowed to do so.

Somehow, Johnson acquired Yukevich's notes. Johnson maintained that they were accidentally given to him by the court reporter. Yukevich insisted that they were taken from his file while only Johnson and plaintiffs' team were in the conference room. As a result, Mitsubishi moved to disqualify plaintiffs' attorneys and experts. The trial court ordered an evidentiary hearing to determine how Johnson obtained the document.

The court reporter was deposed and denied any specific recollection of the Sances deposition. She could not testify what she had done with the deposition exhibits that night and could only relate her general practice. She said she generally collects exhibits and puts them in a plastic covering. She did not remember ever having given exhibits to an attorney. She also testified that she had never seen the document in question. If documents other than exhibits remain on a conference table, she leaves them there. The trial court found that the Sances deposition took place over approximately eight hours. It was a document-intense session and documents were placed on the conference table.

Another member of plaintiffs' legal team submitted a declaration supporting Johnson's assertion that he received the document from the reporter. The court ultimately concluded that the defense had failed to establish that Johnson had taken the notes from Yukevich's file. It thus ruled that Johnson came into the document's possession through inadvertence.

The court found the 12-page document was dated, but not otherwise labeled. It contained notations by Yukevich. Johnson admitted that he knew within a minute or two that the document related to the defendants' case. He knew that Yukevich did not intend to produce it and that it would be a "powerful impeachment document." Nevertheless, Johnson made a copy of the document. He scrutinized and made his own notes on it. He gave copies to his co-counsel and his experts, all of whom studied the document. Johnson specifically discussed the contents of the document with each of his experts.

A week after he acquired Yukevich's notes, Johnson used them during the deposition of defense expert Geoffrey Germane. The notes purportedly indicate that the defense experts made statements at the strategy session that were inconsistent with their deposition testimony. Johnson used the document while questioning Germane, asking about Germane's participation in the strategy session.

Defense Counsel Calfo defended the Germane deposition. Yukevich did not attend. Calfo had never seen the document and was not given a copy during the deposition. When he asked about the document's source, Johnson vaguely replied . . . , "It was put in Dr. Sances' file." Calfo repeatedly objected to the "whole line of inquiry with respect to an unknown document." He specifically said that, "I don't even know where this exhibit came from."

Only after the deposition did Johnson give a copy of the document to Calfo, who contacted Yukevich. When Yukevich realized that Johnson had his only copy of the strategy session notes and had used it at the deposition, he and Calfo wrote to Johnson demanding the return of all duplicates. The letter was faxed the day after Germane's deposition. The next day, defendants moved to disqualify plaintiffs' legal team and their experts on the ground that they had become privy to and had used Yukevich's work product. As a result, they complained, Johnson's unethical use of the notes and his revelation of them to co-counsel and their experts irremediably prejudiced defendants.

The trial court concluded that the notes were absolutely privileged by the work product rule. The court also held that Johnson had acted unethically by examining the document more closely than was necessary to determine that its contents were confidential, by failing to notify Yukevich that he had a copy of the document, and by surreptitiously using it to gain maximum adversarial value from it. The court determined that Johnson's violation of the work product rule had prejudiced the defense and "the bell cannot be 'unrung' by use of in limine orders." Accordingly, the court ordered plaintiffs' attorneys and experts disqualified.

Plaintiffs appealed the disqualification order. The Court of Appeal affirmed. . . .

Plaintiffs contend that the Court of Appeal erred by holding that the entire document was protected as attorney work product. We reject that contention. The Legislature has protected attorney work product under California Code of Civil Procedure section 2018.030, which provides, "(a) A writing that reflects an attorney's impressions, conclusions, opinions, or legal research or theories is not discoverable under any circumstances. (b) The work product of an attorney, other than a writing described in subdivision (a), is not discoverable unless the court determines that denial of discovery will unfairly prejudice the party seeking discovery in preparing that party's claim or defense or will result in an injustice." . . .

Thus, the codified work product doctrine absolutely protects from discovery writings that contain an "attorney's impressions, conclusions, opinions, or legal research or theories." [Citations omitted.] The protection extends to an attorney's written notes about a witness's statements. [Citations omitted.] "[A]ny such notes or recorded statements taken by defendants' counsel would be protected by the absolute work product privilege because they would reveal counsel's 'impressions, conclusions, opinions, or legal research or theories' within the meaning of [the work product doctrine]." [Citation omitted.] When a witness's statement and the attorney's impressions are inextricably intertwined, the work product doctrine provides that absolute protection is afforded to all of the attorney's notes.

Plaintiffs urge that the document is not work product because it reflects the statements of declared experts. They are incorrect. The document is not a transcript of the August 28, 2002 strategy session, nor is it a verbatim record of the experts' own statements. It contains Rowley's summaries of points from the strategy session, made at Yukevich's direction. Yukevich also edited the document in order to add his own thoughts and comments, further inextricably intertwining his personal impressions with the summary. [Citation omitted.] In this regard, the trial court found: "As to the content of the document, although it doesn't contain overt statements setting forth the lawyer's conclusions, its very existence is owed to the lawyer's thought process. The document reflects not only the strategy, but also the attorney's opinion as to the important issues in the case. Directions were provided by Mr. Yukevich as to the key pieces of information to be recorded, and Mr. Yukevich also added his own input as to the important details, by inserting other words in the notes. The attorney's impressions of the case were the filter through which all the discussions at the conference were passed through on the way to the page." . . .

Although the notes were written in dialogue format and contain information attributed to Mitsubishi's experts, the document does not qualify as an *expert's* report, writing, declaration, or testimony. The notes reflect the *paralegal's* summary along with *counsel's* thoughts and impressions about the case. The document was absolutely protected work product because it contained the ideas of Yukevich and his legal team about the case. (§2018.030, subd. (a).)

Because the document is work product we consider what ethical duty Johnson owed once he received it. Plaintiffs rely on *Aerojet-General Corp. v. Transport Indemnity Insurance* (1993), 18 Cal. App. 4th 996 (*Aerojet*), to argue that because the document was inadvertently received, Johnson was duty bound to use the nonprivileged portions of it to his clients' advantage. This argument fails. *Aerojet* is distinguishable because there are no "unprivileged portions" of the document. . . .

In *State Fund*, *supra*, 70 Cal. App. 4th 644, the plaintiff sent defendant's attorney (Telanoff) three boxes of documents that were identical to the documents provided during discovery. Inadvertently, plaintiff also sent 273 pages of forms entitled, "Civil Litigation Claims Summary," marked as "ATTORNEY-CLIENT COMMUNICATION/ ATTORNEY WORK PRODUCT," and with the warning, "DO NOT CIRCULATE OR DUPLICATE." In addition, "[t]he word 'CONFIDENTIAL' [was] repeatedly printed around the perimeter of the first page of the form." When counsel discovered the mistake and demanded return of the documents, Telanoff refused. The trial court, relying on American Bar Association (ABA) Formal Ethics Opinion No. 92-368 (Nov. 10, 1992), imposed monetary sanctions.

The Court of Appeal framed the issue as follows: "[W]hat is a lawyer to do when he or she receives through the inadvertence of opposing counsel documents plainly subject to the attorney-client privilege?" [Citation omitted.] . . . The *State Fund* court went on to articulate the standard to be applied prospectively: "When a lawyer who receives materials that obviously appear to be subject to an attorney-client privilege or otherwise clearly appear to be confidential and privileged and where it is reasonably apparent that the materials were provided or made available through inadvertence, the lawyer receiving such materials should refrain from examining the materials any more than is essential to ascertain if the materials are privileged, and shall immediately notify the sender that he or she possesses material that appears to be privileged. The parties may then proceed to resolve the situation by agreement or may resort to the court for guidance with the benefit of protective orders and other judicial intervention as may be justified." [Citation omitted.] To ensure that its decision was clear in setting forth the applicable standard in these cases, the court explicitly stated that it "declared the standard governing the conduct of California lawyers" in such instances.

The existing *State Fund* rule is a fair and reasonable approach. The rule supports the work product doctrine [citation omitted], and is consistent with the state's policy to "[p]reserve the rights of attorneys to prepare cases for trial with that degree of privacy necessary to encourage them to prepare their cases thoroughly and to investigate not only the favorable but the unfavorable aspects of those cases" and to "[p]revent attorneys from taking undue advantage of their adversary's industry and efforts." . . .

The *State Fund* rule also addresses the practical problem of inadvertent disclosure in the context of today's reality that document production may involve massive numbers of documents. A contrary holding could severely disrupt the discovery process. As amicus curiae The Product Liability Advisory Council, Inc. argues, "Even apart from the inadvertent disclosure problem, the party responding to a request for mass production must engage in a laborious, time consuming process. If the document producer is confronted with the additional prospect that any privileged documents inadvertently produced will become fair game for the opposition, the minute screening and re-screening that inevitably would follow not only would add enormously to that burden but would slow the pace of discovery to a degree sharply at odds with the general goal of expediting litigation."

Finally, we note that "[a]n attorney has an obligation not only to protect his client's interests but also to respect the legitimate interests of fellow members of the bar, the judiciary, and the administration of justice." [Citation omitted.] The *State Fund* rule holds attorneys to a reasonable standard of professional conduct when confidential or privileged materials are inadvertently disclosed.

Here, it is true that Yukevich's notes were not so clearly flagged as confidential as were the forms in *State Fund*. . . . But, as the Court of Appeal observed, "[T]he absence of prominent notations of confidentiality does not make them any less privileged." The *State Fund* rule is an objective standard. In applying the rule, courts must consider whether reasonably competent counsel, knowing the circumstances of the litigation, would have concluded the materials were privileged, how much review was reasonably necessary to draw that conclusion, and when counsel's examination should have ended. . . .

The standard was properly and easily applied here. Johnson admitted that after a minute or two of review he realized the notes related to the case and that Yukevich did not intend to reveal them. Johnson's own admissions and subsequent conduct clearly demonstrate that he violated the *State Fund* rule. . . .

The next question is whether disqualification was the proper remedy. . . .

The *State Fund* court held that "'[m]ere exposure'" to an adversary's confidences is insufficient, standing alone, to warrant an attorney's disqualification. (*State Fund, supra*, 70 Cal. App. 4th at p. 657.) The court counseled against a draconian rule that "'[could] nullify a party's right to representation by chosen counsel any time inadvertence or devious design put an adversary's confidences in an attorney's mailbox.'" However, the court did not "rule out the possibility that in an appropriate case, disqualification might be justified if an attorney inadvertently receives confidential materials and fails to conduct himself or herself in the manner specified above, assuming other factors compel disqualification." . . .

The Court of Appeal properly concluded that such use of the document undermined the defense experts' opinions and placed defendants at a great disadvantage. Without disqualification of plaintiffs' counsel and their experts, the damage caused by Johnson's use and dissemination of the notes was irreversible. Under the circumstances presented in this case, the trial court did not abuse its discretion by ordering disqualification for violation of the *State Fund* rule.

Plaintiffs attempt to justify Johnson's use of the document by accusing the defense experts of giving false testimony during their depositions. Plaintiffs allege that the statements attributed to the experts in the document contradicted their deposition statements and that the experts lied about the technical evidence involved in the case. As an initial matter, we are not persuaded that any of the defense experts ever actually adopted as their own the statements attributed to them. The document is not a verbatim transcript of the strategy session, but Rowley's summary of points that Yukevich directed him to note. Yukevich then edited the document, adding his own thoughts and comments. As the trial court observed, the document was an interpretation and summary of what others thought the experts were saying.

Moreover, we agree with the Court of Appeal that, "when a writing is protected under the absolute attorney work product privilege, courts do not invade upon the attorney's thought processes by evaluating the content of the writing.

. . . We also reject plaintiffs' argument that the crime or fraud exception should apply to privileged work product in this civil proceeding. Under the work product doctrine "[a] writing that reflects an attorney's impressions, conclusions, opinions, or legal research or theories *is not discoverable under any circumstances.* (§2018.030, subd. (a), italics added.) . . . By its own terms, the crime or fraud exception does not apply here.

We affirm the Court of Appeal's judgment.

Questions about the Case

1. What was the nature of the document at issue? Who prepared it? What was it to be used for? What was the role of the paralegal in preparing this document? Was this important?
2. Why did the court decide that the document did not fall strictly into the attorney-client privilege, but was instead protected by the work product rule?
3. What did the plaintiff's lawyer do that was unethical? What should he have done?
4. What would have happened if California followed the current Model Rule on receipt of inadvertently disclosed documents? Would the outcome have been the same? Does the court seem to know that the ABA has reversed its stance on this issue? Does the court care?

In this criminal case, the prosecutor gains access to e-mail communications between a defendant and his lawyer, and the court must decide whether the privilege has been violated and what to do about it.

State v. Lenarz
301 Conn. 417, 22 A.3d 536 (2011)

... As part of its investigation into the incident that formed the basis for the charges in the Simsbury case, the Simsbury police department obtained a search warrant for the defendant's residence. During the search, which took place on November 17, 2004, the police seized a computer, which they sent to the Connecticut Forensic Science Laboratory (state laboratory) to be forensically searched. The next day, at the defendant's arraignment, defense counsel advised the trial court, that certain materials in the computer were subject to the attorney-client privilege and asked the court to fashion orders to protect the defendant's rights. The court ordered that "any communications from [defense counsel] to [the defendant] or from [the defendant] to [defense counsel] remain unpublished [and] unread." The court entered a similar order with respect to communications to and from the defendant's private investigator.

During its examination of the defendant's computer, the state laboratory discovered voluminous written materials containing detailed discussions of the defendant's trial strategy in the Granby cases. The state laboratory read and copied much of this material and transmitted it to the Simsbury police department along with its report. In turn, the Simsbury police department forwarded the materials and the report to the prosecutor. At a meeting between the prosecutor and defense counsel some time in September, 2005, the prosecutor provided defense counsel with a copy of the materials that he had received from the Simsbury police department. Defense counsel immediately requested a meeting with Judge Scheinblum in chambers, at which he advised the judge that the prosecutor had read materials that were subject to the attorney-client privilege. The trial court then ordered the police departments in Simsbury and Granby and the prosecutor to turn over any "questionable material" in their possession to the court and ordered that the material be placed under seal. Although it is unclear from the record how long the prosecutor had been in possession of the privileged communications before the September 2005 meeting, defense counsel represented at a hearing on a motion to suppress the materials seized under the search warrant that the prosecutor had had the materials for six weeks, and the prosecutor did not dispute this claim.

The defendant then filed a motion to dismiss the informations in the Granby cases on the ground that the state had intentionally invaded the attorney-client privilege, thereby depriving the defendant of his right to counsel under the sixth amendment to the United States constitution. The defendant argued that the intrusion had resulted in substantial prejudice to him because the privileged communications contained detailed trial strategy. The state admitted that the prosecutor had read all of the materials and did not dispute that the documents contained trial strategy, but claimed that, because the prosecutor had not conducted any additional investigation and had not interviewed any additional witnesses as a result of reading the materials, the defendant had suffered no prejudice. In addition, the state claimed that the prosecutor had not willfully violated the attorney-client privilege, but had obtained the privileged materials in good faith. Accordingly, the state argued that the appropriate remedy for its allegedly unintentional invasion of the attorney-client privilege was the suppression of the privileged communications. . . .

After an evidentiary hearing, the trial court denied the defendant's motion to dismiss. . . . After a trial, the jury returned a verdict of not guilty on all charges except risk of injury to a child in violation of §53-21 (a) (1) . . . and the trial court rendered judgments in accordance with the verdict. The defendant appealed to the Appellate Court from the judgment of conviction. . . .

The defendant claims on appeal that the trial court improperly denied his motion to dismiss. Specifically, he claims that the trial court's finding that the state had not intentionally invaded the attorney-client privilege when it read the materials taken from his computer was clearly erroneous and that the intentional invasion constituted a per se violation of the sixth amendment right to counsel for which dismissal is the sole appropriate remedy. In addition, the defendant claims that he was irreparably prejudiced by the prosecutor's invasion of the privileged material because it contained trial strategy. The state counters that, because the trial court properly found that the invasion of the privileged documents was unintentional, and because the defendant failed to establish that he was prejudiced by the disclosure, the trial court properly denied the motion to dismiss. The state further contends that, even if the defendant was prejudiced, the appropriate remedy would have been for the trial court to order a prosecutor who had not read the privileged documents to try the case, and the defendant had waived this remedy.

For the reasons that follow, we conclude generally that prejudice may be presumed when the prosecutor has invaded the attorney-client privilege by reading privileged materials containing trial strategy, regardless of whether the invasion of the attorney-client privilege was intentional. We further conclude that the state may rebut that presumption by clear and convincing evidence. Finally, we conclude that, when a prosecutor has intruded into privileged communications containing a defendant's trial strategy and the state has failed to rebut the presumption of prejudice, the court, sua sponte, must immediately provide appropriate relief to prevent prejudice to the defendant.

In the present case we conclude that, because the privileged materials at issue contained the defendant's trial strategy and were disclosed to the prosecutor, the defendant was presumptively prejudiced by the prosecutor's intrusion into the privileged documents. We further conclude that, because, after reviewing the privileged materials, the prosecutor tried the case to conclusion, the taint caused by the state's intrusion into the privileged communications would be irremediable on retrial and the charge of which the defendant was convicted must be dismissed.

We begin our analysis with a review of the law governing governmental interference with the attorney-client privilege. "Connecticut has a long-standing, strong public policy of protecting attorney-client communications. . . . This privilege was designed, in large part, to encourage full disclosure by a client to his or her attorney so as to facilitate effective legal representation." [Citations omitted.] . . .

A number of courts have held that, when the privileged communication contains details of the defendant's trial strategy, the defendant is not required to prove he was prejudiced by the governmental intrusion, but prejudice may be presumed. [Citations omitted.] . . .

Finally, a number of courts have held that the defendant is not required to prove that he was prejudiced by the government's intrusion into attorney-client communications when the intrusion was deliberate and was unjustified by any legitimate governmental interest in effective law enforcement. [Citations omitted.] . . .

We agree with the courts that have held that the burden is not on the defendant to establish that he was prejudiced when the prosecutor has intruded on attorney-client communications that contain information concerning the defendant's trial strategy. Rather, because the disclosure of such information is *inherently prejudicial*, prejudice should be presumed, regardless of whether the invasion into the attorney-client privilege was intentional. The subjective intent of the government and the identity of the party responsible for the disclosure simply have no bearing on that question.

We further conclude that the presumption of prejudice when trial strategy has been disclosed to the prosecutor may be rebuttable. For example, the state may be able to show that no person with knowledge of the privileged communications had any involvement in the investigation or prosecution of the case, the privileged communications contained only minimal information or that the state had access to all of the privileged information from other sources. In light of the important constitutional right at issue, however, we conclude that the state must rebut the presumption of prejudice by clear and convincing evidence. [Citations omitted.] . . .

In the present case, even a cursory review of the materials reveals that the defendant was presumptively prejudiced by the prosecutor's intrusion into the privileged communications taken from the defendant's computer because the privileged materials contained a highly specific and detailed trial strategy. . . .

Having concluded that the defendant was prejudiced by the prosecutor's intrusion into the privileged communications, we turn to the defendant's claim that the trial court abused its discretion when it denied his motion to dismiss. . . . [W]hen a defendant has been prejudiced by governmental intrusions into privileged communications, the remedy must be tailored to cure the prejudice. It follows that, although dismissal of criminal charges is a drastic remedy . . . [Citations omitted.] . . .

Under the circumstances of the present case, however, we conclude that a remand is not appropriate. Even if we were to assume that the state could have proved before trial that a less drastic remedy than dismissal would have been an adequate remedy, now that the case has been tried by the prosecutor who read the privileged communications, it clearly would be impossible to eliminate the potential for prejudice to the defendant with any other sanction. The prosecutor had knowledge of the defendant's trial strategy during the one-and-one-half years preceding trial and, therefore, could use the information in preparing for trial. Indeed, the record strongly suggests that the prosecutor may have revealed the defendant's trial strategy to witnesses and investigators. In addition, consciously or unconsciously, the prosecutor's knowledge of the defendant's trial strategy may have affected his selection and examination of witnesses during trial, which is now a matter of public record. Again, the record strongly suggests that the prosecutor drew on his knowledge of the privileged communications when examining the accusing witness . . . to anticipate and thereby neutralize what otherwise might have been a devastating cross-examination of that witness. . . . Finally, as we have indicated, the information in the privileged communications went to the heart of the defense in that case. Accordingly, even if the case were to be retried by a prosecutor who has not read the privileged communications, it would be impossible for the courts or the defendant to have any confidence that a second trial with a new prosecutor would be untainted by the constitutional violation in the first trial, particularly because the new prosecutor would necessarily have access to the transcript of the original trial. . . .

This is a case in which the prosecutor clearly invaded privileged communications that contained a detailed, explicit road map of the defendant's trial strategy. Compounding the problem, the prosecutor not only failed to inform the defendant and the trial court of the invasion immediately, but also continued to handle the case, to meet repeatedly with witnesses and investigators and ultimately to try the case to conclusion more than one year after the invasion occurred. Under these circumstances, any remedy other than the dismissal of the criminal charge of which the defendant was convicted would constitute a miscarriage of justice. Accordingly, we conclude that the charge of risk of injury to a child in violation of §53-21(a)(1) in Docket No. H12MCR-03-128673 must be dismissed.

The judgment is reversed only with respect to the defendant's conviction of risk of injury to a child and the case is remanded to the trial court with direction to grant the defendant's motion to dismiss that charge and to render judgment thereon; the judgments are affirmed in all other respects. . . .

Questions about the Case

1. What was the subject matter of the communications that were at the heart of this case? Were these communications covered by the attorney–client privilege or the work product rule, or both? Explain.
2. What did the prosecutor do that the court found objectionable? Was this an ethical violation? Under what rule or rules? Was it in violation of a court order? Do you think that the prosecutor should be sanctioned for this action?
3. On what basis did the court decide that the prosecutor's accessing the communication was not acceptable?
4. Once that decision was made, what were the choices of remedies? Why did the court decide on the remedy that it did?

In this case, an appellate court decision addresses the question of the duties owed when a client inadvertently discloses his attorney's privileged email communication.

McDermott Will & Emery LLP v. Superior Court

217 Cal. Rptr. 3d 47, 10 Cal. App. 5th 1083 (2017)

Marilyn H. Hausman and her husband, Richard P. Hausman, Sr. (Dick), had four children, Mary Jo, John, Teri, and Richard P. Hausman, Jr. (Rick). The primary source of the couple's considerable wealth was Marilyn's multi-million dollar investment portfolio. In 2000, Marilyn formed a holding corporation, M. Hausman, Inc. (MHI), to manage her portfolio. Marilyn was MHI's sole shareholder and director, and also served as its president. Dick served as the officer primarily responsible for making and managing MHI's investments, and joined Marilyn as a director in 2002. A few years later, Rick and William J. Cox also became directors of MHI. According to Dick, the value of MHI's portfolio grew to approximately $50 million under his management.

In approximately 2002, Marilyn and Dick hired Gibson, Dunn & Crutcher LLP (Gibson Dunn) and petitioners McDermott Will & Emery LLP and Jonathan C. Lurie (collectively, Defendants) to provide a variety of estate planning services for their family. . . . As part of their representation of the Hausman family, Defendants also represented MHI on corporate, employment, and other miscellaneous matters.

Marilyn died in June 2008, and Dick succeeded her as MHI's president. Rick and Cox also became vice presidents at that time. In 2013, Dick agreed to Rick's request to be named MHI's president so Rick could gain experience in managing MHI, but Dick continued to perform many of the president's essential functions. Soon after becoming president, Rick sought to dramatically increase his and Cox's salaries and other benefits, but Dick objected because he thought the substantial increases were not in MHI's best interests or the best interest of the various trust beneficiaries. A struggle for control of MHI ensued and Dick, Rick, and Cox engaged in protracted discussions attempting to resolve their dispute. To advise him in these discussions and about his options under the various trusts, Dick hired his own attorney, Mark Blaskey.

On August 22, 2013, Dick, Rick, Cox, Blaskey, and Lurie met to discuss their disagreement. Immediately after that meeting, Dick, Blaskey, and Jill Lindsay met to review their options. Lindsay worked for Dick for nearly 40 years, starting as his executive secretary when he was an executive with Allergan and then working personally for him after he left the company. In her capacity as Dick's personal assistant, Lindsay regularly received and maintained correspondence on Dick's behalf.

On August 27, 2013, Blaskey sent Dick a lengthy e-mail summarizing the August 22 meeting and providing legal advice to Dick about his options for resolving the dispute. The following day, Dick forwarded the Blaskey e-mail from his iPhone to "Mr. & Mrs. Gavin Shearer Herbert" at Ninetta Herbert's e-mail address. Dick's transmission did not include any additional text other than "Sent from my iPhone." That same day Ninetta forwarded the e-mail to Gavin at his e-mail address. Gavin was Marilyn's brother and Dick's brother-in-law. Gavin had not been involved in the various Hausman trusts or MHI for many years, but he was attempting to act as an intermediary or informal mediator to resolve the dispute between Dick, Rick, and Cox. Gavin engaged in several discussions with these individuals and also Lurie and Blaskey about the dispute.

Dick testified he did not intend to forward the Blaskey e-mail to Ninetta or Gavin, and did not know he had done so until the forwarded e-mail came to light approximately a year later. Dick was nearly 80 years old when he forwarded the e-mail and he explained multiple sclerosis had limited his physical dexterity. Gavin testified he did not recall receiving the Blaskey e-mail and he had not read it before it was shown to him at his deposition. He further testified that he had no idea why Dick would forward the e-mail to Ninetta, that doing so must have been a mistake, and that he never discussed the e-mail with Dick. Finally, Gavin testified he could not find a copy of the Blaskey e-mail when he was later asked to do so.

Unable to resolve the dispute with Rick and Cox, Dick exercised a power he believed he held under the various trusts to reacquire all of MHI's voting shares and seize control of the company. In October 2013, Dick filed a probate petition to confirm the actions he had taken to reacquire all MHI voting shares under the various Hausman family trusts (hereinafter, Probate Action).

In August 2014, Rick's counsel in the Probate Action, Jason Kirby, discovered a copy of the Blaskey e-mail among Rick's documents as he prepared to respond to Dick's demand to produce documents. Kirby pulled the e-mail and separately sent it to Dick's counsel, Alan Kessel, with a letter explaining the e-mail appeared to be a privileged communication between Blaskey and Dick, but that Dick later waived the privilege by forwarding it to Ninetta and Gavin. The letter further explained that Rick obtained a copy of the e-mail when Gavin handed it out at the September 4, 2013 meeting involving Rick, Cox, Pellizzon, and Gavin. Kirby asked whether Dick's counsel would claim the Blaskey e-mail still was privileged, and if so, for authority supporting that contention. Finally, Kirby assured Dick's counsel he had not used or disclosed the contents of the e-mail. This letter was the first time Dick and his attorney learned the Blaskey e-mail had been forwarded to anyone other than the original recipients, and they did not yet know the e-mail also had been forwarded to Lurie.

Dick's attorney, Kessel, responded that the Blaskey e-mail was a privileged attorney–client communication, and that Dick inadvertently disclosed the e-mail to Ninetta without intending to waive the privilege. Dick's counsel explained that Dick rarely communicated with Ninetta and never talked to her about MHI affairs, and therefore he inadvertently forwarded the e-mail to Ninetta when he was trying to forward it to Lindsay. Based on *State Comp. Ins. Fund v. WPS, Inc.* (1999) 70 Cal. App.4th 644 (*State Fund*) and *Rico v. Mitsubishi Motors Corp.* (2007) 42 Cal.4th 807 (*Rico*), Dick's counsel argued Kirby had an ethical obligation to return the inadvertently disclosed e-mail and destroy any copies. Dick's counsel also asked Kirby to contact any other party he knew had received a copy of the Blaskey e-mail, including Ninetta, Gavin, and Pellizzon, and direct them to destroy their copies.

Kirby argued neither *Rico* nor *State Fund* applied because those cases did not involve a client waiving the privilege by disclosing a communication to third parties before any litigation arose. Nonetheless, Kirby agreed to destroy all copies of the Blaskey e-mail except one, to seal that copy, and only use the copy to resolve the parties' dispute over whether Dick had waived the attorney-client privilege. Kirby also promised not to question anyone about the e-mail's content until the parties resolved the waiver issue. Finally, Kirby asserted he had no obligation to ask third parties to return the Blaskey e-mail. All parties to the Probate Action honored this agreement for several months.

In late July 2015, Defendants produced several thousand pages of documents in the Probate Action based on Dick's subpoena, and that production included a copy of the Blaskey e-mail that Gavin had forwarded to Lurie in September 2013. On August 13, 2015, the parties deposed Lurie in the Probate Action, and James Fogelman of Gibson Dunn represented Lurie in the deposition. When Rick's counsel questioned Lurie about the copy of the Blaskey e-mail that was included in

Defendants' document production, Dick's attorney, Paul George, immediately objected that the e-mail was privileged and should not be used in the deposition. George also explained that Dick's other attorney, Kessel, had asked Rick's counsel to return all copies of the e-mail. This was the first time Dick and his counsel learned the Blaskey e-mail had been forwarded to Lurie.

Fogelman claimed the Blaskey e-mail was not privileged and asserted neither he nor Defendants had ever been asked to return it. To remove any doubt, Dick's counsel therefore requested that Fogelman and his clients return all copies of the Blaskey e-mail because Dick inadvertently disclosed the privileged communication and all attorneys, including Lurie, had an ethical obligation to return or destroy inadvertently disclosed, privileged communications. Fogelman refused to return or destroy the Blaskey e-mail, disputing it was privileged because Dick had disclosed it to third parties, including Ninetta, Gavin, and Lindsay. Fogelman claimed an attorney's ethical obligation to return inadvertently disclosed documents only applied to documents that were inadvertently produced during discovery. Dick's counsel disagreed and the deposition continued. Lurie testified he reviewed the e-mail to refresh his recollection before the deposition, but he did not specifically testify about the e-mail's content.

In May 2015, Plaintiffs filed two malpractice lawsuits against Defendants based on an alleged conflict in representing various members of the Hausman family, the Hausman family trusts, and MHI (collectively, Malpractice Actions). They brought one suit in their individual capacities and as trustees under certain Hausman family trusts. They brought the second lawsuit as a derivative action on MHI's behalf. Dick has different counsel in the Malpractice Actions than he had in the Probate Action, and Defendants are represented in the Malpractice Actions by Fogelman and Gibson Dunn.

In early December 2015, Dick filed a motion in the Malpractice Actions seeking (1) a judicial determination that the Blaskey e-mail was a privileged attorney–client communication that Dick inadvertently disclosed, and (2) an order requiring Gibson Dunn to return all copies of the e-mail and striking those portions of Mary Jo's and Teri's depositions where Fogelman asked questions about the e-mail and read portions of it into the record. Defendants opposed the motion, arguing the Blaskey e-mail never was privileged based on Lindsay's inclusion as an original recipient, and Dick nonetheless waived the attorney–client privilege by disclosing the e-mail to third parties. In support, Defendants filed a copy of the Blaskey e-mail under seal. In March 2016, the trial court granted Dick's motion, and ordered Defendants to seal or return all copies of the Blaskey e-mail and seal the relevant portions of Mary Jo's and Teri's deposition transcripts. Dick served notice of entry of the order on March 15, 2016.

Less than two weeks later, Dick filed a motion to disqualify Gibson Dunn from representing Defendants in the Malpractice Actions based on its use of the Blaskey e-mail and its refusal to return it. Gibson Dunn opposed the motion, arguing it was not readily apparent from the face of the e-mail that it was an inadvertently disclosed, privileged document. Gibson Dunn further argued its disqualification was not warranted because there was no evidence its review and initial failure to return the e-mail would substantially impact the litigation. On May 25, 2016, the trial court granted Dick's motion and disqualified Gibson Dunn from representing Defendants in the Malpractice Actions. The court stayed its ruling for 30 days to allow Defendants to petition this court for relief.

On June 6, 2016, Defendants filed this writ petition seeking a writ of mandate compelling the trial court to vacate (1) its order deeming the Blaskey e-mail privileged, and (2) its order disqualifying Gibson Dunn as Defendants' counsel in the Malpractice Actions. Defendants also sought a stay of all trial court proceedings pending the resolution of this writ petition. We granted the stay request and issued an order to show cause why a writ of mandate should not issue.

Dick contends we should deny Defendants' challenge to the trial court's ruling that the Blaskey e-mail is privileged because Defendants filed their writ petition more than 60 days after Dick served notice of that ruling . . . Although there is no statutory time limit on a common law writ petition, appellate courts generally apply the same 60-day time limit applicable to appeals. But unlike appeals, appellate courts have discretion to decide a writ petition filed after the 60-day period, and typically look to whether there is any prejudice to the opposing party in doing so. (*People v. Superior Court (Lopez)* (2005) 125 Cal.App.4th 1558, 1562-1563.) Here, Dick fails to identify how deciding Defendants' challenge to the privilege ruling will prejudice him.

. . . The attorney–client privilege is a legislative creation, which courts have no power to expand or limit by implying exceptions . . . Based on the privilege, a client may refuse to disclose, and may prevent others from disclosing, confidential communications between a client and his or her attorney. (Evid. Code, §954.)

A "confidential communication between client and lawyer" is statutorily defined as "information transmitted between a client and his or her lawyer in the course of that relationship and in confidence by a means which, so far as the client is aware, discloses the information to no third persons other than those who are present to further the interest of the client in the consultation or those to whom disclosure is reasonably necessary for the transmission of the information or the accomplishment of the purpose for which the lawyer is consulted, and includes a legal opinion formed and the advice given by the lawyer in the course of that relationship." (Evid. Code, §952.)

The attorney–client privilege may be waived, but only by the holder of the privilege . . . A waiver results when the holder, without coercion, (1) has disclosed a significant part of the communication, or (2) has consented to the disclosure made by anyone else. (Evid. Code, §912 . . .)

Under the second method of waiver, "Consent to disclosure is manifested by any statement or other conduct of the holder of the privilege indicating consent to the disclosure, including failure to claim the privilege in any proceeding in which the holder has legal standing and the opportunity to claim the privilege." (Evid. Code, §912, subd. (a).)

. . . Defendants do not dispute the Blaskey e-mail was a privileged attorney–client communication, but contend the trial court erred "as a matter of law" in determining Dick did not waive the privilege. They argue the court "treat[ed] Dick's own post-hoc characterization of his intent as dispositive, while ignoring (or declining to consider) the objective, contemporaneous evidence of Dick's intent." Defendants mischaracterize the trial court's ruling and ignore the substantial evidence supporting the court's conclusion Dick did not waive the privilege.

The trial court concluded Dick did not waive the attorney–client privilege because "[t]here is no basis to find intentional waiver." In support, the court cited Dick's "unequivocal" testimony that he did not intend to forward the Blaskey e-mail to Ninetta, and he did not know how it happened. The court also noted the privilege was not waived by Dick's failure to request that Gavin and Pellizzon return the e-mail or to ask Defendants to return copies of the e-mail they produced in discovery. Finally, the court pointed out the "scenario" this case presented did not fit any of the recognized means for waiving the privilege.

Nothing in the trial court's ruling suggests the court failed to consider all the evidence in reaching its decision, and Defendants do not cite anything in the record to support their contrary contention. We presume the trial court knew and properly applied the law absent evidence to the contrary . . . Moreover, the trial court was not required to make any findings to support its ruling on the privilege motion . . . We therefore review the court's order by inferring it made all favorable findings that are supported by substantial evidence . . .

The critical question is whether there is a genuine likelihood that Gibson Dunn's review and use of the Blaskey e-mail will affect the outcome of the Malpractice Actions . . . The trial court's privilege order prevented Gibson Dunn from using the Blaskey e-mail and the portions of the deposition transcripts that referred to its content. But the court's order could not prevent Gibson Dunn from using the knowledge it acquired by carefully reviewing and analyzing the e-mail even if the e-mail itself is no longer available to the firm.

. . . Substantial evidence supports the finding that disqualification was appropriate to prevent future harm to Dick despite the privilege order because the Blaskey e-mail included information that Gibson Dunn believed it could use to Defendants' advantage. Moreover, the privilege order does nothing to lessen the damage caused to the public's trust in the administration of justice and the integrity of the bar based on Gibson Dunn's previous access and extensive use of the Blaskey e-mail.

The petition for writ of mandate or other appropriate relief is denied. This court's order staying all trial court proceedings is dissolved upon the finality of this opinion. Plaintiffs shall recover their costs for the proceedings in this court.

Questions about the Case

1. What were the facts about the e-mail that is the subject of this case? What factors were cited as a basis for coverage by the attorney–client privilege? Explain.
2. What reasoning do the Defendants offer in support of their belief that the trial court erred in its ruling? Do you agree or disagree?
3. How is a "confidential communication" statutorily defined in this case?
4. Under what circumstances can the attorney–client privilege be waived? What factors will a court look at in deciding whether the privilege was waived?
5. On what basis did the trial court decide that the privilege related to the e-mail communication was not waived? On what basis did the appellate court issue its ruling?

This recent case addresses a discovery dispute concerning a law firm data breach that led to waiver of the attorney-client and work product privileges.

Guo Wengui v. Clark Hill, PLC
338 F.R.D. 7 (D.D.C. 2021)

Plaintiff Guo Wengui has moved to compel Defendant Clark Hill, PLC, his former law firm, to produce "all reports of its forensic investigation into the cyberattack" that led to the public dissemination of Mr. Guo's confidential information. He also asks that the Court mandate that Defendant provide more complete answers to certain interrogatories regarding its investigation into the hack. Plaintiff alleges legal malpractice, breach of fiduciary duty, and breach of contract.

Clark Hill responds that it has turned over all relevant internally generated materials and that the other documents Plaintiff seeks, which were produced by external security-consulting firm Duff & Phelps, are covered by both the attorney-client and work-product privileges. The firm points out that it did not hire Duff & Phelps; instead, the consultants were retained by Defendant's outside litigation counsel, Musick, Peeler & Garrett ("MPG"), to assist in its representation of Clark Hill and to help "prepare for litigation stemming from the attack." The firm also refuses to answer Plaintiff's interrogatories seeking "Clark Hill's understanding of the facts or reasons why" the attack occurred, claiming that "its 'understanding' of the progression of the . . . incident is based solely on the advice of outside counsel and consultants retained by outside counsel" and is therefore privileged. Clark Hill declined to answer the interrogatory regarding the effect of the attack "to the extent it calls for knowledge that Clark Hill obtained as a result of its consultations with outside counsel and consultants retained by outside counsel." Clark Hill also maintains that it cannot respond to Guo's additional requests for "information or documents related to [its] clients other than Plaintiff" who may (or may not) have been affected by the hack at issue, on the grounds that such information is both irrelevant and privileged.

Parties may obtain discovery regarding any nonprivileged matter that is relevant to any party's claim or defense and proportional to the needs of the case." The main question here is whether material concerning the "matter" that Plaintiff has requested in discovery is privileged under either the work-product doctrine or the attorney-client privilege. For both, the party seeking to withhold a document—here, Clark Hill—bears the burden of showing that the privilege applies. See *FTC v. TRW, Inc.*, 628 F.2d 207, 213 (D.C. Cir. 1980) (attorney-client privilege); *United States v. ISS Marine Servs., Inc.*, 905 F. Supp. 2d 121, 134 (D.D.C. 2012) (work-product privilege).

To determine whether a document was "prepared in anticipation of litigation," courts in this circuit apply the "because of" test, asking "whether, in light of the nature of the document and the factual situation in the particular case, the document can fairly be said to have been prepared or obtained because of the prospect of litigation." *United States v. Deloitte LLP*, 610 F.3d 129, 137 (D.C. Cir. 2010) . . . "Where a document would have been created 'in substantially similar form' regardless of the litigation," it fails that test, meaning that "work product protection is not available." *FTC v. Boehringer Ingelheim Pharms., Inc.*, 778 F.3d 142, 149 (D.C. Cir. 2015) (quoting Deloitte, 610 F.3d at 138). For that reason, "the privilege has no applicability to documents prepared by lawyers in the ordinary course of business or for other nonlitigation purposes." *In re Sealed Case*, 146 F.3d 881, 887 (D.C. Cir. 1998) . . . see also *Banneker Ventures, LLC v. Graham*, 253 F. Supp. 3d 64, 72 (D.D.C. 2017) ("Documents that would have been created in the ordinary course of business irrespective of litigation are not protected by the work-product doctrine."); *United States v. Adlman*, 134 F.3d 1194, 1204 (2d Cir. 1998) ("If the district court concludes that substantially the same [document] would have been prepared in any event—as part of the ordinary course of business . . .—then the court should conclude [it] was not prepared because of . . . litigation.").

The Court opined that Clark Hill has not met its burden to show that the Duff & Phelps Report (the "Report"), or a substantially similar document, "would [not] have been created in the ordinary course of business irrespective of litigation." . . . It is therefore more likely than not, if not "highly likely[,] that [Clark Hill] would have conducted an] investigation" into the attack's cause, nature, and effect "irrespective of the prospect of litigation." . . . From the Court's *in camera* review, it is clear that the Report summarizes the findings of such an investigation, and that "substantially the same [document] would have been prepared in any event . . . as part of the ordinary course of [Defendant's] business."

Clark Hill argued that the Report qualifies as being prepared in anticipation of litigation because it was the result of only one half of a "two-tracked investigation of the incident." On one track, Clark Hill's usual cybersecurity vendor, eSentire, worked "to investigate and remediate the attack" so as to preserve "business continuity." . . . ("Over the . . . several weeks [after the attack], Clark Hill engaged with . . . eSentire . . . to ascertain the nature and remediate the effects of the attack."). Clark Hill points out that it has disclosed documents related to eSentire's work . . . On a "separate track from the eSentire work," Defendant insists, was Duff & Phelps, retained by MPG "for the sole purpose of assisting [the firm] in gathering information necessary to render timely legal advice."

Clark Hill claims that it had one "ordinary-course investigation" by eSentire "set up so that [it] could learn how the breach happened and . . . respond to it appropriately"—which did not result in protected work product—while it also engaged a "separate team" to "inform[ ] [its] counsel about the breach so that [they] could provide . . . legal advice and prepare to defend the company in litigation." Id. (finding "information generated along [the latter] track" to be protected work product).

The problem for the defense here is that its two-track story finds little support in the record. The firm offers no sworn statement averring that eSentire conducted a separate "investigation" with the purpose of "learn[ing] how the breach happened" or facilitating an "appropriate[ ]" response . . . The closest it comes is an equivocal statement by Eric Rouseau, its Director of Information Security, that "[b]ecause of eSentire's work, Clark Hill did not need the Duff & Phelps report for business continuity." That is not the same as stating that eSentire conducted its own inquiry to . . . help Clark Hill "ascertain the nature and remediate the effects of the attack." . . . On the contrary, Defendant's own interrogatory answers state that "its understanding of the progression of the September 12, 2017 cyber-incident is based solely on the advice of outside counsel and consultants retained by outside counsel." . . . there is no evidence that eSentire ever produced any findings, let alone a comprehensive report like the one produced by Duff & Phelps, about "the problem that allowed the breach to occur" or any recommendations to "ensure such a breach [cannot] happen again."

The record instead suggests that on September 14, 2017, two days after the cyberattack began, Clark Hill turned to Duff & Phelps instead of, rather than separate from or in addition to, eSentire, to do the necessary investigative work. The firm has pointed to no documents reflecting eSentire's doing investigative or remedial work after September 14, even though, from all indications, the attack was potentially still ongoing and the firm did not yet have a full understanding of its cause or scope. Internal emails also show that Rouseau and Clark Hill's General Counsel, Edward Hood, held a call the morning of the 15th with Duff & Phelps employees, referring to them as "the incident response team." . . . The Report confirms this timeline of Duff & Phelps's involvement. Hood himself admits that the Report was shared not just with outside and in-house counsel, but also with "select members of Clark Hill's leadership and IT team." . . . Hood further avers that the Report was used to "assist[ ] [Clark Hill] in connection with managing any issues, including"—but notably not limited to—"potential litigation . . . related to the . . . cyber incident." . . . Defendant also shared the report with the FBI "as part of the FBI's investigation of the cyber incident." . . . The Report was probably shared this widely, as Plaintiffs persuasively argue, because it "was the one place where [Defendant] recorded the facts" of what had transpired . . . There was no comparable eSentire document. The Report itself, moreover, reveals yet other ways in which Duff & Phelps worked with persons beyond MPG or Clark Hill to help the firm respond to and manage the breach. The fact that "the [R]eport was used for a range of nonlitigation purposes" reinforces the notion that it cannot be fairly described as prepared in anticipation of litigation.

. . . Although engagement letters dated September 14 state that Clark Hill hired MPG in anticipation of litigation and that, on the same day, MPG in turn retained Duff & Phelps, Duff & Phelps's role seems to have been far broader than merely assisting outside counsel in preparation for litigation. Although Clark Hill papered the arrangement using its attorneys, that approach "appears to [have been] designed to help shield material from disclosure" and is not sufficient in itself to provide work-product protection. At a minimum, it is Clark Hill's burden to demonstrate that a substantially similar document to the Duff & Phelps Report would not have been produced in the absence of litigation, and it has fallen well short of doing so. Both the Report and related Materials, referred to by Defendant as "Expert Materials," are accordingly not protected work product.

Although Defendant is not explicit, its unstated argument seems clear enough: the privilege also "can attach to reports of third parties made at the request of the attorney or the client where the purpose of the report was to put in usable form information obtained from the client." TRW, 628 F.2d at 212 (citing *United States v. Kovel*, 296 F.2d 918 (2d Cir. 1961)). The classic example is a report by an accountant who, like a translator, takes the client's tax or financial information and makes it digestible to the attorney . . . Clark Hill's argument, then, is that the Duff & Phelps Report qualifies as privileged per this doctrine. It does not. As the Circuit has explained, the *Kovel* doctrine must be applied narrowly "lest the privilege be construed to engulf 'all manner of services' that should not be summarily excluded from the adversary process." *Linde Thomson Langworthy Kohn & Van Dyke, P.C. v. Resolution Tr. Corp.,* 5 F.3d 1508, 1514–15 (D.C. Cir. 1993) . . . After all, unlike the work-product privilege, which may be overcome by a sufficient showing of need, the attorney-client privilege is absolute. To that end, the *Kovel* court itself made clear that, for instance, "if the advice sought [by the client] is the accountant's rather than the lawyer's, no privilege exists" over the accountant's report. *Kovel,* 296 F.2d at 922 . . .

From the factual record discussed above and the Report itself, the Court concludes that Clark Hill's true objective was gleaning Duff & Phelps's expertise in cybersecurity, not in "obtaining legal advice from [its] lawyer. At a minimum, Defendant has not demonstrated that the opposite is true. Duff & Phelps undertook a full investigation—the only one apparently commissioned by Clark Hill—with the goal of determining how the attack happened and what information was exfiltrated. The Report provides not only a summary of the firm's findings, but also pages of specific recommendations on how Clark Hill should tighten its cybersecurity. And it was shared with both Clark Hill IT staff and the FBI, presumably with an eye toward facilitating both entities' further efforts at investigation and remediation. (Because the Court finds the Report not subject to attorney-client privilege, it does not address Plaintiff's separate argument that Defendant waived the privilege by disclosing the Report to the FBI. For the foregoing reasons, the Duff & Phelps Report and associated materials are not privileged and must be disclosed, and the related interrogatories must be answered.

Defendant separately resists Plaintiff's discovery requests for information relating to the effect of the cyberattack on firm clients other than Guo himself . . . For instance, Plaintiff has served a request for production seeking "[a]ll documents reflecting that the 'hacking' . . . resulted in a third party's obtaining . . . information, data, or material regarding any Clark Hill client other than or in addition to plaintiff." . . . Clark Hill claims that this sort of information is both irrelevant and privileged . . . Here, too, the Court will grant Plaintiff's Motion to Compel: the information is clearly relevant, and appropriate redactions can assuage any privilege or privacy concerns.

. . . the sort of information Plaintiff seeks is directly relevant; and even if it were not, there is a "reasonable likelihood that allowing discovery of the[se] documents will lead to discovery of [other] evidence [that is] relevant," which renders them discoverable under Rule 26. *Food Lion, Inc. v. United Food & Commercial Workers Int'l Union, AFL-CIOCLC,* 103 F.3d 1007, 1013 (D.C. Cir. 1997). The firm also contends that it cannot fully answer interrogatories or turn over documents relating to the hack's effect on its other clients because doing so would reveal that it represents those individuals, and the fact of representation itself is attorney-client privileged. That does not quite state the law accurately. As this Court has previously explained, "Under the general rule, the attorney-client privilege does not protect from disclosure the identity of the client . . . and the general purpose of the work performed." *Cause of Action Inst. v. U.S. Dep't of Justice*, 330 F. Supp. 3d 336, 350 (D.D.C. 2018) . . . On the other hand, "when a client's identity is sufficiently intertwined with the client's confidences," the privilege does apply . . . At this point, Defendant (which bears the burden to demonstrate that the privilege applies) has given the Court no way of knowing whether the latter situation is applicable to any documents at issue.

That said, however, privilege is not the only consideration here. Discovery must be both "relevant" and "proportional to the needs of the case," Fed. R. Civ. P. 26(b)(1), and the Court doubts that the precise identity of any Clark Hill client is relevant to the issues here. To the extent that it is, its germaneness is likely weak enough to be outweighed by the clients' privacy interests. See *Henson v. Turn, Inc.*, No. 15-1497, 2018 WL 5281629, at *5 (N.D. Cal. Oct. 22, 2018) ("Courts and commentators have recognized that privacy interests can be a consideration in evaluating proportionality. . . ."). It thus seems to the Court that Defendant can fully safeguard the identity of its clients and any of their confidences, if applicable, with appropriate redactions in responsive documents and with tailored interrogatory answers. There is no basis, however, for its blanket refusal to respond to Plaintiff's requests for production, and the Court will grant the Motion to Compel that discovery subject to appropriate redactions.

The Court finds that the Report and associated materials are neither protected work product nor attorney-client privileged. It also concludes that Clark Hill must provide the documents requested by Plaintiff regarding the cyberattack's effect on other firm clients, subject to appropriate redactions. The Court, accordingly, will grant Plaintiff's Motion to Compel.

Questions about the Case

1. What was the basis of Plaintiff's Motion to Compel?
2. What two-track process did Defendant employ? What types of investigations did the two-track approach result in? How did this factor into the court's reasoning?
3. What did the court say about Defendant's work product claim? Did Defendant meet its burden that the Duff & Phelps Report would not have been produced in the ordinary course of business? Who did Defendant share the Report with?
4. Did eSentire prepare a report for the Defendant? Do you agree with the Court's contention that Defendant retained Duff & Phelps to supplant the work being performed by eSentire rather than to supplement it with another function?
5. What was the Court's reasoning that the privilege did not apply in this instance?

5

Conflicts of Interest

This chapter explains the rules concerning conflicts of interest that may arise in the representation of clients and how those rules apply to paralegals. Paralegals increasingly face potential conflict situations in today's dynamic legal environment. Chapter 5 covers:

- the foundation on which conflict of interest rules rest
- the rules governing simultaneous and successive representation and their application to paralegals
- special conflict situations and their application to paralegals:
  - being called as a witness
  - business transactions with clients
  - publication rights
  - financial assistance to clients
  - lawyer's interest in litigation
  - gifts from clients
  - agreements with clients limiting lawyer malpractice liability
  - payment of attorneys' fees by third persons
  - conflicts involving family members or relatives
- disqualifications caused by conflicts of interest
- client consent to representation despite a conflict
- screens to protect against disqualification
- conflicts checks and a paralegal's responsibility to maintain records

A. Introduction

Conflicts of interest constitute one of the most troublesome areas of ethics for lawyers, paralegals, and clients. The growth in the size of law firms, the development of branch offices, mergers of firms, the mobility of lawyers and paralegals from firm to firm, and practice specialization have made the potential for conflicts of interest an ever-present concern. Traditional restrictive rules governing conflicts are being modified and adjusted to adapt to the changing environment of law practice and to new kinds of conflicts. Strict conflicts rules can pose an undue hardship on law firms, law firm employees, and clients, as we will see in cases in this chapter. Avoiding conflicts remains one of the critical ethical obligations of lawyers and paralegals.

The principles underlying conflicts of interest are **loyalty and confidentiality**. Both of these duties are threatened when a lawyer or paralegal has an interest that is adverse to a client's. This is true whether the adverse interest is a personal or business one, or relates to the current or past representation of another client. For example, a lawyer who has received confidential information from one client that may help another client may be tempted to divulge that confidential information to help the second client.

Ethics rules governing conflicts of interest have existed since the first codes of lawyer conduct came into being, and conflicts are covered in the ethics rules, cases, and opinions of every jurisdiction. The ethics rules provide the basis for lawyer discipline and are supplemented by court interpretations in cases in which a party has moved to disqualify a law firm because of a conflict of interest. The courts have seen many more conflict dilemmas than have disciplinary bodies and have built a considerable body of law as they have interpreted and applied the rules to increasing numbers and kinds of conflict situations.

The ABA Model Rules of Professional Conduct and state and local rules cover several categories of conflict situations, including:

- simultaneous representation of adverse interests
- representation that is adverse to a former client
- representation of clients whose interests are aligned
- lawyer's financial, personal, or business interests that are or may be adverse to a client.

A critically important aspect of the conflicts rules for paralegals is the principle of imputed or vicarious **disqualification**, a general rule under which the conflict of interest of one person in a firm is imputed to the entire firm, causing the firm to be subject to disqualification from representing the client in question. Some kinds of conflicts are imputed, and others are not. Most states apply the rules of imputation for lawyers to paralegals.

Guideline 7 of the ABA Model Guidelines for the Utilization of Paralegal Services (ABA Model Guidelines) advises lawyers to take **measures to prevent conflicts** resulting from a paralegal's other employment or interests. The comment to this guideline makes it clear that personal and financial interests are covered, as well as interests related to the representation of a client. The comment also discusses the screening of a paralegal from any case in which a conflict exists, a matter covered later in this chapter in Section F. About half the states that have paralegal guidelines refer to paralegal conflicts of interests and call on the lawyer generally to ensure against conflicts impinging on the services rendered to the client. See, for example, Indiana Guideline 9.10(g); Kansas Guideline X; Michigan Guideline 5; New Mexico Guideline VI; North Carolina Guideline 7; South Dakota Guideline 9. Virginia Guideline IX prohibits a paralegal directly from participating in matters where there "may be" a conflict of interest. A few states, such as New Mexico and Connecticut, identify the kinds of conflicts that may "impinge" on services to a client, including "personal, social, business" and "relationship" interests, whereas other states refer only to conflicts arising out of the paralegal's employment (New York State Bar Association Guideline IV). Some state guidelines mention the availability of screening for paralegals (*e.g.*, Pennsylvania), which has been almost universally accepted by the courts, as will be discussed in detail later in this chapter.

The NFPA Model Code includes an extensive section on conflicts of interest (Section 1.6), which acknowledges the different kinds of conflicts that may face paralegals, calls on paralegals to maintain records so that conflicts checks can be conducted, and requires paralegals to adhere to the requirements of screens. The NALA Code of Ethics and Professional Responsibility requires paralegals to disclose "any pre-existing client or personal relationship that may conflict with the interests of the employer or prospective employer and/or their clients." (Canon 8.)

B. Simultaneous or Concurrent Representation

The most clear-cut case of a conflict of interest is ***simultaneous or concurrent representation*** of two clients whose interests are adverse to one another in a lawsuit. It seems absurd to suggest that a lawyer could adequately represent both the plaintiff and the defendant in the same case. However, simultaneous representation problems do arise in situations that are less obvious than a lawyer serving both clients in a contested matter. Many matters that are not litigated have clients with opposing interests, as the following section demonstrates.

Simultaneous or concurrent representation conflict
Where an attorney represents two clients whose interests are adverse to one another.

ABA Model Rule 1.7(a) prohibits concurrent conflicts, which it defines as "directly adverse" interests or interests that carry "a significant risk that the representation of one or more clients will be materially limited by the lawyer's responsibilities to another client, a former client or a third person or by a personal interest of the lawyer." The conflict can be avoided if "(1) the lawyer reasonably believes that [she or he] will be able to provide competent and diligent representation . . . ; (2) the representation is not prohibited by law; (3) the representation does not involve . . . a claim by one client against another client . . . in the same litigation . . . ; and (4) each affected client gives informed consent, confirmed in writing."

To represent the clients in question, the lawyer would have to have both an assurance of **adequate representation** of both clients and **client consent**. Adequate representation of two adverse clients is no small hurdle; it is often quite difficult for a lawyer to demonstrate objectively how they can be equally effective, loyal to, and zealous on behalf of two clients who oppose each other. Even if the lawyer believes that this is possible, it is easy to see how clients would question a lawyer's loyalty if the same firm or lawyer were opposing their interests in another case.

To avoid conflicts, lawyers should have good procedures for **checking for conflicts** when they undertake representation of a new client or hire or retain new personnel. They should decline representation when a conflict is presented that cannot be waived by the clients involved or for which they cannot obtain a consent or establish a screen that will withstand judicial scrutiny. Finally, they should withdraw from representation promptly when an irremediable conflict is discovered after the representation is undertaken. (See more on conducting conflict checks and creating screens later in this chapter.)

The courts generally have treated simultaneous representation as improper on its face and start with the presumption that disqualification is required. The more remote the adverseness, however, the less strictly the rule is applied. For example, it is not considered a conflict of interest *per se* for an attorney to represent business competitors simultaneously in unrelated matters.

Determining whether there has been valid client **consent** (or "waiver" of the client's right to assert the conflict of interest) is also critical. The ABA Model Rules require informed written consent. The Model Rules formulation mandating the consent in writing and has been adopted by most jurisdictions. Some states require consultation for consent to be valid. Consultation means that the lawyer seeking the consent has provided the client with sufficient information to permit the client to appreciate the significance of the conflict. The Model Rules require "informed consent," which means that the lawyer must disclose the "implications of common representation," and the "advantages and risks." (Comment [18] to ABA Model Rule 1.7). For some kinds of conflicts, the lawyer may recommend that the client consult with independent outside counsel to ensure that the client is making a fully informed decision that cannot be challenged later.

General open-ended consents will not ordinarily be upheld. Whether a court honors a client's consent depends on a number of circumstances, including:

- whether the conflict is one that is "consentable"; that is, the lawyer can provide adequate representation
- the extent of the lawyer's disclosure and discussions with the client about the implications of the dual representation
- whether the consent was truly voluntary and not given under pressure from the lawyer or others
- when in the course of the representation the lawyer raised the issue with the client
- the capacity of the client to understand fully the implications of the dual representation and consent
- whether the client consulted with and relied on independent counsel before giving consent
- whether the consent is in writing and signed.

These factors suggest some guidelines that should be followed to ensure that consents will be upheld. Thorough **written disclosures**, which are highly recommended, should state the circumstances giving rise to the potential conflict and the actual and reasonably foreseeable consequences to the client if the lawyer undertakes or continues the representation. If the client consults with **independent counsel**, the lawyer(s) must be truly independent, that is, not from the same firm or recommended by the firm seeking the consent. The written consent should also include:

- consideration for the consent (*i.e.*, future or continued representation)
- procedures to screen appropriately to protect confidentiality
- procedures to follow if a client decides to revoke consent.

Some firms ask clients to consent to **future conflicts**, which is the subject of considerable debate. Whether such consent will be upheld depends on the same factors set forth earlier, especially on whether the particular conflict is "consentable." Other factors include whether the client is an experienced user of legal services, was well informed about the potential future conflict, and/or got advice from independent counsel.

In general, a lawyer cannot withdraw from representing one client to represent the other, more favored client. A court reviewing this situation will ordinarily disqualify the lawyer if representation was concurrent at any time. Improper simultaneous representation generally results in disqualification from representing both clients unless, of course, there is proper consent.

Imputed disqualification rules are usually applied strictly in cases of simultaneous representation involving lawyers. In other words, if one lawyer in a firm has a client-based conflict in an ongoing case without client consent, the entire firm is disqualified. These rules also apply to branch offices of the same firm. A screen to protect against improper access to confidential information will not ordinarily remedy this kind of conflict, as it might in cases involving former clients. Fortunately for paralegals, most courts have been more lenient in applying the vicarious disqualification rules to situations in which the paralegal carries a concurrent conflict to a new firm. See Sections C and F and the cases in this chapter.

Related to direct conflicts in active matters involving clients are *issue or positional conflicts*. An issue conflict occurs when a lawyer is representing two clients in unrelated cases and urging a legal position in one case that would have negative consequences for the other client if the lawyer prevails. It is usually not considered unethical for lawyers to take inconsistent positions, but this scenario can rise to the level of a concurrent conflict if the representation in one case would "materially impair" the representation of the other client in a current case. If this situation arises, the lawyer may seek consent or need to withdraw from one or both matters. (See Comment [24] to ABA Model Rule 1.7.)

Although the Model Rules do not prohibit representation of competitors, some firms have policies against **representing direct competitors** in the same industry. Obviously, clients may have concerns about both loyalty and protection of confidential information if a firm represents competitors. In addition, the potential for being "conflicted out" of representing a client in the case of litigation between competitors is a practical deterrent to law firms. Although not prohibited, lawyers should be especially wary of this kind of conflict if the industry is known for cut-throat competition or if the lawyer possesses confidential information about one client that will damage the other client even if the cases are unrelated.

The Model Rules also prohibit simultaneous representation when the lawyer's responsibilities to one client may "materially limit" representation of another client. For example, a lawyer representing two criminal defendants with conflicting trial dates might have to delay one trial to the detriment of that client. (See Comment [8] to Model Rule 1.7.)

Concurrent conflicts of interests arise in litigation in many ways. One of the most common is dual representation of spouses in a **marital dissolution**. Many marital dissolution matters begin amicably and seem to lend themselves to resolution by one lawyer, for reasons of cost and efficiency, but end up in court. Although the courts are not unanimous, many bar associations and experts advise against representing both parties to a marital dissolution. Sometimes one of the spouses later becomes

---

Imputed disqualification
A conflict of interest involving one person that is attributed to the entire law firm, which is disqualified from representing the party at issue.

Issue conflicts
Occurs when an attorney argues opposing sides of a legal issue, the result of which may be that one client's interests are harmed.

dissatisfied with the property settlement agreement and challenges it in court on the basis that the lawyer had a conflict of interest and favored the other spouse.

Similar problems can arise in representation of **co-parties** in civil litigation. Although aligned initially, co-parties may become adversaries during the course of litigation if cross-claims are filed or another party seeks to realign the parties. One problem area is serving as joint defense counsel in mass litigation, where the interests of all parties may not align perfectly and confidentiality is difficult to maintain. Similarly, a passenger and driver who sue a third party may find themselves adversaries if the passenger learns that the driver was partially at fault and sues the driver. Some jurisdictions, such as California, have decided cases that prohibit any joint representation of a driver and a passenger as an inherent conflict of interest.

ABA Model Rule 1.8(g) prohibits a lawyer who is representing multiple clients from making an **aggregate settlement** of civil claims or a collective plea in a criminal case without informed written consent. Representing seemingly aligned **defendants in criminal cases** is especially risky, as the interests of the defendants are often potentially adverse. In addition to the ethical issues, multiple representation may deprive one or both of the defendants of effective assistance of counsel, which constitutes grounds for appeal of a criminal conviction.

Other less obvious conflict traps can arise in litigation. For example, a firm may be disqualified for retaining an **expert witness** who was previously interviewed by the opposing counsel if confidential information was disclosed to the expert during the course of the interview. Representing both present and future **claimants in class action** suits may also result in an allegation of a conflict if a settlement seems to favor one group over another. Generally, a lawyer may not serve as both named plaintiff and counsel in a class action suit, a conflict that will be imputed to the lawyer's firm.

Although litigation is the most obvious setting for conflicts of interest, many other kinds of legal matters pose potential conflicts. A lawyer may represent more than one party to a **negotiation** if the parties' interests seem aligned but should be aware of the potential for a conflict if negotiations fail or if the resulting contract becomes the subject of a dispute. If litigation is the result, the lawyer may not represent either of the parties against the other and may be subject to suit by a former client for malpractice because of the conflict. For example, entertainment law firms that represent producers, directors, writers, and actors on a single project have been accused of favoring wealthier or more prestigious clients in negotiations on film deals, resulting in less advantageous positions for other clients. Clients of these firms usually consent in writing to the multiple representation; however, parties to the contracts may later complain that there was not full disclosure or that they were pressured into signing consents, as they would have been frozen out of deals if they had sought independent representation.

A conflict of interest may arise in the **drafting of estate plans** for members of the same family, especially if the family members are not in agreement about the disposition of the estate. Similarly, conflicts between an **estate and the heirs** of the estate may prohibit representation of both parties. For other conflicts in a probate setting, see Section E.5, on gifts from clients.

A lawyer who represents a **corporation** may be invited to serve on its board of directors. The ABA Rules advise that lawyers not serve as directors if there is a "material risk that the dual role will compromise the lawyer's independence of professional judgment." (See ABA Model Rule 1.7, Comment [35], and Model Rule 1.13.) Serving on a corporate board increases a lawyer's risk of being sued and threatens the attorney-client privilege as well—remember from Chapter 4 that information that is not treated as confidential and is not communicated for the purpose of obtaining legal advice is not protected. The interests or positions of the board, management, and shareholders may at times diverge. Lawyers serving on boards find themselves in serious conflict situations in shareholder derivative suits, especially when there are allegations of self-dealing or fraud by the board or management. Many law firms restrict or limit service on corporate boards, not only because of the potential for conflicts, but because of the heightened liability of directors under Sarbanes-Oxley. Conflicts may also occur in the corporate setting if a lawyer represents several entities within the corporate family (*e.g.*, parent, subsidiary, affiliate) and these entities find themselves in an adversarial position with one another. Finally, as is also noted in Chapter 4, lawsuits against corporations often result in potential confidentiality and conflict issues when employees or former employees are represented by the same lawyer. See *U.S. v. Nicholas*, 606 F. Supp. 2d 1109 (C.D. Cal. 2009), for a case in point.

Lawyers represent multiple clients whenever they serve more than one party to a **transaction** such as a real estate sale, a mortgage, a loan, or a contract. Several states have advisory opinions on the issue of representing both sides in a real estate transaction, most of which recommend against dual representation except in purely ministerial matters. Some states prohibit dual representation in any complex commercial real estate transaction because of the great potential for conflicts.

A lawyer who has acted as a **judge, law clerk to a judge, mediator**, or other **third-party neutral** in a matter cannot later represent any of the parties involved without informed written consent under Model Rule 1.12. Some cases have held that this kind of conflict is imputed to the law firm where the lawyer works, thereby prohibiting the representation of the client by any lawyer in the firm.

Lawyers who practice in the **bankruptcy** area are subject to special conflict rules. The Bankruptcy Code requires that lawyers for the debtor be "disinterested" and not represent or hold an interest that is adverse to the debtor (11 U.S.C. §327(a)). Lawyers are required to disclose related interests. A lawyer representing a debtor cannot have pre-existing relationships with others who might be involved in the bankruptcy, such as investment bankers involved with a bankrupt corporation or shareholders of the debtor corporation. Such representation would constitute not only an ethical breach, but a violation of federal bankruptcy law, which may result in criminal penalties, as one lawyer learned when he was sent to prison for 15 months and disbarred. Another firm was not awarded fees for its work after it failed to disclose services for another client that conflicted with the interests of the debtor (*In re Prince*, 40 F.3d 356 (11th Cir. 1994)).

C. Successive Representation

The ethics rules also govern the conduct of lawyers who represent a client in a matter that may be adverse to a former client—called ***successive representation***. The ability of clients to be represented by the counsel of their choice and the increasing mobility of lawyers have been significant factors in court decisions that apply conflicts rules in cases of successive representation less rigidly than in the past.

Successive representation conflict
Situation involving a current client whose interests conflict with those of a former client.

The general rule is that a lawyer cannot undertake successive representation if the interests of the former and current clients are **truly adverse** and if the past and current matters are **substantially related**. This formulation presupposes a lawyer-client relationship with the former client in which the lawyer learned confidential information about the new matter. If the current representation relates to the same or a closely related matter, the lawyer would be in a position to breach the duty of confidentiality to the former client by revealing the confidential information to assist the current client. (Remember from Chapter 4 that the duty of confidentiality continues after the termination of the lawyer–client relationship.) Some commentators also cite the duty of loyalty to the former client as a basis for the rule, but others contend that the duty of loyalty, unlike the duty of confidentiality, does not continue after the termination of the lawyer–client relationship. Informed written consent to successive representation is permitted as a way to cure the conflict.

Prior to the provision for successive representation in the Model Rules and in states that followed the Model Code, some courts came to rely on Canon 9 of the ABA Model Code in deciding whether to disqualify a lawyer or firm from successive representation. Canon 9 calls on lawyers to avoid even the **appearance of impropriety**. Most circuits and states, however, do not order disqualification solely on the basis of an appearance of impropriety, but determine whether the confidentiality of the former client's protected communications and information is in jeopardy. Most ethics experts disfavor disqualification predicated solely on the appearance of impropriety; such a finding does not mean that confidential information has been revealed, and the disqualification can severely harm the interests of the client, who loses the right to choose a lawyer.

The ABA Model Rules cover successive conflicts in Rule 1.9(a), which states the general rule that has been followed by most courts: A lawyer may not represent a person in a matter that is "the same or substantially related" to the representation of a former client in which the interests of the potential client are "materially adverse" to the former client, except with informed written consent of the former client.

Paragraph (b) of Rule 1.9 covers the situation in which a lawyer changing firms is faced with the question of whether to represent a new client in a matter that is adverse and substantially related to a matter of a former client of that lawyer's former firm. Such representation is prohibited if the lawyer learned confidential information about the former client in past employment, except with the former client's informed written consent. Rule 1.9(c) reiterates the lawyer's duty not to reveal confidential information of a former client under any circumstances, unless other rules permit or require it or the information has become generally known.

A separate ABA Model Rule applies to **government lawyers**. Model Rule 1.11 allows a former government lawyer to represent a private client in a matter in which the lawyer previously "participated personally and substantially" only with the government agency's informed written consent. It also allows screening to avoid firm disqualification in such a representation. A lawyer who moves into private practice from government service is prohibited from switching sides or from negotiating for private employment with a party or a lawyer with whom the lawyer is dealing on a matter. The flexible approach for government lawyers who wish to move into private practice is predicated on policy reasons: Without this rule, lawyers would be effectively discouraged from entering government and civil service, which is less lucrative than private practice can be, but essential to the public interest. The general acceptance of screening for government lawyers with conflicts is important to paralegals, as these principles have also been applied by some courts to allow screening for paralegal conflicts. See, for example, the *Hayes* case at the end of this chapter.

As the courts rule on an increasing number of motions for disqualification, they face the challenge of applying conflicts rules consistently and fairly to complex fact situations. The courts have been somewhat inconsistent in deciding the question of whether a **substantial relationship** exists between former and current clients' matters. Most courts examine the *facts* of the two matters to see whether it is likely that the attorney would have learned confidential information that relates to both matters. The ABA and other ethics experts favor this approach. A few courts look to the *legal issues* and require a clear or even identical congruence of the past and present issues before ordering disqualification. In either case, if a court finds that the matters are not substantially related, the lawyer and the lawyer's firm will not be disqualified. If the matters are found to be substantially related, a presumption that confidential information was disclosed arises. Some courts have held that this presumption is irrebuttable, thereby precluding evidence to the contrary, such as evidence that the attorney did not learn any confidential information on the prior matter or that the lawyer has been screened. The trend is for the court to find the presumption rebuttable and to allow the lawyer to provide evidence to overcome the presumption that confidential information has been or will be revealed.

D. Attorney as Witness

Another kind of conflict of interest arises when a lawyer or someone in the lawyer's firm is called on to testify in a case in which the lawyer is acting as an advocate.

The rationale for prohibiting lawyers from testifying in cases in which they are an advocate is to protect the client's interest, because the potential exists for such testimony to harm the client's case. This harm may come about in a variety of ways, depending on the nature of the lawyer's testimony. If the testimony is in the client's favor, opposing counsel could discredit it by making the argument that the lawyer is biased in the client's favor. The lawyer may also have an unfair advantage as a witness because a jury may give the lawyer deference and special credibility. Some courts and commentators express concern that opposing counsel will not examine a colleague attorney-witness vigorously out of professional courtesy. Finally, the harm to the client is clear if the lawyer's testimony is not in the client's favor.

ABA Model Rule 3.7 prohibits a lawyer from acting as an "advocate at a trial in which the lawyer is likely to be a necessary witness" unless the testimony relates to an uncontested matter or to the value or nature of legal services in the case, or if disqualification would cause a substantial hardship to the client. The meaning of **necessary witness** is crucial in deciding whether the lawyer can continue as counsel. If testimony would be useful but is not critical, or if other credible evidence could be used to prove the same point, the lawyer's testimony is not "necessary." This rule also limits its application to trial situations, which enables the lawyer to represent the client in non-litigated matters, as well as in pretrial and post-trial matters.

Paralegal as Witness

The rules prohibiting witness-advocate conflicts are applicable to paralegals, who may be potential witnesses in litigation. The rationale stated earlier for this prohibition is not as compelling when a paralegal would be called to testify, as it is based on the advantage that a lawyer has because of their professional status and role as an advocate. The advocate role cannot be attributed personally to a paralegal, who does not argue the client's case in court. A more convincing argument can be made for disqualification if the paralegal's testimony would harm the client's case. Because the conflict would not be imputed to the paralegal's firm, it is unlikely that a court would force disqualification of the whole firm if the paralegal were called to testify, but the firm may decide that the paralegal should not continue to work on the case. An Ohio Ethics Opinion, 87-7 (1987), states that in-house counsel is not required to withdraw because the corporation's paralegal is called as a witness. The opinion specifically cites as a reason that the paralegal's role is not that of advocate.

REVIEW QUESTIONS

1. On what principles are the conflicts of interest rules based?
2. Why are conflicts problems so common?
3. What is the general rule about simultaneously representing two clients whose interests are adverse?
4. Can clients consent to a simultaneous conflict of interest? Under what circumstances may a client consent? What factors would a court consider in deciding whether to honor a consent?
5. What are the requirements for client consent? What should be disclosed in a letter to a client regarding the potential conflict? What should be included in the consent signed by the client?
6. What do the NALA and NFPA ethical rules say about conflicts?
7. What is an issue conflict? Under what circumstances can a lawyer handle two cases that present issue conflicts concurrently?
8. Is it a conflict of interest for a lawyer to represent two clients whose interests were not adverse, but whose trial dates conflict? Why or why not? Would it be a conflict of interest at all if the lawyer could successfully obtain a postponement of one of the trials? Why or why not?
9. Is it ethical for a lawyer to represent both the husband and the wife in an amicable uncontested divorce? Why or why not? Why might it be unwise to undertake this kind of representation?
10. Can a lawyer represent both the passenger and the driver in a lawsuit against another driver? Why or why not?
11. Is it ethical for an attorney to represent codefendants in a criminal case? Why or why not?
12. Can a lawyer represent more than one party to a business transaction? Why or why not?
13. Can a lawyer serve on the board of directors of a corporate client? Why or why not? Can a firm represent both a corporation and its officers? How about employees? What are the considerations and risks?

14. Can a firm represent all the members of a family in creating an estate plan? Why or why not?
15. Can a lawyer with a conflict withdraw from representing one client and continue representing the other client? Why?
16. What is the general rule about representing a client whose interests may be adverse to a former client?
17. What do the ABA Model Rules say about successive conflicts?
18. How and why has Canon 9 been applied in cases of successive representation? Why are courts moving away from this basis for disqualification?
19. How does a court decide if matters in successive representation are "substantially related"? If a court finds that matters are substantially related, is the lawyer or firm automatically disqualified? In what two ways might the lawyer rebut a presumption that the confidentiality of information is at risk?
20. Why is a lawyer generally prohibited from handling a litigated matter in which they will be called to testify? Name the exceptions to the general rule.
21. Do the rules applied to lawyer-witnesses apply equally to paralegals? Explain any differences.

DISCUSSION QUESTIONS AND HYPOTHETICALS

1. If you worked in a law firm and were getting a divorce, would you find it acceptable to have two different lawyers in your firm represent you and your spouse? What if you were getting married and needed a prenuptial agreement?
2. Do you think firms should refuse to handle matters in which there are issue conflicts? What about positional conflicts? Explain your reasoning.
3. Do you think firms should have policies that prevent lawyers from representing clients who are competitors in the same industry? What are the costs and benefits of such a policy? Should a defense firm have a policy that it will not hire paralegals who have worked for plaintiffs' firms?
4. What would you do if you worked for a lawyer who had such a heavy court calendar that they were constantly rescheduling court dates and delaying motions and trials? How might conflicts of interest rules be implicated in this scenario?
5. Under what circumstances might a firm be disqualified because one of its paralegals might be called on to testify against a client in a case? What else might the firm do besides withdraw from representation?

6. What would you do if you knew that your firm had a conflict of interest problem that it was not addressing internally? Would it make any difference in your actions if the firm was knowingly ignoring the problem?
7. May a firm ask a client to consent in advance to future conflicts that might arise? Research this area and see what ethics commentators think. Start with the Comments to Model Rule 1.7.
8. Sean Allen, a lawyer in the Thompson firm, hires two paralegals (Mario and Candy) for the summer to work on intellectual property matters. Both paralegals had worked the previous year at the Hinojosa firm, which represents Future Film Studio (FFS). Sean learned that Mario had billed 1,000 hours to FFS for investigating a film project including sitting in on meetings with the client and conducting legal research, which required the review of confidential client documents. Candy did not work on the film project but billed 10 hours to FFS for generic research on summary judgments. What are the real or potential conflicts that Mario and Candy bring to the Thompson firm? Analyze each separately and be sure to discuss imputation and the potential for screening and/or consent. Discuss whether and how they might be cured.

RESEARCH PROJECTS AND ASSIGNMENTS

1. Draft a letter to a client explaining a recently discovered potential conflict based on your previous employment and prepare a consent form for the client to sign.
2. Locate the federal bankruptcy law that prohibits lawyers from representing a debtor in bankruptcy if the lawyer has preexisting relationships with other possible parties in the bankruptcy matter. How often has this provision been used against lawyers?
3. Check your state's ethics rules and see if they follow the ABA Model Rules exactly or if they deviate from these rules.
4. Check your state and local bar associations' ethics opinions to see if there are any that concern conflicts arising from the employment of nonlawyers or paralegals.
5. Firm ABC represented the Jones Corporation. A lawyer in a branch office files a lawsuit against a subsidiary of Jones. Is this a conflict? What should a court do when faced with a disqualification motion in such a matter? For one court's analysis, see *J.P. Morgan v. Liberty*, 189 F. Supp. 2d 24 (S.D.N.Y. 2002).
6. Can a lawyer represent both a debtor filing for bankruptcy and one of the debtor's creditors? For a case on point, see *U.S. v. Gellene*, 182 F.3d 578 (7th Cir. 1999), in which the offending lawyer was found guilty of fraud and disbarred.

7. A lawyer represents a family in which the grandmother wants to disinherit her wayward granddaughter. Can the lawyer do the estate plan? See ABA Ethics Opinion 05-432 for an analysis of "conflicting economic interests" and "expectant legal rights."
8. Can a child represent one of his parents in a marital dissolution? See the unusual case of *Liapis v. Second Jud. Dist. Ct.*, 128 Nev. Adv. Op. No. 39, 282 P.3d 733 (2012).

E. Other Conflicts in Relationships with Clients

1. Business Transactions with Clients

Business transactions between lawyers and clients have tremendous potential for creating serious conflicts in which lawyers' interests differ from those of the clients and with lawyers' duties to represent the clients. Further, clients rely on lawyers' superior legal knowledge and are generally in a weaker bargaining position on the business deal. The lawyer's duties of loyalty, trust, and zealous representation are implicated whenever a lawyer enters into a business transaction with a client. If the business transaction is personal to the lawyer and does not involve the firm in any way, it is not generally imputed to the firm.

The ABA Model Rules prohibit business transactions between lawyers and clients but provide for an exception with client consent. ABA Model Rule 1.8(a) prohibits a lawyer from entering into a business transaction with a client or acquiring a business interest adverse to a client unless "(1) the transaction and terms . . . are fair and reasonable . . . and are fully disclosed . . . in writing . . . ; (2) the client is advised in writing of the desirability of seeking and is given a reasonable opportunity to seek independent legal counsel . . . ; and (3) the client gives informed consent, in writing, signed by the client, to the essential terms of the transaction and the lawyer's role. . . ."

A client's consultation with independent counsel is of utmost importance. Lawyers must allow the client a reasonable amount of time within which to obtain the opinion of independent counsel and to reflect on whether to sign the consent. Independent counsel must be truly independent; that is, not recommended by or associated with the conflicted lawyer.

In practice, lawyers and clients have many opportunities to enter into business transactions, not all of which are prohibited. Commercial transactions in which clients provide services in a business capacity, such as banking, medical services, products, and utilities, are not prohibited. In these transactions, the lawyer has no advantage over the client.

Examples of business transactions that are generally prohibited include: (1) a lawyer purchasing real estate from a client while also drafting the documents relating to the sale; (2) a lawyer advising clients to make investments in businesses in which he or she has an interest; (3) a lawyer borrowing money from a client while failing to advise the client how to perfect the client's security interest; and (4) a lawyer going into business with a client, forming a corporation for the business that gives the lawyer an ownership interest while continuing to represent the corporation as its lawyer.

One interesting variation of a lawyer-client business relationship is found in firms representing start-up companies with little capital. These firms sometimes take an interest in the new company in exchange for legal services. This kind of arrangement has been upheld as long as the client consented in writing after full disclosure and an opportunity to seek independent legal advice.

Business Transaction Conflicts Involving Paralegals

Conflicts based on business transactions with clients may arise for paralegals as well as lawyers. For example, a paralegal may be invited to invest in a client's business or may own stock in a client's company. Such conflicts are more easily curable for a paralegal than they are for a lawyer because clients rely on the lawyer, not the paralegal, for legal advice, giving the lawyer a potentially unfair advantage over the client. However, paralegals should be aware of the general prohibition on business transactions with clients and take care to avoid dual roles that might create a conflict. Finally, paralegals who purchase stock in client companies must be careful to honor laws prohibiting the use of inside information in buying and selling stock, which were discussed in Chapter 4. In the 1990s, several paralegals were convicted of trading on inside client information. See, for example, *USA v. Gleeman, et al.*, No. 1:92-cr-00878-LMM-3 (SDNY 1992). Many law firms have rules prohibiting lawyers and paralegals from buying stock in corporations that they represent in securities work. All firms should screen for and guard against business conflicts of both lawyers and nonlawyer personnel.

2. Publication, Literary, and Media Rights

A variation of the prohibition on business relationships with clients is the restriction on lawyers entering into an agreement that grants the lawyer publication, literary, or media rights relating to the subject matter of the representation prior to the conclusion of the representation. (See ABA Model Rule 1.8(d).) This rule protects against conflicts that might arise concerning what is best for the client as opposed to what would enhance the value of the "story," that is, the value of the lawyer's interests in the literary or media rights.

In addition to disciplinary action for violation of this rule (which is rare), this kind of conflict may be the basis of a motion to disqualify counsel or an appeal in a criminal case based on ineffective assistance of counsel.

3. Financial Assistance to Clients

Whenever a lawyer loans funds to a client, a new dimension—that of creditor and debtor—is imposed on the lawyer-client relationship. Because of the inherent conflict in both representing the client and being the client's creditor, the ABA Model Rules prohibit most kinds of financial assistance to clients. ABA Model Rule 1.8(e) permits lawyers to advance court costs and expenses, allowing repayment to be contingent on the outcome of the litigation and allowing lawyers to pay litigation costs outright for indigent clients. Some states have not adopted these two aspects of the ABA rules.

Advancing a client funds for living expenses is not allowed under the exception allowing advances for "costs." Doing so is generally regarded as unethical conduct; however, a loan from a lawyer to a client for living expenses may be evaluated separately under the rules relating to business transactions, rather than under the rules about advancing costs.

4. Lawyer's Interest in Litigation

Lawyers are prohibited from acquiring a proprietary interest in litigation in which they are involved under ABA Model Rule 1.8(i). Contingency fees in civil cases and liens to secure fees or expenses are exceptions.

The rule prohibiting a lawyer from obtaining an interest in litigation derives from the old prohibitions on maintenance, **champerty**, and **barratry**. Under English common law, these were crimes relating to "stirring up litigation." Champerty, obtaining a financial interest in the litigation, is still prohibited in some countries where the legal system is based on English law. It was long thought that such conduct encouraged unmeritorious litigation and dishonesty in the courtroom.

Obviously, these old rules have changed in the United States; all jurisdictions allow contingency fees (discussed in Chapter 7) and lawyer advertising (discussed in Chapter 6). The contemporary rules on holding an interest in litigation are founded not so much on concerns about "stirring up litigation," but on the conflict that arises when a lawyer has an interest in a lawsuit and may be tempted to favor his or her own financial interests in the outcome over the best interests of the client.

Champerty
An old common law agreement between a lawyer and a client under which the lawyer undertakes representation and pays costs and is reimbursed and paid out of the recovery; such agreements were outlawed in most states.

Barratry
The common law crime of stirring up lawsuits and disputes.

5. Gifts from Clients

A longstanding rule strongly disfavors gifts made from clients to their lawyers. This rule is especially pertinent when a lawyer drafts a document under which they receive a gift, such as in a will or trust. This scenario is rife with potential for undue influence, fraud, and overreaching, especially because clients in such cases are frequently elderly and may be more vulnerable to overreaching by their attorneys.

Courts frequently void both ***inter vivos*** **and testamentary gifts** in such cases, even without an affirmative showing of undue influence. Some courts allow the lawyer-beneficiary to present evidence showing the legitimacy of the gift. To do so, the lawyer must show that the gift was fair and fully intended by the client, who had the requisite capacity and was not subject to undue influence by the lawyer. One serious additional problem sometimes results from such a gift: It may raise the question of the client's testamentary capacity, potentially voiding the entire estate plan, including the gift.

In addition to the court voiding a gift, a lawyer may be subject to discipline under the state's ethics rules. ABA Model Rule 1.8 prohibits a lawyer from soliciting a substantial gift from a client or preparing a document in which the lawyer or a person related to the lawyer is given a gift, unless the lawyer is related to the client. "Simple gifts" from clients, such as holiday presents or tokens of appreciation, are excepted. (See Comment [6].)

One potential area for abuse arises if a lawyer drafts documents that appoint him or her to perform additional services, such as those of executor or trustee. Although this practice is common, more questionable is the lawyer's drafting of the document nominating him or her to serve as executor or trustee and as counsel. Some states prohibit this arrangement unless the court approves it upon a finding that it is in the best interests of the estate. Comment 8 to Rule 1.8 indicates that a conflict will be found if the lawyer cannot exercise independent professional judgment in the dual role. In these cases, the basic conflict rule (in Model Rule 1.7) would apply, and the lawyer would need to inform the client of the potential conflict and alternatives and to obtain the client's informed consent.

Gifts from Clients to Paralegals

Paralegals also have a potential conflict when a client gives them a gift, especially a valuable gift. As with business transactions, there is less risk of the appearance of undue influence when a gift is bestowed on a paralegal than on a lawyer, but the appearance of impropriety may be present nonetheless. In the case of a substantial gift, especially from an elderly or otherwise vulnerable client, it is advisable for the paralegal's supervising lawyer to recommend that the client consult with independent counsel and for the paralegal to refrain from working on the gift document in any way. For example, see the *In re Estate of Divine* case in Chapter 2.

6. Agreements with Clients Limiting the Attorney's Malpractice Liability

Both case law and the ethics rules prohibit lawyers from attempting to limit their liability for malpractice. In this situation, the lawyer is seeking to protect his or her own interests at the expense of the client. Lawyers cannot ask clients to sign an agreement not to pursue a claim against the lawyer before representation or pressure a client into signing a release after the malpractice has taken place.

ABA Model Rule 1.8(h) prohibits a lawyer from attempting to limit his or her liability prospectively unless the client is represented by independent counsel. It also prohibits a lawyer from settling a malpractice claim unless the client is advised in writing to seek independent counsel and given time to seek independent counsel's advice.

Lawyers cannot circumvent the rule against limiting liability by including in an **engagement letter or retainer agreement** provisions that relieve them from responsibility. For example, a provision that attempted to relieve the lawyer from responsibility if the client failed to inform the lawyer of a new address or phone number has been held to violate ethics rules. Both case law and bar ethics opinions have consistently disallowed such provisions. Equally unacceptable is an endorsement on a check that purports to release the lawyer from liability.

7. Payment of Attorneys' Fees by a Third Party

If someone other than the client pays the lawyer's fees, a conflict may arise over who is guiding the representation, the client or the payor. The lawyer's loyalty and sense of responsibility may be divided and judgment clouded if the person paying the fee wants to be involved in making decisions about the case. The potential for harm to the client is greatest when the interests of the client and the one paying for the representation diverge. Some common instances of third-party payments are a parent paying the fees for a child, a spouse for another spouse, a corporation for a director, and an employer for an employee.

A related conflicts situation arises when the legal fees for the representation of a criminal defendant are paid by an unknown third party who may be the operator of the criminal enterprise for which the defendant worked. In more than one such case, the unnamed third-party payor sought to guide the defense by keeping the client quiet about matters that may have mitigated the client's guilt or lessened the sentence. This situation could not only result in an ethical breach, subjecting the lawyer to a civil suit and disciplinary action, but constitutes grounds for appeal based on ineffective assistance of counsel.

Generally, the ethics rules permit third-party payment of attorney's fees so long as the client consents and the third party does not interfere with the exercise of the attorney's **independent professional judgment** or interfere with the attorney-client relationship and the duties of the attorney that arise from the relationship.

ABA Model Rule 1.8(f) prohibits an attorney from accepting compensation from a third party unless the client gives informed consent, the arrangement does not result in the third party's interference with the attorney's exercise of independent judgment, and confidentiality is protected. Related is Model Rule 5.4(c), which states that lawyers shall not permit the one who pays their fees "to direct or regulate" their professional judgment.

These rules have been applied in employment settings in which paralegals might find themselves. For example, the salary of a lawyer in a public defender's office is paid by a government entity, not by the indigent client whom the lawyer represents. The courts have upheld this arrangement so long as those who have interests that may conflict with a client's do not influence the lawyer's professional judgment and conduct or compensation. The issue is more complicated when a legal advocacy organization that has a political agenda is representing a client whose personal interests may at some time clash with the goals of the organization. The U.S. Supreme Court has endorsed the activities of such organizations and struck down the application of state statutes and ethics regulations that attempted to limit their activities. See *NAACP v. Button*, 371 U.S. 415 (1963), which was based on the First Amendment right of free association. The Court held in *NAACP* that only a compelling state interest could justify regulation that would limit activities of the organization in bringing lawsuits to redress grievances. Nonetheless, the interests of the organization and the client must be in close alignment to avoid a prohibited conflict.

8. Relatives and Close Friends

When married or other closely related lawyers represent adverse interests, the possibility of a conflict that may harm a client clearly exists. Spouses naturally discuss their work with one another, giving rise to the risk of disclosure of confidential information, which can be especially harmful if the spouse who learns the information represents the opposing side in a matter. Duties of loyalty and zealous representation are also implicated; a lawyer may not fight as zealously for a client when the opposing counsel is a spouse or partner. Because spouses have a financial interest in one another's income, the potential to increase the marital funds from a large fee may also influence a lawyer-spouse's sense of loyalty or independent judgment.

Conflicts based on family or other close relationships are not covered explicitly in the language of the conflicts rule; however, Comment 11 to Model Rule 1.7 states that lawyers who are closely related by blood or marriage (e.g., "parent, child, sibling, or spouse") may not ordinarily represent opposing clients in the same matter without informed consent. Family conflicts are not imputed to the lawyer's firm. Some states have more specific prohibitions in this kind of situation, listing the specific relatives who are affected and expanding the scope of the rule to specified nonrelatives.

Relatives of Paralegals

The ethical rules governing conflicts based on family relationships are also applicable to paralegals. The potential for disclosure of protected information is just as great when the conflict involves a paralegal as when it involves a lawyer. Law firms should consider family conflicts when conducting conflicts checks. Paralegals who are related by blood or marriage to someone working in the legal community must be certain to inform their firms fully of their family relationships so that potential conflicts can be identified and addressed.

Two state ethics opinions have addressed the problems created when a paralegal is related to another person involved in a representation. Vermont Ethics Opinion 87-15 (1987) recommended that a law firm could represent clients in a real estate transaction in which the adverse party was the spouse of one of the firm's paralegals so long as the situation was fully disclosed to the client, the paralegal did not work on the matter, and the paralegal was admonished not to reveal client confidences or secrets. Similarly, Michigan Ethics Opinion CI-1168 (1986) found that a legal services organization could represent a plaintiff in an action in which a potential defendant was about to be married to the organization's paralegal and in another action in which the fiancé's father (and paralegal's future father-in-law) was a defendant. The opinion advised full disclosure and consent by the client-plaintiffs. Absent consent, the opinions advised that the organization would be required to withdraw from representation or to terminate the paralegal's employment.

F. Imputed Disqualification

1. Introduction

As mentioned throughout the previous sections, the conflict of one person in a firm may cause the entire firm to be disqualified from representing a client. ***Vicarious or imputed disqualification*** is based mainly on the idea that all the lawyers in a firm know everything about all the clients and cases being handled by the firm. Particularly, the partners in a firm (rather than other employees, whether lawyers or nonlawyers) are believed to share confidential information about clients. Although sharing of information to this extent may not take place in large law firms, it is likely to happen in small law firms. Other grounds for imputing conflicts lie in conflicting financial incentives. Even if confidential information can be protected by careful screening, it may not be possible to protect against the actual or perceived pressure to handle a case in a manner that will most benefit the firm and not necessarily be the most beneficial for the client.

When a firm is disqualified by a court, it may be required to **disgorge fees** paid for the legal services during the representation. This remedy is most often applied when the firm knew or should have known of the conflict and failed to disclose it to the client. A disqualification may also be the basis for a **malpractice** case by the client against the lawyer and firm for breach of fiduciary duty.

The strict application of imputed disqualification rules has created severe problems for law firms, individual lawyers, and clients. Lawyers are much more mobile in their careers than they once were, and clients choose lawyers on a matter-by-matter basis. Law firms merge and dissolve, creating great potential for conflicts. Vicarious disqualification also poses special concerns for paralegals, whose job mobility may be threatened by an overly rigid application of the rules.

Vicarious or imputed disqualification
The imputation of a conflict to others in a firm so that the entire firm is disqualified from undertaking the representation.

2. ABA and State Rules on Imputation of Conflicts and Screening

ABA Model Rule 1.10 distinguishes among different kinds of conflicts. It does not prohibit the firm or lawyer from representing the client if the conflict is personal to the lawyer, namely conflicts covered in Rule 1.8, such as business transactions with and gifts from clients. Part (b) of the Rule covers conflicts that may be created when a **lawyer leaves a firm**. The firm may represent a client whose interests are adverse to those of a former client of the lawyer who left the firm unless the matter is the same or substantially the same, or unless any remaining lawyer has confidential information related to the matter. The rule allows for informed written client consent to conflicts that are imputed to a firm.

Model Rule 1.10(a)(2) allows screening of lawyers with conflicts created when a lawyer changes firms. Lawyers must be screened timely and not apportioned any fees from the matter. Written notice must be given to the former client, indicating the screening procedures and an agreement that the firm will respond to any inquiries or objections from the former client. Upon the former client's request or termination of the screen, the new firm must certify compliance with the screening procedures to the former client. Note that the rule does not require that the firm obtain consent of the former client; however, in practice, consent with screening is preferred.

As noted earlier in this chapter, the Model Rules also have specific provisions for **government lawyers**. Rule 1.11 allows a former government lawyer to represent a client in a matter in which the lawyer participated while employed by the government, with the agency's informed written consent. It further allows another lawyer in the firm to undertake representation when such a conflict exists, provided the former government lawyer is screened from the case and receives no part of the fee, and written notice is given to the government agency. The rule also prohibits a former government lawyer from representing a client against a person about whom the lawyer has damaging confidential information obtained while the lawyer was in government service. Screening and disallowing fee participation in the matter are permitted to enable another lawyer in the former government lawyer's firm to represent such a client. Rule 1.11(d) covers lawyers who are currently employed by the government. It prohibits them from participating in matters in which they were previously involved in private practice and from negotiating for private employment with an opposing attorney or party in a current case.

3. Court Rulings on Imputed Disqualification

Most court decisions on vicarious disqualification were made during the time that the ABA Model Code, which had stricter rules, was followed by nearly all jurisdictions. As a result, the courts have frequently applied a per se rule of imputed disqualification. The trend, however, is toward a more flexible approach, under which the presumption of imputed disqualification may be rebutted by evidence that the disqualified lawyer did not have access to confidential information or that the disqualified lawyer is being properly screened from any involvement in the matter in question. See, for example, *People ex rel. Dept. of Corp. v. Speedee Oil Change Systems, Inc.*, 20 Cal. 4th 1135 (1999). Not all courts are in favor of this trend. Some continue to follow "bright-line" rules requiring disqualification of lawyers and nonlawyers in all simultaneous conflicts where there is not client consent.

4. Use of Screens to Avoid Disqualification

The use of **screening** to overcome disqualification of the entire firm first arose in cases involving former government lawyers. Although the risk of conflicts involving former government lawyers is especially high because of their potential inside knowledge, connections, and influence, the legal community has been concerned about the ability of government lawyers to move into private practice. If disqualification rules are strictly applied, and screens are not allowed to overcome them, government lawyers' employment options are quite limited. Going into government service would become a "permanent" career choice, a significant deterrent to entering government service.

Screening in private law firms, in cases involving lawyer and nonlawyer employees not previously in government service, has become common practice. A screen (which is also called a ***cone of silence*** or ***ethical wall***) isolates the disqualified lawyer or paralegal by setting up procedures to prevent the disqualified person from having access to information about the matter and from being involved in any way in the matter. Screens are often a requirement for a client consent or waiver and are sometimes used when consent cannot be obtained in hopes of avoiding disqualification.

For a court to find that a screen is effective, careful procedures should be followed:

Screen, cone of silence or ethical wall
Isolates a disqualified person by setting up procedures to prevent the affected person from any involvement with or communication about the matter.

- A **memorandum** concerning the affected matter and person involved should be sent to the entire firm, including lawyer and nonlawyer staff, spelling out the restrictions on access to confidential information and on communicating about the matter.
- **Files and documents** should be marked to indicate the limitations on access. Hard copy files should be stored separately in a place that cannot be accessed by the affected person. Blocks of electronic records should be employed to prevent the screened employee from having access to documents on the firm's network.
- Firm and department **e-mails and voice mails** concerning the matter in question should not be communicated to the affected lawyer or paralegal.
- The screen must be erected in a **timely** manner, for example, before the affected person begins employment with the firm or as soon as the conflict is discovered.
- **Physical separation** of the disqualified person from those working on the case is sometimes advisable. In other words, the affected person should not share the same or proximate workspace with others working on the case.

- The affected person should sign an **agreement** vowing not to disclose any confidential information about the matter and not to discuss the matter with anyone at the firm.
- A lawyer who is disqualified should agree not to **share fees** generated by the matter; accounting procedures should be set up to ensure that fees are not shared.
- If the matter extends over a long period of time, the announcements of the screen should be **republished** periodically as a reminder and for the benefit of new employees.

Proving the effectiveness of a screen can be challenging. For the most part, a court evaluating the procedures expects to review affidavits and testimony about the thoroughness and care of the measures taken and the extent to which they are observed. Screening procedures should be routine and careful records must be kept. A court will examine not only the specific procedures in place, but the context of the situation. Is the firm large or small? Does the disqualified attorney or paralegal work in the same department or physical area of the office as the team representing the client in question? Where are the files (including electronic files) relating to the case located? Do the disqualified person and the staff handling the representation work on other matters together? Does the firm have sanctions for breaking the rules relating to the wall? How many other persons in the firm have access to the confidential information?

Firms sometimes use disqualification motions as a **strategy**, to delay a case from proceeding to trial even if they do not reasonably believe that confidential client information has been compromised. Courts look askance at motions that are based on flimsy facts or arguments, especially if they are not made as early as possible in the proceedings or are based on appearance of impropriety rather than on any real danger of harm to a client or a breach of confidentiality. Firms have also been known to use the disqualification rules to prevent another firm from being able to represent a client on a specific matter. For example, a large corporate client may refer minor matters to all the competitor firms in town so that, in the event of major litigation, no other qualified lawyer without a conflict is available to represent the opposing party—that is, all the attorneys are "conflicted out."

As noted above, the ABA Model Rules now support the use of screens, and the trend among states is to endorse this practice as well. At the present time, most states allow screens. (For a court decision exemplifying this trend, see *Kirk v. First American Title Ins.*, 183 Cal. App. 4th 776, 108 Cal. Rptr. 3d 620 (2010).) Advocates of screens as a means to cure an imputed conflict believe not only that the rules are antiquated and impair lawyer mobility and client choice of counsel, but that they discriminate unfairly against private lawyers in favor of government lawyers.

Screening Paralegals and Other Nonlawyer Employees

Many cases in the last decade have addressed the application of the conflict rules to paralegals. The crux of many of these cases is whether a screen can protect a firm from being disqualified because of a conflict of a paralegal. In 1988, the ABA issued Informal Opinion 88-1521, which endorsed the screening of paralegals and which has been followed in most cases decided since that time.

> A law firm that employs a nonlawyer who formerly was employed by another firm may continue representing clients whose interests conflict with the interests of clients of the former employer on whose matters the nonlawyer has worked, as long as the employing firm screens the nonlawyer from information about or participating in matters involving those clients and strictly adheres to the screening process described in this opinion and as long as no information relating to the representation of the clients of the former employer is revealed by the nonlawyer to any person in the employing firm. In addition, the nonlawyer's former employer must admonish the nonlawyer against revelation of information relating to the representation of clients of the former employer.

The opinion distinguishes between using a screen for a lawyer's conflicts and using one for those of a paralegal. At the time this opinion was written, a conflict occasioned by a lawyer's move to another firm would usually result in the disqualification of the new firm, and a screen would not protect the firm from disqualification in most states. However, this advisory opinion found that a paralegal with a similar conflict can be screened, thereby preventing the paralegal's firm's disqualification. The rationale for the more flexible application of screens in cases involving paralegals is expressed in the opinion as follows:

> It is important that nonlawyer employees have as much mobility in employment opportunity as possible consistent with the protection of clients' interests. To so limit employment opportunities that some nonlawyers trained to work with law firms might be required to leave the careers for which they are trained would disserve clients as well as the legal profession. Accordingly, any restrictions on the nonlawyer's employment should be held to the minimum necessary to protect confidentiality of client information.

The ABA Model Guidelines for the Utilization of Paralegal Services also endorse the use of screens for conflicts involving paralegals. The American Law Institute *Restatement of the Law (3rd) of the Law Governing Lawyers* early on endorsed the principle that disqualification rules for lawyers should not limit paralegal job mobility. Comment 4 to Rule 1.10 was added in 2001, stating that imputed disqualification does not apply to nonlawyers, including paralegals, legal secretaries, or law clerks. It also states:

> Such persons, however, ordinarily must be screened from any personal participation in the matter to avoid communication to others in the firm of confidential information that both the nonlawyers and the firm have a legal duty to protect.

Several important state cases decided in the 1990s demonstrate the complexities of this issue and the range of opinions expressed by courts. In an early and influential California case, *In re Complex Asbestos Litigation*, the plaintiff's attorney, a sole practitioner, was disqualified from a number of asbestos cases because his paralegal had previously worked for a firm representing several of the defendants in the case and he had made no attempt to screen this paralegal. The California Court of Appeals endorsed the use of a screening procedure for paralegals to rebut the presumption that confidential information was shared (even though the paralegal in this case was not screened). See this case at the companion website that accompanies this text.

Several Texas cases have fleshed out the rules about paralegal conflicts. The Texas Supreme Court endorsed the use of screens for paralegals in ongoing litigation in the case of *Phoenix Founders, Inc. v. Marshall*, 887 S.W.2d 831 (Tex. 1994), presented later in this chapter. In other cases, courts approved the use of screens but found the procedures employed by the firms to be inadequate. See, for example, *Grant v. Thirteenth Court of Appeals*, 38 Tex. Sup. Ct. J. 12 (1994). In a later case, the Texas Court of Appeals denied a disqualification, citing careful procedures put in place to screen the paralegal from participation in the case (*Rubin v. Enns*, 23 S.W.3d 382 (2000)). In *In re American Home Products Corp.*, 985 S.W.2d 68 (1998), the Court applied the precedents to a complicated situation involving a freelance paralegal and co-counsel. The Texas Supreme Court disqualified the lawyer, holding that the paralegal (who protested that she was not a paralegal and did not have confidential information) had a conflict and that she was not properly screened. The Texas appellate courts have also addressed a conflict that arose when a lawyer worked for opposing counsel as a paralegal prior to becoming a lawyer. Although the court affirmed that the presumption of shared confidences is rebuttable for paralegals, it applied an irrebuttable presumption to these facts and disqualified the firm. *In re TXU U.S. Holdings Co.*, 110 S.W.3d 62 (2002). Finally, two more Texas Supreme Court cases have reaffirmed the screening of paralegals: *In re Columbia Valley Healthcare System*, 320 S.W.3d 819 (Tex. 2010), and *In re Guaranty Ins. Services, Inc.*, 343 S.W.3d 130 (Tex. 2011), which appears at the end of this chapter.

In March 2016, the Texas Supreme Court amended Texas Disciplinary Rule of Professional Conduct 1.06 to add a comment addressing the imputation of conflicts to nonlawyer employees and lawyers who were formerly involved in a matter in a non-lawyer role. Comment [19] provides that with proper screening, the conflict of interest of a non-lawyer, or the conflict of a lawyer that arose before the person became a lawyer, is *not* imputed:

> A law firm is not prohibited from representing a client . . . merely because a nonlawyer employee of the firm, such as a paralegal or legal secretary, has a conflict of interest arising from prior employment or some other source . . . [or] . . . merely because [of] . . . a conflict of interest arising from events that occurred before the person became a lawyer, such as work that the person did as a law clerk or intern. But the firm must ordinarily screen the person with the conflict from any personal participation in the matter to prevent the person's communicating to others in the firm confidential information that the person and the firm have a legal duty to protect.

Cases involving paralegal conflicts have been decided at the appellate level in Florida, but the judicial districts there do not share a single formulation of a rule. See, for example, *Eastrich No. 157 Corp. v. Gatto*, 868 So. 2d 1266 (Fla. App. 2004). Arizona addressed the issue of paralegal conflicts in *Smart Industries Corp. v. Superior Court*, 876 P.2d 1176 (Ariz. App. 1994), and Oklahoma set its standards in *Hayes v. Central State Orthopedic Specialists, Inc.*, 2002 Okla. 30, 51 P.3d 562 (Okla. 2002). A Georgia appellate court upheld the use of screens for paralegals in *Hodge v. Urfa-Sexton*, 322 Ga. App. 534 (Ga. App. 2013). The Rhode Island courts have also decided in favor of the use of screens. In denying a disqualification motion based on a paralegal's conflict, the Rhode Island Superior Court stated:

> Consequently, there is nothing in the record to indicate that disqualification is necessary pursuant to Rule 1.10(c)(1). Although there is a rebuttable presumption that confidential information was disclosed (citations omitted), there is nothing in the record to indicate that there were any improper disclosures of confidential information and, given the fact that [the firm] no longer employs [the paralegal], there is no reason for the Court to believe that any such communications are likely to occur in the future.

Fedora v. Werber, PC/07-6053 (R.I. Super. 2-22-2010).

The Ohio Supreme Court has established an analysis for deciding when a nonlawyer conflict will result in the disqualification of a law firm in *Green v. Toledo Hosp.*, 94 Ohio St. 3d 480, 764 N.E.2d 979 (2002). The Nevada Supreme Court overruled its 1997 decision disallowing screens for paralegals in the case of *Leibowitz v. Dist. Ct.*, 119 Nev. Adv. Op. No. 57, 78 P.3d 515 (2003), overruling in part *Ciaffone v.*

District Court, 113 Nev. 1165, 945 P.2d 950 (1997). See this case at the end of the chapter.

In 2016, Ohio's Board of Professional Conduct issued advice based on Ohio's rules of practice governing certified legal interns, who effectively function as lawyers under clinical supervision while in law school. The Board said:

> The conflicts of a former legal intern, newly employed as a lawyer, are not imputed to the lawyers in a law firm, but necessitate the screening of the lawyer from any matter [for which] he or she had substantial responsibility.

Kansas is the only state whose supreme court has taken a more restrictive view. See *Zimmerman v. Mahaska Bottling Co.*, 270 Kan. 810, 19 P.3d 784 (2001), available at the companion website that accompanies this text. The Alabama State Bar has an ethics opinion that supports disqualification of firms based on paralegal conflicts:

> A nonlawyer employee who changes law firms must be held to the same standards as a lawyer in determining whether a conflict of interest exists. A firm which hires a nonlawyer employee previously employed by opposing counsel in pending litigation would have a conflict of interest and must therefore be disqualified if, during the course of the previous employment, the employee acquired confidential information concerning the case.

Alabama State Bar Association Ethics Opinion 2002-01.

Several bar association ethics opinions have also addressed the issue. See, for example, Florida Advisory Opinion 86-5 (1986); Kentucky Bar Association Ethics Opinion E-308 (1985), which sets forth eight steps (including an effective screen) on the former and employing firm to ensure against breaches of confidentiality; North Carolina Ethics Opinions 74 (1989) and 176 (1994); Philadelphia Ethics Opinion 80-77 (1980); Vermont Bar Association Opinion 78-2 (1978); New Jersey Ethics Opinion 665 (1992) reversing an earlier opinion; Michigan Ethics Opinions RI-115 (1992) and RI-284 (1996); and New York State Bar Association Ethics Opinion 2004-774. The Nebraska State Bar rescinded an ethics opinion that disallowed screens in conflict matters that involve paralegals.

As is evident from the cases in this chapter, the courts have shown sensitivity to the different roles of the lawyer and paralegal and to the problems of job changing in an increasingly mobile legal business. Final note: Because of the differences among states, it is important for paralegals to be up to date on the latest law in the jurisdiction where they practice.

G. Conflicts Checks

Conducting a conflicts check when a firm is considering hiring a new employee, representing a new client, or undertaking a new matter is necessary to identify potential and real conflicts. Comment [3] to ABA Model Rule 1.7 calls for every lawyer to "adopt reasonable procedures, appropriate for the size and type of firm and practice, to determine in both litigation and non-litigation matters the persons and issues involved" so that a determination can be made as to whether a conflict or potential conflict exists.

When a **prospective client** seeks representation by a firm, the lawyer or paralegal who has the initial contact with the person should obtain information necessary to conduct the conflicts check before the prospective client reveals confidential information about the matter for which representation is sought. This early detection process gives greater protection of the confidential information in the event that the firm does not undertake representation and prevents the law firm from inadvertently placing itself in a conflict situation. New client information obtained should relate to the client's activities, other litigation, and the nature of representation sought. If the client is a business client, such as a corporation or partnership, the information should include the names of subsidiaries and other related businesses as well as principal shareholders, officers, directors, partners, and the like. The lawyer and client should discuss the nature of the legal services sought—for instance, whether representation is needed for a single matter such as a lawsuit or negotiation of a business deal or is needed for an array of ongoing legal matters. If a lawsuit is contemplated, the names of potential adversaries should be obtained. Finally, if the client has other legal matters pending, basic information about these matters (such as the names of adversaries and counsel) should be obtained. When an existing client seeks representation on a new matter, information relating to the nature of this matter and potential adversaries should always be obtained. Finally, it is good practice to update information on existing clients regularly—names of officers and directors and the nature of business activities, for instance—to ensure the accuracy and currency of all information.

Similarly, prospective employees, including both lawyers and non-lawyers, must provide the firm with basic information about matters on which they worked in previous employment, major business or financial interests that have the potential to create conflicts, and personal and family relationships that may give rise to conflicts. It is critical in providing this information not to reveal any confidences and to supply the minimum amount of information needed to conduct a conflicts check. ABA Formal Ethics Opinion 09-455 provides guidance to lawyers and paralegals who are changing firms, and to the firms that hope to hire them. It states in part:

Any disclosure of conflicts information should be no greater than reasonably necessary to accomplish the purpose of detecting and resolving conflicts and must not compromise the attorney-client privilege or otherwise prejudice a client or former client. A lawyer or law firm receiving conflicts information may not reveal such information or use it for purposes other than detecting and resolving conflicts of interest. Disclosure normally should not occur until the moving lawyers and the prospective new firm have engaged in substantive discussion regarding a possible new association.

The firm must process the information to determine if any conflicts or potential conflicts exist that would preclude representation or would require consents or the erection of a screen to isolate the disqualified employee. Many firms have computer software programs to conduct conflicts checks quickly and thoroughly. Although a database is an important tool, many firms are finding that using a database alone is not sufficient to identify all potential conflicts. To provide further screening, firms are communicating with daily e-mail alerts about new client matters and using in-house conflicts specialists to follow through on all checks.

Firms also need an established procedure for **evaluating conflicts** that have been identified through the conflicts check. They need to decide how the firm should address a potential conflict: How serious is the conflict? Is it the kind of conflict that would be imputed to the firm? Can the firm provide adequate representation under the circumstances? Can client consent be obtained? Will a screen be effective, and will it be recognized by a court? Some firms have an ethics or conflicts committee or an ethicist-lawyer to advise on these matters. Prompt action on new clients and matters is essential to prevent a client or prospective client from delay in securing counsel and to erect a screen timely if the representation is undertaken. The conflicts committee should evaluate each new client, new matter, and new prospective employee—along with any potential conflicts they carry with them—applying the relevant ethics rules, case law, and firm policies that may have an impact on their decision.

Another way firms are protecting themselves against conflicts is to send very clear and detailed letters to parties with whom they have some contact but are not representing, including prospective clients, parties in joint litigation, and peripheral parties in transactions. These letters explain that the firm is not representing the party. Likewise, engagement letters for clients should be clear about the scope of the representation to keep the firm from being "conflicted out" of representing another client in a different matter that may come up later.

Avoiding conflicts of interest is a critical matter for paralegals. Like lawyers, paralegals have an ethical responsibility to **keep good records** of the matters on which they work and to be forthcoming with this information when appropriate. When a paralegal prepares to change jobs, begins work on a new matter, or engages in freelance work, the record of client matters on which the paralegal worked will be needed. At least one state, New York, requires lawyers to keep records of client matters for this purpose.

For freelance and independent contractor paralegals, every new assignment is a job change; freelancing greatly increases the potential for greater numbers of conflicts. Although it has become common practice for freelance paralegals and lawyers to handle assignments on a temporary, as-needed basis, this practice does necessitate careful monitoring. ABA Formal Opinion 88-356 (1988) endorses the use of temporary lawyers and the agencies that place them in firms but warns that special care is required to guard against conflicts and breaches of confidentiality. These same principles apply to the increasingly common practice of outsourcing legal work.

The NFPA Model Code recognizes the importance of conflicts checks by calling on paralegals to "create and maintain an effective database" to enable the paralegal to identify conflicts, to reveal such information as is necessary to evaluate the existence of an actual conflict, and to comply with screening procedures. NFPA Model Code EC-1.6(e).

REVIEW QUESTIONS

1. What is the general rule about business transactions between lawyers and clients? Give an example of a business transaction between a lawyer and a client. Why do ethics rules prohibit them? Name two conditions necessary for a business transaction to override the ethics rules' prohibitions.
2. What is the general rule about a lawyer being granted publication and media rights? What is the rationale behind it?
3. Are lawyers prohibited from paying clients' costs in a matter? Loaning a client money? Why? What are the circumstances under which a lawyer may cover a client's costs?
4. Why are lawyers prohibited from obtaining an ownership interest in a lawsuit they are handling? How does this rule square with the idea of contingency fees?
5. Under what circumstances are gifts from clients prohibited? Explain the rationale. What steps should be taken to legitimize a gift to an attorney? Do some states have statutes that cover this situation? How and why? Do these rules apply to paralegals?
6. May a lawyer limit his or her malpractice liability to a client in advance of the representation? Why or why not? May a lawyer get a client to settle a malpractice claim in writing? Under what conditions?
7. What potential conflicts arise when a third party pays a client's legal fees? Give two examples of how this can commonly come up. How

might a lawyer accept the fee and guard against the conflicts that might arise from it? How do these rules affect legal aid organizations? Public defenders' offices?
8. What do the ethics rules say about family members representing adverse interests? What family or other relationships are covered? Do these rules apply to paralegals? Do any state's rules cover relationships outside of blood or marriage? Are these conflicts imputed to a paralegal's firm?
9. What is imputed disqualification? What is the basis for this rule? How does the rule apply to paralegals?
10. What do the ABA Model Rules say about imputed disqualification? When does it apply or not apply to different kinds of conflicts?
11. What is the basis for screens being used to prevent disqualification in the case of former government lawyers?
12. What do the ABA rules say about screening of lawyers who change firms? Why is the position of courts and state bar associations changing?
13. What are the elements of a screen that will withstand judicial scrutiny?
14. Why might a court look with disfavor on disqualification motions?
15. What does the ABA say about the use of screens in conflicts cases involving paralegals? Is this policy more flexible than that applied to attorneys? Why?
16. What is the majority position of the states on the use of screens in cases involving paralegal conflicts?
17. How should a conflicts check be conducted when a firm has a new client? A new matter or case? A new employee? On an ongoing basis?
18. Describe a paralegal's obligation to avoid conflicts when changing positions. How does this differ from the requirements for freelance paralegals?
19. What do the ABA Model Guidelines for the Utilization of Paralegal Services say about the screening of paralegals? What do the state guidelines say? How do NALA and NFPA address paralegal conflicts in their ethics codes?

DISCUSSION QUESTIONS AND HYPOTHETICALS

1. Do you think paralegals should be subject to the same rules on conflicts as lawyers? Why or why not? Make a list of the reasons on each side of this argument.
2. Do you think the rules on conflicts of interest are antiquated? Why or why not? How would you change them to make them more responsive to the current and future legal environment?

3. What would you do if a client of a lawyer with whom you work asked you to invest in their business? Buy property from them? Do you think that entering into these transactions would create a conflict of interest? Why or why not? How could you remedy the conflict?
4. Do you think that a paralegal obtaining the rights to a current client's story creates a conflict of interest? Why or why not?
5. Would you loan a client money for living expenses? Why or why not? Would your answer be different if lending the money would keep your client from accepting a low settlement offer because of the client's dire financial condition? What if the client is indigent or unhoused?
6. What would you do if an elderly client wanted to leave you a substantial gift in their will? Would it make any difference if the client had no other living relatives? What if the client wanted to do this because she was estranged from her children?
7. What would you do if a client gave you a valuable piece of jewelry? Would it make a difference if the gift were in thanks for your work on a case? What if the client promised to give you a personal "bonus" if your firm prevailed in the case?
8. What would you do if you worked for a firm that had all new clients sign an engagement agreement limiting the firm's malpractice liability?
9. Do you think the rules prohibiting conflicts among relatives should be limited to parents, children, siblings, and spouses? What about roommates? Long-term live-in relationships? In-laws? Domestic partnerships? Is it any "safer" for closely related lawyers and paralegals to work in the same firm? What kinds of ethical and other problems might this create? Should these conflicts be imputed to the firm?
10. List all the reasons you can think of to justify imputed disqualification. Do these reasons also apply to paralegals? Should the same rules of imputed disqualification apply to paralegals?
11. Knowing how people love to talk about their work, do you think an internal memorandum telling the staff not to discuss a particular case with a certain employee is really an effective method to protect confidentiality? What other measures or sanctions would be more effective?
12. Do you think it is possible to screen an employee in a small law firm; for example, a firm with one lawyer, one paralegal, and one legal assistant? What if the firm had two lawyers, two paralegals, and two legal assistants?
13. Make a list of all the information you would want to conduct a conflicts check on in the case of the following: (1) a new client; (2) a new matter for an existing client; (3) a prospective paralegal employee; (4) a prospective attorney employee; (5) a prospective partner.

14. Who do you think should conduct conflicts checks and decide how to handle conflicts matters within a law firm? Does it make a difference if the firm is a national, multi-office firm or a small, local firm?
15. What kinds of conflicts policies (going beyond the legal ethics rules) do you think a law firm should ideally have? Consider the economic implications of policies that may impose limits on a firm accepting cases.
16. What kind of information should a paralegal keep in their own career conflict database? When should a paralegal give this information to prospective employers? Does supplying this information in itself violate confidentiality rules? What should you do if a firm that has offered you a job does not request this information? (See *Dillman v. Holland & Knight*, 2007 CA 007569 B (D.C. Sup. Ct. 2007).)
17. Should agencies that place paralegals in temporary or freelance jobs do conflicts checks before they send a paralegal to a law firm? Why or why not? Should a paralegal work for an agency that fails to do this? What would you do if you went out on a freelance job and discovered after two days that you had worked on the opposing side of the case the previous week?
18. Bill Brown is a paralegal who works for a large law firm handling the defense in some major products liability litigation. Bill knows that the cases are settling and that he may therefore lose his job. During his employment for this firm, he met a solo lawyer, Mary Maynard, a plaintiff's lawyer who was on the opposition in a few of the products liability cases. He really respected Mary's work. She does family law cases in addition to the litigation that Bill worked on. Can he contact Mary about employment with her? If she offers him a position, can he take it? Are there any restrictions on his work for her firm? Can he check the computer files of the firm to see what cases Mary and his firm have in common? Can he work for Mary on other cases? If so, what measures must be taken to guard against a conflict? Can he go to work for Mary after the products liability cases settle?
19. A law firm represents 600 clients in a class action against a telecommunications company. After negotiating with the company, the firm enters into an agreement under which (1) the company pays the firm $2 million; (2) the firm agrees to persuade the clients to accept expedited mediation procedures to resolve their claims; (3) the company agrees to pay the firm an additional $3.5 million on a sliding scale as the claims are resolved; and (4) the firm agrees to work for the company as a consultant for another two years after the claims are resolved for a fee of $1 million a year. Evaluate each of these aspects of the agreement under the rules in this chapter. Are any of these provisions, or the agreement as a whole, unethical under the rules? Which rules? Are these provisions sanctionable by

the court or the bar? What might be other consequences of this agreement? (See *Johnson v. Nextel Communications, Inc.*, 660 F.3d 131 (2d Cir. 2011).)

RESEARCH PROJECTS AND ASSIGNMENTS

1. What are your state's ethics rules on conflicts of interest? Does your state or local bar association have any special guidelines or ethics opinions on the application of conflict rules to paralegals? Are there any cases in your state involving firm disqualification because of a paralegal conflict of interest? What do they hold and how do they compare with the cases in this chapter?
2. Interview paralegals at five local law firms of different sizes and ask them about their policies and procedures for establishing screens and conducting conflicts checks. Ask the paralegal manager or a senior paralegal if they believe that screens are effective.
3. Draft a form to use for conflicts checks of paralegals and the related policies on how and when checks are done and follow-up procedures.
4. Draft an "I'm not your lawyer" letter to a prospective client that your firm interviewed but decided not to represent.
5. The question of what to disclose when interviewing for a position is sometimes challenging because it pits two ethics principles—avoiding conflicts of interest and protecting client confidences—against each other. For one local bar's guidance on what to do when interviewing with a new firm, see D.C. Ethics Opinion 2002-312. Summarize this opinion for the class.
6. What happens to conflicts when a paralegal becomes a lawyer? Which rules apply? See *In re TXU U.S. Holdings Company*, 110 S.W.3d 62 (2002), for one court's application of the rules.
7. Do the rules about nonlawyer employees apply when a former employee of the opposing party is hired by a law firm? See *In re Bell Helicopter Textron*, 87 S.W.3d 139 (2002).
8. Los Angeles County Bar Association ethics opinion (11-524) on hiring and screening nonlawyer employees (in this instance, law clerks) who may have conflicts contains a footnote that states: "The discussion of nonlawyer employees does not include paralegals, for purposes of this Opinion, as paralegals are subject to the same confidentiality requirements as attorneys under the provisions of Business & Professions Code Section 6453." Look up this code section and share with the class your interpretation of this statement.
9. For an example of a conflict that rises to the level of elder financial abuse, read and analyze *Disciplinary Counsel v. Shaw*, 126 Ohio St.3d 494, 935 N.E.2d 405 (2010). See how many conflicts arise in this case and which rules they violate. Do you think that the sanction was appropriate? Why?

CASES FOR ANALYSIS

The following case is an example of the trend in the courts to permit the use of screens in matters involving a job-changing paralegal.

Phoenix Founders, Inc. v. Marshall
887 S.W.2d 831 (Tex. 1994)

In this original proceeding, we consider whether a law firm must be disqualified from ongoing litigation because it rehired a legal assistant who had worked for opposing counsel for three weeks. We hold that disqualification is not required if the rehiring firm is able to establish that it has effectively screened the paralegal from any contact with the underlying suit. Because this standard had not been adopted in Texas prior to the trial court's disqualification order, we deny mandamus relief without prejudice to allow the trial court to reconsider its ruling in light of today's opinion.

The present dispute arises from a suit brought by Phoenix Founders, Inc. and others ("Phoenix") to collect a federal-court judgment against Ronald and Jane Beneke and others. The law firm of Thompson & Knight represented Phoenix in the original federal-court suit, which began in 1990 and ended in 1991, and has also represented them in the collection suit since its commencement in 1992. The Benekes have been represented in the latter suit by the firm David & Goodman.

In July of 1993, Denise Hargrove, a legal assistant at Thompson & Knight, left her position at that firm to begin working for David & Goodman as a paralegal. While at David & Goodman, Hargrove billed six-tenths of an hour on the collection suit for locating a pleading. She also discussed the case generally with Mark Goodman, the Benekes' lead counsel.

After three weeks at David & Goodman, Hargrove returned to Thompson & Knight to resume work as a paralegal. At the time of the rehiring, Thompson & Knight made no effort to question Hargrove in regard to potential conflicts of interest resulting from her employment at David & Goodman.

Three weeks after Hargrove had returned, counsel for the Benekes wrote to Thompson & Knight asserting that its renewed employment of Hargrove created a conflict of interest. The letter demanded that the firm withdraw from its representation of Phoenix.

Hargrove resigned from Thompson & Knight the next week, after having been given the option of either resigning with severance pay or being terminated. The firm itself, however, refused to withdraw from the case. The Benekes then filed a motion to disqualify. . . .

The disqualification order states that Hargrove possesses confidential information relating to the Benekes, and that all such confidential information was imputed to the firm of Thompson & Knight at the time she was rehired.

This Court has not previously addressed the standards governing a disqualification motion based on the hiring of a nonlawyer employee. With respect to lawyers, however, this Court has adopted a standard requiring disqualification whenever counsel undertakes representation of an interest that is adverse to that of a former client, as long as the matters embraced in the pending suit are "substantially related" to the factual matters involved in the previous suit. [Citation omitted.] This strict rule is based on a conclusive presumption that confidences and secrets were imparted to the attorney during the prior representation. [Citation omitted.]

The Benekes argue that the standards applied to the hiring of lawyers should also apply to the hiring of paralegals. . . . [T]he Benekes urge that the entire firm of Thompson & Knight must be automatically disqualified because of the confidences Hargrove obtained while working at David & Goodman.

We agree that a paralegal who has actually worked on a case must be subject to . . . a conclusive presumption that confidences and secrets were imparted during the course of the paralegal's work on the case. . . .

We disagree, however, with the argument that paralegals should be conclusively presumed to share confidential information with members of their firms. The Disciplinary Rules require a lawyer having direct supervisory authority over a nonlawyer to make reasonable efforts to ensure that the nonlawyer's conduct is compatible with the professional obligations of the lawyer. Tex. Disciplinary R. Prof. Conduct 5.03(a). If the supervising lawyer orders, encourages, or even permits a nonlawyer to engage in conduct that would be subject to discipline if engaged in by a lawyer, the lawyer will be subject to discipline. R. 5.03(b). Thus, to the extent that the Disciplinary Rules prohibit a lawyer from revealing confidential information, R. 1.05(b)(1), they also prohibit a supervising lawyer from ordering, encouraging, or permitting a nonlawyer to reveal such information.

This view is consistent with the weight of authority in other jurisdictions. The American Bar Association's Committee on Professional Ethics has considered whether a law firm that hires a paralegal may continue representing clients whose interests conflict with interests of the former employer's clients on whose matters the paralegal has worked. ABA Ethics Informal Op. 1526 (1988). After surveying case law and ethics opinions from a number of jurisdictions, the Committee concluded that the new firm need not be disqualified, as long as the firm and the paralegal strictly adhere to the screening process set forth in the opinion, and as long as the paralegal does not reveal any information relating to the former employer's clients to any person in the employing firm. Id. A number of courts have since relied on the ABA's opinion to allow continued representation under similar conditions. [Citations omitted.]

Underlying these decisions is a concern regarding the mobility of paralegals and other nonlawyers. A potential employer might well be reluctant to hire a particular nonlawyer if doing so would automatically disqualify the entire firm from ongoing litigation. This problem would be especially acute in the context of massive firms and extensive, complex litigation. Recognizing this danger, the ABA concluded that "any restrictions on the nonlawyer's employment should be held to the minimum necessary to protect confidentiality of client information." ABA Op. 1526 at 2. [Citations omitted.]

We share the concerns expressed by the ABA, and agree that client confidences may be adequately safeguarded if a firm hiring a paralegal for another firm takes appropriate steps in compliance with the Disciplinary Rules. See ABA Op. 1526 at 3. Specifically, the newly-hired paralegal should be cautioned not to disclose any information relating to the representation of a client of the former employer. The paralegal should also be instructed not to work on any matter on which the paralegal worked during the prior employment, or regarding which the paralegal has information relating to the former employer's representation. Additionally, the firm should take other reasonable steps to ensure that the paralegal does no work in connection with matters on which the paralegal worked during the prior employment, absent client consent after consultation. See id.

Each of these precautions would tend to reduce the danger that the paralegal might share confidential information with members of the new firm. Thus, while a court must ordinarily presume that some sharing will take place, the challenged firm may rebut this presumption by showing that sufficient precautions have been taken to guard against any disclosure of confidences.

Absent consent of the former employer's client, disqualification will always be required under some circumstances, such as (1) when information relating to the representation of an adverse client has in fact been disclosed, or (2) when screening would be ineffective or the nonlawyer necessarily would be required to work on the other side of a matter that is the same as or substantially related to a matter on which the nonlawyer has previously worked. . . .

In reconsidering the disqualification motion, the trial court should examine the circumstances of Hargrove's employment at Thompson & Knight to determine whether the practical effect of formal screening has been achieved. The factors bearing on such a determination will generally include the substantiality of the relationship between the former and current matters; the time elapsing between the matters; the size of the firm; the number of individuals presumed to have confidential information; the nature of their involvement in the former matter; and the timing and features of any measures taken to reduce the danger of disclosure.

The ultimate question in weighing these factors is whether Thompson & Knight has taken measures sufficient to reduce the potential for misuse of confidences to an acceptable level. As with any disqualification motion, the trial court must adhere to an exacting standard so as to discourage any use of a disqualification motion as a dilatory tactic. . . .

Because we have modified the controlling legal standard, the writ of mandamus is denied without prejudice to allow the trial court to reconsider the disqualification motion in light of today's opinion. The stay order previously issued by this Court remains in effect only so long as necessary to allow the trial court to act.

Questions about the Case

1. Was the paralegal Hargrove aware of the potential conflict of interest? Did she work on the Phoenix Founders matter at Thompson & Knight, either before she went to David & Goodman or after?
2. Did David & Goodman do a conflicts check?
3. Did Thompson & Knight attempt to screen Hargrove from the Phoenix Founders matter on her return to the firm?
4. What is the standard applied to lawyers in disqualification motions in Texas courts? Does the court apply this same standard to paralegals?
5. What authority does the Texas Supreme Court rely on to make this new rule?
6. What specific steps does the court prescribe to establish an acceptable safeguard against the disclosure of client confidences?
7. Did the Texas Supreme Court here decide whether to disqualify Thompson & Knight?

In this case, the firm knew that the paralegal who had joined the firm had conflicts and attempted to establish an adequate screen.

Lamb v. Pralex Corp.
333 F. Supp. 2d 361 (D.V.I. 2004)

The plaintiff in this case is represented by Lee J. Rohn. . . . Defendants are represented by Kevin Rames, Esq. . . . This motion revolves around Eliza Combie, who worked as a paralegal at the Rames law office from October 30, 2000 to March 26, 2004. Her work at Rames' office involved working with several litigation matters, including this case.

On March 26, 2004, Combie began work with the Rohn law firm. Combie, Rohn and K. Glenda Cameron, Esq., an associate at the firm, assert that they discussed the possible conflicts raised by Combie's possible employment. They also aver that at the initial interview, Combie acknowledged that there were cases in which she was conflicted, at which time she was informed that, should she accept employment with the Rohn firm, she would be barred from contact with those cases.

Rohn and Cameron also state that on Combie's first day of work with Rohn, she submitted the list of cases. The list was circulated to all employees and a memo informing employees to refrain from discussing those cases in her presence was circulated and posted in common areas of the office. Combie, Rohn and Cameron all aver that no one in the office has discussed any of the relevant matters with Combie. They also state that Combie is locked out of the electronic files and does not work in close proximity to them or to Rohn.

Rames invokes ABA Rules of Professional Conduct 5.3, 1.9, 1.16, and 1.10 to argue that Rohn and her entire law firm must be disqualified because during Combie's previous employment with Rames she obtained confidential information regarding pending matters which she may divulge to Rohn. Rohn denies any impropriety and assures the court that no confidences have been disclosed, and that a "scrupulous" screening procedure has been implemented to shield Combie from contact with the conflicted cases. Rames argues that such "self-serving" statements are insufficient to stave off disqualification.

A motion to disqualify counsel requires the court to balance the right of a party to retain counsel of his choice and the substantial hardship which might result from disqualification as against the public perception of and the public trust in the judicial system. . . .

Disqualification issues must be decided on a case by case basis and the party seeking disqualification of opposing counsel bears the burden of clearly showing that the continued representation would be impermissible. [Citation omitted.] Courts are required to "preserve a balance, delicate though it may be, between an individual's right to his own freely chosen counsel and the need to maintain the highest ethical standards of professional responsibility." [Citation omitted.] This balance is essential if the public's trust in the integrity of the Bar is to be preserved. The Court was unable to find a Third Circuit decision on this precise issue. However, several courts have addressed it.

ABA Rule 5.3 addresses the responsibilities of attorneys who employ nonlawyer assistants. It encompasses the protection of client confidences communicated to a nonlawyer assistant, such as a paralegal or secretary. [Citation omitted.] The rule imposes a duty on the supervising attorney to ensure that the non-lawyer adheres to professional obligations. Thus, a trial court has the authority, in a litigation context, to disqualify counsel based on the conduct of a nonlawyer assistant that is incompatible with the lawyer's ethical obligations. *Smart Industries Corp. Mfg. v. Superior Court in and for County of Yuma*, 876 P.2d 1176, 1181 (Ariz. App. Div. 1994). Moreover, such disqualification may be imputed to the entire law firm. *Leibowitz v. The Eighth Judicial District Court of the State of Nevada*, 78 P.3d 515, 523 (Sup. Ct. Nev. 2003).

The issue is whether plaintiff's counsel should be disqualified because a paralegal formerly employed by defendants' attorney and who was involved in litigation concerning defendants is now employed by plaintiff's counsel. The Standing Committee on Ethics and Professional Responsibility, pursuant to the ABA Model Rules of Professional Conduct, hold that a law firm that hires a paralegal formerly employed by another law firm may continue to represent clients whose interests conflict with the interests of clients of the former employer on whose matters the paralegal has worked, so long as the employing firm screens the paralegal, and as long as no information relating to said clients is revealed to the employing firm. *Informal Opinion 88-1526.* . . .

A Court faced with such a motion must first determine whether confidential information has been divulged. Rames claims that Combie participated in all of the cases in which his firm was litigation counsel; that he "shared with Combie litigation strategies and tactics"; and that Combie was "privy to the firm's entire case load as she worked on the vast majority of cases that were and are pending in the Rames law office." Rames maintains that Combie's possession of confidential client information gives Rohn an unfair advantage, and violates the notions of fairness and integrity in the judicial process, requiring disqualification of Rohn and her entire law firm. Combie's affidavit, annexed to Rohn's opposition, counters that Combie "never participated in any discussions or meetings with Attorney Rames," and was never privy to any strategy and tactical deliberation with regard to any opposing counsel. Combie avers that her duties revolved around filing of pleadings and correspondence and that information was transmitted to her on an "as needed" basis. Rames dismisses these statements as self-serving and untrue.

The Court finds that Combie was exposed to confidential information at the Rames law firm. It is reasonable for paralegals to handle confidential client information in order for the law firm employer to render efficient and cost-effective service. Combie is described as an experienced and competent worker. Therefore, it is conceivable that based on her skills, she was given substantial responsibility with the cases, including this case. By virtue of her working on the cases, it is also conceivable that she and Rames shared confidential information regarding them.

However, the fact that Combie has acquired confidential information in a former job is not sufficient by itself to require disqualification of her new employer. [Citations omitted.] . . . The hiring of a nonlawyer who possesses confidential information of an adversary puts such confidential information at risk. As a result, a rebuttable presumption arises that the information will be disclosed to the new employer. [Citations omitted.] The presumption serves to strike a balance between protecting confidentiality and the right to counsel of one's choice. A party is able to rebut the presumption that confidential client information has been used or disclosed, by presenting evidence of effective screening mechanisms to shield the employee from the cases. [Citation omitted.] In other words, the challenged attorney has the burden of showing that the practical effect of formal screening has been achieved and that the employee has not had and will not have any involvement with the litigation or any communication concerning the litigation. [Citation omitted.] In this jurisdiction, the erection of a "Chinese Wall" is recognized in this regard. [Citations omitted.]

Rohn states, and Combie and Cameron aver, that during her interview the parties discussed the fact that she was previously employed with Rames, who is an adversary of Rohn and is opposing counsel in this case. They further state that upon Combie's disclosure of the conflicted cases, "they advised her that were an offer of employment extended, she would be prohibited from and have no access to the electronic or physical files for those cases on which she would be conflicted." A list of the cases was circulated to all employees and posted in common areas; Combie has not been near the files and does not know their location; the employees have been instructed not to discuss the cases in her presence; and she has been locked out of the electronic filing system with regard to those cases.

The evidence of screening provided by Rohn was not directly contradicted by Rames. Although the Court understands his chagrin, more is required before a court will be forced to relieve a litigant of his counsel of choice. A majority of courts have endorsed screening procedures similar to the ones implemented in this case, under similar circumstances. Additionally, Rohn's office employs several individuals and there is little likelihood that Combie will be required to work on the conflicted cases. The Court is satisfied that the procedures employed by Rohn's office to shield Combie from the files supports a finding that any information obtained at the Rames law firm will not be disclosed.

In light of the foregoing, disqualification is not warranted. In addressing ethical problems created by nonlawyers changing employment from a law firm representing one party to a law firm representing an adverse party, courts must fashion rules which strike a balance between the public policy of protecting the confidentiality of attorney-client communications and a party's right to representation by chosen counsel. [Citations omitted.] Accordingly, any restrictions on the nonlawyer's employment should be held to the minimum necessary to protect confidentiality of client information.

A prophylatic rule which requires the employing firm to establish procedures which ensure that confidential information has not and will not be disclosed to the employing firm safeguards the competing interests. The Court finds that plaintiff's counsel has rebutted the presumption of improper disclosure by presenting evidence of the "Chinese Wall" implemented in that regard. Accordingly, disqualification is not warranted and the defendants' motion will be denied at this time.

Questions about the Case

1. Did the lawyers who hired the paralegal in question conduct a conflicts check? When?
2. Did the lawyers screen the paralegal? How? Did the screen have all the components of a screen that are described in this chapter?
3. What reasoning did the court apply in deciding if a disqualification was warranted?
4. Was the screen found to be adequate by the court? Why?
5. How did the court decide? What rule did it establish for the future?

In this case of first impression in Oklahoma, the state's highest court endorses the principle of screening nonlawyer employees and providing an opportunity for the firm being challenged to show that the screen is effective and that no confidences have been revealed.

Hayes v. Central States Orthopedic Specialists, Inc.
2002 Okla. 30, 51 P.3d 562 (Okla. 2002)

From August 1999 until June 2000 April Mendoza worked in Tulsa as a secretary for the firm of Norman Wohlgemuth Chandler & Dowdell, as secretary for John Dowdell and Christina Little . . . , the lawyers primarily responsible for the litigation between Mark Hayes, M.D. and Central States Orthopedic Specialists, Inc. . . . In May Ms. Mendoza gave notice to Norman Wohlgemuth that she was taking a job as secretary for Mr. Frank Hagedorn, a partner in the Tulsa firm of Estill, Hardwick, Gable, Golden & Nelson.

There is significant disagreement between plaintiff and Ms. Mendoza as to the nature and extent of Ms. Mendoza's involvement in the Hayes litigation. Dr. Hayes claims that Ms. Mendoza works on documents containing attorneys' work product and was "intimately familiar" with documents relating to settlement negotiations between the parties. But Ms. Mendoza stated in an affidavit that her duties were purely administrative and she had no recollection of any confidential information relating to the Hayes case. . . .

Dr. Hayes' lawyers sent a letter to Hall Estill requesting that the firm withdraw from the case but Hall Estill declined to do so, and . . . Dr. Hayes filed a motion asking the trial court to require Hall Estill to withdraw. . . .

[T]he trial court filed a written order . . . granting Dr. Hayes' motion and disqualifying Hall Estill. . . .

We begin our discussion of this issue by observing "*Legal practitioners are not interchangeable commodities.*" . . . [Citation omitted.]

A recurring theme in the cases that have recognized waiver as the basis for denying motions to disqualify is that need to insure that such motions are not used for strategic purposes. . . . [D]isqualification is such a drastic measure that it should be invoked if, and only if, the court is satisfied that real harm is likely to result from failing to invoke it.

The undisputed facts here reveal that Dr. Hayes and Mr. Dowdell discussed what to do . . . but decided to take no action whatever for eight months. . . . Although they attempted to explain their inaction on the basis that they were involved in settlement negotiations, it seems to us that this stage of the litigation would have been the very point at which they should have been most worried about Ms. Mendoza's knowledge. . . .

We hold that . . . Dr. Hayes . . . through delay of eight months . . . waived any right he might have had to insist on the harsh remedy of disqualifying Hall Estill. . . . [T]he hardship on Central Orthopedic . . . would likely be significantly greater than any hardship Dr. Hayes will likely suffer. . . .

As a result of our holding . . . it is not strictly necessary for us to address the screening issue. We shall do so, however, because it presents an important question of first impression. . . . The importance of the issue is demonstrated by the *amici curiae* brief filed on behalf of several groups who represent non-lawyers who work as legal assistants in law firms. . . .

The trial court's order relied on *Zimmerman v. Mahaksa Bottling Co.*, 19 P.3d 784 (Kan. 2000), which held, "Screening devices are prohibited under the [Rules of Professional Conduct.]" Thus, despite the undisputed evidence that Ms. Mendoza has not revealed any confidences and was screened from doing so by Hall Estill, the trial court, based on *Zimmerman*, nevertheless disqualified Hall Estill without any inquiry into the effectiveness of the screening. We hold that this was error.

Most authorities recognize that the considerations going into whether screening is proper for lawyers are entirely different than those involving non-lawyer employees. . . .

Rule 1.11 of the Rules of Professional Conduct expressly provide for the use of screening to prevent disqualification of firms who hire former government lawyers, judges, arbitrators, or law clerks. . . .

Contrary to the conclusion of the *Zimmerman* and *Ciaffone* courts, we have found no opinion from any jurisdiction criticizing *Smart Industries* other than *Zimmerman* and *Ciaffone*. . . .

In *Ciaffone*, 945 P.2d at 953, the court relied on an article by M. Peter Moser, *Chinese Walls: A Means of Avoiding Law Firm Disqualification When a Personally Disqualified Lawyer Joins the Firm*, 3 Geo. J. Legal Ethics 399, 403, 407 (1999), to support its conclusion that screening for non-lawyer employees has been "roundly criticized." . . . Moser suggested,

"Greater use of screening mechanism[s such as] so called 'Chinese walls,' should be permitted to protect former clients' confidences from disclosure." [Citation omitted.] Thus, far from showing that the use of devices for non-lawyers had been "roundly criticized," the Moser article stands for the proposition that screening devices for non-lawyers are "generally permitted" and such devices should be more widely used than they are now. . . .

We hold that a *per se* rule that would prohibit a court's examination of the effectiveness of a screening device for a non-lawyer is not appropriate under Oklahoma law. Thus before being disqualified for having hired the non-lawyer employee from its opponent, the hiring firm should be given the opportunity to prove that the non-lawyer employee has not revealed client confidences to the new employer and has been effectively screened from doing so. . . .

ORDER OF THE TRIAL COURT REVERSED AND MATTER REMANDED WITH INSTRUCTIONS TO DENY PLAINTIFF'S MOTION TO DISQUALIFY DEFENDANT'S COUNSEL.

Questions about the Case

1. Did the nonlawyer in this case have a conflict? Did the hiring firm know it? What did the firm do about it?
2. Why did the firm seeking disqualification wait so long to file the motion to disqualify? Was this important in the case?
3. Why did the court act on the matter of screens after finding that it did not need to?
4. Why did a paralegal association (NALA) file an amicus brief?
5. This state is geographically close to which other states that have opinions about screens? What do these other states say? Why did the court not follow Nevada and Kansas?

The following case overrules one part of the *Ciaffone* case mentioned in the previous decision and sets a new rule in the state of Nevada. The case shows the trend of allowing screening of paralegals where a state might not allow screening for lawyers in the same situation.

Leibowitz v. District Court
119 Nev. 523, 78 P.3d 515 (2003)

The law firm of Ecker & Standish was disqualified from representing petitioner Steven Leibowitz pursuant to our decision in *Ciaffone v. District Court*, which addressed imputed disqualification based upon employment of a nonlawyer employee who had access to confidential or privileged information of an adverse party during the course of the employee's prior employment. For the reasons set forth below, we determine that screening is permissible for nonlawyer employees, clarify in part and overrule in part our decision in *Ciaffone* and grant the petition.

This petition for a writ of mandamus arises out of a divorce proceeding. Steven and Deena Leibowitz were married in 1986. The parties later separated, and Deena filed a complaint for divorce in February 2000. Deena hired the law firm of Dickerson, Dickerson Consult & Pocker (DDCP) to represent her. Steven retained the law firm of Ecker & Standish (ES) to represent him in the divorce proceeding. . . .

[T]he district court entered a final judgment resolving all the parties' property, custody, and other divorce issues. . . . Both Steven and Deena appealed the final judgment. . . .

Later in the summer of 2001, while the appeal was pending, Steven filed a motion seeking to modify child custody and visitation. The district court certified its inclination to consider the motion. . . . Steven filed a motion to remand the issues to the district court. Deena opposed the motion.

After filing the motion to remand, ES advised DDCP that ES had hired Haunani Magalianes, a former DDCP employee, as a legal assistant. . . . During discussion regarding possible disqualification, ES discovered that one of its former employees, Pollie J. Baker, worked at DDCP for periods of time between June 2001 and April 2002.

On February 14, 2002 attorney Howard Ecker advised DDCP via letter that ES had hired Magalianes. With respect to the Leibowitz case, Ecker indicated that Magalianes advised Ecker that she did not believe that she had obtained any privileged information as a result of her work in the Leibowitz matter.

DDCP employed Magalianes in its domestic division until May 26, 2000. Thereafter Magalianes transferred to DDCP's civil division until approximately April 2001. According to Magalianes, . . . she had three contacts with the Leibowitz case. First, [she] took the initial phone call from Deena regarding potential representation by DDCP. . . . Second, [she] prepared a short memorandum to attorney Robert P. Dickerson that contained the initial information obtained. . . . Lastly, [she] prepared a substitution of attorney for and a transmittal letter to Deena's former attorney. . . . DDCP asserts Magalianes also participated in a meeting involving a child custody dispute. . . . [She] denies participating in this meeting. DDCP's billing records do not reflect [her] attendance at the meeting, although one of the attorneys present filed an affidavit indicating that [she] was present during a phone call with opposing counsel and at a conference among Deena's counsel after the telephone conversation. . . .

As a condition of her employment, and in the course of her employment with ES, Magalianes was screened from any contact with the Leibowitz case. Specifically, [she] had no access to actual or computer files and was prohibited from conversing with law firm personnel regarding the Leibowitz matter.

ES employed legal assistant Pollie J. Baker from October 2000 until mid-January 2001. Baker worked primarily for ES attorney Ed Kainen. During the period of [her] employment, ES represented Steven in the divorce proceedings. Attorney Thomas J. Standish testified that he did the majority of work on the Leibowitz divorce, but he had some help from Kainen. Baker had access to the Leibowitz files, but Baker averred that she did not have any contact with the Leibowitz case while employed at ES. ES presented evidence that [she] had actual involvement with the case.

Around June 2001, Baker went to work for DDCP and . . . worked there for several months. She left DDCP for a short time and returned in late 2001. Baker ended her relationship with DDCP on April 24, 2002. DDCP indicated that it did not inform ES about Baker's employment at the time because it was unaware of Baker's previous employment with ES. [Her] resume did not disclose her employment with ES. . . .

The district court concluded that *Ciaffone* mandated automatic disqualification whenever a nonlawyer employee had access to an adverse part's privileged or confidential information during employment by that party's attorneys. . . . The district court disqualified ES but declined to disqualify DDCP. . . .

[T]he facts in *Ciaffone* infer that mere exposure to a client's file is sufficient to warrant disqualification. In *Ciaffone*, the nonlawyer's involvement with the prior client's case was limited to some work in a secretarial, word processor capacity. The opinion is silent on whether or not this exposure related to privileged or confidential information. Instead the opinion seems to suggest that any exposure to a client's file is sufficient to invoke imputed disqualification. We there take this opportunity to clarify that the imputed disqualification standards . . . do not apply simply because a nonlawyer employee was exposed, or had access to, a former client's file. The rule only applies when the nonlawyer employee acquires privileged, confidential information.

[In *Ciaffone*, we] concluded that screening was not permitted under the rule for attorneys, and therefore, it should not be permitted for nonlawyers.

Petitioners and amici urge us to overrule that portion of *Ciaffone* and permit nonlawyer screening. They respectfully assert that this court misapprehended the weight of authority on this issue. We agree.

In *Ciaffone*, . . . we rejected [the reasoning of the relevant ABA Ethics Opinion] and said that it was "roundly criticized." We also inferred that a majority of courts had rejected nonlawyer screening and cited a law review article by M. Peter Moser in support of these statements. In fact, Mr. Moser did not criticize nonlawyer screening. He pointed out that a majority of jurisdictions permit nonlawyer screening and argued that screening should also be permitted for lawyers.

As pointed out by the amici's briefs, the majority of professional ethics commentators, ethics tribunals, and courts have concluded that nonlawyer screening is a permissible method to protect confidences held by nonlawyer employees who change employment. Nevada is in the minority of jurisdictions that do not allow screening of nonlawyers moving from private firm to private firm.

Imputed disqualification is considered a harsh remedy that "should be invoked if, and only if, the court is satisfied that real harm is likely to result from failing to invoke it." [Citations omitted.] This stringent standard is based on the client's right to counsel of the client's choosing and the likelihood of prejudice and economic harm to the client when severance of the attorney-client relationship is ordered. It is for this reason that the ABA opined in 1988 that screening is permitted for nonlawyers. . . .

We are persuaded that *Ciaffone* misapprehended the state of the law regarding nonlawyer imputed disqualification. We therefore overrule *Ciaffone* to the extent it prohibits screening of nonlawyer employees.

When a law firm hires a nonlawyer employee, the firm has an affirmative duty to determine whether or not the employee previously had access to adversarial client files. If the hiring law firm determines that the employee had such access, the hiring law firm has an absolute duty to screen the nonlawyer employee from the adversarial cases irrespective of the nonlawyer employee's actual knowledge of privileged or confidential information.

Although we decline to mandate an exhaustive list of screening requirements, the following provides an instructive minimum:

1. The newly hired nonlawyer must be cautioned not to disclose any information relating to the representation of a client of a former employer.
2. The nonlawyer must be instructed not to work on any matter on which he or she worked during the prior employment, or regarding which he or she has information relating to former employer's representation.
3. The new firm should take reasonable steps to ensure that the nonlawyer does not work in connection with matters on which he or she worked during the prior employment, absent client consent . . . after consultation.

In addition, the hiring law firm must inform the adversarial party, or their counsel, regarding the hiring of the nonlawyer employee and the screening mechanism utilized. The adversarial party may then: (1) make a conditional waiver (i.e., agree to the screening mechanisms); (2) make an unconditional waiver (eliminate the screening mechanisms); or (3) file a motion to disqualify counsel.

However, even if the new employer uses a screening process, disqualification will always be required—absent unconditional waiver by the affected client—under the following circumstances:

1. When information relating the representation of the adverse client has been disclosed to the new employer; or, in the absence of disclosure to the new employer,
2. When screening would be ineffective or the nonlawyer necessarily would be required to work on the other side of the matter that is the same or substantially related to a matter on which the nonlawyer has previously worked. . . .

To determine whether screening has been or may be effective, the court should consider: (1) the substantiality of the relationship between the former and current matters, (2) the time elapsed between matters, (3) the size of the firm, (4) the number of individuals presumed to have confidential information, (5) the nature of their involvement with the former matter, (6) the timing and features of any measure taken to reduce the danger of disclosure, and (7) whether the old firm and the new firm represent adverse parties in the same proceeding, rather than in different proceedings. . . .

As to Baker, the record supports the . . . finding that she did not obtain confidential information about Steven's case while employed by ES. . . . [W]e conclude the district court did not err in refusing to disqualify DDCP. . . .

Balancing Deena's interest in preventing possible disclosure of confidential information with Steven's interest in retaining the attorney who has presented him for two years, and the entirety of the divorce proceedings, we conclude that ES should not be disqualified. Magalianes' contacts with Deena were brief and, according to the record, consisted mainly of routine information with some possible confidential information. . . . [T]here is no indication in the record that any confidential information discussed at the conference related to anything but the weekend custody dispute. Although ES is a small firm, there is no evidence that Magalianes would be, by the nature of the firm, forced to work on the Leibowitz matter. Moreover, given the length of time ES represented Steve, the fact that a final judgment has been issued and Magalianes' involvement occurred early in the proceedings, the public's interest in the administration of justice is not significantly impacted. . . . Finally, Steve would suffer extreme prejudice if he had to retain a new attorney this late in the proceedings. . . .

[W]e overrule Ciaffone's prohibition against screening for nonlawyer employees, clarify that mere opportunity to access confidential information does not merit disqualification and conclude that the district court erred in disqualifying the law firm of ES from representing Steven Leibowitz. . . .

LEAVITT, J., with whom AGOSTI, C. J., agrees, dissenting:
I would deny the petition because the district court properly disqualified the law firm of ES.

I would follow the reasoning in *Ciaffone v. District Court* . . . [in which] we held that screening was ineffective to prevent disqualification. . . . [W]e noted . . . "the uncertainty regarding the effectiveness of the screen, the monetary incentive involved in breaching the screen, the fear of disclosing privileged information in the course of proving an effective screen, and the possibility of accidental disclosures."

Questions about the Case

1. What were the facts about the two paralegals in this case? What degree of access did they each have to confidential information in this matter? What was the extent of their work on this matter? Did it make a difference?
2. The court's decision has a clarification of part of the *Ciaffone* case and overrules part of the *Ciaffone* case. What are these two holdings?
3. What should a firm do when it discovers a conflict carried by a new paralegal?
4. What factors will a court look at in deciding whether to disqualify a firm based on a paralegal's conflict?
5. Did the court indicate why it had so misinterpreted the state of the law when it issued the *Ciaffone* opinion?
6. What do you think of the points raised by the dissent?

This is one of several Texas cases that have refined and clarified the rules about conflicts checks and screens for paralegals.

In re Guaranty Ins. Services, Inc.
343 S.W.3d 130 (Tex. 2011)

What happens when a law firm's efforts to screen a conflict fail, permitting a non-lawyer who worked on one side of a case at one firm to work on the other side of the same case at the opposing firm? Here, the trial court disqualified the second firm, reasoning there was a conclusive presumption that the nonlawyer had shared confidential information, despite evidence he had not. A divided court of appeals denied mandamus relief. . . .

The nonlawyer in this story is paralegal Clyde Williams; the two firms are Godwin Pappas Langley Ronquillo, LLP (Godwin Pappas) and Strasburger & Price, LLP (Strasburger). Like many corporate battles, the litigation underlying this mandamus proceeding was a multi-suit affair. The lawsuit from which Strasburger was ultimately disqualified is suit number two in the litigation between Trans-Global Solutions, Inc. (Trans-Global) and Guaranty Insurance Services, Inc. (Guaranty). Trans-Global first sued Guaranty, an insurance agent, for allegedly failing to obtain appropriate insurance. Guaranty prevailed and brought suit number two (the underlying suit), seeking indemnity for the defense costs it incurred in the first suit. Strasburger represents Guaranty in the underlying suit. Trans-Global was first represented by Godwin Pappas in the underlying suit and is now represented by Kane Russell Coleman & Logan, PC (Kane Russell).

In July 2005, Williams began work as a paralegal at Godwin Pappas. While there, he billed a total of 6.8 hours in the underlying suit, reviewing the file to identify persons with knowledge of relevant facts, preparing an initial draft of a response to Guaranty's request for disclosures, assisting in document production, and communicating with opposing counsel. Williams left Godwin Pappas in November 2006. The attorneys handling the case left the firm in August 2008 for Kane Russell, taking the case with them.

In October 2008, Williams applied for a paralegal position at Strasburger. In his Employee Application, he identified Godwin Pappas as one of his previous employers, and Strasburger ran an initial conflicts check, which came back clear. At the firm's request, Williams also identified two potential conflicts due to his previous work on matters in which Strasburger represented another party. Strasburger ran a separate conflicts check on those and restricted his access to documents related to them. Williams attested that he failed to identify the underlying suit as a potential conflict because he did not remember having billed any hours for it.

In addition to the conflicts check, the firm instructed Williams several times prior to his work on this case not to disclose confidential information he gained during his previous employment—specifically during his orientation, and through the Strasburger Employee Information Handbook and a confidentiality agreement. Williams signed the handbook and the agreement. Both required him to notify his supervising attorney immediately if he became aware of a matter on which he previously worked.

Williams started work at Strasburger in January 2009. At that point, the underlying suit was already underway. . . . In July 2009, Williams's supervising attorney at Strasburger asked him to organize the pleadings and discovery in this case. Williams again failed to recognize the conflict and to notify the supervising attorney of its existence. In September 2009, Williams affixed Bates Labels to documents produced to Trans-Global and attached redacting tape to passages highlighted by an attorney. In total, Williams billed about 27 hours on the case at Strasburger.

Emails between Strasburger and Kane Russell regarding routine discovery matters made reference to Williams as a Strasburger legal assistant. A Kane Russell attorney recognized Williams as a former Godwin Pappas employee and notified Strasburger of the conflict. Strasburger immediately instructed Williams to discontinue working on the matter, not to view or access any documents related to the case, and not to disclose any information he had obtained during his employment with Godwin Pappas. Trans-Global moved to disqualify Strasburger. Though Trans-Global disputes this fact before our Court, the record is clear that Trans-Global conceded during the disqualification hearing that no confidences were actually shared. After conducting that hearing, the trial court granted Trans-Global's motion and entered findings of fact and conclusions of law. In brief, it reasoned the journey was irrelevant when the final destination included a nonlawyer on both sides of the same case. It held that evidence Strasburger instituted a screening procedure for nonlawyers was immaterial under Texas law because the screening procedure did not prevent Williams from actually working on the opposite side of the case. Williams's actual work on opposite sides created a genuine threat of disclosure, which meant he was conclusively presumed to have shared confidential information, despite evidence he had not. . . .

While conceding Strasburger's screening procedures were "exemplary," it explained that those procedures, "however thorough, must actually be effective in order to rebut the presumption." 310 S.W.3d at 632 (citing *Phoenix Founders, Inc. v. Marshall*, 887 S.W.2d 831, 833 (Tex. 1994) (orig. proceeding)). It reasoned that "where a paralegal has actually been allowed to work on both sides of the same litigation, even the most exhaustive attempts at screening cannot be deemed effective" and concluded the trial court did not abuse its discretion. *Id.* at 633-634. A dissenting justice took the position that a nonlawyer's actual work on both sides of the case by itself did not mandate disqualification of the second firm. *Id.* at 634 (Waldrop, J., dissenting).

Our conflict-of-interest jurisprudence recognizes distinctions between lawyers and nonlawyers, their duties, and their likelihood of contact with confidential information. We have held that a lawyer who has previously represented a client may not represent another person on a matter adverse to the client if the matters are the same or substantially related. *In re Columbia*, 320 S.W.3d at 824. If the *lawyer* works on a matter, there is an *irrebuttable* presumption that the lawyer *obtained* confidential information during the representation. *Phoenix Founders*, 887 S.W.2d at 833. When the lawyer moves to another firm and the second firm represents an opposing party to the lawyer's former client, a second *irrebuttable* presumption arises—that the lawyer has *shared* the client's confidences with members of the second firm. *Id.* at 834. The effect of this second presumption is the mandatory disqualification of the second firm. *See id.* at 833-834.

But the rule is different for non-lawyers. A *nonlawyer* who worked on a matter at a prior firm is also subject to a *conclusive* presumption that confidences were *obtained*. *In re Am. Home Prods. Corp.*, 985 S.W.2d

68, 74 (Tex. 1998) (orig. proceeding); *Phoenix Founders*, 887 S.W.2d at 834. This rule serves "to prevent the moving party from being forced to reveal the very confidences sought to be protected." *In re Am. Home*, 985 S.W.2d at 74 (quoting *Phoenix Founders*, 887 S.W.2d at 834) (quotation marks omitted). However, the second presumption—that confidences were *shared* with members of the second firm—may be rebutted where nonlawyers are concerned. *Phoenix Founders*, 887 S.W.2d at 835. As applies here, then, there is a conclusive presumption that Williams obtained confidential information, but Strasburger may be free to rebut the presumption that Williams shared those confidences with it. The issue is whether Strasburger can do so in this situation and, if so, whether it has.

The only way to rebut the rebuttable presumption is:

(1) to instruct the legal assistant "not to work on any matter on which the paralegal worked during the prior employment, or regarding which the paralegal has information relating to the former employer's representation," and (2) to "take other reasonable steps to ensure that the paralegal does not work in connection with matters on which the paralegal worked during the prior employment, absent client consent."

In re Am. Home, 985 S.W.2d at 75 (quoting *Phoenix Founders*, 887 S.W.2d at 835). A simple, informal admonition to a nonlawyer employee not to work on a matter on which he worked before is not enough. *In re Columbia*, 320 S.W.3d at 826. And the "other reasonable measures must include, at a minimum, formal, institutionalized screening measures that render the possibility of the nonlawyer having contact with the file less likely." *Id.* Thus, effective screening methods may be used to shield the employee from the matter in order to avoid disqualification. *Id.* at 824 (citations omitted).

But we have never said that ineffective screening measures merited automatic disqualification for nonlawyers. On the contrary, we have explained that in most cases, disqualification is not required provided "the practical effect of formal screening has been achieved." *Phoenix Founders*, 887 S.W.2d at 835, . . .

> The nonlawyer should be cautioned . . . that the employee should not work on any matter on which the employee worked for the former employer. . . . *When the new firm becomes aware of such matters*, the employing firm must also take reasonable steps to ensure that the employee takes no action and does no work in relation to matters on which the employer worked in the prior employment, absent client consent after consultation.

Grant v. Thirteenth Court of Appeals, 888 S.W.2d 466, 467-68 (Tex. 1994) (per curiam) (orig. proceeding) (emphasis added) (quoting ABA Comm. on Ethics and Prof'l Responsibility, Informal Op. 1526 (1988)).

We reiterated the flexibility of this approach as well as the significance of knowledge in *In re Columbia*, which expounded upon the thrust of our prior holdings:

Despite the screening measures used, the presumption of shared confidences becomes conclusive if: (1) information related to the representation of an adverse client has in fact been disclosed, (2) screening would be ineffective or the nonlawyer necessarily would be required to work on the other side of a matter that is the same as or substantially related to a matter on which the paralegal has previously worked; or (3) the non-lawyer has actually performed work, including clerical work, on the matter at the lawyer's directive if the lawyer reasonably should know about the conflict of interest.

320 S.W.3d at 828.

Because Williams actually worked on both sides of this case, the third scenario discussed in *In re Columbia* is implicated. Today we clarify, under that scenario: The presumption of shared confidences is *rebuttable* if the non-lawyer has actually performed work on the matter at a lawyer's directive and the lawyer reasonably should *not* know about the conflict of interest. Put differently, if the nonlawyer has actually worked on the matter, the presumption of shared confidences is *not rebuttable unless* the assigning lawyer should *not* have known of the conflict. . . .

Prior to Williams's discovery by a Kane Russell attorney, there is no evidence Strasburger was ever notified of the conflict. Williams never informed Strasburger that he had worked on the suit. And the fact that he worked less than seven hours on the case certainly supports Williams's claim that he simply forgot he had engaged with the litigation; the fact that he willingly disclosed two other potential conflicts suggests he was not averse to disclosing potential conflicts.

Further, the conflicts check came back clear. Trans-Global argues Strasburger would have discovered the conflict but for its ineffective screening system. We have never required perfection in screening conflicts. And as Strasburger points out, Trans-Global had changed representation, from Godwin Pappas to Kane Russell, since Williams had worked for the other side, and Godwin Pappas had itself changed names several times. Aside from its computerized conflicts check, Strasburger had specifically asked Williams to identify any conflicts of which he was aware. In addition, Trans-Global conceded that Strasburger's system was adequate during the oral hearing on the motion to disqualify, at one point stating, "we have no complaints about their screening procedure," and remaining mum when the trial court stated that Trans-Global had conceded that Strasburger's screening methods were sufficient to meet the *Phoenix Founders* and *In re American Home* standards. The failure of a screening method to actually screen a tainted party will not translate into disqualification where "the practical effect of formal screening has been achieved." *Phoenix Founders*, 887 S.W.2d at 835 (citation omitted). That effect was achieved here because there is no evidence the supervising attorney reasonably should have known about the conflict.

The screening was also effective under the fact-intensive, multi-factor inquiry of *Phoenix Founders*. . . . Almost two years passed between Williams's exit from Godwin Pappas and his application to Strasburger; another three months after that passed before he gained employment there; and another six months after that went by before he actually worked on the case. Only one person—Williams—is presumed to have confidential information, and Williams's minimal work on the case (less than 34 hours across both firms) also suggests effective screening. Finally, the evidence indicates that Strasburger took numerous measures, discussed below, to prevent and later to address the danger of disclosure.

Strasburger clears the hurdles to presumption-rebuttal erected by *In re American Home* and *Phoenix Founders*. At the outset, via his orientation, the Strasburger Employee Information Handbook, and the confidentiality agreement, Strasburger instructed Williams not to engage with matters on which he had worked previously. Those documents also directed Williams to notify his supervising attorney immediately if he realized a conflict. Strasburger also took other reasonable steps to ensure Williams did not work on matters from his prior employment. Specifically, it had in place formal, institutionalized screening procedures, which even the court of appeals noted were "nothing if not thorough." 310 S.W.3d at 633. The trial court similarly noted Strasburger had "presented evidence that it had instituted a screening procedure for nonlawyers," and even Trans-Global itself stated "we have no complaints about their screening procedure." Strasburger also presented evidence that it strictly adhered to its formal screening process when it hired Williams. When Williams identified two closed matters on which he had worked and in which Strasburger had also been involved, Strasburger removed his access to those files. Strasburger also ran a conflicts check based on Williams's previous employers, and it revealed no additional conflicts. Williams signed a confidentiality agreement, certifying that he disclosed the existence of any conflict of interest of which he was aware at the time. He also acknowledged receiving, reading, and signing the Employee Information Book, which informed him of his duty to keep confidential information obtained during his previous employment.

Further, Williams attested that upon discovering the conflict, Strasburger instructed him not to work further on this case, not to access related documents, and not to disclose any information. While such a restriction is not a stand-alone requirement for rebutting the presumption, these additional steps further distinguish this case from other's where we have disqualified firms for a nonlawyer's actual work on both sides of a case. For example, in *In re Columbia*, the paralegal had similarly performed limited work on both sides of the same case. 320 S.W.3d at 823. But the second law firm did not have any formal screening measures in place and, upon realizing a conflict existed, did not immediately remove the nonlawyer's access to the case. *Id.* In fact, the supervising attorney asked the nonlawyer to work on the case even after the conflict came to light. *Id.* Strasburger's efforts after discovering the conflict parallel and reinforce its thorough attempts to preempt the conflict in the first place.

For these reasons, and without hearing oral argument, . . . we conditionally grant mandamus relief and direct the trial court to vacate its order granting the motion to disqualify. . . .

Questions about the Case

1. What was the nature of the work that the paralegal did that led to the conflict?
2. Why was the conflict not revealed in the conflicts check? What did the court say about the effectiveness of the conflicts check procedures?
3. How did the conflict come to light? What did the employing firm do about the conflict then? What did the court say about these procedures?
4. Was any confidential information revealed? Did this matter to the court?
5. What is the difference between the rules on conflicts that govern lawyers and paralegals in Texas?

In this case, a New Mexico federal court magistrate judge granted disqualification of defendants' counsel from 11 consolidated employment cases after the firm hired a paralegal from the firm representing the plaintiffs.

Ullman v. Denco, Inc., et al.
No. 14-cv-843-SMV-GBW (D. N. Mex. 2015)

Since September 30, 2013, Joelle Gonzales ("Gonzales") was the only full-time employee and paralegal of attorney Ben Furth at The Furth Law Firm PA ("Furth"). Furth is Plaintiffs' counsel in this case and the related cases. Gonzales worked extensively on this case and the related cases. Plaintiffs' counsel shared his mental impressions and litigation strategies with Gonzales. Gonzales had access to all the clients' files, interviewed most of the clients, worked on Plaintiffs' damage models, worked with one expert in the case, and possesses extensive information regarding Plaintiffs' legal strategies and "bottom line" settlement numbers. Consequently, Gonzales possesses significant confidential, privileged, and proprietary information regarding Plaintiffs' litigation strategy and work product in this case and the related cases.

On or about March 3, 2015, Holt, Mynatt & Martinez, P.C. ("HMM") contacted and interviewed Gonzales. Damian Martinez

("Martinez"), an attorney of record in this case and Director of HMM, met with Gonzales during the interview process. Gonzales was hired the same day with a start date of March 17, 2015. Later that day, Gonzales informed Furth of the hiring and gave her two-weeks notice. That evening, Furth called Martinez to discuss the ethical issues regarding HMM hiring Gonzales. During the call, Furth informed Martinez that Gonzales had confidential, privileged, and work product information regarding this litigation and the other related cases. Furth suggested that HMM wait until after the mediation scheduled for April 8, 2015, to begin Gonzales' employment. On March 5, 2015, HMM electronically sent Furth a letter refusing to delay hiring Ms. Gonzales. However, HMM laid out the screening mechanisms it intended to use to prevent the disclosure of any confidential information possessed by Gonzales:

1. Ms. Gonzales will be physically separated from the actual file in our office as she will be working upstairs and the file — and the attorneys handling the file — will be located downstairs.
2. The file will be housed in Mr. Fitch's office which is a locked office.
3. All file management will be handled downstairs, including mail and other documents, and will be routed directly to Mr. Fitch rather than being routed through our normal mail handling process.
4. All electronic documentation will be password-protected on our server. Ms. Gonzalez will not have access to the password.
5. There will be an office-wide admonition to all employee: They will not communicate with Ms. Gonzales regarding this matter at any point in time.
6. There will be an admonition to the attorneys handling the matter not to speak openly about the case but rather to hold all conferences inside an office or in our conference room.
7. There will be an admonition to Ms. Gonzalez to avoid any conversation regarding the file whether initiated by her or by someone else.
8. Ms. Gonzales will also be admonished not to disclose any information regarding the file to anyone at HOLT MYNATT MARTÍNEZ P.C. irrespective of whether it is considered "confidential" or not.
9. We would be willing to institute a third-party notification to Mr. Briggs Cheney by Ms. Gonzales if any breach of the ethical wall occurs in any form.
10. Ms. Gonzales will not be allowed to work on the file or have any contact with the file whatsoever.

The letter also advised Furth that "based upon our business need to have another legal assistant start as soon as possible we are going to move forward with the hiring and the employment of Ms. Gonzales at the earliest available time." Soon thereafter, HMM moved Gonzales' start date from March 17th to March 9th. Plaintiffs subsequently filed a motion to disqualify HMM as opposing counsel in this case, and eleven (11) related cases involving Defendants' failure to pay its hourly paid employees earned wages.

There can be no argument that, if Gonzales were an attorney, HMM would have to be disqualified. This result is dictated by the interaction of New Mexico's conflict of interest rule, Rule 16-109, and rule of imputation, Rule 16-110. Rule 16-109(A) states: "A lawyer who has formerly represented a client in a matter shall not thereafter represent another person in the same or a substantially related matter in which that person's interests are materially adverse to the interests of the former client unless the former client gives informed consent, confirmed in writing." HMM does not dispute that, were she an attorney, Gonzales' involvement in this matter on behalf of Plaintiffs would prohibit her involvement in the matter on behalf of Defendants. Given this conflict, the general rule of imputation in Rule 16-110(A) establishes that, were Gonzales an attorney, the conflict would also prevent HMM from representing Defendants. However, in cases where the conflict arrives with a newly hired attorney, an exception to the general rule exists where "(1) the newly associated lawyer has no [confidential] information that is material to the matter; or (2) the newly associated lawyer did not have a substantial role in the matter [and] is timely screened from any participation in the matter. . . ."

N.M. R. PROF'L CONDUCT 16-110(C).

In *Roy D. Mercer, LLC, v. Reynolds*, 292 P.3d 466 (N.M. 2012), the New Mexico Supreme Court addressed these rules and the availability of screening as a potential remedy. The Court held that the plain reading of the rules established that the hiring firm could not avoid disqualification by screening their newly hired attorney unless one of the two conditions of Rule 16-110(C) could be met. *Id.* at 470-471. In the instant case, HMM does not argue that Gonzales does not possess confidential information or did not have a substantial role in the matter when she worked for Plaintiffs' counsel. Thus, if she was an attorney, screening could not avoid the disqualification of HMM because of Gonzales' conflict.

But, of course, Gonzales is not an attorney. Plaintiff argues that this distinction is irrelevant given the rules governing a lawyer's responsibilities regarding non-lawyer assistants, Rules 16-503 and 20-114. Rule 16-503 states:

> With respect to a non-lawyer employed or retained by or associated with a lawyer:
> A. a partner and a lawyer who individually or together with other lawyers possesses comparable managerial authority in a law firm shall make reasonable efforts to ensure that the firm has in effect measures giving reasonable assurance that the person's conduct is compatible with the professional obligations of the lawyer;

B. a lawyer having direct supervisory authority over the non-lawyer shall make reasonable efforts to ensure that the person's conduct is compatible with the professional obligations of the lawyer; and

C. a lawyer shall be responsible for conduct of such a person that would be a violation of the Rules of Professional Conduct if engaged in by a lawyer if:

(1) the lawyer orders or, with the knowledge of the specific conduct, ratifies the conduct involved; or

(2) the lawyer is a partner or has comparable managerial authority in the law firm in which the person is employed, or has direct supervisory authority over the person, and knows of the conduct at a time when its consequences can be avoided or mitigated but fails to take reasonable remedial action.

Rule 20-114 similarly provides that a "lawyer has an affirmative obligation to ensure that a legal assistant, paralegal, or other non-lawyer support staff for whose work the lawyer is responsible does not engage in any activities which, if engaged in by the lawyer, would constitute a violation of the Rules of Professional Conduct."

This dispute is about the independent conduct of HMM attorneys—specifically whether they can represent Defendants notwithstanding the prohibition against Gonzales working on the matter. In other words, is Gonzales' conflict of interest as a paralegal imputed to the entire firm?

Imputation of conflicts is governed by Rule 16-110. By its terms, that rule imputes only the conflicts of "lawyers." *See* N.M. R. PROF'L CONDUCT 16-110 . . . ; *see also* N.M. R. PROF'L CONDUCT 16-109 (consistently referring to "lawyer"); *cf. Mercer*, 292 P.3d at 469 (premising opinion on lawyer's continuing duty of confidentiality and undivided loyalty to his clients). The comments to the rule also support this plain reading: "The rule stated in Paragraph A also does not prohibit representation by others in the law firm where the person prohibited from involvement in a matter is a nonlawyer, such as a paralegal or legal secretary." N.M. R. PROF'L CONDUCT 16-110, Comment 4. Though Furth at times confided in Gonzales as he would another attorney, were the Court to interpret "lawyer" to include "non-lawyer" in the present case, the distinction established by the Rules would be obliterated. Not only would there be no meaningful way of confining such an interpretation to the Rules at issue in this case so that "lawyer" would not thereafter also include "non-lawyer" in other circumstances, Rules 16-503 and 20-114 would be rendered superfluous as the means for addressing non-lawyer conduct because the Rules would simply apply directly to non-lawyers as they do to lawyers.

It is undisputed that Gonzales acquired confidential information about Plaintiffs' case. Were she an attorney, the disclosure of any such information would constitute a violation. Therefore, "[o]nce a district court determines that a non-lawyer employee acquired confidential information about a former client, the district court should grant a motion for disqualification unless the district court determines that the screening is sufficient to safeguard the former client from disclosure of the confidential information." *Leibowitz v. Eighth Judicial Dist. Court of Nev. ex rel. Cnty. of Clark*, 78 P.3d 515, 521 (Nev. 2003). When considering the sufficiency of a screen in a particular case, the "court is faced with the delicate task of balancing competing interests," such as:

(1) the individual right to be represented by counsel of one's choice,
(2) each party's right to be free from the risk of even inadvertent disclosure of confidential information,
(3) the public's interest in the scrupulous administration of justice, and
(4) the prejudices that will inure to the parties as a result of the district court's decision.

Id.

Considering the factors as a whole, and the balance of interests the factors represent, the court concluded that Defendants have failed to meet the burden of proving that the screen will be effective.

For the foregoing reasons, the court concludes that HMM must be disqualified from representing Defendants in this and the related cases, and barred from having any role in the cases going forward. Nonetheless, the court finds no basis for, and hereby deny, Plaintiffs' request for an award of fees and costs.

Questions about the Case

1. What conduct did Gonzales engage in that the court alleges resulted in a conflict of interest? Did Gonzales possess any confidential information about these cases? How did she obtain it?
2. What conduct did HMM engage in that violated the conflict of interest rules? Does it matter that the initial contact was made by HMM and not by Gonzales? Why or why not?
3. Why did Furth object to HMM hiring Gonzales? Identify the reasons cited by Furth in objecting to HMM's employment of Gonzales.
4. Did the court properly grant Furth's motion for disqualification of HMM as counsel? What was the court's reasoning for its decision?
5. Which rules and case law did the court primarily rely on in reaching its opinion?
6. Can Gonzales be sanctioned for her conduct that led to the conflict of interest? Can Furth or HMM be sanctioned? By whom?

7. What should HMM have done to guard against this disqualification? What about Furth?

In this recent case, the California Supreme Court found that the waiver signed by a law firm client was not effective because the law firm failed to disclose a known conflict with a current client.

Sheppard, Mullin, Richter & Hampton, LLP v. J-M Manufacturing Co.
6 Cal.5th 59 (2018)

In 2006, a qui tam action was filed against J-M Manufacturing Company, Inc. (J-M), a pipe manufacturing company, in federal court in California. John Hendrix, the relator in the action, alleged that J-M had misrepresented the strength of polyvinyl chloride pipe it had sold to approximately 200 public entities around the country for use in their water and sewer systems. In early 2010, the complaint was unsealed, and many of these public entities intervened in the case.

As these events were unfolding, J-M began to consider replacing the law firm that had been representing it in the action. In February 2010, shortly after the complaint was unsealed, J-M's general counsel, Camilla Eng, invited attorneys from the law firm of Sheppard, Mullin, Richter & Hampton, LLP (Sheppard Mullin), to discuss taking over the representation from the other law firm. The attorneys, Bryan Daly and Charles Kreindler, ran a conflicts check to determine whether Sheppard Mullin had represented any of the public entities identified as the real parties in interest in the qui tam action. The conflicts check revealed that another Sheppard Mullin attorney, Jeffrey Dinkin, had done employment-related work for a public entity intervener, South Tahoe Public Utility District (South Tahoe), on and off since at least 2002, and most recently in November 2009. South Tahoe had, however, signed an advance waiver of conflicts in cases unrelated to the employment matters on which Dinkin had provided assistance. After internal consultation, Sheppard Mullin's general counsel opined that because of this advance conflict waiver, the firm could take on representation of J-M in the qui tam action.

On March 4, 2010, Sheppard Mullin and J-M signed an engagement agreement. Under the heading "Scope of Representation," the agreement recited that Sheppard Mullin was engaged to represent J-M in the qui tam action. The agreement provided that the representation would terminate on completion of the lawsuit and "any related claims and proceedings," unless the law firm agreed separately to provide J-M other legal services. The agreement recited the terms of the representation, including payment of fees, and provided that these terms would also apply to other engagements for J-M that Sheppard Mullin might undertake, except as the parties otherwise agreed. The engagement agreement also contained a conflict waiver much like the one South Tahoe had signed. The waiver provision provided:

> "Conflicts with Other Clients. Sheppard, Mullin, Richter & Hampton LLP has many attorneys and multiple offices. We may currently or in the future represent one or more other clients (including current, former, and future clients) in matters involving [J-M]. We undertake this engagement on the condition that we may represent another client in a matter in which we do not represent [J-M], even if the interests of the other client are adverse to [J-M] (including appearance on behalf of another client adverse to [J-M] in litigation or arbitration) and can also, if necessary, examine or cross examine [J-M] personnel on behalf of that other client in such proceedings or in other proceedings to which [J-M] is not a party *provided* the other matter is not substantially related to our representation of [J-M] and in the course of representing [J-M] we have not obtained confidential information of [J-M] material to representation of the other client. By consenting to this arrangement, [J-M] is waiving our obligation of loyalty to it so long as we maintain confidentiality and adhere to the foregoing limitations. We seek this consent to allow our Firm to meet the needs of existing and future clients, to remain available to those other clients and to render legal services with vigor and competence. Also, if an attorney does not continue an engagement or must withdraw therefrom, the client may incur delay, prejudice or additional cost such as acquainting new counsel with the matter."

Although Eng revised certain portions of the engagement agreement before signing, she made no changes to the conflict waiver provision. Sheppard Mullin did not tell J-M about its representation of South Tahoe before or at the time the engagement agreement was signed. The engagement agreement also contained an arbitration clause, providing that any dispute over fees or charges that was not resolved through voluntary arbitration under the auspices of the California State Bar, and any other type of dispute between the parties, would be settled by "mandatory binding arbitration" conducted in accordance with the California Arbitration Act (CAA; Code Civ. Proc., § 1282 et seq.). The arbitration clause also stated the agreement would be governed by California law.

Dinkin, the Sheppard Mullin employment partner, again began actively working for South Tahoe later in March 2010, a few weeks after Sheppard Mullin began representing J-M. Over the course of the following year, Sheppard Mullin billed South Tahoe for about 12 hours of work. During this period, South Tahoe's attorneys in the qui tam action became aware that Sheppard Mullin was now representing J-M in that action. In March 2011, South Tahoe's attorneys in the qui tam action wrote to Sheppard Mullin asking for an explanation for the firm's failure to inform South Tahoe of the adverse representation. Sheppard Mullin responded by reminding South Tahoe of its earlier conflicts waiver. Dissatisfied with this response, South Tahoe filed a motion to disqualify Sheppard Mullin in the qui tam proceeding.

In July 2011, the district court granted the disqualification motion, ruling that Sheppard Mullin's simultaneous representation of South Tahoe and J-M had been undertaken without adequately informed waivers in violation of rule 3-310(C)(3) of the Rules of Professional Conduct.

During its representation of J-M, Sheppard Mullin performed approximately 10,000 hours of work in the qui tam action and a related state court action. According to Sheppard Mullin attorney Kreindler, the firm's billings totaled more than $3 million, of which more than $1 million remained unpaid.

Sheppard Mullin sued J-M for the unpaid fees. J-M cross-complained for breach of contract, an accounting, breach of fiduciary duty, and fraudulent inducement; it also sought disgorgement of fees previously paid to Sheppard Mullin, as well as exemplary damages.

Sheppard Mullin petitioned for an order compelling arbitration under Code of Civil Procedure section 1281.2. J-M opposed the order, asserting that Sheppard Mullin's conflict of interest had rendered the parties' entire agreement illegal and unenforceable. Overruling J-M, the superior court granted the petition to compel arbitration.

The arbitrators ruled in Sheppard Mullin's favor. They observed that "the better practice" would have been for the firm to disclose its representation of South Tahoe and seek J-M's specific waiver of the conflict. But the arbitrators concluded that, even assuming Sheppard Mullin's failure to disclose the conflict constituted an ethical violation, the violation was not sufficiently serious or egregious to warrant forfeiture or disgorgement. The arbitrators observed that Sheppard Mullin's representation of South Tahoe involved matters unrelated to the qui tam action and that the conflict of interest had not caused J-M damage, prejudiced its defense of the qui tam action, resulted in communication of its confidential information to South Tahoe, or rendered Sheppard Mullin's representation less effective or less valuable. The arbitrators awarded Sheppard Mullin more than $1.3 million in fees and interest.

Sheppard Mullin petitioned the superior court to confirm the award, but J-M petitioned to vacate it, renewing its contention that the parties' engagement agreement was illegal and unenforceable due to Sheppard Mullin's simultaneous representation of adverse interests in violation of rule 3-310(C)(3) of the Rules of Professional Conduct. Again overruling J-M's objection, the superior court confirmed the award. Citing *Moncharsh v. Heily & Blase* (1992) 3 Cal.4th 1 (*Moncharsh*), the court held that a violation of the Rules of Professional Conduct does not render a retainer agreement unenforceable. The court concluded that the arbitrators therefore did not exceed their powers in awarding the contractual fees. (Code Civ. Proc., § 1286.2, subd. (a)(4).)

The Court of Appeal reversed. The court explained that California law, unlike federal law, treats a challenge to the legal enforceability of a contract as a matter for the court to decide, regardless of whether the contract contains an arbitration clause. The appellate court concluded that here, Sheppard Mullin's concurrent representation of J-M and South Tahoe violated rule 3-310(C)(3) of the Rules of Professional Conduct, notwithstanding the scope of the conflict waivers in the parties' respective engagement agreements. This violation, the court concluded, both rendered the engagement agreement with J-M unenforceable and disentitled Sheppard Mullin from any fees for representing J-M while it was simultaneously representing South Tahoe in other matters. For fee calculation purposes, the court remanded to the superior court to determine when precisely Sheppard Mullin's representation of South Tahoe began. The court granted Sheppard Mullin's petition for review.

The petition presents three questions: (1) whether a court may invalidate an arbitration award on the ground that the agreement containing the arbitration agreement violates the public policy of the state as expressed in the Rules of Professional Conduct, as opposed to statutory law; (2) whether Sheppard Mullin violated the Rules of Professional Conduct in view of the broad conflicts waiver signed by J-M; and (3) whether any such violation automatically disentitles Sheppard Mullin from any compensation for the work it performed on behalf of J-M.

The Court ruled as follows:

We conclude that Sheppard Mullin's concurrent representation of J-M and South Tahoe violated rule 3-310(C)(3) and rendered the engagement agreement between Sheppard Mullin and J-M unenforceable. Our conclusion rests on three subsidiary points: First, at the time Sheppard Mullin agreed to represent J-M in the qui tam action, the law firm also represented a client with conflicting interests, South Tahoe; second, because Sheppard Mullin knew of that conflicting interest and failed to inform J-M of it, J-M's consent was not "informed" within the meaning of the Rules of Professional Conduct; and third, Sheppard Mullin's unconsented-to conflict of interest affected the whole of its engagement agreement with J-M, rendering it unenforceable in its entirety.

Because rule 3-310(C)(3) embodies a core aspect of the duty of loyalty, the disclosure required for informed consent to dual representation must also be measured by a standard of loyalty. To be informed, the client's consent to dual representation must be based on disclosure of all material facts the attorney knows and can reveal . . . An attorney or law firm that knowingly withholds material information about a conflict has not earned the confidence and trust the rule is designed to protect. Assessed by this standard, the conflicts waiver here was inadequate. By asking J-M to waive current conflicts as well as future ones, Sheppard Mullin did put J-M on notice that a current conflict *might* exist. But by failing to disclose to J-M the fact that a current conflict *actually* existed, the law firm failed to disclose to its client all the "relevant circumstances" within its knowledge relating to its representation of J-M. (Rules Prof. Conduct, rule 3-310(A)(1).)

Because this case concerns the failure to disclose a current conflict, we have no occasion here to decide whether, or under what circumstances, a blanket advance waiver . . . would be permissible. We conclude, rather, that without full disclosure of existing conflicts known to the attorney, the client's consent is not informed for purposes of our ethics rules. Sheppard Mullin failed to make such full disclosure here.

As explained . . . violation of a Rule of Professional Conduct in the formation of a contract can render the contract unenforceable as against public policy. That is what happened here when Sheppard Mullin agreed to represent J-M in the qui tam action, while also representing South Tahoe on other matters, without obtaining J-M's informed consent. It is true that Sheppard Mullin rendered J-M substantial legal services pursuant to the agreement, and J-M has not endeavored to show that it suffered damages as a result of the law firm's conflict of interest. But the fact remains that the agreement itself is contrary to the public policy of the state. The transaction was entered under terms that undermined an ethical rule designed for the protection of the client as well as for the preservation of public confidence in the legal profession. The contract is for that reason unenforceable.

As an alternative to contractual recovery, Sheppard Mullin has sought recovery under the equitable doctrine of quantum meruit—a doctrine that has sometimes been applied to allow attorneys "to recover the reasonable value of their legal services from their clients when their fee agreements are found to be invalid or unenforceable." (*Huskinson & Brown v. Wolf* (2004) 32 Cal.4th 453, 462 (*Huskinson*), citing cases; see Rest.3d Law Governing Lawyers, *supra*, § 39.) The Court of Appeal, however, held that Sheppard Mullin's conflict of interest disentitles it from either receiving or retaining any compensation for the approximately 10,000 hours it worked on the qui tam matter, even on a theory of quantum meruit. Relying on a series of California cases in which courts denied compensation in the face of serious ethical breaches, the Court of Appeal held that an attorney may never recover compensation for services rendered while it labored under an improperly waived conflict of interest.

The Restatement instructs, and we agree, that the egregiousness of the attorney's conduct, its potential and actual effect on the client and the attorney-client relationship, and the existence of alternative remedies are all also relevant to whether and to what extent forfeiture of compensation is warranted . . . The law takes these case-specific factors into account because forfeiture of compensation is, in the end, an equitable remedy. As California courts have often noted, the rule governing attorney forfeiture derives primarily from the general principle of equity that a fiduciary's breach of trust undermines the value of his or her services . . . Forfeiture also serves as a deterrent to misconduct, and it avoids putting clients to the task of proving the harm stemming from the lawyer's conflict of interest when the extent of the harm may be difficult to measure.

When a law firm seeks fees in quantum meruit that it is unable to recover under the contract because it has breached an ethical duty to its client, the burden of proof on these or other factors lies with the firm. To be entitled to a measure of recovery, the firm must show that the violation was neither willful nor egregious, and it must show that its conduct was not so potentially damaging to the client as to warrant a complete denial of compensation. And before the trial court may award compensation, it must be satisfied that the award does not undermine incentives for compliance with the Rules of Professional Conduct. For this reason, at least absent exceptional circumstances, the contractual fee will not serve as an appropriate measure of quantum meruit recovery . . . Although the law firm may be entitled to some compensation for its work, its ethical breach will ordinarily require it to relinquish some or all of the profits for which it negotiated . . . On the limited factual record before us, however, we cannot conclude that the existence of an improperly waived conflict of interest, by itself, presents an absolute bar to the award of reasonable compensation for services rendered.

We affirm the judgment of the Court of Appeal insofar as it reversed the superior court's judgment entered on the arbitration award. We reverse the judgment of the Court of Appeal insofar as it ordered disgorgement of all fees collected, and remand for further proceedings consistent with our opinion.

Questions about the Case

1. Did Sheppard Mullin, the law firm in this case, have a conflict? Was the firm aware of it?
2. What steps could Sheppard Mullin have taken to prevent a potential conflict of interest?
3. How does this case address the rules on simultaneous (dual) representation as outlined in this chapter?
4. What did Sheppard Mullin's waiver provision say about conflicts with other clients?
5. What did the court say about the enforceability of the engagement agreement based on the conflict of interest?
6. Which ethical rule was violated? What were the resulting consequences?
7. How did the court rule about compensation to Sheppard Mullin for services rendered? What was the court's reasoning for its decision?

6

Advertising and Solicitation

This chapter covers the rules governing lawyer advertising and direct solicitation of clients, tracing the continued development of these rules since restrictions on advertising were banned by the U.S. Supreme Court 45 years ago. Chapter 6 covers:

- key U.S. Supreme Court cases on the regulation of advertising and solicitation
- current practices in legal advertising and marketing
- ethics rules governing advertising
- application of rules to paralegals
- ethics rules prohibiting direct solicitation of clients
- application of the rules in the online environment

A. Advertising

1. Background and History

In 1977, the landmark case of *Bates v. State Bar of Arizona*, 433 U.S. 350, upset decades of ethics rules prohibiting lawyer advertising, which dated back to the first state codes and first American Bar Association (ABA) model rules, the 1908 Canons. The early rules prohibited virtually every form of advertising except business cards. Later, inclusion of biographical information on approved lists of lawyers was permitted.

The political and social environment surrounding the *Bates* decision was one of growing consumer protection coupled with the growing recognition that most citizens did not have access to legal services. During the late 1960s and throughout the 1970s, new nontraditional methods of increasing access to legal services were being developed. Legal aid clinics and public interest law firms began opening their doors. The first prepaid legal insurance plans were established. Storefront legal clinics handled common legal problems at a lower cost than traditional firms. The organized bar and the public shared the realization that citizens of modest incomes were unable to afford an attorney and did not know how to find one.

The ABA Code of Professional Responsibility (ABA Model Code) adopted in 1969 contained the **traditional restrictions on lawyer advertising**. Only business cards, announcements of lawyer personnel changes within the firm, new locations and addresses, and holiday cards to existing clients were permitted. The ABA made some slight modifications in these rules in the mid-1970s to accommodate the special role of legal aid organizations and prepaid legal insurance plans. However, it was not until *Bates* that sweeping changes were made in the ethics codes of every jurisdiction.

In the *Bates* case, two Arizona lawyers advertised low-cost legal services in a local newspaper and were disciplined by the state bar. Their challenge to restrictions on lawyer advertising was ultimately heard by the U.S. Supreme Court, which struck down the restrictions as violative of the First Amendment. The Court held that lawyer advertising—like other forms of commercial speech—was protected, and states could prohibit advertisements only in limited ways—for example, for false, misleading, or deceptive ads and by means of reasonable time, place, and manner restrictions.

The *Bates* case (included at the end of this chapter) outlines very clearly the arguments on both sides of the lawyer advertising issue. The legal profession's resistance to lawyer advertising at the time was tremendous, because lawyers believed that advertising would de-professionalize and commercialize law practice. Although opposition to advertising still exists, most lawyers engage in some form of advertising that would have been prohibited before *Bates*.

Legal advertising and marketing have become pervasive. Firms have strategic marketing plans that include advertising and often try to create a firm image or brand with a logo, vision statement, and other elements. Studies also show that although many lawyers attribute the declining image of the legal profession to advertising, the public does not. The public considers advertising a source of information and only begins to perceive it as objectionable when it becomes "invasive." Studies also show that advertising works—increasing numbers of people find a lawyer through advertising. The use of the Internet for marketing of legal services has expanded dramatically and created new ethical issues, which are discussed later in this chapter. Studies show that millions of people have used the Internet to find legal services. All large law firms, and even most smaller ones, have their own websites. Firms of all sizes also utilize social media networks.

Some firms are using nonlawyer sales and **business development** consultants or in-house personnel to help them reach prospective clients. Many firms produce sophisticated and well-designed brochures and webpages that describe the backgrounds of attorneys, explain the nature of their services, and highlight prominent matters that they have handled; publish electronic newsletters for clients, updating them on the latest firm triumphs and informing them of changes in the law; hold social events and educational seminars for clients; and have contact through social media to announce accomplishments—for example, when the firm wins an important case or a prestigious new partner joins the firm.

Firms publish e-newsletters on industry issues, such as banking or corporate securities; sponsor blogs; offer webinars; and post videos and podcasts on their websites and social media pages. Websites dedicated to illnesses or medical conditions that have resulted in class action suits against pharmaceutical companies are common. Online legal referral services, lawyer–client matching sites, legal advice sites, chat rooms, sponsored links, and even mass e-mail marketing have been tried. (See Section A.4 for more on the ethics of using electronic communications.)

Law firms place a high value on lawyers who can bring in business. "Rainmakers" who attract business, work well with clients, and keep them satisfied are essential to the success of a firm. Many law firms establish a positive public image by donating funds to worthy causes, participating in community and civic activities, taking *pro bono* cases, and encouraging lawyers to participate in a wide variety of community and civic activities outside the firm. Some firms sponsor in-house seminars to train lawyers how to better market their services and to enhance client relations. Many firms give seminars at professional conferences and trade shows sponsored by industries from which they draw clients.

Some large firms use client surveys to assess the attitudes, needs, and levels of satisfaction of their clients. These surveys aim to identify the importance of various factors in meeting clients' needs and to find out how the firm's responsiveness, communication, services, and fee structure are perceived. Some firms find that client relations are improved simply by virtue of conducting such surveys, and the information gained may be used to enhance services and to remedy weaknesses. Sophisticated research is used to identify issues and trends in areas of practice.

Smaller firms also engage in advertising. The more traditional firms use the same kinds of marketing activities as large firms. But many small firms are specialized, handling one or two kinds of legal matters and seeking a clientele that might not otherwise have a ready referral to a lawyer. Personal injury firms have led the way in lawyer advertising, most visibly with television and radio spots, but also with billboards, flyers placed on cars or doorknobs, posters on telephone poles, and even ads on the back of grocery store receipts. Firms that handle immigration, family law, workers' compensation, Social Security matters, and bankruptcy frequently utilize these techniques. Direct-mail and e-mail advertising is used to target persons who may need specific kinds of legal services, such as foreclosure prevention. Some lawyers use 900 numbers to dispense legal advice, and others include catchy 800 numbers in their print, radio, or television ads. A growing number of small firms and solos advertise in directories published by local churches and civic organizations.

Paralegals play an important role in marketing by serving clients efficiently, emphasizing the cost savings to the client from the use of paralegals, identifying sources for referrals, alerting lawyers to opportunities for rainmaking, and helping to develop marketing plans and client surveys.

2. Case Law on Advertising

Several Supreme Court decisions that followed *Bates* made it clear that the Court will not look favorably at restrictions on lawyer advertising. In *In re R.M.J.*, 455 U.S. 1991 (1982), the Court held that a practitioner could advertise the areas of law in which he practiced in language other than that specified in the state ethics code because the language the lawyer used was not misleading and the code was unnecessarily restrictive. The court also allowed the lawyer to state in the ads the jurisdictions in which he was licensed to practice. In *Zauderer v. Office of Disciplinary Counsel of Supreme Court of Ohio*, 471 U.S. 626 (1985), the Supreme Court reversed the state supreme court's ruling that disciplined a personal injury lawyer for placing a newspaper ad that pictured the intrauterine device that was the subject of litigation. The Court held that the lawyer had the right to publish ads directed at readers with specific legal problems so long as the ads were **accurate and not misleading**. In 1988, the Supreme Court in *Shapero v. Kentucky Bar Association*, 486 U.S. 466, held that state ethics codes could not prohibit truthful and non-deceptive direct-mail advertising. The language it found unconstitutional in the Kentucky code was identical to ABA Model Rule 7.3, which had to be extensively revised. Prior to this case, ethics rules had classified direct-mail advertising as unethical direct solicitation, which was prohibited. In *Peel v. Attorney Registration and Disciplinary Commission of Illinois*, 496 U.S. 91 (1990), the Court struck down state prohibitions on statements carried on a lawyer's letterhead that indicated the lawyer's certification as a specialist. Although the certifying agency here—the National Board of Trial Advocacy—was not one authorized by the state, it had objective and verifiable criteria for the certification of civil trial specialists. This ruling resulted in changes in several state codes that had restrictions similar to those of Illinois.

Peel was followed by another case endorsing the use of a designation by an organization not approved by a state agency. In *Ibanez v. Florida Dept. of Business and Professional Regulation*, 512 U.S. 136 (1994), the Court held that an attorney/certified public accountant who advertised her certified public accountant (CPA) and certified financial planner (CFP) designations could not be reprimanded by the Florida Board of Accountancy for false, deceptive, and misleading advertising because the ad was truthful and the designations were publicly recognized by potential clients.

The pattern of the court striking down state prohibitions on lawyer advertising was finally broken in 1995 in the case of *Florida Bar v. Went For It, Inc.*, 515 U.S. 618 (1995). In this landmark case, the Supreme Court upheld **restrictions on targeted direct mail** advertising sent to accident and disaster victims. The Florida Bar, like the bars in many other jurisdictions, had a rule prohibiting such ads from being sent within 30 days of the incident. In upholding the prohibition, the Court cited heavily to bar studies that showed how negatively such letters were viewed by the public, which saw the lawyers' conduct as an invasion of privacy designed to take advantage of vulnerable people in tragic circumstances. No major Supreme Court decisions on lawyer advertising have come down since that time, although challenges to regulations continue to be made in the courts. The *Went For It* case can be accessed at the companion website that accompanies the text.

For many years after Bates, states attempted, with varying degrees of success, to impose specific kinds of restrictions on lawyer advertising. Several challenges to these restrictions were brought by Public Citizen, a national group that represents more than 100,000 lawyers. The results have been split. In *Public Citizen, Inc. v. Louisiana Attorney Bd.*, 632 F.3d 212 (5th Cir. 2011), the appellate court affirmed a lower court decision upholding several provisions, but struck down restrictions concerning past results, portrayals of judges and juries, and disclaimers, which were found to be unduly burdensome. In *Alexander v. Cahill*, 598 F.3d 79 (2d Cir. 2010), the court struck down "content-based" restrictions, with the exception of portrayals of fictitious law firms, and imposed a **30-day moratorium** on targeted advertising following a specific incident.

In *Harrell v. Florida Bar*, 608 F.3d 1241 (11th Cir. 2010), practitioner Harrell, who had been in constant discussions with the bar over his advertising for several years, filed suit as a co-plaintiff with Public Citizens when the bar determined that he could not use the **slogan**, "Don't settle for less than you deserve." The appellate court summed up the current state of affairs in lawyer advertising:

> The present version of the rules reflects a long and undeniable trend towards increasingly restrictive measures to control attorney advertising. The goal of these measures is to protect the public from misleading advertising and to preserve the reputation of the legal profession in the face of what some perceive as increasingly unscrupulous advertisements. Thus, for example, in 1990, the Florida Supreme Court adopted a range of new rules and explanatory comments that prohibited forms of advertising content such as slogans, jingles, references to past "results obtained," testimonials, statements that "describ[e] or characterize] the quality of the lawyer's services," statements that would be considered true for most lawyers practicing in Florida, statements of comparison like "one of the best" or "one of the most experienced," depictions that "create suspense" or contain "exaggerations" or "call[s] for legal services," and "audio or video portrayal[s] of an event or situation." [Citations omitted.]

The case was reversed in part and affirmed in part, and remanded to the lower court to adjudicate some of the plaintiffs' challenges to the rules on the grounds of vagueness.

Several cases now specifically address technology-mediated advertising. The U.S. District Court in New Jersey upheld a provision of the New Jersey ethics rules that was found to prohibit a lawyer from quoting on his website excerpts of judicial opinions that praised his work (*Dwyer v. Cappell* (D.N.J. 6-26-13)). The Virginia State Bar upheld provisions of the state's professional conduct code for lawyers regarding advertising rules that apply to social media and other new forms of electronic communications (*Hunter v. Virginia State Bar* (Record No. 121472 2-28-13)).

3. Ethics Rules on Advertising

All states have adopted rules similar to the ABA Model Rules, and, as noted above, some have attempted, with varying degrees of success, to be more restrictive than the ABA rules. ABA Model Rule 7.1 prohibits lawyers from making false or misleading communications about themselves or their services. A communication is considered "false or misleading if it contains a material misrepresentation of fact or law, or omits a fact necessary to make the statement considered as a whole not materially misleading." Comment 3 to the rule indicates that facts that create unjustified expectations and unsubstantiated comparisons with other lawyers can be misleading, and suggests that appropriate disclaimers may mitigate such concerns.

Many states have adopted variations on this rule. Some states specifically prohibit ***testimonials***, contending that they are inherently misleading, create unjustified expectations, or are self-laudatory. A growing number of jurisdictions allow testimonials, usually with the requirement that they include information about payment to the endorser or the status of the endorser as a client, or have disclaimers to avoid unjustified expectations. Dramatizations in radio and television ads are also disfavored by many in the organized bar, but are becoming increasingly common and have generally been tolerated. Several states permit them, usually with disclaimers that advise the viewers that the ad is a dramatization and does not guarantee similar results.

The ABA Model Rules do not require ads to be "dignified." The evaluation of what is "dignified" is completely subjective and would not meet the tests established by *Bates* and its progeny. Some state bars encourage dignity in lawyer advertising through aspirational goals that recommend against "the use of inappropriately dramatic music, unseemly slogans, hawkish spokespersons, premium offers, slapstick routines or outlandish settings," which undermine public confidence in the legal profession. But the number of ads that employ these techniques continue to grow.

Some states prohibit all lawyer **comparison advertising**. Other states prohibit statements regarding past performance on the grounds that they are inherently misleading and create false expectations. Several states specifically prohibit predictions of success; these claims would probably be found to be misleading even without a specific prohibition in the code. Claims about quality are generally prohibited, as they cannot be objectively measured. Fee information and comparisons are generally permissible, although some states have adopted specific language regarding descriptions of fees.

ABA Model Rule 7.2(a) permits lawyers to advertise through **written, recorded, or electronic media**. Rule 7.2(b) prohibits payment to a person for recommending legal services except for the cost of ads, charges for legal service organizations or lawyer referral services, or payment when a lawyer buys another lawyer's practice. Rule 7.2(c) adds the requirement that at least one lawyer's name and office address must be included in the ads.

Related ABA Model Rule 7.3(c) requires lawyers to include the words "Advertising Material" at the beginning and end of written, recorded, or electronic communications soliciting employment and on the outside of the envelope of a direct-mail ad. Most states have similar rules about labeling on advertising. Many states require lawyers to keep copies of ads and records on when and where they were used, whatever the method of advertising, for two years or for longer periods, and some require copies of ads to be sent to a specific state agency. Most require specifically worded disclaimers in ads. A few states have a review committee that passes on ads

> **Testimonial advertisements**
> Ads in which a client or person acting as a client explains how valuable the lawyer's services were.

before they are used. Rule 7.3 has also been interpreted to allow counsel for plaintiff and defense in class actions to contact putative members of the class (ABA Formal Op. 07-445).

Some states have restrictions on contacting accident victims through advertising within a 30- to 60-day period after an accident. Federal law also prohibits lawyers and their agents from making unsolicited communications concerning possible causes of action to victims or their relatives for 45 days after an accident involving an air carrier (49 U.S.C. §1136(g)(2)). This ban covers both advertising (e.g., by direct mail) and in-person or phone solicitation.

ABA Model Rule 7.4 allows lawyers to communicate the fact that they practice in a particular field of law and to advertise their certification by an organization approved by a state regulatory authority or the ABA. Lawyers may also indicate that they are licensed as patent attorneys or are engaged in admiralty practice. Most jurisdictions have adopted Rule 7.4, but some jurisdictions prohibit the use of the word "specialize" to describe an attorney's area of expertise (unless they are certified by the state as specialists) and allow terms such as "limited to" or "concentrated in" in particular areas of practice.

Finally, ABA Model Rule 7.5 covers **firm names and letterheads**. Under this rule, a lawyer's letterhead must meet the standards set forth in Model Rule 7.1, that is, not be false or misleading. Trade names are permitted under this rule so long as they do not imply a connection to a government agency or legal services organization. Some states have strict limits on the use of trade names. Firms with multi-jurisdictional practices may use the same firm name but must show limits on listed lawyers' licenses to practice. Lawyers in public office cannot be listed in the firm name or on its letterhead unless the lawyer is actively and regularly practicing with the firm. Finally, lawyers cannot state or imply that they practice with a partnership or organization unless they do this in fact. For example, lawyers who share office space but are not partners cannot hold themselves out as partners by means of their firm name or letterhead.

A debate has arisen about whether lawyers can advertise their designation as a "Super Lawyer" or "Best Lawyer," a designation usually made by a publication based on the votes of peers. The question is whether there should be a total ban on these designations as inherently misleading, or whether narrower restrictions can be applied. Arizona, Connecticut, Iowa, Michigan, and New Jersey have ethics opinions that allow the designation within carefully drawn parameters, such as requirements that the ratings be peer-based and not predicated on the lawyer advertising in the publication. Others also require a disclaimer. (See, for example, New Jersey Supreme Court Committee on Attorney Advertising, "Notice re Attorney Advertising of Awards, Honors and Accolades that Compare a Lawyer's Services to Other Lawyers' Services," issued in May 2016, which requires that the basis for comparison must be verified, the organization must have made an adequate inquiry into the individual's lawyer's fitness, and language explaining the designation must be provided.)

As indicated in Chapter 3, **paralegals' names and titles** may be listed on letterhead and business cards in most jurisdictions. Earlier restrictions on nonlawyers being listed on letterhead and having business cards have been revised because of changes in the rules on lawyer advertising brought about by *Bates* and the cases that followed it. For example, Indiana and South Dakota guidelines that were adopted in the early 1990s and an opinion of a 1994 New Jersey Committee on Attorney Advertising condone the use of paralegals' names and titles on letterhead and in newspaper advertisements (Opinion 16 issued in 1994). Two ethics opinions specifically endorse the use of "CLA" and "CLAS" on letterhead and business cards (Mississippi Bar 95-223 and New York State Bar Association 97-695).

Paralegals must use titles that accurately reflect their nonlawyer status. For example, New York State Bar Association Committee on Professional Ethics Opinion 640 (1992) endorsed the use of "paralegal" and "senior paralegal," which unambiguously convey nonlawyer status, but recommended against the use of several other titles: legal associate, paralegal coordinator, public benefits specialist, legal advocate, family law advocate, housing law advocate, disability advocate, and public benefits advocate. The committee objected to these titles on the grounds that they are likely to be confusing to the public, which would be misled about the nonlawyer status of someone with one of these titles.

A final concern about letterhead and business cards relates to their use, which should be carefully monitored by the law firm. Several ethics opinions advise against allowing clients to use lawyers' letterhead to send correspondence without lawyer review. Business cards, of course, must not be used for unethical solicitation.

Ethics rules on advertising and solicitation continue to be debated. At one end of the opinion spectrum are attorneys who favor a wide-open and unrestricted environment to demystify the legal profession, to promote greater access to legal services, and to encourage a more competitive climate among lawyers, which might lead to lower fees. At the other end are more traditional lawyers who believe that strong prohibitions are essential to preserve the good reputation and status of the legal profession and to protect the public from unscrupulous practitioners.

4. Application of the Rules to Electronic Communications

Lawyers in all legal settings use various kinds of electronic communications to reach prospective clients. Most firms have websites, which, like firm brochures, provide background information on lawyers in the firm and areas in which the firm practices and may include newsworthy articles about legal issues of interest to clients. Some lawyers have blogs, participate in chat groups, use social networking, advertise on Craigslist and similar sites, post on Facebook, LinkedIn, YouTube, and other social networking sites, and use direct e-mail to reach prospective clients. The efficacy of electronic advertising and social media in marketing legal services is still being studied, with some surveys showing that prospective clients prefer to find a lawyer through a colleague's or friend's recommendation. However, a 2013 ABA survey showed that lawyers were getting clients through blogging, micro-blogging, and **social networking.** Since that time, microblogging through social media has become more competitive with traditional blogging. A 2022 ABA survey found that 37 percent of respondents have blogs; 45 percent of those with blogs said this has led to additional clients. The use of social media continues to increase: 87 percent of survey respondents from all law firm sizes reported having a LinkedIn presence; 62 percent were on Facebook; and 82 percent personally maintain a presence on social media for professional purposes. Firms that effectively utilize digital marketing and social media reported a rise in rankings and increased revenue generation. Lawyers are clearly utilizing technology to market. One report showed that law firms are spending nearly $1 billion a year in advertising, much of it through electronic media and television.

Several companies operate "matching" services, in which prospective clients submit a form explaining their legal problem, providing the locality and time frame for retaining counsel, and sometimes indicating the fee that they are willing to pay. The network of lawyers registered with the service can then communicate with the client and offer their services. Some firms attract and serve clients entirely over the Internet, operating "virtual" law practices.

As the use of electronic media has grown, so too have the challenges to the rules and the frequency of sanctions imposed on lawyers who break those rules. Recent examples of sanctions related to advertising include a lawyer who was reprimanded for stating on his website that he had over twenty years in practice when in fact he had seven, and for stating he had "numerous trained and experienced lawyers" on his staff when in fact his firm had only two recent law school graduates; and a firm offering free tee shirts with the firm's name and logo, and then posting photos of the recipients wearing the tee shirts on the firm's social media page.

The use of web-based communications has raised ethical issues that fall in many areas of the ethics rules. Is direct e-mail to prospective clients advertising or solicitation, and which rules apply? Is a website more like a television ad or a firm brochure? If an attorney states a legal opinion in a chat group, is the attorney forming an attorney-client relationship with the person posing the question? Is the attorney violating unauthorized practice rules in states in which they are not licensed to practice but where the opinion is read? Is it inherently misleading to advertise on the

Internet when the attorney is not licensed in all the states where the ad may be read? Can a lawyer pay a referral fee to an Internet service that matches lawyers and clients?

Concerns about confidentiality and conflicts of interest also arise in the online environment. In communicating with a prospective client, the duty of confidentiality is triggered once the lawyer has a discussion with the client about representation. So, what is the duty of the lawyer when a prospective client sends unsolicited confidential information to the lawyer? When does a prospective client have a reasonable expectation that the lawyer would be willing to discuss representation? Can this expectation arise from the nature of the lawyer's site or other electronic communication? What happens if the lawyer already represents the opposing side? Once the confidential information is given to the lawyer, is the lawyer prohibited from representing the opposing party? Most experts indicate that the lawyer is conflicted out of representing the opposing party if the lawyer has obtained confidential information that would be harmful to the person who revealed it.

The ABA and state ethics authorities are gradually addressing these many questions through ethics opinions. A few early opinions found it ethical to operate a firm **website** and to post ads to electronic newsgroups so long as the material complies with existing rules on advertising, including those prohibiting false and misleading statements, requiring the lawyer to maintain copies of the material for review by disciplinary authorities, and mandating specific disclaimers. Some states require lawyers with websites to file a copy with the bar and to pay a filing fee, just as they would with any other lawyer advertisement, and other states have review committees that examine websites before they are posted.

An innovative marketing tactic led to three ethics opinions endorsing the use of "Groupons," "deal of the day," and other kinds of **online coupons** for marketing so long as the lawyer follows all the other ethics rules (ABA Formal Opinion 465 (2013)); New York State Bar Association Committee on Professional Ethics, 2011-897; North Carolina Bar Association Formal Opinion 2011-10, and South Carolina Bar Association Advisory Opinion 11-05. The North Carolina Bar has also endorsed the use of live chat support services on a law firm website, with the caution that other ethics rules in this kind of communication must be carefully followed (North Carolina Bar Association Formal Ethics Opinion 2011-8).

The Philadelphia Bar has provided guidelines about online communications with potential clients, stating:

> [I]t is appropriate for a lawyer who encounters persons "blogging" about complaints, indicating they might need legal assistance, to attempt to communicate with them via the blog or via any other electronic method, provided it is not real-time electronic communication in which the prospective clients are compelled to respond immediately. This would mean,

for example, that the lawyer observing this discussion via a blog could submit a "post" to the blog or could send an e-mail if the posters to the blog have supplied their e-mails, and the lawyer could invite the bloggers to visit the lawyer's firm's website.

Philadelphia Bar Association, Opinion 2010-6.

See also State Bar of California Formal Opinion 2012-186, which clarifies the kind of statements that will be considered advertising when posted on a social media website and Florida Advisory Advertising Opinion A-00-1 (Revised) 1-29-16, which modified the Florida State Bar's opinion related to the solicitation of prospective clients through Internet chat rooms. The issue of whether a lawyer has consulted with a client or formed a **lawyer-client relationship** through an online communication caused the ABA to revise comments to Rule 1.18 (Duties to Prospective Clients) to clarify that a relationship is not formed if a person merely responds to a general advertisement but that a consultation has occurred if the lawyer specifically "invites the submission of information about a potential presentation without clear and reasonably understandable warnings. . . ." (See Comment [2] to Model Rule 1.18.)

Cases and ethics opinions on participation in social networking media, such as **LinkedIn**, **blogs**, **and chat groups**, are starting to emerge. Most authorities, including the ABA, find that these forms of communication are akin to in-person solicitation only if they are live and two-way. Most find that they are not solicitation, as they are not "in person" as required by the ethics rules. Even in states that do not classify these communications as solicitation, lawyers are warned to guard against inadvertently forming a lawyer-client relationship or giving legal advice in a jurisdiction where they are not licensed to practice.

Some bars have considered **direct e-mail advertising** and found that it is not direct solicitation because it is not "live"; the reader can choose not to read it and can reflect on its contents before responding. Direct e-mail marketing lacks the immediacy and confrontational aspects of in-person and telephone communication. However, a few states have disciplined lawyers for "soliciting" clients on the Internet, in part because potential clients located in jurisdictions where the lawyers were not licensed to practice could read the ads and be misled about the lawyer's right to practice in that jurisdiction.

A few states prohibit lawyers from being listed in lawyers' **directories** on the Internet. Several states classify fee-charging directories as profit-making **referral services** that lawyers are prohibited from using unless they are approved by the state bar. Generally, the ethical concern with such referral services is that the lawyer is paying a referral fee to a nonlawyer or is fee splitting with a nonlawyer. (See more on these prohibitions in Chapter 7.) Most states allow online lawyer matching services. As noted earlier, these services invite a prospective client to submit a form that indicates the nature of the legal problem; lawyers who are members of the service in the relevant jurisdiction can respond. A few states prohibit lawyers from participating on these sites, considering them to be unapproved lawyer referral services, but others (New York, Rhode Island, North Carolina, and South Carolina) allow them as a form of advertising. Texas allows participation as long as the matching is automated and not done by nonlawyers running the service. The Federal Trade Commission supports these sites as an effective method for providing access to affordable legal services.

The use of the Internet to communicate about legal services is evolving rapidly and regional differences in applying the ethics rules are quite evident. A few generalizations can be made about the ethics of electronic advertising and solicitation:

- It is acceptable for lawyers and law firms to have **websites** that provide information about the firm so long as the ethics rules on advertising are followed, including those prohibiting false and misleading statements, requiring that lawyers maintain copies of the material for review, specifying language about certifications, and mandating that the lawyer's name and address be included.
- A lawyer's website must state the **jurisdiction(s)** in which the lawyers in the firm are licensed to practice law and should contain disclaimers to warn prospective clients that they can practice only in those states to prevent the communication from being misleading and to guard against UPL.
- In most jurisdictions, Internet advertising, including direct e-mail advertising, constitutes **advertising**, not solicitation, so that lawyers can utilize the Internet to advertise so long as the existing ethics rules on advertising are followed. Presumably, this advertising also permits sponsored links and the use of "pay per click" services. (See, for example, New York State Bar Ass'n Ethics Opinion 1049 (2015), which finds it permissible to post on a website seeking clients for particular kinds of representation and considers these communications to be advertising.)
- Services that match up lawyers with clients may be classified as **referral services**, which must have relevant approvals, or as advertisements, which are permitted as long as other ethics rules on advertising are honored.
- The majority of jurisdictions treat **blogs and chat groups** as advertising, not in-person solicitation, which is subject to the more rigorous restrictions than advertising. Some states, including California, find that chat rooms are not the same as solicitation as the contact is not "in person." Blogs, which are usually one-way communication, are subject to ethics rules on advertising if the rules classify them as advertising, which is increasingly the case. (See, for example, State Bar of California Formal Opinion Interim No. 12-0006 (2014) and Formal Opinion 2016-196 (2016), which hold that blogging about legal matters is an advertisement if the blog directly or implicitly expresses the lawyer's availability for employment.)

- Lawyer **directories on the Internet** are generally permitted, even if lawyers pay for the entries, just as regular hard copy directories would be permitted.
- The categorization of **social media posts** as advertising or solicitation largely depends on the jurisdiction and how the account is utilized. States such as New York and Virginia examine each communication individually. In 2012, California issued an ethics opinion that considered five hypothetical statements from a "hybrid" social media account (used for both personal and professional purposes) to determine whether they would fall under attorney advertising rules or be considered solicitation. (See State Bar of California Formal Opinion 2012-186.) In 2020, Florida revised its guidelines to state that lawyers' personal networking accounts are not subject to legal advertising rules as long as they are not used for the "purpose of marketing legal services." Accounts used primarily "for the purpose of retention of the lawyer or law firm" are subject to the rules on advertising and solicitation. (See Florida Bar's Advertising Guidelines for Networking Sites.)
- The proliferation of **legal marketing** by law firms continues to be a viable advertising opportunity for business development. During the COVID-19 pandemic, legal events targeted towards potential and current clients went virtual. While in-person events have resumed, virtual options will continue to be available. Law firms customarily use digital platforms (Teams, Zoom, Webex, ON24) for client access to webinars and QR codes for distributing external event materials. In recent years, a number of law firms have rebranded for repositioning in the marketplace and enhanced cultural reflection. This includes improved web site functionality to facilitate business development. Law firms largely utilize social media, including podcasting, to provide interpretive analyses of current legal issues. Technology also allows law firms to more efficiently manage client data as well as automate requests for proposals. Ethics violations in legal marketing by law firms may carry serious consequences in the form of fees, expensive domain name changes, and malpractice claims. Lawyers are required to remain aware of their state's ethics rules for legal marketing and ensure that legal marketing professionals they employ adhere to these rules. States vary when it comes to legal marketing ethics requirements, but most states mirror the ABA's Model Rules, with modifications, including the prohibition against making "a false or misleading communication about the lawyer or the lawyer's services." (See ABA Model Rule 7.1 Communications Concerning a Lawyer's Services.)

Disclaimers
A statement denying a person's claim or right.

Disclaimers associated with web-based communications are increasingly important in protecting lawyers against ethical pitfalls. Most lawyers have disclaimers on their websites, indicating that information provided there is not "legal advice" and that no lawyer-client relationship is established by virtue of the prospective client sending a lawyer an e-mail.

Disclaimers should also warn that such communications are not privileged and should ask that prospective clients not send confidential information to the firm's mailbox. Disclaimers should state the jurisdictional limits of the lawyer's practice. Such disclaimers should also be included on electronic ads and other forms of web-based communications like e-newsletters. They should be written in plain English so that the general public can understand them. Good practice suggests that the prospective clients be required to sign a statement indicating that they have read the disclaimers before they proceed to send any information to the lawyer. Disclaimers should be placed where they will be seen by users and not buried several clicks away from the page where the e-mail contact link is provided. See ABA Formal Ethics Opinion 10-457 for more advice on ensuring that the use of websites does not lead to ethical violations.

Through disclaimers and careful site construction, lawyers can discourage prospective clients from providing confidential information in unsolicited e-mails. Sites can invite the prospective client to first send their name, the nature of the claim, and the names of other possible parties so that the lawyer can conduct a conflicts check before any confidential information is revealed. This process protects both the prospective client and the lawyer.

Some commentators have called for **uniform national ethics rules** concerning electronic communications, although little progress has been made to achieve uniformity. The great variation among states in their handling of advertising and solicitation exacerbates this already difficult area of ethics. A lawyer may be in compliance with the local jurisdictional rules but will clearly be in violation of the rules in another state where the communication is read. Further, the lawyers in states with more restrictive advertising rules believe that they are at a competitive disadvantage because they are more limited in what they can say, how they can say it, and where they can say it. Differences in rules on advertising in directories, how one's areas of expertise can be described, whether testimonials can be used, and whether extensive disclaimers are required make advertising on the Internet especially challenging for lawyers in restrictive jurisdictions. And because the current advertising rules were adopted before the extensive use of electronic media, many are calling for a wholesale revision of the rules, including the Association of Professional Responsibility Lawyers, which proposed extensive revisions in 2016. In 2018, the ABA adopted amendments to its legal advertising rules to "focus enforcement on false and misleading ads."

B. Solicitation

The changes in ethics rules and practice relating to advertising have not had much impact on the rules restricting the conduct of lawyers in soliciting clients directly, either in person or by telephone. The foundation for these

Solicitation
A targeted communication initiated by a lawyer that is directed to a specific person and offers to provide legal services.

Runners and cappers
Agents of lawyers who solicit clients in violation of ethics rules.

restrictions is strong and virtually unquestioned by the profession. The rules related to *solicitation* reflect concerns about the intimidation, undue influence, and unfair bargaining position that lawyers may have when they confront a prospective client face-to-face, on the phone, or otherwise in "real time." The legal profession has a long-standing prohibition against "ambulance chasers" or *runners and cappers*—agents of lawyers who prey on accident victims by soliciting them directly at the scene of an accident or while they are in a hospital as the result of an accident. This kind of overreaching conduct, especially when it is directed toward clients who are vulnerable and not in a position to make a rational or well-thought-out choice about selecting counsel, clearly offends most lawyers and the public.

Several cases have addressed this issue. The leading case upholding restrictions on direct solicitation is *Ohralik v. Ohio State Bar Association*, 436 U.S. 447 (1978), included at the end of this chapter. This case involved a lawyer who solicited an accident victim both by telephone and in person. Aggravating the solicitation violation was the lawyer's refusal to stop the solicitation after the potential "client" refused representation.

The U.S. Supreme Court case, *Edenfield v. Fane*, 507 U.S. 761 (1993), caused speculation that the Court might strike down some of the restrictions on direct solicitation by lawyers. In that case, a Florida certified public accountant sought relief from regulations that prohibited direct solicitation of clients. The Court held that such restrictions are a violation of free speech in a business context where prospective clients are sophisticated and experienced business executives.

An exception to rules against direct solicitation of clients is made in cases involving organizations that seek to represent plaintiffs in cases that further a specific political principle, such as freedom of speech or association, or civil rights. Examples of such organizations are the National Association for the Advancement of Colored People and the American Civil Liberties Union. The leading cases in this area are *NAACP v. Button*, 371 U.S. 415 (1963), and *In re Primus*, 436 U.S. 412 (1978).

ABA Model Rule 7.3 prohibits direct solicitation in person, by live telephone, or by real-time electronic contact. This last category of direct solicitation was added to address concerns about solicitation over the Internet (Comment [3]). Exceptions are carved out for contact with other lawyers, family members, close personal relationships, and prior professional relationships. A lawyer must cease solicitation if someone in the excepted categories objects or if the solicitation of that person involves "coercion, duress or harassment." The public interest exception to the ABA Model Rule also appears in the comments.

Some states have adopted additional provisions that prohibit any direct or written solicitation of persons who are in a vulnerable physical, emotional, or mental state or if made at the scene of an accident or en route to a health care facility or in a hospital. Most jurisdictions classify **prerecorded telephone messages** as advertising, not solicitation, because it is not real-time live communication.

The application of the advertising and solicitation rules to class actions also poses some interesting questions. Before a class is certified, lawyers for both plaintiffs and defendants can communicate with prospective members of the class who are not represented by counsel. Once the class is certified, defense counsel cannot communicate with putative members of the class. (See ABA Formal Opinion 07-445.)

A lawyer who attempts to use **agents or intermediaries** to circumvent rules against solicitation will be held responsible in a disciplinary action for the conduct of their agents, under general principles of agency law as well as ethics rules (ABA Model Rule 8.4(a)). Despite these very clear rules, instances of unethical solicitation are not that uncommon, especially by lawyers using agents. For example, agents of lawyers, including accident investigators, have been found soliciting business at the scene of airline crashes and industrial accidents or to persons whose homes are being foreclosed on. (See *Cincinnati Bar Association Mullaney* in Chapter 3 for an example.) Some states are attempting to overcome the difficulties inherent in stopping unlawful solicitation by creating disaster response teams of volunteer and staff lawyers who go to the scenes of major accidents and disasters to warn victims about unlawful solicitation and to deter lawyers from engaging in such conduct.

A few ethics opinions address situations in which nonlawyers solicited legal work for lawyers. The Illinois State Bar Association found it improper for an attorney's employee, designated a "tax representative," to conduct work independently, referring back to the attorney clients that he believed needed further assistance from a lawyer (Illinois State Bar Association 94-8). And the Rhode Island Bar found fee-splitting and unlawful solicitation in a collection agency owned by a nonlawyer who sold forms and legal services, paying the attorney who provided the legal services a percentage of the fees collected (Rhode Island Bar 95-47). Some personal injury lawyers offer a referral fee to anyone who brings a new case to the firm, often accomplished through the agent's unethical in-person or telephone solicitation. In this scenario, the violation is often coupled with the unethical practice of paying a fee for the referral (see Chapter 7).

The NALA and NFPA ethics codes do not address advertising and solicitation directly but prohibit a paralegal from engaging in any act that is unethical. (See NALA Canon 4, NALA Guideline 1, and NFPA Model Disciplinary Rule 1.3.) Likewise, the ABA Model Guidelines for the Utilization of Paralegal Services require the lawyer to ensure that the paralegal's conduct is compatible with ethical rules. (See Guideline 1 and ABA Model Rule 5.3.)

REVIEW QUESTIONS

1. When were prohibitions on lawyer advertising lifted? Under what leading U.S. Supreme Court case? What was the ruling in the case?
2. How did the recognition that many Americans do not have access to legal services affect the movement toward acceptance of lawyer advertising?
3. What kinds of restrictions may states place on lawyer advertising after the *Bates* case?
4. Why do some lawyers dislike lawyer advertising?
5. What kinds of advertising do lawyers most commonly use?
6. What do the key court decisions since *Bates* say about lawyer advertising?
7. What are the general provisions about advertising found in the ABA Model Rules?
8. What kinds of restrictions do some states have that the ABA Rules do not have?
9. Do lawyer ads have to be "dignified"? Is this restriction constitutional?
10. What are the rules governing lawyer advertising of specializations and certifications?
11. Are states permitted to place time restrictions or moratoriums on direct-mail ads to accident victims? Why or why not?
12. Are law firms allowed to use trade names? Under what circumstances?
13. What information about paralegals may law firms include on their letterhead? Their business cards? Websites?
14. Are lawyers prohibited from soliciting clients in person? On the telephone? Why?
15. What are the exceptions to the direct solicitation rule?
16. May lawyers use paralegals to solicit clients directly?
17. How common are violations of the ban on direct solicitation?
18. What job titles for paralegals are and are not acceptable?
19. What role can a paralegal play in marketing?
20. What do ethics rules say about various forms of electronic communication, such as e-newsletters, matching sites, blogs, chat rooms, social media, and websites? Is the use of these media considered advertising or solicitation?
21. What do NALA's and NFPA's ethics codes say about advertising and solicitation?

DISCUSSION QUESTIONS AND HYPOTHETICALS

1. Using the *Bates* case, make a list of the reasons that support banning lawyer advertising and of those that support little restriction of lawyer advertising. Which side of the argument do you find more persuasive?

2. Do you think advertising has hurt or helped the public image of lawyers? Has it made legal services more accessible?
3. Do you think that dramatizations should be restricted? Why or why not? How?
4. Do you think testimonials should be prohibited? Why or why not?
5. Is there anything objectionable about an ad that states that a lawyer is an experienced trial attorney and an expert in personal injury cases when the lawyer has only been in practice a year and all her cases have settled out of court?
6. An ad says, "No recovery, no fee." The fact is that the client is liable for the costs even if he loses. Is this objectionable? Under what rule?
7. May an ad say that an attorney is an "expert"? "Highly qualified"? "Competent"? Why or why not? What about buying an ad in a special magazine called *Super Lawyers* and getting an entry as a "Super Lawyer" as a result?
8. May an ad say that a firm specializes in "quickie divorces"? "Guaranteed visas"? Why or why not?
9. May an ad say the fee is $250 an hour without any additional information? Why or why not?
10. May a firm in a jurisdiction that allows trade names have the name "Public Law Firm"? "Legal Defenders"? "Foreclosure Recovery Center"?
11. May a law firm print its name and phone number on pens that are given out to clients? On shirts donated to the local Little League team? On city maps sent to new residents?
12. Consider the following communications and see how they measure up under the ethics rules and guidelines in this chapter:
    a. Spam e-mail that says in the subject line, "Retain top-notch attorneys for pennies a day."
    b. An e-mail ad that says in the body, "Whether it's a simple speeding ticket or an extensive child custody case, we cover ALL areas of the legal system."
    c. An e-mail that says, "Legal Services for Less than a Penny a Day" and goes on to offer "a top law firm in your area" to produce a "will for you, absolutely FREE, with your membership."
    d. What if the ad in (c) above also indicated, "Why pay $200 or more an hour when you can get the same first-rate service for less than $1 per day?"
    e. A television ad that shows a lawyer called "Action Jackson" talking about his services.
    f. A television ad with a well-known actor saying, "Call the Johnson law firm, RIGHT NOW."
    g. A television ad with O. J. Simpson suggesting that people call a lawyer referral service.

h. A mailing of realistic-looking black plastic grenades with business cards saying that the prospective business client needs to be "armed" against lawsuits.
i. A television ad with a personal injury plaintiff lawyer in a boxing ring fighting against "insurance defense firms."
j. A URL for a lawyer website that reads, "topcorporatelawyer.com."
k. A TV commercial featuring a pit bull in a spiked collar and a telephone number that spells PIT-BULL.
l. Internet ads that say, "Don't settle for less than you deserve."
m. A 10-second Spanish-language radio ad that says, "If you have had an automobile accident, by law you have the right to receive at least $15,000 for your case."
n. A billboard ad that says, "The only woman-led personal injury law firm in the city."
o. A video on YouTube that has the lawyer talking about the services of the firm and areas of expertise.
p. A lawyer with billboards picturing him and a website called "mybaldlawyer.com."

13. How is in-person solicitation different from advertising? How is telephone solicitation different from advertising? Is targeted, personalized, direct-mail advertising more like an online ad or a telephone call? Why or why not?
14. Should political and public interest organizations be excused from restrictions on in-person solicitation? Why or why not?
15. Suppose a corporation called "Foreclosure Fighters" was organized to represent people (for a fee) whose homes were being foreclosed on. Would it be allowed to solicit clients directly under the exception for public interest causes? What if it is nonprofit? Is the name acceptable?
16. What would you do if you were asked to go to the hospital to visit a friend who had been in a car accident to try to get the friend to hire your firm to represent him or her?
17. Can a criminal defense lawyer have flyers about her services handed out at the courthouse? Why or why not? What rules are relevant?
18. A television ad says, "It's not your fault you were hurt on the job, but I know you're afraid to file a job injury claim. You're afraid your boss won't believe you're really hurt—or worse, that you'll be fired. We'll protect you against these threats—these accusations—and work to protect your job. I'm not an actor, I'm a lawyer. I'm Joe Smith. Call me and we'll get you the benefits you deserve." Is this ad acceptable under the ABA Model Rules? See *In re Anonymous Members of the S.C. Bar*, 385 S.C. 283, 684 S.E.2d 560 (2009).
19. Do you think that lawyers should be responsible for endorsements about them (*e.g.*, on LinkedIn) or reviews about them (*e.g.*, on Yelp)? What ethics rules would apply?

RESEARCH PROJECTS AND ASSIGNMENTS

1. Locate the rules governing advertising and solicitation in your jurisdiction. Compare them with the ABA Model Rules.
2. Collect examples of as many different kinds of lawyer ads as you can find in your area. Check the Internet, billboards, television, radio, and so on. Rate these ads according to their (1) usefulness and information value; (2) effectiveness in recruiting clients to a firm; and (3) degree of dignity or offensiveness. Present to the class.
3. Review five local law firms in online newsletters and blogs, website home pages, Internet ads, social media, and other advertising materials and rate them the same way you did the ads in question 2.
4. Does your jurisdiction have any ethics opinions on advertising and solicitation on the Internet? Find and summarize them, comparing them to the ethics rules and leading cases in this chapter.
5. Write an ethics rule that covers advertising and solicitation on the Internet and is constitutional under *Bates* and its progeny.
6. Search the Internet for a site that matches lawyer services with prospective clients. How does it work? What kinds of disclaimers does it have? Are lawyers who use it operating ethically within the rules of your jurisdiction?
7. Search the Internet for a law firm site that offers information about a drug that has been the subject of class action litigation. What kinds of disclaimers and other information are provided to ensure that the lawyers are acting within the bounds of the ethics rules?
8. A client submits a form on the lawyer's website indicating that she needs a divorce and is seeking a property settlement agreement and sole custody of her child. She sends financial information and asks if an extramarital affair that she had will affect the settlement. The statement at the bottom of the form indicates that by sending this information the prospective client is not forming an attorney-client relationship. The lawyer who receives the form already represents the other spouse. What are the issues presented by this scenario? How should they be resolved under the rules set forth in this chapter? See California State Bar Ethics Opinion 2005-168 for guidance.
9. Since the 1980s, California has seen repeated insurance fraud rings that involved staged car accidents and were run by groups of doctors, chiropractors, and lawyers filing and settling the claims. Many cases have involved allegations of "capping" and unauthorized practice of law. See *People v. Zanoletti*, 173 Cal. App. 4th 547 (2009). How was this ring organized? What crimes were committed? What ethics rules are implicated?
10. For an interesting case involving the use of electronic media by a lawyer who joined the American Association of Motorcycle Injury

Lawyers, Inc., which uses the trademark "Law Tigers," read and brief *In the Matter of Anonymous,* 6 N.E.3d 903 (2014).

CASES FOR ANALYSIS

In the following landmark case, the U.S. Supreme Court struck down restrictions on lawyer advertising under the First Amendment. As you read, take note of the arguments for and against such restrictions and how the Court deals with each one.

Bates v. State Bar of Arizona
433 U.S. 350, 97 S.Ct. 2691 (1977)

Justice BLACKMUN delivered the opinion of the Court.

As part of its regulation of the Arizona Bar, the Supreme Court of that State has imposed and enforces a disciplinary rule that restricts advertising by attorneys. This case presents two issues: whether §§1 and 2 of the Sherman Act, 15 U.S.C. §§1 and 2, forbid such state regulation, and whether the operation of the rule violates the First Amendment, made applicable to the States through the Fourteenth.

Appellants John R. Bates and Van O'Steen are attorneys licensed to practice law in the State of Arizona. As such, they are members of the appellee, the State Bar of Arizona. After admission to the bar in 1972, appellants worked as attorneys with the Maricopa County Legal Aid Society.

In March 1974, appellants left the Society and opened a law office, which they call a "legal clinic," in Phoenix. Their aim was to provide legal services at modest fees to persons of moderate income who did not qualify for governmental legal aid. In order to achieve this end, they would accept only routine matters, such as uncontested divorces, uncontested adoptions, simple personal bankruptcies, and changes of name, for which costs could be kept down by extensive use of paralegals, automatic typewriting equipment, and standardized forms and office procedures. More complicated cases, such as contested divorces, would not be accepted. Because appellants set their prices so as to have a relatively low return on each case they handled, they depended on substantial volume.

After conducting their practice in this manner for two years, appellants concluded that their practice and clinical concept could not survive unless the availability of legal services at low cost was advertised and, in particular, fees were advertised. Consequently, in order to generate the necessary flow of business, that is, "to attract clients," appellants placed an advertisement (reproduced in the Appendix to this opinion, infra, [at 221]), in the *Arizona Republic,* a daily newspaper of general circulation in the Phoenix metropolitan area. As may be seen, the advertisement stated that appellants were offering "legal services at very reasonable fees," and listed their fees for certain services.

The issue presently before us is a narrow one. First, we need not address the peculiar problems associated with advertising claims relating to the *quality* of legal services. Such claims probably are not susceptible of precise measurement or verification and, under some circumstances, might well be deceptive or misleading to the public, or even false. Appellee does not suggest, nor do we perceive, that appellants' advertisement contained claims, extravagant or otherwise, as to the quality of services. Accordingly, we leave that issue for another day. Second, we also need not resolve the problems associated with in-person solicitation of clients—at the hospital room or the accident site, or in any other situation that breeds undue influence—by attorneys or their agents or "runners." Activity of that kind might well pose dangers of overreaching and misrepresentation not encountered in newspaper announcement advertising. Hence, this issue also is not before us. Third, we note that appellee's criticism of advertising by attorneys does not apply with much force to some of the basic factual content of advertising: information as to the attorney's name, address, and telephone number, office hours, and the like. . . ,

The heart of the dispute before us today is whether lawyers also may constitutionally advertise the *prices* at which certain routine services will be performed. Numerous justifications are proffered for the restriction of such price advertising. We consider each in turn:

1. *The Adverse Effect on Professionalism.* Appellee places particular emphasis on the adverse effects that it feels price advertising will have on the legal profession. The key to professionalism, it is argued, is the sense of pride that involvement in the discipline generates. It is claimed that price advertising will bring about commercialization, which will undermine the attorney's sense of dignity and self-worth. The hustle of the marketplace will adversely affect the profession's service orientation, and irreparably damage the delicate balance between the lawyer's need to earn and his obligation selflessly to serve. Advertising is also said to erode the client's trust in his attorney: Once the client perceives that the lawyer is motivated by profit, his confidence that the attorney is acting out of a commitment to the client's welfare is jeopardized. And advertising is said to tarnish the dignified public image of the profession.

We recognize, of course, and commend the spirit of public service with which the profession of law is practiced and to which it is dedicated. . . , But we find the postulated connection between advertising and the erosion of true professionalism to be severely strained. At its core, the argument presumes that attorneys must conceal from themselves and from their clients the real-life fact that lawyers earn their livelihood at the bar. We suspect that few attorneys engage in such self-deception. And rare is the client, moreover, even one of modest means, who enlists the aid of an attorney with the expectation that his services will be rendered free of charge. . . .

Moreover, the assertion that advertising will diminish the attorney's reputation in the community is open to question. Bankers and engineers advertise, and yet these professions are not regarded as undignified. In fact, it has been suggested that the failure of lawyers to advertise creates public disillusionment with the profession. The absence of advertising may be seen to reflect the profession's failure to reach out and serve the community: Studies reveal that many persons do not obtain counsel even when they perceive a need because of the feared price of services or because of an inability to locate a competent attorney. . . .

It appears that the ban on advertising originated as a rule of etiquette and not as a rule of ethics. Early lawyers in Great Britain viewed the law as a form of public service, rather than as a means of earning a living, and they looked down on "trade" as unseemly. Eventually, the attitude toward advertising fostered by this view evolved into an aspect of the ethics of the profession. But habit and tradition are not in themselves an adequate answer to a constitutional challenge. In this day, we do not belittle the person who earns his living by the strength of his arm or the force of his mind. Since the belief that lawyers are somehow "above" trade has become an anachronism, the historical foundation for the advertising restraint has crumbled.

2. *The Inherently Misleading Nature of Attorney Advertising.* It is argued that advertising of legal services inevitably will be misleading (a) because such services are so individualized with regard to content and quality as to prevent informed comparison on the basis of an advertisement, (b) because the consumer of legal services is unable to determine in advance just what services he needs, and (c) because advertising by attorneys will highlight irrelevant factors and fail to show the relevant factor of skill.

We are not persuaded that restrained professional advertising by lawyers inevitably will be misleading. Although many services performed by attorneys are indeed unique, it is doubtful that any attorney would or could advertise fixed prices for services of that type. The only services that lend themselves to advertising are the routine ones: the uncontested divorce, the simple adoption, the uncontested personal bankruptcy, the change of name, and the like—the very services advertised by appellants. Although the precise service demanded in each task may vary slightly, and although legal services are not fungible, these facts do not make advertising misleading so long as the attorney does the necessary work at the advertised price. . . .

The second component of the argument—that advertising ignores the diagnostic role—fares little better. It is unlikely that many people go to an attorney merely to ascertain if they have a clean bill of legal health. Rather, attorneys are likely to be employed to perform specific tasks. . . . The third component is not without merit: Advertising does not provide a complete foundation on which to select an attorney. But it seems peculiar to deny the consumer, on the ground that the information is incomplete, at least some of the relevant information needed to reach an informed decision. The alternative—the prohibition of advertising—serves only to restrict the information that flows to consumers. Moreover, the argument assumes that the public is not sophisticated enough to realize the limitations of advertising, and that the public is better kept in ignorance than trusted with correct but incomplete information. We suspect the argument rests on an underestimation of the public. . . .

3. *The Adverse Effect on the Administration of Justice.* Advertising is said to have the undesirable effect of stirring up litigation. The judicial machinery is designed to serve those who feel sufficiently aggrieved to bring forward their claims. Advertising, it is argued, serves to encourage the assertion of legal rights in the courts, thereby undesirably unsettling societal repose. There is even a suggestion of barratry.

But advertising by attorneys is not an unmitigated source of harm to the administration of justice. It may offer great benefits. Although advertising might increase the use of the judicial machinery, we cannot accept the notion that it is always better for a person to suffer a wrong silently than to redress it by legal action. As the bar acknowledges, "the middle 70% of our population is not being reached or served adequately by the legal profession." ABA, Revised Handbook on Prepaid Legal Services 2 (1972). Among the reasons for this underutilization is fear of the cost, and an inability to locate a suitable lawyer. Advertising can help to solve this acknowledged problem: Advertising is the traditional mechanism in a free-market economy for a supplier to inform a potential purchaser of the availability and terms of exchange. The disciplinary rule at issue likely has served to burden access to legal services, particularly for the not-quite-poor and the unknowledgeable. A rule allowing restrained advertising would be in accord with the bar's obligation to "facilitate the process of intelligent selection of lawyers, and to assist in making legal services fully available." ABA Code of Professional Responsibility EC 2-1 (1976).

4. *The Undesirable Economic Effects of Advertising.* It is claimed that advertising will increase the overhead costs of the profession, and that these costs then will be passed along to consumers in the form of increased fees. Moreover, it is claimed that the additional cost of practice will create a substantial entry barrier, deterring or preventing young attorneys from penetrating the market and entrenching the position of the bar's established members.

These two arguments seem dubious at best. . . . The ban on advertising serves to increase the difficulty of discovering the lowest cost seller of acceptable ability. As a result, to this extent attorneys are isolated from competition . . . the incentive to price competitively is reduced. . . . It is entirely possible that advertising will serve to reduce, not advance, the cost of legal services to the consumer.

The entry-barrier argument is equally unpersuasive. In the absence of advertising, an attorney must rely on his contacts with the community to generate a flow of business. In view of the time necessary to develop such contacts, the ban in fact serves to perpetuate the market position of established attorneys. Consideration of entry-barrier problems would urge that advertising be allowed so as to aid the new competitor in penetrating the market.

5. *The Adverse Effect of Advertising on the Quality of Service.* It is argued that the attorney may advertise a given "package" of service at a set price, and will be inclined to provide, by indiscriminate use, the standard package regardless of whether it fits the client's needs.

Restraints on advertising, however, are an ineffective way of deterring shoddy work. An attorney who is inclined to cut quality will do so regardless of the rule on advertising. And the advertisement of a standardized fee does not necessarily mean that the services offered are undesirably standardized. Indeed, the assertion that an attorney who advertises a standard fee will cut quality is substantially undermined by the fixed-fee schedule of appellee's own pre-paid Legal Services Program. Even if advertising leads to the creation of "legal clinics" like that of appellants'—clinics that emphasize standardized procedures for routine problems—it is possible that such clinics will improve service by reducing the likelihood of error.

6. *The Difficulties of Enforcement.* Finally, it is argued that the wholesale restriction is justified by the problems of enforcement if any other course is taken. Because the public lacks sophistication in legal matters, it may be particularly susceptible to misleading or deceptive advertising by lawyers. After-the-fact action by the consumer lured by such advertising may not provide a realistic restraint because of the inability of the layman to assess whether the service he has received meets professional standards. Thus, the vigilance of a regulatory agency will be required. But because of the numerous purveyors of services, the overseeing of advertising will be burdensome.

It is at least somewhat incongruous for the opponents of advertising to extol the virtues and altruism of the legal profession at one point, and, at another, to assert that its members will seize the opportunity to mislead and distort. We suspect that, with advertising, most lawyers will behave as they always have: They will abide by their solemn oaths to uphold the integrity and honor of their profession and of the legal system. . . .

In holding that advertising by attorneys may not be subjected to blanket suppression, and that the advertisement at issue is protected, we, of course, do not hold that advertising by attorneys may not be regulated in any way. We mention some of the clearly permissible limitations on advertising not foreclosed by our holding.

Advertising that is false, deceptive, or misleading of course is subject to restraint. [Citation omitted.] . . . For example, advertising claims as to the quality of services—a matter we do not address today—are not susceptible of measurement or verification; accordingly, such claims may be so likely to be misleading as to warrant restriction. Similar objections might justify restraints on in-person solicitation. We do not foreclose the possibility that some limited supplementation, by way of warning or disclaimer or the like, might be required of even an advertisement of the kind ruled upon today so as to assure that the consumer is not misled. In sum, we recognize that many of the problems in defining the boundary between deceptive and nondeceptive advertising remain to be resolved, and we expect that the bar will have a special role to play in assuring that advertising by attorneys flows both freely and cleanly.

As with other varieties of speech, it follows as well that there may be reasonable restrictions on the time, place, and manner of advertising. [Citation omitted.] Advertising concerning transactions that are themselves illegal obviously may be suppressed. And the special problems of advertising on the electronic broadcast media will warrant special consideration.

The constitutional issue in this case is only whether the State may prevent the publication in a newspaper of appellants' truthful advertisement concerning the availability and terms of routine legal services. We rule simply that the flow of such information may not be restrained, and we therefore hold the present application of the disciplinary rule against appellants to be violative of the First Amendment.

The judgment of the Supreme Court of Arizona is therefore affirmed in part and reversed in part. It is so ordered.

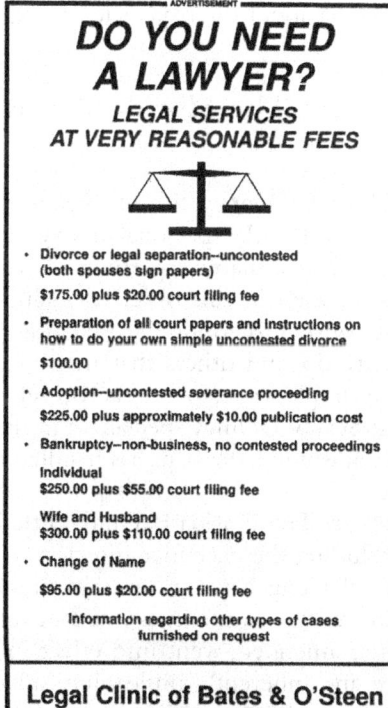

Questions about the Case

1. Examine the ad that is the subject of this litigation and evaluate whether it:

   a. is false or misleading;
   b. is undignified;
   c. is offensive to you personally;
   d. denigrates the image of the legal profession;
   e. would be helpful to someone seeking a lawyer.

2. Make a list of the bar's justifications for prohibiting advertising and summarize how the court refutes each one. Do you agree with the bar's arguments or the Court's rationale on each?
3. What kinds of restrictions may be placed on lawyer advertising after *Bates*?
4. What kind of guidance does this opinion give about other forms of advertising, such as e-mail and television?

In this case, the court enjoined enforcement of a Florida Bar rule that prohibited the plaintiffs from making truthful statements on a website, blog, or social media about their specialty or expertise.

Searcy v. The Florida Bar, *et al.*
140 F.Supp.3d 1290 (2015)

The plaintiff Searcy Denney Scarola Barnhart & Shipley PA is a Florida law firm that handles personal-injury cases. The individual plaintiffs are the firm's five named partners. The firm has included on its website (a term used in this order to include blogs and social-media materials), and wishes to continue to include on its website, some statements that clearly do, and others that may, violate the challenged rules, including, for example, a statement that tort reform benefits insurers and a statement that Searcy Denney specializes in mass-tort and unsafe-product cases. As is undisputed, the firm has handled many mass-tort and unsafe-product cases.

The defendants are The Florida Bar and, in their official capacities, four Bar officers, including the executive director.

The plaintiffs challenge two rules that are part of the Rules Regulating The Florida Bar (sometimes cited in this order as "Florida Bar Rules") which as amended, went into effect in 2013. Rule 4-7.13 prohibits "deceptive and inherently misleading" advertisements, defines that term, and, in Rule 4-7.13(b)(2), gives as a specific example of prohibited material "references to past results unless such information is objectively verifiable." Rule 4-7.14(a) (4) prohibits "a statement that a lawyer is board certified, a specialist, an expert, or other variations of those terms," unless the lawyer has been certified under The Florida Bar's certification plan, another state's comparable plan, or another certification plan accredited by The Florida Bar or the American Bar Association.

The plaintiffs assert that the rules violate the First Amendment, both on their face and as applied. They also initially asserted that Rule 4-7.13 is unconstitutionally vague.

The Bar has established a three-step procedure under which an attorney may obtain an opinion on whether a statement in an advertisement or on the attorney's website violates the rules. The first step is review of the statement by the Bar's Ethics and Advertising Division. The second step is review of the Ethics and Advertising Division's opinion by the Bar's Standing Committee on Advertising. The third step is review by the Bar's Board of Governors.

When invoking this process, an attorney may submit discrete materials from a website but must not submit the entire website. See Florida Bar Rule 4–7.19(d). In accordance with these procedures, Searcy Denney submitted 13 pages from its website (from the thousands of pages on the website as a whole), its LinkedIn profile page (which included a client's unsolicited, favorable comments), and materials from the firm's blog.

The Bar's Ethics and Advertising Division and the Bar's Standing Committee on Advertising provided rather remarkable responses, opining, for example, that Searcy Denney could not include on its website the following statements (deemed not to be objectively verifiable and thus to be forbidden): the days "when we could trust big corporations . . . are over"; "Government regulation of Corporate America's disregard of consumer safety has been lackadaisical at best"; and "when it comes to 'tort reform,' there is a single winner: the insurance industry." In defense of this lawsuit, the Bar has backed away from these obviously unconstitutional positions; the Bar no longer asserts it can prohibit an attorney from making political statements like these.

The Ethics and Advertising Division and the Standing Committee on Advertising also said Searcy Denney could not say it has "32 years of experience handling mass tort cases, resulting in justice for clients in a wide variety of circumstances," or that it was "one of the few law firms in the country to successfully represent innocent victims of dangerous herbal supplements." The theory was that "justice" and "successfully" are not objectively verifiable. The Bar has not renounced these positions. Searcy Denney could have obtained review by the entity that has authority to bind the Bar: the Board of Governors. But Searcy Denney did not do so. Instead, Searcy Denney and its named partners filed this lawsuit.

The first issue is the extent to which the plaintiffs' challenge to these provisions is ripe for adjudication despite Searcy Denney's failure to obtain an opinion from the Board of Governors. The law of the circuit on this issue is set out at length in *Harrell v. The Florida Bar*, 608 F.3d 1241, 1261 (11th Cir. 2010). *Harrell* establishes that a First Amendment challenge to a Bar rule may go forward on the merits when three things are all true. First, the attorney has made statements, and unless prohibited from doing so will continue to make statements, that may violate the challenged rule. Second, the attorney faces a credible threat of disciplinary action if the attorney continues to make the statements. And third, nothing would be gained by requiring the attorney to obtain a more-definitive administrative interpretation of the rule, because the rule's application is clear on its face. *Harrell*, 608 F.3d at 1261–62.

The opinions of the Bar's Ethics and Advertising Division and Standing Committee on Advertising are enough to show that the first two conditions are met. The critical issue, then, is the third: whether application of the challenged rules to Searcy Denney's statements is clear on the face of the rules. As set out below, this condition is not met for the first challenged rule (Rule 4-7.13) but is met for the second (Rule 4-7.14).

Rule 4-7.13 provides in relevant part:

> A lawyer may not engage in deceptive or inherently misleading advertising.
>
> (a) Deceptive and Inherently Misleading Advertisements. An advertisement is deceptive and inherently misleading if it:
>
> (1) contains a material statement that is factually or legally inaccurate;
>
> (2) omits information that is necessary to prevent the information supplied from being misleading; or
>
> (3) implies the existence of a material nonexistent fact.
>
> (b) Examples of Deceptive and Inherently Misleading Advertisements. Deceptive or inherently misleading advertisements include, but are not limited to advertisements that contain:
>
> (1) statements or information that can reasonably be interpreted by a prospective client as a prediction or guaranty of success or specific results;
>
> (2) references to past results unless such information is objectively verifiable, subject to rule 4-7.14;
>
> (3) comparisons of lawyers or statements, words or phrases that characterize a lawyer's or law firm's skills, experience, reputation or record, unless such characterization is *objectively verifiable*.

Florida Bar Rule 4-7.13 (emphasis added).

The difficulty for the plaintiffs in the current lawsuit, though, is that the rule does not explicitly prohibit such a statement. Searcy Denney can hardly be criticized for fearing the worst, based on the Bar's "long and undeniable trend towards increasingly restrictive measures to control attorney advertising," *Harrell*, 608 F.3d at 1248, the many inconsistent and sometimes indefensible positions the Bar has taken in other instances . . . and the opinions of the Bar's Ethics and Advertising Division and

Standing Committee on Advertising in response to Searcy Denney's inquiry in this very case.

The result is different for Rule 4-7.14, which provides in relevant part:

> A lawyer may not engage in potentially misleading advertising.
> (a) Potentially Misleading Advertisements. Potentially misleading advertisements include, but are not limited to: . . .
> (4) a statement that a lawyer is board certified, *a specialist, an expert, or other variations of those terms* unless:
> (A) the lawyer has been certified under the Florida Certification Plan as set forth in chapter 6, Rules Regulating the Florida Bar and the advertisement includes the area of certification and that The Florida Bar is the certifying organization;
> (B) the lawyer has been certified by an organization whose specialty certification program has been accredited by the American Bar Association or The Florida Bar as provided elsewhere in these rules. A lawyer certified by a specialty certification program accredited by the American Bar Association but not The Florida Bar must include the statement 'Not Certified as a Specialist by The Florida Bar' in reference to the specialization or certification. All such advertisements must include the area of certification and the name of the certifying organization; or
> (C) the lawyer has been certified by another state bar if the state bar program grants certification on the basis of standards reasonably comparable to the standards of the Florida Certification Plan set forth in chapter 6 of these rules and the advertisement includes the area of certification and the name of the certifying organization.

Fla. Bar Rule 4–7.14 (emphasis added).

The application of this rule is clear: Searcy Denney cannot say it specializes or has expertise in mass-tort or unsafe product cases, or even in personal-injury cases, even though the firm undeniably has expertise in these areas. Nor can any individual attorney claim to specialize or have expertise in mass-tort or unsafe-product cases, even if the attorney handles only cases of that kind, and even if the attorney has successfully handled many such cases. The challenge to this rule thus is ripe.

The controlling First Amendment standards have been set out in a series of decisions, many specifically addressing statements by lawyers. "Lawyer advertising is a constitutionally protected form of commercial speech, but like any other form of commercial speech, a state may regulate it to protect the public." *Mason v. Fla. Bar*, 208 F.3d 952, 955 (11th Cir. 2000) (citing *Bates v. State Bar of Ariz.*, 433 U.S. 350, 383–84, 97 S.Ct. 2691, 53 L.Ed.2d 810 (1977)). Courts review the constitutionality of a state's restrictions on lawyer advertising based on the test originally adopted by the Supreme Court in *Central Hudson Gas & Electric Corp. v. Public Service Commission of N.Y.*, 447 U.S. 557, 563–66, 100 S.Ct. 2343, 65 L.Ed.2d 341 (1980).

Under *Central Hudson*, a restriction on commercial speech is valid only if (1) the asserted governmental interest in restricting the speech is substantial; (2) the challenged restriction directly advances the asserted governmental interest; and (3) the restriction is not more extensive than is necessary to serve that interest . . . The Bar's ban on truthful statements about a lawyer's or law firm's specialty or expertise, at least as applied to websites, fails all three prongs of the *Central Hudson* test.

This analysis is confirmed by *Abramson v. Gonzalez*, 949 F.2d 1567 (11th Cir. 1992). When that case was decided, Florida licensed psychologists but did not prohibit the practice of psychology without a license. Even so, a Florida statute prohibited unlicensed psychologists from advertising that they were "psychologists." The state's theory was that the public would wrongly assume that a "psychologist" was licensed—much as the Bar asserts that the public will assume a "specialist" is board-certified , , , Here, as in *Abramson*, the state cannot prevent a person from advertising a lawful specialty, even if the state's own definition of the specialty is different.

For these reasons,
IT IS ORDERED:

1. The plaintiffs' summary-judgment motion, as amended . . . is granted in part and denied in part.
2. The defendants' summary-judgment motion . . . is denied.
3. The defendants . . . in their official capacities as employees of the Florida Bar, are enjoined from enforcing Rules Regulating The Florida Bar, Rule 4–7.14(a)(4), to prohibit the plaintiffs from making truthful statements on a website, blog, or social medium about their specialty or expertise. This injunction binds these defendants and their officers, agents, servants, employees, and attorneys—and others in active concert or participation with any of them—who receive actual notice of this injunction by personal service or otherwise.
4. The plaintiffs' other claims are dismissed without prejudice for lack of jurisdiction because the claims are not ripe.

SO ORDERED on September 30, 2015.

Questions about the Case

1. What did the Florida Bar claim that the firm did to violate the state's advertising rules? What did the plaintiffs claim about the state's amended advertising rules?

2. Identify the three-step procedure under which a lawyer may obtain an opinion on whether a statement in an advertisement or on the lawyer's website violates the rules.
3. How did the Bar determine that many of the submitted statements on the firm's website violated the "*objectively verifiable*" requirement?
4. How does the *Central Hudson* case determine the validity of a restriction on commercial speech? What does the court say about the Bar related to the *Central Hudson* case?
5. What was the court's ruling regarding enforcement of the amended advertising rules? Was the ruling extended beyond the named defendants?

The following is an example of the role a paralegal can play in lawyer advertising, but in this instance, the paralegal is not familiar with the restrictions on lawyer advertising that have been set forth in this chapter.

In the Matter of Cartmel
676 N.E.2d 1047 (Ind. 1997)

The Disciplinary Commission alleges that the respondent, Thomas O. Cartmel, violated the *Rules of Professional Conduct for Attorneys at Law*. . . .

The Commission's *Verified Complaint* is in three counts. Pursuant to Count II, the parties agree that on May 1, 1994, the respondent's then-legal assistant placed an advertisement in the *Indianapolis Star*. The advertisement read as follows:

PAST CREDIT PROBLEMS

Our law firm will have incorrect, obsolete or unverifiable negatives removed from your credit report! Our attitude is this: If you are wanting the cheapest fee in town . . . call our "Competitors"! (We don't accept everyone we talk to. . . . We don't have to!) If you are wanting:

- 29 years in practice
- 100% results
- Reestablished credit
- The absolute best company to deal with your personal needs

Call us to set up an appointment. . . . If we take your case, you'll be among the numerous individuals we've given a second chance to!

Upon learning of the advertisement (after it had been published approximately five times), the respondent promptly cancelled it, realizing that its contents were objectionable.

Pursuant to our *Rules of Professional Conduct*, lawyers are responsible for the professional actions of a legal assistant performing legal assistant services at the lawyer's direction and should take reasonable measures to insure that the legal assistant's conduct is consistent with the lawyer's obligations. . . . We find that the legal assistant's placement of the advertisement violated Prof. Cond. R. 7.1(b). . . .

The advertisement contained misleading, unfair, and self-laudatory language prohibited by the rule.

We also find that the placement of the advertisement violated Prof. Cond. R. 7.1(d)(2) and (4). . . .

The advertisement contained a prediction of future success and a statement as to the quality of services offered. . . .

[The court also found that the lawyer violated obligations to hold client funds separately to complete work on a client matter in Count II.]

. . . [A] client hired the respondent to clear her negative credit history and paid him his quoted fee of $600. During the ensuing year, the client dealt exclusively with one of the respondent's legal assistants, Jeff. Between May 1993 and early 1995, the client periodically spoke with Jeff about the status of her pending credit repair. He informed her several times that he was working to clear her credit history. In early 1995, the client began dealing with the respondent's new legal assistant, Dan, who informed the client that Jeff had done little work on her file. Thereafter, the client contacted Dan once or twice a month regarding the status of her credit. . . . [T]he client wrote the respondent and requested that her case be completed. Dan responded to the letter, stating that his review of her credit report revealed that she has successfully applied for credit and that, therefore, the respondent's obligation to her was terminated. . . .

By failing to ensure that his nonlawyer staff's conduct was compatible with the respondent's professional obligation to diligently pursue client matters and keep the client accurately informed about the status of her affairs, the respondent violated Prof. Cond. R. 5.3(b). . . .

We accord some extenuating weight to the agreed mitigating factors. However, it is clear that the respondent abdicated many of the day-to-day functions of his legal practice to legal assistants without adequately supervising their work product or activities. Lawyers should give their legal assistants appropriate instruction and supervision concerning legal aspects of their employment, taking into account the fact that they do not have legal training. . . . The respondent's failure to take such steps resulted in the publishing of a clearly inappropriate legal advertisement. . . .

It is therefore ordered that the respondent be suspended from the practice of law for a period of sixty (60) days. . . .

Questions about the Case

1. What did the paralegal do in this case concerning the ad? What did the paralegal do concerning the client?

2. What should the lawyer have done to meet his ethical duties here?
3. What was objectionable about this ad? Do you think it would fail the requirements of the current ABA Model Rules?
4. Do you think it is common for a paralegal to have the responsibility for writing and placing an ad?
5. Do you think the discipline was appropriate?
6. What did the court say about paralegals' education? Do you agree?

The following case was decided just after *Bates.* In it, the Court addresses the question of restrictions on in-person solicitation of clients by attorneys. Pay close attention to the Court's reasons for the distinction between advertising and solicitation.

Ohralik v. Ohio State Bar Association
436 U.S. 447, 98 S.Ct. 1912 (1978)

Justice POWELL delivered the opinion of the Court.

In *Bates v. State Bar of Arizona*, 433 U.S. 350 (1977), this Court held that truthful advertising of "routine" legal services is protected by the First and Fourteenth Amendments against blanket prohibition by a State. The Court expressly reserved the question of the permissible scope of regulation of "in-person solicitation of clients—at the hospital room or the accident site, or in any other situation that breeds undue influence—by attorneys or their agents or 'runners.'" Id., at 366. . . .

Appellant, a member of the Ohio Bar, lives in Montville, Ohio. . . . On February 13, 1974, while picking up his mail at the Montville Post Office, appellant learned from the postmaster's brother about an automobile accident that had taken place on February 2 in which Carol McClintock, a young woman with whom appellant was casually acquainted, had been injured. Appellant made a telephone call to Ms. McClintock's parents, who informed him that their daughter was in the hospital. Appellant suggested that he might visit Carol in the hospital. Mrs. McClintock assented to the idea, but requested that appellant first stop by at her home.

During appellant's visit with the McClintocks, they explained that their daughter had been driving the family automobile on a local road when she was hit by an uninsured motorist. Both Carol and her passenger, Wanda Lou Holbert, were injured and hospitalized. In response to the McClintocks' expression of apprehension that they might be sued by Holbert, appellant explained that Ohio's guest statute would preclude such a suit. When appellant suggested to the McClintocks that they hire a lawyer, Mrs. McClintock retorted that such a decision would be up to Carol, who was 18 years old and would be the beneficiary of a successful claim.

Appellant proceeded to the hospital, where he found Carol lying in traction in her room. After a brief conversation about her condition, appellant told Carol he would represent her and asked her to sign an agreement. Carol said she would have to discuss the matter with her parents. She did not sign the agreement, but asked appellant to have her parents come to see her. Appellant also attempted to see Wanda Lou Holbert, but learned that she had just been released from the hospital. He then departed for another visit with the McClintocks.

On his way appellant detoured to the scene of the accident, where he took a set of photographs. He also picked up a tape recorder, which he concealed under his raincoat before arriving at the McClintocks' residence. Once there, he re-examined their automobile insurance policy, discussed with them the law applicable to passengers, and explained the consequences of the fact that the driver who struck Carol's car was an uninsured motorist. Appellant discovered that the McClintocks' insurance policy would provide benefits of up to $12,500 each for Carol and Wanda Lou under an uninsured-motorist clause. Mrs. McClintock acknowledged that both Carol and Wanda Lou could sue for their injuries, but recounted to appellant that "Wanda swore up and down she would not do it." The McClintocks also told appellant that Carol had phoned to say that appellant could "go ahead" with her representation. Two days later appellant returned to Carol's hospital room to have her sign a contract, which provided that he would receive one-third of her recovery.

In the meantime, appellant obtained Wanda Lou's name and address from the McClintocks after telling them he wanted to ask her some questions about the accident. He then visited Wanda Lou at her home, without having been invited. He again concealed his tape recorder and recorded most of the conversation with Wanda Lou. After a brief, unproductive inquiry about the facts of the accident, appellant told Wanda Lou that he was representing Carol and that he had a "little tip" for Wanda Lou: the McClintocks' insurance policy contained an uninsured-motorist clause which might provide her with a recovery of up to $12,500. The young woman, who was 18 years of age and not a high school graduate at the time, replied to appellant's query about whether she was going to file a claim by stating that she really did not understand what was going on. Appellant offered to represent her, also, for a contingent fee of one-third of any recovery, and Wanda Lou stated "O.K."

Wanda's mother attempted to repudiate her daughter's oral assent the following day, when appellant called on the telephone to speak to Wanda. Mrs. Holbert informed appellant that she and her daughter did not want to sue anyone or to have appellant represent them, and that if they decided to sue they would consult their own lawyer. Appellant insisted that Wanda had entered into a binding agreement. A month later Wanda confirmed in writing that she wanted neither to sue nor to be represented by appellant. She requested that appellant notify the insurance company that he was not her lawyer, as the company would not release a check to her until he did so. Carol also eventually discharged appellant. Although another lawyer represented her in concluding a settlement with the insurance company, she paid appellant one-third of her recovery in settlement of his lawsuit against her for breach of contract.

Both Carol McClintock and Wanda Lou Holbert filed complaints against appellant with the Grievance Committee of the Geauga County Bar Association. The County Bar Association referred the grievance to appellee, which filed a formal complaint with the Board of Commissioners on Grievances and Discipline of the Supreme Court of Ohio. After a hearing, the Board found that appellant had violated Disciplinary Rules (DR) 2-103 (A) and 2-104 (A) of the Ohio Code of Professional Responsibility. The Board rejected appellant's defense that his conduct was protected under the First and Fourteenth Amendments. The Supreme Court of Ohio adopted the findings of the Board, reiterated that appellant's conduct was not constitutionally protected, and increased the sanction of a public reprimand recommended by the Board to indefinite suspension.

The decision in *Bates* was handed down after the conclusion of proceedings in the Ohio Supreme Court. We noted probable jurisdiction in this case to consider the scope of protection of a form of commercial speech, and an aspect of the State's authority to regulate and discipline members of the bar, not considered in *Bates*. 434 U.S. 814 (1977). . . .

The solicitation of business by a lawyer through direct, in-person communication with the prospective client has long been viewed as inconsistent with the profession's ideal of the attorney-client relationship and as posing a significant potential for harm to the prospective client. It has been proscribed by the organized Bar for many years. . . .

Appellant contends that his solicitation of the two young women as clients is indistinguishable, for purposes of constitutional analysis, from the advertisement in *Bates*. Like that advertisement, his meetings with the prospective clients apprised them of their legal rights and of the availability of a lawyer to pursue their claims. . . .

In-person solicitation by a lawyer of remunerative employment is a business transaction in which speech is an essential but subordinate component. While this does not remove the speech from the protection of the First Amendment, as was held in *Bates* and *Virginia Pharmacy*, it lowers the level of appropriate judicial scrutiny.

As applied in this case, the Disciplinary Rules are said to have limited the communication of two kinds of information. First, appellant's solicitation imparted to Carol McClintock and Wanda Lou Holbert certain information about his availability and the terms of his proposed legal services. In this respect, in-person solicitation serves much the same function as the advertisement at issue in *Bates*. But there are significant differences as well. Unlike a public advertisement, which simply provides information and leaves the recipient free to act upon it or not, in-person solicitation may exert pressure and often demands an immediate response, without providing an opportunity for comparison or reflection. The aim and effect of in-person solicitation may be to provide a one-sided presentation and to encourage speedy and perhaps uninformed decision-making; there is no opportunity for intervention or countereducation by agencies of the Bar, supervisory authorities, or persons close to the solicited individual. The admonition that "the fitting remedy for evil counsels is good ones" is of little value when the circumstances provide no opportunity for any remedy at all. In-person solicitation is as likely as not to discourage persons needing counsel from engaging in a critical comparison of the "availability, nature, and prices" of legal services. . . .

It also is argued that in-person solicitation may provide the solicited individual with information about his or her legal rights and remedies. In this case, appellant gave Wanda Lou a "tip" about the prospect of recovery based on the uninsured-motorist clause in the McClintocks' insurance policy, and he explained that clause and Ohio's guest statute to Carol McClintock's parents. But neither of the Disciplinary Rules here at issue prohibited appellant from communicating information to these young women about their legal rights and the prospects of obtaining a monetary recovery, or from recommending that they obtain counsel. DR 2-104(A) merely prohibited him from using the information as bait with which to obtain an agreement to represent them for a fee. The Rule does not prohibit a lawyer from giving unsolicited legal advice; it proscribes the acceptance of employment resulting from such advice. . . .

The State's perception of the potential for harm in circumstances such as those presented in this case is well founded. The detrimental aspects of face-to-face selling even of ordinary consumer products have been recognized and addressed by the Federal Trade Commission, and it hardly need be said that the potential for overreaching is significantly greater when a lawyer, a professional trained in the art of persuasion, personally solicits an unsophisticated, injured, or distressed lay person. Such an individual may place his trust in a lawyer, regardless of the latter's qualifications or the individual's actual need for legal representation, simply in response to persuasion under circumstances conducive to uninformed acquiescence. Although it is argued that personal solicitation is valuable because it may apprise a victim of misfortune of his legal rights, the very plight of that person not only makes him more vulnerable to influence but also may make advice all the more intrusive. Thus, under these adverse conditions the overtures of an uninvited lawyer may distress the solicited individual simply because of their obtrusiveness and the invasion of the individual's privacy, even when no other harm materializes. Under such circumstances, it is not unreasonable for the State to presume that in-person solicitation by lawyers more often than not will be injurious to the person solicited.

The efficacy of the State's effort to prevent such harm to prospective clients would be substantially diminished if, having proved a solicitation in circumstances like those of this case, the State were required in addition to prove actual injury. Unlike the advertising in *Bates*, in-person solicitation is not visible or otherwise open to public scrutiny. Often there is no witness other than the lawyer and the lay person whom he has solicited, rendering it difficult or impossible to obtain reliable proof of what actually took place. This would be especially true if the lay person were so distressed at the time of the solicitation that he could not recall specific details at a later date. If appellant's view were sustained, in-person solicitation would be virtually immune to effective oversight and regulation by the State or by the legal profession, in contravention of the State's strong interest in regulating members of the Bar in an effective, objective, and self-enforcing manner. It therefore is not unreasonable, or violative of the Constitution, for a State to respond with what in effect is a prophylactic rule.

On the basis of the undisputed facts of record, we conclude that the Disciplinary Rules constitutionally could be applied to appellant. . . . Accordingly, the judgment of the Supreme Court of Ohio is affirmed.

Questions about the Case

1. Why do you think the Court felt compelled to decide this case?
2. What exactly did attorney Ohralik do to break the ethics rules? Did you find his conduct objectionable?
3. What is the basis for the different rules on in-person solicitation and advertising? Do you find this reasoning convincing?
4. What general rule can you derive from this case? Do the ethics rules in your state comport with this decision? Do they carve out any exceptions?

This case concerns the application of state ethics rules on lawyer advertising to a blog and is one of the first state supreme court cases to address such issues.

Hunter v. Virginia State Bar
285 Va. 485, 744 S.E.2d 611 (2013)

Horace Frazier Hunter, an attorney with the law firm of Hunter & Lipton, PC, authors a trademarked blog[1] titled "This Week in Richmond Criminal Defense," which is accessible from his law firm's website, www.hunterlipton.com. This blog, which is not interactive, contains posts discussing a myriad of legal issues and cases, although the overwhelming majority are posts about cases in which Hunter obtained favorable results for his clients. Nowhere in these posts or on his website did Hunter include disclaimers.

As a result of Hunter's blog posts on his website, the VSB launched an investigation. During discussions with the VSB about whether his blog constituted legal advertising, Hunter wrote a letter to the VSB offering to post *a disclaimer* on *one page* of his website. . . . However, the negotiations stalled and no disclaimers were posted at that time.

On March 24, 2011, the VSB charged Hunter with violating Rules 7.1, 7.2, 7.5, 2 and 1.6 by his posts on this blog. Specifically, the VSB argued that he violated rules 7.1 and 7.2 because his blog posts discussing his criminal cases were inherently misleading as they lacked disclaimers. The VSB also asserted that Hunter violated Rule 1.6 by revealing information that could embarrass or likely be detrimental to his former clients by discussing their cases on his blog without their consent.

In a hearing on October 18, 2011, the VSB presented evidence of Hunter's alleged violations. The VSB presented a former client who testified that he did not consent to information about his cases being posted on Hunter's blog and believed that the information posted was embarrassing or detrimental to him, despite the fact that all such information had previously been revealed in court. The VSB investigator testified that other former clients felt similarly. The VSB also entered all of the blog posts Hunter had posted on his blog to date. At that time, none of the posts entered contained disclaimers. Of these thirty unique posts, only five discussed legal, policy issues. The remaining twenty-five discussed cases. Hunter represented the defendant in twenty-two of these cases and identified that fact in the posts. In nineteen of these twenty-two posts, Hunter also specifically named his law firm. One of these posts described a case where a family hired Hunter to represent them in a wrongful death suit and the remaining twenty-one of these posts described criminal cases. In every criminal case described, Hunter's clients were either found not guilty, plea-bargained to an agreed upon disposition, or had their charges reduced or dismissed.

At the hearing, Hunter testified that he has many reasons for writing his blog—including marketing, creation of a community presence for his firm, combatting any public perception that defendants charged with crimes are guilty until proven innocent, and showing commitment to criminal law. Hunter stated that he had offered to post a disclaimer on his blog, but the offered disclaimer was not satisfactory to the VSB. Hunter admitted that he only blogged about his cases that he won. He also told the VSB that he believed that using the client's name is important to give an accurate description of what happened. Hunter told the VSB that he did not obtain consent from his clients to discuss their cases on his blog because all the information that he posted was public information.

Following the hearing, the VSB held that Hunter violated Rule 1.6 by "disseminating client confidences" obtained in the course of representation without consent to post. . . . The VSB further held that he violated Rule 7.2 by "disseminating case results in advertising without the required disclaimer" because the one that he proposed to the VSB was insufficient. The VSB imposed a public admonition with terms including a requirement that he remove case-specific content for which he has not received consent and post a disclaimer that complies with Rule 7.2(a)(3) on all case-related posts.

Hunter appealed to a three-judge panel of the circuit court and the court heard argument. . . . This appeal followed. . . .

Rule 7.1(a)(4), which is the specific portion of the Rule that the VSB argued that Hunter violated, states:

> (a) A lawyer shall not, on behalf of the lawyer or any other lawyer affiliated with the lawyer or the firm, use or participate in the use of any form of public communication if such communication contains a false, fraudulent, misleading, or deceptive statement or claim. For example, a communication violates this Rule if it . . . (4) is likely to create an unjustified expectation about results the lawyer can achieve, or states or implies that the lawyer can achieve results by means that violate the Rules of Professional Conduct or other law.

The VSB also argues that Hunter violated the following subsection of Rule 7.2(a)(3):

> (a) . . . an advertisement violates this Rule if it: . . . (3) advertises specific or cumulative case results, without a disclaimer that (i) puts the case results in a context that is not misleading; (ii) states that case results depend upon a variety of factors unique to each case; and (iii) further states that case results do not guarantee or predict a similar result in any future case undertaken by the lawyer. . . .

In response to these allegations, Hunter contends that speech concerning the judicial system is "quintessentially 'political speech'" which is within the marketplace of ideas. Hunter asserts that the Supreme Court of the United States has twice declined to answer whether political speech is transformed into commercial speech simply because one of multiple motives is commercial. Specifically, he argues that his blog posts are not commercial. . . . However, when speech that is both commercial and political is combined, the resulting speech is not automatically entitled to the level of protections afforded political speech. [Citations omitted.] . . .

Thus, we must examine Hunter's speech to determine whether it is commercial speech, specifically, lawyer advertising. Here, Hunter's blog posts, while containing some political commentary, are commercial speech. Hunter has admitted that his motivation for the blog is at least in part economic. The posts are an advertisement in that they predominately describe cases where he has received a favorable result for his client. He unquestionably references a specific product, i.e., his lawyering skills as twenty-two of his twenty-five case related posts describe cases that he has successfully handled. Indeed, in nineteen of these posts, he specifically named his law firm in addition to naming himself as counsel.

Moreover, the blog is on his law firm's commercial website rather than an independent site dedicated to the blog. [Citation omitted.] The website uses the same frame for the pages openly soliciting clients as it does for the blog, including the firm name, a photograph of Hunter and his law partner, and a "contact us" form. The homepage of the website on which Hunter posted his blog states only:

> **Do you need Richmond attorneys?**
> Hunter & Lipton, CP [sic] is a law practice in Richmond, Virginia specializing in litigation matters from administrative agency hearings to serious criminal cases. As experienced Richmond attorneys, we bring a genuine desire to help those who find themselves in difficult situations. Our partnership was founded on the idea that everyone, no matter what the circumstance, deserves a zealous advocate to fight on his or her behalf.
>
> People make mistakes, and may even find themselves in situations not of their own making. And for these people, the system can be extraordinarily unforgiving and unjust — but you do not have to face this system alone.
>
> **If you find yourself in a difficult legal situation, the Richmond attorneys of Hunter & Lipton, LLP would consider it a privilege to represent you. Please contact our office with any questions or to schedule a consultation.**

This non-interactive blog does not allow for discourse about the cases, as non-commercial commentary often would by allowing readers to post comments. . . . Instead, in furtherance of his commercial pursuit, Hunter invites the reader to "contact us" the same way one seeking legal representation would contact the firm through the website.

Thus, the inclusion of five generalized, legal posts and three discussions about cases that he did not handle on his non-interactive blog, no more transform Hunter's otherwise self-promotional blog posts into political speech, "than opening sales presentations with a prayer or a Pledge of Allegiance would convert them into religious or political speech." [Citation omitted.] Indeed, unlike situations and topics where the subject matter is inherently, inextricably intertwined, Hunter chose to comingle sporadic political statements within his self-promoting blog posts in an attempt to camouflage the true commercial nature of his blog. . . . When considered as a whole, the economically motivated blog overtly proposes a commercial transaction that is an advertisement of a specific product.

Having determined that Hunter's blog posts discussing his cases are commercial speech, we must determine whether the expression is protected by the First Amendment. For commercial speech to come within that provision, it at least must concern lawful activity and not be misleading. Next, we ask whether the asserted governmental interest is substantial. If both inquiries yield positive answers, we must determine whether the regulation directly advances the governmental interest asserted, and whether it is not more extensive than is necessary to serve that interest. *Central Hudson Gas & Elec. Corp. v. Public Serv. Comm'n*, 447 U.S. 557, 566 (1980); *Adams Outdoor Advertising v. City of Newport News*, 236 Va. 370, 383, 373 S.E.2d 917, 923 (1988)....

Of the thirty posts that were on his blog at the time of the VSB hearing, twenty-two posts named himself as counsel and discussed cases that he handled. With one exception, in all of these posts, he described the successful results that he obtained for his clients. While the States may place an absolute prohibition on inherently misleading advertising, "the States may not place an absolute prohibition on certain types of potentially misleading information, . . . if the information also may be presented in a way that is not deceptive." *In re R.M.J.*, 455 U.S. 191, 203 (1982). Here, the VSB's own remedy of requiring Hunter to post disclaimers on his blog posts demonstrates that the information could be presented in a way that is not misleading or deceptive. . . .

[T]he VSB has a substantial governmental interest in protecting the public from an attorney's self-promoting representations that could lead the public to mistakenly believe that they are guaranteed to obtain the same positive results if they were to hire Hunter. . . . The VSB's regulations permit blog posts that discuss specific or cumulative case results but require a disclaimer to explain to the public that no results are guaranteed. (Rules 7.1 and 7.2). This requirement directly advances the VSB's governmental interest. . . .

The disclaimers mandated by the VSB shall precede the communication of the case results. When the communication is in writing, the disclaimer shall be in bold type face and uppercase letters in a font size that is at least as large as the largest text used to advertise the specific or cumulative case results and in the same color and against the same colored background as the text used to advertise the specific or cumulative case results. (Rule 7.2(a)(3)). This requirement ensures that the disclaimer is noticeable and would be connected to each post so that any member of the public who may use the website addresses to directly access Hunter's posts would be in a position to see the disclaimer. Therefore, we hold that the disclaimers required by the VSB are "not more extensive than is necessary to serve that interest." *Central Hudson*, 447 U.S. at 566.

Rule 1.6(a) states, that with limited exceptions,

> [a] lawyer shall not reveal information protected by the attorney-client privilege under applicable law or other information gained in the professional relationship that the client has requested be held inviolate or the disclosure of which would be embarrassing or would be likely to be detrimental to the client unless the client consents after consultation,

except for disclosures that are impliedly authorized in order to carry out the representation. . . .

[T]he VSB's interpretation of Rule 1.6 involves two types of information: 1) that which is protected by the attorney-client privilege, and 2) that which is public information but is embarrassing or likely to be detrimental to the client. Hunter is charged with disseminating the later type of information. In response to these allegations, Hunter argues that the VSB's interpretation of Rule 1.6 is unconstitutional because the matters discussed in his blogs had previously been revealed in public judicial proceedings and, therefore, as concluded matters, were protected by the First Amendment. Thus, we are called upon to answer whether the state may prohibit an attorney from discussing information about a client or former client that is not protected by attorney-client privilege without express consent from that client. We agree with Hunter that it may not. . . .

To the extent that the information is aired in a public forum, privacy considerations must yield to First Amendment protections. In that respect, a lawyer is no more prohibited than any other citizen from reporting what transpired in the courtroom. Thus, the circuit court did not err in concluding that the VSB's interpretation of Rule 1.6 violated the First Amendment. . . .

For the foregoing reasons, we hold that Hunter's blog posts are potentially misleading commercial speech that the VSB may regulate. We further hold that circuit court did not err in determining that the VSB's interpretation of Rule 1.6 violated the First Amendment. Finally, we hold that because the circuit court erred in imposing one disclaimer did not fully comply with Rule 7.2(a)(3), we reverse and remand for imposition of disclaimers that fully comply with that Rule.

Affirmed in part, reversed in part, and remanded.

Questions about the Case

1. What kinds of material and communications appeared on Mr. Hunter's blog? Was this information classified as solicitation or advertising or something else? Describe.
2. Why did Hunter argue that the speech was political, not commercial? What difference would it have made if the court had found that it was political speech?
3. What did the court say about whether Hunter's blog met the requirements for being accurate and honest? Do you agree? Why or why not?
4. What did Hunter have to do to continue to run his blog?
5. What kind of information did Hunter publish about his cases and clients? What did the court say about Hunter's duty to protect client

information? How did the client seem to feel about his posts? How would you feel if you were a client of Hunter's?

This case involves the application of the state ethics rules on advertising to the domain name of a lawyer's website and blog.[1]

Gibson v. Texas Dept. of Ins. Div. of Workers' Comp.
700 F.3d 227 (5th Cir. 2012)

John Gibson is an attorney who represents plaintiffs in workers' compensation claims and contested cases in Texas. Pursuant to this practice, Gibson maintains a website under the domain name of "texasworkerscomplaw.com" in which he discusses matters related to Texas workers' compensation law. He also uses the website to advertise and disseminate information about his law practice.

On February 7, 2011, Gibson received a cease and desist letter from the Texas Department of Insurance, Division of Workers' Compensation ("DWC"), requesting that he no longer use the above-stated domain name. The letter alleged that Gibson's website violated §419.002 of the Texas Labor Code, which states:

> (a) Except as authorized by law, a person, in connection with any impersonation, advertisement, solicitation, business name, business activity, document, product, or service made or offered by the person regarding workers' compensation coverage or benefits, may not knowingly use or cause to be used:
> (1) the words "Texas Department of Insurance," "Department of Insurance," "Texas Workers' Compensation," or "division of workers' compensation";
> (2) any term using both "Texas" and "Workers' Compensation" or any term using both "Texas" and "Workers' Comp"; . . .

Tex. Labor Code §419.002. Although DWC's letter requested a response, Gibson did not provide any written response, nor did he request any form of procedural review from DWC.

Instead, Gibson filed the instant suit, alleging that the regulation violates various constitutional provisions including the First Amendment's guarantee of freedom of speech, the Fourteenth Amendment's

---

1. A "blog" is a shortened, colloquial reference for the term "weblog," and is defined as "'a website that contains an online personal journal with reflections, comments, and often hyperlinks provided by the writer; *also*: the contents of such a site.'" *White v. Baker*, 696 F.Supp.2d 1289, 1310 (N.D.Ga.2010) (quoting Merriam-Webster Online Dictionary, http://www.merriam-webster.com/dictionary/blog (last visited January 31, 2013)).

guarantees of equal protection and due process, and the Fifth Amendment's prohibition on takings. Gibson sought declaratory and injunctive relief pursuant to 28 U.S.C. §2201 and 42 U.S.C. §1983 as well as attorneys' fees pursuant to 42 U.S.C. §1988. The district court dismissed Gibson's Fifth and Fourteenth Amendment claims under Federal Rule of Civil Procedure 12(b)(6), along with Gibson's First Amendment as-applied challenge. The district court declined to consider Gibson's First Amendment facial challenge. Gibson appealed. . . .

The United States Supreme Court has recognized that commercial speech is protected by the First Amendment. [Citations omitted.] However, "[t]he Constitution . . . accords a lesser protection to commercial speech than to other constitutionally guaranteed expression." *Cent. Hudson Gas v. Pub. Serv. Comm'n*, U.S. 557, 562-63, 100 S.Ct. 2343, 65 L.Ed.2d 341 (1980). Regulations on commercial speech are permissible as long as they satisfy the four-part test set forth in *Central Hudson*:

> At the outset, we must determine whether the expression is protected by the First Amendment. For commercial speech to come within that provision, it at least must concern lawful activity and not be misleading. Next, we ask whether the asserted governmental interest is substantial. If both inquiries yield positive answers, we must determine whether the regulation directly advances the governmental interest asserted, and whether it is not more extensive than is necessary to serve that interest.

Id. at 566, 100 S.Ct. 2343. . . .

This brings us to the crux of the question presented by Gibson: whether the district court erred in finding that the statute (a) prohibits commercial speech, and (b) is a valid prohibition of commercial speech under the test set forth in *Central Hudson*.

We agree with Gibson that his domain name and blog may do "more than propose a commercial transaction." [Citation omitted.] The domain name may nevertheless be considered commercial speech if (i) it is an advertisement of some form; (ii) it refers to a specific product; and (iii) the speaker has an economic motivation for the speech. . . . As with many new issues involving the Internet, the proper method of analysis to determine whether a domain name is commercial speech or a more vigorously protected form of speech is *res nova*. A domain name, which in itself could qualify as ordinary communicative speech, might qualify as commercial speech if the website itself is used almost exclusively for commercial purposes. This is an issue we need not reach or decide in this appeal without a record of all of the surrounding facts and circumstances involving the website's domain name. As discussed in more detail below, even if the domain name amounts to commercial speech, Gibson has nevertheless stated a claim under the First Amendment. Therefore, we reverse and remand the case for further proceedings on that basis. But we also reserve to Gibson his right in those proceedings to argue for and adduce evidence in support of stronger protection of his domain name as ordinary, communicative speech, and not merely as commercial speech.

Even if we assume without deciding that the domain name is commercial speech, we must still evaluate whether the statute presents a valid restriction on commercial speech under the test set forth in *Central Hudson*. To answer this question, we first look to whether the speech restricted by the statute is "false, deceptive, or misleading[.]" *Bates v. State Bar of Ariz.*, 433 U.S. 350, 383, 97 S.Ct. 2691, 53 L.Ed.2d 810 (1977). If so, it is not entitled to First Amendment protection. *Id*. The Supreme Court and this circuit have distinguished between two types of misleading speech: that which is "inherently likely to deceive," and that which is only "potentially misleading." *Pub. Citizen, Inc. v. La. Attorney Disciplinary Bd.*, 632 F.3d 212, 218 (5th Cir. 2011) (citing *In re R.M.J.*, 455 U.S. 191, 202-03, 102 S.Ct. 929, 71 L.Ed.2d 64 (1982)). In order for speech to fall outside of the First Amendment's protection, the speech must either be "inherently likely to deceive," or "the record [must] indicate[] that a particular form or method of advertising has in fact been deceptive." *R.M.J.*, 455 U.S. at 202, 102 S.Ct. 929.

Appellees primarily argue that the Texas statute is constitutional because Gibson's domain name amounts to inherently misleading speech. In support of this proposition, they cite to a series of cases in which courts have held that domain names that use trademarks to misidentify the source of a product are outside the reach of the First Amendment. The case law cited by Appellees, however, is unique to the field of trademark infringement. . . . Cases involving trademark infringement involve inherently deceptive speech because they contain a significant risk that an infringing party will freeload on the goodwill that has been created by the original trademark. *See Friedman*, 440 U.S. at 11-16, 99 S.Ct. 887. No such risk is present here. Texas has made no showing that its own talents and energy contributed to the creation of any goodwill in the name "texasworkerscomplaw.com." [Citation omitted.] Instead, the regulation at issue is forward-thinking; intended to prohibit confusion for individuals seeking information from the government agency. . . . Accordingly, the case law cited by Appellees is inapposite.

Other than cases involving trademarks, inherently deceptive speech has been found in essentially one other area: attorney solicitation of prospective clients. *See, e.g., Ohralik v. Ohio State Bar Ass'n*, 436 U.S. 447, 460-62, 98 S.Ct. 1912, 56 L.Ed.2d 444 (1978). In *Ohralik*, the Court specifically noted that "[t]he substantive evils of [attorney] solicitation have been stated over the years in sweeping terms: stirring up litigation, assertion of fraudulent claims, debasing the legal profession, and potential harm to the solicited client in the form of overreaching, overcharging, under-representation, and misrepresentation." *Id.* at 461, 98 S.Ct. 1912. Given the history of in-person solicitation, the Court was convinced that these risks were inherently likely to occur in future solicitations, and such solicitation could therefore be prohibited. *Id.*

The same risks are simply not attendant in the speech at issue here. First, there is no history upon which a court could conclude that speech covered by this statute, and domain names similar to the one at issue, are inherently deceptive. While Texas fears that Gibson's domain name may confuse the public, there is no showing that the domain name is incapable of being viewed in a non-deceptive manner. *See Pub. Citizen*, 632 F.3d at 219. Second, there have been no factual findings to support an allegation that the domain name is actually deceptive. *See, e.g., R.M.J.*, 455 U.S. at 202, 102 S.Ct. 929; *Joe Conte Toyota, Inc. v. La. Motor Vehicle Comm'n*, 24 F.3d 754, 756 (5th Cir. 1994). Therefore, the domain name at issue is entitled to some First Amendment protection.

Although Texas cannot show that the domain name is inherently misleading, that is not the end of our inquiry. Under the *Central Hudson* test, commercial speech that is not inherently misleading may nevertheless be regulated as long as the regulation directly advances a substantial state interest, and is no more extensive than necessary to serve that interest. *Cent. Hudson*, 447 U.S. at 563, 100 S.Ct. 2343; *Pub. Citizen*, 632 F.3d at 218. The chosen regulation does not need to be the least restrictive method for achieving the government's goal. [Citations omitted.]

The court below found the law to be constitutional because its intent is to prevent misuse of the DWC's names and symbols. [Citation omitted.] However, Texas concedes that it has not yet compiled the record necessary to demonstrate satisfaction of the *Central Hudson* test as a matter of law. Although a factual record is not necessarily required for Texas to demonstrate that the regulation fits the *Central Hudson* test . . . the district court nevertheless erred by basing its decision on the legislative record without the benefit of briefing on this issue. . . . Because Texas has made no serious attempt to justify this regulation as narrowly tailored to a substantial state interest, the district court's order dismissing Gibson's as-applied challenge was in error, and this case is remanded to allow Texas the opportunity to develop additional factual findings to support the statute's constitutionality. . . .

In addition to his First Amendment claims, Gibson also alleges that the Texas law is unconstitutional under the Fourteenth Amendment's guarantees of equal protection and due process, and under the Fifth Amendment's prohibition of taking without just compensation. None of these allegations are meritorious.

To state a claim under the Equal Protection Clause, a §1983 plaintiff must either allege that (a) "a state actor intentionally discriminated against [him] because of membership in a protected class[,]" *Williams v. Bramer*, 180 F.3d 699, 705 (5th Cir.1999) [citation omitted], or (b) he has been "intentionally treated differently from others similarly situated and that there is no rational basis for the difference in treatment." *Vill. of Willow-brook v. Olech*, 528 U.S. 562, 564, 120 S.Ct. 1073, 145 L.Ed.2d 1060 (2000). Gibson makes no allegation that this law discriminates, either facially or in its application, against members of any protected class. Nor does he make any serious allegation that this law has been applied to him in a manner different from other similarly situated individuals.

Gibson instead argues that this law subjects him to controls not placed on similarly situated businesses or individuals. The mere fact that a law impacts different individuals in different ways does not subject it to constitutional challenge unless Gibson can show that Texas's law is so extreme as to lack a rational basis. . . .

Gibson also alleges that §419.002 deprives him of procedural due process because there is no means or procedure for hearing, and no possibility of appeal from a determination of a violation of that section. Gibson admits that the regulation permits an affected party to provide a written response to the cease and desist letter, which he did not do. . . . [The regulation about hearings] gives Gibson sufficient notice and an opportunity to be heard prior to any deprivation, and it is difficult to determine any additional procedures that would further reduce his risk. [Citation omitted.] Accordingly, we affirm the district court's dismissal of Gibson's due process claim.

Finally, Gibson cannot succeed on his Fifth Amendment takings challenge because his claim is not yet ripe for adjudication. A takings claim becomes ripe only when "(1) the relevant governmental unit has reached a final decision as to how the regulation will be applied . . . and (2) the plaintiff has sought compensation for the alleged taking through whatever adequate procedures the state provides." [Citations omitted.] Because neither of these steps has occurred in the instant case, we affirm the district court's dismissal without prejudice of Gibson's takings claim.

We affirm the district court's dismissal of Gibson's Fifth and Fourteenth Amendment claims. We also affirm the district court's ruling that the regulation at issue is content-neutral and does not amount to a prior restraint. We reverse the district court's finding that the law is constitutional as applied to Gibson, and remand to permit the parties to more fully develop the record on this issue.

Questions about the Case

1. What was the name of the lawyer's website and what was the name of the agency involved? Do you find this website name to be inherently confusing or not? That is, if you came across this website, would you think it was a state agency or a private lawyer?
2. What were the lawyer's legal arguments for keeping his domain name?
3. On which argument or arguments did he prevail? Why?
4. Are lawyers allowed to indicate that they practice or specialize in workers' compensation law? What rules apply? Is there a parallel to this fact situation?
5. What will happen when the case is remanded?

Fees and Client Funds

This chapter examines the ethics rules relating to financial matters in the representation of clients, including a range of issues from fees and billing to client trust funds. Chapter 7 covers:

- the various kinds of fee arrangements made with clients, including fixed fees, contingency fees, and hourly fees
- the growing use of alternative fee arrangements
- factors considered in determining if a fee is unethically excessive
- billing practices and abuses
- fee agreements with clients
- attorneys' fees under fee-shifting statutes and the compensation in fee awards for paralegal time
- fee splitting and referral fees
- ethics rules prohibiting lawyers from entering into partnerships with paralegals
- duties in handling client funds and client trust accounts

A. Fee Arrangements with Clients

Several different methods are used to charge clients for legal services. The method selected depends mostly on the nature of the services being rendered. The most common methods of billing are fixed fees, contingency fees, and hourly fees.

1. Fixed Fees

Fixed fee
Fee for legal services based on a set amount.

Fixed fees (also known as **flat fees**) usually are used for routine legal services, ones for which the lawyer knows in advance the length of time needed to complete the work. In this instance, the client is paying for the lawyer's expertise as much as for the time expended. Typical services for which a fixed or flat fee is charged are filing a default divorce, forming a basic corporation or partnership, and handling a simple consumer bankruptcy.

A variation on the fixed fee is a fee that is based on the percentage of the worth of the matter being handled, either by statute or by practice. In probate matters, for example, the fee usually is based on a percentage of the value of the estate, according to statute. It is common practice in some states for a lawyer to charge a percentage of the value of a real estate transaction. Although calculated as a percentage, these kinds of fees are not to be confused with contingency fees used in civil litigation matters, in which the lawyer's fee is paid as a percentage of the recovery in the cases and the lawyer does not collect a fee if they lose the case.

2. Contingency Fees

Contingency fee
Fee depends on the successful outcome of a case and is based on a percentage of the recovery.

Contingency fees are usually based on a percentage of the recovery in a case. Sometimes a fixed fee is made contingent on the outcome in a case, giving it the most important attribute of a contingency fee—risk. Contingency fee arrangements typically are utilized by plaintiffs' lawyers in civil litigation matters such as personal injury cases. The risk to lawyers who handle cases on contingency is that they will lose the case and receive no compensation for the time and effort expended.

Although the contingency fee is now well accepted in the United States (it is not used in England or Canada), it was resisted by American lawyers and courts until early in the twentieth century. Contingency fees were thought to stir up litigation and to encourage lawyers to engage in unethical conduct to win cases. Gradually, the bar came to recognize the value of the contingency fee as a means to provide access to legal services to those who have a legal claim but who cannot otherwise afford legal services.

Despite the widespread use of contingency fees in personal injury and medical malpractice cases, ethics rules still place some limitations on this kind of fee arrangement. Contingency fee arrangements are not permitted in any state in **criminal cases** because they are thought to encourage corruption and to discourage plea bargaining. ABA Model Rule 1.5(d)(2). Most jurisdictions also have rules prohibiting contingency fees in **marital dissolution, divorce, and separation** cases and related support and property settlements because they are thought to discourage reconciliation and settlement. ABA Model Rule 1.5(d)(1). In addition, a contingency arrangement in such cases may not be necessary to provide access to legal services as the court may award attorneys' fees to the spouse without the means to pay them.

Other limits on contingency fee arrangements have been codified into state ethics rules or statutes that restrict the **percentage of the fee**. For example, federal law (28 U.S.C. §2678) places the maximum fee at 20 percent of a settlement or 25 percent of a judgment. Some state statutes, such as California Business and Professions Code §6146, limit the percentage that can be collected in medical malpractice cases against health care providers.

The ABA Model Rules (Rule 1.5(c)) and most jurisdictions have special ethics rules relating to the communication with the client of the terms of a contingency fee arrangement. Under these rules, contingency fee agreements must be **in writing and signed** by the client even though other fee agreements are not required to be in writing. (Communication of fee agreements is discussed in the next section of this chapter.) Some states have rules requiring ads that mention contingency fees to disclose that clients are liable for costs even if they lose their case. These rules were upheld in *Zauderer v. Office of Disciplinary Counsel of the Supreme Court of Ohio*, 471 U.S. 626 (1985). Finally, contingency fees are subject to special judicial scrutiny for reasonableness and are disallowed if the percentage is considered exorbitant or the fee is well out of proportion to the work done or the risk taken by the attorney. (See also ABA Model Rule 1.5(a).)

Contingency fees continue to be the subject of some debate within the legal profession. However, they have gained in popularity as clients explore alternative fee arrangements. For example, more corporate clients are requesting contingency arrangements in business litigation, even on the defense side. This kind of arrangement is believed to incentivize lawyers to settle or win in order to earn the fee, or a larger one if they prevail even more quickly and efficiently.

A typical contingency fee in a personal injury matter is one-third of the recovery, but many lawyers charge on a sliding scale that reflects both the amount of risk and the time and effort expended as the case moves forward. For example, a lawyer might charge 25 percent if the case settles before trial, one-third if it goes to trial, and 40 percent if it is appealed.

3. Hourly Fees

Hourly fees
Fees based on hourly rates and the amount of time actually expended.

Hourly fees are the most common method of billing in matters other than civil litigation on the plaintiff side. Charging for time was not always so common in the legal profession but has become deeply ingrained in law practice during the past 40 years. Most large firms bill mainly by means of hourly rates, with every lawyer and paralegal keeping close track of the time spent on client matters, usually in increments of either six or ten minutes.

Hourly rates are based on the expertise and other qualifications of the person billing, the nature and complexity of the services performed and, of course, the market in which the lawyer practices. Lawyers and paralegals in New York, Washington, D.C., and the San Francisco Bay area command higher rates than other parts of the country, in part because of the cost of living in those areas and in part because of the complexity of the legal matters that arise in those areas, e.g., securities work and complex transactions. Hourly lawyer rates nationwide in 2022 ranged from $150 an hour to $2,500 an hour. Paralegal rates range from about $60 to $350 an hour.

There is much discussion in the legal profession about shifting away from the practice of billing by the hour, and many law firms have started to do this, developing alternative methods of charging for their services. Part of the impetus for this move is the increased efficiency of law firms through specialization and the use of technology. Firms that have developed highly valuable expertise and means of producing documents quickly and efficiently want to avoid being penalized for their efficiency and to be fairly compensated not just for their time but also for the "value" of their services. Some commentators have decried the billable hour because they believe that the practice encourages lawyers to do work less efficiently, has led to billing abuses, and results in lawyers working unacceptably long hours. Studies also show that the quality of work starts to degrade after a person has worked about 40 hours in a week. Clients, especially corporate clients that use legal services extensively, want changes in the way that legal services are priced as they seek ways to lower legal fees and to structure fee agreements that allow them to plan and budget more accurately and to assess the value and productivity of the services provided.

4. Alternative Fee Arrangements

The trend toward the use of alternative billing arrangements has accelerated in the last few years as more big law firms have adopted new billing models. Large corporate clients favor flat fees and discounts for volume work, and firms need to rethink their billing methods and business model. Firms would rather avoid having clients question every entry on their bills and demand discounts after the work has been done. Clients find these flat fees and other alternatives attractive because they are predictable, which helps with budgeting and planning and control costs. Some new firms are touting their refusal to bill by the hour as a way to attract prospective clients. Business-savvy clients also know that billing rates are negotiable — about 90 percent of law firms charge different rates to different clients.

Many firms are utilizing an array of alternative methods of structuring fee arrangements, such as charging a percentage of the value of a transaction, charging a premium for achieving results that are especially beneficial to a client, or charging a fixed fee that reflects the value of the services to the client without regard to the time expended. Capping of fees at a predetermined amount, discounted hourly rates for major clients, blended hourly rates arrived at by averaging rates for all firm lawyers and/or paralegals, contingency fees in defense matters, and hybrids of several different billing methods are all commonly used now.

Another method is **task-based billing**, in which clients are charged an agreed-on predetermined flat rate for specific functions, such as taking a deposition or representing a client at a particular kind of hearing. Some small firms charge for pieces of legal work as matters proceed, which is similar to the principle of "unbundling" legal work. Finally, some firms that represent start-up companies are doing legal work in exchange for a percentage interest in the new corporation's stock. This kind of fee arrangement raises a potential conflict of interest because the lawyers have a dual role as investors, but is acceptable if certain conditions are met, including informed written client consent. (See ABA Ethics Opinion 00-418 and Chapter 5 on business relationships with clients.) Most firms that engage clients using these alternative fee arrangements only do so for a relatively small proportion of their clients. Only a few firms have shifted entirely away from hourly billing.

5. Billing for Paralegal Time

Billing practices will continue to evolve as law practice responds to market forces and to changes in the nature of legal work and law practice. The effect on paralegals is significant: Paralegals must be proficient in technology and demonstrably efficient and productive in all their work. Paralegal managers and supervising lawyers must be certain that paralegals are well trained and are assigned to perform work that matches their degree of expertise.

It is well accepted that paralegal time may be charged directly to clients just as lawyer time is. When utilized properly, paralegals are engaged in professional work that would otherwise have to be done by a lawyer. And because paralegal time is billed to clients at lower rates than lawyer time is, the cost of the overall legal services to the client is lower.

Guideline 8 of the ABA Model Guidelines for the Utilization of Paralegal Services (ABA Model Guidelines) provides that lawyers may charge for paralegal services. Most state guidelines also specifically endorse this customary practice, which was acknowledged by the U.S. Supreme Court in *Missouri v. Jenkins*, 491 U.S. 274 (1989) (with regard to statutory fee awards). (Section C later in the chapter covers this topic further.)

Note that nonlawyer legal service providers who do not work under lawyer supervision are not covered by this principle. Some states have statutes that prohibit nonlawyers from receiving fees for providing legal services. (See, for example, Illinois's Attorney Act (705 Illinois Compiled Statutes, 205/1, eff. 2000) and the California Business and Professions Code section 6450.) (See Chapter 2.)

Several state supreme courts have created new job classifications and amended their ethics rules to authorize nonlawyers to directly represent clients on a limited basis. These professionals are also authorized to charge for their services. (See Chapter 2 for further information on limited practice legal professionals.)

6. Ethics Rules on Fees

The ethics rules covering fees prohibit fees that are **illegal, excessive, unconscionable, or unreasonable**. A fee is usually found illegal if it exceeds statutory limits such as those mentioned earlier. It may also be illegal if the legal services were sought for an illegal purpose, such as a criminal enterprise. The ABA Model Rules set standards for judging whether a fee is unethical. The earlier Model Code indicated that fees were unethical if "clearly excessive," whereas the ABA Rules prohibit "unreasonable" fees; however, both contain the same eight factors used to determine whether a fee is unethically high:

(1) the time and labor required, the novelty and difficulty of the questions involved, and the skill requisite to perform the legal service properly;
(2) the likelihood, if apparent to the client, that the acceptance of the particular employment will preclude other employment by the lawyer;
(3) the fee customarily charged in the locality for similar legal services;
(4) the amount involved and the results obtained;
(5) the time limitations imposed by the client or by the circumstances;
(6) the nature and length of the professional relationship with the client;
(7) the experience, reputation, and ability of the lawyer or lawyers performing the services; and
(8) whether the fee is fixed or contingent.

ABA Model Rule 1.5(a)(1)-(8).

Some states, such as California and Texas, set the standard for excessive fees at the "unconscionable" level, which differs in degree from both the ABA Model Code and Model Rules standards. (See California Rules of Prof'l Conduct R. 4-200 and Texas Disciplinary Rules of Prof'l Conduct R. 1.04.)

The reasonableness of fees has been litigated extensively, mainly in cases involving statutory fee awards (discussed below in Section C). Guidelines can be drawn from litigation over fees and from disciplinary cases. Although all the factors on the ABA list may be considered by courts and disciplinary bodies in determining if a fee is unethical, the amount of **time spent** tends to be the most important and serves as a starting point in the analysis of reasonableness of a fee. In fee dispute cases and disciplinary matters, the client's understanding of the fee agreement is also a critical factor.

Probably the most widespread ethical problem relating to fees is one that is not addressed directly by either ethics codes or case law, but nonetheless is one that paralegals are likely to face during the course of their careers. That problem encompasses several activities that constitute **billing fraud or abuse**, such as the practice of inflating the time spent on client matters that are billed by the hour.

The pressure to bill an ever-increasing number of hours in firms that use the hourly billing method is tremendous. The value of a fee-generating lawyer or paralegal is measured largely by how much revenue that person produces for the firm. Expectations for billable hours have risen dramatically over the last 30 years. In the early 1980s, 1,200 billable hours a year was common in a large firm; now, the expectation is 1,800 to 2,400 hours a year for associates in many large firms. This standard means that a person must perform billable work at the rate of about nine hours a day, every working day of the year. It is estimated that to bill nine hours of time requires a workday of 11 to 12 hours.

Most of the pressure to bill falls on highly compensated associates trying to make partner. Several studies have shown that most associates believe that the pressure to bill time hurts their personal lives. Paralegals feel this pressure, too. Many large firms have strict guidelines on paralegal billable hours that require 1,500 to 1,800 hours a year. The pressure to bill incentivizes improper billing practices, such as double billing, billing full rates for recycled work product, overbilling, overstaffing, such as sending two or three lawyers to hearings unnecessarily, billing for overhead costs, padding hours, doing unnecessary work for clients, and spending excessive amounts of time on matters that do not warrant it.

An ongoing parade of cases involving lawyers who have engaged in **overbilling** and **billing of personal expenses** to clients is found in legal publications, periodicals, and blogs. In recent years, for example, lawyers in Georgia, New York, and Pennsylvania were suspended or disbarred for incidents of billing substantial amounts of time for work that they did not perform. A lawyer in D.C. was suspended after he was found to have double billed for his time on 163 occasions over four years. A South Carolina lawyer was sanctioned for billing for 20 meetings that were not held. A court-appointed public defender in West Virginia was caught for billing more than 24 hours a day on 173 occasions. A former partner of a prominent Chicago firm was sentenced to six years in prison for overbilling a city client more than $100,000 for work he never performed. A Texas lawyer was sanctioned after seeking attorneys' fees in a contingency case for work not performed and after being fired by the client. Several clients in Arizona sued a firm after discovering that the firm had charged them for the time of nonlawyer law clerks as though they were lawyer associates. In a lawsuit brought by a major law firm to collect a fee, emails were discovered in which the lawyers referred to the matter as "that bill shall know no limits" and bragged about assigning "random" people to work full-time on research to "churn" the bill. One lawyer was disciplined for charging her client $125 an hour for running errands with him and another for billing her criminal defense clients for her time watching reality-crime shows on television. One out-of-control lawyer in a big law firm in New Jersey was disbarred for creating phony time records, having sex with a client, and submitting expense vouchers to his firm for dinners with his girlfriend. In one of the most outrageous examples, a Minnesota lawyer was sanctioned for engaging in a sexual relationship with a vulnerable client and for billing the client for this time.

Reported cases have involved billing for the time of nonprofessional staff such as secretaries and legal assistants; **overcharging** for legal research and driving time to an unnecessarily distant library; and doubling the costs of process servers and independent contractors. One lawyer was found to have charged three hours of time for reading one sentence. In yet another case, a firm charged eight hours of paralegal time for buying and serving lunch at a meeting. Some firms that have agreed to blended rates or another alternative form of billing have found that these forms are not profitable. A few have remedied this problem by multiplying the time spent by specific factors to ensure a profit, for example, charging 1.5 times the actual time spent. An Illinois lawyer was sanctioned for billing clients for court-imposed sanctions for his own mishandling on a discovery matter.

A growing number of courts are refusing to allow fees as they look deeply into the records. One bankruptcy judge reduced a large fee because of the use of personnel beyond what was needed to handle the case and inflated expenses like first-class airfares and stays at luxury hotels. A federal judge in Boston found that firms in a class action suit had overbilled by $4 million and double counted 9,000 hours. One contractor in the case was paid $30 an hour and charged at $425.

Corporate clients have taken proactive steps to prevent themselves from becoming the victims of unscrupulous billing practices and high legal bills. Many clients ask firms to make **proposals for services**, establish budgets for legal work beyond which a firm may not bill, and demand task-based billing, which provides detailed information on the cost of services from which clients can evaluate services and negotiate future billing arrangements. Many corporations also **restrict the costs** they will pay. For example, they reimburse for coach airfare and standard business accommodations only and will not pay surcharges on computerized legal research or for secretarial overtime or computer use. Even the federal government got involved in uncovering billing abuse when it audited the bills of a large firm that was providing services under the Troubled Asset Relief Program (TARP) and found that the billing arrangements were not sufficiently detailed and that the bills showed unacceptable block billing, vague and inadequate descriptions of work, and other objectionable practices that should have led to the bills being questioned. Finally, client concerns led to the development of new software that allows clients to track billing and legal work in real time.

An ABA formal ethics opinion that addresses billing abuses has been widely cited and followed throughout the country. The abuses highlighted in the opinion are **double billing** (that is, billing more than one client for the same hours—such as billing twice for travel time when making court appearances for more than one client in the same day), **surcharges** on services contracted with outside vendors, such as expert witnesses, and charges beyond reasonable costs for in-house services such as photocopying and computer searches. The opinion calls for **full disclosure** of the basis for charges when the fee agreement is made and subsequently when the client is billed. Further, the opinion emphasizes that the charges must also be reasonable, that is, no charges for unnecessary work or for hours not actually expended (ABA Formal Opinion 93-379). Also see California State Bar Ethics Opinion 147 (1996), which is in accord.

Bar associations have publicly acknowledged the inherent hazards in judging a lawyer's or paralegal's performance solely by the amount of time billed and have pushed firms to consider the quality of life for employees of firms as well as the potential for billing abuse. One ethically dubious practice is **block billing**, which consists of stating several tasks with one hourly amount, such as, "reviewed letter, talked with opposing counsel, conducted research for hearing: 6 hours." Insurance companies, financial institutions, and many corporate clients do not allow this kind of billing and want each task and time itemized. Another is using unrealistically large minimum units for billing. Most firms use 6- or 10-minute increments (i.e., a tenth or sixth of an hour); some use 15-minute blocks. This increment is objectionable, in part because many small routine tasks, such as a phone call or e-mail, do not take a quarter of an hour, so a firm will end up billing for far more than an hour's work if handling many small tasks in that hour are billed at 15 minutes each. Some courts have found the 15-minute increment unacceptable and have reduced fee awards when this billing unit was used.

Paralegals have been implicated in some highly publicized cases. For example, paralegals in one case billed deposition summaries at the rate of four to five pages an hour, about a fourth of the average speed. In another case, a paralegal billed 43 hours in one day. In some cases, paralegal billing rates have been double the market rate, or the time was billed for routine clerical work, such as copying and filing. A few well-publicized cases in the insurance industry have forced insurance defense firms to reconsider what work they assign to paralegals because their clients refuse to pay paralegal rates for work they consider to be clerical.

Billing abuses are not only dishonest and unethical but also detrimental in the long term to the law firm and its relationships with clients. Good firms do not send bills to clients without first examining them to ensure that the amount fairly reflects the services rendered. If the bill is excessive, the partner who is responsible for billing the client will adjust it down, "writing off" excessive time. The written-off time will be allocated back to the one who billed it and may be deducted from his or her total billable hours.

The firm that does not **review bills** or adjust them in this fashion is running the risk of having dissatisfied clients. Some commentators believe that excessive legal fees caused by dishonest billing practices have been a leading factor in the revolt by clients against the high cost of legal services and in the low esteem in which the public holds lawyers.

Paralegals should not themselves engage in such unethical billing practices and have an obligation to report others who do to a supervising lawyer. A paralegal should not continue to work in a firm that encourages such conduct. The NFPA Model Code calls attention to the proper paralegal role in billing under Canon 1.2. Ethical Considerations advise paralegals to prepare thorough, accurate, honest, and complete timekeeping and billing records and tell paralegals not to knowingly engage in fraudulent billing practices, such as inflating hours, misrepresenting the nature of the work that was done for a client, or submitting false expenses. (Also see NFPA Ethics Opinion 95-4, which discusses the ethics of billing for tasks that may be considered nonprofessional clerical work.)

B. Terms and Communication of Fee Arrangements with Clients

As soon as possible after a lawyer and client agree to representation, the lawyer should fully explain the terms of the fee agreement to the client. It is good practice—required in some cases—to put the agreement in writing.

ABA Model Rule 1.5(b) states that lawyers should communicate to the client, "preferably in writing," within a reasonable time after commencing representation, "the scope of representation and the basis or rate of the fee and expenses. . . ." Changes in rates and fees must also be communicated. Contingency fee agreements must be in writing and include the method and percentage(s) by which the fee is to be calculated and provision for payment of costs (i.e., whether they are deducted before or after calculation of the fee). A written statement showing the calculations is required at the conclusion of the matter (Model Rule 1.5(c)). Some states have more stringent requirements about what kinds of fee agreements must be in writing, and many states now require all fee agreements with new clients to be in writing.

Written fee agreements are favored because they promote clear communication between the lawyer and client and can prevent disputes over the fee. In addition, they protect both parties in the event of a dispute — especially lawyers, who will have any misunderstanding about the fee arrangements construed against them. Some state bars have standard engagement forms that lawyers are encouraged to use.

As indicated in Chapter 3 on the unauthorized practice of law, paralegals should be aware that they are prohibited from establishing the attorney-client relationship and setting the fee to be charged in a matter. Only the lawyer can agree to represent a client and in doing so make the appropriate fee arrangement and explain it to the client. The role of the paralegal as a liaison with the client may include answering questions about fees and costs but should not include entering into the contractual agreement with the client on the lawyer's behalf. The paralegal can, of course, relay information back and forth between the lawyer and the client concerning the representation and the fee agreement.

The ABA Model Guidelines state that **establishing a fee** is one of the few specified functions that a lawyer cannot delegate to a paralegal. Guideline 3(b) advises that a lawyer may not delegate "responsibility for establishing the amount of a fee to be charged for a legal service." The comment emphasizes the importance of attorney-client communication and cites state guidelines that also prohibit paralegals from "setting fees" or accepting cases. (See also ABA Informal Opinion 875 (1965), which provides that lay employees may not make fee arrangements or agree to undertake representation on the lawyer's behalf.) The National Association of Legal Assistants (NALA) Code of Ethics and Professional Responsibility provides in Canon 1(b) that paralegals "must not establish an attorney-client relationship [or] set fees."

Written fee agreements or engagement letters should cover:

- the scope of the firm's services;
- the responsibilities of the client and the firm;
- details regarding the method of determining the fee (*i.e.*, hourly, fixed, contingency, or some other method);

- if hourly billing is used, the rates or ranges of rates of all potential billers, including paralegals, should be specified;
- the costs the client is obligated to pay and when they are paid (*e.g.*, in advance or out of the client's recovery after the attorney's fee is calculated in the case of contingency arrangements or at specified regular billings);
- termination rights and responsibilities of both parties;
- method and time of fee payment; and
- procedure for and frequency of billings, if applicable.

The agreement should contain a provision indicating that the agreement is privileged. It is also wise to include language indicating that the firm is not guaranteeing a particular result. If the client does not speak or read English proficiently, the agreement should be in a language that the client understands. The signature clause should include an acknowledgment that the client has read and understood the terms of the agreement. The client should also be given sufficient time to read and reflect on the agreement before signing it. Fee agreements may also contain provisions about how disputes between the lawyer and client are handled (*e.g.*, by mediation or arbitration). Finally, an ABA opinion addresses the issue of changing fee arrangements during representation, which can be done only if reasonable and agreed to by the client (ABA Formal Opinion 11-458).

Some lawyers and bar associations advocate the "unbundling" of **legal services** as a means to increase access to legal services for clients who cannot afford to have a lawyer handle all aspects of their legal matters. Lawyers who unbundle their services often handle divorce, small business matters, and some litigation this way. If this kind of representation is undertaken, the limits on the lawyer's role in representing the client must be very carefully and clearly laid out so that the understanding about what the lawyer will and will not do is very clear. Otherwise, the client may later seek damages from the lawyer if the legal matter is not resolved satisfactorily. The ABA and other bar associations have been progressive in promoting unbundling as a way to increase access to and decrease the cost of legal services. ABA Model Rule 1.2(c) allows lawyers to limit their representation as long as it is "reasonable under the circumstances and the client gives informed consent."

For some kinds of legal work, attorneys may require a ***retainer*** or ***advance fee***, which is paid at the commencement of the agreed-upon work. Although frequently called retainers, advance fees are usually refundable, in that the attorney earns the fee as the work progresses and refunds to the client whatever portion is unearned when, for whatever reason, the services stop. Retainer fees are in whole or in part nonrefundable, in essence acting as a minimum fee regardless of the amount of work done and as a guarantee that the lawyer will be available to

Retainer
Nonrefundable fee paid at the commencement of agreed-on work to ensure the availability of the lawyer to handle specified matters.

Advance fee
Fee paid for legal services in advance, which is refundable if not earned.

handle whatever comes up during the period covered by the retainer. A nonrefundable retainer is ethically acceptable so long as the client fully understands the arrangement and the fee is not excessive, considering the factors noted above and set forth in Model Rule 1.5. Advances must be deposited into the client trust account until earned, while nonrefundable retainers may be deposited directly into a firm operating account. (Client trust accounts are discussed later in Section E.) Both advance fees and retainer fees should be explicitly defined in a written fee agreement.

Hourly billing carries the potential for misunderstandings with clients because, without an estimate of the number of hours a project will take, the client will have no idea what the ultimate bill for services might be. It is good practice for the lawyer to provide the client with an estimate, if at all possible, and to update the estimate if it changes as the matter proceeds.

Payment of **costs** requires special clarity in fee agreements as clients may not expect to pay or may resent paying many additional charges when they are already paying what they believe are high fees. The kind of costs billed directly to clients varies somewhat from firm to firm. As a rule, all lawyers expect clients to pay direct expenses that the firm incurs on behalf of the client. These costs include filing fees with courts and governmental bodies, deposition and trial transcripts, expert reports and testimony, out-of-town travel expenses, outside printing, messengers, process servers, and outside litigation technology. Firms may also charge for copying done within the firm and for long-distance telephone calls. Some firms may also charge clients for costs that might ordinarily be thought of as part of overhead, such as secretarial or legal assistant overtime, in the event the firm must work extra evenings and weekend hours for a particular client. Costs should be itemized on a client's bill. Clarity about costs is key, as clients may challenge bills that include costs like third-party research and copies that clients believe are more appropriately considered part of the lawyer's overhead. (Also see Chapter 5 for conflicts of interest rules relating to advancing costs and other expenses for clients.)

Most jurisdictions permit lawyers to accept payment of legal fees by **credit card**. This practice was first approved by the ABA in its Formal Opinion 338 (1974) with several limitations, including one that lawyers not increase fees to cover expenses of participating in such a plan. Some states also permit lawyers to help clients work out financing for the payment of fees with a bank, a practice endorsed by ABA Formal Opinion 338 (1974). Some lawyers accept property in payment of fees. When doing so, they must be aware of the value of the property and reasonableness of the fee. **Discounting of fees** is also ethical so long as ads or coupons with discounts are honored for the relevant time frame. (See Connecticut Ethics Opinion 94-23, South Carolina Ethics Opinion 96-27, and Texas Ethics Opinion 452 (1998).)

C. Court-Awarded Attorneys' Fees

As a general rule, litigants in the United States must pay their own attorneys' fees. This practice is different from that in England, Canada, and most European countries, which have widespread policies for fee shifting. In England and Canada, for example, all or part of the attorneys' fees in litigation are awarded to the prevailing party.

Efforts have been made to reform the American system with court decisions, contracts, and legislation. Courts have awarded lawyers' fees in cases in which a common fund that benefits persons other than the parties was created as a result of the litigation; in which the litigation resulted in a common benefit to the public or some portion of the public, even though no fund was created; similarly, in which the plaintiff acted as a "private attorney general" vindicating a legal right that also benefits others and for which the plaintiff's actual damages are relatively small; and, finally, in actions for malicious prosecution, for abuse of civil process, or those taken in bad faith. This last category of fee shifting is also supported by legislation in some states. Contract provisions for lawyers' fees are relatively common and are generally enforced by the courts.

Fee-shifting statute
A law that allows a court to award attorneys' fees to one of the parties.

Fee-shifting statutes have proliferated, and hundreds of state and federal statutes provide for the award of attorneys' fees in specified types of litigation. These fee-shifting statutes generally apply to the types of litigation that the legislature wants to encourage as a matter of public policy (for example, protecting civil rights) and award fees only to prevailing plaintiffs, not defendants. Like contingency fees, statutory fees enable plaintiffs who might not otherwise be able to afford a lawyer to bring legal action to vindicate their rights. And like contingency fees, the lawyer is accepting the risk of not being compensated if they do not prevail.

Conflicts of interest may arise in cases involving statutory fees when the interests of the client clash with the interest of the lawyer in maximizing the fee award. For example, an offer to settle may satisfy the client but not include sufficient fees for the lawyer or may satisfy the lawyer as to the fee award but not the client, who wants a larger recovery. The tort reform movement cites this kind of conflict as a reason for legislating against class actions and other kinds of lawsuits, especially noting large attorney fee awards in suits in which the members of the class get only a small sum of money or no monetary recovery at all. Lawyers must always be aware of the potential for a conflict in cases with court-awarded fees and keep the client's best interests in mind when advising whether to accept a settlement offer. For example, see *Johnson v. Nextel Communications, Inc.*, 660 F.3d 131 (2nd Cir. 2011).

One of the most important court decisions concerning paralegals is in the area of statutory fees. The landmark decision of *Missouri v. Jenkins*, 491 U.S. 274 (1989) upheld an award of lawyer's fees that included **compensation for paralegal time** under the federal civil rights statute. The lower court had awarded fees that included compensation for paralegal time at hourly market rates. But the state of Missouri contended, first, that the statute provided only for attorneys' fees, not paralegal fees, and second, that if paralegal time were to be compensable, it should be compensated at cost, not at a market rate that covered overhead and included a profit to the law firm. In upholding the award, the Court construed the attorneys' fee statute broadly, finding that it did include paralegal fees, and followed the long-standing measure of market rates as the appropriate one for setting paralegal fees. In an important case that was decided more recently, *Richlin Security Service Co. v. Chertoff*, 553 U.S. 571 (2008), the U.S. Supreme Court applied *Missouri v. Jenkins* to a case brought under the federal Equal Access to Justice Act. In that case, the appeals court for the Federal Circuit had disallowed compensation for paralegal time at market rates, pointing to the fact that the federal statute was not the same as the one in *Missouri v. Jenkins*. Both cases are included later in this chapter, as are several other cases in which paralegal fees were at issue.

Missouri v. Jenkins was a critical case for paralegals; a court decision that had gone the other way would have acted as a disincentive to the utilization of paralegal services by firms that work on cases for which attorneys' fees may be awarded and may have called into question the common practice of billing for paralegal time at market rates. Thousands of cases awarding paralegal fees as part of attorneys' fee awards have been decided in state and federal trial courts since *Missouri v. Jenkins*. This case was also the first U.S. Supreme Court decision in which the role of paralegals was discussed at any length; the court endorsed the practice as a praiseworthy innovation and an effective means of containing the costs of legal services. Finally, this case gave guidance in what had been in dispute throughout the country; several state and some federal appeals courts had interpreted attorney fee statutes contrary to the holding in *Missouri v. Jenkins*, some finding the statutes not to include paralegal fees at all, and some applying the cost, not market measure, to calculate the award.

After *Missouri v. Jenkins*, several states amended **statutes and/or court rules** to clarify that attorney fee awards include paralegal fees at market rates (*e.g.*, Alaska, Arizona, California, Florida, New Jersey, Illinois, Indiana, New York, Oklahoma, and Ohio). State courts have also ruled that lawyer fee awards in administrative agencies may include compensation for paralegal time at market rates. See, for example, *Schroff, Inc. v. Taylor-Peterson*, 732 A.2d 719 (R.I. 1999), and *Vitac Corp. v. Workers' Compensation Appeals Board*, 854 A.2d 481 (Pa. 2004). Many state supreme courts have followed the lead of the U.S. Supreme Court in *Missouri v. Jenkins* in interpreting their own fee award statutes. See, for example, *Blair v. Ing.*, 31 P.3d 184 (Haw. 2001), *Riemers v. State*, 2008 N.D. 101, 750 N.W.2d 407 (2008), and *Crawford v. City of New London*, No. 3:11-cv-1371 (D. Conn, 3-12-2015).

A few courts have also tied the award of fees to **prequalifying the paralegal**, such as probate courts that require paralegals to be registered with the court by providing background information and certification by the supervising lawyers that the paralegal has appropriate training, education, and work experience. (See, *e.g.*, Franklin County Probate Court, Franklin County, Ohio, Local Rule 75.5.) In a California case, a court determined a fee petition that included compensation for paralegal time would not cover the time of employees who did not meet the statutory minimum qualifications for paralegals. Although this is an important case tying paralegal regulation to fee awards, other California courts have not always followed this reasoning and appellate decisions have not definitively addressed this issue.

Most states that disallowed compensation for paralegal time in fee awards did not object conceptually to the notion that paralegal time is compensable, but asserted that the legislature, not the courts, should make the determination of whether attorneys' fees should also cover paralegal work. Further, some states have found that not all fee award statutes were intended to compensate lawyers for the time of paralegals. For example, many states have statutes that allow one or two lawyers to be appointed to handle criminal cases, particularly capital cases, at the state's expense. Some courts have held that these statutes do not authorize an additional expense for paralegal time. (See, for example, *Moncier v. Ferrell*, 990 S.W.2d 710 (Tenn. 1998).)

Federal courts have interpreted federal statutes to allow paralegal fees under *Missouri v. Jenkins*. And several **federal attorney fee statutes** have been amended to provide for the award of paralegal fees, including the U.S. Bankruptcy Code (11 U.S.C. §330); the Sherman Antitrust Act and Clayton Act (15 U.S.C. §1); and the Surface Mining Control and Reclamation Act of 1977 (30 U.S.C. §1270). After the decision in *Richlin*, it is doubtful that any federal courts would refuse to apply the reasoning of *Missouri v. Jenkins* to fee awards under other federal statutes.

Some federal bankruptcy courts have disallowed fees for paralegal time to bankruptcy trustees, who are entitled to compensation under the Bankruptcy Code, which compensation is capped. One of the definitive cases on the subject is *In re Jenkins*, 130 F.3d 1335 (9th Cir. 1997), which affirmed a Bankruptcy Appellate Panel decision that bankruptcy courts may award compensation for trustee duties performed by paralegals employed by the trustee, provided that the total compensation does not exceed the statutory cap. See also *In re Garcia*, 335 B.R. 717 (9th Cir. BAP 2005). See *Perez v. Cate* at the end of this chapter for an appellate court decision applying the cap to paralegal fees in a case brought under the Prison Litigation Reform Act.

An important issue in statutory **fee petitions** involves the kind of information that must be supplied to the court to justify the award of compensation for paralegal work. Some trial courts have denied or reduced paralegal fees on the grounds that the work done by paralegals was clerical in nature and not the kind of work intended to be covered by an award of attorneys' fees. Others have objected when the fee request did not contain adequate information about the qualifications of the paralegals or the nature of their work. Some courts have reduced the amounts requested for paralegal fees because the petitions were not sufficiently documented, or the reported time was duplicative or excessive. Some courts request more information about the customary practice of billing clients separately for paralegal time and about the market rates charged for their services.

Some statutes or court rules set forth requirements that paralegals must meet to qualify for compensation in attorney fee awards. For example, local court rules for bankruptcy courts in the Northern District of California require that the services would have to have been performed by a lawyer if not done by the paralegal and that the paralegal be "specially trained" or a law student and "not primarily a secretary or clerical worker."

In general, documentation supplied to a court when seeking fees should include:

- **credentials and experience** of the paralegal, including college education and degrees granted; formal paralegal education; years of legal and other related work experience and nature of that experience; and certification or compliance with statutory, court rule, or bar guidelines for paralegals.
- **detailed descriptions** of the work performed, including the number of hours spent (in small increments) and the exact nature of the work, which must be professional in nature and not clerical (*i.e.*, would have been done by a lawyer if it were not for the paralegal).
- information on **firm and market practices and rates**, including paralegal compensation, overhead allocated to paralegals, hourly rates, and comparison data on practices and rates in the legal community.

Additionally, it is preferable for a firm to have a **range of rates** for paralegals, just as they do for lawyers, depending on their experience and the level of work they are performing. As with lawyer work, not all paralegal work requires the same level of sophistication and expertise. If key matters are not covered in fee petitions, courts may deny the award or reduce the amount of the time or fee. For example, courts have objected to paralegals being charged at a rate that was slightly higher than the rate charged for new associates.

Another caution concerns alternative fee agreements and statutory fee awards. A court may not allow a firm to use **blended rates** in its request for fees. See, for example, *Dept. of Trans. v. Robbins and Robbins, Inc.*, 700 So. 2d 782 (Fla. App. 5th Dist. 1997). In reversing a lower court decision on a fee award, the court said:

> [T]he trial court improperly included the paralegal hours as part of the attorneys' hours to get a "blended" effective hourly rate. The trial court

counted the paralegal hours and attorneys' hours to obtain the lodestar. Instead of separately awarding paralegal time, ordinarily billed at $75 per hour, the trial court mixed paralegal and attorney time, then awarded the firm more than $300 per hour for paralegal time. . . .

[T]his court has never held that paralegal time can be "blended" with attorney time to set a reasonable attorney rate. Further, it is not logical to use a paralegal to help on a client's case because it is cheaper for the client, then seek to recoup the paralegal time at an attorney rate. . . . Coupling that with the admission that the paralegal would not reap the benefit of this windfall shows that this "blending" is simply another method to increase the attorneys' fees in the case. Upon remand, the trial court will separate out the paralegal time . . . and multiply the number of paralegal hours by the hourly rate of $75.

Finally, a few but growing number of courts have **reduced fee awards** for lawyer time when the work billed at the lawyer's rate could have been done by a paralegal. This line of cases demonstrates the growing appreciation within the judiciary of the contribution paralegals make to improving the cost-effectiveness of and access to legal services. See, e.g., *In re Music Merchants, Inc.*, 208 B.R. 944 (9th Cir. BAP 1997) and *Interfaith Community Org. v. Honeywell Int'l, Inc.*, 336 F. Supp. 2d 270 (U.S.D.C., D.N.J. 2004), where the court said that a lawyer should not be compensated for clerical work at paralegal rates and, likewise, that a lawyer should not be compensated for "merely clerical tasks such as moving furniture or stacking boxes." See *Metro Data Systems, Inc. v. Durango Systems, Inc.*, 597 F. Supp. 244 (1984); *Lipsett v. Blanco*, 975 F.2d 934 (2d Cir. 1992); *Rodriguez-Hernandez v. Miranda-Vales*, 132 F.3d 848 (1st Cir. 1998); *Moralez v. Whole Foods Market*, No. C 12-01072 CRB (N.D. Cal. 7-30-2013); *Santiago v. Equable Ascent Financial Co.*, 2013 WL 3498079 (N.D. Cal. 7-12-2013); and *Beaulieu v. Colvin*, No. 2016 WL 675646 (D. Me. 1-28-2016). In a case that follows this line, the court stated,

> Plaintiffs stated that the Magistrate Judge should have utilized the standard identified by the United States Supreme Court in *Missouri v. Jenkins*, 491 U.S. 274 (1989), that if certain work performed by attorneys could have (or should have) been performed by paralegals, the proper method of awarding fees is to award those hours at the paralegal rate. (Id. (citing *Jenkins*, 491 U.S. at 288 n. 10).) As a result, Plaintiffs asserted that the court should award Myers fees at the paralegal rate for those tasks deemed appropriate for a paralegal and award her attorney rate for work normally performed by associate attorneys. (Id. at p. 15.) After careful review of Plaintiffs' attorneys' time submissions . . . , the court agrees with the Magistrate Judge that Plaintiffs' attorneys expended more hours than reasonably necessary to litigate this matter.

Glidewell v. Greenville, Civil Action No. 6:09-01932-JMC (D.S.C. 3-20-2012).

In one rare decision, a court refused to reduce the fee award on this basis in a case brought under the Age Discrimination in Employment Act, reasoning that the lawyer was a sole practitioner and did not employ anyone to whom he could delegate paralegal work. See *Jordan v. CCH, Inc.*, 230 F. Supp. 2d 603 (U.S.D.C., E.D. Pa. 2002).

The American Bar Association has endorsed fee awards and billing for paralegal time. In 1993, the American Bar Association House of Delegates adopted a resolution "support[ing] the award of legal assistant/paralegal fees to law firms or attorneys who represent prevailing parties in a lawsuit where statutes or current case law allow for the recovery of attorney fees." This resolution supports Guideline 8 of the ABA Model Guidelines for the Utilization of Paralegal Services, which endorses both recovery for paralegal time in statutory attorney fee matters and the billing of clients for paralegal time.

REVIEW QUESTIONS

1. What are fixed fees? For what kinds of work are they typically used?
2. What are contingency fees? When are they usually used?
3. What are the traditional objections to contingency fees? What are the most important modern limitations on contingency fees? What is a sliding-scale contingency fee?
4. What are hourly fees? In what kinds of legal matters are they typically used? Is this kind of fee on the rise or decline? Why?
5. What is the authority for paralegal time to be billed separately to clients? What is the advantage to the client?
6. Why are some firms starting to use alternatives to hourly billing? What kinds of new fee arrangements are being developed as firms diverge from hourly billing?
7. What factors may be taken into account in determining if a fee is unreasonable or excessive?
8. What is an illegal fee? Give an example.
9. What kinds of billing abuses sometimes take place in law firms, and why? What can happen to lawyers who engage in improper billing practices?
10. What is double billing? Is it ethical?
11. What kinds of expenses can be billed to clients?
12. What are a lawyer's duties relating to the fee arrangement when he or she undertakes representation?
13. Under what circumstances must a fee arrangement be in writing? What should be covered in the fee agreement?
14. Can a paralegal tell a client what the firm's fees are? Can a paralegal negotiate a fee arrangement with a client? What is the paralegal role with regard to fees?

15. What is the difference between a retainer and an advance fee? How are these fees treated when received by the firm?
16. What is unbundling of legal services, and how should it be reflected in a fee agreement?
17. What is the purpose of "fee shifting"?
18. Give some examples of fee-shifting statutes.
19. What was the holding in *Missouri v. Jenkins?* Why is this decision so important for paralegals? What was the decision in *Richlin?* Why is this decision important?
20. What information should be included in a request to the court for paralegal fees as part of an award of attorneys' fees?
21. What are three reasons that the amount for paralegal fees in a court-ordered fee might be denied or reduced?
22. Can a lawyer's fee request be reduced if the lawyer does paralegal work? Clerical work? Why or why not?

DISCUSSION QUESTIONS AND HYPOTHETICALS

1. Do you believe that the special restrictions on contingency fees (for example, in criminal and divorce cases) are warranted? Why or why not?
2. Do you believe the ethics rules should require all fee agreements to be in writing? Why or why not?
3. Should the percentage of attorneys' fees in contingency cases be limited by statutes or ethics codes? Why or why not? What do you think is the reason for limiting the amount of contingency fees in medical malpractice cases? Do you agree with this reasoning?
4. Do you think the trend toward using alternative methods of fee structures — for instance, task-based, value, or premium billing — in lieu of traditional hourly rates is a good one? Why or why not? How do you think that the divergence from time-based billing will affect the use of paralegal services?
5. What would you do if you became aware that several associates in your firm were padding their hours? What if paralegals were doing this?
6. What would you do if your firm expected you to bill 1,800 hours annually (on a calendar billing year), and you knew by September of that year that your hours were going to fall short?
7. What would you do if your firm expected you to bill 1,500 hours a year, but you were not being delegated enough work to keep you busy for that many hours?
8. What would you do if you discovered that you and an associate were doing the same work on a case, and the client was being billed for the duplicative work?

9. In an article in the *ABA Journal*, lawyer-author Scott Turow said: "Who ever says to a client that my billing system on its face rewards me at your expense for slow problem solving, duplication of effort, featherbedding the workforce and compulsiveness—not to mention fuzzy math?" Do you agree with this assessment of the hourly billing model? Why or why not?
10. What would you do if your supervising lawyer continually wrote off your time as excessive, diminishing your billable hours?
11. What would you do if a client called and wanted to know the firm's hourly rates to handle certain kinds of legal work?
12. What would you do if you worked for a sole practitioner, and a prospective personal injury client with a good case came into the office seeking representation, but the lawyer was out of town for two weeks?
13. What would you do if you discovered that a lawyer was inflating the costs on clients' bills by charging for expenses that were not related to the matter or had not been agreed upon by the client?
14. You are flying across the country for client X and en route do some work for client Y. How do you bill your time?
15. What will a court do if it gets a fee petition showing that a lawyer did paralegal work and is requesting lawyer's billing rates for this time? What if two paralegals did the same work and requested fees for all the time spent?
16. Would a court award paralegal fees for time spent filing documents? Organizing documents? Drafting documents? Summarizing documents? What is the basis for your conclusion?
17. Analyze the definitions of "unreasonable" and "unconscionable." What is the difference? What do you think the most appropriate ethical standard should be for legal fees? (For a start on this discussion, see Diener, K. W., A Battle for Reason: The Unconscionable Attorney-Client Fee Agreement, *Journal of The Professional Lawyer* 129 (2016).
18. Do you think the United States should have the kind of two-way fee shifting that England and Canada have? Why or why not?

RESEARCH PROJECTS AND ASSIGNMENTS

1. In a fee dispute, the client, who does not want to pay the whole bill, refuses to pay for paralegal time because it was not covered in the fee agreement. What should the outcome be if the matter is decided by a court? For one court's opinion, see *Updike, Kelly & Spellacy v. Beckett*, 269 Conn. 813, 850 A.2d 145 (2004).
2. Outline the arguments in the *Missouri v. Jenkins* majority opinion and dissent on the award of paralegal fees in attorney fee awards. Which side do you find more convincing, and why? Outline the arguments for charging paralegal fees at market rate as opposed to cost. Which do you find more convincing, and why?

3. Were there cases on paralegal fees in your state and your federal circuit before *Missouri v. Jenkins?* Are they supportive of paralegal fees awards or not? Have there been any cases on paralegal fee awards in your jurisdiction since *Missouri v. Jenkins?*
4. Are there any statutes or court rules in your jurisdiction that provide for paralegal fee awards as part of attorney fees awards? Check the Probate Code, for example.
5. If you are interested in paralegals who work in administrative practice, read the *Vitac* and *Schroff* decisions cited earlier in this chapter and brief them for the class. Do the same principles that apply in civil litigation also apply to fee awards in administrative agencies?
6. A federal district court judge said in one fee award case, "Assigning two partners to prepare the same witness for deposition approaches the definition of 'chutzpah.'" For an amusing read about the ways in which courts examine fee petitions, see *Microsoft Corp. v. United Computer Resources of NJ, Inc.*, 216 F. Supp. 383 (N.J. 2002). Be sure to read footnote 13, which defines "chutzpah" and cites other famous judges who have used this Yiddish term.
7. Do any of the state and local bars in your jurisdiction have ethics rules on billing practices? If so, what do these opinions suggest?
8. Do you think that firms should be compensated for paralegal time that was initially volunteered? What are the arguments on both sides? See *Sundance v. Municipal Court*, 192 Cal. App. 3d 268, 237 Cal. Rptr. 269 (1987) and *Rickley v. Goodfriend*, 207 Cal. App. 4th 1528, 145 Cal. Rptr. 13 (2012).
9. Would a court award fees to a "paralegal" who is not working under the supervision of a lawyer? See *Gross v. Perrysburg Exempted Village School*, 306 F. Supp. 2d 716 (U.S.D.C., N.D. Ohio 2004), where the court made this distinction in a decision under the Individuals with Disabilities Act fee-shifting provision.
10. Do you think that sole practitioners who do not employ paralegals should have their fees reduced in fee awards if they petition for compensation for paralegal work they have done at lawyers' rates? What are the arguments for and against? What if they cannot afford to hire paralegals? Read the relevant cases cited in this chapter where lawyers' hourly rates were reduced because they were doing paralegal work and see what patterns you find.
11. It is said in many fee award cases that paralegal fees are recoverable only to the extent that the paralegal performs work that would otherwise have to be done by a lawyer. Do you agree with this reasoning? Why or why not? What kinds of tasks might not be strictly "lawyer" work but are not clerical either? Is this classification about the nature of legal work immutable, or might it change over time? For guidance, see *Williams v. R.W. Cannon, Inc.*, 657 F. Supp. 2d 1302 (S.D. Fla. 2009), and *Gross v. Perrysburg Exempted Village School Dist.*, 306 F. Supp. 2d 726 (N.D. Ohio 2004).

12. Lawyers who do not delegate or supervise effectively can find their fee awards reduced when there is duplicative work or excessive time spent on projects. For an example of too much time spent researching by a paralegal, see *In re Arabia*, 270 Kan. 742, 19 P.3d 113 (2001). What does this case tell you about how you need to interact with your supervisor?

D. Fee Splitting, Referral Fees, and Partnerships Between Nonlawyers and Lawyers

Ethics rules in every state carefully control the way in which lawyers and nonlawyers are compensated from fees that are collected by lawyers. These rules are designed with a number of important policies in mind: to prevent the unauthorized practice of law; to guard against interference with the lawyer's independent professional judgment about client matters; and to discourage unethical direct solicitation of clients by agents of the lawyer.

Ethics codes have long limited the **splitting of fees** between or among lawyers who are not members of the same firm. ABA Model Rule 1.5(e) permits a division of fees if (1) the division is in proportion to services, or the client agrees in writing and the lawyers assume joint responsibility; (2) the client agrees to the arrangement, including the share that each receives, and the agreement is confirmed in writing; and (3) the fee is reasonable. Some states require only that the client be informed and not object to the arrangement. (For more analysis of lawyer-to-lawyer referral fees, see ABA Formal Opinions 474 and 475 (2016).)

The earlier ABA Model Code was more conservative, and several states followed it, interpreting it to mean that a lawyer may not pay a **referral fee** or a portion of a client's fee to another lawyer simply for referring a case. Referral fees like these have long been thought to be unprofessional and to increase the cost to the client. However, a growing number of states (California, Connecticut, Kansas, Massachusetts, Pennsylvania, and Texas, for example) have rules that permit "forwarding fees" or that exclude the requirement that the fee division be proportionate to services, thereby effectively allowing referral fees. Proponents of referral fees say that they serve the client's interests by encouraging a thoughtful referral to a competent lawyer and point out that clients are protected by the part of the rule that requires the fee to be reasonable. One practice that is questionable under the rules has been used by the company Avvo, which collects fees for services on a flat rate and pays the lawyer a small portion of the fee. (See South Carolina Bar Ethics Advisory Opinion 16-06, which states that this practice violates Rules 5.4 and 7.2.)

Referral fees involving nonlawyers are prohibited under ABA Model 7.2(b), which prohibits payment for recommending the lawyer's services except for payment for advertising and to qualified legal service plans or referral services. All states prohibit referral fees paid to nonlawyers, including paralegals, and prohibit fee-splitting between lawyers and nonlawyers, including paralegals. ABA Model Rule 5.4(a) is similar, specifically prohibiting the sharing of fees between lawyers and nonlawyers. This provision also prohibits lawyers from being influenced in making professional judgments by one who recommends their employment. Exceptions to fee splitting are allowed for lawyers to pay for the purchase of the practice of a deceased, disabled, or disappeared lawyer and for lawyers to share court-awarded fees with a nonprofit corporation that retained or recommended the lawyer.

Most important for paralegals is the provision that allows nonlawyer employees to be included in **compensation and retirement plans** based in whole or in part on profit sharing (Model Rule 5.4(a)(3)). The ABA Model Guidelines follow the standard prohibitions against fee splitting with nonlawyers in Guideline 9. As noted in the comment to that guideline, virtually all states that have adopted guidelines on paralegals have acknowledged the ethics rule on fee splitting. State guidelines use different language to interpret this restriction, making some profit-sharing plans acceptable in some states and not in others. Most emphasize that retirement plans and bonuses based in part on a firm's overall profitability are acceptable. Some are specific, prohibiting profit sharing that "by advance agreement is contingent on the profitability" of the practice. This language means that a firm cannot pay a paralegal from a profit-sharing plan that was agreed on at the time of hire to include a bonus if the firm has a profitable year. States sometimes couple this prohibition with language indicating that a paralegal may be paid a bonus based on the value of their contribution to the firm's practice. Most states are more flexible, allowing profit sharing as long as it is not tied to a specific case or the paralegal's role in bringing in the case.

An early ABA ethics opinion endorsed the inclusion of nonlawyers in profit-based compensation and retirement plans (ABA Informal Opinion 1440 (1979)). Several opinions give advice on compensation plans that are tied to profitability. For example, Mississippi Ethics Opinion 154 (1989) endorsed a bonus plan that compensated paralegals and associates whose billable hours exceeded a set minimum. Iowa Ethics Opinion 90-9 (1990) allows firms to pay paralegals a percentage of total firm income as an incentive. Virginia Ethics Opinion 885 (1987) endorses paralegal compensation based on a percentage of profits from collections plus a base salary. Virginia Ethics Opinion 806 (1986) endorses secretarial bonuses based on annual firm profits. The Utah bar endorses compensation plans based on profit sharing, but not with freelance paralegals (Utah Ethics Opinion 02-07). Oregon Ethics Opinion 505 (1985) and Maryland Ethics Opinion 84-103 (1984) advise that lawyers may not compensate paralegals on a contingent basis or only when fees are collected from a client. Maryland and New York warn that profit-sharing plans may not be tied to referrals or solicitation of clients (New York State Bar Association 733 (2000) and Maryland Ethics Opinion 86-57). See also Philadelphia Ethics Opinion 80-14 (1980) and Virginia Ethics Opinion 767 (1986).

Maryland Ethics Opinion 84-103 (1984) prohibits compensation calculated on a percentage of the recovery in a case. New York's Nassau County Ethics Opinion 87-38 (1987) states that a lawyer may not split fees with a paralegal who brings in clients, interviews them, and prepares legal documents under attorney supervision. The Oregon State Bar Legal Ethics Committee states that compensation may not be calculated on a contingency basis or paid only when fees are recovered (Oregon Ethics Opinion 505 (1985)).

The ethics rules and the court cases and ethics opinions interpreting them make it clear that it is not acceptable for an attorney to pay a nonlawyer for **referring a case**, by means of a direct bonus, increase in compensation, or payment of a portion of a fee received from the client. They also make it clear that a lawyer may not pay a nonlawyer, under any circumstances, a percentage of a fee from a specific client or case. A "bonus" tied to a particular client or case is not acceptable. However, it is appropriate for a firm to increase compensation, to pay bonuses, and to establish a retirement or other deferred compensation plan based on the firm's *overall* profitability. This kind of arrangement breaks the direct link between the payment and a specific client, eliminating concerns about unauthorized practice and incentives to solicit clients or to settle cases even when it is not in the best interests of the client. Bonus plans are commonly used by firms to reward paralegals for their contribution to making the firm profitable.

A few **exceptions** to the prohibition against fee splitting with nonlawyers do exist. As mentioned earlier, fees may be paid to the estate of a deceased lawyer. A lawyer may pay a fee to an approved lawyer referral service. Lawyer referral services are regulated by ethics rules and usually must be approved by the state bar or some other entity. Many are run by local bar associations. Lawyer referral services charge either a flat fee or a percentage of fees. Another exception is the prepaid legal plan, under which a member pays a fee for entitlement to a range of services, and the fee is divided between the lawyer and the plan sponsor. All jurisdictions permit such fee splitting when the plan is nonprofit; some specifically prohibit lawyer participation in profit-making prepaid legal services plans. Remember from Chapter 6 that some states prohibit a lawyer from using unapproved Internet services that match lawyers and clients under the principles against fee splitting.

The same theories underlying the prohibitions on fee splitting with nonlawyers form the basis for rules prohibiting lawyers from entering into **partnerships with nonlawyers**. ABA Model Rule 5.4(b) prohibits a lawyer from forming a partnership with a nonlawyer "if any of the activities of the partnership consist of the practice of law." This rule is sometimes implicated when lawyers are disciplined for aiding in the unauthorized practice of law, fee splitting, and unlawful solicitation if the arrangement with the nonlawyer looks like a partnership or business venture where the nonlawyer has an equal or greater voice in the operation of the firm.

The District of Columbia allows nonlawyer partnerships for other professionals (not paralegals) and the State of Washington allows Limited License Legal Technicians (LLLTs) to be partners in law firms. Most states that have guidelines for the utilization of paralegals reiterate the rule prohibiting a lawyer from forming a partnership with a nonlawyer. See Illinois Guideline (D), Kansas Guideline VII, Kentucky Supreme Court Rule 3.700 Sub-Rule 5, Michigan Guideline III(3), Missouri Guideline II(b), New Hampshire Supreme Court Rule 35 Sub-Rule 5, New Mexico Guideline V, North Carolina Guideline 8, and Rhode Island Guideline VIII.

Because of the changing nature of law practice, the lack of such restrictions in other countries, and the desire of some law firms, especially large law firms, to be full-service providers for their large corporate clients, a movement to modify this prohibition took off in the 1980s. The District of Columbia adopted its own version of Rule 5.4 in 1990, providing that "a lawyer may practice law in a partnership or other form of organization in which a financial interest is held or managerial authority is exercised by an individual nonlawyer who performs professional services which assist the organization in providing legal services to clients. . . ." The rule has specified limitations and the comment makes it clear that paralegals are not eligible to become partners. The comment differentiates between nonlawyer "assistants" and nonlawyer "professionals," specifically naming economists, psychologists or psychiatric social workers, lobbyists, certified public accountants, and professional managers and executive directors as examples of acceptable participants under the rule. The movement to allow "alternative business structures" that would allow nonlawyer ownership, management, and/or investment and permit "multi-disciplinary practice" has picked up some steam in the last year, as the organized bar seeks to develop new ways to deliver legal services. In April 2016, the ABA Commission on the Future of Legal Services published an issues paper on ***alternative business structures***. This paper cites the lack of evidence for harm in these structures and seeks comments before developing recommendations for changes to the ethics rules that currently prohibit this business model.

Two states have recently established alternative business structures. In 2020, the Utah Supreme Court voted to begin regulating nontraditional legal businesses (alternative business structures or ABS) and legal service providers (alternative legal providers or ALP) in Utah's legal regulatory sandbox, enabling entities to develop and test innovative legal

Alternative business structure
An entity that provides legal services and has nonlawyer ownership, managers, or decision-makers in the business.

services methods that are considered the unauthorized practice of law or could not otherwise be offered under the state's existing Rules of Professional Conduct. All ABS and ALP entities must be approved by the Utah Supreme Court. The Utah legal regulatory sandbox is currently authorized through 2027. (See Utah Supreme Court Standing Order No. 15.) In 2021, Arizona adopted a similar but more restrictive model. The Arizona Supreme Court established an Alternative Business Structure (ABS) program that allows a business entity to include nonlawyers who have an economic interest or decision-making authority in a firm and provide legal services in accord with Arizona Supreme Court Rules 31 and 31.1(c). The Arizona ABS program is "rooted in the idea that entrepreneurial lawyers and nonlawyers would pilot a range of different business forms" that will ultimately improve access to justice and the delivery of legal services. Complaints against Arizona ABS entities are received, investigated, and prosecuted by the State Bar of Arizona in the same manner as complaints against lawyers. (See Arizona Code of Judicial Administration §7-209.)

E. Client Funds and Property

The mishandling of client funds is one of the leading causes of disciplinary sanctions imposed on lawyers. The typical scenario is a sole practitioner with cash-flow problems who "borrows" funds from a client trust account to pay operational expenses. Sometimes, a shortfall in a client trust account is the result of sloppy accounting and management practices. In either case, when clients cannot get their money promptly, they may file a complaint with the state or local bar and maybe even the local prosecutor's office.

The most important ethics rule related to client funds is the requirement to keep the client's money separate from the lawyer's, in other words, not to commingle client and law firm funds. The rule against commingling also applies to funds from third parties held by the lawyer. This rule means that lawyers must have a separate bank account that contains only client funds. Some clients may warrant having their own individual **client trust account** if the lawyer handles large amounts of funds or transactions for them. See ABA Model Rule 1.15(a).

Lawyers hold client funds for many reasons. Client trust accounts may contain estate or trust distributions, funds to be distributed at a real estate closing or on settlement of a matter, advance fees, and awards of which the attorney is owed a portion under a fee agreement.

If funds are to be divided between the client and the lawyer, the funds must remain in the client trust account until the lawyer earns them and an accounting is prepared for the client, indicating how the funds are to be divided under the fee agreement. In the event a dispute over the

Client trust account
Bank account set up by a lawyer in which funds are kept that belong to one or more clients.

fee arises, the amount in dispute must be kept in the client trust account until the dispute is resolved. See ABA Model Rule 1.15(e). A minority of jurisdictions allow advance fees to be deposited into a lawyer's operating account. Remember that advances are different from retainers, which are nonrefundable.

Most jurisdictions have detailed guidelines or rules on handling client trust accounts, including what kinds of journals, ledgers, accounting, fee agreements, bills, registers, and other records must be maintained. The ABA has Model Rules on Client Trust Account Records, which have been adopted by several jurisdictions.

Most states have a program under which the interest on certain client trust accounts is used to fund the bar disciplinary system, client security fund, or legal services for the poor, specified by the state's bar, legislature, or supreme court. Well over $100 million a year is raised annually through these programs, known as **IOLTA** (Interest on Lawyers' Trust Accounts). IOLTA programs can be mandatory, voluntary, or "opt-out." A voluntary program means that a lawyer must affirmatively decide to participate; an opt-out program means that all lawyers participate unless they affirmatively declare *not* to. The plans ordinarily cover only client funds that are too small in amount or are to be held for too brief a period to earn interest for the client. Most jurisdictions have voluntary or opt-out plans, or some hybrid of the two. A growing number of plans are being converted to mandatory status.

The funds collected from IOLTA plans are substantial. Each state has its own rules about how these funds are expended. For example, Minnesota's plan allocates the funds to "the poor, law-related education and projects to improve the administration of justice." North Carolina designates its funds for lawyer referral services, attorney grievance and discipline, and a client security fund to reimburse clients for losses caused by the dishonest conduct of lawyers when no other recourse is available. Arizona, New York, Ohio, and Washington State utilize the interest on IOLTA funds for civil legal aid programs.

The constitutionality of IOLTA programs has been upheld after a series of challenges. Those who disputed the legitimacy of the plans asserted that clients have property rights in the interest generated in these accounts, which rights are violated when the interest income, however small, is not paid to the clients. In *Brown v. Legal Foundation of Washington*, 538 U.S. 216, 123 S. Ct. 1406 (2003), the U.S. Supreme Court upheld the constitutionality of the Washington IOLTA plan, finding that there was not a "taking" under the clause of the Constitution that allows for the state to confiscate private property for public use. Further, the Court found that if there were a taking, the interest income that was "confiscated" was clearly being used for a valid public purpose. Finally, the Court went on to say that the amount of just compensation that the client should get was nothing because the amount earned on an individual deposit was either extremely small or nothing.

IOLTA
Interest on Lawyers' Trust Accounts. A program under which the interest from lawyers' client trust accounts, which is too small to pay to clients, is collected by banks and used by bar associations and/or courts to fund law-related programs.

E. Client Funds and Property

Commingling of funds is a basis for disciplinary action, as is ***conversion of funds***, a much more serious breach. Commingling refers only to mixing client funds with those of the lawyer and does not require any intent to harm the client or actual harm to the client. Conversion is the misappropriation of the client's funds for the lawyer's use. Conversion takes place when a lawyer draws funds from the client trust account for personal use or for payment of firm expenses.

Disciplinary bodies are not sympathetic to the defenses that lawyers sometimes use in such cases, including the intention to return the funds or even the actual restoration of the funds. A lawyer's personal or financial problems or the mismanagement of the firm are also not legitimate excuses; in fact, they may be considered aggravating circumstances because they indicate that the lawyer may not be able to handle financial matters well and could repeat this kind of conduct.

Lawyers and paralegals also have a duty to **protect client property** other than money. This duty to safeguard usually requires that property be placed in a safe deposit box. Property covered by these rules typically includes titles to real estate or valuable personal property, jewelry, and securities. If a safe deposit box is shared with other clients, the items must be identified and labeled. ABA Model Rule 1.15(a).

Lawyers have a duty to keep **accurate and complete records** of client funds and property. The ABA Model Rule provides for a specific number of years (five) that records must be kept. Model Rule 1.15(a). Several states have different periods (usually six or seven years) and more specific provisions on recordkeeping. A few jurisdictions provide for random audits of client trust accounts and some for annual certification or verification of compliance with recordkeeping rules. Many states provide for audits in conjunction with disciplinary actions. The State Bar of California recently implemented the Client Trust Account Protection Program (CTAPP) to improve oversight and regulation of client trust accounts, including mandatory reporting requirements for lawyers. Failure to comply with the CTAPP accounting and reporting obligations will lead to mandatory corrective action and repeated noncompliance can result in disciplinary action. During the first half of 2023, 1,600 California lawyers were administratively suspended and enrolled with the State Bar as "inactive," meaning they are not allowed to practice law. (See California Rules of Professional Conduct Rule 1.15.)

Duties specified in the ethics rules are **to notify the client of the receipt of funds** or property, **to deliver client funds or property promptly**, and **to provide a full accounting** to the client on request. ABA Model Rule 1.15(d). The duties to notify, to deliver, and to account for client funds are most often breached because of lax office procedures, but sometimes are a result of a more egregious violation, such as conversion of client funds. If a third party has a claim on client funds held by the lawyer, the lawyer may have a duty not to turn over the funds to the client until the various parties' rights are clarified. The notion of

Commingling of funds
The mixing of client funds with lawyers' funds.

Conversion of funds
The tortious deprivation of another's property without justification or authorization.

what is "prompt" delivery is sometimes an issue in disciplinary actions. The best practice certainly requires action within the month in which funds are received, if not more quickly. Regular periodic accountings to clients (monthly or quarterly) are advisable, rather than accountings only on client request.

All jurisdictions also have some special rules that require attorneys to turn over documents, funds, money, and unearned advanced fees on **termination of representation**. ABA Model Rule 1.16(d) so provides, emphasizing the lawyer's obligation to protect the client's interests and extending the lawyer's duty after representation ends.

One final matter in this area is the handling of a client file after work on the matter is completed. Firms should have policies on **retention of files**, turning files over to clients, destroying files, and ensuring security for files maintained in off-site storage. The client file is generally considered to be the property of the client; therefore, the lawyer cannot destroy old files without first informing the client and getting permission or giving the client the chance to keep the file. Destruction practices should be specified in policies, to guard against the destruction of important documents that should be retained, such as long-term legal agreements, wills, deeds, securities, and tax returns, and to ensure that all copies of documents meant for destruction are in fact destroyed—sometimes a challenge when one is working with electronic documents. It is good practice to include a provision about the handling of client files in the agreement for representation. The material in client files can also protect a lawyer if a malpractice suit is filed, so the statute of limitations should guide the length of time that detailed records of the legal work are kept. Finally, while most documents in legal practice are now in electronic form, converting hard copy files to electronic format requires the approval of the client in some jurisdictions. Care should be taken when doing this kind of conversion to preserve hard copies of critical legal documents like wills and deeds that have original signatures. For guidance, see ABA Formal Opinion 471 (2015), on duties when representation is terminated before a matter is completed, and District of Columbia Bar Association Ethics Opinion 357 (2010) about converting documents to electronic form.

The rules governing the handling of client funds and property are especially important to paralegals in small law firms, where they often must implement instructions relating to client funds and may be delegated substantial responsibility for handling these matters. Checks or property often come directly to the lawyer, who will instruct the paralegal on how to handle the money or property. In small firms, a paralegal may perform some of the accounting and recordkeeping functions. Paralegals must know the rules well enough to identify improprieties and either to rectify them or to inform the supervising attorney. There is a split of authority on whether a paralegal may serve as signatory on client trust accounts; some states allow this practice and others do not. The ABA Model Rules on Client Trust Account Records require that it be the lawyer "or a person under the direct supervision of the lawyer" to sign (Rule 2(a)).

It is not unusual for a lawyer in trouble to blame a nonlawyer employee for poor office practices that resulted in the mishandling of client funds or commingling of client and lawyer funds. As noted above, most courts and disciplinary bodies are unsympathetic to this defense, as lawyers are expected to supervise nonlawyers and are responsible for their conduct. Reports of cases appear every year about paralegals or office managers embezzling money from lawyers, including a case in Florida a few years ago in which a lawyer (now disbarred) and his paralegal used $72,000 for personal expenses and vacations. NALA's Code does not address this area directly, but NFPA's ethics rules call on paralegals to be "scrupulous, thorough and honest" in handling client assets. NFPA Model Code of Ethics Professional Responsibility, EC-1.2(e).

REVIEW QUESTIONS

1. What are the rules about referral fees? What is the basis for these rules? Do the same rules apply to lawyers and paralegals?
2. What are the rules about fee splitting? Give several examples of payments to paralegals that violate these rules.
3. What kinds of retirement, bonus, and profit-sharing plans are permitted for paralegals under the ethics rules?
4. Why do the ethics rules prohibit lawyers from being partners with paralegals in a law practice?
5. What is the basis for the District of Columbia rules permitting nonlawyer partners? May paralegals become partners under this rule? Why or why not?
6. What led to the implementation of alternative business structures in Arizona and Utah?
7. What is a client trust account? What do the ethics rules require concerning client trust accounts?
8. What is IOLTA? What is a client security fund?
9. Describe the difference between the commingling and the conversion of funds. Which is more serious?
10. How might a paralegal violate ethics in the handling of client funds?
11. When a lawyer receives a check for a judgment or settlement and the case was taken on contingency, what should the paralegal working for the lawyer do with the check?
12. Do the facts that a lawyer is very busy, has high staff turnover, and has not had a bookkeeper in months mitigate against charges that the lawyer commingled funds?
13. What are the duties related to handling of client funds, files, and property when representation ceases?

> **DISCUSSION QUESTIONS AND HYPOTHETICALS**

1. Do you think the rules prohibiting fee splitting are well-founded? Why or why not? Do you think the rules should be different for lawyers and nonlawyers?
2. Do you think the rules prohibiting referral fees are well-founded? Why or why not?
3. Can a personal injury firm pay a $500 bonus for every case you bring in? Can you be paid one-third of the fee when the case settles?
4. What are the policy reasons behind the rule in most states prohibiting paralegals from becoming partners in law firms? Is this antiquated thinking? Is it fair? Do you think this rule should be changed? Why or why not?
5. What would you do if an attorney handed you a settlement check in a contingency case and asked you to deposit it in the firm's operating account?
6. Where should you keep the deed of trust to a client's real estate? In your desk? In the client file? Under the floorboard in your attic? Why or why not? What if the property were a valuable diamond ring? Stock certificates?
7. What would you do if you found out your firm was having temporary cash-flow problems because of uncollected receivables and had borrowed from client trust accounts to make the payroll?
8. What is wrong with a lawyer putting client funds in the firm's account if he or she plans to replace them in two days? Would it make any difference if the period were two weeks? If the client owed fees to the attorney? What if the lawyer was doing this for the benefit of another client and it did not benefit them in any way?
9. What would you do if your lawyer-employer, who was very careful about handling client funds, kept no records other than bank reports and withdrawal slips?
10. What would you do if you discovered that a settlement check had come in and been deposited six months ago but that the client had never been notified?
11. What would you do if you found several months-old checks from clients, insurance companies, and others in the bottom of a desk drawer?
12. Find the ABA Commission on the Future of Legal Services issues paper on alternative business structures and do an analysis and report for the class on its research and ideas. Research the history and development of the alternative business structure programs in Utah and Arizona. Which ethical rules in these states were amended to allow these new types of legal service providers?
13. Paralegal Helena Hill works for the Aston law firm on black lung cases. After prevailing in a case, the firm submits a fee petition that, among other things, shows the Altman Weil market rates for lawyers.

The petition includes a request for Helena's time and includes data about fees awarded in previous decisions. Time details were provided to the court. Aston keeps track of time in quarter-hour increments. What will the court decide about the fee award for Helena's time? (See *Eastern Associated Coal Corp. v. Dir., Office of Workers Compensation Programs*, Nos. 11-2038, 11-2380 (4th Cir. 2013).)

14. Paralegal Jorge Escobedo works for a personal injury firm. He is paid a salary and overtime plus a bonus that is based on the following formula: three-tenths of one percent of the gross recovery of cases that he works on. Is this bonus plan acceptable under the ethics rules? (For a case in point, see *In re Weigel*, 342 Wisc.2d 129, 817 N.W.2d 835 (2012).)

RESEARCH PROJECTS AND ASSIGNMENTS

1. Does your jurisdiction allow lawyers to pay or receive referral fees? Is it common practice?
2. Ask some lawyers and practicing paralegals what they think about lawyers forming partnerships with nonlawyers. Has your jurisdiction considered adopting a rule like the District of Columbia's or considered adopting rules that would allow multidisciplinary practice?
3. What kind of IOLTA does your state have—voluntary, opt-out, or mandatory? How do lawyers pay into the fund? What are the funds used for? How much money is currently in the fund?
4. Does your state have a client security fund? How is it funded? How much money is in the fund? What kinds of payments have been made from the fund?
5. Draft a provision for a client engagement letter on handling of client files after the matter is closed and on storing documents electronically.
6. Does your state or local bar have a requirement or an opinion on how long lawyers should retain client files? If so, what is the period?
7. Do you think it is unethical under the rules on unreasonable fees to charge a client for the work of a paralegal intern who is not being paid? Why or why not? See New York State Bar Ass'n Ethics Opinion 1090 (2016) for one opinion.
8. Read and brief the case of *In the Matter of Hear*, 755 N.E.2d 579 (Ind. 2001). In this case, a nonlawyer working for a lawyer with a debt collection business was disciplined when the nonlawyer embezzled funds that belonged to clients.
9. For an example of a lawyer who was suspended with probation for conversion and failure to maintain required trust accounting records, see *In re Salgado*, M.R. 030538, 2019PR00073 (Mar. 16, 2021). Read this case and brief it, paying special attention to the several ethics violations. Have any such cases been published in your jurisdiction?
10. In Chapter 3 we read *In re Morin*, which involved a lawyer who over-delegated work relating to trusts. For a case where a lawyer also engaged in this kind of work violated rules on fee splitting with nonlawyers, see

In re Flack, 272 Kan. 465, 33 P.3d 1281 (2001). Exactly what kind of agreement is described in this case? Is this the kind of situation that the rules on fee splitting were intended to prevent? Why or why not? How does this compare with *In re Hear*, 755 N.E.2d 579 (Ind. 2001), in which the lawyer went into the debt collection business?

11. In *Sanford v. GMRI, Inc.* (also known as the Red Lobster case, found at the end of this chapter), a federal court disallowed the inclusion of paralegal time in a fee award for paralegals who did not meet the statutory requirements to use the title "paralegal." See *Hawkins v. Berkeley Unified School District*, No. C-07-4206 (U.S.D.C., N.D. Cal. 2008), for a contradictory ruling. What does the California statute (Business and Professions Code 6450, et seq.) say about paralegal fee awards? What would you argue on each side of this issue?

12. Consider the relationship of lawyer to the "paralegal" involved, the number of clients affected, the seriousness of the violations, and so on. What can you learn from this comparison? What was the difference in the outcome. Why?

13. For an interesting case that covers UPL and fees, see *Long v. Ethics and Disc. Com. of the Utah Supreme Ct.*, 2011 UT 32, 256 P.3d 206 (2011), also mentioned in the hypotheticals in Chapter 3.

14. Research the methods that are used to finance new law firms. On what basis can law firms get loans to start or run a firm? What is the collateral? Can law firms use crowdfunding to finance a firm or a lawsuit? (You might want to start your research with New York State Bar Ass'n Ethics Opinion 1062 (2015).)

CASES FOR ANALYSIS

In the following landmark case, the U.S. Supreme Court held that attorney fee's awards under the Civil Rights Act may include paralegal fees at market rates. Pay close attention to both issues—the payment of fees for paralegal time and the basis on which the fee should be calculated.

Missouri v. Jenkins
491 U.S. 274 (1989)

Justice BRENNAN delivered the opinion of the Court.

This is the attorney's-fee aftermath of major school desegregation litigation in Kansas City, Missouri. We granted certiorari, 488 U.S.—, 109 S. Ct. 218, 102 L. Ed. 2d 209 (1988), to resolve two questions relating to fees litigation under 42 U.S.C. §1988. First, does the Eleventh Amendment prohibit enhancement of a fee award against a State to compensate for delay in payment? Second, should the fee award compensate the work of paralegals and law clerks by applying the market rate for their work?

I

This litigation began in 1977 as a suit by the Kansas City Missouri School District (KCMSD), the School Board, and the children of two School Board members, against the State of Missouri and other defendants. The plaintiffs alleged that the State, surrounding school districts, and various federal agencies had caused and perpetuated a system of racial segregation in the schools of the Kansas City metropolitan area. They sought various desegregation remedies. KCMSD was subsequently realigned as a nominal defendant, and a class of present and future KCMSD students was certified as plaintiffs. After lengthy proceedings, including a trial that lasted 7 months during 1983 and 1984, the District Court found the State of Missouri and KCMSD liable, while dismissing the suburban school districts and the federal defendants. It ordered various intradistrict remedies, to be paid for by the State and KCMSD, including $260 million in capital improvements and a magnet-school plan costing over $200 million.

The plaintiff class has been represented, since 1979, by Kansas City lawyer Arthur Benson and, since 1982, by the NAACP Legal Defense and Educational Fund, Inc. (LDF). Benson and the LDF requested attorney's fees under the Civil Rights Attorney's Fees Awards Act of 1976, 42 U.S.C. §1988.[1]

Benson and his associates had devoted 10,875 attorney hours to the litigation, as well as 8,108 hours of paralegal and law clerk time. For the LDF the corresponding figures were 10,854 hours for attorneys and 15,517 hours for paralegals and law clerks. Their fee applications deleted from these totals 3,628 attorney hours and 7,046 paralegal hours allocable to unsuccessful claims against the suburban school districts. With additions for post-judgment monitoring and for preparation of the fee application, the District Court awarded Benson a total of approximately $1.7 million and the LDF $2.3 million.

In calculating the hourly rate for Benson's fees the court noted that the market rate in Kansas City for attorneys of Benson's qualifications was in the range of $125 to $175 per hour, and found that "Mr. Benson's rate would fall at the higher end of this range based upon his expertise in the area of civil rights." It calculated his fees on the basis of an even higher hourly rate of $200, however, because of three additional factors: the preclusion of other employment, the undesirability of the case, and the delay in payment for Benson's services. The court also took account of the delay in payment in setting the rates for several

---

1. Section 1988 provides in relevant part:

In any action or proceeding to enforce a provision of sections 1981, 1982, 1983, 1985, and 1986 of this title, title IX of Public Law 92-318 [20 U.S.C. 1681 et seq.], or title VI of the Civil Rights Act of 1964 [42 U.S.C. 2000d et seq.], the court, in its discretion, may allow the prevailing party, other than the United States, a reasonable attorney's fee as part of the costs.

of Benson's associates by using current market rates rather than those applicable at the time the services were rendered. For the same reason, it calculated the fees for the LDF attorneys at current market rates.

Both Benson and the LDF employed numerous paralegals, law clerks (generally law students working part-time), and recent law graduates in this litigation. The court awarded fees for their work based on Kansas City market rates for those categories. As in the case of the attorneys, it used current rather than historic market rates in order to compensate for the delay in payment. It therefore awarded fees based on hourly rates of $35 for law clerks, $40 for paralegals, and $50 for recent law graduates. The Court of Appeals affirmed in all respects.

II

Our grant of certiorari extends to two issues raised by the State of Missouri. Missouri first contends that a State cannot, consistent with the principle of sovereign immunity this Court has found embodied in the Eleventh Amendment, be compelled to pay an attorney's fee enhanced to compensate for delay in payment. . . .

To summarize: We reaffirm our holding . . . that the Eleventh Amendment has no application to an award of attorney's fees, ancillary to a grant of prospective relief, against a State. It follows that the same is true for the calculation of the *amount* of the fee. An adjustment for delay in payment is, we hold, an appropriate factor in the determination of what constitutes a reasonable attorney's fee under §1988. An award against a State of a fee that includes such an enhancement for delay is not, therefore, barred by the Eleventh Amendment.

III

Missouri's second contention is that the District Court erred in compensating the work of law clerks and paralegals (hereinafter collectively "paralegals") at the market rates for their services, rather than at their cost to the attorney. While Missouri agrees that compensation for the cost of these personnel should be included in the fee award, it suggests that an hourly rate of $15—which it argued below corresponded to their salaries, benefits, and overhead—would be appropriate, rather than the market rates of $35 to $50. According to Missouri, §1988 does not authorize billing paralegals' hours at market rates, and doing so produces a "windfall" for the attorney.[7]

---

7. The Courts of Appeals have taken a variety of positions on this issue. Most permit separate billing of paralegal time. Some courts, on the other hand, have considered paralegal work "out-of-pocket expense," recoverable only at cost to the attorney. At least one Court of Appeals has refused to permit any recovery of paralegal expense apart from the attorney's hourly fee. *Abrams v. Baylor College of Medicine*, 805 F.2d 528, 535 (CA 1986).

We begin with the statutory language, which provides simply for "a reasonable attorney's fee as part of the costs." 42 U.S.C. §1988. Clearly, a "reasonable attorney's fee" cannot have been meant to compensate only work performed personally by members of the bar. Rather, the term must refer to a reasonable fee for the work product of an attorney. Thus, the fee must take into account the work not only of attorneys, but also of secretaries, messengers, librarians, janitors, and others whose labor contributes to the work product for which an attorney bills her client; and it must also take account of other expenses and profit. The parties have suggested no reason why the work of paralegals should not be similarly compensated, nor can we think of any. We thus take as our starting point the self-evident proposition that the "reasonable attorney's fee" provided for by statute should compensate the work of paralegals, as well as that of attorneys. The more difficult question is how the work of paralegals is to be valued in calculating the overall attorney's fee.

The statute specifies a "reasonable" fee for the attorney's work product. In determining how other elements of the attorney's fee are to be calculated, we have consistently looked to the marketplace as our guide to what is "reasonable." . . . A reasonable attorney's fee under §1988 is one calculated on the basis of rates and practices prevailing in the relevant market, i.e., "in line with those [rates] prevailing in the community for similar services by lawyers of reasonably comparable skill, experience, and reputation," and one that grants the successful civil rights plaintiff a "fully compensatory fee," comparable to what "is traditional with attorneys compensated by a fee-paying client."

If an attorney's fee awarded under §1988 is to yield the same level of compensation that would be available from the market, the "increasingly widespread custom of separately billing for the services of paralegals and law students who serve as clerks" must be taken into account. All else being equal, the hourly fee charged by an attorney whose rates include paralegal work in her hourly fee, or who bills separately for the work of paralegals at cost, will be higher than the hourly fee charged by an attorney competing in the same market who bills separately for the work of paralegals at "market rates." In other words, the prevailing "market rate" for attorney time is not independent of the manner in which paralegal time is accounted for.[8] Thus, if the prevailing practice in a given community were to bill paralegal time separately at market rates, fees awarded the attorney at market rates for attorney time would not be fully compensatory if the court refused to compensate hours billed by paralegals or did so only at "cost." Similarly, the fee awarded would be too high if the court accepted separate billing for paralegal hours in a market where that was not the custom.

---

8. The attorney who bills separately for paralegal time is merely distributing her costs and profit margin among the hourly fees of other members of her staff, rather than concentrating them in the fee she sets for her own time.

We reject the argument that compensation for paralegals at rates above "cost" would yield a "windfall" for the prevailing attorney. Neither petitioners nor anyone else, to our knowledge, have ever suggested that the hourly rate applied to the work of an associate attorney in a law firm creates a windfall for the firm's partners or is otherwise improper under §1988, merely because it exceeds the cost of the attorney's services. If the fees are consistent with market rates and practices, the "windfall" argument has no more force with regard to paralegals than it does for associates. And it would hardly accord with Congress' intent to provide a "fully compensatory fee" if the prevailing plaintiff's attorney in a civil rights lawsuit were not permitted to bill separately for paralegals, while the defense attorney in the same litigation was able to take advantage of the prevailing practice and obtain market rates for such work. Yet that is precisely the result sought in this case by the State of Missouri, which appears to have paid its own outside counsel for the work of paralegals at the hourly rate of $35.[9]

Nothing in §1988 requires that the work of paralegals invariably be billed separately. If it is the practice in the relevant market not to do so, or to bill the work of paralegals only at cost, that is all that §1988 requires. Where, however, the prevailing practice is to bill paralegal work at market rates, treating civil rights lawyers' fee requests in the same way is not only permitted by §1988, but also makes economic sense. By encouraging the use of lower-cost paralegals rather than attorneys wherever possible, permitting market-rate billing of paralegal hours "encourages cost-effective delivery of legal services and, by reducing the spiraling cost of civil rights litigation, furthers the policies underlying civil rights statutes."[10]

---

9. A variant of Missouri's "windfall" argument is the following: "If paralegal expense is reimbursed at a rate many times the actual cost, will attorneys next try to bill separately—and at a profit—for such items as secretarial time, paper clips, electricity, and other expenses?" The answer to this question is, of course, that attorneys seeking fees under §1988 would have no basis for requesting separate compensation of such expenses unless this were the prevailing practice in the local community. The safeguard against the billing at a profit of secretarial services and paper clips is the discipline of the market.

10. It has frequently been recognized in the lower courts that paralegals are capable of carrying out many tasks, under the supervision of an attorney, that might otherwise be performed by a lawyer and billed at a higher rate. Such work might include, for example, factual investigation, including locating and interviewing witnesses; assistance with depositions, interrogatories, and document production; compilation of statistical and financial data; checking legal citations; and drafting correspondence. Much such work lies in a gray area of tasks that might appropriately be performed either by an attorney or a paralegal. To the extent that fee applicants under §1988 are not permitted to bill for the work of paralegals at market rates, it would not be surprising to see a greater amount of such work performed by attorneys themselves, thus increasing the overall cost of litigation.

Of course, purely clerical or secretarial tasks should not be billed at a paralegal rate, regardless of who performs them. What the court in *Johnson v. Georgia Highway Express, Inc.*, 488 F.2d 714, 717 (CA5 1974) said in regard to the work of attorneys is applicable by analogy to paralegals:

> It is appropriate to distinguish between legal work, in the strict sense, and investigation, clerical work, compilation of facts and statistics and other work which can often be accomplished by non-lawyers but which a lawyer may do because he has no other help available. Such non-legal work may command a lesser rate. Its dollar value is not enhanced just because a lawyer does it.

Such separate billing appears to be the practice in most communities today.[11] In the present case, Missouri concedes that "the local market typically bills separately for paralegal services," and the District Court found that the requested hourly rates of $35 for law clerks, $40 for paralegals, and $50 for recent law graduates were the prevailing rates for such services in the Kansas City area. Under these circumstances, the court's decision to award separate compensation at these rates was fully in accord with §1988.

IV

The courts below correctly granted a fee enhancement to compensate for delay in payment and approved compensation of paralegals and law clerks at market rates. The judgment of the Court of Appeals is therefore

Affirmed.

Justice MARSHALL took no part in the consideration or decision of this case.

Justice O'CONNOR, with whom Justice SCALIA joins, and with whom THE CHIEF JUSTICE joins in part, concurring in part and dissenting in part.

I agree with the Court that 42 U.S.C. §1988 allows compensation for the work of paralegals and law clerks at market rates, and therefore join Parts I and III of its opinion. I do not join Part II, however, for in my view the Eleventh Amendment does not permit enhancement of attorney's fees assessed against a State as compensation for delay in payment. . . .

Chief Justice REHNQUIST, dissenting.

I agree with Justice O'CONNOR that the Eleventh Amendment does not permit an award of attorney's fees against a State which includes compensation for delay in payment. Unlike Justice O'CONNOR, however, I do not agree with the Court's approval of the award of law clerk and paralegal fees made here.

Section 1988 gives the district courts discretion to allow the prevailing party in an action under §1988 "a reasonable attorney's fee as part of the costs." 42 U.S.C. §1988. The Court reads this language as authorizing recovery of "a 'reasonable' fee for the attorney's work product," which, the Court concludes, may include separate compensation

---

11. *Amicus* National Association of Legal Assistants reports that 77 percent of 1,800 legal assistants responding to a survey of the association's membership stated that their law firms charged clients for paralegal work on an hourly billing basis. Brief for National Association of Legal Assistants as *Amicus Curiae* 11.

for the services of law clerks and paralegals. But the statute itself simply uses the very familiar term "a reasonable attorney's fee," which to those untutored in the Court's linguistic juggling means a fee charged for services rendered by an individual who has been licensed to practice law. Because law clerks and paralegals have not been licensed to practice law in Missouri, it is difficult to see how charges for their services may be separately billed as part of "attorney's fees." And since a prudent attorney customarily includes compensation for the cost of law clerk and paralegal services, like any other sort of office overhead—from secretarial staff, janitors, and librarians, to telephone service, stationery, and paper clips—in his own hourly billing rate, allowing the prevailing party to recover separate compensation for law clerk and paralegal services may result in "double recovery."

The Court finds justification for its ruling in the fact that the prevailing practice among attorneys in Kansas City is to bill clients separately for the services of law clerks and paralegals. But I do not think Congress intended the meaning of the statutory term "attorney's fee" to expand and contract with each and every vagary of local billing practice. Under the Court's logic, prevailing parties could recover at market rates for the cost of secretaries, private investigators, and other types of lay personnel who assist the attorney in preparing his case, so long as they could show that the prevailing practice in the local market was to bill separately for these services. Such a result would be a sufficiently drastic departure from the traditional concept of "attorney's fees" that I believe new statutory authorization should be required for it. That permitting separate billing of law clerk and paralegal hours at market rates might "reduc[e] the spiraling cost of civil rights litigation" by encouraging attorneys to delegate to these individuals tasks which they would otherwise perform themselves at higher cost may be a persuasive reason for Congress to enact such additional legislation. It is not, however, a persuasive reason for us to rewrite the legislation which Congress has in fact enacted.

I also disagree with the State's suggestion that law clerk and paralegal expenses incurred by a prevailing party, if not recoverable at market rates as "attorney's fees" under §1988, are nonetheless recoverable at actual cost under that statute. The language of §1988 expands the traditional definition of "costs" to include "a reasonable attorney's fee," but it cannot fairly be read to authorize the recovery of all other out-of-pocket expenses actually incurred by the prevailing party in the course of litigation. Absent specific statutory authorization for the recovery of such expenses, the prevailing party remains subject to the limitations on cost recovery imposed by Federal Rule of Civil Procedure 54(d) and 28 U.S.C. §1920, which govern the taxation of costs in federal litigation where a cost shifting statute is not applicable. Section 1920 gives the district court discretion to tax certain types of costs against the losing party in any federal litigation. The statute specifically enumerates six categories of expenses which may be taxed as costs: fees of the court clerk and marshal; fees of the court reporter; printing fees and witness fees; copying fees; certain docket fees; and fees of court-appointed experts and interpreters. We have held that this list is exclusive. Since none of these categories can possibly be construed to include the fees of law clerks and paralegals, I would also hold that reimbursement for these expenses may not be separately awarded at actual cost.

I would therefore reverse the award of reimbursement for law clerk and paralegal expenses.

Questions about the Case

1. Do you agree that the language of the statute "[c]learly . . . cannot have been meant to compensate only work performed by members of the bar"? Is the Court's reasoning on this point persuasive?
2. Why does the Court hold that attorneys' fees generally should be calculated according to prevailing market rates?
3. Do you agree with the Court that attorneys should be able to make a profit from their paralegals' work in cases like this? Why or why not?
4. Do you agree with the Court's comment in footnote 9 about the "discipline of the market"? Why or why not?
5. What is the most convincing argument that the Court makes for using market rates to calculate paralegal fee awards?
6. What does the Court say about the nature of paralegal work that can be compensated in fee awards? Do you think that time spent numbering documents should be compensated as paralegal time? What about organizing documents? Summarizing depositions? Inputting data into a computer?
7. Summarize the points made by the dissent. Do you think any of them are valid?

In the following case, the Supreme Court had to decide whether to adhere to its interpretation of attorney fee statutes set forth in *Missouri v. Jenkins* or to follow a different path in interpreting a different federal statute.

Richlin Security Service Co. v. Chertoff
553 U.S. 571, 128 S.Ct. 2007 (2008)

[After prevailing against the Government on a claim originating in the Department of Transportation's Board of Contract Appeals, petitioner (Richlin) filed an application with the Board for reimbursement of attorney's fees, expenses, and costs, pursuant to the Equal Access to

Justice Act (EAJA). The Board concluded, *inter alia*, that Richlin was not entitled to recover paralegal fees at the rates at which it was billed by its law firm, holding that EAJA limited such recovery to the attorney's cost, which was lower than the billed rate. In affirming, the Federal Circuit concluded that the term "fees," for which EAJA authorizes recovery at "prevailing market rates," embraces only the fees of attorneys, experts, and agents. . . .]

Justice ALITO delivered the opinion of the Court. . . .

The question presented in this case is whether the Equal Access to Justice Act (EAJA), 5 U.S.C. §504(a)(1) (2006 ed.) and 28 U.S.C. §2412(d)(1)(A) (2000 ed.), allows a prevailing party in a case brought by or against the Government to recover fees for paralegal services at the market rate for such services or only at their cost to the party's attorney. The United States Court of Appeals for the Federal Circuit limited recovery to the attorney's cost. 472 F.3d 1370 (2006). . . .

EAJA permits an eligible prevailing party to recover "fees and other expenses incurred by that party in connection with" a proceeding before an administrative agency. 5 U.S.C. §504(a)(1). EAJA defines "fees and other expenses" as follows:

> "[F]ees and other expenses" includes the reasonable expenses of expert witnesses, the reasonable cost of any study, analysis, engineering report, test, or project which is found by the agency to be necessary for the preparation of the party's case, and reasonable attorney or agent fees. (The amount of fees awarded under this section shall be based upon prevailing market rates for the kind and quality of the services furnished, except that (i) no expert witness shall be compensated at a rate in excess of the highest rate of compensation for expert witnesses paid by the agency involved, and (ii) attorney or agent fees shall not be awarded in excess of $125 per hour unless the agency determines by regulation that an increase in the cost of living or a special factor, such as the limited availability of qualified attorneys or agents for the proceedings involved, justifies a higher fee.) §504(b)(1)(A).

In this case, Richlin "incurred" "fees" for paralegal services in connection with its contract action before the Board. Since §504(b)(1)(A) awards fees at "prevailing market rates," a straightforward reading of the statute leads to the conclusion that Richlin was entitled to recover fees for the paralegal services it purchased at the market rate for such services.

The Government resists this reading by distinguishing "fees" from "other expenses." The Government concedes that "fees" are reimbursable at "prevailing market rates," but it insists that "other expenses" (including expenses for "any study, analysis, engineering report, test, or project") are reimbursable only at their "reasonable cost." And in the Government's view, outlays for paralegal services are better characterized as "other expenses" than as "fees." The Government observes that the second sentence of

§504(b)(1)(A), which explains how to calculate awards for "fees," refers to attorneys, agents, and expert witnesses, without mentioning paralegals. From this omission, the Government infers that Congress intended to treat expenditures for paralegal services not as "fees" but as "other expenses," recoverable at "reasonable cost."

We find the Government's fractured interpretation of the statute unpersuasive. Contrary to the Government's contention, §504(b)(1)(A) does not clearly distinguish between the rates at which "fees" and "other expenses" are reimbursed. Although the statute does refer to the "reasonable cost" of "any study, analysis, engineering report, test, or project," Congress may reasonably have believed that market rates would not exist for work product of that kind. At one point, Congress even appears to use the terms "expenses" and "fees" interchangeably. . . . There is no indication that Congress, in using the term "expenses" in one place and "fees" in the other, was referring to two different components of expert remuneration.

Even if the dichotomy that the Government draws between "fees" and "other expenses" were supported by the statutory text, it would hardly follow that amounts billed for paralegal services should be classified as "expenses" rather than as "fees." The Government concludes that the omission of paralegal fees from §504(b)(1)(A)'s parenthetical (which generally authorizes reimbursement at "prevailing market rates") implies that the recovery of paralegal fees is limited to cost. But one could just as easily conclude that the omission of paralegal fees from the litany of "any study, analysis, engineering report, test, or project" (all of which are recoverable at "reasonable cost") implies that paralegal fees are recoverable at market rates. Surely paralegals are more analogous to attorneys, experts, and agents than to studies, analyses, reports, tests, and projects. . . .

But even if we agreed that EAJA limited a prevailing party's recovery for paralegal fees to "reasonable cost," it certainly would not follow that the cost should be measured from the perspective of the party's attorney. To the contrary, it would be anomalous to measure cost from the perspective of the attorney rather than the client. . . . Such an interpretation would be tough to square with the statutory language. Section 504(a)(1) provides that an agency shall award to a prevailing party "fees and other expenses *incurred by that party*." . . . That language leaves no doubt that Congress intended the "reasonable cost" . . . to be calculated from the perspective of the litigant. That being the case, we find it hard to believe that Congress, without even mentioning paralegals, intended to make an exception of them by calculating their cost from the perspective of their employer rather than the litigant. . . .

To the extent that some ambiguity subsists in the statutory text, we need not look far to resolve it, for we have already addressed a similar question with respect to another fee-shifting statute. In *Missouri v. Jenkins*, 491 U.S. 274 (1989), we considered whether litigants could recover paralegal fees under the Civil Rights Attorney's Fees Awards Act of 1976, 42

U.S.C. §1988. Section 1988 provides that "the court, in its discretion, may allow the prevailing party, other than the United States, a reasonable attorney's fee as part of the costs." We concluded that the term "attorney's fee" in §1988 "cannot have been meant to compensate only work performed personally by members of the bar." 491 U.S., at 285. Although separate billing for paralegals had become "increasingly widespread," *id.*, at 286 (internal quotation marks omitted), attorney's fees had traditionally subsumed both the attorney's personal labor and the labor of paralegals and other individuals who contributed to the attorney's work product, see *id.*, at 285. We were so confident that Congress had given the term "attorney's fees" this traditional gloss that we declared it "self-evident" that the term embraced the fees of paralegals as well as attorneys. *Ibid.*

We think *Jenkins* substantially answers the question before us. EAJA, like §1988, entitles certain parties to recover "reasonable attorney . . . fees." 5 U.S.C. §504(b)(1)(A). EAJA, like §1988, makes no mention of the paralegals, "secretaries, messengers, librarians, janitors, and others whose labor contributes to the work product for which an attorney bills her client." *Jenkins, supra,* at 285. And we think EAJA, like §1988, must be interpreted as using the term "attorney . . . fees" to reach fees for paralegal services as well as compensation for the attorney's personal labor. The Government does not contend that the meaning of the term "attorney's fees" changed so much between §1988's enactment in 1976 and EAJA's enactment in 1980 that the term's meaning in one statute must be different from its meaning in the other. Under the reasoning of *Jenkins*, we take it as "self-evident" that when Congress instructed agencies to award "attorney . . . fees" to certain parties prevailing against the Government, that term was intended to embrace paralegal fees as well. Since §504 generally provides for recovery of attorney's fees at "prevailing market rates," it follows that fees for paralegal services must be recoverable at prevailing market rates as well.

The Government contends that our decision in *Jenkins* was driven by considerations arising from the different context in which the term "attorney's fee" was used in §1988. At the time *Jenkins* was decided, §1988 provided for the recovery of attorney's fees without reference to any other recoverable "expenses." The Government insists that *Jenkins* found paralegal fees recoverable under the guise of "attorney's fee[s]" because otherwise paralegal fees would not be recoverable at all. Since EAJA expressly permits recovery (albeit at "cost") for items other than attorney, agent, and expert witness fees, the Government sees no reason to give EAJA the broad construction that *Jenkins* gave §1988.

The Government's rationale for distinguishing *Jenkins* finds no support either in our opinion there or in our subsequent decisions. Our opinion in *Jenkins* expressed no apprehension at the possibility that a contrary decision would leave the claimant empty-handed. This omission is unsurprising, since our decision in *Jenkins* did not rest on the conviction that recovery at market rates was better than nothing. Our decision rested instead on the proposition—a proposition we took as "self-evident"—that the term "attorney's fee" had historically included fees for paralegal services.

Indeed, the Government's interpretation of *Jenkins* was rejected by this Court just two years after *Jenkins* was handed down. . . .

The Government parries this textual and doctrinal analysis with legislative history and public policy. We are not persuaded by either. . . . We find the Government's policy rationale for recovery at attorney cost likewise unpersuasive. The Government argues that market-based recovery would distort litigant incentives because EAJA would cap paralegal and attorney's fees at the same rate. See 5 U.S.C. §504(b)(1)(A) ("[A]ttorney or agent fees shall not be awarded in excess of $125 per hour unless the agency determines by regulation that an increase in the cost of living or a special factor, such as the limited availability of qualified attorneys or agents for the proceedings involved, justifies a higher fee."). The Government observes that paralegal rates are lower than rates for attorneys operating in the same market. If EAJA reimbursed both attorney time and paralegal time at market rates, then the cap would clip more off the top of the attorney's rates than the paralegal's rates. According to the Government, a market-based scheme would encourage litigants to shift an inefficient amount of attorney work to paralegals, since paralegal fees could be recovered at a greater percentage of their full market value.

The problem with this argument, as Richlin points out, is that it proves too much. The same reasoning would imply that agent fees should not be recoverable at market rates. If market-based recovery of paralegal time resulted in excessive reliance on paralegals, then market-based recovery of agent time should result in excessive reliance on agents. The same reasoning would also imply that fees for junior attorneys (who generally bill at lower rates than senior attorneys) should not be recoverable at market rates. . . . Yet despite the possibility that market-based recovery of attorney and agent fees would distort litigant incentives, §504 unambiguously authorizes awards of "reasonable attorney or agent fees . . . [at] prevailing market rates." 5 U.S.C. §504(b)(1)(A). The Government offers no persuasive reason why Congress would have treated paralegal fees any differently. . . .

We also question the practical feasibility of the Government's interpretation of the statute. The Board in this case relied on the Internet for data on paralegal salaries in the District of Columbia, but the Government fails to explain why a law firm's cost should be limited to salary. The benefits and perks with which a firm compensates its staff come out of the bottom line no less than salary. The Government has offered no solution to this accounting problem, and we do not believe that solutions are readily to be found. Market practice provides by far the more transparent basis for calculating a prevailing party's recovery under EAJA. It strains credulity that Congress would have abandoned this predictable, workable framework for the uncertain and complex accounting requirements that a cost-based rule would inflict on litigants, their attorneys, administrative agencies, and the courts. . . .

For these reasons, we hold that a prevailing party that satisfies EAJA's other requirements may recover its paralegal fees from the Government at prevailing market rates. The Board's contrary decision was error, and the Federal Circuit erred in affirming that decision. The judgment of the Federal Circuit is reversed, and this case is remanded for further proceedings consistent with this opinion.

It is so ordered.

Questions about the Case

1. What federal fee award statute is the subject of interpretation in this case? What fee award statute was the subject of *Missouri v. Jenkins*? How does the wording of the two statutes differ? Why is this wording important in this case?
2. What did the appellate court decide about the fees? No award? Award at cost? Award at market rate?
3. Explain the argument in favor of awarding paralegal fees as "expenses." What are three reasons that the Supreme Court does not agree with this interpretation?
4. What would have been the possible consequences for paralegals and law firms if the court had upheld the appellate court decision?

In this case, the Supreme Court of Oklahoma determined that attorney's fees may also include paralegal work and addressed the issues of the proper rate for paralegal time and of the nature of the work that is compensable.

Taylor v. Chubb
1994 Okla. 47, 874 P.2d 806 (Okla. 1994)

The United States District Court for the Northern District of Oklahoma certified questions of state law to this Court under the Oklahoma Uniform Certification of Questions of Law Act, 20 O.S. 1991 §§1601, et seq. The federal court asks two interrelated questions:

(1) Whether the phrase "attorneys fees," when used in Oklahoma statutory or case law providing for the award of costs to a prevailing party, should be interpreted to encompass all work product of an attorney, including fees for services performed by legal assistants or paralegals?

(2) If the preceding question is answered in the affirmative, whether the decision of the Oklahoma Supreme Court should be applied retroactively to provide for the award of fees in the present litigation?

. . . The Taylors' attorney fee application included time charges for services performed by a legal assistant, who was designated by the National Association of Legal Assistants as a Certified Legal Assistant and Civil Litigation Specialist. The legal assistant's services were performed under the supervision of counsel, were non-clerical in nature, and provided meaningful support to counsel in his handling of the case. The Taylors' lawyers practice in Tulsa, where the prevailing community practice is for lawyers to bill legal assistants' time to clients.

I

We first consider whether charges for legal assistants' time are included in the term "attorney fees," as that term is used in 36 O.S. 1991 §3629.B. This is a question of first impression. . . .

The parties have stipulated that the legal assistant's services were valuable to the Taylors during the litigation. They have also stipulated that the "prevailing practice in the community is for attorneys to bill legal assistant or paralegal time to clients." Under these circumstances we see no reason to ignore such charges. We believe the legislature would have said so had it intended the term "attorney fees" to except charges for the time of legal assistants in communities where the "prevailing practice" is to charge for such time.

The United States Supreme Court considered this issue in *Missouri v. Jenkins*, 491 U.S. 274, 109 S. Ct. 2463, 105 L. Ed. 2d 229 (1989). Seven of the eight justices participating agreed that hourly charges for paralegals and law clerks must be considered in setting an attorney's fee under federal civil rights statutes. . . .

Separately charging for the time of legal assistants has grown in larger communities in response to clients' desire to keep the average hourly rate as low as possible, consistent with competent handling of cases. The U.S. Supreme Court said that to the extent fee applicants for statutory attorney's fees "are not permitted to bill for the work of paralegals at market rates, it would not be surprising to see a greater amount of such work performed by attorneys themselves, thus increasing the overall cost of litigation." *Missouri v. Jenkins*, 491 U.S. at 288. . . .

There is no reason to exclude charges for the time of legal assistants in computing statutorily mandated attorney fees where such charges are customarily made to clients and the legal assistant's services are useful to the client. A contrary holding would require us to assume that the legislature intended the term "attorney fee" to mean something different from the meaning that the stipulation of the parties shows attorneys and clients give it. This we decline to do.

Our holding today, that the time of paralegals is properly includable as a component to be considered in the trial court's assessment of the total value of services rendered, is limited to charges for work performed, *which otherwise would have had to have been performed by a licensed attorney at a higher rate.* There are several charges in the Taylors' attorneys' billings, however, that apparently fail to satisfy this requirement. The billings reflect a charge for the legal assistants' time in court at the same rate, $150.00 per hour, as the licensed attorney charged for his own time. Charges were made for time spent in copying documents and in doing other secretarial tasks, rather than substantive legal work. Such charges are *not* includable in attorneys' fees awarded under §3629.B. The only charges for nonlawyers' time that properly fall within the definition of "attorney fees," under §3629.B are those that are clearly shown to have been made (1) for the delegated performance of substantive legal work, that (2) would otherwise have to be performed by a lawyer, (3) at a rate higher than that charged for the nonlawyers' time....

As its pattern of proof, a party seeking attorney fees must plead and prove that the charges made for non-lawyer's time covered work that a lawyer would have had to perform but for the performance of such services by a legal assistant. In addition, the total charges made for the legal assistant's services must be less than the total charges would have been, had a lawyer performed the services.

Among other tasks, a legal assistant may:

- interview clients
- draft pleadings and other documents
- carry on legal research, both conventional and computer aided
- research public records
- prepare discovery requests and responses
- schedule depositions and prepare notices and subpoenas
- summarize depositions and other discovery responses
- coordinate and manage document production
- locate and interview witnesses
- organize pleadings, trial exhibits, and other documents
- prepare witness and exhibit lists
- prepare trial notebooks
- prepare for the attendance of witnesses at trial
- assist lawyers at trials

II

... Here, our conclusion that the term "attorney fees" includes time charges for legal assistants represents only a clarification of the law, not a change. Our holding is supported by the overwhelming weight of authority. Thus, today's pronouncement changes no preexisting rule of Oklahoma law. We see no reason to apply it prospectively only. We therefore answer yes to Certified Question number (2).

CERTIFIED QUESTIONS ANSWERED.

Questions about the Case

1. What were the credentials of the legal assistant whose time was at issue in this case?
2. What is the prevailing practice of attorneys in Oklahoma concerning billing of paralegal time?
3. Does this court limit its decision to the particular fee award statute in this case? What other kinds of statutes have such provisions?
4. What limitations are placed by the court on compensation for paralegal time?
5. What are some of the tasks that the court acknowledges that legal assistants perform?
6. What should paralegal rates be relative to attorney rates?
7. Does the court find this decision to be a "change" in the law? How does the court describe the ruling?

In this case, brought under federal ERISA law, the attorney fee award was deemed excessive on several grounds, including the charging of lawyers' fee rates for paralegal work.

Mogck v. UNUM Life Insurance Company of America
289 F. Supp. 2d 1181 (S.D. Cal. 2003)

The facts underlying this lawsuit arise from a March 25, 1993 motor vehicle accident in which Plaintiff sustained serious injuries. At the time of the accident, Plaintiff was insured for long-term disability benefits under an insurance policy issued by Defendant UNUM Life Insurance Company of America. Defendant paid Plaintiff occupational long-term disability benefits for two years, from June 25, 1993 to June 25, 1995, and then terminated payment by letter dated June 1, 1995. The letter explained that Defendant would not extend benefits past June 25, 1995 as Defendant had determined that Plaintiff no longer met the definition of disability. . . .

On remand, the parties participated in a Settlement Conference . . . , which resulted in a settlement agreement dated November 13, 2002. The terms of the settlement included separate lump-sum payments to Plaintiff and Plaintiff's attorneys' firm, Miller, Monson. (Settlement Agreement and Release of Claims at 1.) The parties and Magistrate Judge Stiven agreed that Plaintiff's request for statutory attorneys' fees and costs would be submitted to the Court by formal motion. . . .

The long-term disability contract at issue in this case is governed by the Employee Retirement Income Security Act of 1974 (ERISA), 29 U.S.C. §1001 *et seq.* In an ERISA action, a court in its discretion may award attorneys' fees and costs to either party. . . .

Defendant did demonstrate bad faith in its handling of Plaintiff's disability claim. As Defendant points out, however, the parties never litigated the merits of Plaintiff's claim, and thus the propriety of Defendant's claims decision was never adjudicated. Accordingly, the Court does not find evidence that Defendant acted in bad faith in this matter. This factor weighs against awarding attorneys' fees to Plaintiff. . . . Defendant concedes that it has the ability to satisfy a fee award. Thus, this factor weighs in favor of awarding attorneys' fees to Plaintiff. . . . [Deterrence as a] factor requires the Court to consider whether an award of fees against Defendant would deter others from similar conduct in the future. The Court finds that this factor weighs neither in favor of nor against an award of attorneys' fees to Plaintiff. . . . Although Plaintiff brought this suit to benefit himself, the Court agrees that Plaintiff's suit, and appeal, could benefit ERISA plan participants and beneficiaries by helping to resolve contractual statute of limitations and contractual language interpretation issues. . . . Therefore, this factor weighs in favor of awarding attorneys' fees to Plaintiff. . . . [T]his Court exercises its discretion and awards Plaintiff his reasonable attorneys' fees as set forth below. . . .

Plaintiff requests fees in the amount of $351,217.20, consisting of 175.3 hours of work by Attorney Monson at $350.00 per hour, 868.8 hours of work by Attorney Horner at $325.00 per hour, 63.6 hours of paralegal time at $65.00 per hour, and 153.1 hours of secretary time at $22.00 per hour. In addition, Plaintiff seeks additional fees for "approximately two days' work" to compensate Plaintiff for filing the reply and objections to evidence regarding the instant motion, as well as for three hours spent reviewing the papers for confidential information and resubmitting the reply brief. Defendant contends that the amount of fees sought [is] "excessive and patently unreasonable."

Attorneys' fees in ERISA actions are calculated using a hybrid lodestar/multiplier approach. [Citation omitted.] The court first determines the "lodestar" amount by multiplying the number of hours reasonably expended on the litigation by a reasonable hourly rate. The party seeking a fee award must submit evidence supporting the hours worked and the rate claimed. The court may then adjust the lodestar upward or downward using a "multiplier" based on factors not subsumed in the initial calculation of the lodestar. . . .

Plaintiff claims that his attorneys are entitled to recover the "market rates" of $350.00 per hour for Monson and $325.00 per hour for Horner. In support of his claim, Plaintiff submits declarations from eight ERISA attorneys who practice in the Ninth Circuit to demonstrate that Monson's and Horner's actual fees of $295.00 and $250.00, respectively, are below prevailing market rates. Defendant argues that Plaintiff's counsels' normal hourly rates, not the "market rates," should be used. . . .

[T]he Court finds that the rates of $350.00 per hour for Monson and $325.00 per hour for Horner are reasonable attorneys' rates in this case. Monson's and Horner's actual rates indeed appear to be *below* prevailing market rates. Although the Court recognizes that the "relevant community," when determining appropriate attorneys' rates, is generally the one in which the district court sits [citations omitted], it is appropriate to consider the declarations of attorneys in other jurisdictions because ERISA cases involve a national standard, and attorneys practicing ERISA law in the Ninth Circuit tend to practice in different districts. Furthermore, the Court observes that ERISA cases are often considered to be complex, ERISA plaintiff cases are often undesirable, and Plaintiff's attorneys possess extensive experience in ERISA law. . . .

In determining reasonable hours, the party requesting fees bears the burden of submitting detailed time records justifying the hours claimed to have been expended. [Citation omitted.] Those hours may be reduced by the court where documentation of the hours is inadequate, if the case was overstaffed and hours are duplicated, or if the hours expended are deemed excessive or otherwise unnecessary. . . .

[The court reviewed the hours to determine if they were excessive and declined to reduce the hours except for the time spent by one lawyer listening to the oral arguments. The court also denied the Defendant's request to deny fees for all "block-billed" entries.]

Defendant argues that Horner's billing of 77.8 hours to prepare a chronology of documents in this case should be billed at Miller, Monson's $65.00 per hour paralegal rate rather than Horner's attorney rate. Attorney Horner describes the preparation of the chronology as "reviewing of the documents and selecting the pertinent facts and information." The Court agrees that this is a paralegal task. "[W]hen a lawyer spends time on tasks that are easily delegable to non-professional assistance, legal service rates are not applicable." *New Mexico Citizens for Clean Air and Water v. Espanola Mercantile Co., Inc.,* 72 F.3d 830, 835 (10th Cir. 1996). However, the Court finds that Horner spent 49.6 hours, not 77.8 hours, on the chronology. Thus, the Court reduces the fee award by $12,896.00 (49.6 hours × $260 per hour).

In addition to preparing a chronology, Horner engaged in other tasks that would have been easily delegable to either a paralegal or secretary. For example, on 9/7/00, Horner billed .1 hours to "Calendar rescheduled pre-trial conference." On 12/17/01, she billed for calling the Ninth Circuit regarding "page limit and style and cover color." And, on 11/14/01, Horner's billing entry included making "reservations for travel to Pasadena." Other paralegal/secretarial tasks billed for by Horner include creating files, reorganizing files, preparing tables of contents and tables of authorities, and preparing indexes. . . . Therefore, the Court reduces Horner's requested hours by 3%. . . .

Fees for secretarial time may be included in an award for attorneys' fees. See, e.g., D'Emanuele v. Montgomery Ward & Co., Inc., 904 F.2d 1379, 1387 (9th Cir. 1990), *overruled on other grounds by* Burlington v. Dague, 505 U.S. 557 (1992). However, like attorney time, secretarial time must be sufficiently documented. *D'Emanuele*, 904 F.2d at 1387. Miller, Monson's billing entries for secretarial time do not include any information describing the tasks performed. Although Attorney Monson provides a general description of the secretarial tasks performed, including "telephone contact[s] . . . , assisting attorneys and paralegals with finalizing and filing of motion papers, typing letters . . . , and contact with the client," this generalized description provides insufficient support for the secretarial fees requested. Thus, the Court reduces the requested secretarial fees by 25%.

Although not raised by Defendant, the Court finds that there are additional reasons to reduce Plaintiff's attorneys' bills. First, the Court finds that Monson and Horner billed an inordinate amount of time for interoffice conferences. In reviewing Miller, Monson's bills, the Court has noted numerous occasions in which Attorneys Monson and Horner consulted and coordinated with one another. Although it has been recognized that "the participation of more than one attorney does not necessarily constitute an unnecessary duplication of effort" [citation omitted], the Court believes that Monson and Horner inappropriately billed for communicating with one another and delegating tasks to office personnel. . . . This Court doubts that Miller, Monson would have charged Plaintiff for all of Monson's and Horner's consultations with one another (it is not Plaintiff's [nor Defendant's] fault that Miller, Monson chose to staff the case with two attorneys), and thus, as discussed further below, Plaintiff's requested attorney hours will be reduced accordingly.

Additionally, the Court finds that Monson's and Horner's billing entries reflect, at times, double-billing and/or a duplication of effort. For example, on 2/21/00, Monson and Horner each billed for reviewing Defendant's objection to Plaintiff's expert designation. On 6/10/02 and 6/11/02, Monson and Horner each billed for reviewing the Ninth Circuit's opinion in this case. On 11/5/02, both attorneys billed for reviewing Magistrate Judge Stiven's settlement recommendation. These entries provide further support for a reduction in Plaintiff's requested attorney hours, as these hours were not "reasonably expended." [Citation omitted.]

Finally, the Court notes that some of Plaintiff's attorneys' billing entries were vague and thus do not support the hours claimed. See, e.g., 2/10/00 billing entry for "continued work on case." See also 2/21/01 billing entry for "research of issues." Additionally, Plaintiff's attorneys billed for correcting errors previously made. See, e.g., 5/10/01 billing entry, in which Horner billed 2.1 hours for "Telephone call from Mr. Wong at 9th Circuit re: font in footnotes; call to office; review for corrections and review brief format and pagination." Defendant should not be required to pay for Plaintiff's attorneys to fix their own errors.

Pursuant to the above, the Court reduces Monson's and Horner's requested hours by 10% each. . . .

For the reasons set forth above, this Court hereby **GRANTS IN PART** Plaintiff's Motion for Attorneys' Fees and Costs. The Court awards Plaintiff $285,869.00 in attorneys' fees (151.8 hours at $350 per hour for Monson, 755.8 hours at $325 per hour for Horner, minus $12,896.00), $4,134.00 in paralegal fees (63.6 hours at $65.00 per hour), $2,525.60 in secretarial fees (114.8 hours at $22.00 per hour), and $3,246.39 in costs for a total of $295,774.99. . . .

Questions about the Case

1. How did the case get to this point? Did the plaintiffs go to trial and prevail?
2. The court initially analyzes whether attorneys' fees are appropriate. What kinds of factors does the court consider? What did it decide about the fairness of awarding fees?
3. What is the lodestar method? Did the court find the rates reasonable?
4. What tasks did the attorney Horner perform that the court found to be paralegal tasks? Do you agree with this finding? What was the consequence of this finding in terms of the fee award?
5. What does this court say about fee awards for secretarial time?
6. The court reduces the award for inter-office conferences and communications among lawyers and with staff. Do you think it is common practice to bill clients for these communications? If so, is it fair for the court to reduce the fee award given that the fees are based on market rates?
7. Do you agree that fees should not be awarded for time spent correcting the law firm's mistakes?

In the following case, the Iowa Supreme Court strikes down cap on paralegal fees.

GreatAmerica Leasing v. Cool Comfort Air Conditioning and Refrigeration, Inc.
691 N.W.2d 730 (Iowa 2005)

GreatAmerica Leasing Corporation sued Cool Comfort Air Conditioning and Refrigeration, Inc., after Cool Comfort breached a lease for a telephone system. GreatAmerica was partially successful in the suit and obtained a judgment against Cool Comfort for a little less than $17,000.

Pursuant to a fee-shifting clause in the parties' written contract, GreatAmerica asked the district court to require Cool Comfort to reimburse it approximately $35,000 for attorney fees it had expended in the suit. This request included about $5000 in litigation expenses for paralegal work. In support of its motion, GreatAmerica attached a copy of a bill it had received from its law firm. The bill indicated the firm had charged GreatAmerica $80 per hour for paralegal work. Cool Comfort resisted GreatAmerica's motion for attorney fees. Cool Comfort argued GreatAmerica should not recover expenses that were unsuccessful.

The district court granted GreatAmerica almost $19,000 in attorney fees. The district court awarded GreatAmerica less than it had requested for two reasons. First, the court noted GreatAmerica was only partially successful in the suit. For this reason, the court nearly halved the award. [Citations omitted.] Second, the court subtracted an additional $1880 from the amount GreatAmerica had claimed in litigation expenses for paralegal work. The court stated it was

> troubled that regular, licensed attorneys defending felony defendants in criminal cases in Iowa are paid only $50 an hour for what can be more complex litigation [that requires] a license to practice law with substantial trial ability and experience. In this court's view, a paralegal fee assessed against another party should not exceed what the State of Iowa pays for indigent defense. . . . Because no evidence rebuts the necessity of the hours devoted to the case, this court will not reduce the number of hours compensated. However, the award will be at the rate of $50 per hour.

GreatAmerica appealed the district court's award of attorney fees. It challenges only the reduction in litigation expenses due to the capping of the paralegal's hourly rate. Cool Comfort did not cross-appeal and has not filed a brief in this matter. . . .

The sole issue is whether the district court abused its discretion in reducing the amount of attorney fees for GreatAmerica's litigation expenses. We begin with the Iowa Code, which provides:

> When judgment is recovered upon a written contract containing an agreement to pay an attorney's fee, the court shall allow and tax as a part of the costs a reasonable attorney's fee to be determined by the court.

Iowa Code section 625.22 (2003).

A reasonable attorney fee is not limited to the hourly fee charged by lawyers. The concept includes certain litigation expenses, including the cost of paralegals. See, e.g., *Schaffer v. Frank Moyer Constr., Inc.*, 628 N.W.2d 11, 23 (Iowa 2001) (litigation expenses, including the cost of hiring a paralegal, allowed as part of a reasonable attorney fee); [citations omitted]; cf. *Missouri v. Jenkins*, 491 U.S. 274, 284-89, 109 S. Ct. 2463, 2469-72, 105 L. Ed. 2d 229, 241-44 (1989) (construing 42 U.S.C. §1988 to permit reimbursement for paralegal expenses). The district court is considered an expert in what constitutes a reasonable attorney fee, and we afford it wide discretion in making its decision. [Citations omitted.] The district court should consider a number of factors, including:

> the time necessarily spent, the nature and extent of the service, the amount involved, the difficulty of handling and importance of the issues, the responsibility assumed and results obtained, the standing and experience of the attorney in the profession, and the customary charges for similar service.

The court also correctly recognized it was required to "look at the whole picture and, using independent judgment with the benefit of hindsight, decide on a total fee appropriate for handling the complete case." [Citation omitted.]

In its analysis, however, the district court did not consider the *Schaffer* factors nor look at the whole picture. Instead the court focused upon the fact that the State only pays some criminal defense attorneys $50 per hour. . . . Although there is a blush of fairness in the district court's logic that paralegals should not earn more than attorneys, this analysis ignores the fact that the markets for criminal defense attorneys and paralegals in civil litigation are different. To the extent the district court adopted a per se rule capping all pay for paralegals at $50 per hour, the court abused its discretion. Iowa Code section 625.22 contains no such requirement, and to the extent the district court invented one its ruling was based on untenable grounds. Such a fixed policy is the antithesis of discretionary decision making. [Citation omitted.]

The appropriate remedy is to reverse and remand for "a fresh consideration" of a reasonable attorney fee. [Citation omitted.] On remand, the court shall look at the whole picture and determine a reasonable amount for GreatAmerica's litigation expenses. The *Schaffer* factors, although explicitly designed for attorneys, apply by analogy. See *Cont'l Townhouses E. Unit One Ass'n v. Brockbank*, 152 Ariz. 537, 733 P.2d 1120, 1128 (Ct. App. 1986) ("The trial judge . . . may . . . consider the value of services rendered in a case by . . . paralegals, applying the same standards as are used in evaluating lawyers' time."). . . . [Citations omitted.] The fundamental question, however, is simply whether the claimed litigation expenses are reasonable and thus part of a reasonable attorney's fee. [Citation omitted.]

GreatAmerica bears the burden to prove its request was reasonable. [Citations omitted.] As framed in this case, the crux of the dispute revolves around the paralegal's hourly rate. On remand, the district court will have to determine whether $80 per hour is consistent with market rates and practices for similar work in the community. . . . [Citations omitted.] The market rate for the paralegal's services is not necessarily the rate of pay plaintiff's counsel billed its client. Billing sheets provided by the firm, although little evidence of the prevailing rate of pay for similarly situated paralegals, may be considered by the court. [Citation omitted.] In this case GreatAmerica did not offer the district court any additional evidence. While such evidence is not necessary to prevail . . . it would have helped the court reach a decision. . . . In its absence, the district court, as an expert in calculating the local going rate, may settle matters itself. . . .

Nothing in this opinion should be construed as an endorsement or rejection of any particular rate for reimbursement of paralegal expenses.

REVERSED AND REMANDED.

Questions about the Case

1. What was the basis for the limitation on the paralegal fees in the lower court case? Do you find this reasoning about the cap to be persuasive?
2. Why did this court reverse this decision?
3. How does the lower court reasoning conflict with the principles of *Missouri v. Jenkins*?
4. Compare the reasoning of the lower court with the reasoning of the court in the *Richlin* opinion concerning the cap on lawyer fees under EAJA. Do you understand the problem posed by these caps? How would you suggest that this issue be addressed so that it does not recur?

In this case, the court had to decide whether a statutory cap on attorneys' fees in actions under the Prison Litigation Reform Act applied to paralegals.

Perez v. Cate
632 F.3d 553 (9th Cir. 2011)

Carlos Perez and the class of all current and future California inmates housed at one of California's thirty-three state prisons brought an action under 42 U.S.C. §1983 against California prison officials, alleging that they violated the Eighth Amendment in their provision of dental care. The parties settled the action and entered into a remedial plan which provided, among other things, that plaintiffs would monitor the prison officials' implementation of the plan. The parties agreed that plaintiffs were entitled to attorney's fees as the prevailing party, limited to the "billing rates [set forth under] 42 U.S.C. §1997e(d) of the PLRA," including "fees and costs incurred in connection" with monitoring the implementation of the remedial plan. The District Court for the Northern District of California approved the plan in August 2006.

On April 10, 2007, the court entered a stipulated order for the periodic payment of plaintiffs' attorney's fees and costs. During 2007, the prison officials paid the attorney's fees amounts requested by plaintiffs, including the rates charged by plaintiffs for paralegal services.

In 2008, plaintiffs submitted attorney's fees statements asking for payment for paralegal services at a rate of $169.50 per hour. The prison officials refused to pay plaintiffs the requested hourly rate, offering $135 per hour instead. At a hearing on this dispute before the district court, the prison officials claimed that, under the PLRA, plaintiffs were entitled to seek a maximum of $82.50 per hour for paralegal services. The district court disagreed and determined that plaintiffs' proposed hourly rate of $169.50 was reasonable for the work performed and was below the market rate for paralegals in the Bay Area. Therefore, the court ordered prison officials to pay plaintiffs $3,553, the full amount in dispute. Prison officials timely appealed, arguing that the $169.50 per hour rate exceeded the rate for paralegal fees allowed under the PLRA. . . .

In order to determine whether the $169.50 per hour rate approved by the district court for paralegals was permissible under the PLRA, we begin by examining the plain language of the statute. *McDonald v. Sun Oil Co.*, 548 F.3d 774, 780 (9th Cir. 2008).

The PLRA governs prisoners' legal actions "with respect to prison conditions." *See* 42 U.S.C. §1997e(a). Limitations on attorney's fees are set forth in §1997e(d). Among other limitations, §1997e(d)(3) provides that "[n]o award of attorney's fees in an action [brought by prisoners in which attorney's fees are authorized under 42 U.S.C. §1988] shall be based on an hourly rate greater than 150 percent of the hourly rate established under section 3006A of Title 18, United States Code for payment of court-appointed counsel." 42 U.S.C. §1997e(d)(3). In other words, the district court has authority to award attorney's fees up to 150 percent of the hourly rate for counsel established in the Criminal Justice Act, 18 U.S.C. §3006A.

Section 3006A requires every district court, with the approval of the judicial counsel of the relevant circuit, to furnish representation for criminal defendants who lack the financial capacity to hire an attorney themselves. Relevant here, the statute sets forth the maximum hourly rate for payment of court-appointed counsel. . . . It also allows the Judicial Conference to raise the maximum hourly rate above $75 per hour from time to time pursuant to a complex formula set forth in the statute. Further, it requires the Judicial Conference to "develop guidelines for determining the maximum hourly rates for each circuit . . . with variations by district, where appropriate."

In 2000, the Judicial Conference increased the maximum hourly rate for court-appointed counsel to $113 in all ninety-four judicial districts, effective April 1, 2002. (Citations omitted.) Accordingly, reading the PLRA and the Criminal Justice Act together, the PLRA allows an award of attorney's fees in the Northern District of California based on an hourly rate up to 150 percent of $113, or $169.50.

We must next determine how the $169.50 per hour cap on attorney's fees applies to paralegal fees. Although the PLRA does not directly address paralegal fees, the Supreme Court has provided guidance on this issue in two opinions, *Jenkins*, 491 U.S. 274, 109 S.Ct. 2463, and *Richlin Security Service Co. v. Chertoff*, 553 U.S. 571, 128 S.Ct. 2007, 170 L.Ed.2d 960 (2008).

In *Missouri v. Jenkins*, the Court was tasked with interpreting the Civil Rights Attorney's Fees Awards Act of 1976, which provides for a "reasonable attorney's fee as part of the costs." 42 U.S.C. §1988(b); *Jenkins*, 491 U.S. at 276, 109 S.Ct. 2463. This is the same statute referenced in the PLRA. . . . The Court viewed as "self-evident" that a "reasonable attorney's fee" could not have been "meant to compensate only work performed personally by members of the bar." *Jenkins*, 491 U.S. at 285, 109 S.Ct. 2463. Instead, the Court explained, "reasonable attorney's fee" refers to a "reasonable fee for the work product of an attorney," including the work of "secretaries, messengers, librarians, janitors, and others whose labor contributes to the work product for which an attorney bills her client," as well as "other expenses and profit." *Id.*

Because there was no basis for distinguishing paralegals from librarians, the only "question [was] how the work of paralegals [was] to be valued." *Id.* The Court reasoned that an attorney could include paralegal work as part of the attorney's hourly fee and thus charge a higher rate to cover the value of the paralegal's services. *Id.* at 286-87, 109 S.Ct. 2463. Alternatively, the attorney could bill separately for the paralegal's services at market rates. *Id.* Concluding that the latter option did not give the attorney a windfall but actually made "economic sense" and could result in cost-savings, the Court held attorney's fees under §1988(b) can include separately billed paralegal fees, so long as these fees "are consistent with market rates and practices." *Id.* at 287-88, 109 S.Ct. 2463.

The Court affirmed the continued vitality of *Jenkins* in *Richlin*, which held that separately billed paralegal fees were compensable under the Equal Access to Justice Act. 553 U.S. at 590, 128 S.Ct. 2007. This act permits an eligible prevailing party to recover "fees and other expenses incurred by that party in connection with a proceeding before an administrative agency." *Id.* at 576, 128 S.Ct. 2007. . . . The Court explained that "[u]nder the reasoning of *Jenkins*, we take it as 'self-evident' that when Congress instructed agencies to award 'attorney . . . fees' to certain parties prevailing against the Government, that term was intended to embrace paralegal fees as well." *Jenkins* and *Richlin* thus make clear that where, as here, a party is entitled to attorney's fees under 42 U.S.C. §1988, they include separately billed paralegal fees at the market rate. Our conclusion in this regard is buttressed by the fact that the PLRA post-dates *Jenkins*. [Citation omitted.]

Therefore, because the PLRA allows an award of attorney's fees in the Northern District of California based on an hourly rate up to

$169.50, and because attorney's fees include separately billed paralegal fees, we conclude that the PLRA allows an award of paralegal fees up to $169.50 per hour. As the parties do not dispute that $169.50 per hour is below the paralegal market rate in the Bay Area, the district court did not abuse its discretion in awarding plaintiffs $169.50 per hour in this case.

The prison officials make a three-part argument as to why we should read the PLRA as capping paralegal fees at a lower hourly rate than the rate for court-appointed counsel. First, the prison officials note that §3006A requires the Judicial Conference to "develop guidelines for determining the maximum hourly rates for each circuit . . . with variations by district, where appropriate." 18 U.S.C. §3006A(d)(1). Second, they assert that the Judicial Conference has discharged this obligation by promulgating the *Guide to Judiciary Policy* (citation omitted). Section 320.70.50 of Volume 7 of the *Guide* provides that for services of paralegals, among other non-secretarial support personnel, "the court will determine a reasonable hourly compensation rate that may not exceed the lesser of the rate paid to counsel under the CJA or the rate typically charged by counsel to a fee-paying client for such services." *Id.*§320.70.50(a). The prison officials assert that this section constitutes a delegation of authority to district courts to determine hourly rates for paralegals. Third, the prison officials assert that the Northern District of California has exercised this delegation in its General Order No. 2 and its Criminal Justice Act Panel Attorney Manual, which provide that the hourly rate for paralegals may not exceed $55 per hour for contract paralegals or the salaried hourly rate, plus costs of employer-paid basic benefits, for paralegals who are employees. *See* United States District Court for the Northern District of California, *Criminal Justice Act Panel Attorney Manual* (citation omitted). Accordingly, the prison officials conclude that the PLRA limits paralegal fees to no more than 150 percent of the $55 hourly rate established under the *Manual*, or $82.50.

We disagree with this analysis. First, by its terms, the PLRA establishes that the rate for attorney's fees will be 150 percent of a single, benchmark rate: the "hourly rate established under section 3006A of title 18, United States Code, for payment of court-appointed counsel." 42 U.S.C. §1997e(d)(3). The PLRA does not authorize a court to award attorney's fees based on any rate other than this benchmark amount; therefore, a court making the calculation required by the PLRA is not limited by the hourly rates suggested by the Judicial Conference or established by the Northern District of California for payment of paralegals under the Criminal Justice Act. Second, although the prison officials make much of the direction in 18 U.S.C. §3006A to develop guidelines for determining the maximum hourly rates for attorney's fees, such guidelines are not binding on a court tasked with determining the maximum allowable hourly rate under the PLRA, because such guidelines do not themselves constitute the Judicial Conference's determination of the rate that is justified for a circuit or district. Rather, §3006A makes clear that the fees for court-appointed counsel mandated by that section are either $60 per hour or the higher amount determined by the Judicial Conference, and here the Judicial Conference has determined that $113 is justified for the Northern District of California. . . .

Finally, the prison officials argue that their interpretation of the PLRA is consistent with Congress's intent in enacting a statute limiting fees in prisoner cases, namely "to curtail frivolous prisoners' suits and to minimize the costs—which are borne by taxpayers—associated with those suits." *Madrid v. Gomez*, 190 F.3d 990, 996 (9th Cir. 1999). But as plaintiffs argue, Congress could have reasonably decided that placing a strict cap on attorney's fees, linked to the rate established under the Criminal Justice Act for court-appointed counsel, was sufficient to further this policy. The prison officials also note the incongruity of authorizing payment for paralegals at the same hourly rate as attorneys. Plaintiffs, however, explain that this anomaly is the result of a steady increase in both paralegal and attorney rates from 2002 to 2008, when the Criminal Justice Act failed to increase the hourly rate for court-appointed counsel. As a result, both the $113 per hour maximum rate for attorneys under the Criminal Justice Act, and even 150 percent of that rate as allowed under the PLRA, are below the market rate for attorneys and, now, paralegals. According to plaintiffs, this anomaly has diminished now that the Judicial Conference has raised the maximum hourly rate for court-appointed counsel to $142 (150 percent of which totals $213) per hour. [Citation omitted.]

Notwithstanding these policy considerations, we are bound by the plain language of the statute, and must "presume that [the] legislature says in a statute what it means and means in a statute what it says there." [Citations omitted.] Because the PLRA limits courts to an hourly rate that is 150 percent of the rate established for court-appointed counsel under the Criminal Justice Act and does not set a separate benchmark rate for paralegal fees, we affirm the district court's order granting plaintiffs' motion to compel payment of $3,553 in paralegal fees.

Questions about the Case

1. What is a cap on court-awarded legal fees? How is this mandated? How is the rate set?
2. Did the court follow the rulings of earlier Supreme Court cases? What were those cases and what did they hold?
3. What did the court decide about the application of the cap on the paralegal portion of the fee request?

4. What amount per hour was awarded for the paralegal time? What amount was awarded for the lawyers' time? How did this come about? Did this create any issues for the parties or the court?
5. What were the defendants' arguments and what did the court say about them?

This Florida case addresses the question of whether a "multiplier" should be applied to the paralegal fees.

St. Farm Mutual Automobile Ins. Co. v. Edge Family Chiropractic
41 So. 3d 293 (Fla.App. 1 Dist. 2010)

Respondents initiated the underlying [Personal Injury Protection] PIP cases after Petitioner stopped paying medical bills for injuries sustained by Respondents in separate motor vehicle accidents. One of the cases went to trial, resulting in a judgment for Respondents; the other two cases settled with Petitioner agreeing to resume paying the medical bills. Respondents thereafter sought an award of attorney's fees and costs in each case pursuant to section 627.428, Florida Statutes.

Petitioner did not contest Respondents' entitlement to attorney's fees, but because the parties were unable to agree on the amount of the award, the county court held an evidentiary hearing on the issue. At the hearing, the parties stipulated to the hourly rate ($95.00/hour) and number of hours to be awarded for paralegal work. The parties presented conflicting evidence as to the reasonable hourly rate and number of hours for Respondents' attorney and as to the justification for applying a multiplier to the award.

In detailed orders, the county court resolved the conflicts in the evidence and found that the reasonable hourly rate for Respondents' attorney was $350.00/hour and that a 1.5 multiplier was justified in one of the cases and that a 2.0 multiplier was justified in the other two cases. The county court applied the multipliers to the entire fee award, including the paralegal fees. Petitioner appealed the county court's orders to the circuit court, raising the same two issues stated above. The circuit court consolidated the cases and *per curiam* affirmed the county court's orders. Petitioner timely petitioned this court for a writ of certiorari.

The scope of our review in this second-tier certiorari proceeding is limited to determining whether the circuit court afforded due process or departed from the essential requirements of law. . . .

The parties have not cited, nor have we been able to locate, any controlling authority as to whether the multiplier is to be applied only to attorney's fees or whether it may also be applied to paralegal fees.

Relying primarily on two federal district court decisions, Petitioner argues that the multiplier is to be applied only to attorney's fees and that the circuit court departed from the essential requirements of law in affirming the county court's application of the multipliers to the paralegal fees. In response, Respondents cite section 57.104, Florida Statutes, which provides:

> In any action in which attorney's fees are to be determined or awarded by the court, the court shall consider, among other things, time and labor of any legal assistants who contributed nonclerical, meaningful legal support to the matter involved and who are working under the supervision of an attorney.

Respondents argue that based upon this statute, the county court properly included the paralegal fees in the attorney's fee award to which the multipliers were applied and that the circuit court did not violate any "clearly established law" in affirming the county court's orders. Respondents also argue that the failure to apply a multiplier to paralegal fees would compel attorneys to assign paralegal tasks to associate attorneys or perform the work themselves at much higher rates, which would substantially increase the attorney's fees paid by insurers and other responsible parties.

Section 57.104 was enacted in 1987 in response to this court's decision in *Bill Rivers Trailers, Inc. v. Miller*, 489 So.2d 1139 (Fla. 1st DCA 1986). The statute was intended to "reverse" that decision and "specifically provide that an award of attorney's fees would include an award for the services of a legal assistant employed by the attorney." . . .

Bill Rivers Trailers involved a suit over commissions on the sale of refrigerated trailers. 489 So.2d at 1140. The dispute was submitted to arbitration and was resolved in favor of the plaintiff, Miller. *Id.* at 1141. Miller subsequently moved for an award of attorney's fees and costs as the prevailing party. *Id.* The trial court granted the motion and, among other things, awarded fees for the substantive legal work performed by a legal assistant. *Id.* On appeal, this court affirmed the trial court's determination that Miller was the prevailing party, but reversed the fee award because only the attorney's fees (and not the legal assistant's fees) were recoverable. *Id.* at 1143. The court remanded for a determination of a reasonable fee "based upon all appropriate factors having no direct arithmetical relation to the number of hours expended by legal assistants who are not attorneys." *Id.*

Judge Joanos dissented from the reversal of the fees awarded for the work of the legal assistant. . . . In his view, it was appropriate to separately itemize and include the legal assistant's fee as part of the attorney's fee award. Judge Joanos also observed that it was unrealistic to require work needing less expertise and experience to be performed by the attorney in order to be compensated and he pointed out that a legal assistant, performing delegated work under the supervision of counsel and for which counsel is responsible, was "a less expensive way of doing things rather than for the attorney to have done all of the work himself." These observations are borne out by the facts of this case, which reflect that a significant amount of the legal work was done by the paralegal at an hourly rate that was less than one-third of the attorney's hourly rate.

Judge Joanos' observations and section 57.104 are consistent with the prevailing view that an attorney's fee award may include paralegal fees because the paralegal's work is a component of the attorney's work product. In *Missouri v. Jenkins*, 491 U.S. 274, 109 S.Ct. 2463, 105 L.Ed.2d 229 (1989), for example, the Court held that the term "reasonable attorney's fee" in 42 U.S.C. §1988 encompasses not only the work of the attorney, but also that of paralegals whose labor contributes to the attorney's ultimate work product. . . . The Court also observed that the use of lower cost paralegals rather than attorneys encourages cost-effective delivery of legal services and reduces the cost of litigation because, if paralegal fees were not recoverable as part of the attorney's fee award "it would not be surprising to see a greater amount of such work performed by attorneys themselves, thus increasing the overall cost of litigation." *Id.* at 288 n. 10, 109 S.Ct. 2463.

The Court recently reaffirmed *Jenkins* in *Richlin Security Service Co. v. Chertoff*, 553 U.S. 571, 128 S.Ct. 2007, 170 L.Ed.2d 960 (2008), where it held the term "attorney's fees" in another federal statute included fees for paralegal services as well as compensation for the attorney's own labor. As in *Jenkins*, the Court declared that it was "self-evident" that the statute embraced not only attorney's fees, but also paralegal fees. *Id.* at 2014-15.

Although none of these cases involved the application of a multiplier to paralegal fees, the cases (and section 57.104) clearly establish the principle that the paralegal's work is a component of the attorney's ultimate work product. This, in turn, provides support for the application of the multiplier to paralegal fees because the purpose of the multiplier is to enhance the fee calculated under the lodestar methodology to take into account the fact that an attorney working on a contingent fee contract is generally not compensated for any of the services provided to a client when the client does not prevail. (Citation omitted.) Because the potentially uncompensated legal services provided to the client include not only the attorney's work, but also the paralegal's work, it is appropriate to apply the multiplier to the paralegal fees included in the award. Stated another way, because the paralegal's work is part of the legal services provided to the client, there is no principled reason to treat paralegal fees any different from attorney's fees in regards to the application of the multiplier. *Cf. Jenkins*, 491 U.S. at 287, 109 S.Ct. 2463 (rejecting the argument that awarding paralegal fees at the prevailing market rate, rather than the cost to the attorney, would result in a windfall to the attorney because that same argument would apply to associate attorneys and it has never been suggested that the hourly rate applied to the work of an associate attorney in a law firm creates a windfall for the firm's partners or is otherwise improper).

The federal district court cases cited by Petitioner do not compel a contrary decision. First, the cases are not binding precedent; they are, at most, persuasive authority. [Citation omitted.] Second, one of the cases [citation omitted] pre-dated *Jenkins* and section 57.104, and the other case [citation omitted] is not even published in the official reports. Third, neither of the cases includes any analysis supporting the decision not to apply the multiplier to paralegal fees; the cases merely make a blanket statement that the paralegal fees are not to be increased by a multiplier. . . .

In sum, because there is no "clearly established law" prohibiting the application of a multiplier to paralegal fees that are included as part of an attorney's fee award, and because section 57.104 clearly supports the inclusion of the paralegal fees as attorney's fees, we conclude that the circuit court did not depart from the essential requirements of law in affirming the county court orders at issue in this case. Accordingly, the petition for writ of certiorari is DENIED.

Questions about the Case

1. What is a multiplier and when is it applied? What is the public policy reason for it?
2. How much would the multiplier increase the lawyer and paralegal fees?
3. What were the arguments against applying the multiplier?
4. What U.S. Supreme Court cases were cited? For what principles?
5. What was the court's decision and why?

In this California case, a federal court refuses to award fees for paralegal time if the paralegals are not qualified under the California statute regulating paralegals.

Sanford v. GMRI, Inc.
CIV-S-04-1535 DFL CMK, 2005 WL 4782697
(E.D. Cal. 2005)

Plaintiff James Sanford ("Sanford") moves for attorneys' fees and costs in the amount of $18,268.09 following the settlement of his ADA accessibility lawsuit against defendant GMRI, Inc. ("GMRI"). GMRI challenges the reasonableness of the requested fee award. For the following reasons, the court awards $8,132.67 in attorneys' fees and costs.

Sanford, a quadriplegic, filed his lawsuit on August 5, 2004, claiming that he experienced numerous access barriers on his visits to GMRI's Red Lobster restaurant. On August 18, 2005, the parties filed a settlement agreement and the case was dismissed. Sanford released all of his equitable relief claims in exchange for $8,000 in monetary damages and GMRI's promise to remove or remedy the remaining architectural barriers. The resolution of the attorneys' fees issue was left for this motion.

The ADA provides that a court "in its discretion, may allow the prevailing party . . . a reasonable attorney's fee, including litigation expenses, and costs." 42 U.S.C. §12205. . . .

Sanford requests $18,268.09 in attorneys' fees and costs. This amount includes $11,300 in attorney and paralegal fees for 61.45 billed hours and $6,968.09 in litigation expenses and costs. The bulk of the requested litigation expenses consists of $5,513.75 in expert's fees. While conceding that Sanford is the prevailing party, GMRI challenges the hours requested on several grounds. In addition, GMRI argues that Sanford's request for expert witness fees should be denied as insufficiently documented. . . .

GMRI argues that the lodestar figure should be reduced to reflect Sanford's limited success. One of the factors courts must consider in determining the lodestar figure is the "results obtained" in the litigation, especially where a plaintiff did not succeed on some of his claims. . . . Because Hubbard's time entries cannot be easily divided between the successful and unsuccessful claims, the court reduces Sanford's fee award by one-third to account for his limited success. . . .

GMRI also challenges the appropriateness of Hubbard's requested hours, asserting that many of them are unnecessary, excessive, and/or redundant. . . . First, it argues that many of Hubbard's requested hours were unnecessary because Hubbard expended resources on claims which he knew Sanford lacked standing to pursue. However, this is already accounted for in the reduction addressed above. Second, GMRI argues that Hubbard's fees are excessive. For example, GMRI argues that Hubbard's bill for 0.80 hours for preparation of his boilerplate settlement demand letter was unreasonable. Hubbard responds that the amount of time spent drafting the settlement letter was not excessive as he also reviewed the file and associated documents. . . . GMRI makes similar arguments as to other entries, challenging a total of 2.25 hours. The court is not persuaded that these hours were excessive or unnecessary and declines to strike them. The court notes that these hours will be reduced by one third in any event.

In addition to the above charges, GMRI challenges the time billed for plaintiff's motion to compel a site inspection. . . . The court agrees with defendant that these hours were not reasonably expended and should not be awarded.

Similarly, GMRI challenges the time Hubbard took to read its responses and objections to discovery requests. It submitted the same responses and objections in the two previous cases filed against it by

Hubbard, so it argues that it should have only taken 0.50 hours, not 3.65 to review the responses here. The court agrees that these hours are excessive given the repetitive nature of the litigation prosecuted by plaintiff's counsel. The court will reduce these hours to 1 hour.

Third, GMRI challenges the reasonableness of Sanford's claimed paralegal fees. Sanford seeks to recover paralegal-level rates for individuals that Hubbard has previously categorized as legal assistants. Under California Business & Professional Code §6450(c), a person is qualified as a paralegal if: (1) she possesses a certificate of completion of a paralegal program from an ABA-approved or other accredited post-secondary institution; (2) she possesses a baccalaureate degree and has completed one year of law-related experience under the supervision of a qualified attorney; or (3) she possesses a high school diploma or GED and has completed three years of law-related experience under the supervision of a qualified attorney before December 31, 2003. GMRI challenges each of the five individuals listed as paralegals.

First, it alleges that Sanford must present the court with a "written declaration . . . stating that [each individual] is qualified to perform paralegal tasks." Cal. Bus. & Prof. Code §6450(c)(3). Hubbard's declaration generally states that each of the individuals is qualified to perform paralegal tasks. Therefore, Sanford has met this requirement.

Next, GMRI challenges each of the individuals based on her failure to meet the §6450 requirements listed above. Sanford concedes that Christa Duncan will not be a qualified paralegal until she receives her certificate of completion from a paralegal program. In addition, it appears that Alisha Petras is not a qualified paralegal because: (1) she does not have a baccalaureate degree or paralegal certification; and (2) Sanford has not shown that she completed three years of law-related experience under a qualified attorney before December 2003. Finally, MeLisa Dotson and Elva Garcia hold baccalaureate degrees, but they did not complete their one year of law-related service under a qualified attorney until June of this year. Therefore, any time attributed to Dotson and Garcia before June 2005 should not have been billed at a paralegal rate.

On the other hand, GMRI's challenge to Bonnie Vonderhaar should fail. GMRI argues that Vonderhaar does not qualify because Sanford fails to present evidence that she completed one year of legal experience under the supervision of a qualified attorney. However, she satisfies §6450(c) because she holds a paralegal certificate from a NALA-approved institution. Therefore, she is a qualified paralegal in California.

In sum, Duncan and Petras should have been categorized as legal assistants for the entire case, and Dotson and Garcia should have been categorized as legal assistants for any time billed before June 2005. Sanford does not provide a proposed fee for legal assistants. Therefore, Sanford can only recover paralegal rates for Vonderhaar's time and Dotson's and Garcia's time post–June 2005. The resulting fee award is $225.00 out of the total $1,680.00 billed, or a reduction of $1,455.00. . . .

Based on the foregoing discussion, Sanford is awarded $4,957.50 for attorneys' fees, calculated as follows:

***Attorneys/Assistants	Hours	Rate	Total
Lynn Hubbard (attorney)	27.50	$250	$6,875.00
Scott Hubbard (associate)	1.90	$175	$ 332.50
Paralegals	3.00	$75	$ 225.00
Sub-Total:			$7,432.50
Limited Success Reduction (1/3):			$4,957.50

In addition, the court awards Sanford's requested litigation expenses and costs minus a portion of the requested expert witness fees, totaling $3,175.17. In sum, the court awards Sanford $8,132.67 in attorneys' fees and costs. . . .

Questions about the Case

1. Under what statute did the lawyer seek attorneys' fees? Was there any discussion of whether or not attorneys' fees under this statute should include paralegal time at market rates?
2. What was the basis for reducing the paralegal fees?
3. Given what you learned in this chapter about fee petitions, what should the lawyer herein have done to ensure that he would get fully compensated for paralegal time?
4. Is there such a thing as a "NALA-approved" paralegal program? What does the statute really say about the entities that approve paralegal programs?
5. What message does this case send to lawyers in California who might be seeking attorneys' fees under federal statutes?

See other related cases with the same name for additional findings about compensation for paralegal time in fee awards.

In this recent case, the Ohio Supreme Court sanctioned a lawyer for failure to supervise a paralegal regarding the distribution of settlement proceeds.

Cincinnati Bar Assn v. Kathman
165 Ohio St. 3d 283, 178 N.E.3d 484 (2021)

In June or July 2015, attorney Edward Kathman hired Jillian Gorman to work as a paralegal in his law practice. Gorman's job duties were related to Kathman's representation of personal-injury plaintiffs and included preparing contingent-fee agreements using the form that

Kathman had adopted in his practice, corresponding with insurance companies on Kathman's behalf, and collecting information related to clients' damages and medical expenses. Kathman also authorized Gorman to prepare closing statements after a client had settled a personal-injury claim and to write—but not sign—checks on Kathman's IOLTA to distribute the settlement proceeds to the client. Kathman did not give Gorman authority to enter into contingent-fee agreements on his behalf or to sign checks on his operating account.

In February 2016, Gorman witnessed an accident in which Jeffrey Welch was injured, and at the scene, she recommended that Welch hire Kathman. The parties stipulated that Welch would have testified at Kathman's disciplinary hearing that he had met with Gorman and Kathman within two weeks of the accident and signed papers so that Kathman could prosecute a claim on his behalf. But Kathman disputes that such a meeting occurred. Kathman maintains that he never discussed any aspect of Welch's case, including its value, with Gorman or Welch before October 2016. Kathman has no records of his representation of Welch, and he has no knowledge whether any such documentation was stored on the laptop he had provided to Gorman. Kathman stipulated that Gorman invited Welch to her house in October 2016, where she discussed a settlement amount of $20,000 with him. Kathman testified that he spoke with Welch on the phone a few times and invited Welch to meet with him at his office. On November 29, 2016, Welch signed a release and settlement agreement during a meeting with Kathman and Gorman.

Neither Gorman nor Kathman provided Welch with a copy of the release and settlement agreement, and Welch never received the settlement amount. At a subsequent meeting with Kathman, Welch asked about the status of a $20,000 settlement check that had been issued by the insurance company in his case. When Kathman inquired into the issuance of a $20,000 check by the insurance company in connection with the Welch case, he learned that Gorman had forged his signature on the back of the check. The parties stipulated and the board found that Kathman's conduct violated Prof. Cond.R. 5.3(a) (requiring a lawyer possessing managerial authority in a law firm to make reasonable efforts to ensure that the firm has in effect measures giving reasonable assurance that the conduct of a nonlawyer employed by the firm is compatible with the professional obligations of the lawyer) and 5.3(b) (requiring a lawyer having direct supervisory authority to take reasonable efforts to ensure that a nonlawyer employee's conduct is compatible with the professional obligations of the lawyer).

Kathman provided improper financial assistance to clients on five occasions . . . before settling their cases. He later reimbursed himself out of their settlement proceeds. With respect to these occurrences, the parties stipulated and the board found that Kathman violated Prof.Cond.R. 1.8(e) (prohibiting a lawyer from providing financial assistance to a client in connection with pending or contemplated litigation except in certain limited circumstances).

Prof.Cond.R. 1.15(a) requires attorneys to hold the property of clients in an interest-bearing client trust account, separate from the lawyer's own property, and to create and maintain certain records regarding the client funds held in their IOLTA. Kathman used his IOLTA to mainly receive and disburse settlement proceeds from personal-injury cases. Instead of creating a separate record for the account itself indicating the date, amount, and client affected for each debit and credit, Kathman relied on the account's check register. Kathman stipulated that he also failed to maintain a copy of the individual deposit receipts or slips for each of the deposits he made into the account and that he did not perform and retain a monthly account reconciliation. On these facts, the parties stipulated and the board found that Kathman violated Prof.Cond.R. 1.15(a)(3) (requiring a lawyer to maintain a record for the lawyer's client trust account, setting forth the account balance and the name of the account, the date, the amount, and the client affected by each credit and debit), 1.15(a)(4) (requiring a lawyer to maintain all bank statements, deposit slips, and canceled checks, if provided by the bank, for each bank account), and 1.15(a)(5) (requiring a lawyer to perform and retain a monthly reconciliation of the funds held in the lawyer's client trust account).

Kathman stipulated that between February 1, 2016, and March 31, 2020, he consistently kept more than a minimal amount of his own funds in the IOLTA—indeed, for a three-month period he kept at least $150,000 of his own funds in the account. The parties stipulated and the board found that by doing so, Kathman violated Prof.Cond.R. 1.15(b) (prohibiting a lawyer from depositing his or her own funds in a client trust account except to pay or obtain a waiver of bank service charges). The board also found by clear and convincing evidence that this conduct resulted in the improper commingling of personal and client funds in violation of Prof.Cond.R. 1.15(a) (requiring a lawyer to hold the property of clients in an interest-bearing client trust account, separate from the lawyer's own property). The board found that Kathman committed additional violations of Prof.Cond.R. 1.15(a) and 1.15(b) with respect to several specific clients. In multiple instances, Kathman provided payees with checks from his IOLTA, allowing them to cash the checks and secure the IOLTA funds before Kathman's bank had collected or finally received payment on the checks that provided the source of the amounts paid out . . . The record also shows and the parties have stipulated that on at least two occasions, Kathman accepted or held funds in his IOLTA for a "friend," although the funds had no relationship to a legal matter.

Based on these stipulations regarding improper use of the IOLTA and commingling of Kathman's personal funds with client funds, the board found additional violations of Prof.Cond.R. 1.15(a) and 1.15(b).

Kathman stipulated that at some point, he had permitted a client to pay him through PayPal for legal services he was retained to provide. Kathman provided the PayPal account information to the client and, when Kathman received the client's payment into that account, he linked the PayPal account to his IOLTA. Thereafter, without Kathman's permission or — initially — knowledge, someone gained access to his PayPal account and, through that, to the IOLTA. That person effected various payments out of the IOLTA that were unrelated to the interest of any of Kathman's clients or Kathman himself and were unauthorized by Kathman or any client.

No client suffered any loss as a result of these unauthorized transactions, because the bank paid all the charges out of Kathman's personal funds that were on deposit in the IOLTA. Because Kathman's initial efforts to remedy the unauthorized use of his IOLTA through PayPal failed, the unauthorized use continued over a prolonged period of time. Finally, Kathman cured the problem by opening a new IOLTA through which future transactions would be conducted while leaving the earlier IOLTA open to allow outstanding transactions to be completed. In light of these stipulations, the board found that Kathman "fail[ed] to safeguard funds of his clients or third persons" and that he thereby violated Prof. Cond.R. 1.15(a).

Gorman carried out her assigned duties with minimal or no oversight. Kathman gave her a laptop and permitted her to work outside of his small office, but the laptop was not linked or networked with his office computer. Kathman discovered Gorman's wrongdoing during the week of July 3, 2017, while Gorman was on vacation: he opened a bank statement related to his client trust account and discovered that certain checks had cleared that were out of numerical sequence. After inquiring with the bank, he discovered that the checks had been made payable to Gorman herself. He demanded that Gorman return the computer but concluded that it was "inoperable" and did not recover any data from it.

Kathman terminated Gorman's employment and reported her actions to the police. Gorman pleaded guilty to one count of theft and one count of forgery, was sentenced to five years of community control, and was ordered to make restitution in the amount of $200,000. *State v. Gorman*, Hamilton C.P. No. B 1701441 (Feb. 28, 2018). As of October 13, 2020, Gorman had made only $2,535 in restitution.

With respect to mitigating factors, the board accepted the parties' stipulation that Kathman exhibited a cooperative attitude toward the disciplinary proceedings. *See* Gov.Bar R. V(13)(C)(4). Additionally, the board found that Kathman acted without a selfish or dishonest motive, made a timely, good-faith effort to make restitution or to rectify the consequences of his misconduct, and presented evidence of good character or reputation in the form of 13 letters. *See* Gov.Bar R. V(13)(C)(2), (3), and (5).

As for aggravating factors, the board found that Kathman had prior discipline that resulted in an actual suspension from the practice of law and committed multiple offenses. *See* Gov.Bar R. V(13)(B)(1) and (4). Kathman's failure to supervise Gorman, together with the trust-account violations and the multiple instances of advancing money to clients, warrants an actual suspension, particularly in light of his prior disciplinary offense.

. . . Accordingly, we suspend Kathman from the practice of law for one year, with six months of that suspension stayed on the conditions that Kathman engage in no further misconduct and that he pay the cost of these proceedings. If Kathman violates any of these conditions, the stay will be lifted and Kathman will serve the full one-year suspension from the practice of law. Prior to his reinstatement to the practice of law, Kathman shall complete a minimum of 24 hours of CLE on the topics of professional ethics and law-office management. And upon reinstatement to the practice of law, he shall serve a one-year term of monitored probation pursuant to Gov.Bar R. V(21), during which he shall accept the appointment by relator of an attorney monitor who shall provide guidance to Kathman on professional ethics, personnel management, law-office management, and compliance with the IOLTA and record-keeping requirements of the Rules of Professional Conduct.

Questions about the Case

1. What were the specific duties for which Gorman, the paralegal, was hired in this case?
2. What conduct did Kathman engage in related to client trust accounts? What did the court say about this?
3. What steps should Kathman have taken to ensure that Gorman did not act in violation of the ethical rules?
4. Which ethical rules did the court contend were violated?
5. What are the mitigating and aggravating factors that were considered in the court's decision?

8
Competence

This chapter addresses the issue of competence, an essential element of ethical conduct in every profession. Lack of professional competence in legal practice is grounds for both legal remedies and disciplinary sanctions. Chapter 8 covers:

- definitions of lawyer and paralegal competence
- key components of paralegal competence, including:
  - knowledge
  - skills
  - thoroughness and preparation
  - diligence and promptness
  - communication with clients
- sanctions for incompetence, including disciplinary actions and malpractice suits
- malpractice actions, including trends and patterns
- common dilemmas confronting paralegals in the area of competence, including those related to delegation, supervision, and attorney review of work
- factors in the work environment that affect competence

A. Introduction

Lawyers are obligated to represent clients competently by both ethics codes and the common law rules of tort liability for professional negligence. A lawyer's duty to represent a client competently also makes the lawyer responsible for the work of paralegals and others in the law firm; the ultimate responsibility for the competent handling of a client matter rests with the lawyer.

Paralegals must perform competently and hold competence as one of their highest values, both because they desire professional status and treatment and because they share with the lawyer the moral and ethical responsibility for providing quality legal services. As discussed in Chapter 2, paralegals should also be mindful of their own personal tort liability — clients may name paralegals in malpractice actions against lawyers.

Acting competently encompasses knowledge, skills, and their application. As a starting point, most definitions of competence begin with legal knowledge and skill.

B. Legal Education

The knowledge required for lawyer competence generally begins with, at a minimum, a law school education of three or four years followed by passing a bar examination, which tests substantive legal knowledge and judgmental-analytical ability. In many states, bar exams also include a section that requires the candidate to apply legal knowledge and skills to a hypothetical legal matter that simulates real life. As law schools have sought to make legal education more relevant to practice, clinical programs, lawyering skills, and trial techniques courses have been added to the traditional law school curriculum in most law schools. Virtually all schools offer internship and externship programs, many for course credit. Periodically, there are calls for mandatory apprenticeships as a prerequisite to bar admission to ensure that lawyers get practical training before they serve clients. Lawyers learn on the job from more experienced lawyers in the firms that hire them. Some of this training is informal: learning by example, using model forms and documents available in the firm, and improving skills through trial and error under another lawyer's oversight. Some is more formal, by means of in-house training programs, associate professional development and career progression pathways, and mentoring by more experienced lawyers.

Lawyers must continue to develop their legal knowledge and skills throughout their careers. Formal continuing education programs are an important aspect of this. All states have mandatory continuing legal education, usually about 12-15 hours a year. Beyond these mandates, continuing one's professional development is a matter of commitment and integrity, driven by the sense of personal satisfaction derived from doing one's job well, appreciating the ever-changing nature of law and procedure, and valuing the important service that lawyers provide to clients and society at large.

The significant changes in the delivery of legal services and the related ebb and flow in law school enrollments have disrupted legal education in ways not seen for many decades. In this environment, some law schools are closing or merging with other educational institutions, and others are attempting to reinvent themselves. Among the changes they are making are offering more law-related non-JD degree programs and placing more emphasis on practice preparation in the JD programs. The ABA and some law schools have acted on the recommendations of the ABA Task Force on the Future of Legal Education, which has acknowledged the problem created by rising tuition and student debt, the shrinking applicant pool, and the declining number of jobs for new lawyers. This task force has also called for "new or improved frameworks for licensing or otherwise authorizing [nonlawyer] providers of legal services" to increase access to justice. This now also includes nonlawyer legal practitioners. (See more on the discussion of nonlawyer legal service providers and nonlawyer legal practitioners in Chapter 3.)

C. Paralegal Education

Paralegals share lawyers' commitment to education and skill development. Because paralegals in many jurisdictions do not have to comply with minimum educational standards, the responsibility for achieving and maintaining competence through education and skill development rests firmly with paralegals and the lawyers who employ them.

Paralegal education programs are as new as the profession itself—only about 55 years old. The first programs were established around 1970, an estimated half dozen scattered across the country. At last count, there are as many as a thousand paralegal programs situated in a wide variety of institutions, including traditional two- and four-year colleges (both public and private), multidisciplinary and freestanding proprietary institutions (some of which are vocationally oriented), and online schools.

Unlike the law school curriculum, paralegal curricula are not standardized, and offerings vary widely in length, content, format, level of sophistication, and degree of specialization. Good programs teach an appropriate balance of substantive law and practical job skills, have access to a good library collection that includes legal research databases, hire and train well-qualified faculty, and provide services to help students achieve their goal of finding an appropriate paralegal position upon graduation.

More than 260 paralegal programs are currently approved by the American Bar Association (ABA), having met guidelines on curriculum, admissions, faculty, administration, staff, facilities, finances, library, and support services, such as counseling and placement. ABA approval, first granted in 1975, is the only kind of specialized recognition of paralegal educational programs available. It is purely voluntary and is not formally recognized by the federal government; the ABA has never sought such recognition. The standards for paralegal education are set forth in the American Bar Association Guidelines for the Approval of Paralegal Education Programs. The American Association for Paralegal Education, representing more than 300 paralegal programs, also supports paralegal educators to develop and offer quality educational experiences for their students.

Formal paralegal education has become the recognized pathway for entry into the paralegal profession, although firm hiring standards vary throughout the country. Some firms do not require formal paralegal education but favor candidates who have formal training over those who do not. In some cities, a baccalaureate degree alone is the hiring standard in large law firms, while a baccalaureate degree and a paralegal certificate has become the hiring standard in large law firms in other locations. Smaller firms often require previous legal work experience.

Guideline 1 of the ABA Model Guidelines for the Utilization of Paralegal Services (ABA Model Guidelines), in stating the lawyer's responsibility for the actions of paralegals, emphasizes the importance of paralegal education. The comment to the Guideline states that a lawyer should ensure that a paralegal is competent to perform assigned tasks based on the paralegal's education, training, and experience. This Guideline builds on ABA Model Rule 5.3, which requires lawyers to make reasonable efforts to ensure that the conduct of nonlawyer employees is compatible with the lawyer's professional obligations. This rule and the common law rules of tort liability are discussed in Chapter 2. It should be noted that some states set minimum educational requirements and require continuing education. (See Chapter 2.) Several state guidelines on paralegals note that lawyers should ensure that paralegals are competent to do the work they are assigned, and some have a guideline that reflects the paralegal's duty of competence. Several states have a guideline on continuing education for paralegals. The voluntary certification programs that now exist in a few states also set requirements for entry-level and ongoing education. Guideline 10 of the ABA Model Guidelines advises lawyers to encourage continuing education for their paralegals to assure competence.

Whether or not employers require it, paralegals should acquire appropriate formal education to meet their professional obligation of competence. This education should include not only a basic paralegal education but also regular and frequent continuing education to update areas of expertise and to develop skills and higher levels of expertise. Continuing education is available to paralegals in many forms. Paralegals can take courses designed for lawyers or courses designed specifically for paralegals. Continuing education for lawyers and paralegals is readily available through state and local bar associations and independent providers. Paralegal-specific continuing education is provided by paralegal programs; local, regional, and national paralegal associations; and a few independent organizations.

Both major national organizations, the National Association of Legal Assistants (NALA) and the National Federation of Paralegal Associations (NFPA), promote competence and provide continuing education to their members. NALA's Code of Ethics Canon 6 requires paralegals to maintain a high degree of competency. NALA has translated this ideal into action by offering its **Certified Paralegal** examination and its advanced certification examinations, discussed in Chapter 2. Educational or experience requirements must be met to sit for the exams, and CPs must meet continuing education requirements to maintain their certified status. The NFPA Model Code contains a strong statement concerning competence and education in Canon 1.1. It states that "[p]aralegals shall achieve and maintain a high level of competence," through education, training, and work experience. The Code also recommends that paralegals participate in a minimum of 12 hours of continuing education a year and complete all assignments promptly and efficiently. NFPA requires PACE **Registered Paralegals** to participate in continuing education and monitors compliance as NALA also does for CPs. Both NALA and NFPA have annual national educational conferences and encourage their local chapters to provide frequent continuing education seminars.

> **Certified Paralegal**
> Certification for paralegals offered by NALA for passing the Certified Paralegal Examination.

> **Registered Paralegal**
> Certification offered by NFPA for passing the Paralegal Advanced Competency Examination.

D. A Definition of Competency

Competence cannot be defined solely in terms of formal education and professional skill. These are essential preconditions to competence, but competence has full meaning only when it is applied to the tasks at hand—to the specific legal work to be done.

The ABA Model Rules define competence in Model Rule 1.1, which states that competent representation requires "the legal knowledge, skill, thoroughness and preparation reasonably necessary for the representation." Model Rule 1.3 adds two more elements by requiring lawyers to "act with reasonable diligence and promptness." Finally, Rule 1.4 adds that lawyers must communicate effectively, meaning that they must inform clients promptly when a matter requires their informed consent, must reasonably consult with clients, must keep them "reasonably informed" and explain matters to "permit the client to make informed decisions," and must "promptly comply with reasonable requests for information."

These ethics rules and the cases interpreting them can be synthesized into a list of qualities that comprise competence for lawyers and paralegals alike.

1. Knowledge

Both lawyers and paralegals must have appropriate formal education, both legal and general, that enables them to communicate well, in both oral and written form; that provides them with knowledge of substantive law and procedure; that has developed their analytical and judgmental abilities; and that has provided them with the information and skills needed to resolve legal issues presented by clients.

The body of knowledge needed by the lawyer and the paralegal differs somewhat because the lawyer exercises independent professional judgment about how to advise and serve clients, while the paralegal participates in the practical steps both preliminary to these decisions (*e.g.*, interviewing clients, conducting legal and factual research) and later in implementing plans for handling a client matter (*e.g.*, drafting a document, preparing for trial). Further, lawyers represent clients as advocates in courts, which paralegals do not do.

The legal knowledge needed to be competent is highly specialized. As the law has become increasingly complex, most practitioners emphasize no more than a few areas of practice. The trend away from "general practice" is reflected in specialized certification programs offered for lawyers by most states, by the departmentalization of large firms, and by the widespread existence of "boutique" firms that devote themselves to highly specialized areas of law. Lawyers have a duty to refer highly complex, specialized cases to another attorney with appropriate expertise if they do not have the necessary expertise.

Paralegals usually specialize in one practice area, working in areas like civil litigation, estate planning, corporate law, family law, real estate, and bankruptcy. Most paralegal programs' curricula include required specialty courses, and most paralegal continuing education programs are devoted to specialized or advanced courses.

Orientation and formal on-the-job training have become important elements of legal training. Large law firms and government agencies often have formal in-house training programs for lawyers and paralegals, which not only orient them to the firm's "way of doing things" but also teach substantive knowledge and skills. Many firms have in-house training for paralegals on functions such as legal research, technology-based discovery management, and document productions.

2. Professional Skills

Skills are acquired through formal education and through training and experience on the job. Skills include both intellectual skills, such as analytical reasoning and communicating effectively, and the job-specific skills needed for the execution of tasks and the implementation of plans for handling a client matter into action. Professional job-specific skills needed most by paralegals include drafting documents, analyzing documents, summarizing information, handling procedural matters, gathering information, conducting legal and factual research, and technology acumen. Lawyers need different skills, such as trial advocacy and negotiating.

3. Thoroughness and Preparation

In applying knowledge and skills to a legal problem, both lawyers and paralegals must be thorough in their information gathering, analysis, application of judgment, and actions. Neglecting to learn all the facts, to fill out forms properly, or to be meticulous about every detail can have devastating consequences for the client. Because paralegals are especially valued for their knowledge of the facts in the cases they work on and for their attention to detail, thoroughness is one of the most critical aspects of paralegal competence.

Related is preparation. Most successful lawyers and paralegals credit their success in large part to their careful and thorough preparation. Paralegals are often delegated considerable responsibility for preparation, for example, by organizing documents and other information before a trial or by drafting and organizing documents for a real estate or corporate closing. To be effective, the paralegal and lawyer must work together as a team in preparation.

4. Diligence and Promptness

Legal knowledge and skills are worthless unless they are applied to a client matter in a timely and attentive manner. "Diligence" means persistent attention to the legal matter to ensure that it is resolved with the best possible outcome for the client. A lack of diligence or promptness can lead to delays that harm a client's case or cause the client unnecessary anxiety. Examples of failure to act diligently and promptly include missing court dates and appointments, frequently needing continuances, missing a statute of limitations or other filing deadline, not pursuing discovery timely, or taking an unnecessarily long time to act. The duty of diligence requires lawyers and paralegals to be well organized and managed to guard against the missing of critical deadlines, scheduling of conflicting court dates, and so forth. Often these important organizational tasks are delegated to paralegals. (See the *Pincay* case at the end of this chapter for an instance of a missed deadline.)

5. Communication with Clients

The importance of clear communication with clients cannot be overstated. The good work of competent lawyers and paralegals will not be recognized if clients are not kept fully informed about the status of their cases. Lawyers and paralegals must return clients' phone calls and respond to their e-mails promptly. Lawyers must keep clients informed and not make key decisions on the handling of their matters without consultation. Ongoing communication with clients is often an important duty of paralegals. Many lawyers are too busy in court and meetings to return clients' calls as promptly as clients would like and to make regular reports on how matters are proceeding. Paralegals are ideally situated to handle this kind of communication.

E. Consequences of Failure to Act Competently

Malpractice
Improper conduct in the performance of duties by a professional, either intentionally or through negligence.

Failure to act competently can be fatal to a client's rights and to a lawyer's or a paralegal's career. Professional negligence in the handling of a case is the most common basis for ***malpractice*** actions against attorneys. Professional negligence is defined as the failure to exercise the standard of care commonly observed in other professionals. The remedy is compensation for the loss of the client's legal rights, in other words, damages for the losses attributable to the error, *e.g.*, the damages that the client would have been awarded in a case where the client would have prevailed if the lawyer had acted competently. Some cases also permit recovery to third persons who are damaged by a lawyer's failure to act competently (discussed in more detail in the next section). Finally, lawyers found to have been negligent can have the fees they collected in the underlying matter disgorged in addition to being required to pay damages to the injured client or party.

As discussed in Chapter 2, paralegals may be named in malpractice actions against lawyers, including independent contractor paralegals working under the direction of a lawyer. Most lawyers carry malpractice insurance that covers the actions of their employees; such insurance is mandatory in some states. Paralegals should be certain the firm they work for has adequate malpractice coverage that covers paralegals. The most common areas of practice in which malpractice claims are made include real estate; family law; estate, trust and probate; and collections and bankruptcy. The most common kinds of errors are substantive errors, administrative errors, and poor client relations/communications.

Lack of competence is also grounds for **disciplinary action.** The failure to act competently is usually severe or repeated for serious sanctions to be imposed. Frequently the incompetence is coupled with other ethical violations, such as commingling of funds or conversion of client trust account funds or failure to turn over client documents after representation is terminated. Lawyers have been disciplined for competence-related violations involving paralegals, including failing to supervise paralegals properly and aiding in the unauthorized practice of law by allowing paralegals to give legal advice and to prepare legal documents without supervision or review.

Because paralegals are not subject to discipline by the bar and not usually named in malpractice suits, the most likely consequence of a paralegal's failing to act competently is losing one's job, reputation, and employability.

Many malpractice and disciplinary cases involving competence relate to procrastination or to a lack of promptness, thoroughness, or communication. Typical scenarios include missing statutes of limitations, failing to proceed on a client's case after agreeing to representation, and not returning phone calls or responding to emails for an extended period, often because the lawyer has not taken the necessary steps to address a matter. These allegations are sometimes tied to financial improprieties, such as not returning advanced fees, not turning over a settlement check or client's file promptly, or "borrowing" from a client trust account. Some cases of this type are the result of mismanaged law offices; some, troubled attorneys. Personal problems—such as financial, marital, substance abuse, and health problems—often interfere with an attorney's ability to function competently.

Some examples of failure to be thorough include failing to include a bonus in calculating a spouse's legal share of the other spouse's compensation; providing incomplete tax advice on a real estate trust that led to payment of huge tax bills, including interest and penalties; and recommending a settlement in a case that resulted in the client accepting a much smaller settlement than the case was worth. One firm was hit with a $16 million verdict for including the wrong provision in an agreement, as the result of a cut-and-paste error. Recently, two New York lawyers were sanctioned for submitting a legal brief that included six fictitious case citations generated by an artificial intelligence chatbot, ChatGPT.

Keeping abreast of changes in law and practice is critical in the application of technology. It is especially easy to make errors when working with technology, such as selecting the wrong electronic form; not using the correct provisions; changing some but not all names, numbers, or provisions; and misdirecting e-mail. For example, lawyers have been charged with not meeting standards of competence for failing to protect the confidentiality of client information when using electronic repositories for documents and not submitting documents to the court in the proper electronic portal. Other concerns address the proper use of social media, which was emphasized in the New York State Bar Association's Social Media Ethical Guidelines (June 2015), stating, "A lawyer has a duty to understand the benefits and risks and the ethical implications associated with social media." Noted is the potential for errors in research and electronic discovery. (See, for example, State Bar of California Formal Opinion 11-004 on a lawyer's duties in the handling of discovery of electronically stored information.) Other experts have called on lawyers to be competent in cybersecurity, internet-based investigations, and internet-based marketing. (See Perlman, A., The Twenty-First Century Lawyer's Evolving Duty of Competence, 22 *The Professional Lawyer* 4 (2014) and Facciola, J. M., A Judicial Perspective: Technological Competence and Law Schools, *ABA Journal of the Professional Lawyer* 119 (2015).)

A large proportion of lawyers with disciplinary records have **alcohol or drug dependency problems** or emotional and personal problems that impair their ability to function in an ethical and effective manner. Most state and many local bar associations now have programs to help lawyers with these problems. Lawyers can participate voluntarily or be required to participate as part of an agreement or sanction for a violation of the ethics rules. Studies show that as many as 20 percent of lawyers have alcohol or substance abuse problems and that at least 20 percent of disciplinary matters stem from these problems. Lawyers have been found to have some of the highest depression rates among the professions. One of four lawyers has elevated feelings of distress, and half of lawyers feel that they do not have enough time for their families. Paralegals should be alert to the symptoms of substance abuse and addiction in colleagues so that they can intervene as needed. Among the common symptoms are missed work, lateness to work, procrastination, missed deadlines, blaming others, withdrawing from relationships at work, deterioration in appearance, memory loss, erratic behavior, and losing control in work or social settings.

Several cases involving mistakes of paralegals are found at the end of this chapter. In addition, see *Musselman v. Willoughby Corp.* in Chapter 2, which involves a lawyer's failure to exercise adequate oversight of paralegals who made substantive errors that harmed clients.

F. Current Developments and Issues re: Competence

Third-party claims
Claims by non-clients against lawyers who, in representing clients, may have caused harm to the third person.

Lawsuits against lawyers have increased nearly 60 percent in the last 25 years. Some of the increase in claims against lawyers is from ***third-party claims*** by non-clients who were harmed by the actions of clients from whom they can no longer recover. Not all states allow such third-party claims. See Can Lawyers be Sued by Non-Clients?, *Professional Liability Legal Malpractice* (July 2012).

An attorney may owe a duty to a third party if the attorney was hired for the purpose of benefitting a third party. See *MacLeish v. Boardman & Clark LLP*, 924 N.W.2d 799 (Wis. 2019) (non-client named as a beneficiary in a will has standing to sue attorney for malpractice if beneficiary can demonstrate attorney's negligence impeded testator's intent); see also Ronald E. Mallen and Jeffrey M. Smith, *Legal Malpractice* §7.10, at 379 (3d ed., 1993) ("the vast majority of modern decisions have favored expanding privity beyond the confines of the attorney-client relationship where the plaintiff was intended to be the beneficiary of the lawyer's retention").

Examples of third-party liability are found in corporate securities work, where additional duties to the purchasers of securities are imposed by federal law. Under securities law, lawyers may be held liable if material false or misleading statements are included in offerings. Private investors in all kinds of investments see lawyers as potential defendants when promoters have misled investors or when the investors depended on opinion letters or other documents prepared by lawyers.

The principles underlying third-party liability were broadly applied during the savings and loan crisis in the 1990s in lawsuits by the federal government against lawyers who represented failed thrift institutions. Cases have involved claims against lawyers who provided opinion letters to banks about the viability of companies seeking to borrow funds. When the companies later became insolvent, the lawyers were sued. The failure of large companies in the 1990s, such as Enron and WorldCom, led to many such lawsuits, which claimed that the law firms gave legal advice that allowed these companies to defraud investors and lenders. A multi-million-dollar verdict was rendered against lawyers in a case where third parties sued the lawyers who had approved an illegal tax shelter. During the economic downturn that began in 2007, bankruptcy trustees and large investors sued lawyers for fraud and for aiding and abetting breaches of fiduciary duty.

Another practice area where third-party liability may arise is **estate planning.** When a gift to an intended beneficiary fails because of a lawyer's negligence, the intended beneficiary may seek damages from the attorney, even though the attorney represented the testator, not the beneficiary. Other cases hold that a lawyer has a duty to the beneficiaries of an estate to ascertain a client's testamentary capacity. (For example, see *Moore v. Anderson Ziegler*, 109 Cal. App. 4th 1287, 135 Cal. Rptr. 2d 888 (2003); *Fickett v. Superior Court*, 27 Ariz. App. 793, 558 P.2d 988 (1976), where a lawyer was held liable not only to the guardian-client but also to his ward; *Johnson v. Sandler*, 958 S.W.2d 42 (Mo. Ct. App. W.D. (1997). See also *Calvert v. Scharf*, 619 S.E.2d 197 (W.Va. 2005), which found that the intended beneficiaries of a will can sue the lawyer who prepared the will when they can show the testator's intent was frustrated by the negligence of the lawyer, resulting in the loss of the beneficiaries' interest under the will.)

Similar cases have held lawyers who represented sellers in **real estate transactions** liable to buyers for making misleading statements that the buyer relied on in making the purchase. (See the *Motors Liquidation* case at the end of this chapter for an example.) Similarly, a law firm that represented defendants in a lawsuit against its insured was held liable to the plaintiff in that lawsuit for making a fraudulent statement about coverage under the policy at issue. (See *Shafer v. Berger, Kahn*, 107 Cal. App. 4th 54, 131 Cal. Rptr. 2d 777 (Cal. Ct. App. 2003).)

Further extensions of third-party liability are expected, especially in areas heavily regulated by the government, such as environmental and securities law. Civil lawsuits have been brought by insurance companies against the lawyers who represented their insureds and lost; jurisdictions are split on whether such actions are permitted. An example in family law is a case in which a spouse was allowed to sue her ex-husband's lawyer for helping him to prepare a second set of books that led to the undervaluation of his business and a lower than called-for settlement for his wife.

More malpractice cases are being brought against lawyers for breaches of confidentiality and **conflict of interest**, in some instances where a firm represented two clients that ultimately became adversaries. Some cases concern conflicts that arose when a lawyer did business with clients or served on a corporate client's board of directors. In one case, a multimillion-dollar verdict was rendered against a law firm that advised the client-beneficiary to make a large donation to a foundation represented by the firm. In another case, a client sued and prevailed when a conflict screen was not honored.

Malicious prosecution cases against lawyers are also on the rise. In these cases, a lawyer can be held liable civilly for initiating a lawsuit without probable cause or continuing to prosecute a case after learning that there is no probable cause.

Discovery abuse includes various means of using the discovery process to delay, harass, or wear down an opposing party. Parties who engage in discovery abuse can be reprimanded by the court, held in contempt, and sanctioned. Sanctions can range from the cost of attorneys' fees for the opposing party to a fine for every day they are out of compliance. Penalties can also be imposed against parties as well as lawyers and law firms for lack of cooperation. See *Abbott Laboratories, et al., v Adelphia Supply USA* at the end of this chapter, where the defendants engaged in a "calculated pattern of pervasive misconduct" replete with "bad faith conduct" that "started early on and continued even after defendants were caught red-handed," leading to severe sanctions.

As mentioned above, one area of particular concern to practitioners now is the degree to which lawyers and paralegals must have the latest information available through technology. The standard of care for lawyers in doing **research** is based on what was readily available at the time the research was performed and what could be found by standard research techniques. Lawyers are expected to conduct reasonable research to identify controlling law and to make decisions based on that law. Lawyers use electronic research services that provide access to the latest opinions that are not yet available in hard copy. Electronic research is the "standard" that lawyers are required to meet.

Some states allow lawyers to be sued under **consumer fraud statutes** that provide for damages for deceptive practices or fraud. Such statutes may apply even where the client could not prevail in a malpractice case. Other states specifically refuse to apply such statutes to lawyers, holding to the traditional separation of powers interpretations that give exclusive authority over the practice of law to the courts (as was discussed in Chapter 1). Of the states that do allow such actions, some apply consumer protection statutes only to the entrepreneurial or commercial aspects of law practice, such as advertising and fee setting. Louisiana, Texas, Connecticut, Washington, and Colorado allow lawyers to be sued under consumer protection statutes. (See *Reed v. Allison & Perrone*, 376 So. 2d 1067 (La.App. 4 Cir. 1979); *Heslin v. Conn. Law Clinic*, 190 Conn. 510, 461 A.2d 938 (1983); *Short v. Demopolis*, 103 Wn.2d. 52, 691 P.2d 163 (1984); *Crowe v. Tull*, 126 P.3d 196 (Colo. 2006); *Latham v. Castillo*, 972 S.W.2d 66 (Tex. 1998).) The states that have held that lawyers are not subject to these statutes include Florida, Illinois, New Jersey, Georgia, New Hampshire, Pennsylvania, and Delaware. (See, for example, Office Atty. Gen. v. Shapiro 59 So.3d 353 (Fla.App. 4 Dist. 2011); *Rousseau v. Eshleman*, 128 N.H. 564, 519 A.2d 243 (1986); *Cripe v. Leiter*, 184 Ill.2d 185, 703 N.E.2d 100 (1998); *Jamgochian v. Prousalis*, No. 99C-10-022, 2000 WL 1610750 (Del. Super. 2000); *Averill v. Cox*, 145 N.H. 328, 761 A.2d 1083 (2000); *Macedo v. Russo*, 178 N.J. 340, 840 A.2d 238 (2004); *Beyers v. Richmond*, 594 Pa. 654, 937 A.2d 1082 (2007); *State v. Hanna*, 287 Ga. 289, 695 S.E.2d 612 (2010).)

Providing legal information or services over the Internet creates issues about the establishment of the **attorney-client relationship**. As discussed in both Chapters 3 and 6, lawyers who give their opinions in chat rooms or on websites that provide "legal information" run the risk of inadvertently establishing a lawyer-client relationship that may end in a malpractice suit if the "client" is dissatisfied with the outcome of the matter.

G. Avoiding Malpractice

The following is a summary of advice on avoiding malpractice claims.

1. Lawyers should use carefully drafted **letters of engagement** and **letters terminating or declining representation**. These documents

should spell out and limit the scope of representation, the expectations and responsibilities of the law firm, and those of the client. Engagement letters should clearly indicate that the lawyer is not guaranteeing a particular outcome.

2. **Clients should be selected carefully**. Difficult personalities and questionable cases should not be accepted. Lawyers should learn about the client before accepting a case, checking for a history of fraud, a record of many legal problems or changing lawyers, criminal activity, and so on. Clients' stories should be verified before the lawyer takes action.

3. Lawyers and clients should enter into complete and well-drafted **fee agreements** for each representation that cover all the terms noted in Chapter 7. Fee agreements should be entered into as soon as possible in the representation, be clear about the scope of the services, and be followed meticulously.

4. Clients should be charged **reasonable fees** that are in accord with fee agreements. Bills should be detailed and should be reviewed before being sent. Excessive, duplicative, or inappropriate charges should be removed before sending bills. Billing should be prepared and sent regularly and timely.

5. Clients' **phone calls and e-mails should be returned promptly**, preferably the same day. Lawyers and paralegals should take the time to educate the client about the law and legal process and show that they care about clients' concerns. Clients should be sent copies of documents and work product. Correspondence and other materials from clients should be promptly acknowledged.

6. Lawyers and paralegals should **listen to clients** carefully and try to understand their goals and expectations. Unrealistic expectations should be addressed immediately and thoughtfully. Lawyers should follow the client's lead in determining a course of action.

7. Lawyers should exercise **independent judgment** on clients' behalf and should **respect clients' decisions.**

8. Law firms should have **good management systems** and **well-trained personnel** in place, especially concerning the following matters:

   - conflicts checks and screens
   - protection of client confidentiality
   - calendaring deadlines, court dates, and the like
   - billing and time keeping
   - handling client property
   - client trust accounts
   - the use of technology.

9. Lawyers and paralegals should be scrupulous in the handling of **clients' funds** in keeping with the rules set forth in Chapter 7. Client trust accounts and related records must be perfectly maintained

with no commingling or other irregularities. Client files must be turned over promptly upon termination and settlements must be paid promptly after receipt.
10. If a client asks for advice on an **unsettled area of law**, the lawyer should be sure that the client understands that the area of law is unsettled and that the lawyer is making a judgment about the likely state of the law, not a guarantee.
11. Paralegals and lawyers should be meticulous about checking for **conflicts of interest** and, when appropriate, obtaining consents and establishing screens.
12. Lawyers and paralegals should know the **limits of their competence** and should seek guidance and consultation when in doubt about how to proceed on a matter. Lawyers should not accept cases for which they do not have the necessary expertise and should not "dabble" in these areas. Likewise, paralegals should seek guidance and support when venturing into a new area of practice.
13. Firms should provide **education** for lawyers and paralegals and have mentors for employees to consult for **support** when challenged by an assignment.
14. The **culture** of the firm and its commitment to high standards can deter the kind of sloppy work that leads to malpractice actions.
15. The firm management should also be alert to employees who may have **personal or substance abuse problems** that could interfere with their work.

Paralegals can help firms avoid malpractice. Communication with clients is greatly improved when lawyers give paralegals responsibility for keeping clients informed. When clients call and the lawyer is unavailable, the paralegal can take or return calls promptly. Keeping accurate and detailed time records and alerting the lawyer to potential problems in time and billing can prevent problems with clients. Paralegals often have responsibility for monitoring deadlines and handling client funds, especially in small law firms.

H. Factors Affecting Paralegal Competence

Paralegals must be cognizant not only of the meaning of competence and how it is embodied in their work, but also of the factors that may either enhance their competence or detract from it. Because paralegals work under the direction and supervision of lawyers, they are not in a position to set the quality standards or determine firm values and culture. However, paralegals can influence firm standards and culture and can seek employment with firms that have high standards of quality and encourage competence and professionalism.

Paralegals face some common competence-related issues. Perhaps the most common is being asked to perform a task that the paralegal does not have the requisite knowledge or skill to perform. This scenario presents an especially difficult dilemma for paralegals, who want to do challenging, interesting work and who know their value is in relieving lawyers from tasks that they would otherwise have to perform. A new paralegal, like a lawyer just out of law school, must learn on the job. With a strong education, good research and drafting skills, self-confidence, and motivation, a paralegal can learn how to perform assigned tasks by conducting research, finding models in firm files, and consulting with a mentor or more experienced colleague in the firm. When paralegals accept new and challenging assignments, they should make the supervising lawyer aware whether they are experienced in performing the task, so that the lawyer exercises an appropriate or heightened level of delegation and review.

A related concern is the proper **delegation**, supervision, and review of paralegal work by lawyers. The ethics and agency rules discussed earlier and in Chapter 2 make it clear that the lawyer is ultimately responsible for the work of the paralegal. For a variety of reasons, lawyers do not always carry out their supervisory responsibilities as well as they should. Many lawyers are not skilled delegators; they often do not give adequate information and instructions when assigning work. Many lawyers are overloaded and simply do not take the time to delegate thoughtfully and to review thoroughly. Proper delegation requires selecting the appropriately skilled person for the task and giving sufficient direction to see that the finished product meets expectations. The information that must be given to the one performing the task includes background on the matter or reference to appropriate files that contain relevant information; an exact description of the end product desired; references to sources that may be of assistance; deadline dates; and, if possible, an estimate of the time the task should take. Paralegals given assignments without this information may end up spending too much time, creating an end product that was not desired, or missing the expected due date. The paralegal who works for a poor delegator must take the responsibility for getting information and instructions necessary to complete projects correctly and on time by asking the appropriate questions, repeating instructions to make sure that they have been understood, and reducing oral instructions to writing, which can be done in a short confirming e-mail.

Paralegals also find that lawyers do not always **review** their work as carefully as they should, especially when the paralegal is a long-term, trusted employee whose competence has been proven. Even if the paralegal is confident in their work product, the lawyer must review it. If a paralegal is aware that the lawyer is not adequately reviewing their work, the paralegal should discuss the matter with the lawyer to encourage more careful review. The problem of inadequate review is exacerbated when a paralegal is working for an inexperienced lawyer or one who does not have expertise in the relevant area of practice. If the paralegal is very experienced, the lawyer may rely too heavily or even completely on the paralegal's expertise. For an example of a nonlawyer employee not being properly supervised, read *De Vaux v. American Home Assurance Co.* at the companion website that accompanies this text.

A **heavy workload** often interferes with the performance of lawyers, paralegals, and other law firm employees. Intense work demands and the importance of billable hours can lead to serious consequences—stress, depression, and burnout—and mistakes. Workplace demands were also exacerbated by the COVID-19 pandemic. In 2022, the ABA commissioned its *Practice Forward: The New Normal* survey to help lawyers navigate the legal profession as it transitioned beyond the pandemic. The survey found that 59 percent of lawyers work more than 40 hours a week and more than 22 percent average more than 50 hours of work a week. As the legal profession evolves post-pandemic under the "new normal," the vast majority of lawyers surveyed (87%) said their workplace allowed lawyers to work remotely. About 30% of lawyers work from home almost all the time. Another 30% work in the office nearly 100% of the time. Most lawyers reported that working remotely or on a hybrid basis has not adversely impacted the quality of their work, productivity, or billable hours. This is particularly true for women lawyers, 56% of whom said that remote or hybrid working increased their ability to balance work and family obligations. However, the remote work environment began to shift in mid-2023, as some of the largest law firms moved to mandate as many as 4 days of in-office work per week for lawyers and paralegals.

Ethics opinions advise lawyers not to accept a court appointment if their workload is too heavy and to request to be withdrawn if the overload situation arises after the appointment. Many factors determine whether one's caseload is too heavy, including not only the number of cases, but their complexity, the degree of support provided, the lawyer's ability and experience, and the lawyer's other duties, including the obligation not to overload other lawyers and staff (ABA Formal Opinion 06-441).

Signs of a lawyer with an unreasonably heavy workload include taking on too many cases, being poorly organized or managed, and not having adequate staff. Sometimes, especially in litigation, temporary crises occur before and during trial that require everyone involved in a case to work long hours for extended periods. Paralegals need to be assertive enough in their dealings with lawyers to avoid taking on more work than they can competently handle. Too heavy a workload causes a decline in productivity and quality and increases the likelihood of shortcuts being taken and mistakes being made. A firm that continually operates in this crisis mode is not a good place to work—the stress is unhealthy, people do not feel personally or professionally satisfied, and mistakes will be made. Paralegals should avoid working for law firms characterized by excessive workloads. They also should be aware of the potential problems created by a temporary heavy workload. When a project or group of projects requires long hours and creates high pressure over an extended period, measures should be taken to remedy the situation. For example, retaining additional support may alleviate the workload, making it possible for everyone to function more effectively.

Paralegals should have a realistic perception of their own level and areas of competence and, while striving to learn and develop, should not get so far ahead of their knowledge and skills that they are no longer acting competently. Continuing education, in-house training programs, and mentoring can help paralegals develop and maintain long and satisfying careers.

An honest **self-assessment** will identify personal characteristics that affect competence. Experienced paralegals know what talents and qualities they do and do not possess, and optimize their strong points and compensate for their weaknesses. Paralegals should work on improving skills in areas of weakness, strengthen their natural abilities, and seek work that matches their attributes. For example, a paralegal who is not a good writer should strive to improve those skills. A paralegal who works well with people should seek a position that will make use of that ability, such as one that involves supervision of others or frequent client contact.

Paralegals with **personal, health, or family problems** must consider how these problems affect their work. No one functions effectively when troubled, worried, or distracted. A paralegal who has difficulties outside the office must be alert to the potential for a decline in productivity and accuracy. Paralegals with problems should take special care to ensure that the quality of their work is maintained during stressful periods by double-checking work, getting support from colleagues in the office, and taking time off to address their problems. If problems are serious or ongoing, the paralegal should discuss them with a supervisor for emotional and practical support. Paralegals with substance abuse problems should seek professional help, and their colleagues and friends in the workplace should encourage them to do so.

REVIEW QUESTIONS

1. What are the elements of competence?
2. Are lawyers responsible for the conduct of their paralegals? Cite the relevant ABA Model Rule and the relevant section of the ABA Model Guidelines.

3. Can paralegals be disciplined for their failure to act competently? Can they be sued? What is the motivation for paralegals to be competent? Give as many reasons as you can.
4. Describe and compare legal and paralegal education.
5. What are three good sources of paralegal continuing education?
6. What do the NALA and NFPA ethics guidelines say about competence?
7. How do the ABA Model Rules define competence?
8. Do lawyers and paralegals need to have the same knowledge and skills to be competent? How do their knowledge and skills differ? What knowledge and skills might they both need?
9. How does legal specialization affect lawyer and paralegal competence?
10. What role do law firms' in-house training and orientation programs play in developing competence?
11. How does a paralegal demonstrate competence in preparing a case?
12. What does diligence mean? What is the paralegal's role in ensuring diligence?
13. Give three examples of common problems associated with a lack of diligence or promptness.
14. Why is communication with clients included in the definition of competence? What role can a paralegal play in this area?
15. What are three possible consequences of a lawyer's failure to act competently? What are the possible consequences of a paralegal's incompetence?
16. Give five examples of common grounds for malpractice claims.
17. What is third-party liability? Give two examples of third-party claims against lawyers.
18. Besides negligence, what ethical duties can form the basis for a malpractice claim?
19. What is malicious prosecution and how is it used?
20. Can lawyers be sued under state consumer protection statutes? What are the theories behind whether lawyers should or should not be subject to these statutes?
21. Name five steps that a firm can take to prevent malpractice claims.
22. How should a paralegal respond if they are asked to perform a function in which they have no expertise?
23. What steps should a paralegal take if their supervising attorney gives incomplete instructions on a project?
24. What should a paralegal do if the supervising attorney is not carefully reviewing the paralegal's work?
25. What should a paralegal do if their workload is too heavy and cannot be handled in a timely and effective manner?
26. What might a paralegal do upon learning that another paralegal in the firm has a substance abuse problem that is affecting their work?

27. What are some ways that paralegals might fail to act competently when using technology? When conducting legal research?

DISCUSSION QUESTIONS AND HYPOTHETICALS

1. Do you think states should set minimum levels of education for paralegals? Why or why not?
2. What would your model of paralegal education be if you were required to set minimum standards? Consider how much college education and paralegal education should be included. Think about a model that is ideal, as well as one that is based on minimum standards.
3. Do you think paralegals should have to take a licensing exam to demonstrate their competence before they are allowed to work as a paralegal? Why or why not? What should such an exam cover?
4. Are there any other elements that you think should be added to the definition of competence given in the ABA Model Rules 1.1, 1.3, and 1.4?
5. How can you tell whether a law firm encourages competence and quality?
6. What would you do if on your first day on the job, right out of paralegal school, a lawyer asked you to draft an antitrust complaint for filing the next day in federal court? Assume that your specialties in school were probate and real estate.
7. What would you do if you were an independent probate paralegal and were asked to do work for a lawyer who admittedly knew nothing about probate?
8. What would you do if a lawyer passed you in the hall, handed you a phone message, and told you to call the client back and draft whatever documents the client asked for?
9. Describe the extent to which a lawyer should review the following work:

    a. form complaint
    b. form will and trust
    c. form demurrer
    d. form patent application
    e. articles of incorporation
    f. promissory note
    g. a trial notebook
    h. answers to interrogatories
    i. documents for a complex real estate transaction
    j. bankruptcy schedules of assets and liabilities
    k. appellate appendix or record on appeal
    l. abstracts of documents in a computerized retrieval system.

10. What would you do if you worked for a firm that was always in an overworked, crisis mode?
11. What would you do if you knew that a lawyer in your firm frequently took shortcuts, such as not gathering facts carefully or not researching legal issues thoroughly?
12. Name three personal strengths that may help you in your career. Name three weaknesses that might interfere with your competence or success. Considering these, what should you do to maximize your strengths and minimize your weaknesses? What kind of work are you best suited for? What kind of work environment?
13. What would you do if your best paralegal friend at work was having a personal problem and asked you to cover for their tardiness, long personal phone calls, incessant texting, and so forth? What if you could see that this friend was making a lot of mistakes at work? Would it make any difference if the friend were a lawyer? Your supervising lawyer?
14. As mentioned in the section on legal education, many bar leaders are seeking to reform legal education. Some are calling for more attention to "core competencies." Among the core competencies discussed in these articles are oral communication, writing, strategic thinking, project management, service orientation, self-awareness, team building and inclusion, and drive to learn and improve. Are these competencies learned in law school or in paralegal school? Should they be? Where else might one develop or learn them? Should law school and paralegal education give more attention to them? Or screen applicants for them?

RESEARCH PROJECTS AND ASSIGNMENTS

1. Check the local ethics code in your jurisdiction to see what provisions it contains on competence. Compare these with the ABA Rules.
2. Check the listings of lawyers who were recently disciplined in your jurisdiction. What kinds of competence-related issues do you see? What proportion of the sanctions relate directly to issues of competence, as opposed to other kinds of ethical breaches?
3. Contact paralegal instructors for referrals to find out:
   a. law firm hiring standards for paralegals
   b. if they have in-house orientation or training programs for paralegals
   c. if they have paralegal managers or supervisors
   d. if they have a mentoring program for paralegals
   e. if they pay the cost for their paralegals to take continuing education or other job-relevant courses.
4. Call your local paralegal association and get a listing of its continuing education programs for the upcoming year. What kinds of programs

do they offer? Are they specific to paralegals or are they also open to lawyers?
5. Obtain the current informational materials on NALA's CP program and NFPA's PACE program. What are the requirements to take these exams? What is tested on these exams? How many paralegals in your area are certified by one of those organizations? Ask five paralegals who are certified why they took the exam and how it has affected their careers.
6. Does your jurisdiction have a certified specialist program for lawyers? In what areas of law? How many lawyers are certified? Do most paralegals in your area "specialize"?
7. Interview five paralegals who work in five different areas of practice, asking them to list the functions that they perform and the functions that their attorney-supervisors perform. Compare the lists and look for functions in common. Is there a difference in the competence needed by lawyers and paralegals? What generalities can you draw about the differences and common elements?
8. Does your state or local bar association have a lawyer assistance program to help lawyers who have alcohol or substance abuse problems? What does it do? Does it cover nonlawyer employees such as paralegals?
9. Does your jurisdiction have any cases or statutes about a lawyer's duties to third parties? You can start with the cases cited in this chapter and see what other cases or statutes they cite. If so, what do these cases hold? Do they lean toward expanding or restricting a lawyer's duties to those who are not clients?
10. Does your jurisdiction have any cases interpreting whether consumer protection statutes apply to lawyers? Start with the cases in this chapter on this topic and see what you find. Do the decisions in your jurisdiction allow lawyers to be sued under these statutes? Describe the bases for the conflicting interpretations about whether these statutes should be used to sue lawyers. Which position do you support and why?
11. For a case in which a former client sues a law clerk, read *Busch v. Flangas*, 837 P.2d 438 (Nev. 1992).
12. For a case where a lawyer is disciplined for failure to act competently because of the misdeeds of his secretary, see *Mahoning County Bar Association v. Lavelle*, 107 Ohio St. 3d 92, 836 N.E.2d 1214 (2005). What did the secretary do with regard to each of the two clients who complained? What should the lawyer have done to guard against this conduct? What ABA Model Rule was implicated and how? Also see *Disciplinary Counsel v. Maley*, 119 Ohio St. 3d 217 (2008) for a case where a secretary filed multiple bankruptcy cases without any lawyer supervision.
13. Find the final report of the ABA Task Force on the Future of Legal Education on the ABA website and research how law schools and the ABA are addressing the recommendations.

14. Read and brief this malicious prosecution case in which a plaintiff was allowed to bring an action against a group of lawyers who had sued him for securities fraud; see *Cole v. Patricia A. Meyer*, 206 Cal. App. 4th 1095, 142 Cal. Rptr. 3d 646 (2012).
15. Another case involved a paralegal who left the state before she completed assigned work on a critical document to be filed with a court. To see what the court did about dismissing the case, see *Henderson v. Pacific Gas*, 187 Cal.App.4th 215, 113 Cal.Rptr. 3d 692 (2010).
16. One new way that bar associations and courts are seeking to prevent misconduct and malpractice is through "Proactive Management-Based Regulation." Read about this on the ABA and state bar websites and report to the class on its purposes, level of adoption nationwide, and efficacy.
17. Read and report to the class on the findings and recommendations from this Australian study, published online: Michalak, R. T., Causes and Consequences of Work-Related Psychosocial Risk Exposure: A Comparative Investigation of Organisational Context, Employee Attitudes, Job Performance and Wellbeing in Lawyers and Non-Lawyer Professionals (2015).
18. Read and report to the class on the findings from an interprofessional team study of American lawyers, published online: Krill, P. R., Johnson, R., Albert, L., "The Prevalence of Substance Use and Other Mental Health Concerns Among American Attorneys," 10 *J. Addict. Med.* 1 (January/February 2016).
19. Read and report to the class on the findings and recommendations from this Canadian study, published online: Keet, M., Heavin, H. & Sparrow, S., Anticipating and Managing the Psychological Cost of Civil Litigation, *Windsor Yearbook of Access to Justice*, 34(2) (2017).

CASES FOR ANALYSIS

In this disciplinary matter, a lawyer was sanctioned for incompetence and other violations arising out of an improper relationship with nonlawyers.

In re Gillaspy
640 N.E.2d 1054 (Ind. 1994)

Respondent Joseph M. Gillaspy was charged by Verified Complaint for Disciplinary Action with numerous violations of the *Rules of Professional Conduct for Attorneys at Law*. . . . Rothfuss referred Hamilton and Hamilton's wife to James Wilson ("Wilson") of JNW Management Corporation for the purpose of filing a petition for bankruptcy, pursuant to Chapter 13 of the United States Bankruptcy Code. Like Rothfuss, Wilson was not a lawyer. On August 1, 1991, a voluntary petition for bankruptcy was filed in United States Bankruptcy Court, Southern Division, Indianapolis, on behalf of Hamilton and his wife. The petition listed Respondent as the attorney of record, even though Wilson had prepared the paperwork relative to the petition. On November 7, 1991, Hamilton and his wife attended the first meeting of creditors, pursuant to Section 341 of the bankruptcy code. At this meeting, Hamilton met Respondent for the first time.

Hamilton did not pay Respondent for the legal services. Respondent received a check for $300.00 from Benefit Planners as payment for the legal services he rendered on behalf of Hamilton. Rothfuss, as president of Benefit Planners, signed the check. Respondent undertook to represent other individuals in bankruptcy matters under circumstances similar to those in the Hamilton bankruptcy.

The agreed facts clearly and convincingly establish that Respondent violated Ind. Professional Conduct Rule 1.4(b) since, having never even met Hamilton or his wife prior to the filing of the bankruptcy petition, Respondent did not explain matters to them to the extent reasonably necessary to permit them to make informed decisions regarding the representation. Because he abdicated the factual and legal analysis of this matter to non-lawyers Rothfuss and Wilson, Respondent failed to provide competent representation and therefore violated Prof. Cond. R. 1.1. Respondent violated Prof. Cond. R. 1.8(f) by accepting compensation from Rothfuss for representing Hamilton, while non-lawyers Rothfuss and Wilson exercised what should have been Respondent's independent professional judgment and confidential lawyer-client relationship between Respondent and the Hamiltons. By sharing fees with Rothfuss and Wilson, allowing them to direct and regulate his professional judgment in rendering legal services, and by assisting Rothfuss and Wilson in activity which constituted the unauthorized practice of law, Respondent violated Prof. Cond. R. 5.4(a), 5.4(c), and 5.5(b). . . .

We are inclined to accept the agreed sanction, noting that Respondent's fee-sharing arrangement with non-lawyers clearly threatened Respondent's independent professional judgment and competence. However, we are also cognizant of the fact that none of the bankruptcy petitioners filed grievances relating to any unprofessional or incompetent representation by Respondent; that Respondent ceased his affiliation with Benefit Planners immediately upon learning that there were ethical problems with the arrangement; and that Respondent was completely cooperative and truthful during the Commission's investigation of this matter. The Commission and Respondent characterize Respondent's dealings with Benefit Planners as resulting from professional naïveté, rather than from a willful scheme to take advantage of clients. . . .

It is, therefore, ordered that Respondent, Joseph M. Gillaspy, is suspended from the practice of law for a period of not less than ninety (90) days, beginning November 14, 1994, with automatic reinstatement to occur immediately after the conclusion of the suspension period. . . .

Questions about the Case

1. Who prepared and filed the bankruptcy case? Who appeared at the hearing?
2. What functions did the lawyer Gillaspy and the nonlawyer involved perform in this legal matter? Which constituted the practice of law?
3. Why did the representation here amount to "incompetence"?
4. Who did the clients pay? How was Gillaspy paid?
5. What were the mitigating factors in setting the sanction? What was the sanction? Do you believe that it was an appropriate sanction?

The following case involves a lawyer being disciplined for the conduct of her paralegal, who had been in prison, and addresses an array of competency and supervision issues.

Mississippi Bar v. Thompson
2007-BA-00556-SCT, 5 So. 3d 330 (Miss. 2008)

Gail Thompson employed Robert Tubwell, a former inmate at the Mississippi State Penitentiary at Parchman, as a paralegal at the Thompson Law Firm in Tunica County. Thompson hired Tubwell based, in part, on his reputation as a successful writ writer while at Parchman, and his potential ability to generate business for Thompson's firm.

Mario McGaughy, an inmate serving a life sentence without the possibility of parole, met Tubwell while the two were at Parchman. When McGaughy learned that Tubwell was working as a paralegal, he wrote Tubwell at Thompson's law office. McGaughy sought to hire a lawyer to file his petition for post-conviction relief. A series of communications then ensued between Tubwell and McGaughy, McGaughy's mother, and McGaughy's stepfather.

On February 1, 2002, Tubwell wrote McGaughy on Thompson Law Firm letterhead. The letter stated that Tubwell had consulted with Thompson and that she had agreed to work with him on McGaughy's case. Tubwell stated that everything would be reviewed by an attorney and quoted McGaughy a fee of $500 for the preliminary work. He also requested that McGaughy send future correspondence to his Southaven apartment address, and provided McGaughy his personal home and cellular phone numbers.

It is somewhat unclear whether the $500 payment was made, and if so, to whom such payment was directed. McGaughy stated that his father paid $550 via money order, but could not confirm whether the payment was made to the Thompson Law Firm or to Tubwell himself. Tubwell acknowledged that he received fifty dollars for travel-related expenses, but claimed that he never received the $500 money order. Thompson also denied ever receiving anything from McGaughy. Regardless, the complaint tribunal found implicitly that the $500 payment was made.

On March 18, 2002, Tubwell again wrote McGaughy on Thompson Law Firm letterhead. Tubwell advised McGaughy that he had a strong case and that there was a seventy-percent chance that this Court would reverse and grant a new trial.

Tubwell eventually obtained McGaughy's court records and mailed McGaughy his files, along with a pro se petition for post-conviction relief. Per Tubwell's instructions, McGaughy signed and had notarized the necessary documentation without realizing that he was filing pro se. This Court ultimately denied McGaughy's pro se petition for post-conviction relief.

Thereafter, Tubwell informed McGaughy that the next step would be to file a writ of habeas corpus in federal court. Tubwell later wrote McGaughy to inform him that he had begun work on filing the habeas corpus petition. But a petition for habeas corpus was never filed on McGaughy's behalf.

On November 18, 2004, McGaughy, on the belief that he had hired Thompson's law firm to represent him on his application for post-conviction relief and his federal habeas corpus petition, filed an informal complaint against Thompson with the Mississippi Bar. . . .

A hearing was held on March 14, 2006, in which Thompson testified that she was unaware of Tubwell's correspondence with McGaughy, and claimed that he had taken advantage of her. Thompson stated that she trusted Tubwell and had instructed him that any cases he was working on had to come through her office. Yet she admitted that additional safeguards should have been implemented.

In addition to the McGaughy matter, the Bar inquired about Thompson's handling of client files after she moved her law office from Oxford to Tunica in 2000, and when she closed her Tunica practice in 2003. When Thompson moved her practice from Oxford to Tunica in 2000, she left some client files in a storage facility in Oxford. She admitted that those files had been lost. In 2003, Thompson closed her Tunica office after being suspended from the practice of law for a period of eighteen months. After closing the Tunica office, Thompson kept two file drawers of client files in a storage unit in Tunica. She testified that those file drawers were later moved to the home/office of Oxford attorney Alvin Chambliss. She explained that those file drawers remain locked because she lost the keys.

After hearing testimony and arguments, the complaint tribunal issued its opinion on March 16, 2007. . . . Aggrieved by the complaint tribunal's ruling, the Bar appeals to this Court. . . .

The complaint tribunal found that Thompson failed to adequately safeguard client property by losing or misplacing client files. Rule 1.15 requires lawyers to hold the property of others with the care required of a professional fiduciary. M.R.P.C. 1.15, cmt. The loss of client files constitutes a violation of Rule 1.15. [Citations omitted.] Thompson admitted to losing client files that she had placed in an Oxford storage unit. Although Thompson said that she returned important documents to clients "most times," she could not say that she had done so every time. We find that Thompson violated Rule 1.15. . . .

The complaint tribunal found that Thompson did not violate Rule 1.6 because there was no proof that she divulged any confidential client information. With certain exceptions, Rule 1.6 generally prohibits the disclosure of information relating to the representation of a client, absent the client's informed consent. M.R.P.C. 1.6. While Thompson admitted to losing the client files in Oxford, there is no evidence that any of those files were divulged. Likewise, there is no evidence that any of the client files from her Tunica office were disclosed. We find that there is insufficient evidence to show that Thompson violated Rule 1.6.

The complaint tribunal found that Thompson had not violated Rule 1.2(a) or 1.3 because no attorney-client relationship existed between Thompson and McGaughy. The Bar contends that Tubwell, acting as an agent for Thompson, communicated Thompson's consent to act as McGaughy's lawyer, and that Thompson should have known of McGaughy's reliance. Rule 1.2(a) provides that a lawyer shall abide by a client's decisions concerning the objectives of representation and shall consult with the client as to the means by which they are pursued. M.R.P.C. 1.2(a). Rule 1.3 requires a lawyer to act with reasonable diligence and promptness in representing a client. M.R.P.C. 1.3. For either rule to be implicated, an attorney-client relationship must exist.

The existence of an attorney-client relationship depends upon the circumstances and may be a question of fact. M.R.P.C., SCOPE. . . . A lawyer's consent to represent a client need not be made by the lawyer himself. "An agent for the lawyer may communicate consent, for example, a secretary or paralegal with express, implied, or apparent authority to act for the lawyer in undertaking a representation." Restatement (Third) of the Law Governing Lawyers §14, cmt. e (2000).

Thompson hired Tubwell to do legal research and draft briefs. He was told not to independently communicate with clients. Thus, Tubwell lacked express authority to communicate Thompson's consent to represent a client. Tubwell also lacked implied authority because communicating Thompson's consent to represent a client was not "necessary, proper, and usual," in the exercise of his express duties. [Citations omitted.]

Apparent authority is "authority that the principal has by words or conduct held the alleged agent out as having." [Citation omitted.] Apparent authority requires "(1) acts or conduct of the principal indicating the agent's authority, (2) reasonable reliance on those acts, and (3) detrimental change in position as a result of reliance." [Citations omitted.] A principal is "bound if the conduct of the principal is such that persons of reasonable prudence, ordinarily familiar with business practices, dealing with the agent might rightfully believe the agent to have the power he assumes to have."

The Bar cites *De Vaux v. American Home Assurance Co.*, 387 Mass. 814, 444 N.E.2d 355 (1983), for support. In *De Vaux*, an individual called the attorney's office seeking legal advice. The attorney's secretary returned this person's phone call and rendered some legal advice, arranged for a medical examination, and instructed the person to write a letter requesting the attorney's assistance. This person delivered a letter to the attorney's office, but the secretary misfiled the letter. As a result, the attorney failed to discover the letter until after the statute of limitations had expired. The person then filed a malpractice suit against the attorney based, in part, on a theory that the secretary had apparent authority to establish an attorney-client relationship on behalf of the attorney. The plaintiff claimed that the attorney had placed the secretary in a position in which prospective clients might reasonably believe that she had the authority to establish an attorney-client relationship. The Supreme Judicial Court of Massachusetts held that "[i]t is a question for the jury whether the attorney allowed his secretary to act as she did, and whether he knew what she was doing."

Thompson stated that Tubwell had not been given authority independently to communicate with clients and had been instructed not to sign any letters. She told Tubwell that any cases he worked on had to come through her office. Thompson included Tubwell's name on the law firm letterhead, but identified him as a paralegal. Furthermore, she disclaimed any knowledge of Tubwell's correspondence with McGaughy or his work on McGaughy's case. We find insufficient evidence to support that Thompson, by her words, actions, or conduct, indicated that Tubwell had authority to communicate her consent to undertake the representation of a client.

We also find that no attorney-client relationship was established by Thompson's failure to communicate her lack of consent to represent McGaughy. Thompson had no knowledge of McGaughy's case or Tubwell's correspondence with McGaughy, and therefore, could not reasonably have known about McGaughy's reliance on her services. Because no attorney-client relationship existed, we find that Thompson did not violate Rules 1.2(a) and 1.3. . . .

The complaint tribunal found that Thompson had violated Rule 5.3 by failing to implement adequate safeguards to give reasonable assurance that Tubwell's conduct complied with the professional obligations of a lawyer. The tribunal concluded that Thompson's lack of supervision had permitted Tubwell to engage in the unauthorized practice of law.[10]

---

10. "The practice of law includes the drafting or selection of documents, the giving of advice in regard to them, and the using of an informed or trained discretion in the drafting of documents to meet the needs of the person being served. So any exercise of intelligent choice in advising another of his legal rights and duties brings the activity within the practice of the legal profession." [Citations omitted.]

Rule 5.3 provides that a lawyer with managerial authority in a law firm "shall make reasonable efforts to ensure that the firm has in effect measures giving reasonable assurance that the [non-lawyer's] conduct is compatible with the professional obligations of the lawyer. . . ." Thompson testified that she had total control of the firm's post office box and that she reviewed all mail that came into the firm, including any letters addressed to Tubwell. McGaughy stated that every letter he wrote to Tubwell was addressed to the Thompson Law Firm in Tunica. While it is unclear from the record exactly how many letters McGaughy sent to Tubwell, six letters from Tubwell to McGaughy acknowledged, either directly or implicitly, the receipt of an earlier letter from McGaughy. Nevertheless, Thompson said she could not recall seeing any letters from McGaughy.

While Thompson set forth some general instructions and procedures, she admitted that she had not done enough. When asked what steps she had put into place to ensure that Tubwell was not independently working on cases that he had handled while in prison, Thompson answered:

> Other than trusting him and, you know, telling him that any cases that, you know, we have, any cases that you have that you're working on, it's got to come through my office. . . . And, you know, had I—I guess had the foresight or just had—[he] didn't give me any reason to distrust him. You know, I wouldn't have—you know, I would have put other, I guess, precautions in place.

Furthermore, while she knew about Tubwell's armed robbery conviction at the time she hired him, she was unaware of his prior conviction for forgery until she read his deposition in this matter.

We find that Thompson violated Rule 5.3 by failing to make sufficient efforts to supervise Tubwell's work. This is especially true in light of Tubwell's criminal past and Thompson's awareness of the fact that Tubwell might have continued to work on cases from his earlier days as a writ writer. While Thompson's ill-advised choice of an untrustworthy paralegal may bear upon the degree to which she could foresee Tubwell's actions, it does not excuse her violation of the rules of professional conduct. [Citation omitted.]

The complaint tribunal held that there was insufficient evidence to find that Tubwell had violated Rule 5.5(b). The tribunal determined that there was not enough evidence to show that Thompson knew or should have known that Tubwell was holding out himself or her firm as attorneys for McGaughy. The Bar, however, asserts that a lawyer can assist a non-lawyer in the unauthorized practice of law by giving him all the necessary resources to practice law, and then failing to supervise him.

Rule 5.5(b) prohibits a lawyer from assisting a non-lawyer in the unauthorized practice of law. While a lawyer may employ paralegals and delegate duties to them, the lawyer must supervise the delegated work and retain responsibility for it. The Bar cites *In re Gaff*, 272 Ga. 7, 524 S.E.2d 728 (2000), to support its argument that a Rule 5.5 violation can occur as a result of a lawyer's failure to supervise. In *In re Gaff*, Gaff opened a second law office in another town and allowed a disbarred attorney, Ellis, to work there unsupervised as a paralegal. *Gaff*, 524 S.E.2d. at 728. Gaff failed to implement procedures to insure that Ellis did not have contact with Gaff's clients. Ellis engaged in forgery, theft, and met with and assisted clients on his own. The Supreme Court of Georgia held that Gaff had assisted Ellis in the unauthorized practice of law by failing to supervise him and failing to establish precautionary policies and procedures. . . .

While Tubwell took advantage of his position in Thompson's firm and engaged in the unauthorized practice of law without her direct knowledge, her failure to supervise and enforce necessary precautions allowed his actions to go unnoticed. . . . Accordingly, we find that Thompson assisted Tubwell in the unauthorized practice of law by giving him the position and resources necessary to practice law, and then failing to adequately supervise him. Therefore, we find that Thompson violated Rule 5.5(b). . . .

Rule 8.4(a), (d), provides that it is professional misconduct to violate or to attempt to violate the rules of professional conduct and to engage in conduct that is prejudicial to the administration of justice. M.R.P.C. 8.4(a), (d). Whenever there is a violation of any other rule, there will always be a violation under Rule 8.4. [Citation omitted.] Having found that Thompson violated Rules 1.15, 5.3, and 5.5(b), we necessarily find that she violated Rule 8.4(a) as well. Furthermore, Thompson's conduct was prejudicial to the administration of justice, because McGaughy was deprived of his right to file a habeas corpus petition and paid for non-existent representation. Therefore, we find that Thompson violated Rule 8.4(a), (d). . . .

We affirm the complaint tribunal with regard to its finding that Thompson violated Rules 1.15, 5.3, and 8.4(a), (d). We find that Thompson also violated Rule 5.5(b), and therefore, reverse the complaint tribunal's finding as to that issue. . . . [W]e reverse the one-year, retroactive suspension and remand this case to the tribunal for consideration of the appropriate sanction(s) in light of these factors.

Questions about the Case

1. What was the relationship of the lawyer Thompson and her paralegal Tubwell? Why did she hire Tubwell? Was he qualified to work as a paralegal? What kinds of background checks or conditions should lawyers insist on when hiring a paralegal?

2. What were the ways in which Tubwell acted unethically or incompetently in this case? What should Thompson have done to prevent these breaches?
3. What did you learn about protecting the records of clients? What other ethical issues are raised by Thompson's conduct concerning the files?
4. Do you agree with the court's analysis about apparent authority? Do you think that the facts here are substantially different from those in *DeVaux?*
5. Do you agree that Thompson aided in UPL? Why or why not? What was the UPL? Could Thompson have prevented it?
6. Given the factors to be considered in setting the sanction, as cited in the case, what do you think is an appropriate sanction?

In this disciplinary matter, a lawyer fails to supervise a paralegal and is held accountable for her many errors.

People v. Smith
74 P.3d 566 (Colo. O.P.D.J. 2003)

During the relevant time period from 1999 to 2001, Smith was a sole practitioner. He handled a large-volume practice with approximately half of the practice devoted to domestic law. Jeanette Ross ("Ross") worked as Smith's legal assistant from 1996 to 2001. During the period of her employment, Smith put measures in place to assure that all communications, oral and written, were brought to his attention. Ross was required to receive, open, and sort mail and record telephone messages. Ross would review incoming mail and place matters requiring prompt attention on Smith's desk with the client file. Less critical communication was placed in sorted stacks for Smith's review. Smith would then review his mail or telephone messages and instruct Ross what action to take on a given case. It was Smith's practice to review all court orders. Smith did not utilize computer software to track deadlines in cases. Smith and Ross did, however, manually record dates on two calendars. In addition, Smith allowed Ross to prepare form pleadings, prepare and send correspondence, docket court appearances, communicate with clients by phone, and handle settings with the court. Smith periodically reviewed case files to determine if cases were properly advancing.

Smith did not give Ross permission to sign his name to pleadings. Ross was permitted to write checks on Smith's operating account and utilize his signature stamp on operating account checks without prior authorization from Smith. Ross testified that she signed Smith's name to routine pleadings. Ross's testimony that Smith permitted her to sign his name to pleadings was not credible. . . .

8. Competence

In late 1998, Roy Reynolds, Jr. ("Reynolds") retained Smith to represent him in an uncontested divorce and paid him $800. . . . On January 27, 1999, Smith filed Reynolds' Petition for Dissolution of Marriage together with a Summons for Dissolution of Marriage or Legal Separation and Temporary Injunction. . . . On the same day, the court issued a form order entitled "Domestic Case Management and Delay Reduction Order" requiring that Smith take specified actions by a certain date. The order required Smith to provide a copy to Mrs. Reynolds. Although Smith did not see the order, he was fully aware of the routine procedure in uncontested divorces and knew what deadlines were imposed by the court as a matter of course. Smith did not set a Temporary Orders Hearing or engage in the pre-hearing conference as required by the court's order. Smith knew that Mrs. Reynolds was pregnant and he felt it necessary to wait for the birth of the child before requesting that the court enter child support orders. Smith did not file a plan for alternative dispute resolution by the stated deadline due to his unconfirmed belief Reynolds' desired to forestall the divorce.

Thereafter, Mrs. Reynolds, who resided in Kansas, signed a Waiver and Acceptance of Service and Affidavit with Respect to Financial Affairs prepared by Smith, and returned both documents to Smith's office. Mrs. Reynolds did not obtain counsel at that time.

Between January and May, Smith and Reynolds were in communication. In May 1999, Smith drafted a Settlement Agreement and gave it to Reynolds to review. Reynolds took the Separation Agreement prepared by Smith to Kansas for Mrs. Reynolds to sign, and she signed it on June 16, 1999, had it notarized and gave it back to Reynolds. Reynolds gave it back to Ross shortly thereafter. Reynolds failed to sign it. Smith was unaware that Reynolds had returned the Separation Agreement to his office.

On May 20, 1999, Ross filed a Notice to Set regarding a hearing on Permanent Orders. Ross affixed Smith's signature to the Notice to Set. Thereafter, she neglected to call the court at the appointed time to set the hearing.

On June 7, 1999, the court issued a form Status Order notifying the parties that the Reynolds case would be dismissed unless Smith took certain specific actions. Smith did not see the Status Order, did not take any of the actions the court directed him to take, and did not provide a copy of the Order to the parties. Smith believed that the case was proceeding on course and that he was waiting for a return of the signed Separation Agreement by the parties.

Ross, in an effort to cover her failure to follow through on the Notice to Set, filed another Notice to Set on June 10, 1999. Smith signed the notice but did not confirm with Ross that she set the hearing. A hearing was not set.

Ross attempted to contact Reynolds but was unable to do so. Smith told Ross to send a letter to Reynolds and advise him that the case may be dismissed if the Separation Agreement was not filed. Smith believed Ross did so, but did not check the file to confirm that she had. Ross did not send a letter to Reynolds.

During July and August 1999, Reynolds attempted to contact Smith several times but was able to only speak to Ross. The calls were not routed to Smith, and Smith was not advised that Reynolds was attempting to reach him.

On August 11, 1999, the court dismissed the case on the grounds that the parties had not complied with the court's June 7, 1999 Status Order and required Smith to provide a copy of the order to the parties. Smith did not see the order and therefore did not comply with it. Smith continued to believe that Reynolds had lost interest in pursuing the divorce.

In October, Ross contacted the court to set the matter for a Permanent Orders hearing. It was at this point that she discovered the case had been dismissed. She determined to conceal this fact from Smith. On October 25, 1999, without Smith's knowledge or approval, Ross filed a Notice to Set Uncontested Permanent Orders, an Affidavit With Respect to Financial Affairs and the Separation Agreement both of which Mrs. Reynolds had signed on June 16, 1999. Ross hoped that the court would reopen the case. Nothing further occurred . . . in [the][c]ase. . . .

In early 2000, due to the lack of communication with Smith, Reynolds came to Smith's office to inquire about the status of his case. Reynolds never spoke directly with Smith; rather, he believed at the time that Ross was his lawyer. Reynolds confronted Ross with the court order dismissing the case in August 1999 which he first saw when he reviewed the court file at the courthouse. Ross told Reynolds the court had lost the paperwork and it would be necessary to file a new case. Ross did not tell Smith about Reynolds' visit to the office.

On March 6, 2000, without Smith's knowledge or approval, Ross commenced a new action on behalf of Reynolds by filing a Summons for Dissolution of Marriage and Temporary Injunction in Arapahoe County District Court. . . . Ross affixed Smith's signature to the documents. Ross falsely notarized a Waiver and Acceptance of Service and affixed Mrs. Reynolds' signature without her knowledge or authority.

The next day, without informing Smith, Ross sent a letter to Reynolds enclosing financial affidavits, a Separation Agreement and Child Support Worksheets. After receiving these documents, Reynolds came to the office and was angry with Ross. Ross did not inform Smith that Reynolds had visited the office. Smith believed the case was closed because Reynolds had not signed the Separation Agreement. Smith had no communication with Reynolds in 2000.

On March 20, 2000, Ross filed a Petition for Dissolution of Marriage and affixed Smith's name to the pleading.

In July 2000, Mrs. Reynolds believed the divorce had been finalized. She contacted Smith's office and spoke to Ross numerous times and to Smith once, asking for a copy of the decree. Ross informed her she would inquire into the status of the case and get back to her. Later Ross told Mrs. Reynolds she was not sure why there was no decree and that there was some confusion in Smith's office. After receiving a call from Mrs. Reynolds' father, Smith asked Ross about the status of the case. Ross said that Reynolds came in to sign the Separation Agreement and that they were waiting to receive a decree from the court. Smith then told Mrs. Reynolds that he was waiting for a decree from the court and that he would get back to her. Smith did not get back to Mrs. Reynolds.

On July 15, 2000, Ross drafted a second Separation Agreement. She affixed the signatures of Smith as counsel for Reynolds, Mrs. Reynolds, and the attorney's name who shared Smith's office as counsel for Mrs. Reynolds. Ross notarized the signatures stating that she witnessed the signatures in Adams County, even though Mrs. Reynolds continued to reside in Kansas. Ross filed it with the court. Neither Smith, Mrs. Reynolds, nor the attorney who was purportedly signing as counsel for Mrs. Reynolds knew that Ross had affixed their signatures to the document. Ross knew at the time that Smith would not condone her drafting the Separation Agreement and affixing signatures to it.

In August 2000, Ross filed an Affidavit for Decree Without Appearance of Parties with the court. She affixed the signatures of Smith and the attorney who shared Smith's office as counsel for Mrs. Reynolds without their knowledge or approval. Ross knew the court would rely on the document as containing valid signatures and knew at the time she filed the document that she was making a false statement to the court.

Finally, in the spring of 2001, Mrs. Reynolds hired an attorney in Kansas to commence a new divorce proceeding at a cost of $1,500. On April 3, 2001, Ross sent a letter to Mrs. Reynolds' attorney in Kansas stating that the dissolution of marriage action in Arapahoe County had not been dismissed. She wrote the letter on behalf of Smith and affixed his signature to the letter without his knowledge. On the same date, she notified the clerk of the district court in Shawnee County, Topeka, Kansas, that the matter had not been dismissed, and again affixed Smith's name to the letter without his knowledge.

On April 12, 2001, a Decree of Dissolution of Marriage issued from Arapahoe District Court in [the second case]. The Magistrate entered the Decree unaware that it had been presented by Ross with falsified signatures of the attorneys and parties.

Shortly thereafter, the divorce proceeding in Kansas was completed and Mrs. Reynolds obtained a decree.

Smith acknowledged that he was responsible for Ross's actions, but also believed that his actions were based on his belief that Reynolds had decided not to go forward with the divorce. Smith also believed that were it not for Ross's actions as an "intervening cause," he would have been aware of the court's orders and of Reynolds' communication with Ross.

Both parties suffered harm as a result of the delay in obtaining the divorce: Mrs. Reynolds applied for but could not obtain financial aid because she was required to include Mr. Reynolds' income on her application, and she paid additional attorneys' fees to resolve the divorce. Mr. Reynolds was required to resolve child support issues in another jurisdiction. Both parties suffered personal inconvenience and stress for over one and one half years.

Smith refunded the $800 Reynolds paid to him.

The Complaint filed in this matter alleges that Smith's conduct violated Colo. RPC 1.3 (an attorney shall act with reasonable diligence and promptness in representing a client) in claim one; Colo. RPC 1.4(a) (an attorney shall keep a client reasonably informed about the status of a matter and promptly comply with reasonable requests for information) and Colo. RPC 1.4(b) (an attorney shall explain a matter to the extent reasonably necessary to permit the client to make informed decisions regarding the representation) in claim two; Colo. RPC 5.3(a) (partner in a law firm shall make reasonable efforts to ensure that the firm has in effect measures giving reasonable assurance that the person's conduct is compatible with the professional obligations of the lawyer) and Colo. RPC 5.3(b) (a lawyer having direct supervisory authority over the nonlawyer shall make reasonable efforts to ensure that the person's conduct is compatible with the professional obligations of the lawyer) in claim three, and Colo. RPC 1.16(d) (upon termination an attorney takes steps to the extent reasonably practicable to protect a client's interests) in claim four.

Colo. RPC 5.3 provides:

> With respect to a non-lawyer employed or retained by or associated with a lawyer:
>> (a) a partner in a law firm shall make reasonable efforts to ensure that the firm has in effect measures giving reasonable assurance that the person's conduct is compatible with the professional obligations of a lawyer;
>> (b) a lawyer having direct supervisory authority over the non-lawyer shall make reasonable efforts to ensure that the person's conduct is compatible with the professional obligations of the lawyer. . . .

Smith entered into an attorney/client relationship with Reynolds, thereby forming an obligation to perform the agreed-upon professional services, including obtaining a divorce for Reynolds through the entry of permanent orders. By agreeing to perform the requested services, Smith inherently agreed that he would perform the services in accordance with the Colorado Rules of Professional Conduct. The Complaint alleges that Smith did not have measures in place which would give reasonable assurance that Ross's conduct was compatible with the obligations of a lawyer. The evidence presented, however, revealed that Smith did have measures in place to reasonably assure that all communications with his office were promptly brought to his attention and that Ross would conduct herself in such a manner as was compatible with his professional responsibilities. Ross didn't follow those measures. Since such measures were in place, the charged violation of Colo. RPC 5.3(a) is dismissed.

The charged violation of Colo. RPC 5.3(b) requires a different consideration. Colo. RPC 5.3(b) focuses upon whether the attorney having direct supervisory authority over a non-lawyer adequately supervises that individual. Smith had direct supervisory authority over Ross in this case. He delegated substantial responsibility to her and failed to review her work. Indeed, although the client file was in his office for the entire period of time the events were unfolding, he did not review that file to determine if Ross was, in fact, attending to the case as she described to him. Smith's failure to adequately supervise Ross allowed her to conceal the court's orders requiring that Smith take specific action on Reynolds' behalf, including setting a temporary orders hearing, engaging in alternative dispute resolution or informing the court that none was necessary, calendaring all deadlines set by the court, confirming that Smith's office was in contact with the client, and confirming the correct status of the case. A simple examination of the Reynolds file would have disclosed Ross's activities and alerted Smith of the problems developing in the case.

Smith's failure to adequately supervise Ross resulted in her engaging in the unauthorized practice of law. Smith's acting as Ross's direct supervisor but failing to fulfill his professional obligations with regard to that supervision violated Colo. RPC 5.3(b). Allowing a non-lawyer assistant to engage in the unauthorized practice of law by failing to supervise the non-lawyer is grounds for discipline. *People v. Reynolds*, 933 P.2d 1295, 1298-99 (Colo. 1997); *People v. Stewart*, 892 P.2d 875, 877-78 (Colo. 1995).

Smith argues that but for Ross's failing to advise him of Reynolds' attempts to contact him, her failing to provide him with the court's orders, and her failing to advise him that the case had been dismissed, he would not have neglected the client's case. Smith's argument is without merit.

Other jurisdictions have examined this issue. The Restatement (Third) of Law Governing Law §11 (2003) concerning a lawyer's duty of supervision, provides:

Supervision is a general responsibility of a principal. A . . . lawyer with authority to direct the activities of another lawyer or nonlawyer employee of the firm is such a principal. Appropriate exercise of responsibility over those carrying out the tasks of law practice is particularly important given the duties of lawyers to protect the interests of clients and in view of the privileged powers conferred on lawyers by law. The supervisory duty, in effect, requires that such additional experience and skill be deployed in reasonably diligent fashion.

Lack of awareness of misconduct by another person, either lawyer or nonlawyer, under a lawyer's supervision does not excuse a violation of this Section. To ensure that supervised persons comply with professional standards, a supervisory lawyer is required to take reasonable measures, given the level and extent of responsibility that the lawyer possesses. Those measures, such as an informal program of instructing or monitoring another person, must often assume the likelihood that a particular lawyer or nonlawyer employee may not yet have received adequate preparation for carrying out that person's own responsibilities. . . .

After initially pursuing the Reynolds matter and drafting a separation agreement, Smith lost contact with Reynolds and failed to inform himself of the status of the case. He failed to comply with the court's January 27, 1999 and June 7, 1999 orders. Even if as Smith asserts he did not see the court orders and therefore could not comply with them, he was fully aware of the procedures and deadlines set forth by the court in a divorce proceeding. Smith failed to make every effort to locate the client and acquire his signature on the Separation Agreement, and failed to take adequate measures to confirm the status of the case. Instead, he relied on Ross to oversee the file. Smith's failing to take the required steps to resolve the Reynolds matter constitutes neglect in violation of Colo. RPC 1.3.

Although Smith's conduct clearly constitutes neglect, it does not, however, rise to the level of abandonment. To find abandonment rather than mere neglect, the evidence must objectively indicate that counsel deserted, rejected, and/or relinquished his professional responsibilities. In the present case, although Smith should have taken measures to locate Reynolds, Ross did not inform Smith that Reynolds had come to the office inquiring about the status of the case. Smith continued to believe that Reynolds had lost interest in pursuing the divorce. Ross fostered Smith's lack of awareness of Reynolds' numerous attempts to contact him. He did not, therefore, desert, reject, or relinquish his professional responsibilities. Smith's actions did not terminate the attorney–client relationship with Reynolds and the provisions set forth in Colo. RPC 1.16(d) were not triggered. Accordingly, claim four alleging a violation of Colo. RPC 1.16(d) is dismissed.

Initially, for approximately the first four months of representation, Smith stayed in adequate contact with Reynolds and kept him informed of the case status. Thereafter, however, for a period of a year and a half, Smith violated Colo. RPC 1.4(a) by failing to keep Reynolds reasonably informed about the status of the divorce proceeding. Smith violated Colo. RPC 1.4(b) by failing to explain the procedural status of the case to Reynolds to the extent reasonably necessary to permit the client to make informed decisions. His failure to inform himself of the status of the case does not abrogate his responsibility to keep the client reasonably informed.

Smith's conduct regarding the Reynolds matter resulted in injury to Reynolds: his divorce matter was dismissed, both parties suffered considerable distress not knowing whether they were divorced over a considerable period of time, and Reynolds must suffer the inconvenience of pursuing his legal rights in another jurisdiction.

MATTHEW S. SMITH . . . is suspended from the practice of law for a period of nine months. . . . Smith shall pay the costs in conjunction with this matter. . . .

Questions about the Case

1. Make a list of all the mistakes the paralegal made in this case. Sort them as failing to meet standards of competence and intentional acts.
2. On what basis did the court find the lawyer Smith responsible for the paralegal's actions?
3. Did the court find that the paralegal had committed UPL? On what basis, and under what definition of the practice of law? Was the lawyer held responsible for aiding in the unauthorized practice?
4. What should the lawyer have done to avoid this situation? Did he "over-delegate"?
5. What could the paralegal have done?
6. Was there a basis here for a malpractice action against Smith and Ross?
7. Was the sanction appropriate?

The mistake in this appeal was the result of a paralegal failure to calendar a deadline properly.

Pincay v. Andrews
389 F.3d 853 (9th Cir. 2004)

This appeal represents a lawyer's nightmare. . . .

The underlying dispute began in 1989 when Laffit Pincay, Jr. and Christopher McCarron (Pincay) sued Vincent S. Andrews, Robert L. Andrews, and Vincent Andrews Management Corp. (Andrews) for financial injuries stemming from alleged violations of the Racketeer Influenced and Corrupt Organizations Act (RICO) and California law. In 1992, a jury returned verdicts in Pincay's favor on both the RICO and the California counts. Pincay was ordered to elect a remedy, and he chose to pursue the RICO judgment. This judgment was reversed on appeal on the ground that the RICO claim was barred by the federal statute of limitations. [Citation omitted.] On remand, Pincay elected to pursue the remedy on his California law claim. Judgment was entered in his favor on July 3, 2002.

Andrews's notice of appeal was due 30 days later, but a paralegal charged with calendaring filing deadlines misread the rule and advised Andrews's attorney that the notice was not due for 60 days, the time allowed when the government is a party to the case. *See* Fed. R. App. P. 4(a)(1)(B). Andrews's counsel learned about the error when Pincay relied upon the judgment as being final in related bankruptcy proceedings, and Andrews promptly tendered a notice of appeal together with a request for an extension within the 30-day grace period. By that time the matter had been in litigation for more than 15 years. Everyone involved should have been well aware that the government was not a party to the case, and any lawyer or paralegal should have been able to read the rule correctly. The misreading of the rule was a critical error that, had the district court viewed the situation differently, would have ended the litigation then and there with an irreparably adverse result for Andrews. The district court, however, found the neglect excusable and granted the motion for an extension of time to file the notice of appeal.

Pincay appealed to this court, and a majority of the three-judge panel concluded that Andrews's attorney had improperly delegated the function of calendaring to a paralegal, and held that the attorney's reliance on a paralegal was inexcusable as a matter of law. *Pincay v. Andrews*, 351 F.3d 947, 951-52 (9th Cir. 2003). It ordered the appeal dismissed. The dissent would have applied a more flexible and deferential standard and affirmed the district court. *Id.* at 952-56. . . .

A majority of the active non-recused judges of the court voted to rehear the case en banc to consider whether the creation of a per se rule against delegation to paralegals, or indeed any per se rule involving missed filing deadlines, is consistent with the United States Supreme Court's leading authority on the modern concept of excusable neglect. [Citation omitted.] . . . The *Pioneer* decision arose in the bankruptcy context and involved the "bar date" for the filing of claims. The Court in *Pioneer* established a four-part balancing test for determining whether there had been "excusable neglect" within the meaning of Federal Rule of Bankruptcy Procedure 9006(b)(1). The Court also reviewed various contexts in which the phrase appeared in the federal rules of procedure and made it clear the same test applies in all those contexts. The *Pioneer* factors include: (1) the danger of prejudice to the non-moving party, (2) the length of delay and its potential impact on judicial proceedings, (3) the reason for the delay, including whether it was within the reasonable control of the movant, and (4) whether the moving party's conduct was in good faith. 507 U.S. at 395, 113 S. Ct. 1489.

In this case, the district court analyzed each of the *Pioneer* factors and correctly found: (1) there was no prejudice, (2) the length of delay was small, (3) the reason for the delay was carelessness, and (4) there was no evidence of bad faith. It then concluded that even though the reason for the delay was the carelessness of Andrews's counsel, that fact did not render the neglect inexcusable. . . .

Because the panel majority decided the case in part on the issue of delegation of calendaring to a paralegal, we consider that issue first. This issue was not presented to the district court, and it was raised sua sponte by the three-judge panel.

In the modern world of legal practice, the delegation of repetitive legal tasks to paralegals has become a necessary fixture. Such delegation has become an integral part of the struggle to keep down the costs of legal representation. Moreover, the delegation of such tasks to specialized, well-educated non-lawyers may well ensure greater accuracy in meeting deadlines than a practice of having each lawyer in a large firm calculate each filing deadline anew. The task of keeping track of necessary deadlines will involve some delegation. The responsibility for the error falls on the attorney regardless of whether the error was made by an attorney or a paralegal. *See* Model Rules of Prof'l Conduct R. 5.5 cmt. 2 (2002) ("This Rule does not prohibit a lawyer from employing the services of paraprofessionals and delegating functions to them, so long as the lawyer supervises the delegated work and retains responsibility for their work."). We hold that delegation of the task of ascertaining the deadline was not per se inexcusable neglect.

The larger question in this case is whether the misreading of the clear rule could appropriately have been considered excusable. Resolution of that question requires some effort to try to distill any principles that have evolved in the 10 years since *Pioneer*. In *Pioneer* itself, the Court adopted a broader and more flexible test for excusable neglect. A narrower test existed in many circuits before *Pioneer* that limited excusable neglect to situations that were beyond the control of the movant for an extension as, for example, the messenger being hit by a truck on the way to the court clerk's filing desk. *See Pioneer*, 507 U.S. at 387-88 & n. 3, 113 S. Ct. 1489.

The district court followed our decision in *Marx*, where we acknowledged that *Pioneer* had worked a change in our circuit's law as to what constitutes excusable neglect. 87 F.3d at 1053-54. As we explained in *Marx*, our "strict standard," which required both a showing of extraordinary circumstances that prevented timely filing and injustice resulting from denying an extension gave way to an equitable determination that involves consideration of the four *Pioneer* factors. We therefore affirmed the district court's grant of an extension of time to file a notice of appeal in *Marx* because the district court correctly considered the *Pioneer* factors. . . .

Our court, in other cases, has also described *Pioneer*'s flexible approach, saying, for example, "we will ordinarily examine all of the circumstances involved rather than holding that any single circumstance in isolation compels a particular result regardless of the other factors." [Citations omitted.]

We seemed to take a more narrow approach in *Kyle v. Campbell Soup Co.*, 28 F.3d 928 (9th Cir. 1994). In that case our court reversed the district court's finding of excusable neglect. We emphasized the fact that the attorney had made a mistake in interpreting rules that were not ambiguous and we focused on the particular facts of *Pioneer*, including a "dramatic ambiguity" in the notice of the filing deadline at issue.

Our circuit's confusion is not isolated. The authorities interpreting *Pioneer* in a number of circuits are in some disarray. In fact, the confusion begins with *Pioneer* itself, and various subsequent circuit opinions have cited similar portions of *Pioneer* to support their respective but differing conclusions. . . .

In this case the mistake itself, the misreading of the Rule, was egregious, and the lawyer undoubtedly should have checked the Rule itself before relying on the paralegal's reading. Both the paralegal and the lawyer were negligent. That, however, represents the beginning of our inquiry as to whether the negligence is excusable, not the end of it. The real question is whether there was enough in the context of this case to bring a determination of excusable neglect within the district court's discretion.

We therefore turn to examining the *Pioneer* factors as they apply here. The parties seem to agree that three of the factors militate in favor of excusability, and they focus their arguments on the remaining factor: the reason for the delay. Appellee Andrews characterizes the reason for the delay as the failure of a "carefully designed" calendaring system operated by experienced paralegals that heretofore had worked flawlessly. Appellant Pincay, on the other hand, stresses the degree of carelessness in the failure to read the applicable Rule.

We recognize that a lawyer's failure to read an applicable rule is one of the least compelling excuses that can be offered; yet the nature of the contextual analysis and the balancing of the factors adopted in *Pioneer* counsel against the creation of any rigid rule. Rather, the decision whether to grant or deny an extension of time to file a notice of appeal should be entrusted to the discretion of the district court because the district court is in a better position than we are to evaluate factors such as whether the lawyer had otherwise been diligent, the propensity of the other side to capitalize on petty mistakes, the quality of representation of the lawyers (in this litigation over its 15-year history), and the likelihood of injustice if the appeal was not allowed. Had the district court declined to permit the filing of the notice, we would be hard pressed to find any rationale requiring us to reverse.

We are also mindful that Rule 4 itself provides for leniency in limited circumstances. It could have been written more rigidly, allowing for no window of opportunity once the deadline was missed. Many states' rules provide for an extension of the time for filing a notice of appeal under few, if any, circumstances. . . .

We understand several of our sister circuits have tried to fashion a rule making a mistake of law per se inexcusable under Rule 4. [Citations omitted.] . . . We agree that a lawyer's mistake of law in reading a rule of procedure is not a compelling excuse. At the same time, however, a lawyer's mistake of fact, for example, in thinking the government was a party to a case and that the 60-day rule applied for that reason, would be no more compelling.

We are persuaded that, under *Pioneer*, the correct approach is to avoid any per se rule. *Pioneer* cautioned against "erecting a rigid barrier against late filings attributable in any degree to the movant's negligence." There should similarly be no rigid legal rule against late filings attributable to any particular type of negligence. Instead, we leave the weighing of *Pioneer*'s equitable factors to the discretion of the district court in every case.

We hold that the district court did not abuse its discretion in this case. Therefore, the district court's order granting the defendant's motion for an extension of time to file the notice of appeal is AFFIRMED. . . .

KOZINSKI, Circuit Judge, with whom Judges RYMER and MCKEOWN join, dissenting . . .

At bottom, what the sophisticated-calendaring-system excuse comes down to is that the lawyer didn't bother to read the rule; instead, he relied on what a calendaring clerk told him. While delegation may be a necessity in modern law practice, it can't be a lever for ratcheting down the standard for professional competence. If it's inexcusable for a competent lawyer to misread the rule, it can't become excusable because the lawyer turned the task over to a non-lawyer. Errors made by clerks performing lawyerly functions are probably less excusable than those made by the lawyer himself; they certainly can't be more so.

The majority may be right that any competent lawyer or clerk should have been able to read the rule correctly, but that is quite different from saying that a lawyer and a non-lawyer would be equally likely to *mis*-read the rule. Studying and practicing law develops certain skills and habits of mind that, one hopes, make lawyers more careful than non-lawyers about reading rules. When a lawyer turns this function over to a non-lawyer, it increases the likelihood an error will be made. Had the lawyer in this case read the rule himself, rather than relying on what a clerk told him, he doubtless would have gotten it right. Indeed, the 30-day rule for appeals in federal court is so well known among federal practitioners that, had the lawyer but *thought* about the rule, rather than relying entirely on the calendaring clerk's representation, he would surely have realized that the 60-day period is wrong. Instead, the lawyer delegated the calendaring issue to the calendaring "system," which is made up entirely of non-lawyers. If turning large chunks of law practice over to para-professionals can itself be an excuse for misreading rules, then we'll probably see more such delegation and misreading. It is the cold logic of the marketplace that conduct that is rewarded will be repeated. . . .

I would hold that the error here—whether made by the lawyer, the calendaring clerk or the candlestick-maker—is inexcusable and dismiss the appeal as untimely. . . .

Questions about the Case

1. What was the paralegal's error? Did the work that the paralegal was doing require a sophisticated knowledge of the law? What competencies mentioned in this chapter did it require?
2. What did the court say about establishing a rule for mistakes made by paralegals? Is this good or bad for paralegals?
3. What is "excusable neglect"? Was the neglect here found to be excusable? If so, why?
4. What should the lawyer and the paralegal have done to prevent this error?
5. What might have been the consequences if the decision had gone the other way?
6. What do you think about the dissent's opinion?

In this case, a paralegal who worked without lawyer supervision was engaged in the unauthorized practice of law.

Tegman v. Accident & Medical Investigations
107 Wn. App. 868, 30 P.3d 8 (2001)

. . . Between 1989 and 1991, plaintiffs Maria Tegman, Linda Leszynski, and Daina Calixto were each injured in separate and unrelated automobile accidents. After their accidents, each plaintiff retained G. Richard McClellan and Accident & Medical Investigations, Inc. (AMI) for legal counsel and assistance in handling their personal injury claims. McClellan and AMI purported to represent each plaintiff in seeking compensation from insurance companies for their injuries. Each plaintiff signed a contingency fee agreement with AMI, believing that McClellan was an attorney and AMI a law firm. McClellan has never been an attorney in any jurisdiction.

McClellan and AMI employed Camille Jescavage and Lorinda Noble, both licensed attorneys. Jescavage and Noble learned that McClellan entered into contingency fee agreements with AMI's clients and that McClellan was not an attorney. They settled a number of cases for AMI, and learned that McClellan processed settlements of AMI cases through his own bank account. Noble resigned from AMI in May 1991, after working there approximately six months.

In July 1991, McClellan hired Deloris Mullen as a paralegal. Mullen considered Jescavage to be her supervising attorney though Jescavage provided little supervision. Jescavage resigned from AMI in the first week of September 1991. McClellan told Mullen that her new supervising attorney would be James Bailey. Mullen did not immediately contact Bailey to confirm that he was her supervising attorney. He later told her he was not.

While at AMI, Mullen worked on approximately 50-60 cases, including those of plaintiffs Tegman, Leszynski, and Calixto. Mullen was aware of some of McClellan's questionable practices and knew that there were substantial improprieties involved with his operation. Mullen stopped working at AMI on December 6, 1991, when the situation became personally intolerable to her and she obtained direct knowledge that she was without a supervising attorney. When she left, she did not advise any of the plaintiffs about the problems at AMI.

After Mullen left, McClellan settled each plaintiff's case for various amounts without their knowledge or consent, and deposited the funds in his general account by forging their names on the settlement checks.

In 1993, Calixto, Leszynski, and Tegman each individually sued McClellan, AMI, Mullen, and Jescavage. Tegman also sued Noble. Their complaints sought damages on various theories. The cases were consolidated. Discovery took place between 1993 and 1998. In the interim, McClellan pleaded guilty to mail fraud in United States District Court in 1997 and was sentenced to two years imprisonment. Also, this court affirmed a judgment by the same trial court in another case where McClellan settled a client's case without authorization and stole the proceeds. *Bullard v. Bailey*, 91 Wn. App. 750, 959 P.2d 1122 (1998). That judgment apportioned 20-percent fault to attorney James Bailey who, like Noble and Jescavage, had associated himself with AMI and failed to warn his clients of McClellan's improprieties.

In the present matter, the court entered summary judgment against McClellan and AMI on the issue of liability. After a six-day trial, the court held Mullen, Noble, and Jescavage liable for negligence and legal negligence, and awarded damages. Only Mullen and Noble appeal. Their appeals have been consolidated. . . .

Mullen, a paralegal, contends the court erred in finding her negligent. To establish the elements of an action for negligence, a plaintiff must show: (1) the existence of a duty owed, (2) breach of that duty, (3) a resulting injury, and (4) a proximate cause between the breach and the injury. [Citation omitted.]

Non-attorneys who attempt to practice law will be held to the same standards of competence demanded of attorneys and will be liable for negligence if these standards are not met. [Citations omitted.] In *Bowers*, sellers sold property to buyers who had persuaded a non-attorney escrow agent to prepare an unsecured promissory note in favor of the sellers. After the deed was delivered to the buyers, the sellers learned the significance of the fact that the note was unsecured. . . . The sellers sued the escrow agent and obtained summary judgment on liability for negligence. Our Supreme Court affirmed, holding the escrow agent to an attorney's standard of care. The escrow agent breached a duty to inform the sellers of the advisability of obtaining independent counsel. *Bowers*, 100 Wn. 2d at 590. That duty was owed because the escrow agent, by preparing the closing documents, was engaging in the practice of law.

The "practice of law" clearly does not just mean appearing in court. In a larger sense, it includes "legal advice and counsel, and the preparation of legal instruments and contracts by which legal rights are secured." [Citations omitted.]

Mullen contends that her status as a paralegal precludes a finding that she was engaged in the practice of law. She argues that a paralegal is, by definition, someone who works under the supervision of an attorney, and that it is necessarily the attorney, not the paralegal, who is practicing law and owes a duty to the clients. Her argument assumes that she had a supervising attorney. The trial court's determination that Mullen was negligent was dependent on the court's finding that Mullen knew, or should have known, that she did not have a supervising attorney over a period of several months while she was at AMI. "Had Mullen been properly supervised by an attorney at all times 'uring her employment with AMI, plaintiffs presumably would have no case against her. Rather, her supervising attorney would be responsible for any alleged wrongdoing on her part."

We agree with the trial court's observation. The label "paralegal" is not in itself a shield from liability. A factual evaluation is necessary to distinguish a paralegal who is working under an attorney's supervision from one who is actually practicing law. A finding that a paralegal is practicing law will not be supported merely by evidence of infrequent contact with the supervising attorney. As long as the paralegal does in fact have a supervising attorney who is responsible for the case, any deficiency in the quality of the supervision or in the quality of the paralegal's work goes to the attorney's negligence, not the paralegal's.

In this case, Mullen testified that she believed James Bailey was her supervising attorney after Jescavage left. The court found Mullen was not justified in that belief. Mullen assigns error to this finding, but the evidence supports it. Mullen testified that she had started to distrust McClellan before he informed her that Bailey would be her supervising attorney. Mullen also testified that she did not contact Bailey to confirm that he was supervising her. Bailey testified at a deposition that he did not share Mullen's clients and she did not consult him regarding any of her ongoing cases. He also said that one of the only conversations he remembers having with Mullen with respect to AMI is one where he told her that he was not her supervising attorney after she raised the issue with him. This testimony amply supports the trial court's finding that Mullen was unjustified in her belief that Bailey was her supervising attorney.

In *Hunt*, a paralegal appealed a criminal conviction for the unauthorized practice of law based on his conduct in running a claim settlement company. Among other things, Hunt failed to inform his clients of his activities, did not inform clients of the full amount of settlements, reached settlements without consulting his clients, and filed incomplete or improper documents in court. In a constitutional challenge to the unauthorized practice of law statute, RCW 2.48.180, Hunt argued that his status as a paralegal prevented a finding that he was engaged in the practice of law. The Court of Appeals disagreed and affirmed his conviction: "It is the nature and character of the service performed which governs whether given activities constitute the practice of law, not the nature or status of the person performing the services." Hunt, 75 Wn. App. At 802 (citing in part *WSBA*, 91 Wn. 2d at 54). As in Hunt, Mullen's status as a paralegal did not preclude the trial court from concluding that Mullen had engaged in the practice of law.

Contrary to Mullen's argument, such a conclusion does not require evidence that the paralegal called herself an attorney, entered appearances, or charged fees. Mullen testified that she negotiated settlements on behalf of the plaintiffs. She sent a letter rejecting, without Tegman's knowledge, a settlement offer made to Tegman. She continued to send out demand and representation letters after Jescavage left AMI. Letters written by Mullen before Jescavage's departure identify Mullen as a paralegal after her signature, whereas letters she wrote after Jescavage's departure lacked such identification. Even after Mullen discovered, in late November 1991, that Bailey was not her supervising attorney, she wrote letters identifying 'this office' as representing the plaintiffs, neglecting to mention that she was a paralegal and that no attorney was responsible for the case. This evidence substantially supports the finding that Mullen engaged in the practice of law.

Mullen contends that she cannot be held liable for negligence because the statute that prohibits the unauthorized practice of law was not in effect at the time she worked for AMI. The trial court dismissed the plaintiffs' claims that were based on the alleged statutory violation, but this does not prevent Mullen from being liable on the negligence claim.

Under *Bowers*, the duty arises from the practice of law, not from the statute. Mullen points out that an attorney-client relationship is an element of a cause of action for legal malpractice. [Citation omitted.] The trial court did not find that she had an attorney-client relationship with any of the plaintiffs, and she contends that as a result it is illogical to hold her to the standard of care of an attorney.

Mullen, because she is not an attorney, could not have attorney-client relationships. Nevertheless, as *Bowers* demonstrates, a layperson can logically be held to the standard of care of an attorney in a negligence action. The duty arises from the attempt to engage in the practice of law rather than from the professional status of the defendant. The trial court, covering all bases, held Mullen liable both for negligence and legal negligence. While the "legal negligence" label may have been incorrect, any such error is immaterial because the negligence theory produces the same result and, as the trial court observed, for practical purposes the allegations are the same.

Accordingly, we conclude the trial court did not err in following *Bowers* and holding Mullen to the duty of an attorney. The duty of care owed by an attorney is that degree of care, skill, diligence, and knowledge commonly possessed and exercised by a reasonable, careful, and prudent lawyer in the practice of law in Washington. [Citation omitted.]

Mullen challenges, as unsupported by the evidence, the trial court's key finding as to the duties that Mullen owed and breached. The court found that the standard of care owed by an attorney, and therefore also by Mullen, required her to notify the plaintiffs of: (1) the serious problems concerning the accessibility of their files to persons who had no right to see them, (2) the fact that client settlements were not processed through an attorney's trust account, but rather McClellan's own account, (3) the fact that McClellan and AMI, as non-lawyers, had no right to enter into contingent fee agreements with clients and receive contingent fees, (4) the fact that McClellan was, in fact, engaged in the unlawful practice of law, and that, generally, (5) the clients of McClellan and AMI were at substantial risk of financial harm as a result of their association with AMI. Mullen breached her duty to her clients in all of these particulars.

The finding rests on the testimony of attorney Charles Nelson Berry III, an expert witness for the plaintiffs. The trial court found Berry's testimony to be "thoughtful and well-considered" and significantly, unrebutted.

Mullen argues that the finding must be stricken because Berry improperly derived the standard of care from the Rules of Professional Conduct. In testifying that an attorney's conduct violated the legal standard of care, an expert witness may base an opinion on an attorney's failure to conform to an ethics rule, and may testify using language found in the Rules of Professional Conduct, as long as the jury is not led to believe that the ethical violations were actionable. [Citation omitted.] Berry's testimony, phrased in terms of breach of the standard of care, stayed within this constraint. We conclude the finding is supported by substantial evidence. Accordingly, the trial court did not err in concluding that Mullen was negligent. . . .

All three plaintiffs testified that they hired McClellan and AMI to legally represent them and believed that McClellan was an attorney whom they trusted and relied upon to handle their respective claims. They found out that he was not an attorney only after their claims had been settled. Mullen did not advise any of the plaintiffs that McClellan was not a lawyer; that AMI was not a law firm; that she, as a paralegal, had no real supervision; or that client funds did not go through a trust account. These omissions by Mullen sufficiently link her to the plaintiffs' later injury to establish cause in fact. It was reasonable for the trial court to infer that if Mullen had properly advised the plaintiffs of the problems at AMI, more likely than not they would have withdrawn their cases from AMI in time to avoid being harmed by McClellan's fraudulent acts.

Legal causation turns on a policy question of how far the consequences of a defendant's acts should extend. [Citations omitted.] Mullen contends that her connection to the plaintiffs' injuries is too remote because she did not render direct legal advice and that it is unjust to hold her, an employee paralegal, responsible for the criminal, intentional acts of her employer. The *Bullard* court rejected a similar argument asserted by Bailey, an attorney who allowed himself to become associated with McClellan. . . .

Although Mullen was a paralegal, she is held to an attorney's standard of care because she worked on the plaintiffs' cases during a period of several months when she had no supervising attorney. The fact that she did not render legal advice directly does not excuse her; in fact, her failure to advise the plaintiffs of the improper arrangements at AMI is the very omission that breached her duty. Under these circumstances it is not unjust to hold her accountable as a legal cause of the plaintiffs' injuries.

As all the elements of negligence have been established, we affirm the judgment against Mullen.

The trial court entered judgment against Mullen and Noble, McClellan, and AMI jointly and severally for compensatory damages. . . . The court entered judgment against McClellan and AMI for substantial additional sums, including attorney fees, for criminal profiteering and Consumer Protection Act violations. Mullen and Noble object to being held jointly liable for the compensatory damages. They ask that the judgments be revised so that they are responsible for only that portion of the compensatory damages corresponding to the percentages of fault the trial court attributed to them. . . .

[T]he trial court determined that Mullen was 10 percent at fault in each of the three cases; attorney Jescavage was 10 percent at fault in each of the three cases; and Noble was five percent at fault in Tegman's case. The court determined that McClellan and AMI had the remaining percentages in each case. The court then concluded that each of the plaintiffs was not at fault, and held all defendants jointly as well as severally liable in accordance with the statute. . . .

The judgments are affirmed.

[*Postscript:* On appeal, the Washington Supreme Court held that "Noble is jointly and severally liable only for those damages caused by 'fault' of the defendants, and to this extent she is jointly and severally liable with all the defendants. She is not, however, liable for damages that result from intentional acts or omissions. We remand for segregation of that part of the damages due to intentional conduct from those damages due to negligence." See *Tegman v. Investigations, Inc.*, 150 Wn. 2d 102, 75 P.3d 497 (2003).]

Questions about the Case

1. What specifically did the paralegal do that the court construed as being negligent?
2. To what standard of care was she held? Why?
3. What should the paralegal have done to avoid malpractice?
4. Did the paralegal also engage in UPL? What effect does the finding have on the outcome of the case?
5. What was the issue relating to the expert witness? How did the court decide?
6. What proportion of the damages did the paralegal have to pay?
7. Under what act was the principal of the company convicted of a crime? What does this chapter say about the application of similar statutes to lawyers?

In the following case, a paralegal's clerical error makes its way to the California Supreme Court.

Zamora v. Clayborn Contracting Group, Inc.
28 Cal. 4th 249, 121 Cal. Rptr. 2d 187, 47 P.3d 1056 (2002)

... Pablo Zamora (Zamora), doing business as Creative Engineering and Fabrication, filed suit against Clayborn Contracting Group, Inc. (Clayborn), alleging breach of contract and other related claims. The complaint alleged that Clayborn failed to pay for road signs produced and supplied by Zamora and sought approximately $143,000 in damages plus attorney fees. Clayborn answered and filed a cross-complaint. Although the cross-complaint did not specify the amount of damages sought, Clayborn sent Zamora an invoice for approximately $157,000 before filing the cross-claim.

Less than two months before trial, Zamora's counsel mailed Clayborn a section 998 offer. Although Zamora apparently intended to offer to settle for a judgment in his favor in the amount of $149,999, the actual offer sent to Clayborn stated: "Plaintiff Pablo Zamora aka Pablo

Iniguez dba Creative Engineering and Fabrication hereby offers to have judgment *taken against himself and for* defendant Clayborn Contracting Group, Inc. . . . pursuant to Section 998 of the Code of Civil Procedure for the sum of $149,999. . . ."

Clayborn filed a notice of acceptance of the offer approximately three days after reviewing it. One week later and two days after learning about the mistake in the offer, Zamora's counsel advised the court of his intention to file a motion to set aside "the judgment based on mistake, inadvertence and excusable neglect." After obtaining an order shortening the time for hearing the motion, Zamora filed a motion to set aside the section 998 offer or to vacate entry of judgment pursuant to the discretionary relief provision of section 473, subdivision (b).

In support of the motion, Zamora submitted declarations from himself, his counsel, the legal assistant who typed the section 998 offer and other litigants in related cases. Zamora averred that he *only* authorized his attorney to settle for a judgment in his favor in the amount of $149,999 and never authorized his attorney to agree to any judgment in favor of Clayborn.

Zamora's counsel declared that he, by phone, instructed his legal assistant to prepare a document offering to settle for a judgment against Clayborn in the amount of $149,999 pursuant to section 998. Zamora's counsel, per office policy, authorized his legal assistant to send the document with his stamped signature even though he had not reviewed it, because he was out of town and time was of the essence. He further stated that, before making this offer, Zamora had never offered to settle the matter for less than $150,000 *from* Clayborn. His legal assistant largely corroborated his story and claimed that she "mistakenly typed the word 'against' as opposed to the phrase 'in favor of' Pablo Zamora."

Zamora's counsel also stated that, after accepting the section 998 offer, Clayborn unilaterally cancelled depositions and took pending motions to coordinate this action with other actions and to amend the cross-complaint off calendar without informing Zamora or other interested parties. A declaration from another litigant involved in the coordination motion corroborated these statements.

In opposition, Clayborn submitted declarations claiming that it acted in good faith and believed the offer was correct as written. Clayborn claimed that the proposed amount of the settlement — $149,999 — was consistent with the amount stated in its latest invoice to Zamora — approximately $157,000. Clayborn's counsel further stated that he had told Zamora's counsel that Clayborn would not give Zamora any money and had suffered significant damages due to Zamora's conduct. Finally, Clayborn identified two tax levies against Zamora for approximately $31,000, as grounds for its failure to question the validity of the offer.

After a hearing, the trial court found that Zamora's counsel made a ministerial or clerical error and granted the motion to set aside the judgment pursuant to the discretionary relief provision of section 473, subdivision (b). The Court of Appeal affirmed. After ordering the trial court to "enter judgment, nunc pro tunc as of February 17, 2000, pursuant to the section 998 offer filed that date," the court concluded that: (1) Section 473, subdivision (b) permitted relief from a judgment entered in accordance with a section 998 settlement for "mistake, inadvertence, surprise, or excusable neglect"; and (2) the trial court did not abuse its discretion by granting Zamora relief from the section 998 settlement. . . .

As relevant here, the discretionary relief provision of section 473, subdivision (b) provides that: "The court may, upon any terms as may be just, relieve a party or his or her legal representative from a judgment, dismissal, order, or other proceeding taken against him or her through his or her mistake, inadvertence, surprise, or excusable neglect." According to Clayborn, this provision applies only to involuntary judgments or dismissals; therefore, Zamora could not obtain relief from the voluntary judgment. . . . We disagree.

Our analysis begins with the statutory language. [Citation omitted.] The discretionary relief provision of section 473, subdivision (b) applies to *any* "judgment, dismissal, order, or other proceeding." Ostensibly, this statutory language does not limit the application of the discretionary relief provision to involuntary judgments or dismissals. Indeed, our courts have interpreted the provision in this manner for over a century.

The Legislature first enacted the discretionary relief provision found in section 473, subdivision (b) in 1872, and the language of this provision has not changed appreciably since then. [Citations omitted.] . . . Since 1872, California courts have consistently applied the discretionary relief provision of section 473 to voluntary judgments or dismissals. For example, as early as 1901, this court affirmed an order setting aside a voluntary dismissal entered pursuant to a settlement agreement. . . .

California courts have long held that "[e]ven after a voluntary dismissal with prejudice has been filed, the trial court *has jurisdiction* to vacate the judgment of dismissal under Code of Civil Procedure section 473 where it has been entered as a result of the plaintiff's 'mistake, inadvertence, surprise, or excusable neglect.'" [Citations omitted.] . . . In accordance with these principles, California courts have consistently held that parties may obtain relief from judgments, dismissals, or stipulations voluntarily entered into pursuant to a voluntary agreement through the discretionary relief provision of section 473. In fact, Clayborn cites no majority decision to the contrary.

Indeed, this longstanding interpretation of the discretionary relief provision of section 473 comports with its underlying purpose. . . . "It is well settled that appellate courts have always been and are favorably disposed toward such action upon the part of the trial courts as will permit, rather than prevent, the adjudication of legal controversies upon their merits." . . .

The recent addition of a mandatory relief provision to section 473 for attorney fault also does not dictate a contrary result. . . . In enacting this exception, the Legislature, however, made no changes to the discretionary relief provision of section 473, and the legislative history indicates no intent to alter the scope of this provision. Indeed, the Legislature has *never* substantively altered the statutory language at issue here despite the long line of California cases permitting discretionary relief from judgments entered pursuant to a settlement agreement . . . even though it has amended section 473 many times. Thus, the Legislature has apparently adopted this longstanding interpretation of the provision. [Citation omitted.]

Having established that Zamora may avail himself of the discretionary relief provision of section 473, subdivision (b), we now consider whether the trial court properly applied it. "A ruling on a motion for discretionary relief under section 473 shall not be disturbed on appeal absent a clear showing of abuse." [Citation omitted.] . . . "A party who seeks relief under section 473 on the basis of mistake or inadvertence of counsel must demonstrate that such mistake, inadvertence, or general neglect was excusable because the negligence of the attorney is imputed to his client and may not be offered by the latter as a basis for relief." [Citation omitted.] In determining whether the attorney's mistake or inadvertence was excusable, "the court inquires whether 'a reasonably prudent *person* under the same or similar circumstances' might have made the same error." [Citation omitted.] In other words, the discretionary relief provision of section 473 only permits relief from attorney error "fairly imputable to the client, i.e., mistakes anyone could have made." [Citation omitted.] "Conduct falling below the professional standard of care, such as failure to timely object or to properly advance an argument, is not therefore excusable. To hold otherwise would be to eliminate the express statutory requirement of excusability and effectively eviscerate the concept of attorney malpractice."

The party seeking relief under section 473 must also be diligent. [Citation omitted.] Thus, an application for relief must be made "within a reasonable time, in no case exceeding six months, after the judgment, dismissal, order, or proceeding was taken." (§473, subd. (b).)

Where the mistake is excusable and the party seeking relief has been diligent, courts have often granted relief pursuant to the discretionary relief provision of section 473 if no prejudice to the opposing party will ensue. [Citations omitted.] In such cases, the law "looks with [particular] disfavor on a party who, regardless of the merits of his cause, attempts to take advantage of the mistake, surprise, inadvertence, or neglect of his adversary." [Citation omitted.] Here, the trial court reasonably concluded that the mistake made by Zamora's counsel was excusable. The erroneous substitution of the word "against" for the phrase "in favor of" is a clerical or ministerial mistake that could have been made by anybody. While counsel's failure to review the document before sending it out was imprudent, we cannot say that his imprudence rendered the mistake inexcusable under the circumstances. Indeed, appellate courts have routinely affirmed orders vacating judgments based on analogous mistakes made by an attorney or his or her staff. For example, courts have set aside judgments where: (1) The attorney mistakenly checked the "with prejudice" box instead of the "without prejudice" box; (2) an associate misinterpreted the instructions of the lead attorney and gave incorrect information at a hearing; and (3) the attorney's secretary lost the answer to be filed. [Citations omitted.]

In addition, Zamora was diligent in seeking relief, and Clayborn suffered no apparent prejudice. Finally, the record suggests that Clayborn took unfair advantage of the mistake. We find it hard to believe that Clayborn had no inkling that the section 998 offer was a mistake when the uncontroverted record established that: (1) Zamora's complaint sought over $140,000 in damages; (2) Zamora had never offered to settle for less than $150,000 from Clayborn prior to making the offer; (3) the section 998 offer proposed to settle the matter for almost the same amount ($149,999) as Clayborn's entire claim for damages (approximately $157,000); and (4) Clayborn knew Zamora was having financial difficulties and had failed to pay approximately $31,000 in tax levies. Clayborn's rush to get approval of the settlement and its abrupt cancellation of depositions and hearings on pending motions with no notice to the parties involved cast further doubt on its claim of innocence. Under these facts, the trial court did not abuse its discretion by granting relief to Zamora pursuant to section 473, subdivision (b). . . .

Finally, in reaching this holding, we do not offend the public policies favoring the private resolution of civil disputes. Although the law favors settlements [Citation omitted], it only favors *authorized* settlements. . . .

Our holding also does not circumvent longstanding principles of contract law. Even if, as Clayborn contends, Zamora was limited to the contractual defense of unilateral mistake, ample evidence supports the trial court's decision. As noted above, the undisputed facts strongly suggest that Clayborn "had reason to suspect that a mistake had been made." [Citation omitted.] Moreover, even assuming Clayborn had no knowledge of Zamora's mistake, enforcement of the section 998 settlement would still arguably be unconscionable. . . . Thus, requiring Zamora to file a separate action in order to rescind his section 998 offer would not promote the sanctity of contract law. It would only waste judicial resources.

In any event, we are confident trial courts will exercise this discretionary power to vacate judgments entered pursuant to a settlement agreement both carefully and sparingly. . . . Indeed, courts have been exercising this power for over a century with no apparent ill effects. Most cases still settle, and courts rarely set aside settlement agreements. Our holding today should not change that.

We affirm the judgment of the Court of Appeal.

Questions about the Case

1. What was the error that the paralegal made in this case? How did the lawyer compound the error?
2. What did the opposing counsel do in response to the error? What should he have done? (See Chapter 9 for duties in litigation for more background.) Could the opposing counsel have been sanctioned for this conduct?
3. What was the basis for the court's decision?
4. How does the California Supreme Court's analysis of "excusable neglect" in this case compare with that of the U.S. Court of Appeal in the *Pincay* case above?
5. What system could be put into place in a law firm to prevent this kind of mistake from being made?

In this high-profile case, a mistake by a paralegal that went undiscovered by any of the lawyers involved in the transaction erased a $1.5 billion security interest in a loan made by JPMorgan Chase to General Motors.

Official Comm. of Unsecured Creditors of Motors Liquidation Co. v. JPMorgan Chase Bank, N.A. (In re Motors Liquidation Co.)
777 F.3d 100 (2d Cir. 2015)

In October 2001, General Motors entered into a synthetic lease financing transaction (the "Synthetic Lease"), by which it obtained approximately $300 million in financing from a syndicate of lenders including JPMorgan Chase Bank, N.A. ("JPMorgan"). General Motors' obligation to repay the Synthetic Lease was secured by liens on twelve pieces of real estate. JPMorgan served as administrative agent for the Synthetic Lease and was identified on the UCC-1 financing statements as the secured party of record.

Five years later, General Motors entered into a separate term loan facility (the "Term Loan"). The Term Loan was entirely unrelated to the Synthetic Lease and provided General Motors with approximately $1.5 billion in financing from a different syndicate of lenders. To secure the loan, the lenders took security interests in a large number of General Motors' assets, including all of General Motors' equipment and fixtures at forty-two facilities throughout the United States. JPMorgan again served as administrative agent and secured party of record for the Term Loan and caused the filing of twenty-eight UCC-1 financing statements around the country to perfect the lenders' security interests in the collateral. One such financing statement, the "Main Term Loan UCC-1," was filed with the Delaware Secretary of State and bore file number "6416808 4." It "covered, among other things, all of the equipment and fixtures at 42 GM facilities, [and] was by far the most important" of the financing statements filed in connection with the Term Loan. *Official Comm. of Unsecured Creditors of Motors Liquidation Co. v. JPMorgan Chase Bank, N.A. (In re Motors Liquidation Co.)*, 486 B.R. 596, 603 n.6 (Bankr. S.D.N.Y. 2013).

In September 2008, as the Synthetic Lease was nearing maturity, General Motors contacted Mayer Brown LLP, its counsel responsible for the Synthetic Lease, and explained that it planned to repay the amount due. General Motors requested that Mayer Brown prepare the documents necessary for JPMorgan and the lenders to be repaid and to release the interests the lenders held in General Motors' property.

A Mayer Brown partner assigned the work to an associate and instructed him to prepare a closing checklist and drafts of the documents required to pay off the Synthetic Lease and to terminate the lenders' security interests in General Motors' property relating to the Synthetic Lease. One of the steps required to unwind the Synthetic Lease was to create a list of security interests held by General Motors' lenders that would need to be terminated. To prepare the list, the Mayer Brown associate asked a paralegal who was unfamiliar with the transaction or the purpose of the request to perform a search for UCC-1 financing statements that had been recorded against General Motors in Delaware. The paralegal's search identified three UCC-1s, numbered 2092532 5, 2092526 7, and 6416808 4. Neither the paralegal nor the associate realized that only the first two of the UCC-1s were related to the Synthetic Lease. The third, UCC-1 number 6416808 4, related instead to the Term Loan.

When Mayer Brown prepared a Closing Checklist of the actions required to unwind the Synthetic Lease, it identified the Main Term Loan UCC-1 for termination alongside the security interests that actually did need to be terminated. And when Mayer Brown prepared draft UCC-3 statements to terminate the three security interests identified in the Closing Checklist, it prepared a UCC-3 statement to terminate the Main Term Loan UCC-1 as well as those related to the Synthetic Lease.

No one at General Motors, Mayer Brown, JPMorgan, or its counsel, Simpson Thacher & Bartlett LLP, noticed the error, even though copies of the Closing Checklist and draft UCC-3 termination statements were sent to individuals at each organization for review. On October 30, 2008, General Motors repaid the amount due on the Synthetic Lease. All three UCC-3s were filed with the Delaware Secretary of State, including the UCC-3 that erroneously identified for termination the Main Term Loan UCC-1, which was entirely unrelated to the Synthetic Lease.

The mistake went unnoticed until General Motors' bankruptcy in 2009. After General Motors filed for Chapter 11 reorganization,

JPMorgan informed the Committee of Unsecured Creditors (the "Committee") that a UCC-3 termination statement relating to the Term Loan had been inadvertently filed in October 2008. JPMorgan explained that it had intended to terminate only liens related to the Synthetic Lease and stated that the filing was therefore unauthorized and ineffective.

On July 31, 2009, the Committee commenced the underlying action against JPMorgan in the United States Bankruptcy Court for the Southern District of New York. The Committee sought a determination that, despite the error, the UCC-3 termination statement was effective to terminate the Term Loan security interest and render JPMorgan an unsecured creditor on par with the other General Motors unsecured creditors. JPMorgan disagreed, reasoning that the UCC-3 termination statement was unauthorized and therefore ineffective because no one at JPMorgan, General Motors, or their law firms had intended that the Term Loan security interest be terminated. On crossmotions for summary judgment, the Bankruptcy Court concluded that the UCC-3 filing was unauthorized and therefore not effective to terminate the Term Loan security interest. *In re Motors Liquidation Co.*, 486 B.R. at 647–48.

On appeal to this Court, the parties offered competing interpretations of UCC §9-509(d)(1), which provides that a UCC-3 termination statement is effective only if "the secured party of record authorizes the filing." JPMorgan reasoned that it cannot have "authorize[d] the filing" of the UCC-3 that identified the Main Term Loan UCC-1 for termination because JPMorgan neither intended to terminate the security interest nor instructed anyone else to do so on its behalf. In response, the Committee contended that focusing on the parties' goal misses the point. It interpreted UCC §9-509(d)(1) to require only that the secured lender authorize the act of filing a particular UCC-3 termination statement, not that the lender subjectively intend to terminate the particular security interest identified for termination on that UCC-3. The Committee further argued that even if JPMorgan never intentionally instructed anyone to terminate the Main Term Loan UCC-1, JPMorgan did literally "authorize the filing"—even if mistakenly—of a UCC-3 termination statement that had that effect.

In our prior certification opinion we recognized that this appeal presents two closely related questions. . . . Recognizing that the first question—what is it that the UCC requires a secured lender to authorize—seemed likely to recur and presented a significant issue of Delaware state law, we certified to the Delaware Supreme Court the following question:

> Under UCC Article 9, as adopted into Delaware law by Del. Code Ann. tit. 6, art. 9, for a UCC-3 termination statement to effectively extinguish the perfected nature of a UCC-1 financing statement, is it enough that the secured lender review and knowingly approve for filing a UCC-3

purporting to extinguish the perfected security interest, or must the secured lender intend to terminate the particular security interest that is listed on the UCC-3?

In re Motors Liquidation Co., 755 F.3d at 86. The second question—whether JPMorgan granted the relevant authority—we reserved for ourselves, explaining that "[t]he Delaware Supreme Court's clarification as to the sense in which a secured party of record must authorize a UCC-3 filing will enable us to address . . . whether JPMorgan in fact provided that authorization." *Id.* at 86-87.

In a speedy and thorough reply, the Delaware Supreme Court answered the certified question, explaining that if the secured party of record authorizes the filing of a UCC-3 termination statement, then that filing is effective regardless of whether the secured party subjectively intends or understands the effect of that filing . . . Before a secured party authorizes the filing of a termination statement, it ought to review the statement carefully and understand which security interests it is releasing and why. . . .

Official Comm. of Unsecured Creditors of Motors Liquidation Co., 2014 WL 5305937, at *3-5.

The Delaware Supreme Court has explained the sense in which a secured party must "authorize . . . the filing" of a UCC-3 termination statement. What remains is to answer the question we reserved for ourselves in our prior certification opinion: Did JPMorgan authorize the filing of the UCC-3 termination statement that mistakenly identified for termination the Main Term Loan UCC-1?

In JPMorgan's view, it never instructed anyone to file the UCC-3 in question, and the termination statement was therefore unauthorized and ineffective. JPMorgan reasons that it authorized General Motors only to terminate security interests related to the Synthetic Lease; that it instructed Simpson Thacher and Mayer Brown only to take actions to accomplish that objective; and that therefore Mayer Brown must have exceeded the scope of its authority when it filed the UCC-3 purporting to terminate the Main Term Loan UCC-1.

What JPMorgan intended to accomplish, however, is a distinct question from what actions it authorized to be taken on its behalf. Mayer Brown prepared a Closing Checklist, draft UCC-3 termination statements, and an Escrow Agreement, all aimed at unwinding the Synthetic Lease but tainted by one crucial error: The documents included a UCC-3 termination statement that erroneously identified for termination a security interest related not to the Synthetic Lease but to the Term Loan. The critical question in this case is whether JPMorgan "authorize[d] [Mayer Brown] to file" that termination statement.

After Mayer Brown prepared the Closing Checklist and draft UCC-3 termination statements, copies were sent for review to a Managing Director at JPMorgan who supervised the Synthetic Lease payoff and who had signed the Term Loan documents on JPMorgan's behalf. Mayer Brown also sent copies of the Closing Checklist and draft UCC-3 termination statements to JPMorgan's counsel, Simpson Thacher, to ensure that the parties to the transaction agreed as to the documents required to complete the Synthetic Lease payoff transaction. Neither directly nor through its counsel did JPMorgan express any concerns about the draft UCC-3 termination statements or about the Closing Checklist. . . .

. . . it is clear that although JPMorgan never intended to terminate the Main Term Loan UCC-1, it authorized the filing of a UCC-3 termination statement that had that effect. "Actual authority . . . is created by a principal's manifestation to an agent that, as reasonably understood by the agent, expresses the principal's assent that the agent take action on the principal's behalf." Restatement (Third) of Agency §3.01 (2006); accord *Demarco v. Edens*, 390 F.2d 836, 844 (2d Cir. 1968). JPMorgan and Simpson Thacher's repeated manifestations to Mayer Brown show that JPMorgan and its counsel knew that, upon the closing of the Synthetic Lease transaction, Mayer Brown was going to file the termination statement that identified the Main Term Loan UCC-1 for termination and that JPMorgan reviewed and assented to the filing of that statement. Nothing more is needed.

For the foregoing reasons, we REVERSE the Bankruptcy Court's grant of summary judgment for the Defendant and REMAND with instructions to the Bankruptcy Court to enter partial summary judgment for the Plaintiff as to the termination of the Main Term Loan UCC-1.

Questions about the Case

1. Who handled the work related to the UCC searches? Was this work properly delegated? Who handled the work related to the Closing Checklist and the UCC-3 termination statement?
2. What should the associate have done upon receiving the UCC search results from the paralegal? What should the paralegal have done? What was the associate's duty of competence related to the UCC searches?
3. When and how was the mistake discovered? Identify all parties who obtained and reviewed the UCC search results and the UCC-3 termination statement before it was filed.
4. What is JPMorgan's position about the filing of the UCC-3 termination statement? Do you agree or disagree with this argument? Does it make a difference that JPMorgan did not intend to terminate the Main Term Loan UCC-1? What actions did JPMorgan authorize to be taken on its behalf?
5. What did the Delaware Supreme Court say about the effect of a secured party of record authorizing the filing of a UCC-3 termination

statement? Does it matter whether the secured party intended or understood the effect of that filing?
6. How did the Delaware Supreme Court sum up the lesson this case provides in its answer to the certified question?

In this recent and highly contentious case, the defendants were severely sanctioned for repeated and pervasive discovery abuse.

Abbott Laboratories, et al. v. Adelphia Supply USA
15-CV-05826 (CBA) (LB) (E.D.N.Y. Mar. 24, 2020)

Plaintiffs, Abbott Laboratories, Abbott Diabetes Care Inc., and Abbott Diabetes Care Sales Corp. (collectively "Abbott"), filed a motion for case-ending sanctions against Defendants H&H Wholesale Services, Inc. ("H&H"), Howard Goldman, and Lori Goldman (collectively the "H&H Defendants"). The Court referred Abbott's motion to the Honorable Magistrate Judge Lois Bloom for a report and recommendation pursuant to 28 U.S.C. § 636(b)(1). (D.E. dated January 14, 2019.) The parties submitted briefing, and Magistrate Judge Bloom held oral argument, (D.E. dated February 27, 2019). On May 2, 2019, Magistrate Judge Bloom issued a thorough and well-reasoned report and recommendation recommending that the Court grant Abbott's motion for sanctions and enter a default judgment against the H&H Defendants (the "R&R"). The H&H Defendants timely filed objections to the R&R), and Abbott filed a reply to their objections. The H&H Defendants' objections brief also includes a request that, should the Court find in favor of Abbott, the Court's order be certified for interlocutory appeal. On August 12, 2019, the H&H Defendants supplemented their objections brief, and Abbott responded on August 19, 2019. For the reasons set forth below, the Court adopts Magistrate Judge Bloom's recommendations.

On October 5, 2015, Abbott filed the instant trademark action against the H&H Defendants and hundreds of other defendants, including pharmacies, distributors, importers, and online sellers, alleging that these defendants had violated Abbott's rights by selling the international version of Abbott's FreeStyle diabetes test strips in the United States ("Compl."). On May 25, 2017, Abbott initiated a related action, *Abbott Laboratories et al. v. H&H Wholesale Services Inc. et al.*, 17-cv-03095 (CBA) (LB) (E.D.N.Y.), alleging that the H&H Defendants were selling international FreeStyle test strips repackaged into counterfeit U.S. boxes (hereinafter "*Abbott II*").

Abbott's sanctions motion is based on the discovery conduct of Howard Goldman, President of H&H; Lori Goldman, Howard Goldman's wife and an H&H employee; Andrew Sweet, H&H's general manager who was involved with the response to the Court's discovery orders; and David Gulas, H&H's 30(b)(6) witness and the employee primarily involved with sales of the test strips. The facts underlying this motion are laid out in detail in the R&R. They are summarized below.

On January 13, 2017, Magistrate Judge Bloom held her first of many conferences with the parties to address various discovery issues. (R&R at 2.) On January 17, 2017, Magistrate Judge Bloom ordered all defendants to "review all formal and informal communications regarding [their] purchases and sales of International FreeStyle test strips in 2014, including emails, text messages, purchase orders, delivery invoices, and check/wire transfers." (*Id.*) On January 25, 2017, counsel for the H&H Defendants informed the Court that the H&H Defendants "have conducted a review of all formal and information [*sic*] communications regarding the purchase and sale of International FreeStyle test strips for the year of 2014 . . . . Individual Defendants Howard Goldman and Lori Goldman do not have any responsive documents. As to H&H, there are approximately 6,000 responsive documents[.]" (*Id.*) In light of the H&H Defendants' claim that producing more than one year of responsive documents would be unduly burdensome, Magistrate Judge Bloom, in an order dated January 27, 2017, directed the H&H Defendants to produce only their 2014 documents. (*Id.* at 2-3) ("[D]ue to the disproportionate number of responsive documents identified by defendants H&H Wholesale Services, Inc, Howard Goldman, and Lori Goldman, these defendants need only produce the documents for 2014.") All other defendants were directed to produce responsive documents for the years 2013, 2014, and 2015. (*Id.* at 3.)

The H&H Defendants' production was coordinated by Andrew Sweet, H&H's general manager, and Jason Yert, H&H's counsel from Kerr, Russell and Webber PLC ("Kerr Russell"). (*Id.*) On February 10, 2017, despite their previous assertion that there were 6,000 responsive documents for the year 2014, the H&H Defendants produced only 314 responsive documents. (*Id.*) ("Waters Decl." ¶ 2.) On March 22, 2017, Abbott raised objections to the H&H Defendants' February 10, 2017 production, including that the documents produced were printed "in hard copy, scanning them all together, and produc[ed] . . . as a single, 1,941-page PDF file." (R&R at 3.) On March 24, 2017, Magistrate Judge Bloom ordered the H&H Defendants to "produce an electronic copy of the 2014 emails (1,941 pages)," including metadata. (*Id.*)

On May 24, 2017, the Court entered a seizure order in *Abbott II* that authorized Abbott to seize, *inter alia*, a copy of H&H's email server. (*Id.* at 3-4.) Once Abbott had seized H&H's email server, Abbott "had the proverbial smoking gun" and raised concerns that the H&H Defendants had failed to comply with the Court's order to produce responsive documents in the instant action. (*Id.* at 4.) On July 12, 2017, Magistrate

Judge Bloom ordered the H&H Defendants to "re-run the document search outlined in the Court's January 17 and January 21 [2017] Orders," "produce the documents from the re-run search to Abbott," and produce "an affidavit of someone with personal knowledge" regarding alleged technical errors that affected the earlier production. (R&R at 4).) This time, the H&H Defendants produced 3,569 responsive documents from 2014. (*Id.* (citing Waters Decl. ¶ 3).)

It quickly became clear that the H&H Defendants' initial representation to the Court that they had 6,000 responsive documents from 2014 had been false. (R&R at 8-11 (describing the H&H Defendants' "wholly unsubstantiated serial explanations" regarding why they had provided this incorrect figure to the Court and finding that the H&H Defendants had materially misrepresented the number of responsive documents/pages to the Court").) Providing this inaccurately high number had facilitated their objective: the H&H Defendants were granted a modification of the Court's discovery order, so that they had to produce documents from only 2014 while all other defendants were ordered to produce documents from 2013, 2014, and 2015. (*Id.*)

It also became clear that the search terms the H&H Defendants had used to make their 2014 production—containing only 314 documents—were intentionally deficient, and did not capture the vast majority of the documents the Court had ordered them to produce. (*Id.* at 10-13 (describing the improper search terms used and noting that "both sides agree that H&H's search terms were inadequate and failed to capture the documents responsive to the Court's Orders").)

Even more egregiously, the H&H Defendants had willfully withheld every single document sent by, received by, or referencing Howard Goldman or Lori Goldman in their initial production. (*Id.* at 14-15.) They had also intentionally withheld every document concerning Holland Trading Group, a Dutch company from whom H&H was allegedly purchasing counterfeit test strips. (*Id.* at 13-15; *see also Id.* at 23 ("There is no credible explanation for why the Holland Trading, Howard Goldman, and Lori Goldman documents were not produced except that the documents were willfully withheld.").)

Not only were these documents willfully withheld when they should have been produced, but the H&H Defendants—largely through their then-counsel and through their general manager, Andrew Sweet—proffered serial, inconsistent excuses as to why they were not produced. As explained in the R&R, "the H&H [D]efendants' explanations regarding the Holland Trading, Howard Goldman, and Lori Goldman documents continue to change as the scent becomes too fresh and the trail too hot to risk further non-compliance. . . . The H&H [D]efendants have always had one more excuse up their sleeve in this series of episodes of nonfeasance, which amounts to deliberate tactical intransigence." (*Id.* at 23 (internal quotation marks omitted).) In light of the H&H Defendants' "ever-changing explanations as to [these] withheld documents, Mr. Sweet's inconsistent testimony, and assertions of former counsel," Magistrate Judge Bloom found that the H&H Defendants had "calculatedly attempted to manipulate the judicial process." (*Id.* at 23-24.)

Finally, the R&R describes perjured testimony by David Gulas, who served as H&H's 30(b)(6) witness. (*Id.* at 24-26.) And it details the inconsistent and evasive testimony of Howard Goldman. (*Id.* at 26-27.)

As summarized in the R&R, the misconduct involved in this case "was not an isolated instance of perjury or one withheld document"; rather, "it was a calculated pattern of pervasive misconduct that started early on and continued even after [the H&H] [D]efendants were caught red handed." (*Id.* at 29-30.) Considering the record as a whole, the R&R found that the H&H Defendants perpetrated a fraud upon the Court. (*Id.* at 30.)

Rather than viewing a party's failure to comply with discovery orders in isolation, courts are permitted to analyze such failures under their broader inherent power—a power that "extends to a full range of litigation abuses," including, most importantly, to fraud upon the court. *Chambers v NASCO, Inc.*, 501 U.S. 32, 46 (1991); *see also Skywark v. Isaacson*, No. 96 Civ. 2815 JFK, 1999 WL 1489038, at *14 n.27 (S.D.N.Y. Oct. 14, 1999) (considering defendants' motion "in the more inclusive context of fraud upon the court," rather than solely under Rule 37, because plaintiffs' "fraudulent approach as a whole . . . is not simply covered by any one rule"), report and recommendation adopted by 2000 WL 145465 (S.D.N.Y. Feb. 9, 2000). Indeed, as the Second Circuit has explained:

> [I]t would be excessively formalistic to view the defiance of the order in isolation rather than against the background of [plaintiff's] prolonged and vexatious obstruction of discovery . . . through perjurious testimony of its top officials and false representations to the court by its counsel.

Penthouse Int'l Ltd. v. Playboy Enters., 663 F.2d 371, 388 (2d Cir. 1981). Magistrate Judge Bloom considered the H&H Defendants' conduct under this rubric, and the H&H Defendants expressly note that they do not object to her having done so (H&H Def. Obj. at 10-11 & 11 n.4).

A fraud upon the court occurs where it is established by clear and convincing evidence "that [a party] has sentiently set in motion some unconscionable scheme calculated to interfere with the judicial system's ability impartially to adjudicate the action." *New York Credit & Fin. Mgmt. Grp. v. Parson Ctr. Pharmacy, Inc.*, 432 Fed. App'x 25 (2d Cir. 2011) (summary order) (internal quotation marks omitted) (quoting *Scholastic, Inc. v. Stouffer*, 221 F. Supp. 2d 425, 439 (S.D.N.Y. 2002)); *McMunn v. Mem'l Sloan-Kettering Cancer Ctr.*, 191 F. Supp. 2d 440, 445 (S.D.N.Y. 2002) (noting a party interferes with the "the judicial system's ability impartially to adjudicate a matter by improperly influencing the trier or unfairly hampering the presentation of the opposing party's claim or defense" (internal quotation marks omitted)); *see also Hargrove v. Riley*, 04-cv-04587, 2007 WL 389003, at *11 (E.D.N.Y. Jan. 31, 2007); *Shangold v. Walt Disney Co.*, 03-cv-09522, 2006 WL 71672, at *4 (S.D.N.Y. Jan. 12, 2006) (dismissing plaintiff's case with prejudice where plaintiff fabricated evidence and manipulated the judicial process).

The "essence of a fraud upon the court" is "when a party lies to the court and his adversary intentionally, repeatedly, and about issues that are central to the truth-finding process." *McMunn*, 191 F. Supp. 2d at 445. "[A]n isolated instance of perjury, standing alone, will not constitute a fraud upon the court." *Id.*; *see also Jung v. Neschis*, 01-cv-06993, 2009 WL 762835, at *21 (S.D.N.Y. Mar. 23, 2009); *Skywark*, 1999 WL 1489038, at *14 (describing "persistent misrepresentations"). "Rather, fraud upon the court occurs where a party has acted knowingly in an attempt to hinder the fact finder's fair adjudication of the case and his adversary's defense of the action." *McMunn*, 191 F. Supp. 2d at 445 (quoting *Skywark*, 1999 WL 1489038, at *14).

. . . If it is shown by clear and convincing evidence that a party perpetrated a fraud upon the court, courts consider the following five factors to determine the appropriate sanction: (i) "whether the misconduct was the product of intentional bad faith;" (ii) "whether and to what extent the misconduct prejudiced the injured party;" (iii) "whether there is a pattern of misbehavior rather than an isolated instance;" (iv) "whether and when the misconduct was corrected;" and (v) "whether further misconduct is likely to occur in the future." *McMunn*, 191 F. Supp. 2d at 461. When faced with a fraud upon the court, "[t]he available sanctions at a court's disposal . . . range from the issuance of a jury charge on falsehoods under oath, to the imposition of attorney's fees occasioned by the conduct in question, and finally to the entry of judgment against the offending party." *Skywark*, 1999 WL 1489038, at *14 (citations omitted).

. . . The H&H Defendants assert that Magistrate Judge Bloom failed to consider lesser sanctions on the record before recommending the imposition of case-ending sanctions and thereby committed an abuse of discretion. (H&H Def. Obj. at 8-10.) The H&H Defendants acknowledge that the Second Circuit does not require that district courts "explicitly consider the efficacy of lesser sanctions" before imposing the sanction of default under all circumstances. (*Id.*) But they argue that failing to do so is only appropriate where the sanctioned party has been (1) subjected to a lesser sanction at an earlier phase of the litigation, or (2) repeatedly warned of the potential for such sanctions. (*Id.* at 8-9.) Here, because the H&H Defendants were not previously sanctioned for the non-compliance that is the subject of Abbott's sanctions motion, nor warned of the possibility of default, they argue that the imposition of default without an on-the-record consideration of the efficacy of lesser sanctions was contrary to law and therefore an abuse of discretion. (*Id.* at 9-10.) In the context of this case, this argument is entirely unpersuasive.

. . . it is clear to this Court that lesser sanctions would be ineffective in this case. Given (1) the bad-faith, repeated, and egregious nature of the H&H Defendants' discovery misconduct, (2) their repeated misrepresentations to the Court in an attempt to cover up this misconduct, (3) the fact that their misconduct may never have come to light if not for their having being caught, (4) their continued evasion even after having been caught, (5) the prejudice suffered by Abbott as a result of the foregoing, and (6) the particular stage of the proceedings, lesser sanctions—such as merely awarding attorneys' fees or providing an adverse inference instruction at a potential trial—would not sufficiently punish the H&H Defendants nor deter those who might be tempted to similar conduct. Indeed, the H&H Defendants themselves are unable to suggest any lesser sanctions that might be effective here.

The H&H Defendants also argue that the R&R improperly recommends case-ending sanctions against Howard Goldman and Lori Goldman even though it makes findings of bad faith or willfulness only as to H&H. (H&H Def. Obj. at 10-15.) Specifically, the H&H Defendants contend that the R&R does not find bad faith on a clear and convincing basis against Howard Goldman and Lori Goldman individually but instead improperly imputes to them the bad faith of (1) agents of H&H, including David Gulas and Andrew Sweet, and (2) the company itself. (*Id.*) This objection fails for the reasons set forth below.

. . . This objection fails because the R&R is quite clear that it did not simply impute the bad faith of H&H employees to the Goldmans but rather that it found bad faith as to each of the H&H Defendants, including the Goldmans. There is no dispute that the discovery orders that were violated in this action were directed toward all of the H&H Defendants, including Howard and Lori Goldman, and there is no dispute that they were both individually required to respond . . . There is also no dispute that, like H&H, the Goldmans relied on H&H employees and their counsel to respond to the Court's discovery orders on their behalf, including by producing their individual work emails . . . And they relied on their agents to respond to the Court's subsequent orders to conduct an internal investigation and submit a written report explaining how the original orders were violated in the first place . . . The R&R concludes that "the H&H [D]efendants' bad faith can be inferred from the H&H [D]efendants' deliberate and strategic non-compliance with discovery, their selective withholding of responsive documents, and their perjury as well as deceptive and evasive testimony." (R&R at 29.) Each of the H&H Defendants—including the Goldmans—had a duty to comply with the Court's orders, and each willfully and grossly failed to do so.

. . . the R&R correctly states and applies the law concerning clients' liability for the sanctionable conduct of their agents, and the extensive evidence of bad faith committed by the Goldmans' agents is attributable as a matter of law to each of them individually. It was not improper to consider the conduct of these agents in determining that there is clear and convincing evidence of bad faith as to the Goldmans individually.

... For the reasons stated above, the Court agrees with the thorough, thoughtful, and well-reasoned decision by Magistrate Judge Bloom and affirms its conclusions. The Court grants Abbott's motion for sanctions and enters a default judgment against the H&H Defendants. It denies the H&H Defendants' request to certify this order for interlocutory appeal under 28 U.S.C. § 1292(b).

Questions about the Case

1. What was the underlying dispute between Abbott and the HH Defendants?
2. Why did Abbott file the motion for sanctions?
3. What did the HH Defendants tell the court about their inability to produce documents for 2013, 2014, and 2015, when all other defendants were required to do so? How did Magistrate Judge Bloom rule on this?
4. How many responsive documents did the HH Defendants initially produce in response to Abbott's document request? In what format were they produced? What did Magistrate Judge Bloom say about this?
5. What did Magistrate Judge Bloom's report and recommendation (the "R&R") say about the HH Defendants' conduct during discovery? Was this conduct imputed to HH only? What did the R&R say about the Goldmans?
6. In many jurisdictions, Magistrate Judges handle discovery disputes. Case-ending sanctions such as the court-imposed default judgment levied against the HH Defendants are rare. Do you agree with the R&R's conclusions and the District Court's ruling affirming them? Why or why not?

Special Issues in Advocacy

This chapter describes the many ethical dilemmas that paralegals face when working in litigation. Chapter 9 covers:

- the roles of the lawyer and paralegal in litigation
- the duty to represent clients zealously
- rules about unmeritorious claims, delay, and abuse of discovery
- prohibitions on disruptive courtroom tactics
- sanctions for ethics violations before courts
- duties of candor and honesty
- prohibited relationships and communications with judges
- prohibited contact with jurors
- restrictions on contact with represented parties and unrepresented persons
- contact with witnesses
- rules on trial publicity
- special rules for prosecutors and their paralegals

A. Introduction

The trial lawyer arguing for a client in front of a judge and jury is a common image of a lawyer. In fact, most lawyers are not litigators and do not appear in court regularly. The majority of lawyers in this country do not litigate matters, either civil or criminal, and many lawyers never represent a client in an adversarial proceeding. Areas of practice that do not emphasize litigation include corporate, tax, business transactions, real estate, estate planning, probate, environmental law, entertainment law, intellectual property, and trademark and copyright. Increasingly, even lawyers who practice in areas that are within the purview of the courts, such as family law, resolve matters through negotiation, mediation, and other alternative means that avoid resolution by way of a trial.

Nonetheless, lawyers are often accused of promoting a culture that is "too litigious." People look to the courts to handle disputes that would not have been resolved by lawyers and judges in the past. Some commentators believe that there is a **litigation explosion**; others argue that this claim is not borne out by empirical research. Politicians blame the rising cost of health care and insurance on the growth in litigation against doctors and hospitals. Plaintiff lawyers disagree with this characterization and contend that resolving disputes in court is often the only way to get justice for persons who have been injured by the practices of corporate entities and to force reluctant corporations to change the way they do business. A review of American legal history, especially in the area of tort law, supports this contention.

Court dockets continue to be crowded, courts are underfunded, and the wheels of justice often seem to grind slowly despite reforms intended to streamline litigation by encouraging alternate dispute resolution, limiting discovery, creating fast-track processes of certain kinds of disputes, and instituting more effective trial procedures.

Litigation paralegals must be diligent in their efforts to meet high standards of competence and ethics and keep up with the ever-changing ethics rules and court decisions that govern conduct in litigation. Unlike lawyers, the majority of paralegals, about 75 percent, work in civil litigation. Although lawsuits culminate in a trial (unless they are settled before trial), most of the work in litigation is done out of court, before trial, in the preparation of a case, and during the discovery process. The role of paralegals in litigation is expansive, including gathering facts, interviewing clients and witnesses, drafting pleadings and motions, conducting legal research, drafting discovery requests and motions and responding to discovery, preparing for trial by organizing documents, managing databases of documents, overseeing e-discovery, locating and preparing expert witnesses, and preparing demonstrative evidence and electronic trial exhibits. Many litigation paralegals serve on a team with lawyers, accompanying them to court and assisting in court by managing trial exhibits, taking notes, making observations about jurors' reactions to the proceedings, handling logistics and emergencies, and doing last-minute research. As the discovery experts in a case, paralegals must have a mastery of the facts and evidence. Litigators greatly value the contribution that paralegals make to the team effort that is needed to win. Paralegals are often the ones who find a "smoking-gun" document. Finally, paralegal work enables lawyers to concentrate their full attention on presenting the case, examining and cross-examining witnesses, and making objections.

Because paralegals have such an expansive role in litigation, they need a deep understanding of the ethics rules governing advocacy. Violations of litigation-related rules sometimes occur when a lawyer acts through someone else, such as a paralegal. Related rules have already been covered in this book—paralegals may not make court appearances or give clients legal advice, must disclose to courts and clients their identity as nonlawyers, must avoid conflicts of interest in litigation, and must protect privileged information and material in litigated matters.

The rules on advocacy start with the basic premise that lawyers must represent clients zealously. ABA Model Rule of Professional Conduct 1.3 calls on lawyers to exercise "reasonable diligence and promptness," and comment [1] describes this duty further as "zeal in advocacy. . . ." **Zealous representation** entails exercising one's best efforts on the client's behalf within the boundaries of law and ethics. The duty to represent clients zealously has special meaning in the context of the lawyer's role as an advocate. This duty must be exercised within the constraints created by other ethical duties, legal obligations, and moral imperatives, such as the lawyer's duties of candor to the court, the administration of justice, client confidentiality, and the search for the truth. As stated in the comment, this duty "does not require the use of offensive tactics or preclude the treating of all persons involved in the legal process with courtesy and respect." See, for example, Iowa State Bar Association Ethics Opinion 14-02, which advises that it is an ethical violation to wrongfully accuse another lawyer of unethical conduct, fraud, dishonesty, or deceit to gain a tactical advantage. See also Association of the Bar of the City of New York Ethics Formal Opinion 2015-5. The following sections address the ethics rules on advocacy, with emphasis on the rules that affect paralegals most directly.

B. Unmeritorious Claims, Delay, and Discovery Abuse

The ABA Model Rules prohibit lawyers from bringing **unmeritorious claims and defenses**. ABA Model Rule 3.1 states that lawyers shall not make a claim or defense unless it has a basis in law and fact. This provision allows for the situation where the lawyer is arguing in good faith for an extension, modification, or reversal of the law. Actions that violate this rule are typically called "frivolous."

Violations of this rule most commonly occur when a lawyer brings an unwarranted action to gain some advantage over the opposition, to force a party to expend funds to defend the action, or simply to earn fees. A lawyer who brings an action based on inaccurate information supplied by a client, without conducting any investigation, may also violate this rule. If the action is in fact unmeritorious, the lawyer may be found to have violated ethics rules, court rules, and/or related statutes for failing to investigate. Most jurisdictions hold that the lawyer has a duty to make a reasonable inquiry unless immediate action is necessary to protect the client's interests. An example of an unmeritorious claim is a plaintiff who sues a competitor without grounds under the law merely for the purpose of driving him or her out of business. For example, in one federal case, a law firm and its client were required to pay the opposing party and its lawyer $200,000 for filing a frivolous patent case and for filing a motion for reconsideration when the case was thrown out.

Discovery abuse
Using the discovery process to harass or burden a party.

Related to unmeritorious claims are ***abuses of the discovery process***. Conducting excessive or unnecessary discovery has been employed as a strategy to delay litigation, to burden the opposing counsel, to raise the cost to the opposition and, generally, to wear down the opposing party and counsel. To deter discovery abuse, courts have adopted rules that strictly circumscribe discovery, expedite the pretrial stage, and discourage excessive and unnecessarily lengthy discovery. These rules limit the number of interrogatories that can be posed, establish strict deadlines for completion of discovery, and mandate alternative dispute resolution and pretrial settlement procedures. Rules on e-discovery address some concerns about the issues related to cost and protection of privileged communications in electronic files, but unintended consequences of e-discovery include more complicated trial preparation, increased time and cost, and growth in the number of lawyers sanctioned for e-discovery violations.

ABA Model Rule 3.4(d) specifically forbids making frivolous pretrial discovery requests and failing to comply with proper discovery requests. Violations of this rule occur, for example, when a lawyer requests discovery that is beyond the scope of the case, perhaps by flooding the opposition with irrelevant interrogatories; gives incomplete answers to interrogatories; requests discovery of unnecessary confidential, sensitive, or embarrassing information; and makes unfounded objections to discovery. Lawyers have been known to provide many more documents than requested, seeking to hide a damaging document. In one example of an ethics sanction involving discovery, a legal team removed 2,300 documents from 81 boxes of documents that were ordered produced. In another, the failure to produce a key letter from a doctor in a case involving a disability led to the dismissal of the case.

ABA Model Rule 3.2 requires lawyers to "make reasonable efforts to expedite litigation consistent with" clients' interests. The comment to this rule cites as improper delays that are made for a lawyer's convenience, to frustrate the opposition's legitimate goals, and to realize financial gain. Unethical delays for which attorneys have been sanctioned include refusing to respond to communications of opposing counsel; repeated failure to appear at hearings, settlement conferences, or depositions; unnecessary delays in filing motions to disqualify counsel; and failing to complete discovery in accordance with court rules, court orders, or statutes. Violations of this rule may also have implications for the lawyer's duty to act competently because timeliness in handling client matters is an element of competence.

The most common way that ethical breaches in litigation are addressed is by means of a **court-ordered sanction** against the lawyer. Discipline by state disciplinary authorities for bringing frivolous actions or defenses, abusing discovery, or causing unnecessary delays is relatively rare. When it does occur, it is usually in a particularly egregious case, such as when a lawyer files several frivolous lawsuits or when the ethical violation is coupled with other violations such as incompetence or failure to obey a court order. Sometimes a judge will inform the relevant disciplinary authorities of an ethical breach.

Examples include a case where two law firms were sanctioned with six-figure fines for incorrectly claiming in a bankruptcy filing that their client owned a mortgage that had in fact been reassigned, and another where a prominent New York firm was sanctioned for bringing a "ridiculous, frivolous" lawsuit on behalf of a billionaire client concerning his former father-in-law's estate. The court said that no competent lawyer could have concluded that a lawsuit could be brought upon reading the testamentary documents.

One important remedy available to the victims of such conduct is a civil suit against the client, the lawyer, or both for ***malicious prosecution*** or ***abuse of process***. Grounds for malicious prosecution exist when a civil lawsuit or criminal prosecution has been brought, without probable cause and with malice, after the defendant prevails in the action. Limited immunity for the lawyer exists only if the lawyer acted in good faith. An abuse of process action may be brought when the legal process is misused to achieve other than legitimate legal purposes, such as filing a criminal complaint to force the defendant to pay a debt.

Malicious prosecution/abuse of process
Improper use of a civil or criminal process.

The courts impose sanctions against lawyers who violate the ethics rules and related statutes and court rules under their **contempt power**. This power can be exercised for any kind of lawyer misconduct in a matter before a court, including disobeying a court order (including a discovery order) or acting in a manner that disrupts the proceedings. Contempt is covered in more detail in Section C.

Courts can impose **monetary sanctions**. Under federal statutes and procedural rules and under state court rules or statutes, courts have authority to impose sanctions against lawyers, clients, or both for actions that are unwarranted, delaying, or harassing. Federal Rule of Civil Procedure 11 provides for sanctions against attorneys, clients, or both for filing unwarranted or other objectionable pleadings and papers. Rule 11 is supplemented by Federal Rule of Civil Procedure 37, which provides for sanctions for failure to make or cooperate in discovery. These rules parallel the ethics rules, specifically requiring that court filings be well grounded in fact, and warranted by existing law or a good-faith argument for the extension, modification, or reversal of existing law. Filings for an improper purpose, such as to harass or to cause unnecessary delay or needless expense, are also prohibited. Sanctions may include payment of expenses and attorneys' fees to the opposing party or parties and fines. The most severe sanction, rarely exercised, is the dismissal of an action with prejudice.

Rule 11, adopted to alleviate unnecessary delays and court filings, has been widely used by federal judges. Monetary sanctions can be substantial. Examples of some kinds of cases in which sanctions have been awarded under Rule 11 are using abusive language in a motion, filing an action unwarranted by law for purely political reasons, asking for an inflated amount of damages, delaying the production of specific documents for an extended period without adequate explanation, filing a motion to disqualify counsel purely to delay the proceedings, and lying about the existence of documents sought through discovery.

Rule 11 contains provisions designed to make the application of sanctions uniform and fair. The imposition of sanctions is discretionary, not mandatory. Parties are usually given time to remedy conduct after notification that sanctions will be sought. Nonmonetary sanctions that will deter the wrongful conduct are favored. Law firms, not just individual lawyers, can be held responsible for violations. States have comparable rules and statutes authorizing sanctions, and case law recognizes the inherent authority of a court over its proceedings as the basis for imposing sanctions. See the *Bonda* case at the end of this chapter for an example of sanctions imposed by a trial judge for delays and failure to pursue discovery.

C. Disruption in the Courtroom and Disobeying Court Orders

Trial lawyers are expected to conduct themselves with decorum when they are in court out of respect for the court, the administration of justice, and all the parties involved in the case. Under the Model Rules, a lawyer may not "engage in conduct intended to disrupt" proceedings (ABA Model Rule 3.5(d)).

A tension can exist between this rule and the duty to advocate zealously. Lawyers who are charged with disruptive conduct usually contend that they are just doing their utmost to represent their clients. Sometimes unacceptable conduct in court is designed to influence the jury or to throw the opposing counsel off track. Examples of **disruptive conduct** and **dirty tricks** in the courtroom are raising an unfounded objection to break opposing counsel's train of thought; making faces or gestures to the judge or the jury; asking a question that alludes to evidence known to be inadmissible; insulting a judge or opposing counsel, for example, by calling them names or accusing them of collusion, racism, incompetence, or bias; referring to the proceedings in an insulting or rude manner; making unsupportable, inflammatory, or prejudicial side remarks to the jury; and asking questions of a witness after the judge has warned that the questions are prohibited. In a Florida case, a public defender was sanctioned for pretending to gag while a jailhouse informant was testifying.

Disruptive tactics and violations of the decorum of a proceeding often arise in communications with opposing counsel, both in and outside the courtroom. In a highly publicized Florida case, a judge slashed attorneys' fees in a case where the plaintiff's lawyers, who prevailed in the case, were "overzealous," refusing to shake hands with the opposing counsel and being verbally abusive to them. During trial, they frequently rolled their eyes, looked at the ceiling, and flailed their arms. In another Florida case, a lawyer was removed from a fair labor class action case after he scheduled depositions at Dunkin' Donuts, attended them in T-shirts and shorts, and drew obscene pictures and played Angry Birds during the deposition. In an Oklahoma case, a lawyer was ordered to write an article on civility after he wrote to opposing counsel to "sit quietly in the corner," "be like a potted plant," "spare me your phony sermons," and "please stop the charade," among other insults. A Texas lawyer was sanctioned for calling opposing counsel an "ignorant slut" and "pansy" during a deposition and sending e-mails filled with obscenities and threats. A district court judge ordered a lawyer with a large law firm to make a training video on the impropriety of making unspecified form objections, witness coaching, and excessive interruptions and called the lawyer's conduct "obstructionist" and "costly." Other examples of lawyer misconduct in depositions include a lawyer being sanctioned for flinging coffee at opposing counsel and for threatening opposing counsel with pepper spray and a stun gun. In a federal case, the court sanctioned a lawyer for several ethical violations during discovery, including making sexist remarks to opposing counsel (*Claypole v. County of Monterey*, U.S. District Court, Northern District of California, Case No. 14-cv-02730-BLF (2016)). In another, a lawyer was sanctioned for several offenses, including calling opposing counsel profane and sexist names and making derogatory sexist remarks about her to her face and in front of others (*In re Novoselsky*, Illinois Attorney Registration and Disciplinary Commission, No. 2011PR00043 (2015)).

Other cases involving courtroom misconduct relate to disrespectful interactions with judges. In a California case, a judge mandated that all the lawyers in a defense firm take an ethics course when the judge found that the lawyers had repeatedly misstated the record, made frivolous objections, and mischaracterized the law. A Texas judge found a lawyer guilty of contempt and sentenced him to 90 days in jail after he made a lewd gesture in a criminal proceeding. A Tennessee lawyer was suspended from federal court practice and fined after he repeatedly interrupted and talked over a judge who was questioning him. And a prominent California lawyer was suspended for three years for disruptive conduct, including repeatedly asking identical inadmissible questions, being sarcastic or snide to witnesses, badgering witnesses, and personally attacking opposing counsel. In a Michigan case, a lawyer was held in contempt for repeatedly interrupting a judge every time the judge asked his client a question. A California lawyer was fined after engaging in a 20-minute "shout-fest" with a judge over a scheduling matter. A federal court upheld a sanction imposed by a bankruptcy judge on a lawyer who wrote in a brief that the judge's findings were "half-baked." In a recent North Carolina case, a lawyer faced sanctions for statements in pleadings accusing the judges who had ruled against his client of "overwhelming incompetence and ignorance," being "asinine," and acting like "mentally challenged cheerleaders." A Louisiana lawyer was disbarred for "numerous false, misleading, and inflammatory statements" made about a judge on Twitter.

Disobeying a court order is also an ethical breach and sanctionable (ABA Model Rule 3.4(c)). Violations of this rule most often arise when a lawyer does not comply with a discovery order issued by the court. For example, in a Texas case, a lawyer agreed to pay more than $1 million in fines for violating a court order by failing to produce records from a former client for more than two and a half years. In another case, a California court granted summary judgment when a lawyer failed to participate meaningfully in judicial arbitration. In yet another case, a lawyer was fined for revealing the names of witnesses that were subject to a protective order.

Acts that reflect disrespect for the court may subject a lawyer to disciplinary action and are likely to elicit an immediate response from the judge. Judges may hold an attorney in *contempt* for offensive courtroom conduct. Contempt power is reserved for situations in which the administration of justice and orderly proceedings are immediately and substantially threatened. Generally, the court will warn a lawyer, sometimes repeatedly, before holding the lawyer in contempt. Contempt can be punishable by jail time and is reported to the appropriate disciplinary authorities, which may give rise to disciplinary proceedings.

Judges have sanctioned lawyers in court for many kinds of disruptive conduct such as the ones described above. Other examples are continued argument on a point on which the court has ruled; continued

Contempt
An act that obstructs the administration of justice, impairs the dignity of the court, or shows disrespect for the authority of the court.

mention of inadmissible evidence or prohibited arguments; presentation of false evidence; the use of abusive, vulgar, and obscene language; disrespectful, irrelevant, or unjustified criticism of the court; and absence from or tardiness for scheduled court dates. For example, a lawyer and his client were jailed for four hours when they were 50 minutes late to jury selection. Another lawyer skipped a trial to attend a wedding in Paris and was convicted of misdemeanor contempt after the judge discovered that her excuse of having been in the hospital was not true. Insults, sarcasm, and the like can be punishable by contempt if they disrupt the proceedings.

Most paralegals do not find themselves in situations in which they would be in a position to engage in unethical conduct in court, but issues can arise when they accompany their lawyer-supervisors to court. Many paralegals working in civil litigation and criminal practice attend court proceedings and therefore must be aware of and abide by these rules. NFPA Model Code EC-1.3(a) calls on paralegals to refrain from "conduct that offends the dignity and decorum" of the courts.

D. Candor and Honesty

The ABA Model Rules contain several provisions calling for lawyers to be **honest** in their representation of clients. Candor in communications with the court does not, however, obligate the lawyer to disclose evidence that is prejudicial to the client unless such information is not privileged and is requested through proper discovery, or the lawyer is so obligated by some special rule of law, such as the duty of prosecutors to disclose exculpatory evidence.

The ethics rules specifically prohibit a lawyer from making a **false statement of law or fact** or failing to correct one (ABA Model Rule 3.3(a)(1)); offering **false evidence** or failing to take remedial measures when the lawyer knows it has been offered (Rule 3.3(a)(3)); and **not disclosing adverse controlling authority** when opposing counsel fails to do so (Rule 3.3(a)(2)). A non-client's fraud on the court must be promptly revealed to the court by the lawyer.

Model Rule 3.4 prohibits lawyers from **obstructing access** to evidence; **altering, destroying,** or **concealing evidence**; and **falsifying or allowing others to falsify evidence**. (See the section later on witnesses for more on false testimony by witnesses.) See *Eaton v. Fink* at the end of this chapter, about a paralegal who reveals that false evidence was admitted in a case.

Some examples of violations of the ethics rules on honesty with tribunals may be instructive. In one disciplinary case, a lawyer was censured for failing to disclose to arbitrators that a doctor had changed his diagnosis of the condition of the client. In another case, a court ordered a default judgment against a defendant whose lawyer refused to produce a witness that had avoided service. A federal court ordered a default in a high-profile racial discrimination case against a corporate defendant for altering and destroying key documents, leaving critical information out of affidavits, blocking access in court to relevant information, and intimidating a witness. Other cases have involved lawyers requesting that a client be released from custody to attend his mother's funeral after it had been held; providing false information on the value of a client's property; failing to provide the names of more than 20 known witnesses in a case; and conveying client's property with the intent to defraud a creditor. In a major case against an automobile manufacturer, lawyers were held to be acting improperly for allowing false testimony of an employee several times over a period of years. Defense lawyers were sanctioned for failing to produce relevant reports that the plaintiff's counsel obtained from a federal agency and others were suspended from practice for nine months for intentionally influencing their client to misrepresent the site of the accident that was the subject matter of the case. In a Massachusetts case, a lawyer was reprimanded for omitting references to certain critical facts in a document filed with the court. The judge said, "In as brazen a piece of misrepresentation as we have ever seen, the lawyer deleted certain words, phrases, and sentences without the use of an ellipsis, or any other indication of editing." A New York district attorney was fired and suspended from practice when she falsely stated that the record showed the defendant's blood alcohol level, when the test results were not recorded on the document. In a Louisiana case, a lawyer in a child custody case was disbarred for buying his client shampoo that would eliminate signs of his drug use. In a recent case, two federal prosecutors faced a six-month suspension over claims by local bar regulators that they concealed evidence from defense lawyers in a criminal case 12 years prior.

Perjury
Criminal offense of making false statements under oath.

Client ***perjury*** is a difficult and complex ethical dilemma for lawyers. The courts have not been uniform in their handling of this area, and ethics rules and their interpretations also vary from one jurisdiction to the next. As a general rule, in a civil case, the lawyer who knows that a client intends to commit perjury should not call the client to testify. Most courts recommend or mandate withdrawal from representation or disclosure to the court if the client testifies dishonestly.

Criminal cases in which a client lies present even more serious problems because of the client's right to testify and to be represented by **competent counsel**. The U.S. Supreme Court has held that withdrawal is the appropriate action (*Nix v. Whiteside*, 475 U.S. 157 (1986)). However, withdrawal may not be allowed at the time of trial if the court finds that withdrawal would interfere with a speedy trial and the administration of justice. Authorities are split on whether a lawyer who is not permitted to withdraw should disclose the intended perjury. Some courts endorse allowing the defendant to testify in narrative form without the lawyer's help. After the perjury has occurred, most courts require the lawyer to seek withdrawal. If withdrawal is not granted, some courts require disclosure of the perjury.

Both narrative testimony and withdrawal during trial signal to the jury and the judge that the defendant was lying, highlighting the conflict between the duties of zealous representation and candor to the court.

Some commentators believe that client and witness perjury is widespread. Some examples are: relatives testifying falsely as alibi witnesses; spouses hiding assets in marital dissolution cases; and police lying under oath about the circumstances of an arrest, a search and seizure, a police action, or an informant. In one Silicon Valley case, a defendant in a patent case falsified a notebook that was said to contain his notes on an invention. A paralegal in the case noticed differences in two versions of the same notebook, which the court ultimately found to have been falsified. The client in this case was prosecuted for obstruction of justice and perjury.

The **duty of candor** to the court applies to legal research and use of precedent in documents filed with a court. A paralegal who finds adverse controlling authority while conducting legal research must report the authority to the supervising attorney, who should include it in relevant documents filed with the court. See Model Rule 3.3(a)(1), which prohibits lawyers from making a "false statement of law," and 3.3(a)(2), which requires lawyers to disclose adverse controlling authority. Of course, paralegals and lawyers drafting briefs and motions can cite the adverse authority and seek to distinguish it legally or factually or argue for a change in the law. The *Massey* case later in this chapter illustrates one possible result of controlling adverse authority not being cited.

Remedies for destroying, altering, or suppressing evidence imposed by disciplinary bodies and the courts are supplemented by **obstruction of justice** statutes, at both state and federal levels. In addition to criminal charges being brought against the lawyer, client, or both, statutes provide for sanctions in the pending case, including fines, dismissal, award of legal fees and costs, and civil causes of action by the injured party. Destruction of evidence may also give rise to a civil cause of action for ***spoliation***, in which the injured party can collect damages for substantial interference with the ability to prove a claim or defense because the evidence is no longer available. In some states, courts allow an adverse inference to be drawn from a party's failure to produce the evidence. Questions have arisen in the last few years about what kind of pre-litigation advice a lawyer can give a client about deleting electronically stored material, like emails and social media pages. Ethics opinions say that lawyers can advise clients to change privacy settings and to remove information unless they have a duty to preserve the information under the law. (See New York County Lawyers Association Ethics Opinion 745 (2013), Pennsylvania Bar Association Ethics Opinion 2014-300, Philadelphia Bar Association Opinion 2014-5, and Florida Bar Advisory Opinion 14-1 (2015).) (For an example of a case where counsel advised deletion of the client's emails, see *Premium Pet Health, LLC v. All American Pet Proteins, LLC*, District Court, City and County of Denver, Case No. 2014CV31366 (2015).)

Spoliation
Destruction of evidence that may result in a civil cause of action for damages for interference with the ability to prove a claim or defense.

REVIEW QUESTIONS

1. Why do paralegals need to know about the rules governing advocacy?
2. What is zealous representation, and what other constraints are there on a lawyer's unfettered zeal in representing a client?
3. Define two kinds of unmeritorious claims or defenses, and give an example of each.
4. Under what circumstances can a lawyer make a claim that is not warranted under existing law?
5. Does a lawyer have a duty to investigate a client's story before filing an action?
6. Give three examples of abuses of the discovery process.
7. Give an example of an unethical delay. What other ethics violations might be involved in an unnecessary delay?
8. Name four kinds of remedies or sanctions that might result from bringing unmeritorious claims, abusing discovery, or causing unnecessary delays.
9. Under what circumstances may an action for malicious prosecution be brought? Abuse of process?
10. Give three examples of actions by lawyers that would be disruptive in the courtroom. What do the ethics rules prohibiting such disruptions say? For what reasons might a lawyer be disruptive?
11. What is the most immediate remedy for disruptive conduct in the courtroom or disobedience of a court order?
12. What kinds of actions are prohibited by a lawyer's duty of candor to the court?
13. What must a lawyer do if they discover that false testimony has been given by a non-client witness? What if the false testimony is given by a client in a civil case? In a criminal case?
14. What should a paralegal do if they discover adverse controlling authority in the course of research?
15. What are three things that might happen if a lawyer presents false evidence or permits false testimony in court?

DISCUSSION QUESTIONS AND HYPOTHETICALS

1. Why are there proportionately more paralegals in litigation than there are lawyers working in litigation?
2. Why do you think that lawyers have duties that temper their duty to represent clients zealously? Discuss the tension between the potentially conflicting sets of duties and whether the courts and ethics authorities seem to have found the right balance.

3. What would you do if you interviewed a client who told you a story that you did not fully believe and your supervising lawyer told you to draft and file a complaint on the client's behalf based solely on the client's story?
4. How would you respond if your supervising lawyer asked you to prepare a bankruptcy petition that you knew was designed solely to stop a foreclosure proceeding against your client?
5. What would you do if your supervising lawyer asked you to prepare requests for continuances in virtually every case they handled? What if you knew it was because the lawyer was unprepared and behind in work? What if you knew it was because your client was ill and the lawyer was trying to avoid going to trial before the client's death?
6. What would you do if the supervising lawyer asked you to give nonresponsive or incomplete answers to interrogatories? What if this lawyer asked you not to produce certain documents that you believe were requested in a proper document production request?
7. How would you react if you were asked to draft interrogatories about the opposition's personal affairs, which had no relationship to the case? What about interrogatories requesting information that you knew to be privileged?
8. Why are court-imposed sanctions such a powerful remedy for abuses in pleading and discovery?
9. Suppose you are responsible for handling the discovery in a case, and the supervising lawyer tells you to disregard a court order to complete discovery. What do you do?
10. Suppose you are a litigation paralegal who is accompanying a lawyer to court for an important trial. What would you do if the supervising lawyer kept whispering to you during opposing counsel's examination of witnesses? What if you knew that this conduct was intended to distract the jury?
11. How would you respond if the supervising lawyer asked you to shred documents that you knew were discoverable?
12. How would you use adverse authority in a brief if you believed the authority was not controlling in your jurisdiction?
13. What steps would you take if you knew that a client was planning to lie during testimony? What if you knew a non-client witness was planning to lie? Would your answer depend on whether the supervising attorney knew too?
14. Do you believe that the adversary system encourages perjury? Contact local federal and/or state prosecutors and interview several lawyers for their opinion on this issue. Ask them how many prosecutions for perjury have been brought in recent years.
15. Your client's credibility and reputation are at issue in a lawsuit you are handling for her. Her social media posts are filled with obscenities and references to her sexual exploits. What, if anything, can you advise her about her social media history and use?

RESEARCH PROJECTS AND ASSIGNMENTS

1. Find the rules of civil procedure, court rules, and ethics rules in your jurisdiction about frivolous and unwarranted claims and contentions. How do these rules compare with each other and with the ABA Model Rules? What interesting recent cases have been decided on the basis of these rules? Have any of them involved paralegals?
2. For an interesting high-profile case involving a professional basketball player, see *Sprewell v. Golden State Warriors*, 266 F.3d 979 (9th Cir. 2001), in which the federal appellate court upholds the lower court's decision to dismiss the case, in part, and reverses dismissal of the sanction of the lawyers for conduct discussed in this chapter. Read and brief this case for the class.
3. What are your state's rules on e-discovery? Have the courts in your jurisdiction decided any cases interpreting them? What do they say about destroying e-mails and other electronic evidence? Research if lawyers are being sanctioned frequently for violating the rules. What kinds of violations did you find?
4. New York's trial judges have adopted Uniform Rules Relating to the Conduct of Depositions to promote ethical and civil behavior in taking depositions. Does your jurisdiction have any such rules? Contact three trial lawyers and ask them if bad conduct in depositions is a problem.
5. Read *Hoag v. Amex Assurance Co.*, 953 A.2d 713 (Del. 2008), in which the court upheld a dismissal after the plaintiff failed to comply with four court orders for discovery over a period of three years.
6. In *Wade v. Soo Line Railroad Corp.*, 500 F.3d 559 (7th Cir. 2007), the judge dismissed a case and sanctioned a lawyer for concealing documents in several different ways. Read and brief this case to see what the appeals court decided.
7. For a seminal case addressing the extent and cost of e-discovery, see *Zubulake v. UBS Warburg*, 217 F.R.D. 309 (S.D.N.Y. 2003) and related cases. What is the *Zubulake* Test and how is it applicable to litigation practice? See also *Pension Committee of University of Montreal Pension Plan v. Banc of America Securities*, 716 F.Supp. 220 (S.D.N.Y. 2010), which expounds on *Zubulake* regarding the duty to preserve and produce electronically stored information ("ESI"). What sanctions are available when this duty is breached?
8. For an exceptionally contentious case involving discovery, which contains allegations of bribes and a request for the judge to recuse himself, see *Sentis Groups v. Shell Oil*, 559 F.3d 888 (8th Cir. 2009). In this case, the judge was the one who was accused of inappropriate language, directing profanities at the plaintiffs' counsel more than 15 times. What can happen to a judge who engages in this kind of conduct?

9. Making frivolous claims in an appeal is also sanctionable. For an interesting case, see *In re White*, 121 Cal. App. 4th 1453, 18 Cal. Rptr. 3d 444 (2004). In this case involving three appeals, the lawyer was found to be operating a *habeas corpus* writ mill in which he aided in the unauthorized practice of law and failed to supervise nonlawyers. The appeals he filed were found to be frivolous and he was ordered to refund fees to clients and pay a sanction.
10. Should clients have a right to have their paralegals at counsel table during trial? For one interesting case, see *Finley v. State*, 725 So.2d 226 (Miss. 1998), in which the court held that a trial should not be stopped when a paralegal who had been in court with the legal team was injured in a car accident and could not participate.
11. What are a lawyer's obligations when receiving a subpoena regarding a client? Does the lawyer have to consult the client? Resist the disclosure? What if the lawyer disagrees with the client's decision? What if the client is unavailable? See ABA Formal Opinion 473 (2016).
12. For an interesting case involving a lawyer who was sanctioned by a court for trying to get in information that was prohibited by the judge's earlier orders, see *Martinez v. Cal. Dep't of Transportation*, 238 Cal. App. 4th 559 (2015). In this case, the defense lawyer repeatedly made references to the plaintiff having a Nazi symbol on his motorcycle helmet.

E. Relationships and Communications with Others

As discussed in Chapters 3 and 6, paralegals must take care to disclose their status as a non-lawyer paralegal. When communicating with persons outside their own firms, paralegals can easily be mistaken for lawyers. A third person who assumes that a paralegal is a lawyer may believe that the paralegal intended this impression, giving rise to a claim that the paralegal held themself out as a lawyer. This rule is critical in litigation practice because paralegals communicate frequently with courts, opposing counsel, co-counsel, clients, third parties, experts, and witnesses.

1. Judges

As mentioned in Section C, inappropriate **criticism of judges** in court may give rise to disciplinary action and, if it is disrespectful or disruptive, can lead to immediate sanctions under the judge's contempt power. Ethics rules prohibit lawyers from making false statements about the "qualifications or integrity of a judge. . . ." ABA Model Rule 8.2(a). Lawyers are protected from liability for derogatory statements about a judge unless made with knowledge of the statement's falsity or with reckless disregard (*Garrison v. Louisiana*, 379 U.S. 64 (1964)). In most jurisdictions, courts have held that the First Amendment does not protect lawyers from disciplinary action for criticizing judges inappropriately because of the strong state interest in protecting public officials and in maintaining respect for the courts. However, in a minority of jurisdictions, discipline of lawyers who publicly and harshly criticized judges has been struck down on appeal. In one case, a lawyer called a judge an anti-Semite and a drunk. In the other, a lawyer called a local judge "a midget among giants" in a letter to a newspaper. A Tennessee lawyer was recently given a two-year suspension for saying that a judge "disgrace[d] his judicial office" and that his decision was "a stench in the nostrils of the nation." An Illinois lawyer was suspended for six months for criticizing a judge, calling him at one point "a narcissistic, maniacal mental case." In a Michigan case, a well-known lawyer was brought before the state grievance commission for repeatedly using obscenities in court and calling justices "three jackass court of appeals judges" and "Nazis." In a recent Texas case, a judge ordered three lawyers to complete 30 hours of ethics-related continuing legal education for "baseless attacks on the integrity of this Court" in implying the judge ignored racist and anti-Semitic conduct in the case. In another recent case, the New Mexico Supreme Court indefinitely suspended a lawyer for implying that the judge had intentionally concealed a relationship, ignored the law, and "fixed" the case.

Ethics rules prohibit lawyers from attempting to **influence judges**. Model Rule 3.5(a) prohibits a lawyer from seeking to influence a judge by any illegal means, for example, ***bribery***. Bribery is also a crime punishable under state law. Rule 8.4(f) also prohibits knowingly assisting a judge in violating the law or the rules of judicial conduct. Implying or stating that one can influence a public official, including a judge, is prohibited by Model Rule 8.4(e). It should be noted that judges are governed by their own ethics canons and rules of conduct in every jurisdiction and that these rules parallel those already stated.

Paralegals must also be mindful of rules relating to ***ex parte*** communications with judges. To ensure fairness in the adversarial process, lawyers are prohibited from having contact with the judge in a case without the presence of the opposing counsel. Such secret communications might give the communicating party an unfair advantage or give an appearance of influence or favoritism. The ethics rules that prohibit *ex parte* communications with judges are set forth in Model Rule 3.5(b). Exceptions to these rules are made for special *ex parte* proceedings that do not require opposing counsel's presence, such as petitions for a temporary restraining order. The NFPA Model Code calls attention to the rules regarding *ex parte* communications in EC-1.2(a) and (b).

Bribery
The crime of giving or receiving something of value as payment for an official act.

Ex parte
Action taken by or on behalf of a party without the presence of the opposing party.

2. Jurors

Seeking to influence or having ex parte **communications with jurors** or prospective jurors, before and during trial, is expressly prohibited by ethics rules to prevent influence and bribery. ABA Model Rule 3.5(a) and (b). Lawyers are prohibited from such communications even if they are not involved in the case at issue. A lawyer may not circumvent these rules by using an agent, such as the client or a paralegal.

In addition to disciplinary action for such conduct, a ***mistrial*** is likely to be declared if *ex parte* communications with jurors come to light. The lawyer's intent or lack of intent to influence the juror or jurors is not relevant in such cases. A lawyer's research on prospective jurors by using an investigator to contact them and ask them questions from a standard questionnaire has been held impermissible and, in one case, led to the criminal conviction and disbarment of the lawyer. Lawyers should not attempt to contact prospective jurors through social media. However, lawyers may review a juror's internet presence in advance of or during a trial as long as the lawyer does not attempt to communicate directly with the juror, and may take remedial measures if evidence of misconduct is found online. (See ABA Formal Opinion 466 (2014); Association of the Bar of the City of New York, Committee on Professional Ethics Formal Opinion 2012-2; and New York County Lawyers Association Formal Opinion 743, issued 2011.)

Even simple socializing during a break in the proceedings has been held to be grounds to declare a mistrial. See the *Omaha Bank* case at the end of this chapter for an illustration of what can happen when a lawyer has contact with a juror outside the courtroom. Some courts have also disqualified counsel for such improprieties. In an Oklahoma case, a juror went into a bar after the conclusion of the case and before deliberations, and talked to a lawyer who was not involved in the case about his bias against plaintiffs. This conversation resulted in the defense verdict being reversed.

Jury tampering is, of course, a crime in every jurisdiction and under federal laws. For example, 18 U.S.C. §§1503 and 1504 make it a crime to attempt to influence a juror or judge.

Lawyers and paralegals should also be aware of the rules on the use of cell phones and social media by jurors. Many courts have adopted rules prohibiting the use of electronic media by jurors (*e.g.*, Florida and Texas) and in 2012, the federal Judicial Conference issued model rules that expand prohibitions on juror use of all forms of electronic devices for communications and research. Some states, like California, have passed statutes establishing that jurors can be given jail time for using media to communicate or research. Examples of this kind of juror misconduct include jurors researching the cases or parties involved in cases online, jurors posting on social media or blogging about cases before they were over, looking up the definitions of legal terms and sentencing guidelines, and even "friending" a party or witness. Jurors are being removed from

Mistrial
Trial terminated and declared void prior to the return of a verdict.

jury duty and fined for violations of the rules, and these actions can also lead to a mistrial. In one case in New York, a juror was fined $1,000 and a mistrial was declared after she posted details about her emotional state and jury deliberations on Facebook. In a recent high profile New Mexico criminal case, a judge declared a mistrial after a juror researched the penalty for first-degree murder on their own time and then included that information in a notebook they used during the trial.

Finally, lawyers and paralegals can be sanctioned for misuse of social media in litigation as well. In a recent case in Chicago, a partner in a large law firm was sanctioned for tweeting photos of evidence while observing a federal trial. In another, a lawyer representing a wife in a child custody case was disbarred for promoting a social media campaign that called for signing petitions and sending communications to judges concerning the husband's alleged abuse of the children in the case (*In re McCool*, 172 So. 3d 1058 (La. 2015)). And in another, a trial was delayed and a lawyer sanctioned when she posted a one-sided account of a case on Facebook right before jury selection.

Communicating with jurors after a trial is forbidden in some states. Other states do not prohibit post-trial communications, which attorneys may desire in order to evaluate their presentation, to find out what influenced the jurors, and to ascertain whether the jury deliberated appropriately. ABA Model Rule 3.5(c) allows communication after the jury is discharged unless prohibited by law or court order; if the juror has made known a desire not to communicate; or if the communication involves misrepresentation, coercion, harassment, or duress. General harassment of jurors is also prohibited by the provision on respect for the rights of third persons, found in Model Rule 4.4.

Some states have a rule that obligates lawyers to reveal improper conduct toward or among jurors to the court, although no comparable provision exists in the Model Rules.

3. Parties and Unrepresented Persons

Lawyers are prohibited from communicating directly with **parties who are represented by counsel** and may communicate only with the person's lawyer unless they are authorized by law or a court order or have the other lawyer's consent (ABA Model Rule 4.2). This rule is based primarily on concerns about overreaching conduct that may disrupt the trust between the lawyer and client or may influence the client against the client's interest. Clients are more vulnerable when their counsel is not present and may be more easily persuaded to give information or settle a case against their own interest. Unethical solicitation is also a concern, as described in Chapter 6.

Rules prohibiting communication with represented parties do not apply when represented parties are not truly adverse, are seeking a second opinion or new counsel, or are dissatisfied with their lawyers over the representation or fees and are considering taking action against the lawyer. This prohibition does not restrict the actions of the *parties*, who are free to speak to each other, although most lawyers warn their clients not to do so because of the potential for such conversations interfering with the representation and strategy in the case.

The *Crane* case at the end of this chapter illustrates how a lawyer might break this rule and what consequences might follow. When a violation of this ethics rule takes place during proceedings, remedies include suppression of evidence and disqualification of counsel. Disciplinary sanctions may follow, especially if the conduct involved dishonesty. An example from a recent New Jersey case involved lawyers who were charged with unethical conduct when they had a paralegal in their firm "friend" a litigant on Facebook and access the party's nonpublic pages.

It should be noted that the rules prohibiting lawyers from communicating with represented parties apply to federal prosecutors. For some time in the 1990s, the U.S. Attorney General argued otherwise, but in 1998, Congress passed a law holding federal prosecutors to state ethics rules, which prohibit such contacts in all jurisdictions (28 U.S.C. §530B).

Ethics rules also restrict the communications a lawyer may have with a **party not represented by counsel**. ABA Model Rule 4.3 prohibits a lawyer from stating or implying that the lawyer is "disinterested," requires a lawyer to clear up any misconception that an unrepresented person may have about the lawyer's role, and prohibits the lawyer from giving legal advice to the unrepresented person. The only advice that the lawyer can give such a person is to secure counsel. Paralegals who conduct investigations and talk to prospective witnesses should be keenly aware of these restrictions.

In the corporate setting, determining who a lawyer or paralegal may communicate with during litigation is sometimes difficult. Most cases hold that a lawyer may speak to unrepresented former employees of a corporation on the opposing side of litigation unless the employees were privy to privileged information. Current employees may be classified as "represented persons" if the corporation provides counsel to them. Members of a class in a class action are also considered to be represented parties. An ABA opinion addresses the question of whether a lawyer can communicate with in-house counsel when the corporation is represented by outside counsel. In holding that such communications generally do not require advance approval of outside counsel, the opinion holds that lawyers should not have such a communication if the lawyer is a party to the matter (ABA Formal Opinion 06-443).

The question of whether a lawyer or paralegal may attempt to communicate with non-parties using social media has been addressed by the San Diego County Bar Association, which said that the ethics rules "bar an attorney from making an ex parte friend request of a represented party . . ." and that "the attorney's duty not to deceive prohibits him from making a friend request even of unrepresented witnesses with disclosing the purpose of the request. . . ." (San Diego Cty. Bar Association Ethics Opinion 2011-2; also see Philadelphia Bar Association Ethics Opinion 2009-2 and New York City Bar Opinion 2010-2.).

Because a lawyer may not circumvent the rules on communications by using an agent, a paralegal should not engage in improper communications when working in litigation or other areas of practice. Paralegals frequently have contact with clients, opposing counsel, and witnesses. They must refrain from communicating with persons represented by counsel and from misleading persons not represented by counsel about their interest in a matter. An earlier ABA ethics opinion makes it clear that a lawyer is responsible for the improper *ex parte* contacts of nonlawyers. In the scenario posed by the ABA, a lawyer is responsible for the violations of this rule by an investigator under their supervision who made improper contacts that the lawyer either did not try to prevent, told the investigator to make, or failed to instruct the investigator not to make once the contact came to light (ABA Formal Opinion 95-396). See *In re Ositis* at the end of this chapter for an example of a case in which a lawyer was disciplined for directing his investigator to pose as a journalist to interview a potential party. Many but not all states follow this interpretation and prohibit lawyers from allowing their agents to "pretext" in investigations.

The ABA Guidelines on the Utilization of Paralegal Services and most state guidelines do not make specific reference to paralegals communicating with third parties. The Pennsylvania Bar, in its ethics opinion on paralegals, is the exception, reminding lawyers to warn paralegals not to communicate with represented persons (Penn. Bar Ass'n Formal Opinion 98-75).

4. Witnesses

A few special rules govern lawyers' contact with witnesses. A lawyer is forbidden from advising or causing a witness to flee the jurisdiction or to hide **to avoid testifying** (ABA Model Rule 3.4(a) and (f)). In addition to violating ethics rules, such conduct constitutes obstruction of justice and violates statutes that make it a crime to tamper with a witness or to delay, hinder, or prevent a witness from testifying.

A lawyer may not advise a witness to **testify falsely** or offer an inducement to testify falsely (ABA Model Rule 3.4(b)). Giving false testimony under oath constitutes perjury, and counseling a witness to do so constitutes the crime of ***subornation of perjury***.

Subornation of perjury
Criminal offense of encouraging another to commit perjury.

Lawyers and paralegals interview witnesses in depth to ascertain as exactly as possible the content of the witnesses' testimony, their credibility, and the consistency of their story. Witnesses sometimes change or are unclear about their stories, providing the opposing counsel with a chance to impeach the credibility of the witness.

Ethics rules do not prohibit lawyers from **preparing witnesses**, including clients, to testify effectively. A witness who is familiar with deposition and courtroom procedure and who knows the kinds of questions that counsel and opposing counsel will ask is more likely to be credible and less likely to become confused when questioned by opposing counsel. Lawyers and paralegals who handle witness preparation must be careful not to encourage witnesses to give false testimony or to over-coach witnesses so that their testimony seems "prepared" and they lose credibility. See ABA Formal Opinion 508, *The Ethics of Witness Preparation* (August 5, 2023).

Unethical coaching of witnesses is sometimes discovered and sanctioned. In one large asbestos case, the plaintiffs' lawyers prepared a detailed memorandum to their clients telling them how to testify, including what to say about their injuries. When the defense counsel was inadvertently given a copy of this memorandum, the firm stopped sending it to the plaintiffs and blamed an overzealous paralegal for writing it. In seeking the death penalty in a criminal case against a terrorist, a veteran U.S. attorney coached witnesses and gave them copies of trial transcripts in contravention of a court order, causing the judge to sanction the lawyer and to exclude key witnesses and other evidence. In a case in Chicago, a criminal defense lawyer was prosecuted for several offenses relating to a trial, including giving question-and-answer scripts to witnesses that included untrue statements. In another case, an Ohio prosecutor was suspended after he created a false Facebook page that he used to communicate with witnesses. In a recent case, a lawyer received a 90-day suspension from the Florida Supreme Court after he was accused of coaching a witness via text messages during a telephonic deposition. See *The Florida Bar v. Derek Vashon James*, No. SC-20-128 (2021). Paralegals must be mindful of the line between preparing witnesses to give their testimony effectively and encouraging them to testify untruthfully. Perjury is hard to prove, especially when the witness is also the client, but judges have little tolerance for over-coaching witnesses and juries are usually perceptive about the veracity of witnesses.

General rules about the treatment of third persons serve to prohibit the **harassment of witnesses**, both inside and outside the courtroom. ABA Model Rule 4.4 prohibits lawyers from engaging in any conduct the only purpose of which is to "embarrass, delay, or burden a third person."

Related to these ethical prohibitions are statutes that prohibit the **recording** of a person without his or her permission. Federal statutes provide criminal and civil remedies for interception and disclosure of wire, oral, or electronic communications and prohibit their use as evidence in court. (See, for example, 18 U.S.C. 2511(2)(d).) Not all jurisdictions prohibit secret tape recording of conversations, and some states have actually endorsed the practice. An ABA advisory opinion recommends against secret tape recording on ethical grounds (ABA Formal Opinion

01-422 (2001)). It is advisable to consult state statutes and rules before engaging in such conduct.

Lawyers may **pay witnesses for expenses** related to their testifying. The usual and permissible expenses are travel and lost wages. Payment may be made for time spent in preparation, such as meetings with lawyers and paralegals; however, witnesses must not be paid for the value or efficacy of their testimony. The agreement to pay the witness should meet the standards of the ethics rules and statutes, and should not be kept secret from the court.

Expert witnesses may also be paid a reasonable fee for their professional services. No witness, including experts, may be paid a fee or bonus that is contingent on the outcome of a case, as this would obviously provide an incentive for false testimony. ABA Model Rule 3.4(b) prohibits lawyers from offering an illegal "inducement" to a witness.

As discussed in Section D earlier, with regard to client perjury, a lawyer has special duties to prevent the introduction of false testimony and to take corrective measures if a witness gives false testimony. A lawyer who knows that a witness intends to testify falsely should advise the witness not to do so and should refuse to call the witness if he or she persists in intending to commit perjury. Once false testimony is given by a witness, the lawyer must inform the court (ABA Model Rule 3.3(a)(3)).

F. Trial Publicity

Balancing **the right of free expression and the right to a fair trial** is sometimes challenging. The public interest in criminal and civil cases and the pervasiveness of the modern media have frequently clashed with the smooth administration of the court system and assurance of a fair trial, especially in criminal cases and cases where a jury is involved. This conflict has most noticeably presented itself in sensational cases, especially those in which the press sought to have cameras in the courtroom or in which a judge issued a ***gag order***. Lawyers sometimes meet daily with the media in high-profile cases and are often accused by opposing counsel of "trying the case in the press."

Gag order
Court-imposed order that restricts information or comment about a case.

The original ABA Model Code provisions on trial publicity were quite restrictive, and after being challenged in court as unconstitutional, the ABA revised the rules. Model Rule 3.6(a) contains a general admonition against extrajudicial statements if "the lawyer knows or reasonably should know [that the statement] will be" publicly disseminated "and will have a substantial likelihood of materially prejudicing an adjudicative proceeding." Subsection (b) lists the basic items of information that a lawyer can state publicly in any case. Lawyers are also specifically permitted to make statements to mitigate adverse publicity not generated by the lawyer or the client under subsection (c). All lawyers in a firm involved in a case are covered.

All states have a rule on trial publicity, but the details of the rules vary from jurisdiction to jurisdiction. Some states have retained language from the old Model Code, but most have adopted some version of Model Rule 3.6. A few have established a more permissive standard, prohibiting only statements that create a danger of "imminent and substantial harm" of prejudicing the adjudicative proceeding.

Although disciplinary actions against lawyers for violations of these provisions are relatively rare, they do occur, usually in sensational cases that are closely covered by the media. For example, the lawyer representing criminal underworld figure John Gotti was held in contempt for statements made in his media campaign, particularly for statements intended for potential jurors. The defense lawyers in the O. J. Simpson murder prosecution were investigated for statements made to the media about a frame and cover-up of their client, but no ethics charges were brought. As already noted, some courts issue gag orders to prevent lawyers from making any statements in the interests of a fair trial, but when challenged, these gag orders are sometimes struck down as unconstitutional prior restraints on speech. Lawyer relations with the media in high-profile cases relate not only to legal ethics but to the impact on public opinion of lawyers. Polls have shown that the public views lawyers negatively in part because of their conduct in heavily reported, often scandalous, cases.

ABA Model Rule 3.6(d) specifically prohibits associates in the same firm from commenting on a case but does not specifically refer to nonlawyer "employees"; the general provision in the ABA Model Rules covering a lawyer's responsibility for acts of employees, however, extends the reach of this rule to paralegals (ABA Model Rule 5.3).

G. Special Rules for Prosecutors

As representatives of the government and "the people," prosecutors have a special duty of truth and fairness in the administration of justice. Prosecutors must not seek only to convict but also to **seek justice** and to ensure that all citizens are afforded their rights. A separate rule (Model Rule 3.8) sets forth these obligations, and local laws frequently impose additional obligations.

One critical duty of the prosecutor is not to institute unsupported criminal charges or to continue to pursue an unsupported action. **Probable cause** is required (ABA Model Rule 3.8(a)). This limitation also prevents prosecutors from abusing their discretion in prosecuting cases by singling someone out for prosecution. Prosecutors are also required to **disclose information** that tends to negate or mitigate guilt or to reduce punishment, *i.e.*, exculpatory evidence (ABA Model Rule 3.8(d)). In some states, withholding exculpatory evidence or altering evidence may also be a crime. (See, *e.g.*, California Penal Code Section 141 signed into law in 2016.)

The ABA Model Rules contain additional provisions that require prosecutors to make reasonable efforts to see that the accused **knows of the right to counsel** and has had an opportunity to secure counsel under subsection (b); not to obtain a waiver of rights from an unrepresented accused under subsection (c); and to exercise reasonable care to prevent employees and others involved with the prosecution from making extrajudicial statements that would "heighten public condemnation of the accused" under subsection (f). Finally, ABA Model Rule 3.8(e) limits a prosecutor's right to subpoena a lawyer to testify about a client or former client. A prosecutor may subpoena a lawyer only if the information sought is not privileged, is essential to the case and not otherwise available, and if the prosecutor has prior judicial approval. For additional guidance on ethical issues in the criminal area, see the ABA Standards for Criminal Justice, which include separate sections on the prosecutorial and defense functions.

In addition to disciplinary sanctions for violations of these rules, courts may impose remedies in a pending case if the defendant's constitutional rights have been violated. For example, a court may **reverse a conviction**, **suppress evidence**, **dismiss charges**, **or order a new trial**. For example, a murder conviction was reversed on appeal when the appellate court found extensive prosecutorial misconduct, including misrepresenting the law and the facts and intimidating witnesses. In another case, the prosecutor in closing arguments misstated the defendant's testimony and said that the defendant had been "programmed" and "counseled" to lie. A district attorney was disbarred after it came to light that he had made untrue accusations, influenced the police investigation, attempted to manipulate witnesses, and refused to hear exculpatory evidence in a highly publicized sexual assault case. In several cases, prosecutors have been sanctioned or fired for failure to disclose exculpatory evidence, including cases where the evidence surfaced after the defendants in question were convicted.

H. Electronic Resources

During the COVID-19 pandemic, the legal profession was required to pivot to online and electronic modalities. Court hearings, depositions, and some trials were conducted remotely using web conferencing platforms and related technology resources. These same platforms and resources continue to be used for daily communications with employees who work virtually.

Prior to the pandemic, most discovery was already being conducted through the use of technology. Electronic discovery (e-discovery) of electronically stored information (ESI) is now the norm in legal practice. Section 8 of ABA Model Rule 1.1 states: "To maintain the requisite knowledge and skill, a lawyer should keep abreast of changes in the law and its practice, including the benefits and risks associated with relevant technology, engage in continuing study and education and comply with all continuing legal education requirements to which the lawyer is subject." Seventy-eight percent of states have adopted the ethical requirement for lawyers to maintain technological competence. The responsibility to be technologically competent also extends to paralegals.

Current rules on e-discovery for ESI are largely based on the Sedona Principles, developed by the Sedona Conference®, which sought to apply the principles of discovery to ESI as "a reasonable and balanced approach to the treatment of electronic data." See *The Sedona Principles, Third Edition: Best Practices, Recommendations & Principles for Addressing Electronic Document Production*, 19 Sedona Conf. J. 1 (2018).

The Electronic Discovery Resource Manual (EDRM) is another widely used resource that was issued to guide e-discovery processes. It consists of nine distinct stages that outline what e-discovery activities look like during an investigation: information governance, identification, preservation, collection, processing, review, analysis, production, and preservation. See *EDRM Model 2.0* (2023).

In conjunction with technology resources, courts have carefully deliberated lawyers' ethical responsibility to develop technology acumen. In its Formal Opinion No. 2015-193, the State Bar of California Standing Committee on Professional Responsibility and Conduct applied lawyers' duties of competence, supervision, and confidentiality to their ethical duties in e-discovery. For a more specific example of the requirement to maintain ethical technology standards, see Illinois State Bar Association Advisory Opinion No. 18-01 (January 2018).

In addition to the discovery process, many courts now require that trials be conducted via the use of technology by the utilization of trial specific programs with laptops, tablets, smartphones, and other devices. Paralegals are vital in the management of electronic databases and electronic trial exhibits. Litigation attorneys and paralegals should be conversant in these technology programs and obtain the requisite training to use them effectively.

Lawyers can be subject to misconduct allegations related to e-discovery and trial technology for a general lack of technological sophistication, overzealous conduct, a lack of development of professional duties as an advocate, and legal incompetence.

In recent years, the use of generative Artificial Intelligence (AI) has proliferated. Discussions continue regarding the applicability and viability of AI and ChatGPT, a prototype for public use, in legal practice. A recent survey of law firm lawyers conducted by Thomson Reuters Institute showed that a large majority (82%) of those surveyed said they believe that ChatGPT and generative AI *can* be readily applied to legal work, and a slightly smaller majority (51%) said that ChatGPT and generative AI *should* be applied to legal work.

A myriad of ethical considerations exists related to the use of generative AI and ChatGPT. In a recent article, Nicole Black wrote that "a key part of learning about this emerging technology includes understanding its limitations and risks. Over time, as the technology improves and is incorporated into legal technology products specifically designed with the needs and compliance requirements of legal professionals in mind, the risks will be reduced." See *Leveraging ChatGPT In Legal Practice: Best Practices And Ethical Considerations*, abovethelaw.com (May 2023). At its 2023 midyear meeting, the ABA House of Delegates unanimously adopted a resolution that urged "organizations that design, develop, deploy, and use artificial intelligence ('AI') systems and capabilities to follow certain guidelines" and added that it "urges Congress, federal executive agencies, the Courts, and State legislatures and regulators, to follow these guidelines in legislation, legal decisions, and standards pertaining to AI." See ABA Resolution 604, adopted February 6, 2023.

It is yet to be determined how far generative AI and ChatGPT will be incorporated into daily legal practice, but ethics violations have already occurred. Consequently, a Texas federal judge recently added a requirement that any attorney appearing in his court must attest that "no portion of the filing was drafted by generative artificial intelligence," or if it was, that it was checked "by a human being." See *Mandatory Certification Regarding Generative Artificial Intelligence*, Judge Brantley Starr, United States District Court, Northern District of Texas. This directive was shortly adopted by another court in the same jurisdiction. See *In re Pleadings Using Generative Artificial Intelligence*, General Order 2023-05, United States Bankruptcy Court, Northern District of Texas, June 21, 2023. In a recent, widely reported case, a federal judge imposed $5,000 fines on two New York lawyers and a law firm for their submission of a brief containing fictitious legal research. The lawyers denied they acted in bad faith. In support of the sanction, the judge stated that the lawyers "abandoned their responsibilities when they submitted non-existent judicial opinions with fake quotes and citations created by the artificial intelligence tool ChatGPT, then continued to stand by the fake opinions after judicial orders called their existence into question." See *Mata v. Avianca, Inc.*, Case No. 1:22-cv-01461-PKC, United States District Court, Southern District of New York, June 22, 2023. In order to avoid these and other types of ethical dilemmas, the ABA "urges lawyers to keep informed about new and emerging technologies and protect digital products, systems, and data from unauthorized access, use, and modification." See ABA Resolution 609, adopted August 8, 2023.

REVIEW QUESTIONS

1. What are the three main ethics rules governing lawyers' relationships with judges?
2. What do the ABA Model Rules say about lawyers attempting to influence judges? What crime occurs when a lawyer tries to influence a judge?
3. Under what circumstances can a lawyer give a judge a gift?
4. Why are lawyers and their employees prohibited from having *ex parte* communications with judges?
5. What kinds of contact with jurors are prohibited by the ethics rules and why? What crime might be involved when a lawyer or paralegal tries to influence a juror?
6. What are the general rules about lawyers and their agents having contact with persons who already have a lawyer? Why? What are the exceptions?
7. What is the general rule about contact with persons who are not represented by counsel?
8. Do federal prosecutors follow federal or state ethics rules, such as those prohibiting contact with represented persons? Under what authority?
9. What is prohibited by the ethics rules on lawyers' contact with witnesses? What crimes might be committed in contact between lawyers and witnesses?
10. Is it ethical for a paralegal to prepare a witness for trial? What kinds of things do paralegals need to be careful about when they talk to witnesses?
11. What are the ethical and practical concerns when lawyers and paralegals talk to employees in the corporate setting?
12. What actions might constitute harassing a witness? What crime (or crimes) might be committed in addition to violations of ethics rules?
13. May a lawyer pay a witness to testify? What are the applicable restrictions?
14. May a lawyer pay an expert witness? May the amount be based on the outcome in the case?
15. May a paralegal research a prospective juror on the internet? May the paralegal "friend" the prospective juror on Facebook? What about researching a party or witness? What ethics rules apply?
16. What two important constitutional interests are being balanced in the ethics rules on trial publicity?
17. What kinds of extrajudicial statements are generally permitted by ethics rules? What kinds are prohibited?
18. May a lawyer have a paralegal speak to the press and reveal information about a pending case that the lawyer could not reveal under the ethics rules? Why or why not?

19. Why are prosecutors bound by additional ethics rules? Name four ethical duties that prosecutors have that other lawyers do not have.
20. What sanctions and remedies may be imposed for prosecutorial misconduct?
21. What are the ethical considerations related to the use of Generative Artificial Intelligence and ChatGPT?

DISCUSSION QUESTIONS AND HYPOTHETICALS

1. What would you do if your lawyer-employer asked you to invite a judge who was serving on one of your cases to a social event you were planning?
2. Can you ask a judge who is a friend of yours questions about a pending case? Why or why not?
3. Do you think lawyers and their employees should be prohibited from giving campaign contributions to judges? Why or why not? What restrictions, if any, might mitigate the potential for harm?
4. What would you do if your supervisor asked you to give a sealed note to a juror during a recess? What rules apply?
5. Why are lawyers not involved in a case prohibited from talking to jurors about the case?
6. What would you do if your supervising lawyer asked you to contact the opposing party in a divorce case to see if the spouses could meet without the lawyers present to work out an amicable settlement?
7. What would you do if a co-plaintiff who was not represented by your firm contacted you to discuss changing lawyers? What if the party wanted to discuss the merits of the case? The performance of his or her lawyer?
8. What would you do if you were interviewing a potential witness who did not have a lawyer, and you suddenly realized that she seemed to believe that you and your firm were representing her?
9. Suppose that one of your duties as a litigation paralegal is to prepare witnesses for trial. What would you do if you were preparing a witness and his or her story kept changing? What if the witness seemed to be changing the facts to be more favorable to your side? Suppose the witness, although generally favorable to your client, has some information that is adverse to your client. What do you tell the witness about how to handle this information while he or she is on the stand?
10. What would you do if you discovered that a client was sending anonymous threatening letters to a witness who planned to testify against her? Would it make any difference if you knew the witness's testimony would be false?

11. What would you do if you found out that your firm paid a witness, who was not an expert, a witness fee that was three times his normal salary?
12. Review the rules governing a lawyer's handling of client perjury. Do you think a lawyer should be bound to tell the court if her client commits perjury? Would you answer differently in criminal and civil cases? What does your jurisdiction's ethics rule say? Are there any cases on the issue in your jurisdiction?
13. What would you do if your supervising lawyer asked you to leak information to the press that you know is prohibited by ethics rules? Would it make any difference if you were certain that without press coverage of this information, your client was more likely to be unfairly convicted of a serious crime?
14. Suppose you work for the local prosecuting attorney. What would you do if you uncovered information that proved a criminal defendant in a case was innocent? What if you went to the supervising lawyer and she refused to drop the charges or to turn over the exculpatory evidence to the defendant's counsel?
15. What would you do if your supervisor, the prosecuting attorney, asked you to obtain a statement from a recently arrested person, and in doing so you discovered that the person had not been advised of their right to counsel? What if the accused had been advised of their right to counsel but had not yet been able to reach a lawyer?
16. Can a lawyer advise her client to clean up his Facebook page? What about changing the settings so that more postings are private? What ethics rules are implicated?

RESEARCH PROJECTS AND ASSIGNMENTS

1. Read, brief, and compare these three interesting cases about lawyers who were disciplined for criticizing judges: *Standing Committee v. Yagman*, 55 F.3d 1430 (9th Cir. 1995); *In re Green*, 11 P.3d 1078 (Colo. 2000); and *In re Koven*, 134 Cal. App. 4th 262, 35 Cal. Rptr. 3d 317 (2005). Consider also the reasoning of the federal court that upheld the Kentucky ethics rules on criticism of judges in *Berry v. Schmitt*, 688 F.3d. 290 (6th Cir. 2012).
2. Read and brief the following case on tape recording by a lawyer and compare it with ABA Formal Opinion 01-422 mentioned in this chapter: *Mississippi Bar v. Attorney ST*, 621 So. 2d 229 (Miss. 1993).
3. Read and brief the case of *Dayton Bar Association v. O'Brien*, 103 Ohio St. 3d 1 (2004), in which a lawyer implies to a client in a criminal matter that he could bribe a judge.
4. Does your state have ethics rules that govern communication with jurors after trial? Do you think lawyers should be able to interview jurors after a trial is over? Why or why not?

5. For a case applying the rules about communicating with unrepresented persons in a corporate setting, read *Snider v. Superior Court*, 113 Cal. App. 4th 1187, 7 Cal. Rptr. 3d 119 (2003), in which an order disqualifying a lawyer is vacated on appeal.
6. Does your jurisdiction have a statute that prohibits or limits the tape recording of conversations? What does it say about getting permission from the party or parties? About the admissibility of illegally tape-recorded conversations?
7. Does your state have a statute or court rule that addresses jurors' use of social media to communicate or research during a trial? See, for example, California Assembly Bill 141, adopted in 2011, which amended several sections of the Code of Civil Procedures and Penal Code.
8. What does your jurisdiction's ethics code say about extrajudicial statements or trial publicity? Do you think the rule strikes the right balance between free speech and fair trial? Have any lawyers in your jurisdiction been disciplined under the rule?
9. Obtain a copy of your state judicial canons and compare the relevant provisions to those for lawyers covered in this chapter.
10. Prosecutors were suspended for ripping pages out of opposing counsel's notebook during a deposition so that they could get a handwriting sample. To find out the rest of the facts and see what happened to the lawyers, read and brief *In re Winkler*, 834 N.E.2d 85 (Ind. 2005).
11. For a leading case on pretexting, see *Midwest Motor Sports v. Arctic Sales, Inc.*, 347 F.3d 693 (8th Cir. 2003). This case interprets Model Rule 8.4(c), concerning conduct involving dishonesty, fraud, deceit and misrepresentation, and finds the conduct in this case unethical and the evidence inadmissible. Also see New York Cty. Lawyers Association Formal Opinion 737 (2011), which supports a general prohibition on pretexting but allows some room for exceptions.
12. A California court found that a lawyer did not violate ethics rules when he used an investigator to interview employees who were potential witnesses in a sexual harassment case prior to the time the lawsuit was filed and when none of those interviewed were represented by counsel. *Jorgensen v. Taco Bell Corp.*, 50 Cal. App. 4th 1398, 58 Cal. Rptr. 2d 178 (1996). Do you agree with this ruling? Why or why not? Is there potential for ethics violations in this scenario?
13. Are there any recent cases in your state in which lawyers were disciplined or held in contempt for rudeness to the judge or opposing counsel? For some examples, see *In re McBurney*, 13 A.3d 654 (R.I. 2011) where the lawyer attacked opposing counsel in pleadings and *In re Anonymous*, 392 S.C. 328, 709 S.E.2d 633 (2011) in which a lawyer is issued a private Letter of Caution for an inflammatory e-mail that included a personal attack against a family member of opposing counsel.

14. What are a judge's obligations when using social media? See ABA Formal Opinion 2013-462.
15. What rules might be implicated if a prosecutor provides official letterhead to a debt collection company so that the company can write letters to debtors threatening prosecution? For a complete analysis, see ABA Formal Opinion 469 (2014).
16. How is evidence obtained from the Internet, including social media sites, properly authenticated? For cases on this evolving issue, see *Commonwealth v. Williams*, 926 N.E.2d 1162 (Mass. 2010), and *U.S. v. Vayner*, 769 F.3d. 125 (2d Cir. 2014).
17. Nearly 40 states have formally adopted the revised comment to ABA Model Rule 1.1, which requires lawyers to understand the use of technology as well as the tools necessary to obtain, process, and review information. Two federal court cases highlight the ever-increasing requirements related to minimum technology competency, especially for cases involving e-discovery. See *Branhaven v. Beeftek*, 965 F. Supp. 2d 650 (D. Md. 2013), and *In re Delta/Airtran Baggage Fee Antitrust Litigation*, 846 F. Supp. 2d 1335 (N.D. Ga. 2012).

CASES FOR ANALYSIS

In the following case, the court dismisses the complaint of a litigant who failed to move forward with this case. As you read, consider what conduct by a litigant might warrant this harsh sanction.

Bonda Industrial (HK) Co., Ltd. v. Talbot Group, LLC
08 Civ. 5507 (PKL) (U.S.D.C., S.D.N.Y. 2009)

Bonda initiated this action . . . in New York State Supreme Court alleging breach of contract, conversion, promissory estoppel, and unjust enrichment. Bonda's claims are based upon defendants' alleged failure to pay Bonda for certain clothing Bonda manufactured. Defendants removed the case to this Court. . . .

In their amended answer, defendants denied the majority of plaintiff's allegations and asserted counterclaims against Bonda and Wong for breach of contract, breach of warranty, conversion, and trademark infringement in connection with the promotion, marketing, and distribution of clothing using defendants' trademark.

As this Court explained during the . . . order to show cause hearing, to date, Bonda and Wong have not filed a reply to the counterclaims, due in large part to the fact that their attorney, Dwane Smith, Esq., cannot file pleadings on his clients' behalf as he is neither admitted to this Court, nor admitted to try this particular case *pro hac vice*. In addition, plaintiff has otherwise neglected to prosecute its claims, as demonstrated by its failure to respond adequately to, or to serve, discovery requests, or to otherwise advance this case.

Plaintiff's failure to prosecute is exacerbated by Mr. Smith's repeated misrepresentations to this Court as to his intentions to move the case forward. Time after time, the Court gave Mr. Smith and his client the benefit of the doubt, granting numerous extensions to allow Bonda and Wong time to file a reply to the counterclaims, and to otherwise demonstrate an intent to prosecute plaintiff's claims. As far back as July 21, 2008, Mr. Smith informed the Court by letter that he intended to seek admission *pro hac vice*, and he assured the Court that he would be following up on his application in the upcoming week. Based on this representation, the Court so ordered the parties' stipulation, granting plaintiff an additional twenty (20) days to respond to the counterclaims and for Mr. Smith to appear in the action. Plaintiff's requests for extensions were again granted . . . based upon the Court's understanding that Mr. Smith was trying to gain admission to this Court.

Mr. Smith's representations were not limited to written communications. At both the September . . . and November . . . pre-trial conferences, Mr. Smith assured the Court that he would promptly submit a *pro hac vice* application, and that his client intended to pursue its claims. On both occasions, the Court cautioned Mr. Smith that plaintiff's failure to prosecute this case would be grounds for dismissal under Rule 41(b) and pursuant to the Supreme Court's decision in *Link v. Wabash R.R. Co.*, 370 U.S. 626 (1962), and its progeny.

In a purported effort to address Mr. Smith's failure to gain admission to this Court, on November 10, 2008, Bonnie Mohr, Esq. filed a notice of appearance in this action. The notice provides, "Please take notice that the undersigned hereby appears in the above captioned action as counsel to the Law Offices of Dwane Smith PLLC." Notably, Ms. Mohr did not appear on behalf of Bonda and Wong. Prior to the November 25, 2008 pre-trial conference, Ms. Mohr informed the Court that she would be assisting Mr. Smith with electronic filing, as she was admitted to the Southern District of New York, but that Mr. Smith would continue to represent Bonda and Wong in the case. Ms. Mohr's notice of appearance was not accompanied by an application for Mr. Smith's *pro hac vice* admission, nor did her assistance impact plaintiff's lack of effort in the case.

By order to show cause, Talbot Group and Potamus Holding ask the Court to dismiss the case pursuant to Rule 41(b). Specifically, defendants contend that Mr. Smith's inability to gain admission to this Court or to move his client's case forward in any manner warrants dismissal. In the alternative, Talbot Group and Potamus Holding seek a default judgment against Bonda and Wong for their failure to respond to the counterclaims.

In opposition to defendants' motion, plaintiff's counsel emphasize that plaintiff has not missed any conferences, has not submitted any vexatious or burdensome filings to the Court, and that it is unlikely that defendants have suffered economic loss by plaintiff's delays. In addition, plaintiff's counsel submitted notice of a cross-motion, seeking leave of the Court to extend time to December 12, 2008, to allow Bonda and Wong to serve and file an answer to the counterclaims, to serve supplemental discovery responses, and to serve discovery demands. Moreover, Mr. Smith and Ms. Mohr submitted a signed consent to substitute Ira Meyerowitz, Esq. as attorney of record for Bonda and Wong.

As proposed substituted counsel, Mr. Meyerowitz attended the December 17, 2008 hearing. After reviewing plaintiff's abysmal record in this case, the Court specifically asked Mr. Meyerowitz whether he was prepared to get involved in this case in its current posture. Mr. Meyerowitz informed the Court that he was reluctant to get involved in this "hornet's nest" unless the Court was prepared to consider his participation a "clean break from the past."

Federal Rule of Civil Procedure 41(b) allows a district court to dismiss an action if a plaintiff fails to prosecute the case or fails to comply with orders of that court. The Second Circuit has outlined five factors that a district court must consider to determine whether dismissal pursuant to Rule 41 is appropriate, including: (1) the duration of plaintiff's failure to prosecute the case and/or comply with court orders; (2) whether plaintiff was on notice that further delay and/or continuing to disregard court orders would result in dismissal; (3) whether defendants would likely be prejudiced by further delay; (4) a balancing of the court's interest in managing its docket with plaintiff's right to an opportunity for a day in court; and (5) whether there are other lesser sanctions available to the court to remedy the situation. [Citations omitted.] . . .

In balancing these five factors, the Court is mindful that involuntary dismissal of a plaintiff's case is "a harsh remedy to be utilized only in extreme situations." [Citations omitted.] . . .

The first factor—the duration of plaintiff's delay and/or disregard of Court orders—favors dismissing plaintiff's case pursuant to Rule 41(b). Here, plaintiff's inexcusable behavior provides the Court with two alternative grounds to dismiss: (1) plaintiff and its counsel have failed to comply with specific orders of this Court for an unreasonable amount of time; and (2) there has been a complete lack of prosecution of this case for more than six months.

Without offering a reasonable excuse, plaintiff has failed to comply with the orders of this Court. At the September 4, 2008 pre-trial conference, the Court specifically instructed Mr. Smith to gain admission before this Court and to promptly move plaintiff's case along. The Court reiterated these directives at the November 25, 2008 pre-trial conference. Both orders were completely ignored until defendants brought the instant motion. In opposition to defendants' motion, plaintiff's only explanation for its failure to comply with this Court's orders is that Mr. Smith's financial constraints, the demands of his practice as a solo practitioner, and personal issues he faced impeded his ability to gain admission to this Court and to otherwise proceed with this case. Mr. Smith was responsible for bringing these facts to the Court's attention, rather than misrepresenting his intentions and ignoring the Court's directives. . . . While sympathetic to Mr. Smith's purported difficulties, the Court is not satisfied that Bonda has demonstrated any good faith efforts to comply with the orders that would excuse counsel's behavior. [Citation omitted.]

Moreover, while plaintiff's counsel argued to this Court that he is exclusively to blame for plaintiff's inactivity in this case, it is well established that a client is bound by the actions of his counsel. [Citations omitted.] Further, Bonda has not presented any evidence that its intention to pursue its claims was inhibited by its counsel's neglect. Rather, it appears that plaintiff put its head in the sand, allowing its counsel to file notices of appearance and substitution of counsel, but ignoring the fact that discovery was not served, that the counterclaims were not answered, and that there was no indication plaintiff's claims were progressing. In fact, Mr. Smith's only representations to this Court as to his client's participation in this case indicate difficulties he encountered in getting information from his client due to the fact that he contacted Wong too late, she was traveling, needed more time, and had laser surgery. As defendants argue . . . in opposing this motion to dismiss, Bonda had the opportunity to state clearly its intention to prosecute this case. Bonda's opposition, however, does not demonstrate that counsel's failures alone are to blame for the lack of progress in this suit.

Alternatively, plaintiff's claims must be dismissed because plaintiff has failed to prosecute this case since it has been pending before this Court. [Citation omitted.] For more than six months after the case was removed to this Court, plaintiff has failed to demonstrate any intent to advance its claims, or to defend against the counterclaims. Failing to prosecute these claims for more than six months is unreasonable, and grounds for dismissal. [Citations omitted.]

The Second Circuit has instructed district courts to consider whether plaintiff received notice that its failure to comply with Court orders and/or additional delays would result in dismissal. The Court finds that this factor supports dismissal. This Court emphasized at both the September and November pre-trial conferences that there is clear precedent allowing the Court to dismiss a case when plaintiff fails to prosecute its claims. The Court also reminded Mr. Smith that it was completely unacceptable for him to ignore his duty to gain admission to this Court. At both conferences, the Court cautioned that if plaintiff and its counsel continue to ignore their obligations, plaintiff's claims would be dismissed. As such, only after plaintiff disregarded these explicit warnings did the Court consider dismissing plaintiff's claims. [Citation omitted.] Moreover, the fact that the Court invited defendants to make this motion to dismiss by order to show cause demonstrates that plaintiff was on notice that the Court was contemplating dismissal. [Citations omitted.]

The third factor the Court considers in assessing whether plaintiff's claims should be dismissed is whether defendants would be prejudiced by further delay. Where, as here, delay is unreasonable, prejudice may be presumed as a matter of law. [Citations omitted.] Such a presumption is generally warranted because "delay by one party increases the likelihood that evidence in support of the other party's position will be lost and that discovery and trial will be made more difficult." [Citation omitted.]

While defendants need not show prejudice in this case, in considering this factor, the Court notes that defendants have offered uncontested evidence of the prejudice they have suffered because of plaintiff's behavior. In particular, defendants offered uncontroverted evidence that Wong knew that defendants were trying to finalize a business arrangement, but that the ongoing stalemate in this litigation was preventing the deal [from closing]. . . .

The fourth factor requires the Court to strike a "balance between [its] calendar congestion and the plaintiff's right to an opportunity to be heard." [Citation omitted.] The Court is always reluctant to deprive a plaintiff of a chance to litigate its claims, but finds that this case is an example of a "rare occasion" where such deprivation is warranted. [Citation omitted.] Because of plaintiff's lack of prosecutorial activity in this case, this Court was forced to consider several requests for extensions and to hold three pre-trial conferences discussing plaintiff's failures. Thus, the Court devoted significant time and resources to this case. At no time, however, did plaintiff demonstrate its intent to comply with Court orders or illustrate that it was not burdening this Court's docket with a case that it did not intend to prosecute. [Citation omitted.]

Moreover, plaintiff could have avoided this dismissal if it made any attempt to comply with the orders of this Court and advance this case. Instead, plaintiff's right to its day in court is diminished by plaintiff's and plaintiff's counsel's recalcitrance. [Citations omitted.]

In evaluating the fifth and final factor, the Court considers the appropriateness of alternative sanctions. . . . After considering the option of sanctioning the attorneys and/or plaintiff directly, the Court finds that such sanction would be insufficient to remedy this situation. . . .

Despite Mr. Smith's assurances to the contrary, plaintiff provided no evidence to indicate that it was not complicit in counsel's failures. . . . This Court will not ignore six months of inactivity, misrepresentations, and disregard of Court orders to the defendants' detriment.

The Court is mindful of the fact that sanctioning lawyers directly might be a more appropriate sanction when the delay is occasioned by plaintiff's counsel's disregard of their obligations rather than by plaintiff's own behavior or strategy. [Citation omitted.] Here, however, plaintiff's counsel's egregious behavior in the face of the Court's repeated warnings, coupled with the lack of any evidence of good faith efforts by plaintiff to advance its claims, leaves dismissal as the only possible remedy. [Citation omitted.] This Court will not penalize defendants for plaintiff's failures. [Citation omitted.]

For the foregoing reasons, defendants' motion to dismiss is hereby GRANTED, and plaintiff's claims are DISMISSED with prejudice. Plaintiff's cross-motion for leave of this Court for additional time to supplement discovery responses and to serve discovery demands is DENIED AS MOOT, to the extent those requests pertain to plaintiff's claims. This decision does not, however, dismiss or otherwise limit defendants' counterclaims. To the extent defendants intend to pursue their counterclaims, the parties are ordered to appear before this Court for a pre-trial conference. . . .

Questions about the Case

1. How long was the delay in pursuing this case? Does that seem like a long time to you?
2. What were the five factors that the court considered in deciding whether to dismiss? Which were the most compelling in this case?
3. What does *pro hac vice* mean? What were the roles of the other two lawyers who were involved on the plaintiff's side in this case? Why was their involvement not sufficient to save the case from dismissal?
4. Does the plaintiff have a cause of action against this lawyer? What did this court say about the plaintiff's role in the dismissal?

In the following case, the lawyers on both sides missed the controlling legal authority at the trial court and the matter had to be corrected after an incorrect ruling was made.

Massey v. Prince George's County
907 F. Supp. 138 (D. Md. 1995)

. . . Plaintiff Willie Massey alleges that in the early morning hours of November 4, 1992 he was sleeping in a vacant or abandoned building in Cheverly, Maryland. He contends that all of a sudden he was awakened by Prince George's County police officers who, without warning, set their police dog upon him. Massey says that although he offered no resistance, the animal proceeded to bite him and inflict painful and permanent injury all over his body. In his Third Amended Complaint before the Court, Massey has sued the individual officers for assault and battery under Maryland law and for deprivation of his Fourth Amendment rights, i.e., for use of excessive force, under 42 U.S.C. §1983. The officers have denied liability, claiming that Massey was warned about the dog in a loud voice and that he resisted their efforts to arrest him.

Earlier in these proceedings, Defendants filed a fifteen page Motion for Summary Judgment to which excerpts from depositions of Plaintiff and various officers were appended. With regard to the Section 1983 claims, Defendants argued that their seizure of Plaintiff and the force used by them were reasonable as a matter of law. After citing general Supreme Court law regarding such claims, defense counsel invited the Court's attention to the case of *Robinette v. Barnes*, 854 F.2d 909 (6th Cir. 1988), in which the U.S. Court of Appeals for the Sixth Circuit concluded that the use of a trained police dog in circumstances comparable to those in the case at bar was reasonable as a matter of law. . . .

In the present case, Plaintiff's Response to Defendants' Motion for Summary Judgment consisted of a single page, his Statement of Material Facts in Dispute barely more than two. In these, Plaintiff's counsel cited one case and one alone, namely the *Robinette* case already cited by defense counsel, which Plaintiff's counsel did no more than attempt to distinguish on its facts.

When the matter came on for oral argument, defense counsel again argued the applicability of *Robinette* to the present case, while Plaintiff's counsel again tried to distinguish *Robinette* on its facts, offering no further citation to authority.

At the conclusion of oral argument, largely on the strength of *Robinette*, the Court announced its decision to dismiss the two counts of excessive force, finding the officers' actions reasonable as a matter of law. What remained open, however, was the issue of whether Plaintiff's state law cause of action for assault and battery could survive in the face of the Court's ruling with regard to the two federal constitutional torts. . . .

Defense counsel has now submitted a one-page letter brief in conformity with the Court's request. Plaintiff's counsel has submitted a six-page letter which, while it comports with the Court's directive in part, in effect invites the Court to reconsider its dismissal of the two federal constitutional counts. Plaintiff seems to understand that his request for reconsideration is out of order at this time, but there is a feature of counsel's letter that cannot go unremarked even now. The critical feature is that for the first time Plaintiff's counsel cites legal authority directly on point to the case at bar. The case, *Kopf v. Wing*, 942 F.2d 265 (4th Cir. 1991), is not only an excessive force case involving a police dog, but is the controlling law in this Circuit. As the Court will discuss presently, that case clearly mandates denial of Defendants' Motion for Summary Judgment, which is to say reinstatement of the excessive force claims the Court recently dismissed. But the fact that *Kopf* has been cited for the first time by Plaintiff's counsel in a supplemental letter—well after the filing of his threadbare initial response to Defendants' Motion for Summary Judgment and his equally scant oral argument on the motion—is a cause for considerable concern. At the same time, the fact that this case has never been cited by defense counsel in his initial pleadings, in oral argument or indeed to this day, gives cause for even greater concern. . . .

The parallels between *Kopf* and the case at bar are striking and need little elaboration. The Court accepts without question that, on the authority of *Kopf*, Plaintiff ought to have prevailed as against Defendants' Motion for Summary Judgment. Notwithstanding this, neither Plaintiff's nor Defendants' counsel brought the case to the Court's attention even through oral argument. Thereafter, only Plaintiff's counsel, never defense counsel, cited the case, and then only because the Court had directed briefing on another point of law. . . .

One must assume that had Plaintiff's counsel, in preparing his initial Opposition to the Motion for Summary Judgment, exhibited the same degree of diligence that ultimately permitted him to locate the case in untimely fashion, he could have located the case in timely fashion. Instead, counsel offered only the sketchiest statement of grounds, reflecting a bare minimum of legal research, showing every sign of having been dictated on the run. The net effect of this truncated effort was to consume valuable court time in oral argument and the preparation of supplemental briefs (not to mention preparation of the present Opinion), all of which could have been avoided by earlier diligence on counsel's part. Counsel appears to have forgotten two of the most fundamental rules of professional conduct. First, Rule of Professional Conduct 1.1 provides that:

> [a] lawyer shall provide competent representation to a client. Competent representation requires the legal knowledge, skill, thoroughness and preparation reasonably necessary for the representation. . . .

The other Rule of Professional Conduct counsel has apparently misplaced is Rule 1.3 which holds that "[a] lawyer shall act with reasonable diligence and promptness in representing a client." Failure to pursue applicable legal authority in timely fashion may well constitute a violation of this rule.

The action of defense counsel in this case raises a far more serious concern. It is possible that defense counsel also overlooked the *Kopf* precedent, but if he did, the oversight was glaring and extremely troublesome. *Kopf* not only deals with a claim of excessive force against police where a police dog was involved; individual Prince George's County police officers and the County itself were defendants in that case. Indeed, at least one attorney for Prince George's County in *Kopf*, as shown in the reported case, was an individual, whom the Court judicially notices, was still in the County Attorney's office at the time of the filing of the present Motion for Summary Judgment.

The regrettable inference is that defense counsel in the instant case may in fact have deliberately failed to disclose to the Court directly controlling authority from this Circuit. If so, the action would constitute a clear violation of the Rules of Professional Conduct.

Thus, Rule 3.3(a)(3) provides that "a lawyer shall not knowingly . . . fail to disclose to the tribunal legal authority in the controlling jurisdiction known to the lawyer to be directly adverse to the position of the client and not disclosed by opposing counsel." In federal court, the "controlling jurisdiction" is the circuit in which the district court sits. *Hazard & Hodes, op. cit.* §3.3.207. Particularly disturbing is the type of case encountered here—a litigant who was an unsuccessful party to a directly relevant adverse precedent who has failed to cite that precedent to the court. [Citations omitted.] . . .

Under the circumstances, the Court will direct defense counsel to show cause to the Court in writing within thirty (30) days why citation to the *Kopf* case was omitted from his Motion for Summary Judgment, oral argument, and indeed from any pleading or communication to date.

The Court also recollects that in the last several months counsel for Prince George's County was before the Court in at least one other police dog excessive force case in which a Motion for Summary Judgment in favor of the County was granted. It may be that *Kopf* was omitted from the pleading in that proceeding as well. Accordingly, the Court directs defense counsel and the Office of the Prince George's County attorney, within sixty (60) days to disclose to the Court the status of that case and any and all police dog excessive force cases involving Prince George's County that were pending as of August 9, 1991, the date *Kopf* was decided by the Fourth Circuit, or that have been filed from that date to the present. The Court's Show-Cause Order, entered simultaneously with this Opinion, spells out the information that is to be provided. Any further sanctions that may be imposed by the Court will depend on the County's showing of cause pursuant to this directive.

Enough has been said for now. No formal Motion for Reconsideration need be filed by Plaintiff's counsel since, as indicated, *Kopf* clearly dictates reinstatement of the excessive force claims. In consequence, the state court claim for assault and battery also remains in the case. . . .

Questions about the Case

1. What was the disposition of the case at the hearing on the summary judgment? On what case did the court rely and what did it hold?
2. What was the correct statement of the law? What happened to the case as a result of this ruling?
3. Why does it appear that the plaintiff's counsel did not cite the case? Why did the defense not cite the case?
4. What are the possible ethical violations of both the lawyers involved? Which is most egregious?
5. What remedy is the court likely to impose on the lawyers if they cannot justify their actions? What disciplinary sanction do you think might be appropriate? Why do courts disapprove of this particular ethical violation so strongly?

The following case illustrates how the advocacy rules may apply even when there is no lawsuit pending. The attorney who is being disciplined in this case engages in more than one kind of the prohibited conduct discussed in this chapter. He claims that nonlawyers in his office were partly responsible.

Crane v. State Bar of California
30 Cal. 3d 117, 635 P.2d 163, 177 Cal. Rptr. 670
(1981)

. . . 1. *The Mercury Case*

Representing the sellers of a residence, in April 1978 petitioner sought and obtained from Mercury Savings and Loan Association (Mercury), the beneficiary under a first trust deed, a beneficiary statement describing the status and indebtedness of the underlying loan. Without either the consent or knowledge of Mercury, he then "crossed out" certain printed material included in the statement by Mercury. The deleted language gave notice that Mercury intended to enforce an acceleration clause in the note and deed of trust unless it received an assumption agreement executed by any purchaser of the premises. Petitioner subsequently forwarded the altered statement to the escrow company handling the sale, describing it as "the Beneficiary Statement from the . . . lender on your escrow," and without notifying that company that the deletions were made by him and were wholly unauthorized.

The State Bar Court found petitioner's conduct in this regard to be [willful], improper and a dishonest act under the statute.

2. *The Robinson Case*

In December 1978 petitioner communicated with counsel for Mr. and Mrs. Robinson both by telephone and by mail in connection with the unrecorded claim of petitioner's client to real property which was subject to a trust deed then being foreclosed by the Robinsons. Both orally and in writing, the Robinsons' attorney specifically advised petitioner that he represented the Robinsons. Thereafter, petitioner's office sent two letters directly to the Robinsons without notifying their lawyer. The first—which apparently was a "follow-up" to a still earlier letter sent to the Robinsons before petitioner had been contacted by their lawyer—repeated a request for a beneficiary statement on their trust deed and offered to "waive" the $100 statutory penalty if it was received promptly. The second, sent seven days later, demanded that the Robinsons forward "forthwith" the $100 and the beneficiary statement. It stated further that if the statement was not received within five days, an action would be commenced against the Robinsons to recover both damages and the forfeiture, and that "the Department of Savings and Loan and the Attorney General's office will be requested to assist us in solution." A notation on the last letter indicated that copies were being sent to a named commissioner of the Department of Savings and Loan and to a named deputy attorney general. The letters were on petitioner's legal stationery and purported to be signed by him.

The State Bar Court found that petitioner's direct communication with the Robinsons despite his knowledge that they were represented by a lawyer was a clear violation of rule 7-103 of the Rules of Professional Conduct, and that his final letter to them constituted an impermissible threat in violation of rule 7-104.

Discussion

With respect to the Mercury matter, petitioner admits both his unauthorized alteration of the beneficiary statement and his failure to advise the escrow company that the deletion was his, and not that of the beneficiary or trustee under the trust deed. He denies, however, that he was "dishonest," arguing that he had no intent to deceive the escrow company, but merely sought to prevent Mercury from improperly interfering with the prospective sale by asserting demands which Mercury had no right to make in the beneficiary statement.

We reject petitioner's disavowal of any dishonest intent. Even if we assume for purposes of argument that Mercury endangered the successful closing of escrow by asserting a right which it did not have, any such risk could be removed or minimized *only* if the reader of the statement believed the acceleration language was deleted by Mercury itself. The circumstances of petitioner's unauthorized unilateral alteration were deceptive and known by him to be so. . . .

In the Robinson matter, petitioner also admitted in a stipulation of facts filed with the State Bar Court his "technical violation" of rule 7-103 of the Rules of Professional Conduct by communicating directly with the Robinsons despite his awareness that they were represented by counsel. He now contends, however, that the letters to the Robinsons requesting, and then demanding, the beneficiary statement and statutory penalty, and threatening suit and action by state officials, were not "upon a subject of controversy" and that his client and the Robinsons were not "adverse parties" within the meaning of that rule.

There was substantial evidence to the contrary, however, including testimony of the Robinsons' lawyer that he had discussed with petitioner the adverse interest of the parties in connection with the foreclosure of the trust deed, and beyond that evidence, the contents of the letters themselves belie petitioner's claims.

We similarly reject petitioner's asserted excuse that any violation of rule 7-103 was inadvertent and precipitated by members of his staff. Acknowledging negligence in failing properly to prevent direct contact with represented parties by correspondence on his letterhead and over his purported signature, petitioner contends that the discipline proposed for that negligence is unduly severe. Petitioner's attempt to avoid the blame for his violation of the Rules of Professional Conduct is unconvincing. An attorney is responsible for the work product of his employees which is performed pursuant to his direction and authority. The legal onus for the violation of rule 7-103 rests upon petitioner alone. . . .

Accordingly, it is ordered that Fred R. Crane be suspended from the practice of law in this state for a period of one year. . . .

Questions about the Case

1. Describe the acts that constituted breaches of ethics in the *Mercury* and *Robinson* cases. What ethical principles presented in this chapter do these acts offend?
2. What was attorney Crane's defense in the *Mercury* matter? How did the court handle this defense?
3. What were Crane's defenses in the *Robinson* case? How did the court handle them?
4. Was Crane aware of the correspondence with the Robinsons? Would it have made any difference whether he knew it or not?
5. What sanction was imposed? Do you think it was appropriate?

In the *Omaha Bank* case that follows, an appellate court examines the decision of a lower court that refused to replace a juror after the juror had contact with the defendant's attorneys outside the courtroom. As you read, consider whether this incident might also give rise to a disciplinary action.

Omaha Bank v. Siouxland Cattle Cooperative
305 N.W.2d 458 (Iowa 1981)

Siouxland Cattle Cooperative (Siouxland) appeals from an adverse judgment on its damage claim in a law action for fraud against Omaha Bank for Cooperatives (Omaha Bank) and Robert Zuber, a bank officer, and from the trial court's order for a sheriff's deed to the bank in a foreclosure action. Siouxland claims that the trial court erred in failing to replace a juror with an alternate, in its instructions to the jury, and in ruling that Siouxland has lost a right of redemption from the foreclosure sale. . . .

After a day at trial on March 3, 1980, Omaha Bank's lawyers, Robert J. Banta and Gerald P. Laughlin, stopped for dinner in Merrill, Iowa. After finishing dinner, they entered the bar portion of the restaurant to pay their bill. Juror Adamson was seated at the bar. He offered to buy the lawyers a drink and they declined. Adamson was insistent and offered again. The lawyers then sat at a booth near the bar and received a drink, courtesy of Adamson. Adamson introduced the lawyers to other patrons and they all conversed about various subjects. There is no evidence that the pending trial was discussed.

On March 6 attorney Laughlin informed the court, in the presence of lawyers for other parties, of the contact with juror Adamson. We do not have a transcript of the meeting but apparently the trial court concluded that nothing improper had occurred.

On March 11 Siouxland's attorney, Steven A. Carter, reported to the court that he had advised his client to move for a mistrial because of the misconduct. Carter also stated that Siouxland did not want a mistrial and wanted to proceed with the jury. Because Siouxland would not follow Carter's advice to move for a mistrial, Carter requested the court, before the case was submitted to the jury, to remove Adamson and replace him with an alternate juror under Iowa R. Civ. P. 189, as then in effect. The trial court denied the request, stating, "I said at the time there was nothing wrong with it and found that, and I do now." The court also indicated that a motion for a mistrial was the only proper procedure to follow.

After the jury returned a verdict for the bank and Zuber, Siouxland moved for a new trial because of misconduct by juror Adamson, who had become foreman of the jury. Iowa R. Civ. P. 244(b). The trial court overruled the motion primarily because Siouxland had not moved for a mistrial during trial.

The juror's offer of drinks and the lawyers' acceptance was clearly misconduct by all of them. Adamson, in speaking to the lawyers and offering and buying them drinks, violated the standard admonition given by the court to refrain from contact with the lawyers involved in the case. The bank's lawyers violated their ethical obligation prohibiting communication with a juror during trial unless it is in the course of official proceedings. Iowa Code of Professional Responsibility DR 7-108(B) and (C).

Omaha Bank and Zuber apparently concede that the contact was misconduct but argue that Siouxland has waived any claim for a new trial. The waiver argument is based on Siouxland's refusal to move for a mistrial after discovering the misconduct. A party learning during trial of misconduct by a juror must complain to the trial court rather than wait for the outcome and then move for a new trial after losing.

Siouxland declined to move for a mistrial during trial. The record does not indicate, however, that Siouxland elected to wait until the adverse verdict before complaining to the court about the misconduct. Rather, before the case was submitted for jury decision, Siouxland requested the court to replace Adamson with an available alternate. Iowa R. Civ. P. 189, The Code 1979. We conclude that Siouxland adequately made its record to the court by requesting that an alternate replace the offending juror. . . .

In this case, we conclude that the trial court abused its discretion because there is not substantial evidence to support a finding that the contact was not prejudicial to Siouxland. Adamson and the lawyers did not merely meet and exchange greetings, but rather had an extended conversation. [Citations omitted.] The lawyers accepted a drink and participated with the juror in the gathering in the bar. The circumstances surrounding the contact are the only bases upon which to determine whether the contact may have influenced the juror or the jury.

In addition, we conclude that the fraud claim must be retried to "zealously [guard] the utter independence of jurors." *State v. Carey*, 165 N.W.2d 27, 29 (Iowa 1969). We simply cannot allow a foreman of a jury to purchase drinks during trial for lawyers representing a party. In cases of such gross impropriety, even if the meeting were unintentional, we are not only concerned with injustice to particular litigants but also with the appearance of impropriety that casts doubt on our jury system. Attempts to ingratiate one side to a juror by extended conversation and acceptance of drinks must be condemned. . . .

Questions about the Case

1. What ethics rule did the attorneys violate in this case? Could their acts have been grounds for discipline?
2. Exactly what contact did the bank's attorneys have with the juror Adamson? Who instigated the contact? Did they discuss the case? Does it matter? Why or why not?
3. Why wasn't a mistrial declared when the trial judge discovered the contact? Why wasn't the juror replaced? When was the trial judge informed of this conduct?
4. As the juror and attorneys did not discuss the case, what is the potential prejudice to the other party?
5. What reasons does the court give for reversing the decision of the lower court? With which court do you agree? Why?

This case arises from civil litigation in which a paralegal claims that false evidence was admitted. The court explains how a paralegal has the same duties as a lawyer to prevent false evidence from being admitted in a case and protects the paralegal who revealed the unethical actions of her employer.

Eaton v. Fink
697 N.E.2d 490 (Ind. Ct. App. 1998)

Mark Van Eaton filed a Complaint for Damages for Defamation against Donna Fink. . . .

. . . This suit arises from statements made by Fink in connection with another case, *Kirchoff v. Selby*. . . . Fink worked as a legal assistant for attorney Dean Richards, who represented the Selbys. Attorney Patrick Shoulders represented the Kirchoffs. A jury awarded the Selbys $730,000.00. Before the trial court entered the judgment on the verdict, Fink informed Shoulders that she had manufactured an exhibit on behalf of the Selbys, at Richards' request, in order to rehabilitate Van Eaton's testimony. She also stated that Van Eaton had testified falsely when he claimed, on rebuttal, that he had made notes regarding the differences between Exhibit 10 and Exhibit 12 prior to trial. In addition, Fink claimed that she has assisted Richards in the fabrication of Exhibit 61, a Stock Exchange and Subscription Agreement. After her sworn statement was taken before a notary, Fink sent a copy via facsimile to Richards.

The Kirchoffs filed a motion to correct error based on newly discovered evidence. . . . The trial court granted the Kirchoffs' motion and ordered a new trial. Cross appeals were filed, and we affirmed the trial court's judgment. . . . [T]he case is now pending before our supreme court. . . .

On the same day the Kirchoffs filed their motion to correct error, Van Eaton filed this defamation suit against Fink. Fink responded that her statements were privileged and filed a motion for judgment on the pleadings. . . . The court agreed and granted Fink's motion for summary judgment.

Indiana law affords absolute privilege to statements made in the course of a judicial proceeding. . . . We hold that the rule also applies to communications subsequent to a judicial proceeding, provided that the communication is related to the proceeding, made in good faith and in contemplation of further proceedings before the trial court or on appeal.

Here, although the *Kirchoff v. Selby* trial had ended, the trial court's judgment was not yet final. Fink's statement to Shoulders, which contained allegations that she had falsified a document at the direction of Richards during trial and that Van Eaton had lied regarding the falsified document during cross-examination, was made in contemplation that the Kirchoffs would request a new trial based on that information. Thus, Fink's statement to Shoulders is entitled to absolute privilege.

Fink concedes that the separate defamation that occurred when she separately published the statement via facsimile to Richards is not entitled to absolute privilege. Instead she maintains that qualified privilege applies.

The doctrine of qualified privilege protects "communications made in good faith on any subject matter in which the party making the communication has an interest or in reference to which he has a duty, either public or private, either legal or moral, or social, if made to a person having a corresponding interest or duty." [Citation omitted.] . . .

The defendant has the burden to establish the existence of a privileged occasion for the publication by proof of a recognized public or private interest which would justify the utterance of the words. Once the existence of the privilege is established, the burden shifts to the plaintiff to prove that the defendant abused the privilege. Abuse is shown when: (1) the communicator was primarily motivated by ill will . . . ; (2) there was excessive publication . . . ; or (3) the statement was made without belief or grounds for belief in its truth. [Citation omitted.]

Here, as Richards' legal assistant, Fink was required to conform to the same standards as an attorney. See Rule of Professional Conduct, Guideline 9.10(j) (legal assistant shall be governed by the American Bar Association Model Code of Professional Responsibility and American Bar Association Model Rules of Professional Conduct). An attorney shall not unlawfully obstruct another's parties access to evidence or unlawfully alter, destroy or conceal a document or other material having potential evidentiary value. Ind. Prof. Con. R. 3.4. A lawyer shall not counsel or assist another person to do any such act. Id. A lawyer shall not knowingly make a false statement of material fact to a tribunal or offer evidence the lawyer knows to be false. Ind. Prof. Con. R. 3.3(a)(1) and (2). Fink's statement contained allegations that she and Richards had falsified evidence presented to the court at the trial. Assuming that Fink and Richards had engaged in the conduct described by Fink, Fink and Richards would have corresponding legal, moral, and social duties to correct the injustice that resulted from their behavior. . . .

Still, Van Eaton contends that Fink abused her qualified privilege because her statement was motivated primarily by ill will and without belief in its truth. In support of his contention, Van Eaton directs us to the one-paragraph supplemental affidavit of Richards and claims that it demonstrates that Fink made her statements in an attempt to extort money from the Selbys. The affidavit states:

> That during an argument [Richards] had with Donna Fink . . . she stated that she was going to [accuse Richards and an associate] of raping her and . . . manufacturing false documents. She named numerous documents . . . that she felt could have been manufactured. . . . [S]ome of the documents were Exhibit 12 . . . and Exhibit 61. She mentioned numerous other exhibits that were admitted at the trial. She stated that Mark Van Eaton, Jeff and Diane Selby, Richards [and others] would be in serious trouble.

Van Eaton mischaracterizes the supplemental affidavit. Although the affidavit shows that Fink was upset with Richards, it does not demonstrate that she attempted to extort money from anyone. Further, we cannot infer from the affidavit that Fink's statement was motivated by "ill will" or that she did not believe in the truth of her statements. Rather the supplemental affidavit indicates that she believed that the documents were manufactured. . . . [W]e conclude that the trial court properly granted summary judgment in favor of Fink.

Affirmed.

Questions about the Case

1. What kind of false evidence was presented in this case? If the paralegal Fink is telling the truth, what were the roles of the lawyer Richards, the witness Van Eaton, and herself in this matter?
2. When in the case did Fink raise the issues of the false evidence and testimony? Why does this matter?
3. What happened to the parties to the case where the false evidence was presented?
4. What ethics rules were violated? What could happen to the lawyer? To Fink? To Van Eaton?
5. What was cited by the court in holding that Fink had a duty relating to the false evidence?
6. Why is this case important for paralegals?

In this case, a lawyer is disciplined for directing a nonlawyer, his investigator, to pose as a journalist to interview an unrepresented person likely to be named as an adverse party.

In re Ositis
333 Or. 366, 40 P.3d 500 (2002)

. . . In 1989, the accused represented Hickey, who bought and sold animals for medical research, in proceedings before the United States Department of Agriculture. Hickey's business had been targeted by animal rights activists, and Hickey felt that he was in some personal danger. The accused introduced Hickey to Stevens, a private investigator, who initially was hired to provide security for Hickey and his wife at [a] . . . hearing.

After the hearing, Settlemier, who owned a farm that was directly adjacent to Hickey's business, spoke to television news reporters, and her statements were later televised. Hickey and the accused knew Settlemier, and knew that she strongly opposed Hickey's business. Hickey and the accused believed that Settlemier was permitting animal rights activists to use her property as a base of operations for observing and "raiding" Hickey's facilities. . . .

[O]n November 7, 1989, Stevens, the private investigator, telephoned Settlemier, introduced himself as a reporter for the International

News Services, and asked if Settlemier would answer some questions about Hickey's animal research supply business. . . .

Settlemier agreed to the interview, and Stevens questioned her at length about the factual basis for her comments to the news reporters . . . to the effect that Hickey's business was involved in animal abuse and pet theft. Stevens tape-recorded his conversation with Settlemier without her knowledge and permission. He never informed Settlemier that he was gathering information for Hickey and the accused.

After the interview, Stevens shared what he had learned from Settlemier with the accused. Several years later, Settlemier's tape-recorded statements were used as impeachment evidence in a defamation action that Hickey brought against her. Settlemier's lawyer later complained to the Bar that the accused had violated his ethical duties by participating in a scheme to obtain information from Settlemier by deceitful means. The present disciplinary proceedings against the accused followed. . . .

[Ositis] contends, specifically, that DR 1-102(A)(3) [which says that lawyers may not engage in conduct involving dishonesty, fraud, deceit, or misrepresentation] should not be interpreted to apply to misrepresentations made directly or indirectly by a lawyer that go solely to the lawyer's identity and purpose and that are made for the purpose of gathering information from potential adversaries before the institution of a legal action.

The accused's arguments in that regard focus on the same concerns that this court considered in *In re Gatti*, 330 Or. 517, 8 P.3d 966 (2000). That is, the accused argues that use of this limited sort of misrepresentation is a common and longstanding practice among lawyers, that an exception from the broad disciplinary rule prohibiting misrepresentation is necessary if lawyers are to succeed in discovering and rooting out wrongful conduct, that legal scholars and other jurisdictions have concluded that such limited deception is not unethical, and that the Bar's enforcement practices strongly suggest that identical conduct by government lawyers is ethical. This court rejected those arguments in *Gatti*, noting that ". . . the wording of DR 1-102(A)(3) . . . , and this court's case law does not permit recognition for an exception for any lawyer." . . .

[T]he evidence clearly and convincingly shows that . . . the accused had the undisclosed facts of Stevens's purpose and connection in mind and knew that those facts were material to Settlemier's decision to be interviewed. The ruse was a misrepresentation by nondisclosure. . . .

The accused argues, however, that, even if certain of Stevens's action would—if committed by a lawyer—violate DR 1-102(A)(3), the trial panel erred in concluding that any of Stevens's representations to Settlemier can be attributed to him. In that regard, the accused denies that Stevens was working for him when Stevens interviewed Settlemier or that he otherwise controlled Stevens's actions with regard to the interview. . . .

DR 1-102(A)(1) . . . expands the realm of accountability: It makes lawyers accountable not only if their **own** acts violate the rules, but also if they violate a rule "through the acts of another." . . .

[W]e conclude that the evidence clearly and convincingly shows that the accused made misrepresentations to Settlemier "through the acts of another." . . . Our conclusion arises . . . out of the undisputed fact that the accused suggested a particular line of inquiry to Stevens, knowing that Stevens intended to represent himself to Settlemier as a reporter, not as a private investigator. . . .

The accused is reprimanded.

Questions about the Case

1. Is it clear who the investigator Stevens was working for—the lawyer or the client? Did it make a difference to the outcome?
2. Was the status of the investigator similar to that of a paralegal who might contact a possible adversary?
3. What ethics rules were violated? What is the equivalent rule in the Model Rules?
4. Are there other rules that may have been violated; for example, contact with unrepresented persons?
5. The lawyer seems to think that what he did was a standard investigative technique. Do you agree? What about his claim that lawyers need to be able to use ruses such as this one to investigate thoroughly?
6. Do you think that the tape recording in the case may have been illegal? Why did the court not consider this?

In this case, the lawyers for a paralegal who sues her former firm finds the court objects to the firm's conduct in the case.

Sayhers v. Prugh
560 F.3d 1241 (11th Cir. 2009)

Plaintiff worked as a paralegal at the law firm Prugh, Holliday & Karatinos, P.L. After she left the firm, she retained her own lawyer. Then she sued Prugh, Holliday & Karatinos, P.L. and its named partners (Defendants) for alleged violations of the overtime provisions of the FLSA; she claimed that she was not paid appropriately—at a rate at least 1.5 times her straight-time rate—for hours worked in excess of 40 per workweek. Before filing the suit, Plaintiff made no written demand for payment on Defendants; and her lawyer—before filing the complaint—made no attempt to inform Defendants of her claim or to collect any of the allegedly outstanding sums from them. Plaintiff had instructed her lawyer just to file suit, which he did. Defendants timely answered the complaint and denied all liability.

The complaint set forth only a generic request for damages: no specific dollar amount was demanded. So Defendants served discovery on Plaintiff that asked her to disclose the total number of over-time hours she allegedly worked without sufficient pay and all evidence supporting that calculation. Plaintiff, however, objected to those requests and repeated that she worked in excess of 40 hours per workweek and wanted payment for it. Defendants also engaged in settlement discussions. But those talks proved unhelpful, as Plaintiff asked for significant money damages without offering proof of the amount Defendants actually owed to her.

Sometime after discovery closed, Defendants tendered an offer of judgment under Federal Rule of Civil Procedure 68 for $3,500 plus any attorney's fees and costs to which the district court determined Plaintiff was entitled. Defendants denied all liability in the Rule 68 offer. Plaintiff accepted the Rule 68 offer. The district court entered judgment in favor of Plaintiff and afforded her an opportunity to file a motion for attorney's fees and costs.

Plaintiff, through her lawyer, timely moved for her litigation expenses. She asked the district court to award her $13,800 in attorney's fees and $1,840.70 in costs. Defendants objected.

On its own initiative, the district court scheduled oral argument on the issue. At that hearing, the district court asked Plaintiff's lawyer, among other things, to respond to Defendants' contention that he afforded Defendants no notice of Plaintiff's claim before filing suit. Plaintiff's lawyer admitted that the allegation was true. The lawyer's sole explanation was that he was only following the instructions of his client. After reviewing the parties' briefs and hearing oral argument (allowing the district court to interrogate Plaintiff's lawyer and to observe his demeanor), the district court concluded that Plaintiff had prevailed in the civil action. But the district court denied attorney's fees and costs. The district court wrote that "there are some cases in which a reasonable fee is no fee" and found that this case was such a case. This appeal followed. . . .

In general, a prevailing FLSA plaintiff is entitled to an award of some reasonable attorney's fees and costs. 29 U.S.C. §216(b) [citations omitted]. But the district court treated this case as an exception to that rule by finding that a reasonable fee and cost award here was zero. The district court, in substance, based this exception on its inherent powers to supervise the conduct of the lawyers who come before it and to keep in proper condition the legal community of which the courts are a leading part. Plaintiff criticizes this decision as an abuse of discretion. We disagree.

That federal courts are accorded certain inherent powers is well established. [Citation omitted.] Those powers are not governed by rule or by statute, "but by the control necessarily vested in courts to manage their own affairs so as to achieve the orderly and expeditious disposition of cases." [Citation omitted.] "Because of the potency of those powers, they must be "exercised with restraint and discretion."

. . . A federal court may wield its inherent powers over the lawyers who practice before it. This control derives from a lawyer's role as an officer of the court. [Citation omitted.] It encompasses, among other things, the authority to police lawyer conduct and to guard and to promote civility and collegiality among the members of its bar. . . .

Defendants are lawyers and their law firm. And the lawyer for Plaintiff made absolutely no effort—no phone call; no email; no letter—to inform them of Plaintiff's impending claim much less to resolve this dispute before filing suit. Plaintiff's lawyer slavishly followed his client's instructions and—without a word to Defendants in advance—just sued his fellow lawyers. As the district court saw it, this conscious disregard for lawyer-to-lawyer collegiality and civility caused (among other things) the judiciary to waste significant time and resources on unnecessary litigation and stood in stark contrast to the behavior expected of an officer of the court.[8] The district court refused to reward—and thereby to encourage—uncivil conduct by awarding Plaintiff attorney's fees or costs.

Given the district court's power of oversight for the bar, we cannot say that this decision was outside of the bounds of the district court's discretion.[9]

We strongly caution against inferring too much from our decision today. These kinds of decisions are fact-intensive. We put aside cases in which lawyers are not parties. We do not say that pre-suit notice is usually required or even often required under the FLSA to receive an award of attorney's fees or costs. Nor do we now recommend that courts use their inherent powers to deny prevailing parties attorney's fees or costs. We declare no judicial duty. We create no presumptions. We conclude only that the district court did not abuse its discretion in declining to award some attorney's fees and costs based on the facts of this case.

We affirm the order of the district court. AFFIRMED.

---

8. The customs of professional courtesy were important to the district court. In its written order, the district court used these words: "This Court is not ruling that a pre-suit letter is always required, but in this case, the Plaintiff's lawyer did not even make a phone call to try to resolve the issue before filing suit. The Defendant is a law firm. Prior to filing suit in this local area, it is still reasonable to pick up the phone and call another lawyer so it won't be necessary to file suit. The defense proffered by Plaintiff's lawyer for not doing so is that his client instructed him to file suit first and ask questions later. . . . [T]he Court reminds him that the lawyer is the officer of the Court, not the client. This [C]ourt will not permit lawyers to file unnecessary litigation and palm it off on their clients."

9. We have said that a court may not sanction a lawyer under its inherent powers absent a showing "that the lawyer's conduct constituted or was tantamount to bad faith." *Thomas*, 293 F.3d at 1320 (internal quotation marks omitted). We have assumed that awarding no attorney's fees and costs constitutes some informal sanction. Nevertheless, even if bad faith is required, we conclude that the conscious indifference to lawyer-to-lawyer collegiality and civility exhibited by Plaintiff's lawyer (per his client's request) amounted to harassing Defendants' lawyers by causing them unnecessary trouble and expense and satisfied the bad-faith standard.

Questions about the Case

1. What was the paralegal suing for? Are paralegals non-exempt employees who should be paid overtime under federal law? (See Chapter 10.)
2. What did the paralegal recover? How much overtime does this represent based on average salaries in your area? Did the court find that she had prevailed in the case?
3. What did the lower court decide about attorney fees for her lawyer? What did this court decide?
4. What did the court say that the lawyer did to warrant no fees? Is this conduct covered by the ethics rules? Do other lawyers do what he did?
5. What was the court's authority to decide this way?
6. What does the court say about creating a new precedent?

10
Professionalism

This chapter addresses issues relating to professionalism in the legal field and outlines some of the challenges facing paralegals. Chapter 10 covers:

- the image of the legal profession in our society
- where paralegals "fit" in the legal profession
- definitions and elements of professionalism for paralegals
- current issues for paralegals, including:
  - regulation of the paralegal profession
  - title and definition of legal assistant/paralegal
  - paralegal education
  - utilization of paralegal services
  - overtime compensation
  - gender and other bias issues
- paralegal participation in pro bono activities

A. The State of Professionalism in the Legal Field

A poor **public image** has plagued the legal profession for more than 50 years despite the efforts of the organized bar to overcome it. In the last third of the twentieth century and into the twenty-first, the legal profession fell dramatically in the eyes of the general public. The lack of esteem for the profession can be traced back to the dishonest and manipulative conduct of White House lawyers during the Watergate scandal. The notion that lawyers engage in unscrupulous behavior has been reinforced in succeeding decades by media attention on individual lawyers whose outrageous misconduct has shocked and embarrassed the profession, and major crises like the last recession, when lawyers were seen as enabling the practices that led to massive foreclosures and almost brought down the economy. Film and television images of lawyers are often very negative and depict lawyers as inept or dishonest, including film depictions of lawyers as pathological liars, incompetent alcoholics, and advocates so overly zealous that they will lie and cheat to win a case.

During this period, society has become more **litigious**. The public looks to the law to solve many of its problems, sometimes social and personal ones, which prior to the 1960s would have been dealt with in other ways or not dealt with at all. Lawyers—and what many people consider an oversupply of them—have been blamed for the increase in litigation. The press jumps on the filing of frivolous lawsuits; it rarely reports when those suits are thrown out.

Public opinion polls consistently show that lawyers rate well below most other occupations in several areas, including related to honesty and integrity. A 2017 Gallup poll found that 28 percent of the public rated the "honesty and ethical standards" of lawyers low or very low. A 2013 Pew Research Center poll found that the public rated lawyers the lowest on a list of professions for "contribution to society's well-being." In a 2012 survey by the American College of Trial Lawyers, respondents indicated that they thought 51 percent of lawsuits are frivolous and unnecessary. An earlier ABA survey showed that people perceive lawyers to be greedy, manipulative, and corrupt. Those polled told stories of "lawyers who misrepresent their qualifications, over-promise, are not up front about their fees, charge too much for their services, take too long to resolve matters, and fail to return client phone calls." That survey also showed that Americans believe lawyers have too close a connection to politics, government, and big business and are not effective at policing themselves. Less than one in five surveyed were extremely or very confident in lawyers. Most thought lawyers are more interested in winning and making money than in justice.

High **legal fees** and high incomes earned by some lawyers add to the perception of lawyers as overpaid and greedy. Law firms that base fees on billable hours create great pressure on lawyers to bill for an unrealistically high number of hours. As noted in Chapter 7, this pressure can lead lawyers to inflate or pad bills. Overbilling drives clients away, creating a cycle of competitiveness and ever-higher billable hour requirements. Loyalty within law firms is not high in this environment; 40 years ago, most law school graduates went with a firm and stayed there for their entire career. Lawyers now commonly move three or four times before they stick with a firm. Even name partners leave for more attractive situations. The overwhelming sense of law practice as a business first and a profession second has caused great turnover and instability in firms, which dissolve and merge frequently.

The public perception is that lawyers manipulate the legal process, finding clever ways to **circumvent the law** to prevail. This goal of winning at all costs has made many lawyers seem like devious and overzealous abusers of the system. Many citizens believe that lawyers use "technicalities" to get criminal defendants off and to protect wealthy corporate executives and corporations from accountability for their misdeeds. Lawyers' involvement in highly publicized criminal cases and business-related scandals has validated public opinion that lawyers' knowledge and skills are for sale to the highest bidder and that lawyers will not hesitate to use their talents to line their clients' or their own pockets, whatever the cost to the public. A related client complaint is that lawyers are too chummy with one another; some clients complain when their lawyers extend professional courtesies such as extensions to opposing counsel.

The **competitiveness and zeal** of lawyers has led to abuses of the justice system, such as those described in Chapter 9 on trial advocacy. Admittedly, some lawyers view the litigation process as a game where tactics and strategy are more important than merit and substance. Bringing frivolous cases and motions, flooding an opponent with irrelevant and unwarranted discovery, and behaving discourteously and disrespectfully to opposing counsel and even to judges have become daily methods of operation for some lawyers. An unrelenting series of **high-profile scandals** involving lawyers support these impressions. For example, in the 1990s, tobacco industry lawyers were found to have suppressed evidence of the harmful effects of smoking. The country's leading plaintiff securities class action law firm was indicted for illegal conduct in handling its cases, and its two top partners pleaded guilty to paying kickbacks to plaintiffs and were sentenced to prison and disbarred. In the past two decades, lawyers serving corporate clients have been found guilty of backdating stock options and law firms have misused consumer protection statutes and the ADA to extort fees and damages from small businesses. One New York investment lawyer who was convicted of stealing nearly $400 million from hedge funds and investors through fake investment devices was disbarred and sentenced to 20 years in prison.

Two Florida lawyers who set up a Ponzi scheme bilked investors of $800 million; both were disbarred and one of the lawyers received a 50-year prison sentence. In 2017, a partner in a big law firm was arrested while trying to sell a whistleblower complaint to the company under investigation. During the last recession, lawyers representing banks in foreclosures have been found responsible for some of the internal practices that led to improperly documented and sometimes invalid foreclosures. Worse yet, lawyers defrauded thousands of desperate homeowners seeking loan modifications. These law firms advertised heavily, using names such as "U.S. Loan Auditors" and "U.S. Foreclosure Relief." They collected fees from vulnerable clients for loan modification and forensic audit services and rarely did anything to help people keep their homes.

Misconduct that especially hurts lawyers often involves dishonesty, from "small" offenses like unauthorized use of Westlaw, lying on a resume, and offering to write students' term papers on Craigslist, to serious and even criminal offenses, including insider trading, falsifying financial records, committing tax and insurance fraud, and embezzling client funds. Recently, a high-profile lawyer was convicted of stealing $11 million from clients and sentenced to 14 years in prison. Yet another high-profile and formerly well-regarded lawyer was disbarred and is under indictment for stealing millions of dollars from clients over several decades. Another category of misdeeds that seems to be expanding might be called "lawyers gone wild." In recently reported cases, one lawyer hired a hit man to murder another lawyer; another used his paralegal to set up opposing counsel for a DUI arrest; a lawyer in Illinois pulled a gun on a process server; and more than one lawyer assaulted opposing counsel in a deposition. A lawyer was recently convicted of killing his wife and son to cover up his theft of millions of dollars from clients over a number of years and was disbarred and sentenced to life in prison. (See Chapter 9 for other examples.) Several lawyers have been sanctioned for misconduct involving sex, including lawyers who sexually harassed and assaulted women; a lawyer who had an affair with a client's wife; a lawyer who advertised to hire a secretary who would have sex with him and his partner; and lawyers who had sex with vulnerable clients, including some who were incarcerated. ABA Model Rule 1.8(j), adopted by many states, prohibits lawyers from having sex with clients unless a pre-existing consensual relationship exists. Several lawyers have been disciplined or disbarred for discriminatory treatment of others, including for making racist and sexist statements. One Connecticut lawyer was not disbarred for his treatment of women, but is subject to a court-ordered lifetime ban on representing women.

The positive side of the legal profession rarely makes the daily newspaper, blogs, or the evening news. In fact, lawyers who engage in the conduct that gives the legal profession a bad name are a relative few. Most lawyers are honest and ethical and devote themselves to representing their clients as conscientiously as they can. Many lawyers take on cases at discounted fees and do extensive *pro bono* and public service work. They are regular volunteers in their communities. Studies show that about two-thirds of lawyers engage in *pro bono* and community service work. Lawyers have collectively created vast programs of support for underrepresented populations and have banded together in times of crisis to help victims of natural and other catastrophic disasters. The profession has often been a lone voice protecting constitutional rights, as seen in the lawyers who work on the Innocence Project and represent important causes for free. The images of Perry Mason and Atticus Finch still powerfully project what society wants a lawyer to be—courageous, smart, and steadfast in the quest for justice and fairness.

Historically, lawyer misconduct is usually uncovered and reported to authorities by clients, not other lawyers. Instances where lawyers report misconduct are few despite the **snitch rules** that are contained in most states' ethics rules. Firms usually handle ethical breaches internally and as privately as possible. Some courts have found that lawyers who report violations as required by the codes cannot be fired for these actions and have an action for retaliatory discharge if they are fired. However, not all states have decided this issue and at least one, Illinois, holds that lawyers who report ethical violations and then get fired do not have a cause of action for retaliatory discharge (*Jacobson v. Knepper & Moga*, 185 Ill.2d 372, 706 N.E.2d 491 (1998)). A few states also have **whistleblower statutes** that protect employees from being discharged in retaliation for reporting violations. It should be noted that the NFPA Model Code requires paralegals to report ethical and legal violations. See NFPA Model Code EC-1.3(d) and (f).

The organized bar at the national, state, and local levels has developed initiatives relating to **professionalism** and many, including the ABA, have committees that are intended to promote professionalism and to educate lawyers and the public about it. Disciplinary systems have been reformed and operate more efficiently and openly. Court rules and statutes limit discovery and provide for severe sanctions against lawyers for abuse. Bar associations have public relations campaigns to improve their image and encourage lawyers to engage in *pro bono* work and to support local charities and community activities.

More than a hundred state and local bar associations, and some courts, have adopted **codes of professional courtesy and civility** or **litigation guidelines** that advise lawyers on how to conduct themselves. The general courtesy or professionalism guidelines typically cover client relations (including communicating frequently, advising mediation, resolving matters expeditiously, not overcharging); relations with other lawyers and parties (including acting courteously, not engaging in delay or unmeritorious tactics, cooperating in scheduling and resolving disputes, not disparaging other lawyers, not harassing the opposition); relations with courts (including advocating vigorously but with civility, being punctual, being honest with the court); and duty to the public and

Snitch rules
Rules requiring lawyers to report unethical conduct.

Whistleblower statutes
Laws that protect employees who report violations of law from being retaliated against by employers.

the profession (including keeping current in practice areas, supporting the profession, and upholding the profession's image). Litigation guidelines usually contain rules covering continuances, extensions, service of process, communication with adversaries, discovery, and motions. They specify conduct that is courteous, honest, and not designed to harass or unduly burden opponents.

A strong correlation exists between lawyer disciplinary actions and **substance abuse and emotional problems**. Some studies estimate that at least half the lawyers disciplined for misconduct are "impaired" by some type of substance abuse or mental health problem, such as depression. Lawyers are more likely than persons in most other occupations to be alcoholics or chemically dependent. (See more on this in Chapter 8.) Bar associations have been proactive in developing programs to identify and help lawyers who are impaired before the impairment leads to unethical and destructive conduct. Legal Assistance programs, offered in all jurisdictions, are staffed by professional therapists and peer counselors and provide confidential assistance and referrals. Paralegals should be alert to the signs of mental health and substance abuse problems in themselves and their colleagues, such as arriving to work late or leaving early, missed appointments, last-minute cancellations, irritability, inability to work with others, hostility or avoidance, missed deadlines, and poor judgment. And firms should take action to deal with these issues before they lead to serious breaches of duty to clients or worse.

Among the other recommendations to address concerns about declining professionalism and ethics are requirements to teach ethics and professionalism across the curriculum in law school, more aggressive judicial intervention in litigation, and more *pro bono* and public service or public interest work. Some local bars offer client relations programs that attempt to alter lawyers' attitudes toward and treatment of clients. Some bar associations and firms have formal mentoring programs, designed to imbue law students and new lawyers with the values and culture of the legal profession. Many ethicists and bar leaders have called on lawyers to examine the ethical and moral content of their actions and to avoid separating their values and beliefs as persons from their conduct as lawyers. Increasingly heard are proposals for law firms to end the use of billable time as the primary method of setting legal fees. Lawyers who are sanctioned for unethical conduct are often required to attend "ethics school" as part of their penalty.

Dissatisfaction among lawyers is also high. Many lawyers leave the legal profession because of the problems that characterize law practice today. A 2018 survey found that 60% of lawyers feel stressed either most or all of the time. Some surveys show that as many as half the lawyers in practice would not become lawyers if they had it to do all over again. Firms deal with quality-of-life issues by creating counseling programs for troubled lawyers, providing part-time and flexible scheduling options, encouraging sabbaticals, increasing *pro bono* work, offering stress management programs, and establishing a firm culture that values collegiality and gives employees more time for their lives outside law practice. Many firms have designated an in-house ethics counsel or a committee to help lawyers with ethical dilemmas and have established one-on-one or small group mentoring for new lawyers to mitigate the negative effects of working in isolation and to build collegiality and trust.

Burnout and stress are recognized factors in lawyer dissatisfaction and in ethical misconduct. The pressures of the billable hours, the competitive environment of the legal world, the lack of loyalty among clients and law firms, the constant work of meeting other peoples' needs, and the feeling of not having control contribute to burnout, detachment from relationships with others, loss of job satisfaction, and even chronic anger and anxiety. The long hours alone make the job of a lawyer challenging, especially now that lawyers make themselves available 24-7 through technology that enables them to work wherever they are and at any time of the night or day.

Finally, the huge shifts in the way that law is practiced and legal services are delivered have created both a challenge and an opportunity for the legal profession. New models of law practice are emerging, including multi-disciplinary practice with nonlawyer ownership, virtual law practice, "advice" companies, networks of lawyers who work on short-term projects, and firms that provide services for a monthly subscription price.

Working in this dynamic milieu presents paralegals with choices about how they will navigate and thrive. Concerns about the integrity of the legal profession, voiced both by the public and within the profession, affect the way in which paralegals are viewed and view themselves. Paralegals are not immune from engaging in unethical conduct. In the last few years there have been several publicized cases of paralegal misconduct, including a New Jersey paralegal who was part of a real estate fraud scheme and who pled guilty to making false statements to the Department of Housing and Urban Development; a Canadian paralegal found guilty of embezzling more than $1 million from trust and other counts; and a Connecticut paralegal who pleaded guilty to embezzling $600,000 by paying her bills out of the firm accounts and falsifying accounting records. An Ohio paralegal continued the law practice of a retired lawyer, and a California paralegal "bought" the law practice of an elderly and impaired lawyer for $20 and also persuaded him to make the paralegal and his family the beneficiaries of his estate plan. A California paralegal stole a check written to her firm, altered the amount, and used the proceeds to take a private jet to New York for a spending spree. On the other hand, some paralegals have foiled unethical conduct, like the North Carolina paralegal who told state investigators about a scheme by two district attorneys who were going to hire each other's wives and then not require them to work for their salaries.

Paralegals can be part of the problem—working for firms that use their talents to abuse the legal process, overwork employees to the point of burnout, or engage in unethical and shoddy practices—or part of the solution—working for firms that use their talents to improve efficiency, to perform work competently and ethically, and to lower the cost of legal services. As the problems plaguing the profession and the proposals to solve them continue to shape new models of practicing law, paralegals can contribute to the creation of a profession that is characterized by integrity and honor.

B. Professionalism and the Paralegal

Paralegals are in a sometimes difficult and ambiguous position in the legal profession. Because they are not lawyers, they may not engage in certain activities carved out exclusively for the lawyer. But they do engage in substantive legal work that otherwise would have to be done by lawyers and that is paid for by the client. Although paralegals are part of the professional staff engaging in legal work, not part of the support staff, they can never be full and equal members of the professional team as partners in the firm. Because the paralegal profession is a relatively new occupation, the parameters of job responsibilities remain unclear, continue to evolve, and differ according to the assignment, the supervisor, and the work setting. Also, because of the relative youth of the occupation, the paralegal's role is not universally understood either by those in the legal profession or by the general public. Paralegals frequently must explain what they do to laypersons and must develop their own job descriptions and their role in the legal environment. The dilemma posed by this ambiguity has many ramifications for the daily work lives of paralegals. The overriding question it raises is how paralegals can forge a role for themselves—a professional role that holds them to high standards of ethics and performance while affording them the opportunity for long, satisfying, and challenging careers. Committing to the highest values of professionalism is an essential first step in this process.

Dictionaries define "profession" as an occupation that involves a special education and requires mental rather than manual labor. Sociologists define the term as an occupation whose members have the exclusive right to engage in certain activities that are intellectual in nature and require special education. Professions are bound by codes of ethics and are generally self-regulating. Philosophers tend to define a profession as a calling that requires a special commitment to public service.

Paraprofessional
A person who works within a profession in a subordinate position but with special training and a degree of independence in carrying out duties.

Paralegals usually are classified as ***paraprofessionals***, performing legal work under the supervision of a lawyer, but having special education and sharing in the societal prestige of the lawyer. Analogous are the many paraprofessionals in health care, such as physical therapists, nurse practitioners, and dental assistants. However, it is noteworthy that the health care field has very well-delineated educational and licensing requirements for paraprofessionals, something that is still largely missing and is only beginning to be explored in the legal field.

Limited research has been done on the paralegal field as an occupation. In their excellent book *Paralegals: Progress and Prospects of a Satellite Occupation*, Quintin Johnstone and Martin Wenglinsky analyze how the paralegal occupation fits the sociologist's definition of a profession, emphasizing three main characteristics—**collegiality**, **occupational prestige**, and **overtraining**. Although the first edition is now more than 30 years old and much has changed, this book provides a useful framework for analyzing the development of the paralegal profession.

The authors found many inconsistencies that reinforce the ambiguity that paralegals may feel about their role. For example, some law firms do not require formal paralegal training, creating inconsistent and sometimes low hiring standards in the field. On the other hand, paralegals who have a formal education, frequently a baccalaureate degree and postgraduate certificate, occasionally find themselves "overtrained" for many of the tasks that they perform and need to seek positions that will align with their education and functions. Prestige for paralegals is often found in the reflected, and sometimes shared, prestige of the lawyers with whom paralegals work. This status may be enhanced by the law firm's treatment of paralegals, affording them a meaningful career path and appropriate perquisites, treating them with respect, and acknowledging and rewarding their contributions.

Collegiality also presents dichotomies. Not all paralegals feel a common bond with and loyalty to their paralegal colleagues, not having had a shared educational experience, like lawyers have, and not possessing a common exclusive grant to engage in certain work. Aggravating this lack of bond is the fact that many paralegals view themselves as competitors within the firm for the most interesting work and highest pay. Thus, they often express their primary loyalty to the firm or to their supervising attorney, not to their occupation. Many paralegals work in small or midsized firms where they may be the only paralegal, lending to their feelings of isolation from other paralegals. On the other hand, paralegal associations have been quite successful in building a strong sense of camaraderie and shared interests and responsibilities among their members. However, it is estimated that only about 20 percent of the paralegals in the country belong to such an organization. See Q. Johnstone & M. Wenglinsky, *Paralegals: Progress and Prospects of a Satellite Occupation*, pp. 183 et seq. (1985).

Another interesting analysis of the paralegal occupation traces its evolution from an occupation to a profession, as defined by sociologists who study occupations. Green, D., Snell, J., Corgiat, R., and Paramanith, T., "The Professionalization of the Legal Assistant: Identity, Maturation States and Goal Attainment," 7 *J. Paralegal Educ. & Prac.* 35 (1990). This article cites five stages in the **development of a profession**: diffusion, education, associations, agitation and self-regulation, and formulation of a professional code. The authors found in 1990 that the paralegal field was advancing, although not smoothly, in the second stage (education) and recommended a strengthened and standardized paralegal curriculum.

Since that time, substantial progress has been made in the "professionalization" of the paralegal occupation. Levels of education, both general and specialized paralegal education, are rising, and more law firms are requiring college and paralegal-specific education. Paralegal work has grown and become more sophisticated. It includes more client contact and requires higher levels of organizational, communication, and technology skills. Billing rates and salaries continue to rise. Both NALA and NFPA promote voluntary certification, and several statewide voluntary certification programs have been established, perhaps a precursor to real regulation. Paralegal associations are strong and are having an impact on important issues like certification, regulation, utilization, and attorney's fees.

Given the history and future of the paralegal field, professionalism for paralegals might be viewed as having the following elements.

1. Commitment to Legal Services

Paralegals should always remember that their highest goal is to assist in the delivery of legal services that are delivered ethically, competently, and efficiently. In addition to living this commitment in their daily work, this commitment also requires paralegals to engage in activities that improve access to legal services, such as *pro bono* programs. See Section D later in this chapter.

2. Commitment to Education

Fulfilling this commitment includes participating in formal education, continuing education, and on-the-job learning that enhance knowledge and skills and continually develop the paralegal's potential. Education heightens the paralegal's ability to deliver quality legal services and enriches long-term career satisfaction.

3. Commitment to the Highest Standards of Ethical Conduct

Paralegals should know the rules of ethics that bind lawyers and understand how these rules apply to them. Further, they should internalize the values reflected in these rules and seek to develop their own personal standards of ethics and morality that reach beyond the minimums imposed by law. Paralegals must be scrupulously honest in their relations with clients, courts, attorneys, co-workers, and others in their professional world.

4. Commitment to Excellence

Paralegals should set high standards of performance for themselves and seek to meet those standards in all the work they undertake. They should approach each task with an attitude of seriousness and diligently apply their knowledge, skill, and talent to accomplish their work.

5. Commitment to the Paralegal Profession

Paralegals are part of a distinct profession within the legal field, with interests and goals that are shared by other paralegals. They should engender collegiality among their colleagues, mentor new paralegals, and act as role models and sources of information for those who aspire to the paralegal profession. They should also support paralegal activities organized through professional associations, bar associations, and alumni associations.

6. Commitment to a Strong Work Ethic

Paralegals should strive to do their best on every task and to serve clients diligently. They should be meticulous and thorough, organized, prompt in meeting deadlines, and always do more than the minimum. They should take pride in their work and always produce work that merits that pride.

7. Commitment to Acting with Integrity and Honor

Paralegals should be courteous, respectful, and fair in their dealings with lawyers, other paralegals, support staff, clients, and others both within and outside their firm. They should demonstrate maturity, patience, and thoughtfulness in their actions, avoiding gossip, undue criticism of others, prejudice and bias, and favoritism. This commitment means being sensitive to the needs and talents of others, valuing the differences in people's backgrounds, and recognizing others' achievements.

8. Commitment to Balance as a Person

Paralegals should not become so consumed by their work that they neglect other aspects of their lives, such as family, friends, health, and personal interests and activities. They should seek to be well rounded and should have a variety of interests. Commitment to a profession need not prevent paralegals from leading a full life; in fact, paralegals who narrow their interests to work only will not be as effective in relations with others and can lose the sense of proportion and balance needed to fulfill their commitments as professionals.

9. Commitment to Good Judgment, Common Sense, and Communication

Paralegals should strive to understand and work well with others. They should listen to others carefully and communicate, both orally and in writing, clearly and persuasively.

C. Current Issues in Professionalism

A number of important issues face the paralegal profession. One issue that has always been central to the debate about the evolution of the paralegal field is **regulation**. Discussed in Chapter 2, regulation is a complex question that will not be resolved easily. The debate has raised many difficult questions:

- Is there a need for regulation, *i.e.*, what purposes would regulation serve?
- Who should be regulated?
- Who should do the regulating?
- Should regulation be mandatory?
- What level or kind of regulation is appropriate?
- What educational requirements should be established?
- What kind of examination, if any, should be required?
- What, if any, specific tasks should paralegals be authorized to perform?
- Do paralegals need their own ethics rules?
- Should paralegals be required to meet continuing education requirements?

Resolution of the regulation issue will set the course for the future of the career, defining the extent to which it becomes an independent, self-regulated profession, and the nature and character of the paralegal role and the work that paralegals do.

A related issue has been the use of **the titles "paralegal" and "legal assistant"** to identify persons working in a paralegal capacity. For many years the two titles were used interchangeably, although there were some regional preferences for one title or the other. Some paralegals advocated for one uniform title and definition, which they believed would advance the profession. In the 1990s, many lawyers started to give the title "legal assistant" to personnel who previously would have been called legal secretaries. This enhancement of title for their assistants created conflict with paralegals, who often have specific educational credentials and do billable work for clients. At the same time, a growing number of states have started to reserve both titles for "true" paralegals. Many firms and educational programs have moved away from the title legal assistant to paralegal. In 2003, the ABA changed the name of its entity on paralegals from the Standing Committee on Legal Assistants to the Standing Committee on Paralegals. Local associations affiliated with NFPA all use "paralegal," and NALA now uses Certified Paralegal after many years of adhering to Certified Legal Assistant. The recently adopted state certification programs also use "paralegal" instead of legal assistant in their titles. And in 2020, in recognition of the changes in the legal profession, the ABA adopted the sole title of "paralegal," removed the title "legal assistant" from its formal definition of paralegal, stopped using the titles interchangeably. (See Chapter 2.)

The movement toward one title also has ramifications for the **definition of paralegal**, i.e., whether the term *paralegal* should include nonlawyer legal service providers who do not work under lawyer supervision. Note that the definitions cited in Chapter 2 endorse the view that this title belongs to those persons who work under the supervision of a lawyer. This limitation on the use of the title has been reinforced in states from Maine to California that have statutes and court rules that prohibit the use of the title by persons who act as nonlawyer legal services providers. As noted in Chapter 2, some states give other titles to nonlawyers who provide legal services directly to the public, like Legal Document Assistant, Legal Document Preparer, Limited License Legal Technician, and more recently, Legal Paraprofessional.

Education is another important issue for paralegals. The lack of consistency in hiring standards and the lack of uniformity in the paralegal curriculum have prevented paralegals from having a shared body of knowledge and a shared educational experience, two important characteristics of a profession, which can inhibit the development of collegiality among paralegals. On the other hand, the diversity within paralegal education offerings and the variety of ways that one can enter the field have allowed the paralegal profession to flourish. Paralegals have a continuously expanding bank of job responsibilities, unhindered by a standardized, limiting education that trains everyone to perform the same tasks. The diverse work and life experiences that are brought to the profession by the wide variety of people who become paralegals have enriched both the career possibilities and the legal profession itself. Whereas the ABA and the American Association for Paralegal Education endorse a minimum of two years of college for entry into the paralegal field, the International Practice Management Association, representing corporate counsel offices and large law firms, favors a four-year degree. As noted earlier, levels of educational attainment among paralegals are rising.

The ambiguity that comes with a relatively new and evolving profession continues to result in challenges for paralegals in their work. Even now, more than 50 years after the advent of the modern American paralegal, **utilization of paralegal services** is not universal. Some lawyers do not hire paralegals at all; others are unclear on how to utilize their talents and skills or are reluctant to delegate anything more than routine or repetitive work to them. Although all large law firms and many mid-sized ones employ paralegals, the majority of sole practitioners and small firms do not use paralegal services. Some lawyers and law firms treat their paralegals poorly—by not compensating them fairly, not providing appropriate working conditions and clerical support, or not giving them recognition when deserved—but still expect professional work and loyalty. Not surprisingly, this kind of treatment results in high turnover. Some paralegals leave the profession after a few years, dissatisfied with their treatment, compensation, and the nature of their work.

One important question with which paralegals and their employers struggled was whether paralegals should be classified as **exempt or nonexempt** employees. Nonexempt employees are entitled to overtime compensation under the Fair Labor Standards Act and similar state laws. When the Department of Labor adopted new Wage and Hour Rules and Regulations in 2004, it established the rule that paralegals are not generally exempt from overtime under the category of "exempt learned professional." The Department cited evidence that a four-year degree is not required for entry into the profession, which is considered a minimal prerequisite for classification of an occupation as exempt. The current provision does permit exempt status for paralegals who "possess advanced specialized degrees," such as engineers, and other provisions of the rules allow exempt status for managers and supervisors (see 29 CFR 541.301(e)(7)).

Prior to the adoption of this rule, paralegals were divided on the question of overtime. Some believed that their classification as nonexempt undermined their professional work and status. Others appreciate that they receive higher compensation when paid for overtime work. It appears that most firms are honoring the rules. Some large law firms have career paths that classify the lower rungs of the ladder as nonexempt and the top level or levels as exempt, based on the qualifications of the paralegals, the nature and complexity of specific responsibilities, the degree of independence exercised by the paralegal, and the involvement of the paralegal in management or supervisory work.

The paralegal career continues to be a **female-dominated occupation** that serves a still-male-dominated profession. Other traditionally female-dominated professions such as nursing and teaching have struggled very hard—not always successfully—to achieve parity in status and recognition, fair treatment, good working conditions, and compensation that is based on the value, nature, and difficulty of their work. Women are entering law school in numbers equal to men and now make up about forty percent of the lawyers in this country. However, women lawyers have not yet broken through the glass ceiling into the ranks of partners and judicial officers in proportion to their overall numbers in the profession.

Women lawyers and paralegals continue to experience **harassment and discrimination**. Surveys show that 50 percent of women lawyers believe they have been harassed and almost as many believe that they have been discriminated against in the allocation of work and in salary and promotion decisions. Many women leave the practice of law or leave traditional law firms to move in-house or to start their own firms. A report from the Equal Employment Opportunity Commission showed that discrimination claims (of all types) against legal sector employers have increased in recent years.

Bias against lawyers on the basis of racial/ethnic background, sexual orientation, gender, gender identity, and disability also plagues the legal profession. African-American, Latino/Hispanic, Asian-American, and Native American lawyers are underrepresented in the legal profession and in law schools, with little chance of achieving representation that is proportionate to the general population during our lifetime. Women lawyers and lawyers from these underrepresented groups make less money, are less likely to make partner, are less likely to be appointed to the bench, and are systematically excluded from key firm committees and prestigious practice areas. Some law firms have not been proactive in hiring lawyers from underrepresented groups, and others have a climate that is not conducive to the success of diverse lawyers. Several jurisdictions have anti-bias rules that make it an ethical violation to discriminate in the operation of a practice and/or to disparage or humiliate someone on the basis of race, national origin, sex, sexual orientation, religion, age, or disability. ABA Model Rule 8.4(g) makes it unethical for a lawyer to harass or discriminate on the basis of race, sex, religion, national origin, ethnicity, disability, age, sexual orientation, gender identity, marital status, or socioeconomic status. The Americans with Disabilities Act protects disabled persons, including employees, in their interactions with law firms. Diversity pipeline projects at national and local bar associations seek to bring more underrepresented groups into the legal profession and to support efforts to achieve fairness and parity in law practice. Although it is rare that lawyers are disciplined for harassment or discrimination, these acts sometimes have more immediate consequences.

Finally, paralegals should be aware of the emerging developments in law practice that are designed to challenge the conventional models of operation. Among these are **collaborative law practice**, in which "parties and their lawyers commit to working cooperatively to reach a settlement." (See ABA Formal Opinion 07-447, endorsing this model so long as the client consents.) Another new model is the **virtual law office**, in which lawyers practice entirely online without physical office space, sometimes with the goal of providing more affordable legal services. (See, for example, California State Bar Formal Opinion 2012-184.) Finally, many lawyers and experts believe that law practice as we know it will change dramatically in the coming years, as fewer clients need or can afford to pay for "bespoke" legal services and more services are provided by teams of lawyers and nonlawyers using technology and standardized forms and processes. (See *The End of Lawyers? Rethinking the Nature of Legal Services*, by Richard Susskind, Oxford University Press, 2010 and the ABA Report on the Future of Legal Services in the United States, 2016.)

D. Pro Bono Work

The legal needs of the vast majority of Americans are not being met by our current system. Study after study has proven that most Americans—especially poor and moderate-income persons—do not have access to a lawyer when they need one. Most Americans cannot afford a lawyer; many who actually can afford one believe that they cannot. Most would not know how to go about finding a lawyer.

Pro bono
For free.

To cope with this problem, the organized bar has encouraged individual lawyers to engage in ***pro bono*** work and has sponsored a wide variety of pro bono programs to which lawyers can contribute their time and expertise. Many states and some local bars have aspirational guidelines for lawyers, usually for 50 hours of pro bono work a year. Only a few have rules mandating pro bono work, which can be fulfilled by making a donation in lieu of doing the work. Ten states (Florida, Hawaii, Illinois, Indiana, Maryland, Minnesota, Mississippi, Nevada, New Mexico, and New York) require lawyers to report the amount of time they devote each year to pro bono work. Thirteen states have voluntary pro bono reporting systems in place. Some states count financial contributions as pro bono in lieu of handling actual legal work pro bono. The ABA reports that the total time of pro bono work in these states alone is close to five million hours a year, but that it still does not fill the systemic need for legal services. Some law schools have a requirement for public service or pro bono work, and many law firms have policies that encourage their lawyers to engage in such activities. The ABA Model Rules encourage lawyers to do pro bono work, and an ABA opinion endorses the practice of allowing a state supreme court judge to sign a letter encouraging lawyers to provide pro bono services. (See ABA Model Rule 6.1 and ABA Formal Opinion 470 (2015).)

Paralegals have an opportunity to help. Participating in pro bono activities as part of one's professional commitment also increases career satisfaction. Some surveys of paralegals show that more than 40 percent participate in some kind of pro bono work, usually through a program with their employer or a paralegal association.

Guideline 10 to the ABA Model Guidelines for the Utilization of Paralegal Services (ABA Model Guidelines) and several states' guidelines encourage lawyers to facilitate paralegal participation in pro bono activities. Lawyers have a duty to provide pro bono services under ABA Model Rule 6.1 and Canon 2 of the ABA Model Code, and the ABA has called on lawyers to fulfill this duty by aspiring to do 50 hours of pro bono work annually.

Many law firms that do pro bono work include paralegals in these activities. Paralegals who do not have an opportunity to become involved in pro bono work through their jobs should seek out activities on their own. Local bar associations and paralegal associations have pro bono projects on which paralegals can work. Legal aid organizations and law clinics are always in need of volunteers.

Pro bono programs have been established in many specialized areas of law, affording paralegals a chance either to exercise their expertise or to develop it in a new area. Examples of the areas some of the programs cover are court-appointed special advocates in juvenile cases; facilitators or mediators in family law; consumer and landlord–tenant matters; major public interest litigation (*e.g.*, housing or employment discrimination, elder abuse, and children's rights); immigration; mental health advocacy; domestic violence counseling; medical advocacy; and homeless projects.

Paralegals who do pro bono work often find themselves working more independently than they do in their law firms, engaged in challenging tasks to which they may not be delegated on their jobs. Paralegals in legal aid settings very often have extensive client contact, handling intake interviews and helping clients directly with matters not requiring a lawyer. They sometimes advocate for clients before administrative agencies, conduct in-depth research, and draft documents and memoranda.

In addition to building their skills, paralegals who do pro bono work derive the ultimate satisfaction of helping someone who needs help and might not otherwise have received that help. Usually the assistance is of the most critical kind—for instance, keeping someone from losing a home or social service benefits—and is a matter of survival to the clients.

The National Federation of Paralegal Associations Model Code of Ethics and Professional Responsibility and Guidelines for Enforcement, Canon 1.4, states that paralegals "shall serve the public interest by contributing to the improvement of the legal system and delivery of quality legal services, including pro bono publico services and community service." In the accompanying Ethical Consideration 1.4(d), the Federation asks its members to aspire to contribute 50 hours of pro bono services and/or community service annually. Excellent materials on paralegal involvement in pro bono activities are available through local bar associations, the National Federation of Paralegal Associations, the National Association of Legal Assistants, and their local chapters and affiliates.

REVIEW QUESTIONS

1. Give five reasons why the public image of lawyers is so poor. Is this image warranted?
2. Give five examples of the kinds of lawyer misconduct that contributes to the public image of lawyers.
3. What are lawyers doing to improve their public image?
4. How can information about the positive endeavors of lawyers be disseminated to the public?
5. What is a code of professional courtesy or civility? What kinds of conduct does it cover?
6. What can a paralegal do to improve professionalism and the public image of the legal field?
7. Why are paralegals in a somewhat ambiguous position in the legal environment? Give at least three reasons. What can paralegals do about it?
8. How is "profession" defined?
9. What is a paraprofessional?
10. What is collegiality? Why might maintaining collegiality be challenging for paralegals?
11. Describe the nine professional commitments that paralegals should make.
12. Name and discuss three issues facing today's paralegals.
13. What is the basis for classifying a paralegal as an exempt or nonexempt employee? What is the current law concerning overtime pay for paralegals?
14. Does the fact that paralegals are predominately female affect the career? How?
15. To what extent is the legal profession representative of the racial-ethnic diversity in this country? What is being done about that?
16. What are some of the emerging issues related to models of law practice?
17. What is the current state of legal services for poor and middle-income Americans?
18. Have pro bono activities increased or decreased in the last decade?
19. What kinds of pro bono activities do lawyers and paralegals do?
20. What are the benefits to a paralegal of doing pro bono work?
21. How can a paralegal get involved in pro bono work?

DISCUSSION QUESTIONS AND HYPOTHETICALS

1. Do you think the legal profession deserves its poor public image? Why or why not?
2. How can the legal profession overcome its poor image?
3. Do you think lawyers' job mobility is a good or bad thing? Why?
4. What are some of the signs of substance abuse or mental health problems that may affect performance and ethics? What should you do if you learn about problems like this in your work setting?
5. Do you think paralegals should be classified as professionals or paraprofessionals? Is this distinction important to you? Why?
6. Do you think Johnstone and Wenglinsky's three characteristics (collegiality, overtraining, and prestige) are instructive in evaluating the paralegal occupation as a profession? Why or why not? What other characteristics might you add?
7. Do you think standardization in paralegal education would be good or bad for the career? Why?
8. How can paralegals build collegiality? Why is it important?
9. Do you think voluntary certification is good for the paralegal profession? Why or why not? What about mandatory regulation? Why or why not?
10. Looking at the five stages toward professionalization presented by the Green article, where do you think the paralegal occupation fits?
11. Do you agree with the nine professional commitments for paralegals? Why or why not? How would you prioritize their relative importance? What would you add or delete?
12. How can paralegals help overcome lawyers' reluctance to utilize their services? How can paralegals encourage lawyers to utilize their services more effectively and fully?

RESEARCH PROJECTS AND ASSIGNMENTS

1. Read a general interest newspaper every day for a month and collect all the articles that mention lawyers. How many are favorable? What image do they present?
2. Read the local legal newspaper for a month and count the number of articles about lawyers engaged in unprofessional conduct and about good work that lawyers are doing. Does this information align with the information in this chapter?
3. Does your local bar association or court have a code of professional courtesy? Do you think a nonbinding code such as this is appropriate or effective for a court or bar association to have? Why or why not? Should such a code be binding? Why or why not? Do such codes

derogate the lawyer's duty of zealousness? Do they contribute to lawyers' "clubbiness"? Do they work?

4. Contact your local paralegal association and get salary surveys that ask about job satisfaction, career paths, *pro bono* work, and exempt or nonexempt status.
5. Read Krieger, L. S. and Sheldon, K. M., "What Makes Lawyers Happy?: A Data-Driven Prescription to Redefine Professional Success," 83 *George Washington L.R.* 2, 2015. Can you find any studies of what makes paralegals happy in their work? How might the information and recommendations in this article help legal employers to improve not only lawyer job satisfaction, but also paralegal job satisfaction?
6. Contact five paralegals at local law firms and ask them:
   a. if they regard their paralegal career as a profession;
   b. if they are treated as professionals by their employers;
   c. if they plan to continue as a paralegal indefinitely, and if not, what they plan to do and why they are leaving the career;
   d. if they are members of the local paralegal association;
   e. if their firm does pro bono work;
   f. if they do pro bono work;
   g. if their education and training are well utilized;
   h. if they are paid overtime;
   i. if their firms promote diversity;
   j. if they have experienced discrimination.
7. Does your state or local bar association have a program to provide assistance to impaired lawyers? How does it work? How many lawyers participate in it? If the bar has an estimate of how many lawyer disciplinary matters are associated with substance abuse, what does it show?
8. Read and summarize Virginia State Bar Ethics Opinion 1886 (2016) that addresses the duties of a lawyer and law firm when a lawyer in the firm is impaired. Be sure to include the hypothetical scenarios and how they were handled.
9. Does your state or local bar association undertake activities to promote diversity in the legal profession? Find statistics on the proportion of underrepresented groups and women in the legal profession. What kinds of activities does your state or local bar undertake to promote diversity? Is your paralegal class at school more or less diverse than the local bar? Is it more or less diverse than the general population?
10. Contact the local bar and paralegal associations and find out what kinds of pro bono opportunities are available to you.
11. Read ABA Formal Opinion 07-447 on collaborative law practice. Research whether there are collaborative law firms in your area. How widespread is this kind of practice in your area? What areas of law do these lawyers work in? Do they hire or retain paralegals?

12. For a case of a lawyer who was out of control, see *In re Usher*, 987 N.E.2d 1080 (Ind. 2013). This lawyer was suspended for three years after pursuing a romantic relationship with a law clerk and attempting to destroy her legal career. He enlisted a paralegal to help him. What would you have done differently if you were the paralegal?
13. See Utah State Bar Ethics Advisory Opinion 11-03 on whether a lawyer can ask a law student to undertake legal research using the student's free Lexis or Westlaw account. What would you do if you were asked to use your paralegal student account to do research while doing an internship?
14. Read the ABA Commission on the Future of Legal Services 2016 issues paper on alternative business structures (ABS) and report on the status of the ABS movement and the pros and cons of this form of practice. Be sure to consider how it might affect paralegals.
15. Read the UC Hastings WorkLife Law 2015 report on "New Models of Law Practice" by Joan Williams, Aaron Platt, and Jessica Lee, and Mary E. Vandenack's 2021 article published by the ABA, "Evolving Law Firm Models With Innovation: Using Lessons Learned From the Pandemic." What models do you find in your legal community? What do these new models do to improve access to legal services? To improve the satisfaction of lawyers and others who work in law? To improve diversity?
16. Read *Lola v. Skadden, Arps, Slate, Meagher & Flom*, 620 Fed. Appx. 37 (2d Cir. 2015). Should contract lawyers be subject to overtime compensation? Under what circumstances? Was the plaintiff practicing law while working for the defendant as a contract lawyer? Did he exercise any legal judgment in performing his duties? Does document review constitute substantive legal work?

Glossary

Abuse of process   The improper use of a civil or criminal process.
Administrative agency   A government body responsible for the control and supervision of a particular activity or area of public interest.
Advance fee   A fee paid by a client to a lawyer in advance of the work being done, which is earned by the lawyer as the work is done and is refundable if not earned.
Artificial intelligence (also called generative artificial intelligence)   The ability of a computer or other device to perform activities that are normally thought to require human intelligence.
Associate   A lawyer in a law firm who is not a partner but is an employee.
Attorney-client privilege   The rule of evidence that protects confidential communications between a lawyer and client made in the course of the professional relationship.

Barratry   The common law crime of stirring up lawsuits and disputes.
Bribery   The crime of giving or receiving something of value as payment for an official act.

Certification   A form of recognition of an occupation based on a person's having met specified qualifications.
Certified Paralegal   Certification for paralegals offered by NALA for passing the Certified Paralegal examination.
Champerty   An old common law agreement between a lawyer and client under which the lawyer undertakes representation and pays costs and is reimbursed and paid a fee out of the recovery; such agreements were outlawed in most states.

Chat Generative Pre-trained Transformer (ChatGPT) An artificial intelligence (AI) chatbot that uses natural language processing to create humanlike conversational dialogue.

Chinese wall An antiquated term for an ethical/conflicts screen. See **Screen/screening.**

Class action suit A lawsuit brought by a representative of a group of persons on behalf of the group.

Client security fund A fund set aside to reimburse clients whose funds have been converted or misappropriated by lawyers.

Client trust account A bank account set up by a lawyer in which funds are kept that belong in whole or in part to the client; can usually include funds from more than one client.

Commingling The mixing of the funds of a fiduciary, including a lawyer, with those of a client.

Cone of silence The silence imposed on a person with a conflict of interest when a screen is erected to protect against breaches of confidentiality.

Confidentiality agreement An agreement entered into between a law firm and an employee or other agent in which the employee or agent agrees to keep client information confidential.

Contempt An act that obstructs the administration of justice, impairs the dignity of the court, or shows disrespect for the authority of the court.

Contingency fee A fee that is contingent on the successful outcome of a case and based on a percentage of the recovery.

Control group test The test applied by some courts to determine whether communications in a corporate setting are covered by the attorney-client privilege; under this test, communications are privileged only if they are made with the top management and board members.

Conversion The tortious deprivation of another's property without justification or authorization.

Court facilitators Persons employed by the courts to assist laypersons who are representing themselves in their own court matters. Typically employed in family law courts.

Deposition A method of pre-trial discovery that consists of a witness's or party's statement taken under oath in a question-and-answer format and recorded.

Disbarment The rescinding of a lawyer's license to practice law.

Disclaimers A statement denying a person's claim or right.

Discovery Pre-trial procedures designed for the parties to gain information in order to narrow the issues of fact and law.

Discovery abuse Using the discovery process to harass or burden a party.

Document production A form of discovery under which one party must provide copies of specified documents to the other side.

E-discovery Discovery of all types of data maintained in electronic format, such as documents, e-mails, voicemails, texts, images, calendar files, databases, spreadsheets, audio and video files, animations, web sites, and social media.

Electronic discovery reference model (EDRM) Model that outlines a standard approach to the discovery of electronically stored information.

ESI Electronically stored information.

Ethics opinions Written opinions promulgated by bar associations in which the association interprets the relevant ethical precedents in the context of a specific ethical dilemma posed to it.

Ex parte An action taken by or on behalf of a party without the presence of the opposing party.

Extra-judicial An act that takes place outside the presence of the judge or jury.

Fee-shifting statute A law that allows a court to award attorneys' fees to one of the parties.

Fixed fees A fee for legal services based on a set amount, usually used for standardized routine work.

Forwarding fee A fee paid by a lawyer to another lawyer for referring a case.

Freelance paralegals Paralegals who work as independent contractors providing services to lawyers, usually on an as-needed basis, and work under lawyer supervision.

Gag order A court-imposed order that restricts information or comment about a case.

Hourly fees Fees for legal services based on hourly rates and the amount of time actually expended in rendering the services.

Imputed conflict/disqualification A conflict of interest involving one person that is attributed vicariously to the entire law firm, which is disqualified from representing the party at issue; same as vicarious disqualification.

In camera Proceedings held in the judge's chambers without the jury or public present; the examination of documents to determine if there is privileged information is conducted "in camera."

Independent paralegals A term sometimes used by nonlawyer legal service providers and sometimes used by freelance paralegals. See both these terms in this glossary.

Integrated bar A bar association in which the mandatory and voluntary aspects of bar activities are combined, and membership is required.
Inter vivos During life.
IOLTA Interest on Lawyers' Trust Accounts. A program under which the interest from lawyers' client trust accounts, which is too small to pay to clients, is collected by banks and used by bar associations and/or courts to fund law-related programs.
Issue conflict The situation that arises when a lawyer argues opposing sides of a legal issue, the result of which may be that one client's interests are harmed, even though that client is not a party to the matter.

Jailhouse lawyers Prison inmates who assist other prisoners in preparing post-conviction writs and lawsuits.

Legal document assistants/preparers Nonlawyer legal service providers who assist persons in preparing legal documents without giving legal advice under California statutes (LDAs) or Arizona court rules (LPAs).
Legal malpractice Improper conduct in the performance of duties by a legal professional, either intentionally or through negligence.
Legal technicians A term used by some nonlawyer legal service providers.
Licensing Mandatory governmental regulation of a profession requiring that the members meet specified qualifications.
Lien An encumbrance or claim on the property of another as security for a debt or charge.
Limited practice legal professionals Licensed professionals who are not lawyers but are authorized by state statutes and court rules to practice law and represent clients on a limited basis.

Malicious prosecution An action to recover damages resulting from an unsuccessful criminal or civil action that was instituted without probable cause and with malice.
Malpractice Improper conduct in the performance of duties by a professional, either intentionally or through negligence.
Mistrial A trial terminated and declared void prior to the return of a verdict, often because of a jury deadlock.
Multidisciplinary practice A business model under which law firms and other professionals form partnerships to deliver legal and other related services to clients.
Multijurisdictional practice Engaging in the practice of law in more than one state.

Nonlawyer legal service providers Persons not licensed to practice law who provide legal services directly to the public.

Paraprofessional A person who works within a profession in a subordinate position but with special training and a degree of independence in carrying out duties.

Perjury The criminal offense of making false statements under oath.

Pleading Statements in written legal form that set forth the plaintiff's cause of action and the defendant's grounds of defense.

Probation A procedure under which someone found guilty of an offense is subjected to certain conditions and oversight by the entity involved and is released from a more serious sanction contingent on fulfillment of the conditions imposed.

Pro bono For free.

Professional negligence Improper conduct in the performance of duties by a professional, either intentionally or through negligence.

Pro hac vice The permission granted by a court to an out-of-state lawyer to appear in a particular case even though not admitted to practice in that jurisdiction.

Pro per A nonlawyer representing himself or herself in a legal matter.

Pro se A nonlawyer representing himself or herself in a legal matter.

Real estate closing The consummation of the sale of real estate by payment of the purchase price, delivery of the deed, and finalizing collateral matters, such as mortgage, insurance, and taxes.

Registered Paralegal Certification offered by NFPA for passing the Paralegal Advanced Competency Examination.

Reprimand A warning; the least serious sanction that can be placed on a lawyer for unethical conduct; it may be public or private.

Reproval and Admonition Another term for reprimand, used in some states.

Retainer A nonrefundable fee for legal services paid to ensure the availability of the lawyer to handle specified matters whether or not any such matters arise during the retainer period.

Runners and cappers Agents of lawyers who solicit clients in violation of ethics rules.

Screen/screening The isolation of a person from participation in a matter through imposition of procedures within a firm intended to prevent the affected person from revealing information protected under the ethics rules or the attorney-client privilege.

Sedona Principles Concept developed by the Sedona Conference® to apply the principles of discovery to ESI as an approach to the treatment of electronic data.

Self-representation The act of representing oneself in legal proceedings before a tribunal.

Simultaneous representation/conflict The representation of clients in current legal matters where their interests are adverse.

Snitch rules Rules requiring lawyers to report unethical conduct.

Solicitation Direct unrequested contact with a prospective client for the purpose of obtaining employment.

Spoliation Destruction of evidence that may result in a civil cause of action for damages for interference with the ability to prove a claim or defense.

Subject matter test The test applied by some courts to determine whether communications in a corporate setting are covered by the attorney-client privilege; under this test, confidential communications with corporate employees are privileged if they were made for the purpose of enabling the lawyer to render legal services.

Subornation of perjury The criminal offense of encouraging another to commit perjury.

Successive representation/conflict The representation of a client whose interests are adverse to a former client.

Suspension The temporary removal of a lawyer's license to practice law for a stated period.

Testamentary Through a will.

Testimonial advertisements Ads in which a client or person acting as a client explains how valuable the lawyer's services were.

Third-party claims Claims by nonclients against lawyers who, in representing clients, may have caused harm to the third person.

Unconscionable So unreasonable as to render a contract unenforceable, usually because the terms are so favorable to one party; can be applied to legal fee agreements.

Unlawful detainer assistant Title granted by the California legislature to persons who provide legal-clerical services to persons representing themselves in matters relating to evictions.

Vicarious disqualification The imputation of a conflict to others in a firm so that the entire firm is disqualified from undertaking the representation; same as imputed disqualification.

Whistleblower statutes Statutes that protect persons who report violations of the law against retaliation.

Will execution The formal process of signing and witnessing a will.

Work product rule The rule of evidence that protects the work done by a lawyer and his/her employees and agents in the process of representing a client in litigation.

Table of Cases

Principal cases are indicated by italics.

Abbott Laboratories v. Adelphia Supply USA, 445
Ackert; United States v., 141
Alexander v. Cahill, 269
Allstate Ins. Co. v. West Va. State Bar, 82
American Bar Ass'n v. FTC, 3
American Home Prods. Corp., In re, 223
American Tobacco Co. v. Florida, 134
Amobi v. District of Columbia, Dep't of Corr., 171
Anonymous, In re, 482
Anonymous, Matter of, 286
Anonymous Members of the S.C. Bar, In re, 284
Arabia, In re, 337
Arons, In re, 64
Asousa Partnership v. Smithfield Foods, 157
Attorney Grievance Comm'n of Md. v. Hallmon, 74
Averill v. Cox, 399

Baird v. Koerner, 131
Bates v. State Bar of Ariz., 91, 266, 286, 299
BDO Seidman; United States v., 141
Beaulieu v. Colvin, 332
Bedwell v. Fish & Richardson P.C., 158
Bell Helicopter Textron, In re, 232
Benninghoff v. Superior Court, 29
Berry v. Schmitt, 481
Beyers v. Richmond, 399
Birbower, Montalbano, Condon & Frank, P.C. v. Superior Court, 63
Blair v. Ing, 329
Bloss v. Ford Motor Co., 137
Board of Comm'rs of the Utah State Bar v. Petersen, 61, 98

Bonda Indus. (HK) Co. v. Talbot Grp., 483
Branhaven v. Beeftek, 483
Brockey v. Moore, 73, 115
Brown v. Legal Found. of Wash., 342
Busch v. Flangas, 408
Button; NAACP v., 216, 280

Calvert v. Scharf, 397
Cartmel, In the Matter of, 284, 297
Cavanaugh v. Cardinal Local Sch. Dist., 64
Central Hudson Gas & Elec. Corp. v. Public Serv. Comm'n, 297
Ciaffone v. District Court, 224-225, 247
Cincinnati Bar Ass'n v. Foreclosure Solutions, 125
Cincinnati Bar Ass'n v. Kathman, 381
Cincinnati Bar Ass'n v. Mullaney, 61, 63, 78, 84, 121, 281
Cincinnati Bar Ass'n v. Telford, 95
Claypole v. County of Monterey, 459
Coito v. Superior Court, 158
Cole v. Meyer, 409
Columbia Valley Healthcare Sys., In re, 223
Commonwealth v. Williams, 483
Condon; Doe v., 63
Crane v. State Bar of Cal., 492
Crawford v. City of New London, 329
Cripe v. Leiter, 399
Crowe v. Tull, 399

Davies v. Unauthorized Practice Comm. of State Bar of Tex., 65
Dayton Bar Ass'n v. O'Brien, 481

Table of Cases

Dayton Supply v. Montgomery Bd. of Rev., 64
Delta/Airtran Baggage Fee Antitrust Litigation, In re, 483
Denver Bar Ass'n v. P.U.C., 87
Department of Corp., People ex rel. v. Speedee Oil Change Sys., Inc., 219
Department of Trans. v. Robbins and Robbins, Inc., 331
DeVaux v. American Home Assurance Co., 403
Dillman v. Holland & Knight, 231
Disciplinary Counsel v. Maley, 408
Disciplinary Counsel v. Shaw, 232
Divine, In re Estate of, 52, 215
Doe v. *see name of opposing party*
Dowd, In re, 71
Drake v. Superior Court of San Diego County, 60
Dwyer v. Cappell, 270

Eastern Associated Coal Corp. v. Director, Off. of Workers Comp. Programs, 347
Eastrich No. 157 Corp. v. Gatto, 224
Eaton v. Fink, 459, 497
Edenfield v. Fane, 280
Eizenga v. Unity Christian School, 136
Ellis; United States v., 141

Faretta v. California, 68, 80
Federal Election Comm'n v. Christian Coalition, 133
Fedora v. Werber, 224
Fickett v. Superior Court, 397
Finch, In re, 60, 100
Finley v. State, 467
Flack, In re, 63, 348
Florida Bar, State ex rel. v. Sperry, 98
Florida Bar v. Abrams, 50
Florida Bar v. Derek Vashon James, 473
Florida Bar v. Neiman, 78, 95
Foster; State v., 70, 95
Fry v. Napoleon Comm. Sch., 64

Garcia, In re, 330
Garrison v. Louisiana, 468
Gellene; United States v., 210
Genovese v. Provident Life Ins. Co., 162
Gibson v. Texas Dep't of Ins. Div. of Workers' Comp., 309
Gillaspy, In re, 409
Gleeman; United States v., 212
Glidewell v. Greenville, 332
Goldberger & Dubin; United States v., 141
Grand Jury Matter, In re, 141
Grand Jury Subpoena Duces Tecum, In re, 141
Grand Jury Subpoena for Attorney Representing Reyes-Requena, In re, 141

Grand Jury Subpoenas, In re, 140
Grant v. Thirteenth Court of Appeals, 223
Great Am. Leasing v. Cool Comfort Air Conditioning & Refrigeration, Inc., 367
Green, In re, 481
Green v. Toledo Hosp., 224
Gross, In re, 111
Gross v. Perrysburg Exempted Vill. Sch., 336
G.S., F.S.; In re Grand Jury Proceedings, 134
Guaranty Ins. Serv., Inc., In re, 223, 247
Guo Wengui v. Clark Hill, PLC, 131, 191

Haines v. Liggett Grp. Inc., 134
Hanna; State v., 399
Hansen v. Hansen, 61
Harrell v. Florida Bar, 269
Hawkins v. Berkeley Unified Sch. Dist., 348
Hayes v. Central State Orthopedic Specialists, Inc., 224, 240
Hear, In the Matter of, 347, 348
Hecker, In the Matter of, 39
Heintz v. Johnson, 3
Henderson v. Pacific Gas, 409
Heslin v. Connecticut Law Clinic, 399
Hickman v. Taylor, 137
HLC Props., Ltd. v. Superior Court, 129
Hoag v. Amex Assurance Co., 466
Hodge v. Urfa-Sexton, 224
Holmes v. Petrovich Dev. Co., 131, 158
HPD Labs., Inc. v. Clorox Co., 129, 159
Hrones, In re, 85
Hunter v. Virginia State Bar, 270, 303

Ibanez v. Florida Dep't of Bus. & Prof'l Regulation, 269
Interfaith Comm. Org. v. Honeywell Int'l, Inc., 332

Jackson v. United Artists Theatre Circuit, Inc., 81
Jacobson v. Knepper & Moga, 509
Jamgochian v. Prousalis, 399
Jasmine Networks, Inc. v. Marvell Semiconductors, Inc., 157
Jenkins, In re, 330
Johnson v. Avery, 72, 81
Johnson v. Nextel Commc'ns, Inc., 232, 328
Johnson v. Sandler, 397
Jordan v. CCH, Inc., 333
Jorgensen v. Taco Bell Corp., 482
J.P. Morgan v. Liberty, 210

King v. First Capital Fin. Servs. Corp., 95
Kirk v. First Am. Title Ins., 221
Klitsch, In re, 14
Koen Book Distribs. v. Powell, Trachtman, 142

Table of Cases

Kovel; United States v., 140
Koven, In re, 481

Lake v. City of Phoenix, 155
Lamb v. Pralex Corp., 236
Landlords Prof'l Servs.; People v., 112
Latham v. Castillo, 399
Leibowitz v. Dist. Ct., 224, 242
Lenarz; State v., 181
Lenz v. Universal Music Corp., 141
Lewis v. Casey, 72
Liapis v. Second Judicial Dist. Ct., 211
Lipsett v. Blanco, 332
Little Compton, In re Town of, 85
Lola v. Skadden, Arps, Slate, Meagher & Flom, 525
Long v. Ethics & Disc. Comm'n of the Utah Supreme Ct., 82, 348
Los Angeles County Bd. of Supervisors v. Superior Court, 142

Macedo v. Russo, 399
Mack v. Baker, 134
MacLeish v. Boardman & Clark, 397
Mahoning Cmty. Bar Ass'n v. Lavelle, 408
Martin Marietta Corp., In re, 133
Martin; United States v., 135
Martinez v. Cal. Dep't of Transportation, 467
Massey v. Prince George's County, 488
Mata v. Avianca, Inc., 478
McBurney, In re, 482
McCool, In re, 470
McDermott Will & Emery LLP v. Superior Court, 185
Merits Incentives, LLC v. Eighth Judicial District Court of Nevada, 171
Metro Data Sys., Inc. v. Durango Sys., Inc., 332
Microsoft Corp. v. United Computer Res. of N.J., Inc., 336
Midwest Motor Sports v. Arctic Sales, Inc., 482
Mississippi Bar v. Attorney ST, 481
Mississippi Bar v. Thompson, 85, 111
Missouri v. Jenkins, 320, 328, 329, 330, 334, 335, 336, 348, 355, 360, 370
Mogck v. UNUM Life Ins. Co. of Am., 363
Moncier v. Ferrell, 330
Moore v. Anderson Ziegler, 397
Moralez v. Whole Food Mkt., 332
Morin, In re, 62, 76, 118, 347
Motors Liquidation Co., In re, 440
Music Merchants, Inc., In re, 332
Musselman v. Willoughby Corp., 37, 40, 41, 80, 396

NAACP v. *See name of opposing party*
Newman v. Highland Sch. Dist. No. 203, 135
Nicholas; United States v., 135, 204
Nix v. Whiteside, 462

North Carolina St. Brd. of Dental Examiners v. FTC, 40
Novoselsky, In re, 459

Office Atty. Gen. v. Shapiro, 399
Official Comm. of Unsecured Creditors of Motors Liquidation Co. v. JPMorgan Chase Bank, 440
Ohio State Bar Ass'n v. Burdzinski, Brinkman, Czarzasty & Lanwehr, Inc., 85
Ohralik v. Ohio State Bar Ass'n, 280, 299
Omaha Bank v. Siouxland Cattle Coop., 494
Oregon State Bar v. Taub, 66
Ositis, In re, 472, 499

Peel v. Attorney Registration & Disciplinary Comm'n of Ill., 269
Pension Committee v. Banc of America Securities, 466
People v. *see name of opposing party*
Perez v. Cate, 330, 370
Phillips, In re, 46, 62, 63, 80, 158
Phoenix Founders, Inc. v. Marshall, 223, 233
Pincay v. Andrews, 424
Premium Pet Health v. All American Pet Proteins, 463
Primus, In re, 280
Prince, In re, 205
Public Citizen, Inc. v. Louisiana Attorney Disciplinary Bd., 269

Reed v. Allison & Perrone, 399
Regents of the Univ. of Cal. v. Superior Court, 142
Reynoso, In re, 72, 109
RFF Family P'ship LP v. Burns & Levinson, 140
Richlin Sec. Serv. Co. v. Chertoff, 329, 334, 355, 370
Rickley v. Goodfriend, 336
Rico v. Mitsubishi Motors Corp., 174
Riemers v. State, 329
Ritchie; United States v., 141
R.M.J., In re, 268
Rodriguez-Hernandez v. Miranda-Vales, 332
Rousseau v. Eshleman, 399
Rubin v. Enns, 223

Salgado, In re, 347
Samaritan Found. v. Superior Court, 129
Sanford v. GMRI, Inc., 25, 348, 378
Santiago v. Equable Ascent Fin. Co., 332
Sayhers v. Prugh, 501
Schroff, Inc. v. Taylor-Peterson, 329, 336
Scott, In re, 29, 85
Searcy v. Florida Bar, 292

Table of Cases

SEC v. Bernard L. Madoff Investment Securities LLC, 134
Sentis Grps. v. Shell Oil, 466
Shafer v. Berger, Kahn, 398
Shapero v. Kentucky Bar Ass'n, 268
Shaw v. Murphy, 72
Sheppard, Mullin, Richter & Hampton, LLP v. J-M Manufacturing Co., 258
Short v. Demopolis, 399
Smart Indus. Corp. v. Superior Court, 224
Smith; People v., 417
Snider v. Superior Court, 482
Sperry v. Florida, 87
Sprewell v. Golden State Warriors, 466
Standing Comm. v. Yagman, 481
State Bar v. Lang, 11
State Compensation Ins. Fund v. WPS, Inc., 154
St. Farm Mut. Auto. Inc. Co. v. Edge Family Chiropractic, 375
St. Simons Waterfront, LLC v. Hunter, Maclean, Exley & Dunn, 140
State. *See name of opposing party*
Statewide Grievance Comm. v. Zadora, 82
Stewart; United States v., 158
Styles v. Mumbert, 141
Sundance v. Municipal Court, 336
Supreme Court of Ariz. v. Struthers, 37, 44
Swidler & Berlin v. United States, 141

Taylor v. Chubb, 360
Tegman v. Accident & Med. Investigations, 429
TXU U.S. Holdings Co., In re, 223, 232

Ullman v. Denco, Inc., 253
Unauthorized Practice of Law Comm., State Bar of Texas v. Cortez, 88
Unauthorized Practice of Law Comm. v. State Dep't of Workers' Comp., 8, 87

United States v. *See name of opposing party*
Updike, Kelly & Spellacy v. Beckett, 335
Upjohn Co. v. United States, 135
Usher, In re, 525

Vayner; United States v., 483
Victor Stanley, Inc. v. Creative Pipe, Inc., 134, 153, 165
Vitac Corp. v. Workers' Comp. Appeals Board, 329, 336
VLT, Inc. v. Lucent Technologies, Inc., 133

Wade v. Soo Line R.R. Corp., 466
Wal-Mart Stores, Inc. v. Dickinson, 158
Weigel, In re, 347
Welch, In re, 65
White, In re, 467
Whitehead v. Town House Equities, Ltd., 60
Whitehouse v. U.S. Dist. Ct., 141
Williams v. R.W. Cannon, Inc., 336
Williams v. Sprint/United Mgmt. Co., 158
Winkelman v. Parma City Sch. Dist., 64
Winkler, In re, 482
Wolff v. McDonnell, 72

Zamora v. Clayborn Contracting, 435
Zanoletti; People v., 285
Zauderer v. Office of Disciplinary Counsel of the Supreme Court of Ohio, 268, 317
Zimmerman v. Mahaska Bottling Co., 225
Zubulake v. UBS Warburg, 466

Index

AAfPE (American Association for Paralegal Education), 20, 22, 390, 517-518
ABA. *See* American Bar Association
ABS (Alternative business structures), 340-341
Abuse of process, action for, 457
Access to legal services
   advertising and, 273, 276-277
   barriers to, 29
   contingency fees and, 316
   limited nature of, 29, 520
   nonlawyer service providers, 59-63, 72-73
   technology and, 61-62
   unbundling of services, 326
Accident victims, solicitation of, 269, 272, 280
Accounting for client funds and property, 343
ADA (Americans with Disabilities Act), 519
Administrative agencies, 86-88
Administrative Procedure Act, 86-87
Admonition of lawyers, 6
Advance fees, 326-327
Advanced Certified Paralegal (ACP) credential, 21
Adverse controlling authority, disclosure of, 461
Advertising, 266-279
   accident victims, solicitation of, 269, 272, 280
   case law, 268-270
   certification or specialization, including in, 272
   current ethics rules, 270-273
   current issues and trends in, 267, 273-279
   dignity of, 271
   direct-mail, 268
   disclaimers, 278-279
   e-mail, 268, 274-275, 276
   ethics rules, 270-273
   false or misleading, 270-271, 278, 279
   historical perspective, 266-268
   Internet, 267, 273-279
   Model Rules, 4
   solicitation, 279-281
   statements regarding past performance or comparison, 271
   Supreme Court decisions, 268-269
   targeted to accident and disaster victims, 269, 272
   testimonials, 271
   trade names in, 272
   types of, 267-268
Advice. *See* Legal advice
Advocacy, 454-478. *See also* Litigation process; Zealous representation
Advocate-witness conflict, 207
Affirmation of Responsibility (NFPA), 35
Age Discrimination in Employment Act, 333
Agents, attorney's, 129, 279-281, 472
Aggravating and mitigating factors, sanctions decisions and, 6
AI (Artificial Intelligence), 477-478
Alabama, 4, 155, 225
Alaska, court-awarded paralegal fees, 329
Alcohol dependency. *See* Substance abuse
Alternative business structures (ABS), 340-341
Alternative legal service providers. *See* Nonlawyer legal service providers
"Ambulance chasers," 280
American Association for Paralegal Education (AAfPE), 20, 22, 390, 517-518
American Bar Association (ABA). *See also* Model Code of Professional Responsibility; Model Guidelines for the Utilization of Paralegal Services; Model Rules of Professional Conduct
   blogs, social networking, and chat groups, 274

Index

American Bar Association (ABA) (*continued*)
    Canons of Professional Ethics (1908), 4, 266
    curriculum for paralegals, guidelines for, 20, 389-390, 517
    definition of paralegal, 27
    endorsement of paralegal concept, 20
    ethics opinions. *See* American Bar Association ethics opinions
    fee-splitting, 337, 338
    Guidelines for the Approval of Paralegal Education Programs, 390
    House of Delegates, 27, 61, 333, 478
    licensing of paralegals, stance on, 27-28
    model codes, generally, 4-5
    Model Rules on Client Trust Account Records, 344-345
    overview, 3-5
    paralegal programs approved by, 389-390
    partnerships with nonlawyers, 339-340
    Practice Forward survey, 403
    Special Committee on the Unauthorized Practice of Law, 59
    Standards for Criminal Justice, 476
    Standing Committee on Paralegals, 20, 27, 517
    Task Force on the Future of Legal Education, 30
    technology use, 478
    unauthorized practice of law, 61
American Bar Association ethics opinions
    advertising (Formal Opinion 07-445), 272
    billing abuses (Formal Opinion 93-379), 323
    class actions, communication with prospective members (Formal Opinion 07-445), 281
    collaborative law practice (Formal Opinion 07-447), 520
    conflicts checks (Formal Opinion 09-455), 226-227
    counsel (Formal Opinion 06-443), 471
    credit card payments (Formal Opinion 338), 327
    defined, 5
    disclosure of paralegal status (Informal Opinion 1367), 89-90
    fee arrangements (Formal Opinion 11-458), 326
    fee arrangements (Informal Opinion 875), 325
    financing for payment of fees (Formal Opinion 338), 327
    improper ex parte contacts of nonlawyers (Formal Opinion 95-396), 472
    inadvertent receipt of privileged information (Formal Opinions 92-368, 94-382, and 06-440), 154
    lawyer workloads (Formal Opinion 06-441), 403
    letterhead, paralegals on (Informal Opinion 1527), 91
    metadata (Formal Opinion 06-442), 150
    paralegal use of business cards (Informal Opinions 909 & 1185), 90
    profit-based compensation and retirement plans (Informal Opinion 1440), 338
    prohibition of paralegals to set fees (Informal Opinion 875), 325
    screening of paralegals (Informal Opinion 88-1521), 222
    social media use by juror, lawyer review of (Formal Opinion 466), 469
    temporary lawyers (Formal Opinion 88-356), 228
    use of technology (Formal Opinion 11-459), 149
    use of unencrypted e-mail (Formal Opinion 99-413), 150
    Web-based communication issues, 275, 279
    witness preparation (Formal Opinion 508), 473
American Civil Liberties Union (ACLU), 280
Americans with Disabilities Act (ADA), 519
Anti-virus software, 149
Appearance in court. *See* Court appearances
Appearance of impropriety, conflicts of interest and, 205-206
Apprenticeships, 388
Arbitration. *See* Mediation and arbitration
Arizona
    alternative business structure, 341
    attorney-client privilege, 129
    billing issues, 322
    computer programs for form preparation, 72
    conflicts of interest, 224
    court-awarded paralegal fees, 329
    IOLTA plans, 342
    lawyer advertising, 272
    legal document preparers, 31
    legal help for inmates, 72
    limited practice legal professionals, 32, 69
    metadata, use of, 155
    paralegal representation in court, 69
    practice of law, defined, 66
    regulation of paralegals, 25
    unauthorized practice of law, 61, 62
Artificial Intelligence (AI), 477-478
Association for Legal Professionals (NALS), 22, 23
Association of Professional Responsibility Lawyers, 280
Associations, paralegal, 20-22. *See also individual associations*
Attorney-client privilege, 73-74, 128-136
Attorney-client relationships
    Internet advice and inadvertent establishment of, 73, 275, 276, 399
    successive representation and, 205-207
    unauthorized practice of law and, 73-74
Attorneys. *See* Lawyers
Attorney's fees. *See* Fees
Audits, 135, 343

Bankruptcy, 60, 204-205, 330
Bankruptcy Code, 330

Bar associations. *See also specific states*
  American Bar Association. *See* American Bar Association (ABA)
  efforts to improve image of lawyers, 509-510
  pro bono work encouraged by, 520
  state, 2-3
  unauthorized practice of law and, 58, 59
Barratry, 213
"Best Lawyer" designations, 272
Bias and discrimination, 518-519
Billable hours, 318, 322-323, 507
Billing fraud or abuse, 321
Black, Nicole, 478
Block billing, 323
Blogs, 267, 274, 276. *See also* Social media
Board of directors of corporate client, serving on, 204, 398
Bonuses, 338-339
Borrowing from clients, 212
Bribery, 468
Brochures, law firm, 267
Bureau of Indian Affairs, 87
Bureau of Labor Statistics, paralegal careers, 21
Burnout, 511
Business cards, 90, 273
Business relationships with clients. *See also* Corporate clients
  conflicts of interest and, 211-212, 398
  malpractice claims, 398
  nonlawyer legal service providers, regulation of, 29-31
  regulation of lawyers in, 3
  testamentary gifts from clients, 214

California
  advertising, 278
  billing issues, 323
  certification of paralegals, 27
  Client Trust Account Protection Program, 343
  computer programs for form preparation, 72
  confidentiality and technology, 149
  conflicts of interest, 223
  court-awarded paralegal fees, 329, 330
  disbarred lawyers as paralegals, 29
  disciplinary sanctions, 476
  disobeying a court order, 460
  disruptive conduct of lawyers, 459-460
  legal document assistants, 31, 73
  legal representation by spouse, 69
  nonlawyer fees for legal services, 320
  paralegal appearance before administrative agencies, 87
  referral fees, 337
  regulation of paralegals, 24-25
  Rules of Professional Conduct, 29
  social media as solicitation, 276
  solicitation by lawyers, 277
  Statements of Principle for nonlawyer service providers, 59
  technological competence, 477
  titles for paralegals, 89
  unauthorized practice of law, 63
California Business and Professions Code, 317
Canada, 26, 328
Candor to the court, duty of, 463
Canons of Professional Ethics, ABA (1908), 4, 266
Cappers and runners, 280
Cellular telephones, confidentiality and, 148
Certification
  ABA stance on, 27
  advertising of lawyer, 269, 272
  defined, 23
  designations and titles, 89, 272, 516-517
  examinations, 22, 26, 391
  programs for paralegals, 20-21, 22-23, 391
  specialized, for lawyers, 392
  state-specific, 26-27
  trends, 23
Certified Paralegal/Advanced Certified Paralegal (CP/ACP) program, 20-21, 22, 23
Champerty, 213
Chat groups, 73, 274, 276
ChatGPT, 395, 478
Civil suits
  malicious prosecution/abuse of process, 457
  representation of co-parties, 203
  third-party malpractice claims, 396-397
  unauthorized practice of law, 59, 66
Claim or defense, unmeritorious or frivolous, 455-458
Class action suits
  class members as represented parties, 471
  conflicts of interest in representation, 203, 328
  solicitation exception for, 272, 281
Claw-back agreements, 132-133
Clayton Act, 330
Client files. *See* Files, client
Client funds and property, 341-345, 400-401
Client perjury, 461-462, 474
Clients
  business transactions with, 211-212
  communication with, 394, 400
  conferences with, 146
  consent to potential conflict of interest, 200-201
  contact with by paralegals, 71-72, 394, 400, 404
  disclosure of identity or whereabouts, 131
  prospective, conflicts checks, 200, 226, 279
  selection of, 400
  unlawful solicitation of, 63
Client security funds, 342
Client surveys, 267-268
Client Trust Account Protection Program (CTAPP), 343
Client trust accounts, 341-342, 344-345

539

Cloud computing, 148
Coaching witnesses, 473
Code of Ethics and Professional Responsibility, NALA
   Canon 3(b), 325
   Canon 4, 281
   Canon 5, 91
   Canon 6, 391
   Canon 7, 144
   Canon 9, 199
Code of Ethics and Professional Responsibility, NFPA, 35
Codes of ethics, generally, 4-5, 35. *See also* Code of Ethics and Professional Responsibility, NALA; Model Code of Ethics and Professional Responsibility, NFPA; Model Code of Professional Responsibility, ABA; Model Rules of Professional Conduct, ABA
Collaborative law practice, 519-520
Collegiality, 511, 513, 515
Colorado
   computer programs for form preparation, 72
   consumer protection, 399
   disbarred lawyers as paralegals, 29
   guidelines for paralegal use, 34
   limited practice legal professionals, 33-34
   unauthorized practice of law, 76
Commingling of funds, 343
Commission on the Evaluation of Professional Standards (Kutak Commission), 4
Communications
   with clients, 394, 400
   with judges, 468
   with jurors, 469-470
   with parties represented by counsel, 470-471
   with unrepresented parties, 471-472
   with witnesses, 472-474
Competence, 388-404
   duty of, 388
   education and training, 388-391
   factors affecting, 401-404
   incompetence, sanctions for, 394-396
   knowing limits of, 401
   qualities comprising, 392-394, 399-401, 454-455
   questioning of by clients, disclosure of privileged information and, 134
   technological, 477
Computer programs, 72, 149-150, 227
Computers, measures to protect confidentiality of, 145, 146, 148-150
Concurrent representation, 199-205. *See also* Simultaneous representation
Cone of silence (screen), 220
Confidentiality, 142-155. *See also* Attorney-client privilege
   agreements, 147
   breaches of, 398
   cloud computing, 148
   conflicts of interest and duty of, 198

   ethics rules, 142-143
   inadvertent disclosure of information, 132-134, 153-154
   malpractice claims, 398
   paralegals and, 142-155, 228
   policies and procedures, 144-147
   principle of, 128
   successive representation and, 205-207
   technology, special issues relating to, 147-152
   use of information for gain, 147
   Web-based communications, 275, 279
   work product doctrine, 137
Conflicts of interest, 198-228
   appearance of impropriety, 205-206
   business transactions with clients, 211-212, 398
   conflicts checks, 200, 226-228, 279, 401
   consent to future conflicts, 201
   duty of confidentiality and, 198
   financial assistance to clients, 213
   generally, 198-199
   gifts from clients, 214-215
   imputed disqualification for, 198-199, 202, 218-225
   issue conflicts, 202
   malpractice claims, 398
   malpractice liability, agreements with clients, 215
   motions to disqualify counsel, 7, 206-207, 213, 221
   proprietary interest in litigation, 213
   publication, literary, and media rights, 212-213
   relatives and friends, 216-217
   simultaneous or concurrent representation, 199-205
   statutory fees and, 328
   successive representation, 205-207
   third-party payment of fees, 215-216
   Web-based communications and, 275, 279
Connecticut
   consumer protection, 399
   guidelines for paralegal use, 34
   lawyer advertising, 272
   referral fees, 337
   screening paralegals from cases, 199
   unauthorized practice of law, 76, 77
Consent, 200-201, 211, 217
Constitutional rights, prosecutorial violation of, 476
Consumer fraud suits against lawyers, 399
Contempt power of courts, 7, 457, 460
Contingency fees, 213, 316-317, 325
Continuing education, 388-389, 390
Control group test, corporate setting, 135
Conversation, disclosure of confidential information in, 145-146
Conversion of client funds, 343
Co-parties to litigation, simultaneous representation of, 203
Cordless telephones, confidentiality and, 148

Corporate clients
   attorney-client privilege and, 135-136
   billing practices, steps to prevent abuses, 322-323
   conflicts of interest arising with, 202, 204
   internal audits and attorney-client privilege, 135
   malpractice claims for securities work, 397
Corporate officers, legal representation by, 63-64
Corporate setting, 471
Correspondence, signing of by paralegals, 89-90
Costs of litigation. *See* Expenses
Counseling programs, 510
Court appearances, 68-71, 458-461
Court facilitators, 73
Court order, disobeying, 460
Court-ordered disclosure and attorney-client privilege, 136
Craigslist, 274
Credit card, payment of legal fees by, 327
Crime, future, 134
Criminal cases
   charges against lawyers, 6
   charges for unauthorized practice of law, 59
   client perjury, 461-462
   contingency fees and, 317
   disclosure of privileged information and, 134
   representation of multiple defendants, 203
   special rules for prosecutors, 475-476
   third-party payment of attorneys' fees for defendants, 215-216
   unauthorized practice of law, 66
Criminal evidence, attorney-client privilege and, 132
Criticism of judges, inappropriate, 467-468
CTAPP (Client Trust Account Protection Program), 343

Databases, protection of information in, 146
Defendants, paralegals as, 36
Defense or claim, unmeritorious or frivolous, 455-458
Delaware, 27, 399
Delaying litigation, unethically, 456, 458
Delegation of duties, 402
Department of, U.S. *See name of specific department*
Depositions, 69-70
Depression rates, 396, 510
Destruction of evidence, 461, 463
Digital courier services, 150
Direct e-mail advertising, 276
Direct-mail advertising, 268, 269, 271-272
Directories, online, 276-277, 278
Dirty tricks in the courtroom, 459
Disabled employees, 519
Disaster victims, direct-mail advertising targeting, 269

Disbarment
   billing abuses, 321-322
   candor, 462
   discrimination, 508
   illegal conduct and fraud, 507-508
   jurors, research on, 469
   lawyers working as paralegals following, 29
   misuse of client funds, 345, 508
   overview, 5
   for pre-existing relationships in bankruptcy, 205
   prosecutorial misconduct, 476
   social media use, 470
   statements about judges, 460
   unauthorized practice of law following, 67
Disciplinary actions. *See also* Disbarment
   for commingling and conversion of funds, 343
   disclosure of privileged information in, 134
   disrespect for the court, 459-460
   for ethical misconduct of lawyers, 5-6, 457-458, 507-508
   generally, 3
   for Internet solicitation of clients, 275
   sanctions for incompetence, 394-396
   trial publicity violations, 474-475
Disclaimers in advertising, 278-279
Disclosure of paralegal status, 88-91, 455, 467
Discounting of fees, 318-319, 327
Discovery
   abuses of, 398, 456, 458
   blanket privilege, 136
   e-discovery, 456, 477
   electronic databases and documents, use of, 137
   failure to comply, 459
   inadvertent disclosure of information, 152
   paralegal involvement in, 153, 454-455
   work product doctrine and, 137
Discriminatory practices, 519
Dismissal of charges, 458, 463
Disobeying a court order, 460
Disqualification of counsel
   appearance of impropriety and, 205-206
   for communicating with represented parties, 471
   for contact with jurors, 469
   disgorgement of fees, 218
   imputed disqualification, 198-199, 202, 218-225
   motions to disqualify, 7, 206-207, 213, 221
   screening to avoid, 220-225
   for simultaneous or concurrent representation, 200, 201-202
Disruptive conduct in the courtroom, 458-461
Dissolution of marriage. *See* Divorce
District of Columbia, 155, 321-322, 340
Divorce, 60, 202-203, 317
Document production, 132-134, 137, 153
Do-it-yourself legal kits, 59, 72
Double billing, 321, 323
Drug dependency problems. *See* Substance abuse

541

Education and training
  lawyers, 30, 388-389, 392, 401
  paralegals, 22, 389-391, 401, 513, 514, 517-518
800 telephone numbers, law firms with, 268
Electronically stored information (ESI), 477
Electronic Discovery Resource Manual (EDRM), 477
Electronic identification cards (smart cards), 149
Electronic newsgroups, 275
Electronic records, confidentiality of, 145, 147-152
Electronic resources, use of, 61-62, 72, 398-399, 456, 476-478
Electronic social networking. See Social media
E-mail
  advertising, 268, 274-275, 276
  confidentiality and, 150-152, 279
  policies and procedures, 151-152
  prompt response to client, 394, 400
  solicitation by, 274-275, 276
Embedded metadata, 150, 154-155
Employment discrimination, 519
Encryption software, 150
Engagement letters, 399-400
England, fee shifting in, 328
Equal Access to Justice Act, 329
ESI (Electronically stored information), 477
Estate planning. See Probate matters; Wills
Ethical wall (screen), 220
Ethics, teaching, 510
Ethics opinions
  ABA. See American Bar Association ethics opinions
  generally, 5, 35
  state bar associations. See specific states
Europe, fee shifting in, 328
Evidence, 132, 461, 463, 476
Executor, naming lawyer as, 214
Exempt status of paralegals, 518
Ex parte communications, 468-469, 471-472
Expenses, 213, 325-327, 474
Expert witnesses, 203, 474

Facebook, 152, 274, 470, 471
Fair Labor Standards Act, 518
Fair trial, right to, 474
False or misleading advertising, 270-271, 278, 279
False testimony, 461, 472, 474
Falsification of evidence, 461
Family law advertising, 30, 59, 268, 273, 454
Family relationships, 69, 216-217
Fax communications, confidentiality and, 147-148
Federal Electronic Communications Privacy Act, 148
Federal Rules of Civil Procedure, 137, 458
Federal Rules of Evidence, protection against loss of attorney-client privilege, 132-133, 154

Federal Trade Commission, 62, 76
Fees, 316-341
  adjustment, 324
  alternative arrangements, 318-319
  attorney-client privilege and, 131-132
  billing abuses, 320-324, 507
  blended rates, 331-332
  capping, 319
  commingling and conversion of funds, 343
  court-awarded, 328-333
  discounts, 318-319, 327
  disgorging, on disqualification of counsel, 218
  establishing, 324-327
  ethics rules, 320-324
  expert witnesses, 474
  federal statutes, 330
  fee-shifting statutes, 328
  fee-splitting, 63, 337-341
  financing of, 327
  full disclosure, 323
  illegal, 320
  liens to secure, 213
  limited practice legal professionals, 320
  for paralegal services, 319-320
  partnerships with nonlawyers, 340-341
  petitions to the court for paralegal fees, 330-332
  prequalification of, 330
  property as payment of, 327
  reduction, 332-333
  reform efforts, 328
  seizure of fee paid with assets obtained through illegal activities, 131-132
  setting, 74, 325
  sharing of, 32, 219
  statutory awards, 320, 321, 328-333
  third-party payment of, 215-216
  types of. See Fees, types of
  unauthorized practice of law and setting of, 58, 63, 74
  unreasonable or excessive, 320-321, 400
  written agreements, 317, 324-326, 400
Fees, types of
  advance, 326-327
  contingency, 213, 316-317, 325
  estimated, 327
  fixed, 316
  forwarding, 337
  hourly, 318, 322
  percentage-based, 317, 319
  referral, 281, 337, 339
  retainers, 326-327
  task-based, 319
Fiduciary relationship of lawyer and client. See Client funds and property; Fees
Files, client
  handling of, 144-147, 344, 401
  retention policies, 344
  screening, 220
  shredding, 145

Financial assistance to clients, 213
Financing for payment of fees, 327
Firewalls, 150
Fixed fees/flat fees, 316
Fleeing, advising witnesses on, 472
Florida
   advertising, 278
   computer programs for form preparation, 72
   conflicts of interest, 224, 225
   consumer protection, 399
   court-awarded paralegal fees, 329
   disruptive conduct of lawyers, 459
   lawyer advertising, 269, 276
   metadata, use of, 155
   pro bono work, 520
   regulation of paralegals, 25
   unauthorized practice of law, 71, 77
   voluntary certification program for paralegals, 26-27
   witness coaching, 473
Foreclosure consultants, 61, 268
Foreclosures, 508
Forwarding fees, 337
Fraud, 134, 320-324, 399
Free association, right of, 216
Free expression, right of, 474
Freelance paralegals
   client confidentiality and, 144
   conflicts checks, 228
   screening of, 223
   use of, 21, 30, 92-93
Frivolous claims or defenses, asserting, 455-458
Future crime or fraud, attorney-client privilege and, 134

Gag orders, 474, 475
Gender-related issues, 403, 518-519
Georgia
   billing issues, 321
   conflicts of interest, 224
   consumer protection, 399
   guidelines for paralegal use, 34
   unauthorized practice of law, 76, 78
Gifts from clients, 214-215
Government (administrative) agencies, 86-88
Government lawyers, 206, 219
Groupons, 275

Harassment, 470, 519
Hawaii, 26, 520
History, 20-23, 58-64
Honesty, duty of, 461-463
Hourly fees, 318, 322
Hybrid work schedule, 403

Idaho, guidelines for paralegal use, 34
IDEA (Individuals with Disabilities Education Act), 64

Identity of client, attorney-client privilege and, 131
Illinois
   confidentiality issues, 144
   court-awarded paralegal fees, 329
   disbarred lawyers as paralegals, 29
   guidelines for paralegal use, 34
   lawyer misconduct, 508
   nonlawyer fees for legal services, 320
   partnerships with nonlawyers, 340
   solicitation, 281
   technological competence, 477
   unauthorized practice of law, 62, 76
Immigration law, nonlawyer service providers, 60, 62
Imputed disqualification, 198-199, 202, 218-225
Inadvertent disclosure of information, 132-134, 152-155
In camera examination, 136
Incidental legal services test, 65
Incompetence. *See* Competence
Independent contractors. *See* Freelance paralegals
Independent counsel, consultation with, 201, 211
Indiana
   court-awarded paralegal fees, 329
   disbarred lawyers as paralegals, 29
   guidelines for paralegal use, 34
   lawyer advertising, 273
   paralegal representation in court, 69
   pro bono work, 520
   screening paralegals from cases, 199
Individuals with Disabilities Education Act (IDEA), 64
Influencing judges, attempts at, 468
In-house training programs, 392
Injunctive relief for unauthorized practice of law, 66
Inmates, nonlawyer assistance by, 72
Insider trading, 147, 212
Instagram, 152
Insurance, 266, 323, 394
Insurance companies, 137, 398
Integrated bar associations, 2. *See also* Bar associations
Interest on Lawyers' Trust Accounts (IOLTA), 342
Intermediaries, solicitation by, 281
Internal Revenue Service, 87, 131
International Practice Management Association (IPMA), 21, 22, 27, 518
Internet
   advertising, 267, 273-279
   directories and referral services, 276-277, 278
   legal information or advice on, 73, 274, 277-279, 399
   social networking, 152, 274, 276
   statement of jurisdiction on Web sites, 277
   virtual law office, 520
Interstate Commerce Commission, 87

Index

Inter vivos gifts from clients, 214
IOLTA (Interest on Lawyers' Trust Accounts), 342
Iowa
  confidentiality issues, 144
  depositions conducted by paralegals, 70
  guidelines for paralegal use, 34
  lawyer advertising, 272
  profit-based compensation, 338
  titles used by paralegals, 89
  unauthorized practice of law, 76
IPMA. *See* International Practice Management Association
Issue conflicts, 202

Jailhouse lawyers, 72
Job opportunities for paralegals, 21-23
Judges, 204, 467-468
Judiciary, 2-3. *See also* Supreme Court decisions
Jurisdiction, 63, 277
Jurors, 469-470
Justice, duty to seek, 475
Justice, U.S. Department of, 62, 64, 76

Kansas
  conflicts of interest, 225
  guidelines for paralegal use, 34
  partnerships with nonlawyers, 340
  referral fees, 337
  screening paralegals from cases, 199
Kentucky
  conflicts of interest, 225
  guidelines for paralegal use, 34
  lawyer advertising, 268
  partnerships with nonlawyers, 340
  voluntary certification program for paralegals, 27

Labor, U.S. Department of, 518
Laptop computers, confidentiality measures for, 150
Law clerks, conflicts of interest, 204
Law firms
  alternative business structure, 340-341
  changing, screening and, 219
  conflicts checks, 226-228
  imputed disqualification, 198-199, 202, 218-225
  multidisciplinary practices, 340, 511
  nonlawyer interest in, 31, 32
  trade names, 272
Law school education, 388-389, 510
Law students, representation in court by, 69
Lawyers
  advocate-witness conflict, 207
  burnout and stress, 510-511
  collaborative law practice, 519-520
  commingling and conversion of funds, 343
  delegation of duties, 402
  depression rates, 396, 510
  dissatisfaction of, 510-511
  education and training, 30, 388-389, 392
  employment discrimination, 519
  erroneous possession of privileged documents, 153-154
  establishing fees, 324-327
  estate of deceased lawyer, fees paid to, 339
  hired by nonlegal service providers, 63
  inadvertent receipt of privileged information, 153-154
  large-volume practices, 63
  networks, 511
  practice of law, defined, 64-66
  pressure to bill, 321
  public image, 506-509
  in public office, 272
  relationship with clients. *See* Attorney-client relationships
  review of paralegal work, 402-403
  salaries, 507
  skills required, 393
  solicitation by, 279-281
  specialized certification, 392
  subpoena of, 476
  substance abuse by, 396
  supervision by. *See* Supervisory or managerial authority of lawyers
  utilization of paralegals, 63, 67-68, 92-93, 518
  virtual law office, 520
  workload issues, 318, 321, 403-404
  zealous representation, duty of, 455
LDAs. *See* Legal document assistants
LDPs. *See* Legal document preparers
Legal advice
  communicating via correspondence, 89-90
  disclaimers, 278-279
  prohibition of nonlawyers from giving, 71-74, 88
  trends in services, 511
  to unrepresented persons, 471
  on Web sites, 73, 274, 277, 399
Legal advocacy organizations, 216
Legal aid organizations, 21, 266
"Legal assistance" programs, 510
Legal Assistant Management Association, 21. *See also* International Practice Management Association (IPMA)
Legal assistants, 20, 24, 25, 89, 516-517
Legal costs, types of, 327
Legal document assistants (LDAs), 31, 73
Legal document preparers (LDPs), 31, 73
Legal marketing. *See* Advertising
Legal Paraprofessionals (LP), 32-33, 69
Legal secretaries, 89, 517
Legal Services Corporation, funding of, 20, 59
Legal technicians, 31
Letterhead, 90-91, 272-273
Liability, 35-37

Licensed Legal Paraprofessional (LLP) program, 33-34
Licensing, 23, 27-34
Liens to secure fees or expenses, 213
Limited License Legal Technicians (LLLTs), 31
Limited licensing, 30-34
Limited practice legal professionals, 31-34, 320
Limited Practice Rule for Limited License Legal Technicians, 31
LinkedIn, 152
Literary rights, 212-213
Litigation process
 abuses of, 457, 507-508
 court-awarded attorney's fees, 328-333
 delaying, 456-457
 disclosure of confidential information, 137
 disruptive conduct, 458-461
 mistrials, 469-470
 paralegal involvement in, 70, 454-455
 proprietary interest in, 213
 reform efforts, 454
 technology use, 477
 trial publicity, 474-475
 unmeritorious claims or defenses, 455-458
 zealous representation. *See* Zealous representation
Litigiousness of society, 454, 506
Living costs, advancing to a client, 213
Living trusts, preparation of, 62
Loan modification agencies, 61, 508
Location of client, attorney-client privilege and, 131
Louisiana, 27, 269, 399, 460
Loyalty, duty of, 198, 200, 205, 211, 217

Maine, 24, 155
Malicious prosecution, 398, 457
Malpractice insurance, 394
Malpractice suits
 advice for avoiding, 399-401
 agreements with clients limiting lawyer's liability, 215
 for breach of attorney-client privilege, 136
 disclosure of privileged information in, 134
 disqualification as basis for, 218
 malpractice, defined, 6
 medical malpractice cases, fees in, 317
 paralegals as defendants, 36, 394-395
 sanctions for incompetence, 394-396
 securities work, 397
 third-party liability, 396-397
 trends in, 396-399
Management by lawyers. *See* Supervisory or managerial authority of lawyers
Marital relationship. *See* Spouses
Marketing. *See* Advertising
Maryland
 attorney supervision of freelance lawyers, 144
 metadata, use of, 155

nonlawyer practitioners, 73
 pro bono work, 520
 profit-based compensation, 338-339
Massachusetts, 29, 337
MDP (Multidisciplinary practice), 340, 511
Media, lawyer relations with, 474-475
Media rights, 212-213
Mediation and arbitration, 3, 454
Medical malpractice cases, fees in, 317
Mental health issues
 disciplinary action and, 510
 substance abuse, 3, 396, 401, 404, 510
Mental impressions and work product doctrine, 137
Metadata, embedded, 150, 154-155
Michigan
 attorney-client privilege, 129
 conflicts of interest, 217, 225
 disruptive conduct of lawyers, 460
 guidelines for paralegal use, 34
 lawyer advertising, 272
 partnerships with nonlawyers, 340
 screening paralegals from cases, 199
Minnesota
 billing issues, 322
 IOLTA plans, 342
 limited practice legal professionals, 32-33
 pro bono work, 520
 regulation of paralegals, 26
Mississippi, 89, 273, 338, 520
Missouri, 34, 340
Mistrials, 469-470
Mobility of attorneys, 205-207, 218-225
Model Code of Ethics and Professional Responsibility, NFPA
 Canon 1.1, 391
 Canon 1.2, 324
 Canon 1.4, 521
 DR 1.5, 144
 DR 1.6, 199
 DR 1.7, 91
 EC 1.2, 468
 EC 1.3, 461
 EC l.2(e), 345
 EC l.4(d), 521-522
 EC l.6(e), 228
Model Code of Professional Responsibility, ABA
 advertising by lawyers, 266
 Canon 2, 521
 Canon 9, 205
 DR 3-101(A), 67
 EC 3-5, 64
 generally, 4
Model Disciplinary Rules, NFPA, 281
Model Guidelines for the Utilization of Paralegal Services, ABA
 communications with third parties, 472
 generally, 34
 Guideline 1, 67, 281, 390
 Guideline 2, 67-68

Model Guidelines for the Utilization of
  Paralegal Services, ABA (*continued*)
  Guideline 3, 74
  Guideline 3(b), 325
  Guideline 4, 88-89
  Guideline 6, 143-144
  Guideline 7, 199
  Guideline 8, 320, 333
  Guideline 9, 338
  Guideline 10, 390, 521
  paralegals listed on letterhead, 91
Model Rules of Professional Conduct, ABA
  conflicts of interest, categories of, 198
  generally, 4
  informed written consent to conflict of
    interest, 200-201
  Rule 1.1, 391, 477
  Rule 1.2(c), 326
  Rule 1.3, 391, 455
  Rule 1.4, 391-392
  Rule 1.5, 327
  Rule 1.5(a), 320
  Rule 1.5(b), 324-325
  Rule 1.5(c), 317, 325
  Rule 1.5(d)(2), 317
  Rule 1.5(e), 337
  Rule 1.6, 142-143, 152
  Rule 1.7, 200, 202, 204, 214, 217, 226
  Rule 1.7(a), 200
  Rule 1.8(a), 211
  Rule 1.8(b), 218-219
  Rule 1.8(c), 214
  Rule 1.8(d), 212-213
  Rule 1.8(e), 213
  Rule 1.8(f), 216
  Rule 1.8(g), 203
  Rule 1.8(h), 215
  Rule 1.8(i), 213
  Rule 1.8(j), 508
  Rule 1.9, 206
  Rule 1.9(a), 206
  Rule 1.9(b), 206
  Rule 1.9(c), 206
  Rule 1.10, 218, 222-223
  Rule 1.10(a)(2), 219
  Rule 1.11, 206, 219
  Rule 1.11(d), 219
  Rule 1.12, 204
  Rule 1.13, 204
  Rule 1.15(a), 341, 343
  Rule 1.15(d), 343-344
  Rule 1.15(e), 342
  Rule 1.16(d), 344
  Rule 1.18, 276
  Rule 3.1, 455
  Rule 3.2, 457
  Rule 3.3(a), 461, 463, 474
  Rule 3.4, 461
  Rule 3.4(a), 472
  Rule 3.4(b), 472, 474
  Rule 3.4(c), 460
  Rule 3.4(d), 456
  Rule 3.4(f), 472
  Rule 3.5(a), 468
  Rule 3.5(b), 468
  Rule 3.5(c), 470
  Rule 3.5(d), 458
  Rule 3.6, 475
  Rule 3.6(a), 474
  Rule 3.6(b), 474
  Rule 3.6(c), 474
  Rule 3.6(d), 475
  Rule 3.7, 207
  Rule 3.8, 475
  Rule 3.8(a), 475
  Rule 3.8(b), 476
  Rule 3.8(c), 476
  Rule 3.8(d), 475
  Rule 3.8(e), 476
  Rule 3.8(f), 476
  Rule 4.2, 470
  Rule 4.3, 471
  Rule 4.4, 470, 473
  Rule 4.4(b), 154, 155
  Rule 5.3, 25, 36, 92, 143, 281, 390, 475
  Rule 5.3(b), 67
  Rule 5.4, 67, 74
  Rule 5.4(a), 338
  Rule 5.4(b), 339-340
  Rule 5.4(c), 216
  Rule 5.5, 63
  Rule 6.1, 521
  Rule 7.1, 270, 272, 278
  Rule 7.2(a), 271
  Rule 7.2(b), 271
  Rule 7.2(c), 271
  Rule 7.3, 272, 280
  Rule 7.3(c), 271-272
  Rule 7.4, 272
  Rule 7.5, 272
  Rule 8.2(a), 468
  Rule 8.4(a), 281
  Rule 8.4(e), 468
  Rule 8.4(f), 468
  Rule 8.4(g), 519
Model Standards and Guidelines for the
  Utilization of Legal Assistants (NALA), 35
Monetary sanctions, 394, 457-458
Montana, regulation of paralegals, 26
Motions to disqualify counsel. *See*
  Disqualification of counsel
Multidisciplinary practice (MDP), 340, 511
Multiple clients. *See* Simultaneous representation

NALS, the Association for Legal Professionals,
  22, 23
National Association for the Advancement of
  Colored People (NAACP), 280
National Association of Legal Assistants (NALA)
  attorney-client relationships, 74
  certification examination, 27, 391

Certified Legal Assistant (CLA)/Certified
    Paralegal (CP) program, 20-21, 22, 517
Certified Paralegal/Advanced Certified
    Paralegal (CP/ACP) program, 23
code of ethics. *See* Code of Ethics and
    Professional Responsibility, NALA
contact information, 35
disclosure of paralegal status, 91
educational requirements for paralegals, 391
Guideline V.1, 144
history, 20
membership, 22
Model Standards and Guidelines for the
    Utilization of Legal Assistants, 35
pro bono work, 522
titles used by paralegals, 517
National Federation of Paralegal Associations
    (NFPA)
    Affirmation of Responsibility, 32
    certification examination, 22, 391
    contact information, 35
    disclosure of paralegal status, 91
    educational requirements for paralegals, 391
    ethics opinions, issuance of, 35
    history, 20
    membership, 22
    pro bono work, 521-522
    titles used by paralegals, 517
Nebraska, 34, 225
Necessary witnesses, 207
Negotiations, 77-78, 203
Networks, closed, 150
Nevada, 26, 224, 520
New Hampshire, 34, 155, 340, 399
New Jersey
    billing issues, 322
    conflicts of interest, 225
    consumer protection, 399
    court-awarded paralegal fees, 329
    lawyer advertising, 270, 272, 273
    regulation of paralegals, 26
    voluntary certification program for paralegals, 27
New Mexico
    guidelines for paralegal use, 34
    partnerships with nonlawyers, 340
    pro bono work, 520
    regulation of paralegals, 25
    screening paralegals from cases, 199
New York
    advertising, 278
    artificial intelligence use, 395, 478
    billing issues, 321
    conflicts of interest, 225
    court-awarded paralegal fees, 329
    guidelines for paralegal use, 34
    IOLTA plans, 342
    lawyer advertising, 273, 275, 277
    metadata, use of, 155
    pro bono work, 520
    profit-based compensation, 339
    regulation of lawyers in, 2

screening paralegals from cases, 199
    titles used by paralegals, 89
    unauthorized practice of law, 75-76, 77
Newsgroups, 275
Newsletters, law firm, 267
NFPA. *See* National Federation of Paralegal
    Associations
900 telephone numbers, law firms with, 268
Nonexempt status of paralegals, 518
Nonlawyer legal service providers. *See also*
    Paralegals; Unauthorized practice of law
    (UPL)
    areas of practice, 59-62
    need for, 59-60
    overview, 29-31
    prosecutions against, 60-61
    right to self-representation and, 68, 72
    titles used by, 73, 516-517
North Carolina
    conflicts of interest, 225
    guidelines for paralegal use, 34
    IOLTA plans, 342
    lawyer advertising, 275, 277
    partnerships with nonlawyers, 340
    screening paralegals from cases, 199
    unauthorized practice of law, 71, 76
    voluntary certification program for
        paralegals, 26
North Dakota, 34

Obstruction of justice statutes, 463, 472
Ohio
    conflicts of interest, 225
    court-awarded paralegal fees, 329
    IOLTA plans, 342
    paralegal as witness, 208
    voluntary certification program for
        paralegals, 26
Oklahoma, 224, 329, 459
Online coupons, 275
Online directories, 276-277, 278
Ontario, Canada, regulation of paralegals, 26
On-the-job training, 392
Oregon, 26, 33, 62, 338-339
Orientation training, 392
Overbilling, 322-323, 507
Over-coaching witnesses, 473
Overtime, 518

Paralegal Advanced Competency Examination
    (PACE), 22, 391
Paralegals
    advertising by lawyers, names used in, 273
    business transactions with clients, 212
    certification, 20-21, 22, 23, 27, 391
    codes of ethics. *See* Code of Ethics and
        Professional Responsibility, NALA;
        Model Code of Ethics and Professional
        Responsibility, NFPA

Paralegals (continued)
  common tasks and functions, 75, 454-455
  communication skills, 516
  competence, 391-394, 401-404, 454-455
  confidentiality issues, 142-155
  conflicts of interest, 199, 207-208, 212, 214-215, 217
  contact/communication with clients, 71-72, 394, 400, 401
  court, unethical conduct in, 461
  court appearances in uncontested matters, 69
  definitions of, 23, 25, 27, 517
  depositions conducted by, 69-70
  disclosure of status, 88-91, 455, 467
  education levels, 22, 389-391, 513, 514, 517-518
  employment opportunities and job market, 21-23
  ethical standards, 514
  ex parte communication, 471-472
  examinations, 22, 27, 391
  exempt or nonexempt status of, 518
  family member, representation of, 217
  fees and billing. *See* Paralegals, fees and billing
  freelancing/independent contractors, 21, 30, 92-93
  gender issues, 518-519
  gifts from clients, 214-215
  handling of client funds and property, 343
  history of the profession, 20-23
  integrity and honor, 515
  legal assistants and, 89
  legal service, 514
  liability of, 35-37
  licensing, 23, 27-29
  malpractice actions, 36, 395
  marketing role of, 268
  misconduct of, 511-512
  mistakes by, 396
  number of, 21
  other terms for, 29-31
  performance standards, 514-516
  privileged information disclosed or possessed, 153-154
  pro bono work by, 514, 521-522
  professional commitment, 515
  professionalism, 512-516
  regulation of. *See* Regulation of paralegals
  retirement plans, 338
  role in litigation, 70, 454-455
  screening from cases, 199, 222-225
  self-assessment by, 404
  signing of pleadings, 70-71
  state guidelines for utilization of, 34
  titles used by, 88-91, 273, 516-517
  training programs, 20, 389-391, 401
  trial publicity and, 475
  unauthorized practice of law. *See* Unauthorized practice of law (UPL)
  unrepresented parties, communication with, 472
  utilization of, 34, 63, 67-68, 92-93, 518
  as witnesses, 207-208
  work ethic, 515
Paralegals, fees and billing
  billable hours, 318, 319-320, 328-333
  billing abuses and, 323-324
  bonuses, 339
  compensation at market rates, 328-329, 331
  duties performed for bankruptcy trustees, 330
  federal statutes, 330
  fee splitting, 63, 337-341
  overtime compensation, 518
  petitions to the court for, 330-332
  prequalification of, 330
  profit-based compensation, 338-339
  prohibition against setting, 325
  referral fees, 339
Paraprofessionals, classification of paralegals as, 512-513
Parents, legal representation by, 64, 69
Partnerships with nonlawyers, 63, 337-341, 511
Passwords, computer, 150
Patent Office, 87
Pennsylvania
  billing issues, 321
  certification of paralegals, 27
  communication of paralegals with represented parties, 472
  consumer protection, 399
  depositions conducted by paralegals, 70
  guidelines for paralegal use, 34
  metadata, use of, 155
  referral fees, 337
  screening paralegals from cases, 199
  unauthorized practice of law, 76-77
Perjury, 461-462, 472-473, 474
Personal expenses, billing for, 322
Personal injury firms, 77-78, 268, 281, 317
Personal problems, 396, 401, 404
Pleadings, 70-71, 75, 454
Pleas, collective, 203
Podcasts, 267
Policies and procedures, 144-147, 344-345
Positional conflicts, 202
Post-trial communications with jurors, 470
Practice Forward survey (ABA), 403
Practice of law, 64-66, 511, 520. *See also* Unauthorized practice of law (UPL)
Preexisting documents, attorney-client privilege and, 132
Prejudice, dismissal of action with, 458
Prepaid legal plans, 339
Preparation of witnesses, 473
Prerecorded telephone messages, 281
Press, lawyer relations with, 475
Press kits, 267
Prison Litigation Reform Act, 330
Probable cause requirement, 475
Probate matters
  conflicts of interest, 204

estate of deceased lawyer, fees paid to, 339
executor, naming lawyer as, 214
malpractice claims, 397-398
percentage of worth fees for, 316
wills, 75-76, 136, 204, 214, 397-398
Probation, for lawyers, 5-6
Pro bono work, 267, 508-509, 514, 520-522
Procrastination, 395, 396
Profession, defined, 512
Professional competence. *See* Competence
Professional development, 388-389, 391
Professionalism, 506-522
concerns about, 509-512
current issues, 516-520
elements of, 514-516
of paralegals, 512-516
pro bono work, 267, 514, 520-522
public perception of lawyers, 506-509
Professional judgment test, 64-65
Profit-based compensation, 338-339
Property in payment of fees, 327
Proposals for service, 322
Propria persona. *See* Pro se litigants
Prosecutors, special rules for, 475-476
Pro se litigants, assisting, 60, 72
Public defender's office, 216
Public interest work, 520-522
Public opinion, 475, 506-509
Publication rights, 212-213
Publicity, trial, 474-475

Racial bias, 519
Rainmakers, 267
Real estate transactions
closings, 76-77
conflicts of interest, 204, 212, 217
third-party malpractice claims, 398
Reasonable inquiry, duty to make prior to actions, 456
Recording without permission, 473-474
Record keeping for client funds and property, 344-345
Referral fees, 281, 337-338, 339
Referral services, 276-277, 339
Registered Paralegal designation, 391
Regulation of lawyers, 2-7, 457-458
Regulation of paralegals. *See also* Supervisory or managerial authority of lawyers
codes of ethics and guidelines of paralegal associations, 35
debate about, 27-29, 516
limited licensing, 30-34
state efforts, 24-26, 29-31
state guidelines for the utilization of paralegals, 34
voluntary certification, 26-27
Relatives, 69, 216-217
Remedies. *See* Sanctions and remedies
Remote work, 403

Represented parties, communication with, 470-471
Reprimands of lawyers, 6
Reprovals of lawyers, 6
Research standards, 398-399
Respondeat superior, doctrine of, 36-37
Retainer fees, 326-327
Retention of files, policies, 344
Retirement plans, 338
Rhode Island
conflicts of interest, 224
guidelines for paralegal use, 34
lawyer advertising, 277
partnerships with nonlawyers, 340
solicitation, 281
unauthorized practice of law, 76
Right to counsel, informing accused of, 476
Runners and cappers, 280

Safe deposit boxes, 343
Salaries of lawyers, 507
Sanctions and remedies
aggravating and mitigating factors, 6
artificial intelligence use, 395, 478
disobeying court orders, 460-461
disruption of courtroom, 458-461
for ethical misconduct of lawyers, 5-6, 457-458, 507-508
for incompetence, 394-396
monetary, 394, 457-458
nonmonetary, 458, 476
obstruction of justice, 463
for unauthorized practice of law, 66
Sarbanes-Oxley Act, 3, 135-136, 204
Savings and loan crisis, 397
Scope of representation, limiting, 400
Screen (ethical wall), 220
Screening to overcome conflicts of interest, 199, 219-225
Secret recording, 473-474
Securities and Exchange Commission, 3, 135-136, 147
Securities law, 147, 212, 397
Sedona Principles, 477
Self-assessment, 404
Self-help legal kits, 59, 72
Self-representation, 68, 72
Settlements, 77-78, 203, 328
Sex discrimination, 519
Sexual orientation, discrimination based on, 519
Sherman Antitrust Act, 59, 330
Shredding files, 145
Signing of correspondence by paralegals, 89-90
Simultaneous representation, 199-205
Sliding scale for contingency fees, 317
Small Business Administration, 87
Small claims advisors, 73
Smart cards (electronic identification cards), 149
Snapchat, 152

549

Snitch rules, 509
Social media
 advertising on, 267, 274-279
 confidentiality issues, 152
 jurors and, 469
 legal information or advice on, 73
 misuse of by attorneys and paralegals, 270-271
Social Security Administration, 87
Solicitation, 279-281. *See also* Advertising
South Carolina
 billing issues, 322
 guidelines for paralegal use, 34
 lawyer advertising, 275, 277
 regulation of paralegals, 26
 unauthorized practice of law, 77-78
South Dakota, 24, 34, 199, 273
Spoliation, 463
Spouses, 69, 217
Start-up companies, interests in, 212, 319
State bar associations, 2-3, 58. *See also specific states*
State courts, regulation of lawyers by, 2
Statutory fee awards, 320, 321, 328-333
Stress, 510-511
Subject matter test, corporate setting, 135
Subject matter waivers, 133
Subornation of perjury, 472-473
Subpoena of lawyers, 476
Substance abuse, 3, 396, 401, 404, 510
"Substantial relationship," successive representation and, 206-207
Successive representation, 205-207
Summary ejection proceedings, 73
"Super Lawyer" designations, 272
Supervisory or managerial authority of lawyers
 ABA stance on, 35-37
 delegation of duties, 402
 freelance lawyers, supervision of, 144
 inadequate exercise of, 63, 395, 402
 independent contractor paralegals and, 92-93
 responsibility for, 67
Suppression of evidence, 461, 463, 476
Supreme Court decisions
 advertising by lawyers, 91, 266, 268-269
 conflicts of interest, 216
 direct solicitation by lawyers, 280
 disclosure of confidential material, 135
 interest on client trust accounts held in IOLTA, 342
 legal advocacy organizations, conflicts of interest, 216
 legal/paralegal fees, 330
 statutory fee awards, 320, 328-329, 330
 withdrawal from case involving intended perjury, 462
Surcharges, 323
Surface Mining Control and Reclamation Act of 1977, 330
Suspension of lawyers, 5

Tampering with a jury, 469
Task-based billing, 319
Technology
 cloud computing, 148
 confidentiality issues, 147-152
 ethical issues, 478
 keeping abreast of, 395-396, 477
 legal marketing, changes in, 278
 research standards, 398-399
Tennessee, disruptive conduct of lawyers, 460
Termination of representation, 344, 401
Testamentary gifts from clients, 214
Testimonial advertisements, 271
Texas
 artificial intelligence use, 478
 billing issues, 322
 conflicts of interest, 223-224
 consumer protection, 399
 disobeying a court order, 460
 disruptive conduct of lawyers, 459, 460
 guidelines for paralegal use, 34
 lawyer advertising, 277
 publication of electronic self-help resources, 61
 referral fees, 337
 voluntary certification program for paralegals, 26
Third parties, 204, 215-216, 396-398, 472
TikTok, 152
Titles, paralegal use of, 88-91, 273, 516-517
Tort liability for professional negligence, 394
Trade names in advertising, 272
Traditional areas of practice test, 65
Training programs. *See* Education and training
Trials, 469-470, 474-475. *See also* Litigation process
Trustee, naming lawyer drafting a document as, 214
Trusts, 62, 341-342, 344-345
Typing services for legal documents, 60

Unauthorized practice of law (UPL), 58-93
 administrative agencies, nonlawyer practice before, 86-87
 alternative business structure, 340-341
 conduct that constitutes, 68-74
 court appearances, 68-71
 disclosure of status as paralegal, 88-91
 electronic resources and self-help materials, 61-62
 establishing the attorney-client relationship, 74
 fees, setting, 74
 giving legal advice, 71-74, 88
 history of, 58-64
 immigration law, 60, 62
 independent contractors, paralegals as, 92-93
 jurisdictional issues, 63
 lawyers' responsibilities, 67-68
 living trusts, preparation of, 62

negotiation of settlements, 77-78
nonlawyer legal service providers, 59-63
practice of law, defined, 64-66
prosecutions for, 59, 60-61
real estate transactions, 76-77
remedies, 66
responsibility of lawyer to prevent, 67-68
trends in, 63-64
types of cases, 66
will execution, 75-76
Unbundling of legal services, 326
Unlawful detainer assistants, 73
Unmeritorious claims or defenses, 455-458
Unrepresented parties, contact with, 471-472
Unsettled areas of law, 401
Unwarranted actions, bringing, 455-458
UPL. *See* Unauthorized practice of law
U.S. Department of. *See name of specific department*
U.S. Supreme Court. *See* Supreme Court decisions
Utah
    alternative business structure, 340-341
    guidelines for paralegal use, 34
    limited practice legal professionals, 31-32
    profit-based compensation, 338
    regulation of paralegals, 26
    Rules of Professional Conduct, 32
Utilization of paralegals, 34, 63, 67-68, 92-93, 518

Vermont, 77, 155, 217, 225
Vicarious disqualification. *See* Imputed disqualification
Vicarious liability, doctrine of, 36-37
Videos, Internet, 267
Virginia
    advertising, 278
    guidelines for paralegal use, 34
    lawyer advertising, 270
    profit-based compensation, 338-339
    screening paralegals from cases, 199
    unauthorized practice of law, 77
Virtual law office, 520
Viruses, computer protection against, 149
Visa consultants, 62

Waivers, 133, 200-201, 476
Washington
    consumer protection, 399
    guidelines for paralegal use, 34
    IOLTA plans, 342
    nonlawyer practitioners, 31
    paralegal representation in court, 69
    partnerships with nonlawyers, 340
We the People (WTP), 60
Web sites
    advertising on, 267, 273-279
    providing legal information, 73, 274, 277, 399
    social networking, 152, 274-279
    statement of jurisdiction on, 277
West Virginia, 34, 322
Whereabouts of client, attorney-client privilege and, 131
Whistleblower statutes, 509
Wills. *See also* Probate matters
    attorney-client privilege and, 136
    drafting of, simultaneous representation and, 204
    executing, 75-76
    gifts from clients, 214
    third-party malpractice claims, 397-398
Wisconsin, 26, 77
Withdrawal from representation, 201-202
Witnesses
    advising to hide or avoid testifying, 472
    attorneys as, 207
    conflicts of interest involving, 203
    contact with, rules for, 472-474
    expert, 474
    false testimony, 461
    necessary witness, 207
    paralegals as, 207-208
    payment for expenses, 474
    perjury by, 461-462, 472, 474
    preparing, 473
Witnessing of wills, 75-76
Women. *See* Gender-related issues
Work product doctrine, 137
Workload issues, 318, 321, 403-404
WTP (We the People), 60

YouTube, 274

Zealous representation
    abuse of justice system, 507
    advocacy and, 455
    business transactions with clients, 211
    disruptive conduct in courtroom, 459
    family relationships and, 217
    multiple clients, 200